THE ART
OF THE PLAY

AN ANTHOLOGY OF NINE PLAYS

Alan S. Downer
PRINCETON UNIVERSITY

HOLT, RINEHART AND WINSTON · NEW YORK

To the Memory of
HARLEY GRANVILLE–BARKER

PREFACE

THE DEDICATION of this book is a necessary acknowledgment. Many years ago, in Barker's lectures *On Dramatic Method*, I met for the first time the agreeable proposition that a playwright's work must be approached through the theater of his time rather than the codes of later criticism. And in his celebrated *Prefaces to Shakespeare* he had demonstrated that his various talents and experiences as actor, playwright, director, and scholar collaborated to shed new light on old and much-abused texts. However, it was almost accidentally that the more general value of his understanding of dramatic art was revealed to me.

One blacked-out and comfortless winter night during World War II he was discussing some of the prefaces to Shakespeare that he would never have time to write. Not without a recognition of both irony and the " pathetic fallacy," our conversation turned to *The Tempest*. By coincidence we had both been reading, or rereading, some of the critical essays this last work in the Shakespearean canon had provoked, and were struck by the variety and occasional absurdity of the critical conclusions. Is it a romantic image of the artist surrendering his powers at the end of his career? or a Christian allegory? Can its unity be discovered through the analysis of Freudian symbols? or by applying Marxist dialectic? Or is it, as Dr. Johnson seemed to think, a *mere* exercise of the fancy, and — " of these trifles enough."

Barker was at once intrigued and baffled by these critical propositions, but his bafflement did not proceed from an imperfect sympathy with the premises of the authors. His constant question was, how would such-or-such interpretation be conveyed by Shakespeare's actors in Shakespeare's theater? As the most progressive of producers in his own active years in the English theater he was not of course suggesting a return to the horse-and-buggy conditions of Shakespeare's stage. But he was constantly aware of the drama as an art and of the text of the play as only a partial record of the artistic whole.

To say that the drama is an art is to imply that it does something more than follow the course of events of a narrative, something more than hold a simple reflector up to mankind. In addition to relating human ex-

perience, it interprets human experience, and the interpretation — as in
all arts — is conveyed by signs and symbols and conventions. The recorded dialogue, constituting for most readers the sole experience of the
play, must be considered in the light of the [unrecorded] conventions of
its own theater if the modern reader or producer is not to go astray in
understanding the work. It will then be possible to find in modern theater practice equivalents for conveying the purpose and meaning of the
play. For example, while recognizing the splendor and effectiveness *in itself* of Paul Robeson's performance of Othello, Barker felt that the audience was " jarred by a sudden transportation into the realm of realism: a
real Moor, insistently that, presenting a real Moor. Whisperings round
the theater, ' That's a *real* Moor you know.' A disadvantage to him in his
performance to be on a different plane." The " plane " of Shakespeare's
play is, of course, the plane of symbolic action; the presence of a " real
Moor " injected a social problem into a moral conflict. A seventeenth-cen-
tury tragedy was reworked in the image of a proletarian drama of the
1930's.

As for *The Tempest,* Freud, Marx, and the cultural anthropologists
would be as misleading as the realists or the gaudy showmen. " I fancy,"
he said, " that if you consider it as a *Masque* and not a *play,* and recognize the difference of treatment and tone, it comes out all right." He was
thinking of the problem of presenting the play in a theater, but the same
problem faces any reader who wishes to approximate something like the
full experience intended for him by the artist.

The present volume is intended both for the student of literature as an
introduction to the drama as an art, and for the student of theater as an
introduction to the problems presented by the drama as an historical, literary, and esthetic phenomenon. It is assumed that understanding and
producing drama are very nearly synonymous, and that the end and purpose of seeing and reading a play is to *experience* the work as a whole. It
is further assumed that this experience is available to the trained reader.

Each of the chapters considers one or more elements of the drama —
the tools and conventions with which the playwright works — illustrating them in three key plays: *Prometheus Bound, Dr. Faustus,* and *Ghosts.*
These plays have been chosen as good in themselves, as examples of the
basic forms which the drama has taken in its historical development, and
as providing clear and comprehensible illustrations of the elements under
consideration. The discussion of the tools of the playwright and the
working parts of the drama is followed by a consideration of the larger
aspects of the whole work, with additional plays for study and analysis.

Since this is a book for the beginner rather than the expert, the commentary and editorial matter have been composed with his needs in mind. An effort has been made to explain every point, including those that may seem obvious even to the least experienced readers. The discussion of complex and subtle matters is a sterile pastime if the often tedious examination of primary and simple matters has been slighted. At the expense of ease and grace, therefore, I have permitted myself a good deal of repetition both of detail and conclusions. In the interests of clarity and concreteness, controversial points have been simplified and certain gaps in the historical record filled in with (clearly indicated) hypotheses. Wherever possible, photographs and other illustrations have been introduced to assist the reader in the difficult business of visualizing the play in performance. Footnotes, glossarial and otherwise, to the texts of the plays have been held to a minimum, so that the reader may not be distracted from the main purpose of playreading: to experience the dramatic action.

The book does not pretend that only nine plays in the whole repertory of the theater are worthy of consideration. On the contrary, an effort has been made to introduce references to many plays in illustrating the workings of the art. When possible these references have been made to such plays as *Macbeth,* with which a majority of readers may be presumed to be acquainted; but unfamiliar plays have been introduced without hesitation when they would serve to clarify or demonstrate a point. It is hoped, in fact, that the richness of the dramatic experience may induce the student to wish to read further in dramatic literature, and to this end a number of convenient anthologies have been included in the List of Suggested Readings at the end of the book.

The professional legitimate theater, at least in America, is a minute and geographically restricted operation with which comparatively few Americans come in contact. There is, however, the vast and growing semiprofessional, community, and school theater, as well as the readily available drama of the movie house and television set to provide living and active matter for experience and appreciation. It may be hoped that the present approach to dramatic art may find a usefulness outside the classroom and the professional study. If the drama is an imitation, intensification, and ordering of life, the *experience of drama* makes available to the conscious and sensitive spectator-reader, as Barker put it, " the thing that was at the moment [of its writing] as near to wisdom as it is given to fallible man to attain."

A.S.D.

Princeton University
February 24, 1955

CONTENTS

PART THREE: PLAYS FOR ANALYSIS

Fuente Ovejuna (The Sheep Well) (379–406) — Oedipus Rex
(407–440)

ILLUSTRATIONS

PART ONE

THE TOOLS OF THE PLAYWRIGHT

I

A CHAPTER OF DEFINITIONS

This book is concerned with the peculiar and complex nature of dramatic art. *Peculiar* and *complex* are not, perhaps, very encouraging words to meet at the beginning of a new venture; yet it is well to be clear at once that drama is unlike any other form of narrative communication and that a great many other things besides words will engage our attention.

The beginner may wonder, and properly wonder, whether it is necessary to concern himself with *dramatic* art. He will ask why a play, which is made up of words written on a page, cannot be read as a poem is read, or a short story, or a novel. Of course it can; and that being the case, the reader who is merely interested in narrative might better stick to prose fiction, where readability is a criterion, instead of wrestling with the deliberate discomforts of the format of the printed play — unless he is in search of the special satisfaction a play is designed to yield: the dramatic experience.

That is, a play can be read in search of the author's ideas, but there is a limited number of important ideas available to any artist: you will generally find him affirming one of the Ten Commandments or the Bill of Rights, or condemning one of the Seven Deadly Sins — for these, after all, have been the basic ideas and ideals of many of the civilizations of history. What the dramatist contributes is a special kind of statement of the old ideas, revitalizing and making an immediate part of the spectator's experience those basic facts of life which, taken for granted, have become forgotten, moribund, or ineffective. One of the purposes of any serious playwright — and the word serious does not exclude the authors of comedy — is so to restate a particular human experience as to illuminate human experience in general.

3

In the course of everyday living it is impossible to see the consequences of the choices, the decisions, we are constantly called upon to make. The dramatist, telescoping, concentrating, and intensifying his actions, enables the spectator to see that life (like art) has a beginning, a middle, and an end. He gives us the satisfaction of form, of pattern, which the necessities and circumstances of daily living deny us. And he gives it to us not as words on paper or paint on canvas, but as an arrangement of living, breathing life, the terms that a living, breathing audience can most directly respond to. It is in this sense that the playwright is advised to hold his mirror up to nature; the more recognizably living his materials, the better chance he has of providing his audience with the dramatic experience.

The dramatic experience. Perhaps it is time to attempt a definition. It is the discovery by the audience of a truth about man's life, not through thinking upon the event but through observing it, through sense perception rather than intellection. In a successful play, the illusion of experience is complete. Most of us can remember sitting next to people at the movies who talked back to the characters on the screen, and even the most sophisticated audiences have been known to scream aloud at an unexpected turn of events.

Some years ago, an English play concerned itself with the trials of a wife whose husband had determined to murder her. She finds herself, momentarily and unexpectedly, alone in a cottage with the opportunity to escape. She tries a door; it is locked. She tries a window; it is locked. She tries another window, and another, and another. All are locked. Escape seems impossible. Suddenly she remembers a back entrance, a door she has not tried. With a cry of joy she runs to the door. Fearfully she turns the knob — the door opens slightly. Relief flows over her (and the audience). She flings open the door and rushes — into the arms of her waiting husband.

The play is a thriller and of no consequence to the literature of the drama, but the incident provides a black and white illustration for a playgoer's primer. The cries and gasps and starts which it regularly evoked from audiences are a demonstration of the meaning of *dramatic experience* on its simplest level. The tears and laughter which other situations can evoke from their audiences are further demonstrations of this level of the meaning of the experience of drama. The less obvious reactions called forth by subtler and more complex plays are modifications of the primer illustration.

The exact nature of this aspect of the dramatic experience is a subject for psychologists and mystics — for (and this must be considered later in this chapter) the heart of the drama is a mystery, both in its origin as a form of narrative art and in its continuing power to control and direct the sympathies of its audiences. It is not simply that the spectator " identifies " himself with the heroine of *Love from a Stranger,* or with Hamlet, for not all plays concentrate the audiences' sympathies on a single character (see, for instance, *The Sea Gull*). Nor do audiences, as it were, become children again as they take their uncomfortable and expensive seats, forgetting the realities of the world through which they have just fought their way, and submitting gratefully to an unspoken command from the playwright: " Let's pretend." The ideal playgoer is aware both of the world of the stage and the world of reality; he is aware of the artifice, the conventions. He is not a child reborn; he knows that art is not a game and that the dramatic experience, however delightful, is something more than peterpanaceas.

Coleridge, speaking of the spectator's contribution to the success of a performance, referred to the playgoer's " willing suspension of disbelief." But this is not really an explanation of the ultimate mystery. The playgoer's " suspension of disbelief " is more than willing. In fact, it takes an effort of will to disbelieve while in the playhouse; or rather, belief and disbelief are not involved, except insofar as the playgoer accepts certain conventions, and these in themselves are temporary and change from time to time and from culture to culture.

Convention means, literally, a meeting of minds. In art it is generally defined as an agreement between the artist and his audience that certain modifications or elisions of reality will be accepted by both parties to make communication possible. The most obvious of these, perhaps, is the omniscience granted the novelist that he may move freely from one side of a conflict to the other. The operatic composer is permitted to characterize his hero with a leitmotiv; the director of a movie may show us first the heroine tied to a railroad track and immediately after the hero struggling through a forest fire to reach her. Modern audiences are so accustomed to such treatments of reality that it is unnecessary to remind them of their agreement to accept them as substitutes. But there are other conventions, less obvious or less familiar, underlying each of the arts. The story of any art form is in part the history of its conventions, what they are, their growth, and modification.

The study of any art form, then, may well begin with a discovery of its conventions, of the means by which the artist communicates with his hearers. This is particularly true of the drama, since the playwright has chosen to communicate with a mass audience. He is not directing himself to the perceptive individual who may by a happy combination of circumstances, nerves, and intellect respond to his unique or wayward genius. He is addressing himself to a group, a hundred, a thousand people, and if he would be understood he must speak their language (in the figurative as well as the literal sense), or by speaking their language in part, teach them to understand his special vocabulary.

For the purposes of discussion, the conventions of the drama may be temporarily isolated. But we must be constantly aware that the art itself, the dramatic experience, is organic. The closest examination of an arm or a leg or a liver provides but misleading clues to the nature of Man. Such isolation of the elements of dramatic art is necessary, however dangerous it may be, since the dramatic experience is so habitual, so common an experience that the playgoer frequently needs to be reminded that he has been present at an artistic and created performance. Man is, by nature, both an actor and a spectator. Imitation, which is the basis of acting, is born in him, and communication by gesture and action is present in the most primitive cultures. Indeed, the very word *dramatic* is one employed casually and daily, without any particular reference to the theater or to art. Whatever is startling, striking, or out of the ordinary (and sometimes not very far out of the ordinary at that) is " dramatic." At any rate the term is used in quite a different sense from those related to other forms of narrative communication: *poetic,* for instance, or *fictitious,* which frequently is used to suggest an improbability or something artificial. *Dramatic,* although derived from the most highly artificial of narrative forms, is never used as a synonym for *artificial*. It is for this reason that it is more than usually necessary to insist on the *making* that goes into a dramatic work, in order that we may be prepared to approach and judge it in its proper light, relating it to, but not confusing it with, the life that it so closely imitates.

Drama then is not something read, or heard, or seen; it is something *experienced*. It retains this peculiar quality in common with the church service and other religious rituals to which it is closely associated by its origin. It retains, that is, an element of mystery, an element which defies analysis or definition by the methods available to criticism. But the other elements which go into the makeup of the dramatic experience are all capable of definition, and their contribution can be assessed. They are: the playwright, the playhouse, the player, and the play.

A good many of the terms employed in the discussion of plays and playwrighting will, of course, be similar to the terms employed in the discussion of other narrative arts. However, each of these arts is unique, and the terms must inevitably acquire special shades of meaning adapted to the particular art under discussion. Of drama this is especially

true; it will be well to have in mind, then, the precise meaning of each
term before any attempt is made to consider the function of the elements or tools or conventions involved in the creation of the dramatic
experience as a whole.

The First Plays

Definitions, particularly as they come prefabricated from the dictionary,
have the smell of abstraction about them. The drama, as we have been
insisting, is living, and therefore abhors abstraction. The definition of
terms related to dramatic art should, properly, be living and as concrete
as possible. Definition should somehow derive from dramatic experience.
Here, then, are two plays, the simplest, most primitive dramas of the
ancient and the modern worlds. After they have been " performed," the
definition of terms will be less of an academic exercise.

Every race and every culture creates its special form of dramatic experience; yet, different as the developed or sophisticated forms may be,
they share common origins and intentions, and they are all born of necessity and a common fundamental instinct. Thus the differences in
these two little plays will be at once apparent to the eye of the playgoer,
but their essential likeness will become apparent in the analysis and
definition of the elements that enter into the making of each.

The first play is without date or precise location. It is, in fact, both
anonymous and hypothetical. It is the first " play " to be performed in
ancient Greece, and it must be constructed from the researches and hypotheses of classical scholars and anthropologists and archaeologists. The
time is before the keeping of historical records, and the setting is a field
in the open countryside, near a small village called, perhaps, Ikaria. Near
this village occurred a famous incident in the life of Dionysos, the god
of wine, and as a result his cult was especially active here.

Every December when the more demanding agricultural chores were
over and there was little to do but worry about how the fall planting
of grain would turn out, the Ikarians were accustomed to hold a festival
in honor of their god. At first a group of fifty men and boys assembled
on the flat, circular threshing floor to chant hymns associated with
Dionysos. With the passing decades, the rites became more complex, the
performers (and probably the spectators) consumed large quantities of
the wine which was the god's gift to his followers, and the festival began
to assume a theatrical character. With intoxication came impersonation.
Instead of singing about Dionysos as true believers in contemporary
Ikaria, they came to imagine themselves to be the actual followers of
Dionysos as he went about his mission on earth untold centuries before.

They sang and danced as a group, as a *chorus*, rudely dressed in goat-skins, and circling about a temporary altar erected in the center of the threshing floor. They sang of the adventures of Dionysos, of his miraculous birth from the thigh of Zeus, of his upbringing by the nymphs in Asia Minor, of his mission and ministry in Greece as he distributed gifts or punishments to those tribal kings who accepted or rejected him. Always they sang and acted as a unit, sometimes as the nymphs who nurtured the divine infant, rushing to receive him, cradling him in their arms, dancing to disguise his hiding place or to defend him from pursuers; sometimes they were the women of Thebes, his devotees, driven mad by their king's rejection of him and wreaking a mad bacchantic vengeance on the doubter. As the complexity of the ritual increased, the chorus acquired a leader, a *choragus*, perhaps the local priest of Dionysos, who identified himself with the god and sang exhortations or explanations or commands to his followers. This prototype of drama, called a *dithyramb*, remained essentially a poetic narrative, something like the modern oratorio or cantata, though certainly wilder in its performance and with a more positive suggestion of representation.

On this particular December morning about 560 B.C., the spectators standing about the circular threshing floor are to see an innovation. The ritual begins in customary fashion. To the slow insistent rhythm of a drumbeat, the chorus, robed in skins, enters the ring and circles about the altar. The sound of a flute rises above the regular thump of bare feet on the hardened earth and the drum shifts its marching rhythm to that of the wailing oriental tune. Silence. The chorus suddenly raises its arms above the altar and cries in a high falsetto, " Io, Bacchus," using one of the many names of the god of their idolatry, " Io, Bacchus! "

Now the flute and drum resume, and the chorus, singing and moving in unison in a slow circle, begins a hymn to Dionysos.

> We, we are the Bacchae
> We who brought Bromios
>   God born of god
>   Dionysos
> Home from the hills
> To the cities of Greece
> Who brought Bromios. . . .

On and on the dithyramb continues, growing swifter and wilder in accent and melody, the stamping feet of the chorus following the rapid beats of the drum, and their bodies turning and shuddering in ecstasy. Suddenly a high note is followed by silence as the chorus freezes in position and the choragus enters the ring and walks slowly to the altar. As priest of the cult he is wearing his long religious robe, but no other attempt at costuming or disguising him has been made.

Quietly the chorus resumes, in unison:

> But who is this, fair-haired with fragrant locks,
> The charms of Aphrodite in his eyes?

Raising both arms, the priest chants a long expository speech. He is, he says, Dionysos and he has come from the distant forests of Asia Minor across the seas with his followers to propagate his religion and bestow on men the gift of the vine. And now after long wanderings and perilous adventures he has come to the city of Pentheus. What reception awaits him from Pentheus?

Thus far the spectators standing about the circular performing place have been aware only of beholding a conventional dithyramb; but an innovation awaits them. As the priest finishes his chant, a second figure breaks through the choral ring and approaches him. This is a second priest, Thespis by name, garbed like the first in a flowing ankle-length gown. As the newcomer nears the altar, " Dionysos " turns to his " followers," and sings:

> The king, Pentheus, is coming.
> Let no sound be made, no whisper
> Of my sacred name.

Thespis, impersonating King Pentheus, stops at the side of the other priest. Silently he looks upon the chorus. Then, led by the flute, he begins his chant:

I hear of strange evils abroad in the city, that our women have deserted their houses on pretense of Bacchic rites and are revelling in the dark woods on the mountains, honoring their newfound god Dionysos. But religion covers their lust and liquor. I will hunt them from the mountains and bind them fast in iron.

DIONYSOS. Have you no reverence for the gods?

PENTHEUS. A god! a lawless corrupter of women, destroyer of cities.

DIONYSOS. But savior of men — I bring relief from sorrow.

PENTHEUS. And do you perform your sacred acts by night or day?

DIONYSOS. Mostly by night; there's holiness in the dark.

PENTHEUS. For women there's deceit and corruption.

DIONYSOS. A man may contrive a base deed by daylight.

PENTHEUS. You shall be punished for your dishonest subtlety.

DIONYSOS. And you for your folly and insolence to the god.

PENTHEUS. I will cut off your tresses and seize your wand and imprison you.

DIONYSOS. Dionysos will pursue you with vengeance for this blasphemy.

Dionysos turns from the king and raises his left arm. The drum beats an irregular rhythm and the flute's wailing becomes high and sharp. To the chorus, kneeling about the altar in the presence of the king, he sings:

> Barbarian women, are ye so distraught with fear that ye cower?
> Rise up.

Thespis, " King Pentheus," moves uncertainly from the altar, breaks through the ring of the chorus, and leaves the performing area. Dionysos continues:

Terrible, ah, terrible you are and terrible the fate to which you go. On swift hounds of madness let Justice come, bearing her sword. Let her plunge it in his throat and slay him, the godless, the lawless, the unrighteous, the earth-born. Io, Bacchus!

The cry is picked up by the chorus as it commences a dance, slowly at first, then, led by the drum, faster and faster and wilder and wilder, until it is whirling in ecstatic fury about the god. At its climax, all movement ceases, the instruments are silent, the dancing figures frozen. Then, an instant later, a frenzied cry bursts from their lips, and they rush from the threshing floor in pursuit of the king. The play is over.

It must be remembered that no such play has survived, that what has just been described is a patchwork of fragments literary and archaeological, of hypothesis and of more than a little imaginative reconstitution. For the second illustrative play, although the reader must still call upon his imagination, an historical record exists. The play is usually called *Quem Quaeritis* (*Whom Seek Ye*), and it is generally recognized as the first fruit of the drama of the modern, as opposed to the ancient, world. The performance is recorded by the Bishop of Winchester and dates from around A.D. 975.

While the third lesson is being chanted let four brethren vest themselves. Let one of these, vested in an alb, enter as though to take part in the service, and let him approach the sepulchre without attracting attention and sit there quietly with a palm in his hand, while the third response is being chanted; let the remaining three follow, and let them all, vested in copes, bearing in their hands thuribles with incense, and stepping delicately as those who seek something, approach the sepulchre. These things are done in imitation of the angel sitting in the monument, and the women with spices coming to anoint the body of Jesus. When therefore he who sits there beholds the three approach him like folk lost and seeking something, let him begin in a dulcet voice of medium pitch, to sing, *Quem quaeritis* (Whom seek ye?). And when he has sung it to the end, let the three reply in unison *Ihesu Nazarenum*. So he, *Non est hic, surrexit sicut praedixerat* (He is not here, he is risen as was foretold). *Ite, nuntiate quia surrexit a mortuis* (Go, proclaim that he is risen from the dead). At the word of this bidding let those three turn to the choir and say *Allelulia! resurrexit Dominus!*

This said, let the one, still sitting there and as if recalling them, say the anthem *Venite et videte locum* (Come and examine the spot). And saying this, let him rise, and lift the veil, and show them the place bare of the cross, but only the cloths laid there in which the cross was wrapped. And when they have seen this, let them set down the thuribles which they bare in that same sepulchre, and take the cloth, and hold it up in the face of the clergy, and as if to demonstrate that the Lord has risen and is no longer wrapped therein, let them sing the anthem *Surrexit Dominus de sepulchro* (The Lord is risen from the tomb), and lay the cloth upon the altar. When the anthem is done, let the [choir], sharing their gladness at the triumph of our King . . . , begin the hymn *Te Deum laudamus*. And this begun, all the bells chime out together.

Interesting as the historical study of any art may be, these primitive examples of dramaturgy have been inserted at this point for purposes of definition. The contribution of the history of drama to an understanding of the dramatic experience will be explored later.

Consider first these plays as innovations. Into the established ritual of the dithyramb stepped Thespis, confronting the priest who impersonated Dionysos and *forcing him to become,* not a narrator of events, but a doer, an actor. Into the established ritual of the Mass came the four priests, not reading the Gospel for the day but speaking individual speeches selected and assigned to them by an unknown master. Both Thespis and the unknown master were playwrights, the one traditionally, the other historically, the founders of the craft in their respective cultures.

Playwright

There are several names for the author of a dramatic work: the Greeks called him a poet; later ages have called him a dramatist or playwright. Of these terms, playwright is perhaps the most precise, though to students its orthography is as baffling as its etymology should be illuminating. In English, the suffix *-wright* means maker, as in *shipwright* or *wheelwright;* hence a playwright is not a playwriter but a playmaker, an artisan who, out of many materials and with divers tools, designs, shapes and builds the form of narrative we call a play. To understand the proper spelling of *playwright* is to have constantly in mind a unique characteristic of his art: he works not just with words but with many other tools, all of which must be considered in understanding the dramatic experience.

The poet and the novelist work with words, the musician with notes and sounds, the painter with colors. The playwright works with verbal tools, like the poet and novelist; with human tools, the actors, their bodies and faces, voices and movements; and with mechanical, inorganic tools, the theater and its machinery. Thespis, as playwright, took the tools that were available to him — the threshing floor, the altar, the priest of Dionysos and the chorus of worshippers — and stepped into the situation himself to create the kind of immediacy that constitutes dramatic action. The unknown Christian master, who may or may not have been one of the participating priests, followed the same method and the same inspiration in building or making his play.

Playhouse

The first of the playwright's tools is the theater. That it was born before the drama proper is suggested by the threshing floor which received Thespis, or the great cathedral in which the *Quem Quaeritis* was enacted. It encouraged and controlled the growth of the principal patterns of drama, the focussed and the panoramic; in its various shapes, dimensions, and complexities, it established many of the conventions by which the playwright was able to communicate with his audience, and many of the restrictions through which rebellious artists have broken to create works which speak with a renewed vitality. It has been at various times the temple of accepted ritual and the forum of the individualist. While its classically derived title, *theater*, simply indicates that it is a " seeing-place," its homelier English name, *playhouse*, comes closer to defining its relation to the art of the drama. It is a housing for a play, a home, with all the comforts and discomforts of its domestic counterpart.

Because the playhouse of Thespis was the circular threshing floor around which the audience stood, his play was designed to keep the principal actors in the center, where they would be equally visible to all the spectators. Since a curtain was an impossibility in such a playhouse, the playwright had to take into consideration the problems of getting all his actors on and all his actors off the stage; since the ritual nature of the dithyramb insisted on the presence *throughout* of the chorus and its leader, the kinds of situations and the nature of the action selected had to conform to this fixed condition: inevitably the dramatic scenes would tend to be investigations, debates, conflicts of will. In such a way the primitive Greek playhouse may be said to control the playwright's work.

The medieval cathedral, on the other hand, permitted or encouraged quite another sort of playwrighting. Rectangular in shape, and generally of great length, it welcomed movement, not just to the center, but from place to place. The physical act of seeking was as well adapted to this housing as verbal debate to the Greek circular playing area. The medieval playwright, then, was well advised to make much use of physical movement in telling his stories, and later, but still very early, plays would deal with the journey of the shepherds to Bethlehem, the coming of the wise men and the flight into Egypt, while the action of the oldest surviving Greek play (half a century after Thespis) is confined to a chorus of young ladies seeking protection of a king and his decision to grant their request.

Any playhouse, of course, whether Greek or Christian, is more than the restricting, enclosing walls. The playwright will see it as composed of two main parts, the stage or acting area and the auditorium or spectator's area, each of which provides its special tools for and obstacles to communication. Much of the nature of the playwright's work will depend upon whether or not the stage is equipped with scenery, and whether the scenery is representational or non-representational. The machinery of the stage will also enter into his work — the facilities for the changing of settings, for example, trap doors and elevators, devices for the imitation of fire, clouds, running water. In the modern theater playwrights have learned how to do much with the illustrative and suggestive power of electric lighting, but even the Greeks made dramatic use of the effects possible from natural light.

Compared to his use of the stage, the playwright's use of the auditorium will be subtler, perhaps almost unconscious. Yet even the most basic architectural conditions will influence him: Is the theater roofed, or open to the elements? Does the audience stand, or is it provided with seats? Beyond that he must consider the very hour of day at which his audience assembles. Greek plays began at dawn on a holiday. Modern plays begin after supper and the audience assembles after a full day's work. And so it is that a play written for one type of stage and auditorium emerges as a radically different work when presented in a different " housing."

Player

The second of the playwright's tools is the actor, the player. The group of singers and dancers performing the ancient dithyramb were actors insofar as they felt themselves to be impersonating the followers of a god. But it was not until Thespis took them in hand that they became players in the full meaning of the term. In his primitive play, they not only imitated persons, but persons whom he had involved in an action, persons directed to do something. Perhaps the clearest way to indicate the difference is to consider the Greek terms for the various participants. The singers and dancers were called a chorus — that is, a *group*. The priest was called choragus, *leader* of the group. But Thespis, when he entered the scene, was called an hypokritos, that is, *response-giver*. The actor is not a narrator, but a man who asks questions, who gives answers, who takes a stand. He might more correctly and completely be called a *reactor*. The dithyramb performers simply present a situation; the actor does something as the result of the situation in which he finds himself.

Thus too in the *Quem Quaeritis*. As priests, the performers were accustomed to presenting the situation to their congregations in narrative. As players, they were instructed by the medieval playwright to put themselves into the situation and react to it. The reaction, however, was not left to their own fancy. As instruments of the playwright, they were directed first to step delicately as those who seek something. When they met the angel they were provided with precise words for speaking and a defined reaction to the angel's replies. From the very beginning of playing, in both the classical and the modern world, the actor was not a free agent, but a tool of the playwright, to be manipulated to create the dramatic experience he desired.

Play

These then are the non-literary tools of the playwright: the playhouse with its stage and machinery and auditorium, and the players. The literary tools of the play itself will be more familiar to the experienced reader, yet they also must be considered for their special function in creating the dramatic experience. Like any narrative, a play is based upon a plot, but what the audience sees is never an orderly — that is to say, historical or chronological — presentation of the plot. Instead the playwright selects certain incidents from the total plot to be enacted before the spectators by his players. The remainder of the total plot may be revealed, as much or as little as suits his purpose, in narrative, reminiscence, report, or, when the matter is familiar to the spectators, by suggestion.

Thus even the simplest and briefest of plays may be based on a plot of great complexity. In the description of the dithyramb something was said of the career of Dionysos. When Thespis came to compose his "play," he chose only one incident from that career, the humbling of Pentheus, to reveal to the audience. It is a brief, horrible, almost melodramatic incident. Yet underlying it, giving it stature and significance, is the whole biography of Dionysos, his divine birth, his sufferings, his mission. A second glance at the text shows how the playwright reminded his audience of the past from which the presented incident achieves its meaning: through passages of *exposition* disguised as ritual hymns or as a kind of sermon of the priest to the flock, and in the self-justification of the hero himself. In the *Quem Quaeritis* the exposition is merely suggested. Given the cathedral setting and an audience instructed over many centuries in the stories of the Christian church, it is enough for the playwright to hint, " He is risen, *as it was foretold.*" The expository clause would bring into the mind of the spectator a flood of recollections attesting the wonder of the mystery of Christ. As the drama becomes more sophisticated, as it employs more and more unfamiliar materials (" original plots "), exposition becomes one of the major technical problems of the playwright, and his skill in solving it, in making the exposition an organic part of his work, is a partial measure of his stature as an artist.

Action

Most of the attempts at a definition of drama have turned on its most spectacular element, action. Yet it is not always clear what the term *action* has meant to the definers. While it is obviously possible, and perhaps necessary in the light of the future development of dramatic art, to complicate the meaning of the term and invest it with subtleties, it will be useful as a beginning to attempt a definition on the basis of the two primitive plays already cited.

Action, as opposed to narrative or exposition, means movement performed in a special acting area by specially selected players. It involves impersonation by the players, and agreement on the part of the audience to accept the impersonated movement as a valid means of communication of either a story or an idea, or both. It is not, therefore, idle bustle or movement for its own sake, but movement for the purpose of communication. It is planned, proportioned, and directed for (as the older books of rhetoric used to say) unity, coherence, and emphasis. The playwright creates dramatic action by a selection of incidents from the whole plot and their arrangement into a pattern for impersonation or imitation to serve as a vehicle for his *central idea* or *theme.*

Consider how carefully this has been done by the medieval author of the simplest of Christian plays. His central idea is exultation or rejoicing that the divinity of Christ has been demonstrated, that He is the Savior foretold by the prophets of the Old Testament. Out of all the possible incidents available to him in which the divinity of Christ is suggested, he chooses the moment when the Three Marys approach the tomb of their dead leader — three women, believers and followers, who have come to pay a last tribute to the death of their hopes. Forlornly they move towards the altar, seeking. Wondering, they behold the angel and answer his question (with some courage, considering the circumstances under which the Crucifixion had taken place). But as the angel exhibits the empty grave and empty grave-clothes, their certainty is restored, their faith renewed. Directed to go and tell the news far and wide, they turn to the choir, and the triumphant " Alleluia! " projects their faith and rejoicing to the whole congregation.

This is not, of course, either reality or history. Historical events almost never achieve the simplicity and directness of this incident — and if they do, they are generally labelled dramatic. The missteps and fumblings by the way, the incidental matters that so complicate the simplest of human actions, are ruthlessly eliminated. The playwright sticks steadily to his business, selecting and arranging his facts to create the most unified, coherent, and emphatic presentation of his action, both in the words he assigns his chosen players and the gestures and actions he directs them to employ.

One other quality of dramatic action will be apparent in these early examples. The element of movement has been emphasized in the definition. But dramatic movement, while it includes the entrance and exit of characters and the " seeking " of the Three Marys, has a more general and important aspect. In distinguishing the function of Thespis as an actor from the priest as a choragus, it was pointed out that the actor does not simply exist or narrate, he reacts. The situation at the beginning of a play is more or less fixed — the followers of Dionysos, defying the agnosticism of their king, worshipping their god; the Three Marys preparing to perform the final obsequies for their dead Master — as fixed as the atoms in a chemical element. The actor is a reagent introduced into this fixed element or situation. The situation is at once disturbed, destroyed, or reoriented. The essence of dramatic action is change, and the audience is kept constantly aware of this movement away from one arrangement towards others whose pattern cannot always be anticipated. Dramatic action is constantly " in process," it is " becoming," and it is in this way also that it presents a full and lively image of man's experience.

As the playwright selects and arranges a series of dramatic actions involving change and development as the vehicle for his understanding of life to be performed by players in a given playhouse, he is using all the tools of his craft to hold the mirror up to nature and provide his audiences with a dramatic experience.

Ghosts: A Preliminary Word

Before we can develop our discussion of some of the dramatist's tools defined in the first chapter, we shall need a full-length play to provide exemplary material. *Ghosts*, more precisely titled *Those Who Walk Again*, is a play of great intrinsic interest with a gripping story and a central idea that has not dulled with the passing years. It is also the work of one of the master craftsmen of the modern realistic theater and provides an excellent point of reference for almost any aspect of technique or structure.

Begin by reading the play twice, for it is only with the second reading that the critical process can start to function. The first time, you will be reading for the story, to find out what happens. The second time, with your knowledge of what happens, of " how it all comes out," you can observe the pattern of the play, the selection and arrangement of incidents. This structure is the clue to the meaning the author intends to put in the story he is telling.

Read slowly. A play is a work of great economy; every word, every action must do full duty in revealing the playwright's meaning.

Try your best to visualize the stage setting, the appearance of the characters, their movements about the stage. Ibsen, like most modern playwrights, assists the reader by furnishing specific details and descriptions as clues.

At the end of the text you will find a series of questions. When you have finished your first reading, try to answer the questions before rereading the play; they will help you to sharpen your reactions and focus your attention on dramatic essentials as you reread.

Ghosts, Act III. See page 52. Alla Nazimova as Mrs. Alving, Harry Ellerbe as Oswald. Photo by Vandamm.

GHOSTS

A DOMESTIC DRAMA IN THREE ACTS

by Henrik Ibsen

ᶦᵗᵗ

CHARACTERS

REGINA ENGSTRAND, *Mrs. Alving's companion*
JACOB ENGSTRAND, *a carpenter*
PASTOR MANDERS
MRS. HELENE ALVING, *widow of Captain Alving*
OSWALD ALVING, *her son, a painter*

The action takes place in Mrs. Alving's country home near one of the large fjords in the west of Norway.

Setting. A large room, looking on a garden, with a door in the left wall and two doors in the right. In the middle of the room, a round table with chairs set about it; on the table are books, magazines, and newspapers. At the left front, a window and a small sofa with a sewing table placed before it. At the back of the room an open, somewhat narrower solarium, enclosed by glass set in large panes. To the right of the solarium there is a door leading into the garden. The glass windows reveal a barren, rocky landscape, obscured by a steady rain.

ACT ONE

[Scene I] (*Carpenter* ENGSTRAND *comes in through the door from the garden. His left leg is slightly deformed; the sole of his boot is built up.* REGINA, *with an empty watering pot in her hand, prevents him from coming farther into the room.*)

REGINA. (*Sharply*) What do you want? Stand right where you are. It is positively dripping off you.

ENGSTRAND. This is God's own rain, my child.

REGINA. It's the devil's rain, that's what it is.

ENGSTRAND. Lord! How you talk, Regina. (*Limps a step closer*) What I wanted to say was this —

REGINA. Don't clump so with that foot of yours, man. The young master is asleep upstairs.

ENGSTRAND. Asleep? In the middle of the day?

REGINA. It's none of your business.

ENGSTRAND. I was out on a spree last night —

REGINA. *That* I can believe.

ENGSTRAND. — Yes, for we men are weak, my child —

REGINA. (*Ironically*) Yes, *we* certainly are.

ENGSTRAND. — and temptations are manifold in this world, you see. But all the same,

19

God knows I was hard at work at half-past five this morning.

REGINA. Yes, yes, of course, of course. Now go away; I will not stand here and have *rendezvous* with you.

ENGSTRAND. What is it you won't have?

REGINA. I won't have anyone find you here, so just run along about your business.

ENGSTRAND. (*Limps into the room a few steps.*) Damned if I go before I've had a talk with you. This afternoon I will be finished with my work down at the schoolhouse, and then I'll take the steamer and be off to the city tonight.

REGINA. (*Mutters*) Have a nice trip.

ENGSTRAND. Thank you, my child. To-morrow the Orphanage is to be opened, and then there'll be fancy doings, and plenty of good strong drinks, I don't doubt. And no-body can say of Jacob Engstrand that he can't keep himself out of the way of tempta-tion.

REGINA. Hoh!

ENGSTRAND. You see, there are going to be any number of big guns here tomorrow. Pastor Manders is expected from the city.

REGINA. He's coming today.

ENGSTRAND. There! You see. And I'll be damned careful that he doesn't find out any-thing against me, you can bet.

REGINA. Oh! So that's your game.

ENGSTRAND. My game?

REGINA. (*Looks at him, coldly*) What trick are you going to play on Pastor Manders?

ENGSTRAND. Hush! Hush! Are you crazy? Would *I* want to play any trick on Pastor Manders? Oh, no! Pastor Manders has been far too kind to me for that. But I just wanted to tell you, you know — that I mean to start off for home again tonight.

REGINA. The sooner the better, as far as I am concerned.

ENGSTRAND. Yes. But I want to take you with me, Regina.

REGINA. (*Open-mouthed*) You want me — ? What are you saying?

ENGSTRAND. I said, I want to take you home.

REGINA. (*Scornfully*) Never in this world will you get me in your home.

ENGSTRAND. We'll see about that.

REGINA. We certainly will see about it. I, who have been brought up by a lady like Mrs. Alving! I, who am treated almost as a daughter here! Do you suppose I'm going home with you — to a house like yours? Not likely!

ENGSTRAND. What the devil do you mean? Are you setting yourself up against your fa-ther, girl?

REGINA. (*Without looking at him*) You've said often enough that I was no child of yours.

ENGSTRAND. (*Crosses toward* REGINA) Stuff! Why should you bother about that?

REGINA. Haven't you sworn at me many a time and called me a — *Fidonc!*

ENGSTRAND. Curse me now, if I ever used such an ugly word.

REGINA. Oh! I know well enough what word you used.

ENGSTRAND. Well, but — that was only when I was a bit — hmm. Temptations are manifold in this world, Regina.

REGINA. Ugh!

ENGSTRAND. And when your mother got up on her high horse, I had to find some way of taking her down. She was always setting up as a fine lady. (*Mimics her*) " Let me go, Jacob; let me be. Remember, *I've* been three years in Chamberlain Alving's family at Ro-senvold." (*Laughs*) Damn! She never could forget that the Captain was made a Cham-berlain while she was in service here.

REGINA. Poor mother! You worried her into her grave fast enough.

ENGSTRAND. (*Swinging round*) Oh, sure, I'm to blame for everything.

REGINA. (*Turns away again, half-aside*) Ugh! And that leg, too!

ENGSTRAND. What did you say, girl?

REGINA. *Pied de mouton.*

ENGSTRAND. Is that English, too?

REGINA. Yes.

ENGSTRAND. Oh, you've picked up some learning out here; maybe that'll come in use-ful now, Regina.

REGINA. (*After a short pause*) What do you want with me in town?

ENGSTRAND. Can you ask what a father can want with his only child? Am I not a lonely and forsaken widower?

REGINA. Don't try any nonsense like that. Why did you want me?

ENGSTRAND. Well, I'll tell you: I've been thinking of taking up a new line of business.

REGINA. (*Contemptuously*) You've tried that often enough, and much good has ever come out of it.

ENGSTRAND. Yes, but this time you'll see, Regina! — I've put aside a very tidy little pile from this Orphanage job.

REGINA. Have you? That's good.

ENGSTRAND. Well, how could a man spend his money in this isolated hole?

REGINA. Well, what of it?

ENGSTRAND. So, you see, I thought of investing the money in some paying proposition. I thought of a sort of *sailor's tavern* —

REGINA. Horrid!

ENGSTRAND. Oh, a regular high-class affair, of course; not a low pigsty for common sailors. No! By God, it would be for captains and mates, and — and — the very best people, you understand.

REGINA. And I was to — ?

ENGSTRAND. You are to help, sure. But only for the sake of appearances, you understand. Not a bit of hard work for you, my girl. You shall do exactly as you like.

REGINA. Oh, indeed!

ENGSTRAND. But there must be a skirt in the house. That's as plain as day. For I want to have it lively in the evening, with singing and dancing and the like. You must remember they are weary wanderers on the ocean of life. (*Nearer*) Now don't be foolish and stand in your own way, Regina. What can become of you here? What good is it to you that your mistress has taught you a lot of things? I hear you're supposed to look after the children in the new Orphanage. Is that the sort of thing for you? Huh? Are you so dead set on wearing yourself out for a pack of dirty brats?

REGINA. No, if things go as I want them to, then — well, there's no telling.

ENGSTRAND. What do you mean by " There's no telling "?

REGINA. Never you mind. — Is it a great deal of money you've saved up?

ENGSTRAND. What with one thing and another, a matter of seven or eight hundred crowns.

REGINA. That's not bad.

ENGSTRAND. It's enough to make a start with, my child.

REGINA. Are you thinking of giving me any of that money?

ENGSTRAND. No, I'm damned if I am!

REGINA. (*Rises and takes a few steps towards him*) Not even sending me a scrap of stuff for a new dress?

ENGSTRAND. If you'll come to town with me, you'll soon get dresses enough.

REGINA. Pooh! I can do that on my own if I want to.

ENGSTRAND. No, a father's guiding hand is what you want, Regina. Now, I've got my eye on a tidy house in Little Harbor Street. I won't need much ready money, and it could be sort of a sailor's home, you know.

REGINA. But I will *not* live with you. I will have nothing whatever to do with you. So be off!

ENGSTRAND. You wouldn't remain long with me, my girl. No such luck! If you knew how to play your cards, such a fine big girl as you've become in the last year or two —

REGINA. Well?

ENGSTRAND. It wouldn't be long before some mate came your way, or it might even be a captain —

REGINA. I won't marry anyone of that sort. Sailors have no *savoir vivre*.

ENGSTRAND. What haven't they got?

REGINA. I know what sailors are, I tell you. They're not the sort of people to marry.

ENGSTRAND. Then never mind about marrying them. You can make it pay all the same. The Englishman — the man with the yacht — he gave three hundred crowns, he did; and she wasn't a bit handsomer than you are.

REGINA. Get out — get out of here! Get out, I tell you! (*Forcing him to the garden door*) And don't bang the doors. Young Mr. Alving —

ENGSTRAND. Yes, I know, he's asleep. It's funny how you bother about young Mr. Alving. (*He speaks more softly.*) Oh, it's him, is it —

REGINA. Be off, and quickly! You're crazy, I tell you! No, don't go that way. There comes Pastor Manders. Here, go down through the kitchen stairs.

ENGSTRAND. (*Is talking as he goes*) Yes, yes, I'm going. But just you talk to the Pastor there. He's the man to tell you what a child owes to its father. For I am your father, all the same, you know. I can prove it from the church register. (*He goes out by the door* REGINA *has opened and now closes behind him.* REGINA *glances at herself hastily in the mirror, fans herself with a handkerchief, adjusts the collar of her uniform. Then she resumes watering the flowers.*)

[Scene II]   (PASTOR MANDERS, *in an overcoat, with an umbrella, a small travelling kit hanging from his shoulder, comes through the garden door into the solarium.*)

PASTOR MANDERS. How do you do, Miss Engstrand?

REGINA. (*Pretending to be surprised and pleased*) Oh, how do you do, Pastor Manders? Is the steamer in already?

PASTOR MANDERS. (*Coming into the room*) It's just in. Terrible weather we've been having lately.

REGINA. (*Following him*) It's such blessed weather for the country, sir.

PASTOR MANDERS. Yes, you are quite right. We townspeople think too little about that. (*He starts to take off his coat.*)

REGINA. Oh, let me help you. There! How wet it is! I'll just hang it up in the hall. (*She takes* MANDERS' *things up Left to the hall and hangs them up.*) And your umbrella, too. I'll open it and let it dry. (*She takes the things out through the second door on the Right.* PASTOR MANDERS *takes off his kit and places it and his hat on the table.* REGINA *returns.*)

PASTOR MANDERS. It's a comfort to get safe under cover. Tell me, is all going well?

REGINA. Yes, thank you, sir.

PASTOR MANDERS. You have your hands full, I suppose, in preparation for tomorrow.

REGINA. Yes, there's plenty to do, of course.

PASTOR MANDERS. And Mrs. Alving is at home, I trust?

REGINA. Oh, yes. She's upstairs taking the young master his chocolate.

PASTOR MANDERS. Yes, I heard down at the pier that Oswald had arrived.

REGINA. Yes, he came the day before yesterday. We didn't expect him until today.

PASTOR MANDERS. Quite strong and well, I hope?

REGINA. Yes, thank you, quite; but dreadfully tired with the journey. He came straight from Paris. I believe he came all the way in one train. He is sleeping a little now; so perhaps we'd better talk a little quietly.

PASTOR MANDERS. All right! As quietly as you please.

REGINA. (*Arranging a chair for* MANDERS *beside the table*) Now do sit down Pastor Manders, and make yourself comfortable. (*He sits; she places a stool under his feet.*) There! Is that better, sir?

PASTOR MANDERS. Much, thank you. (*Looking at her closely*) Do you know, Miss Engstrand, I really think you have grown since I last saw you.

REGINA. Do you think so, sir? Mrs. Alving says my figure has filled out, too.

PASTOR MANDERS. Filled out? Well, perhaps a little; just enough. (*There is a short pause.*)

REGINA. Shall I tell Mrs. Alving you are here?

PASTOR MANDERS. Thanks, thanks, there's no hurry, my dear child. By the bye, Regina, my good girl, tell me, how is your father getting along out here?

REGINA. Oh, thank you, he is getting on well enough.

PASTOR MANDERS. He came to see me last time he was in town.

REGINA. Did he, indeed? He's always so glad of a chance to talk with the pastor.

PASTOR MANDERS. And you look in upon him at his work during the day?

REGINA. Oh, of course, when I have time, I —

PASTOR MANDERS. Your father is not a man of strong character, Miss Engstrand. He needs a guiding hand.

REGINA. Oh, yes; that's certainly so.

PASTOR MANDERS. He needs to have someone near him whom he cares for, and whose judgment he has confidence in. He frankly admitted that when he came to see me.

REGINA. Yes, he has said something like that to me. But I don't know whether Mrs. Alving can spare me — especially now, when we have the Orphanage to manage. And then I should be so sorry to leave Mrs. Alving; she has always been so kind to me.

PASTOR MANDERS. But a daughter's duty, my good girl — . Of course, we must first get your mistress's consent.

REGINA. But I don't know whether it would be quite proper for me, at my age, to keep house for a single man.

PASTOR MANDERS. What! My dear Miss Engstrand! We are talking about your own father.

REGINA. Yes, that may be, but all the same — . Now if it was in a *respectable* house, and with a real gentleman —

PASTOR MANDERS. But, my dear Regina —

REGINA. — one I could really love and respect, and take the place of a daughter —

PASTOR MANDERS. Yes, but my dear good girl —

REGINA. Then I should be glad to go to town. Out here it's very lonely and you know yourself, Pastor, what it is to be alone in the world. And I can say this for myself: I am both quick and willing. Don't you know of any such place for me, Pastor?

PASTOR MANDERS. No, I certainly do not.

REGINA. But, dear, dear Pastor, do remember me if —

PASTOR MANDERS. (*Getting up*) Yes, yes, certainly, Miss Engstrand.

REGINA. For if I —

PASTOR MANDERS. Will you be so good as to tell your mistress I am here?

REGINA. I will at once, sir. (*She goes out, Left.*)

[Scene III]   PASTOR MANDERS. (*Takes a few steps up and down the room, stands a moment at the windows looking out into the garden with his hands clasped behind his back. Then he returns to the table, takes up a book and looks at the title page, starts, and looks at several more.*) Hm! — yes, a-ha!

(MRS. ALVING *enters from the Left.* REGINA *follows her, crossing the room and going out through the first door on the Right.*)

MRS. ALVING. (*Shaking his hand*) Welcome, my dear Pastor.

PASTOR MANDERS. How do you do, Mrs. Alving? Here I am, as I promised.

MRS. ALVING. Always punctual to the minute.

PASTOR MANDERS. You may well believe it wasn't so easy for me to get away. With all the boards and committees I belong to —

MRS. ALVING. That makes it all the kinder of you to come so early. Now we can settle our business before dinner. But where is your luggage?

PASTOR MANDERS. (*Quickly*) I left it down at the inn. I shall stay there tonight.

MRS. ALVING. (*Suppresses a smile*) Can't I persuade you, even now, to pass the night under my roof?

PASTOR MANDERS. No, no, Mrs. Alving; but many thanks just the same. I shall stay down there as usual. It's so convenient for starting again.

MRS. ALVING. Well, you must have your own way. But I really should have thought that we two old people —

PASTOR MANDERS. Now you're making fun of me. Ah! To be sure! This is a joyful day for you. You have got tomorrow's festival to look forward to and then you have got Oswald home again.

MRS. ALVING. Yes, you don't know what a delight it is to me. It is more than two years since he was home. And now he has promised to stay with me all winter.

PASTOR MANDERS. Has he really? That's very thoughtful of him. For I can well believe that life in Rome and Paris offers many more attractions.

MRS. ALVING. True. But here at home he has his mother, you see. My own boy, he hasn't forgotten his love for his mother.

PASTOR MANDERS. It would be sad indeed, if absence and working at art and that sort of thing were to blunt his natural feelings.

MRS. ALVING. Yes, you may well say so. But there is nothing of that sort to fear in him. I am quite curious to see if you will recognize him now. He will be down soon. He's upstairs now, resting a little on the sofa. But do sit down, my dear Pastor.

PASTOR MANDERS. Thank you. Then it's quite convenient for you?

MRS. ALVING. Certainly. (*She sits by the table.*)

PASTOR MANDERS. Very well. Then you shall see — (*He goes up to the chair where his case is lying, takes out papers, sits down on the opposite side of the table and looks for a place for his papers.*) Now, to begin with, here is — . Tell me, Mrs. Alving, how do these books come to be here?

MRS. ALVING. These books? They are books I am reading.

PASTOR MANDERS. Do you read this sort of literature?

MRS. ALVING. Certainly I do.

PASTOR MANDERS. Do you feel yourself better or happier for such reading?

MRS. ALVING. I feel that I become, so to speak, more self-reliant.

PASTOR MANDERS. That's strange. How is that?

MRS. ALVING. Well, I seem to find explanation and confirmation of all sorts of things I have been thinking about. For that is really the wonderful part of it, Pastor Manders; there is nothing new in these books, nothing but what most people think and believe. Only most people don't formulate it to themselves or else keep quiet about it.

PASTOR MANDERS. Great heavens! Do you really believe that most people —

MRS. ALVING. I do, indeed.

PASTOR MANDERS. But surely not in this country? Not here with us?

MRS. ALVING. Yes, certainly, with us, too.

PASTOR MANDERS. Well, I really must say —

MRS. ALVING. But what do you object to in these books?

PASTOR MANDERS. Object to? You surely don't believe I waste my time studying such publications?

MRS. ALVING. Then you don't really know what you are condemning?

PASTOR MANDERS. I have read enough *about* these books to disapprove of them.

MRS. ALVING. Yes, but your own opinion —

PASTOR MANDERS. My dear Mrs. Alving, there are many occasions in life where one must rely upon others. It is so in this world; and it is a good thing. How could society get on otherwise?

MRS. ALVING. Well, there you may have a point.

PASTOR MANDERS. Besides I, of course, do not deny that there may be much that is interesting in such books. And I can hardly blame you for wishing to keep up with the intellectual movements which are said to be going on in the outside world — where you have permitted your son to pass so much of his life. But —

MRS. ALVING. But — ?

PASTOR MANDERS. (*Lowering his voice*) But one doesn't talk about that, Mrs. Alving. One is hardly called upon to account to the public for what one reads, or what one thinks within his own four walls.

MRS. ALVING. No, certainly; I believe that, too.

PASTOR MANDERS. Only think of the consideration you owe this Orphanage, which you decided to build at a time when your thoughts about such things were very different from your present ones — as far as I can judge.

MRS. ALVING. Yes, yes, that I freely admit. But — it was about the Orphanage —

PASTOR MANDERS. Oh, yes, it was about the Orphanage we were to speak. All I say is: Prudence, my dear lady! And now we'll get to business. (*He opens his case, removes a number of papers.*) Do you see these?

MRS. ALVING. The documents?

PASTOR MANDERS. All — and in perfect order. I can tell you it was hard work to get them in time. I had to put on strong pressure. The authorities are almost painfully scrupulous when you want them to come to the point. But here they are at last. (*He leafs through the papers.*) Here is the formal deed of gift of the parcel of ground known as Solvik in the Manor of Rosenvold, with all the newly constructed buildings, schoolrooms, master's house, and chapel. And here is the legal sanction for the endowment and for the regulations of the institution. Will you look at them? (*Reads:*) " Regulations for the Children's Home to be known as ' Captain Alving's Memorial.' "

MRS. ALVING. (*Looks at the paper for a long time.*) So there it is.

PASTOR MANDERS. I have chosen the name " Captain " rather than " Chamberlain." Captain looks less ostentatious.

MRS. ALVING. Yes, yes, as you think best.

PASTOR MANDERS. And here you have the bank account showing the capital amount and the interest which covers the current expenses of the Orphanage.

MRS. ALVING. Thank you; but you keep it — it will be more convenient.

PASTOR MANDERS. With pleasure. I think we will leave the money in the bank for the present. The interest is certainly not what we could wish — four percent, and six months' notice of withdrawal. Perhaps a good mortgage and an undoubted security — then we could consider the matter.

MRS. ALVING. Certainly, my dear Pastor. You are the best judge of these things.

PASTOR MANDERS. I will keep my eyes open anyway. But now — there is one more thing I have always meant to ask you.

MRS. ALVING. And what is that?

PASTOR MANDERS. Shall the Orphanage buildings be insured or not?

MRS. ALVING. Of course they must be insured.

PASTOR MANDERS. But just a moment, Mrs. Alving. Let's look into the matter a little more closely.

MRS. ALVING. I have everything of mine insured: buildings, and livestock, and crops.

PASTOR MANDERS. Of course you have — on your own estate. And so have I, naturally. But this, you see, is quite another matter. The Orphanage is to be consecrated, as it were, to a higher purpose.

MRS. ALVING. Yes, but that's no reason —

PASTOR MANDERS. For my own part, I should not see the smallest impropriety in guarding against all eventualities —

MRS. ALVING. I should think not.

PASTOR MANDERS. — but how would the people here, your neighbors, feel about it? You, of course, know better than I.

MRS. ALVING. H'm — the general feeling —

PASTOR MANDERS. Is there any considerable number of responsible people — really responsible — who might be shocked?

MRS. ALVING. What do you mean by really responsible people?

PASTOR MANDERS. Well, I mean people in such independent and influential positions that one cannot ignore their opinion.

MRS. ALVING. There are several people of that sort here who would very likely be shocked if —

PASTOR MANDERS. That's just it. There are many like that in the town. Think of my colleagues alone, and their congregations. People who would be only too ready to interpret our actions as signs that neither you nor I had the right faith in a higher Providence.

MRS. ALVING. But so far as we are concerned, my dear Pastor, you have, at least, the consciousness that —

PASTOR MANDERS. Yes, I know — I know; my conscience will be quite easy, that is true enough. But nevertheless, we should not escape grave misunderstanding. And that might react unfavorably upon the Orphanage, and restrict its usefulness.

MRS. ALVING. Well, in that case then —

PASTOR MANDERS. Nor can I lose sight of the difficult — I may even say painful — position I might get into. In the best circles of the town. People are much interested in the Orphanage. It is founded for the benefit of the town, as well as the country; and it is to be hoped it will considerably lighten our tax for the poor. But since I have been your advisor, and have had control of the business matters, I'm afraid the zealous believers will first and foremost direct their attacks against *me* —

MRS. ALVING. Oh! You mustn't run the risk of that.

PASTOR MANDERS. — Not to speak of the attacks that would undoubtedly be made upon me in certain papers and periodicals, which —

MRS. ALVING. Enough, my dear Pastor Manders. That quite decides it.

PASTOR MANDERS. Then you do not wish the Orphanage insured?

MRS. ALVING. No.

PASTOR MANDERS. (*Leans back in his chair.*) But if a misfortune *were* to happen? Such a thing *can*, of course, occur — would you be able to make good the damage?

MRS. ALVING. No; I tell you plainly, I should do nothing of the kind.

PASTOR MANDERS. Then I must tell you, Mrs. Alving — it is really no small responsibility we are taking upon ourselves.

MRS. ALVING. But do you think we *can* do anything else?

PASTOR MANDERS. No, that's just the thing; we really can't do otherwise. We must not expose ourselves to false interpretation; and we have no right whatever to give offense to our neighbors.

MRS. ALVING. You, as a clergyman, certainly should not.

PASTOR MANDERS. And I really think, too, we may trust that an institution of this kind has good fortune on its side — yes, that it stands under a special Providence.

MRS. ALVING. Let us hope so, Pastor Manders.

PASTOR MANDERS. Shall we consider the matter settled then?

MRS. ALVING. Yes, I believe we may.

PASTOR MANDERS. Good. As you will. (*Writes.*) So — no insurance.

MRS. ALVING. It is rather curious that you should just happen to mention the matter today —

PASTOR MANDERS. I have often thought of asking you about it —

MRS. ALVING. — For we very nearly had a fire down there yesterday.

PASTOR MANDERS. You don't say so.

MRS. ALVING. Oh, it was of no importance. A heap of shavings caught fire in the carpenter's workshop.

PASTOR MANDERS. Where Engstrand works?

MRS. ALVING. Yes. He's often very careless with matches, they tell me.

PASTOR MANDERS. He has so many things in his head, that man — so many temptations. Thank God, he is now striving to lead a decent life, I hear.

MRS. ALVING. Indeed! Who says so?

PASTOR MANDERS. He himself assures me of it. And he is certainly an excellent workman.

MRS. ALVING. Oh, yes; so long as he is sober —

PASTOR MANDERS. Yes, that's a sad weakness. But he is often driven to it by his bad leg, he says. Last time he was in town I was really touched by him. He came to me and thanked me so warmly for having got him work here, so that he might be near Regina.

MRS. ALVING. He doesn't see much of her.

PASTOR MANDERS. Oh, yes. He has a talk with her every day. He told me so himself.

MRS. ALVING. Yes, yes. Perhaps.

PASTOR MANDERS. He feels so clearly that he needs someone to hold him back when temptation comes. That is what I can't help liking about Jacob Engstrand; he comes to you helplessly, accusing himself and confessing his own weakness. The last time he was talking to me — Mrs. Alving — suppose it were a real necessity for him to have Regina home again —

MRS. ALVING. Regina!

PASTOR MANDERS. — You must not set yourself against it.

MRS. ALVING. Indeed, I shall set myself against it. And besides, Regina is to have a position in the Orphanage.

PASTOR MANDERS. But after all, remember he's her father —

MRS. ALVING. I know quite well what sort of father he has been to her. No! She shall never go to him with my consent.

PASTOR MANDERS. (*Crosses to her.*) My dear lady, don't take the matter so warmly. You misjudge Engstrand sadly. You seem to be quite alarmed —

MRS. ALVING. (*More quietly*) It doesn't matter. I have taken Regina into my house, and there she shall stay. (*Listens.*) Hush, my dear Pastor Manders; don't say any more about it. (*Her face lights up with happiness.*) Listen! There is Oswald coming downstairs. Now we will think of no one but him.

[Scene IV] (OSWALD ALVING, *in a light overcoat, with hat in hand and smoking a large meerschaum pipe, comes into the room through the door on the Left.*)

OSWALD. (*In the door*) Oh! I beg your pardon; I thought you were in the study. (*Moving in*) Good afternoon, Pastor Manders.

PASTOR MANDERS. (*Seems slightly amazed.*) Ah —! How strange —!

MRS. ALVING. Well, what do you say to this young man, Mr. Manders?

PASTOR MANDERS. I say — I say — why! Is it really — ?

OSWALD. Yes, it is really the Prodigal Son, sir.

PASTOR MANDERS. My dear young friend —

OSWALD. Well, then, the reclaimed son.

MRS. ALVING. Oswald is thinking of the time when you were so much opposed to his being a painter.

PASTOR MANDERS. To our human eyes many a step seems dubious which afterwards proves — (*They shake hands.*) Anyhow, welcome, welcome home. Why, my dear Oswald — I suppose I may call you by your Christian name?

OSWALD. Yes; what else would you call me?

PASTOR MANDERS. Very good. What I wanted to say was this, my dear Oswald — you must not believe that I utterly condemn the artist's calling. I have no doubt there are many who can keep their inner self unharmed in that profession, as in any other.

OSWALD. Let us hope so.

MRS. ALVING. (*Beaming with delight*) I know one who has kept both his inner and outer self unharmed. Just look at him, Mr. Manders.

OSWALD. (*Moves restlessly across the floor.*) Yes, yes, Mother; let's say no more about it.

PASTOR MANDERS. Why, certainly — it can't be denied. And you have begun to make a name for yourself, already. The newspapers have often spoken of you, and most favorably. By the bye, just lately they haven't mentioned you so often.

OSWALD. (*Near the flowers*) I have not been able to paint so much lately.

MRS. ALVING. Even a painter needs a little rest now and then.

PASTOR MANDERS. I can quite believe it. And, meanwhile, he can be gathering his forces and preparing himself for some great work.

OSWALD. Yes. Mother, will dinner soon be ready?

MRS. ALVING. In less than half an hour. He has a good appetite, thank God.

PASTOR MANDERS. And a taste for tobacco, too.

OSWALD. I found my father's pipe in my room and so —

PASTOR MANDERS. Aha! Then that accounts for it.

MRS. ALVING. For what?

PASTOR MANDERS. When Oswald stood there in the hallway, with the pipe in his mouth, I could have sworn I saw his father, large as life.

Oswald. No, really?

Mrs. Alving. Oh! How can you say so? Oswald takes after me.

Pastor Manders. Yes, but there is an expression about the corners of the mouth — something about the lips that reminds one exactly of Alving; at any rate, now that he is smoking.

Mrs. Alving. Not in the least. Oswald has rather a clerical curve about his mouth, I think.

Pastor Manders. Yes, yes; some of my colleagues do have much the same look.

Mrs. Alving. But put your pipe away, my dear; I don't permit smoking in here.

Oswald. (*Puts the pipe in his pocket.*) With pleasure. I only wanted to try it; because I smoked it once when I was a child.

Mrs. Alving. You?

Oswald. Yes. I was quite small at the time. I remember I came up to Father's room one evening when he was in high spirits.

Mrs. Alving. Oh! You can't remember anything about those days.

Oswald. Yes. I remember distinctly. He took me up on his knee and gave me the pipe. " Smoke, boy," he said. " Smoke away, boy." And I smoked as hard as I could until I felt I was going quite pale, and the perspiration stood out in great drops on my forehead. Then he burst out laughing heartily —

Pastor Manders. That was most extraordinary.

Mrs. Alving. My dear friend, it was only something Oswald has dreamt.

Oswald. No, Mother, I assure you I haven't dreamt it. For — don't you remember? — you came and carried me out into the nursery. Then I was sick, and I saw that you were crying. Did Father often play such pranks?

Pastor Manders. In his youth he overflowed with the joy of life —

Oswald. Yes. Nevertheless he managed to do so much in the world; so much that was good and useful; and he died so young, too.

Pastor Manders. Yes, you have indeed inherited the name of an active and worthy man, my dear Oswald Alving. Let us hope it will be an incentive to you.

Oswald. It ought to, indeed.

Pastor Manders. It was good of you to come home for tomorrow's ceremony in his honor.

Oswald. It was the least I could do for my father.

Mrs. Alving. And I am to keep him here so long! — That is the best of all.

Pastor Manders. Yes, you are going to stay at home through the winter, I hear.

Oswald. My stay is indefinite, sir. But, it is good to be at home again!

Mrs. Alving. (*Beaming*) Yes, isn't it?

Pastor Manders. (*Looks sympathetically at* Oswald.) You went out into the world early, my dear Oswald.

Oswald. I did. Sometimes I wonder whether it was not too early.

Mrs. Alving. Oh, not at all. A healthy lad is all the better for it, especially when he's an only child. He ought not to hang on at home with mother and father and get spoiled.

Pastor Manders. That's a very debatable question, Mrs. Alving. A child's proper place is, and must be, the home of his father.

Oswald. There I quite agree with you, Pastor Manders.

Pastor Manders. Only look at your own son — there is no reason why we shouldn't say it in his presence — what has happened in his case? He is twenty-six or seven and has never had the opportunity of learning what home life really is.

Oswald. Excuse me, Pastor; there you are quite mistaken.

Pastor Manders. Indeed? I thought you had lived almost exclusively in artistic circles.

Oswald. So I have.

Pastor Manders. And chiefly among the younger artists.

Oswald. Certainly.

Pastor Manders. But I thought most of these young fellows could not afford to set up house and support a family.

Oswald. There are many who can't afford to marry, sir.

PASTOR MANDERS. Yes, that's just what I say.

OSWALD. But you can have a home for all that. And several of them have, as a matter of fact; and very well-ordered, comfortable homes they are too. (MRS. ALVING *listens, nods, watching intently.*)

PASTOR MANDERS. But I'm not talking of bachelors' quarters. By a " home " I understand the home of a family, where a man lives with his wife and children.

OSWALD. Yes, or with his children and his children's mother.

PASTOR MANDERS. (*Starts. Claps his hands together.*) But good heavens — !

OSWALD. Well?

PASTOR MANDERS. Lives with — his children's mother!

OSWALD. Yes. Would you have him turn his children's mother out of doors?

PASTOR MANDERS. Then it is illicit relations you are talking about. About these so-called free marriages!

OSWALD. I have never noticed anything particularly irregular about the life these people lead.

PASTOR MANDERS. But how is it possible that a — a young man or young woman with any decent principles can endure to live in that way — in the eyes of all the world!

OSWALD. What can they do? A poor young artist — a poor girl. It costs a lot of money to get married. What are they to do?

PASTOR MANDERS. What are they to do? Let me tell you, Mr. Alving, what they ought to do. They ought to exercise self-control from the first; that's what they ought to do.

OSWALD. Talk like that won't go far with warm-blooded young people over head and ears in love.

MRS. ALVING. No, it wouldn't go far.

PASTOR MANDERS. (*Persisting*) How can the authorities tolerate such things? Allow it to go on in the light of day? Mrs. Alving, was I not right to be deeply concerned about your son, living in circles where open immorality prevails, and has even a sort of prestige — !

OSWALD. Let me tell you, sir, that I have been a regular Sunday guest in one or two such irregular homes —

PASTOR MANDERS. On Sunday of all days!

OSWALD. Isn't that the day to enjoy one's self? Well, never have I heard an offensive word, nor have I ever seen anything that could be called immoral. No; but do you know when and where I have found immorality in artistic circles?

PASTOR MANDERS. No! Thank heavens, I don't.

OSWALD. Well, then, let me tell you. I found it when some of your model fathers and husbands came to Paris to have a look around. They could tell us about places and things we never dreamt of.

PASTOR MANDERS. What? Do you mean to say that respectable men from home here would — ?

OSWALD. Have you never — when these respectable men got home again — haven't you heard them talking about the way immorality was running rampant abroad?

PASTOR MANDERS. Yes, of course —

MRS. ALVING. I have, too.

OSWALD. Well, you may take their word for it. They know what they are talking about. (*With hands pressed to his head*) Oh! That great, free, glorious life out there — that it should be defiled in such a way.

MRS. ALVING. You must not get excited, Oswald.

OSWALD. Yes, you are quite right, Mother. It's not good for me. You see, I'm awfully tired. I'll go for a little walk before dinner. Excuse me, Pastor, I know you can't take my point of view, but I couldn't help speaking out. (*He goes out Left.*)

[Scene V]   MRS. ALVING. My poor boy!

PASTOR MANDERS. You may well say so. Then that's what it has come to with him! (MRS. ALVING *looks at him, but says nothing. He paces up and down.*) He called himself the Prodigal Son. It's only too true! (MRS. ALVING *looks steadily at him.*) And what do you say to this?

MRS. ALVING. I say that Oswald was right in every word.

PASTOR MANDERS. (*Stands still.*) Right! Right! In such principles!

MRS. ALVING. Here, in my loneliness, I have come to the same way of thinking, Pastor Manders. But I have never dared to touch upon the matter. Well! Now my boy shall speak for me.

PASTOR MANDERS. You are much to be pitied, Mrs. Alving. But now I must speak seriously to you. Now it is no longer your business manager and advisor, your own and your late husband's friend, who stands before you. It is the priest — the priest who stood before you in the moment of your life when you needed counsel most.

MRS. ALVING. And what has the priest to say to me?

PASTOR MANDERS. Remember — a little. The time is well chosen. Tomorrow will be the tenth anniversary of your husband's death. Tomorrow the memorial in his honor will be unveiled. Tomorrow I shall have to speak to the whole assembled multitude. But today I will speak to you alone.

MRS. ALVING. Very well, Pastor Manders. Speak!

PASTOR MANDERS. Do you remember that after less than a year of married life you stood on the verge of an abyss? That you forsook your house and home? That you fled from your husband? Yes, Mrs. Alving — fled, fled, and refused to return to him however much he begged and prayed of you?

MRS. ALVING. Have you forgotten how infinitely miserable I was in that first year?

PASTOR MANDERS. It is only the spirit of rebellion that craves for happiness in this life. What right have we human beings to happiness? No, we must do our duty! And your duty was to hold firmly to the man you had once chosen and to whom you were bound by a holy tie.

MRS. ALVING. You know very well what sort of life my husband was leading at that time — what excesses he was guilty of.

PASTOR MANDERS. I know very well what rumors there were about him, and I am the last to approve his conduct as a young man, if the reports about him are true. But a wife is not to be her husband's judge. It was your duty to bear with humility the cross which a Higher Will had, for your own good, laid upon you. But instead of that you rebelliously cast away the cross, deserted the man you should have supported, risked your good name and reputation, and — nearly succeeded in ruining other people's reputations into the bargain.

MRS. ALVING. Other people's? One other person's, you mean.

PASTOR MANDERS. It was unspeakably reckless of you to seek refuge with me.

MRS. ALVING. With our clergyman? With our intimate friend?

PASTOR MANDERS. Especially on that account. Yes, you may thank God that I possessed the necessary firmness — that I dissuaded you from your wild designs, and that it was vouchsafed me to lead you back to the path of duty and home to your lawful husband.

MRS. ALVING. Yes, Pastor Manders, it was certainly your doing.

PASTOR MANDERS. I was but a poor instrument in a Higher Hand. And what a blessing it has been to you all the days of your life that I persuaded you to resume the yoke of duty and obedience! Didn't it all happen as I foretold? Didn't Alving turn his back on his errors as a man should? Didn't he live with you blamelessly from that time? Didn't he become a benefactor to the whole district? And didn't he raise you up to him so that you, little by little, became his assistant in all his undertakings? And an able assistant, too — Oh! I know, Mrs. Alving, *that* praise is due to you. — But now I come to the next serious mistake in your life.

MRS. ALVING. What do you mean?

PASTOR MANDERS. Just as you once denied a wife's duty, so you have since denied a mother's.

MRS. ALVING. Ah — !

PASTOR MANDERS. All your life you have been dominated by your own willfulness. All your impulses have been toward insubordination and lawlessness. You have never been willing to submit to restraint. Everything in life that has weighed upon you you have cast away without care or conscience, like a burden you could throw off at will. It did not please you to be a wife any longer, so you left your husband. You found it troublesome to be a mother, so you put your child out to strangers.

MRS. ALVING. Yes. That's true, I did.

PASTOR MANDERS. And thus you have become a stranger to him.

MRS. ALVING. No! No! I am not.

PASTOR MANDERS. Yes, you are; it can't be otherwise. And how have you got him back again? Think well, Mrs. Alving. You have sinned greatly against your husband — you admit that by building this memorial to him. Now, also, see how you have sinned against your son. There may be time to lead him back from the paths of error. Turn back yourself, and save what may yet be saved in him. For — (*He raises his forefinger.*) it is true, Mrs. Alving, you are a guilty mother! — This I have thought it my duty to say to you.

(*Pause*)

MRS. ALVING. (*Slowly, with self-control*) You have now spoken out, Pastor Manders. And tomorrow you are to speak publicly in memory of my husband. I shall not speak tomorrow. But now I will speak frankly to you, as you have spoken to me.

PASTOR MANDERS. To be sure. You want to bring forward excuses for your conduct —

MRS. ALVING. No, I will only tell you a story.

PASTOR MANDERS. Well?

MRS. ALVING. All that you have just said about me and my husband and our life together after you had brought me back to the path of duty — as you called it — these are all matters about which you know nothing from your own observation. From that moment, you — who had been our intimate friend — never again set foot in our house.

PASTOR MANDERS. You and your husband left town immediately after.

MRS. ALVING. Yes. And in my husband's

lifetime you never came out here to see us. It was business that forced you to visit me when you undertook the affairs of the Orphanage.

PASTOR MANDERS. (*Softly and uncertainly*) Helene — if that is meant as a reproach, I would beg you to bear in mind —

MRS. ALVING. — the regard you owed to your position, yes. And that I was a runaway wife. One can never be too cautious with such unprincipled creatures.

PASTOR MANDERS. My dear — Mrs. Alving, that is an absurd exaggeration —

MRS. ALVING. Yes, yes, yes, suppose it is. All I wanted to say was, that your judgment of my married life is founded upon nothing but current gossip.

PASTOR MANDERS. Well, perhaps. What then?

MRS. ALVING. Well, then, Manders — I will tell you the truth. I have sworn to myself that one day you should know it — you alone!

PASTOR MANDERS. And what is the truth, then?

MRS. ALVING. The truth is that my husband died just as dissolute as he had lived all his days.

PASTOR MANDERS. (*Groping for a chair*) What are you saying?

MRS. ALVING. After nineteen years of marriage, as dissolute — in his desires, at any rate — as before you married us.

PASTOR MANDERS. And Alving's irregularities, his excesses, if you like, you call a " dissolute life "?

MRS. ALVING. Our doctor used the expression.

PASTOR MANDERS. I don't understand.

MRS. ALVING. You don't need to.

PASTOR MANDERS. It almost makes me dizzy. All your married life — the seeming union of all these years was nothing more than a miserable sham.

MRS. ALVING. Nothing more. Now you know.

PASTOR MANDERS. This is — it bewilders me. But how was it possible — ? How could such a state of things be kept dark?

MRS. ALVING. That has been my ceaseless struggle day after day. After Oswald's birth, I thought Alving seemed a little better. But it didn't last long. And then I had to struggle twice as hard, fighting for life or death, so that nobody should know what sort of a man my child's father was. And you know what power Alving had of winning people's hearts. Nobody seemed able to believe anything but good of him. But at last, Manders, — for you must know the whole story — the most repulsive thing of all happened when he brought the scandal within our own walls.

PASTOR MANDERS. Impossible! Here!

MRS. ALVING. Yes, in our own home. (*She indicates the dining room.*) It was in there, in the dining room, that I first came to know of it. I was busy with something in here, and the door was standing ajar. I heard our housemaid come up from the garden with water for the flowers.

PASTOR MANDERS. Well — ?

MRS. ALVING. Soon after I heard Alving come too. I heard him say something softly to her. And then I heard — (*with a short laugh*) Oh! It still sounds in my ears, so heartbreaking and yet so ludicrous — I heard my own servant-maid whisper, " Let me go, Chamberlain! Let me go."

PASTOR MANDERS. What unseemly levity on his part! Ah, it cannot have been more than levity, Mrs. Alving; believe me, it cannot.

MRS. ALVING. I soon knew what to believe. The Chamberlain had his way with the girl; she became a mother, Pastor Manders.

PASTOR MANDERS. (*As if petrified*) Such things in this house! In this house!

MRS. ALVING. I had borne a great deal in this house. To keep him home in the evenings — and at night — I had to make myself his boon-companion in his secret orgies up in his room. There I had to sit with him, clink glasses and drink with him, listen to his silly, ribald talk, and fight to get him to bed —

PASTOR MANDERS. (*Shaken*) And you endured all that?

MRS. ALVING. I had my little son. But when the last insult was added; when my own servant-maid — . Then I swore to myself: this shall come to an end. And so I took charge of the house — the whole charge — over him and over everything. For now I had a hold over him, you see; he did not dare to protest. It was then that Oswald was sent from home. He was seven and beginning to notice and ask questions as children do. I couldn't bear that, Manders. It seemed to me that the child would be poisoned by merely breathing the air in this polluted home. That was why I sent him away. And now you can understand why he was never allowed to set foot inside his home so long as his father lived. No one knows what it has cost me.

PASTOR MANDERS. What a tragic existence! (*He pauses, crosses up Center to steps.*)

MRS. ALVING. I could never have endured it if I had not had my work. Yes, I can boast that I have really worked! All the improvements of the property, all developments, all the new ideas that Alving took credit for — do you think *he* bothered about such things? *He,* who lay the whole day on his couch reading old Official Lists! No; I want you to understand this too: *I* was the one who kept him in line in his lucid moments; *I* had to bear the whole weight when he resumed his bestialities or began to whine about his bad luck.

PASTOR MANDERS. And it is to that man you raise this memorial. (*He indicates the Orphanage.*)

MRS. ALVING. There you see the power of an uneasy conscience.

PASTOR MANDERS. An uneasy — what do you mean?

MRS. ALVING. It has always seemed to me impossible but that the truth would come out and be believed. So the Orphanage exists to deaden all rumors and banish doubt.

PASTOR MANDERS. In that you certainly have not missed your aim, Mrs. Alving.

MRS. ALVING. And besides, I had one other reason. I did not wish that Oswald should inherit anything whatever from his father.

PASTOR MANDERS. Then it is Alving's fortune that — ?

MRS. ALVING. Yes. The sums which I have spent upon the Orphanage, year by year, make up the amount — I have reckoned it precisely — the amount which made Lieutenant Alving a good match in his day.

PASTOR MANDERS. I don't quite understand —

MRS. ALVING. It was my purchase money — . I do not intend that that money should pass into Oswald's hands. My son shall have everything from me — everything —

[Scene VI]   (OSWALD ALVING comes through the door Right; he has removed his hat and coat and left them in the hallway.)

MRS. ALVING. Are you back so soon? My dear, dear son!

OSWALD. Yes. What can a fellow do outdoors in this eternal rain? But isn't dinner nearly ready?

REGINA. (Enters from the dining room with a parcel.) A parcel has come for you, Mrs. Alving.

MRS. ALVING. (With a glance at MANDERS) Probably copies of the ode for tomorrow's ceremony.

PASTOR MANDERS. H'm —

REGINA. And dinner is ready.

MRS. ALVING. Very well. We will come presently. I will just — I will just — (She opens parcel.)

REGINA. (To OSWALD) Oh — would Mr. Alving like red or white wine?

OSWALD. Both, if you please.

REGINA. Bien! Very well, sir. (Exit into dining room.)

OSWALD. I may as well help to uncork it. (Goes into the dining room, leaving the door half open.)

MRS. ALVING. (Has finished opening the parcel.) Yes, I thought so. Here is the ceremonial ode, Pastor Manders.

PASTOR MANDERS. (With clasped hands) How I'm to deliver my discourse tomorrow without embarrassment —

MRS. ALVING. Oh! You'll get through it somehow.

PASTOR MANDERS. (Quietly, so as not to be heard in the dining room) Yes; it would not do to provoke scandal.

MRS. ALVING. (Speaks firmly.) No. And then this long comedy will be ended. After tomorrow it shall be for me as though he who is dead had never lived in this house. No one shall be here but my boy and his mother.

(From the dining room the sound of a chair overturning, followed by voices.)

REGINA'S VOICE. (Hoarsely, but whispering) Oswald! Stop! Are you mad? Let me go!

MRS. ALVING. (Starting in horror) Ah!

(She stares wildly at the half-opened door. OSWALD is heard coughing and humming within. Then the sound of a bottle being uncorked.)

PASTOR MANDERS. What in the world is the matter? What is the matter, Mrs. Alving?

MRS. ALVING. (Quickly) Ghosts! The couple — from the past — (pause) risen again!

PASTOR MANDERS. What! Is it possible! (Pause) Regina? Is she Alving's —

MRS. ALVING. Yes. Come. Not a word — !

(She takes PASTOR MANDERS by the arm and goes towards the dining room, trembling.)

ACT TWO

[Scene I]   (The same room. Rain-mist heavy over landscape. PASTOR MANDERS and MRS. ALVING enter from the dining room.)

MRS. ALVING. (Just inside the door) Velbekomme,[1] Mr. Manders. (She turns back to the dining room and speaks to OSWALD.) Aren't you coming too, Oswald?

OSWALD. No, thank you. I think I shall go out awhile.

MRS. ALVING. Yes. Do. The weather seems brighter now. (She closes dining room doors, goes to the first door on the Right and calls:) Regina!

REGINA. (Outside) Yes, Mrs. Alving.

MRS. ALVING. Go into the laundry and help with the garlands.

---

[1] A conventional after-dinner phrase spoken by the hostess to her guests: "I hope the meal will do you good." Here, of course, with unconscious irony.

REGINA. Very well.

(MRS. ALVING *makes sure that* REGINA *has gone; then she shuts the door.*)

PASTOR MANDERS. I suppose he can't overhear us in there?

MRS. ALVING. Not when the door is shut. Besides, he is going out.

PASTOR MANDERS. I am still quite upset. I can't think how I could get down a bit of dinner.

MRS. ALVING. (*Overwrought, moving up and down*) No more can I. But what is to be done now?

PASTOR MANDERS. Yes, what is to be done? Upon my word, I am so utterly inexperienced in matters of this sort.

MRS. ALVING. I am quite convinced that, so far, no harm has been done.

PASTOR MANDERS. No! Heaven forbid! But it is an unseemly state of things, nevertheless.

MRS. ALVING. The whole thing is an idle fancy of Oswald's, you may be sure of that.

PASTOR MANDERS. Well, as you say, I'm not accustomed to affairs of the kind. But I should certainly think —

MRS. ALVING. Out of the house she must go, and that immediately. It is as clear as daylight —

PASTOR MANDERS. Yes, of course she must.

MRS. ALVING. But where to? It would not be right to —

PASTOR MANDERS. Where to? Naturally, to her father.

MRS. ALVING. To whom did you say?

PASTOR MANDERS. To her — But then, Engstrand is not — Good heavens, Mrs. Alving, how is it possible? You must be mistaken after all.

MRS. ALVING. Alas! I'm mistaken in nothing. Johanna confessed all to me — and Alving could not deny it. So there was nothing to be done but to get the matter hushed up.

PASTOR MANDERS. No, that was all you could do.

MRS. ALVING. The girl left our service at once, and got a good sum of money to hold her tongue for the time. The rest she managed for herself when she got into the town.

She renewed her old acquaintance with Engstrand, the carpenter, gave him to understand, I've no doubt, how much money she got, and told him some tale about a foreigner who put in here with a yacht that summer. So she and Engstrand got married in hot haste. Why, you married them yourself.

PASTOR MANDERS. But how shall I comprehend this — I recollect distinctly Engstrand coming to give notice of the marriage. He was broken down with contrition, and blamed himself so bitterly for the misbehavior he and his sweetheart had been guilty of.

MRS. ALVING. Yes, of course, he had to take the blame upon himself.

PASTOR MANDERS. But such a piece of duplicity on his part! And toward *me* too. I certainly never could have believed it of Jacob Engstrand. Ah! I shall not fail to give him a serious talking to — he may be sure of that. And then the immorality of such a connection! For money — ! What was the sum the girl was given?

MRS. ALVING. It was three hundred crowns.

PASTOR MANDERS. There! Think of that! For a miserable three hundred crowns to go and marry a fallen woman!

MRS. ALVING. Then what have you to say to me? I married a fallen man.

PASTOR MANDERS. But — good heavens! What are you talking about? A fallen man?

MRS. ALVING. Do you think Alving was any purer when I went to the altar than Johanna was when Engstrand married her?

PASTOR MANDERS. Well, but there's a world of difference between the two classes —

MRS. ALVING. Not so much difference after all, except in the price — a miserable three hundred crowns and a whole fortune.

PASTOR MANDERS. How can you compare the two cases? You had taken counsel with your own heart and with your friends.

MRS. ALVING. (*Without looking at him*) I thought you understood where what you call my heart had strayed to at the time.

PASTOR MANDERS. Had I understood anything of the kind, I should not have continued a daily guest in your husband's house.

MRS. ALVING. Well, the fact remains that with myself I took no counsel whatever.

PASTOR MANDERS. Well, then, with your nearest relatives — as your duty bade you — with your mother and both your aunts.

MRS. ALVING. Yes, that is true. Those three cast up the account for me. Oh! It's marvelous how clearly they made out that it would be downright madness to refuse such an offer. If mother could only see me now and know what all that magnificence has come to.

PASTOR MANDERS. Nobody can be held responsible for the result. This, at least, remains clear: your marriage was in accordance with law and order.

MRS. ALVING. (*At the window*) Oh! That perpetual law and order! I often think it is that which does all the mischief in the world.

PASTOR MANDERS. Mrs. Alving, that is a sinful way of talking.

MRS. ALVING. Well, I can't help it; I can endure all this constraint and cowardice no longer. I cannot! I must work my way out to freedom.

PASTOR MANDERS. What do you mean by that?

MRS. ALVING. (*Tapping on the window sill*) I ought never have to concealed the facts of Alving's life. But at the time I dared do nothing else — even for my own sake. I was such a coward.

PASTOR MANDERS. A coward?

MRS. ALVING. If people had come to know anything, they would have said — " Poor man! With a runaway wife, no wonder he kicks over the traces."

PASTOR MANDERS. Such remarks might have been made with a certain show of right.

MRS. ALVING. (*Looking directly at him*) If I were what I ought to be, I should go to Oswald and say, " Listen, my boy. Your father was self-indulgent and vicious — "

PASTOR MANDERS. Merciful heavens — !

MRS. ALVING. And then I should tell him all I have told you — from beginning to end.

PASTOR MANDERS. The idea is shocking, Mrs. Alving.

MRS. ALVING. Yes, I know that. I know that very well. I am myself shocked at it. (*Goes from the window.*) I am such a coward.

PASTOR MANDERS. You call it " cowardice " to do your plain duty? Have you forgotten that a son should love and honor his father and mother?

MRS. ALVING. Don't let us talk in such platitudes. Let us ask: Should Oswald love and honor Chamberlain Alving?

PASTOR MANDERS. Is there no voice in your mother's heart that forbids you to destroy your son's ideals?

MRS. ALVING. Yes, but the truth?

PASTOR MANDERS. Yes, but his ideals?

MRS. ALVING. Ah — ideals! If I were only not the coward I am!

PASTOR MANDERS. Do not despise ideals, Mrs. Alving. They will avenge themselves cruelly. Take Oswald's case; he unfortunately seems to have few enough ideals as it is, but I can see that his father stands before him as an ideal.

MRS. ALVING. You are right there.

PASTOR MANDERS. And this conception of his father you have yourself implanted and fostered in his mind by your letters.

MRS. ALVING. Yes. In my superstitious awe of Duty and Decency, I lied to my boy year after year. Oh! What a coward, what a coward I have been!

PASTOR MANDERS. You have established a happy illusion in your son's heart, Mrs. Alving, and assuredly you ought not to undervalue it.

MRS. ALVING. H'm, who knows whether it is so happy after all — ? But, at any rate, I won't have any goings-on with Regina. He shall not go on and make the poor girl unhappy.

PASTOR MANDERS. No. Good heavens! That would be dreadful!

MRS. ALVING. If I knew he was in earnest, and that it would be for his happiness —

PASTOR MANDERS. What? What then?

MRS. ALVING. But it could not be, for

I'm sorry to say Regina is not a girl to make him happy.

PASTOR MANDERS. Well, what then? What do you mean?

MRS. ALVING. If I were not such a pitiful coward, I would say to him, " Marry her, or make what arrangements you please, only let us have no deception."

PASTOR MANDERS. But, good heavens! Would you let them marry? Anything so dreadful — so unheard of — !

MRS. ALVING. Do you really mean " unheard of "? Hand on heart, Pastor Manders, do you suppose that throughout the country there are not plenty of married couples as closely akin as they?

PASTOR MANDERS. I don't understand you at all.

MRS. ALVING. Oh, yes, indeed you do.

PASTOR MANDERS. Ah, you are thinking of the circumstances where — Yes, sad to say, family life is not always as it should be. But as for the sort of thing you're hinting at, one can't say — not with any certainty. Here, on the other hand — : that you, a mother, would permit your — !

MRS. ALVING. It is not my will. I wouldn't permit it for anything in the world; that is just what I was trying to say.

PASTOR MANDERS. No, because you are a " coward," to use your own term. But if you were not a " coward "! — Good heavens, such a reprehensible connection.

MRS. ALVING. So far as that goes, they say we are all sprung from connections of that sort. And who is it arranged the world so, Pastor Manders?

PASTOR MANDERS. Questions of that sort I must decline to discuss with you, Mrs. Alving. You are far from being in the right frame of mind for them. But that you dare call your scruples " cowardly "!

MRS. ALVING. Let me tell you what I mean. I am timid and half-hearted because I cannot get rid of the ghosts that haunt me.

PASTOR MANDERS. What's that?

MRS. ALVING. Ghosts! — When I heard Regina and Oswald in there, it was as though I saw ghosts before me. But I almost think we are all of us ghosts, Pastor Manders. It is not only what we have inherited from our father and mother that " walks again " in us. It is all sorts of dead ideas, and lifeless old beliefs. They have no vitality, but they cling to us all the same, and we can't get rid of them. — Whenever I take up a newspaper I seem to see ghosts gliding between the lines. There must be ghosts all the country over. They must be as thick as the sands, I think. And then we are all so pitifully afraid of the light.

PASTOR MANDERS. Ah! Here we have the fruits of your reading! And pretty fruits they are, upon my word! Oh! Those horrible, revolutionary, free-thinking books!

MRS. ALVING. You are mistaken, my dear Pastor. It was you yourself who set me thinking, and I thank you for it with all my heart.

PASTOR MANDERS. I?

MRS. ALVING. Yes. When you forced me under the yoke you called Duty and Obligation; when you praised as right and proper what my whole soul rebelled against as something loathsome. It was then that I began to look into the seams of your doctrine. I only wished to pick at a single knot, but when I had got that undone, the whole thing unraveled.

PASTOR MANDERS. (*Quiet; greatly moved*) And was that the result of my life's hardest battle?

MRS. ALVING. Call it, rather, your most pitiful defeat.

PASTOR MANDERS. It was my life's greatest victory, Helene — the victory over myself!

MRS. ALVING. It was a crime against us both.

PASTOR MANDERS. When you left your home and came to me — crying, " Here I am, take me! " — I commanded you, saying — " Woman, go home to your lawful husband." Was that a crime?

MRS. ALVING. Yes, I think so.

PASTOR MANDERS. We two do not understand each other.

MRS. ALVING. Not now, at any rate.

PASTOR MANDERS. Never, never, in my

most secret moments have I ever thought of you except as another's wife.

MRS. ALVING. Oh! Indeed?

PASTOR MANDERS. Helene — !

MRS. ALVING. People so easily forget their past selves.

PASTOR MANDERS. I do not. I am what I always was.

MRS. ALVING. Well, well, well — don't let us talk of old times any longer. You are now over head and ears in Commissions and Boards of Direction, and I am fighting my fight with ghosts both within me and without.

PASTOR MANDERS. Those without I shall help you to lay. After all the shocking things I have heard from you today I cannot in conscience permit an unprotected girl to remain in your house.

MRS. ALVING. Don't you think it would be the best plan to get her provided for? I mean, by a good marriage.

PASTOR MANDERS. No doubt. I think it would be desirable for her in every respect. Regina is just now at the age when — of course, I don't know much about these things, but —

MRS. ALVING. Regina matured very early.

PASTOR MANDERS. Yes! Did she not? I have an impression that she was remarkably well developed, physically, when I prepared her for confirmation. But in the meantime, she must go home, under her father's eye. — Ah! But Engstrand is not — That he — that he could so hide the truth from me! (*There is a knock at the door.*)

MRS. ALVING. Who can that be? Come in!

[Scene II] ENGSTRAND. (*In his Sunday best, standing in the doorway*) I beg your pardon humbly, but —

PASTOR MANDERS. Ah! H'm —

MRS. ALVING. Is that you, Engstrand?

ENGSTRAND. There was none of the servants about, so I took the liberty of just knocking.

MRS. ALVING. Oh! Very well. Come in. Is there anything you want to speak to me about?

ENGSTRAND. (*Coming in*) No. I'm great-ly obliged to you — . It was with the Pastor I wanted to have a word or two.

PASTOR MANDERS. H'm, — indeed! You want to speak to me, do you?

ENGSTRAND. Yes, I should like so very much to —

PASTOR MANDERS. (*Stopping before him*) Well, may I ask what you want?

ENGSTRAND. Well, it was just this, your Reverence — we've been paid off down yonder — My grateful thanks to you, ma'am. And now everything's finished, I've been thinking it would be but right and proper if we that have been working so honestly together all this time — well, I was thinking we ought to end up with a little prayer-meeting tonight.

PASTOR MANDERS. A prayer-meeting? Down at the Orphanage?

ENGSTRAND. Oh, if your Reverence doesn't think it's proper —

PASTOR MANDERS. Oh, yes! I do — but — h'm —

ENGSTRAND. I've been in the habit of offering up a little prayer in the evening myself.

MRS. ALVING. Have you?

ENGSTRAND. Yes, every now and then — just a little exercise, you might call it. But I am a poor, common man, and have little enough gift — God help me! And so I thought, as the Reverend Mr. Manders happened to be here, I'd —

PASTOR MANDERS. Well, you see, Engstrand, I must first ask you a question. Are you in the right frame of mind for such a meeting? Do you feel your conscience clear and at ease?

ENGSTRAND. Oh! God help us! Your Reverence, we'd better not talk about conscience.

PASTOR MANDERS. Yes, that's just what we must talk about. What have you to answer?

ENGSTRAND. Why — one's conscience — it can be bad enough now and then.

PASTOR MANDERS. Ah, you admit that. Then will you make a clean breast of it and tell the truth about Regina?

MRS. ALVING. (*Quickly*) Pastor Manders!

PASTOR MANDERS. Just let me —

ENGSTRAND. About Regina! Lord! How you frighten me! (*Looks at* MRS. ALVING.) There's nothing wrong about Regina, is there?

PASTOR MANDERS. We will hope not. But I mean what is the truth about you and Regina? You pass for her father, eh?

ENGSTRAND. (*Seems uncertain.*) Well, h'm, — your Reverence knows all about me and poor Johanna.

PASTOR MANDERS. Come, no more lying. Your wife told Mrs. Alving the whole story before quitting her service.

ENGSTRAND. Well, then, may — ! Now, did she really?

PASTOR MANDERS. So you are found out, Engstrand.

ENGSTRAND. And she swore and took her Bible oath —

PASTOR MANDERS. Did she take her Bible oath?

ENGSTRAND. No, she only swore; but she did it so earnestly.

PASTOR MANDERS. And you have hidden the truth from me all these years? Hidden it from me! From me, who have trusted you without reserve in everything.

ENGSTRAND. Well, I can't deny it.

PASTOR MANDERS. Have I deserved this of you, Engstrand? Haven't I always been ready to help you in word and deed, so far as it stood in my power? Answer me. Have I not?

ENGSTRAND. It would have looked bad for me many a time but for Pastor Manders.

PASTOR MANDERS. And you reward me thus! You cause me to enter falsehoods in the Church Register, and you withhold from me, year after year, the explanations you owed alike to me and to truth. Your conduct has been wholly inexcusable, Engstrand — And from this time forward all is over between us.

ENGSTRAND. (*With a sigh*) Yes! I suppose it must be.

PASTOR MANDERS. How can you possibly justify yourself?

ENGSTRAND. How could I guess she had made bad worse by talking about it? Will your Reverence just fancy yourself in the same trouble as poor Johanna —

PASTOR MANDERS. I!

ENGSTRAND. Lord bless you! I don't mean so exactly the same. But I mean, if your Reverence had anything to be ashamed of in the eyes of the world, as the saying is. — We men oughtn't to judge a poor woman too hardly, your Reverence.

PASTOR MANDERS. I am not doing so. It is you I am reproaching.

ENGSTRAND. Might I make so bold as to ask your Reverence a bit of a question?

PASTOR MANDERS. Yes, ask away.

ENGSTRAND. Isn't it right and proper for a man to raise up the fallen?

PASTOR MANDERS. Most certainly it is.

ENGSTRAND. And isn't a man bound to keep his sacred word?

PASTOR MANDERS. Why! Of course he is, but —

ENGSTRAND. When Johanna had got into trouble through that Englishman — or it might have been an American or a Russian, as they call them — well, you see, she came into the town. Poor thing! She'd sent me about my business once or twice before, for she couldn't bear the sight of anything but what was handsome, and I'd got this damaged leg. Your Reverence recollects how I ventured into a dancing saloon, where seafaring people carried on, with drink and deviltry, as the saying goes. And then when I was for giving them a bit of an admonition to lead a new life —

MRS. ALVING. (*At the window*) H'm —

PASTOR MANDERS. I know all about that, Engstrand — those ruffians threw you downstairs. You have told me of that affair already. Your injury is a badge of honor.

ENGSTRAND. I am not puffed up about it, your Reverence. But what I wanted to tell was that when she came and confessed all to me, with weeping and gnashing of teeth, I can tell your Reverence I was sore at heart to hear it.

PASTOR MANDERS. Were you indeed, Engstrand? Well, go on.

ENGSTRAND. So I said to her, " The American, he's sailing about on the boundless sea.
And as for you, Johanna," said I, " you've
committed a grievous sin and you're a fallen
creature. But Jacob Engstrand," said I, " he's
got two good legs to stand upon, *he* has — "
You know, your Reverence, I was speaking
figuratively — like.

PASTOR MANDERS. I understand quite well.
Go on.

ENGSTRAND. Well, that was how I raised
her up and made an honest woman of her so
that folks shouldn't get to know how she's
gone astray with foreigners.

PASTOR MANDERS. All that was very good
of you. Only I can't approve of your stooping to take money —

ENGSTRAND. Money? Not a stiver.

PASTOR MANDERS. (*Indicates* MRS. AL-
VING.) But —

ENGSTRAND. Oh! — Wait a minute. Now
I recollect. Johanna had a trifle of money. But
I would have nothing to do with it. " No,"
said I, " that's Mammon; that's the wages of
sin. This dirty gold — or paper money, or
whatever it was — we'll just fling that back
to the American," said I. But he was gone
away, over the stormy sea, your Reverence.

PASTOR MANDERS. Was he really, my good
Engstrand?

ENGSTRAND. Aye, sir. So Johanna and I,
we agreed that the money should go to the
child's education, and so it did. And I can
give you an account for every blessed cent
of it.

PASTOR MANDERS. Why! This alters the
case considerably.

ENGSTRAND. That's just how it stands,
your Reverence. And I make so bold as to
say I've been an honest father to Regina, so
far as my poor strength went, for I'm but a
poor creature, worse luck!

PASTOR MANDERS. Well, well, my good
fellow —

ENGSTRAND. And I've brought up the
child, and lived kindly with poor Johanna,
and ruled over my own house, as the Scripture has it. But I could never think of going up to your Reverence and puffing myself

up and boasting because I, too, had done
something in the world. No, sir, when anything of that sort happens to Jacob Engstrand, he holds his tongue about it. It
doesn't happen so very often, I dare say. And
when I do come to see your Reverence, I
find plenty to say about what's wicked and
weak. For I do say — as I was saying just
now — one's conscience isn't always as clean
as it might be.

PASTOR MANDERS. Give me your hand,
Jacob Engstrand.

ENGSTRAND. Oh, Lord! Your Reverence —

PASTOR MANDERS. Come, no nonsense.
There we are!

ENGSTRAND. And if I might humbly beg
your Reverence's pardon —

PASTOR MANDERS. You? On the contrary,
it is I who ought to beg your pardon.

ENGSTRAND. Lord, no, sir!

PASTOR MANDERS. Yes, certainly. And I
do it with all my heart. Forgive me for misunderstanding you. And I wish I could give
you some proof of my hearty regret and of
my good will toward you.

ENGSTRAND. Would you, your Reverence?

PASTOR MANDERS. With the greatest of
pleasure —

ENGSTRAND. Well, there's the very opportunity now. With the money I've saved
here, I was thinking I might found a Sailors'
Home down in the town.

MRS. ALVING. You want to?

ENGSTRAND. Yes. It, too, might be a sort
of Orphanage, in a manner of speaking.
There are many temptations for seafaring
folk ashore. But in this little house of mine,
a man might feel as under a father's eye, I
was thinking.

PASTOR MANDERS. What do you say to
this, Mrs. Alving?

ENGSTRAND. It isn't much I've got to
start with, the Lord help me! But if I could
only find a helping hand, why —

PASTOR MANDERS. Yes, yes — We'll look
into the matter. I entirely approve of your
plan. But now, go ahead of me and get everything ready. And get the candles lighted

to give the place an air of festivity. And then we will pass an edifying hour together, my dear Engstrand, for now I quite believe you are in the right frame of mind.

ENGSTRAND. Yes, I trust I am. And so I'll say goodbye, Ma'am. And thank you kindly. And take good care of Regina for me — (*He turns and wipes a tear from his eye.*) Poor Johanna's child — H'm, that's an odd thing, now, but it's — but it's just as if she'd grown into the very core of my heart. It is indeed. Yes, indeed. (*He bows and goes out.*)

[Scene III] PASTOR MANDERS. Well, what do you say about that man now, Mrs. Alving? That threw a totally different light on matters, didn't it?

MRS. ALVING. Yes, it certainly did.

PASTOR MANDERS. It only shows you how excessively careful one must be in judging one's fellow creatures. But it's a great joy to discover that one has been mistaken. Don't you think so?

MRS. ALVING. I think that you are, and will remain, a great baby, Manders.

PASTOR MANDERS. I?

MRS. ALVING. (*Putting both hands upon his shoulders*) And I have half a mind to put my arms round your neck and kiss you.

PASTOR MANDERS. (*Steps back hastily.*) No, no; God bless us — What an idea —

MRS. ALVING. (*Smiles.*) Oh! You need not be afraid of me.

PASTOR MANDERS. (*By the table*) You have sometimes such an exaggerated way of expressing yourself. Now I'll just collect all the documents and put them in my bag. (*He picks up bag.*) There, now. And now, goodbye, for the present. Keep your eyes open when Oswald comes back. I shall look in again later. (*He takes his hat and goes out after ENGSTRAND.*)

[Scene IV] MRS. ALVING. (*Sighs, looks a moment out the window, straightens a few things in the room, and starts to go into the dining room. She pauses in the doorway.*) Oswald, are you still at the table?

OSWALD. (*Within*) I am only finishing my cigar.

MRS. ALVING. I thought you had gone for a little walk.

OSWALD. In such weather as this? (*A glass clinks. Mrs. ALVING leaves the door open and sits down with some knitting on the sofa by the window.*) Wasn't that Pastor Manders who went away just now?

MRS. ALVING. Yes, he went down to the Orphanage.

OSWALD. (*The glass and decanter clink again.*) H'm.

MRS. ALVING. (*With an anxious glance*) Oswald, you should be careful with that liqueur. It is strong.

OSWALD. It keeps out the damp.

MRS. ALVING. Wouldn't you rather come in with me?

OSWALD. I can't smoke in there.

MRS. ALVING. You know quite well that you may smoke cigars.

OSWALD. Oh, all right, then, I'll come in. Just a tiny drop more first! There! (*He enters, smoking a cigar, and closes the door behind him. A short pause.*) Where's Manders gone to?

MRS. ALVING. I've just told you; he went down to the Orphanage.

OSWALD. Oh, ah — so you did.

MRS. ALVING. You shouldn't sit so long at the table after dinner, Oswald.

OSWALD. But I find it so pleasant, Mother. Just think what it is for me to come home and sit at Mother's table, in her room, and eat her delicious dinner.

MRS. ALVING. My dear, dear, boy!

OSWALD. (*Impatiently, walking and smoking*) And what else can I do with myself here? I can't set to work at anything —

MRS. ALVING. Why can't you?

OSWALD. In such weather as this? Without a single ray of sunlight the whole day? (*Crossing the floor*) Oh! Not to be able to work!

MRS. ALVING. Perhaps it was not quite wise of you to come home.

OSWALD. Oh, yes, Mother — I had to.

MRS ALVING. Why? I would ten times rather forego the joy of having you here than —

OSWALD. (*Standing by the table*) Now, tell me, Mother, does it really make you so very happy to have me home again?

MRS. ALVING. Does it make me happy?

OSWALD. (*Crumpling a newspaper*) I should have thought it must be pretty much the same to you whether I was in existence or not.

MRS. ALVING. Have you the heart to say that to your mother, Oswald?

OSWALD. But you've got on very well without me all this time.

MRS. ALVING. Yes, I've got on without you. That is true.

(*Silence. The twilight is slowly falling. Os-WALD paces the floor. He has put out his cigar.*)

OSWALD. (*Standing by* MRS. ALVING) Mother, may I sit down on the sofa by you?

MRS. ALVING. (*Making room*) Yes, do.

OSWALD. (*Sits.*) Mother, now I am going to tell you something.

MRS. ALVING. Well?

OSWALD. (*Stares front.*) For I can't go on hiding it any longer.

MRS. ALVING. Hiding what? What is it?

OSWALD. (*As before*) I could never bring myself to write to you about it, and since I've come home —

MRS. ALVING. (*Placing her hand on his arm*) Oswald, what *is* the matter?

OSWALD. Both yesterday and today I have tried to put the thoughts away from me — to get free from them, but it won't do.

MRS. ALVING. (*Rising*) Now, you must speak out, Oswald!

OSWALD. (*Draws her down again to sofa.*) Sit still, and then I will try and tell you. I complained of being tired after my journey —

MRS. ALVING. Well, what then?

OSWALD. But it isn't that that's the matter with me; it isn't any ordinary fatigue —

MRS. ALVING. (*Tries to rise.*) You're not ill, Oswald?

OSWALD. (*Draws her down again.*) Do sit still, Mother. Only, take it quietly. I am not downright ill, either — not what is commonly called "ill." (*Holds his head in both*

hands.) Mother, my mind is broken down — ruined — I shall never be able to work again. (*He throws himself into her lap and sobs.*)

MRS. ALVING. (*Holds his face in her hands*) Oswald, look at me! No, no; it isn't true.

OSWALD. (*Looking up with despairing eyes*) Never to be able to work again. Never, never! It will be like living death! Mother, can you imagine anything so horrible?

MRS. ALVING. My poor boy! How has this horrible thing come over you?

OSWALD. (*Sitting upright again*) That's what I can't possibly grasp or understand. I have never led an unsteady life — never, in any respect. You must not believe that of me, Mother. I have never done that.

MRS. ALVING. I'm sure you haven't, Oswald.

OSWALD. And yet this has come over me just the same — this awful misfortune!

MRS. ALVING. Oh! But it will pass away. It is nothing but overwork. Trust me, I am right.

OSWALD. (*Heavily*) I thought so too at first, but it isn't so.

MRS. ALVING. Tell me the whole story.

OSWALD. Yes, I want to.

MRS. ALVING. When did you first notice it?

OSWALD. It was directly after I had been home last time, and had got back to Paris again. I began to feel the most violent pains in my head — chiefly in the back of my head, I thought. It was as though a tight iron ring was being screwed round my neck and upward.

MRS. ALVING. Well, and then?

OSWALD. At first I thought it was nothing but the ordinary headache I had been so plagued with when I was growing up —

MRS. ALVING. Yes, yes —

OSWALD. But it was not that. I soon found that out. I couldn't work. I wanted to begin upon a new big picture but it was as though my powers failed me; all my strength was crippled; I could not form any definite images; it all swam before me — whirling round and round. Oh! It was an awful state.

At last I sent for a doctor, and from him I got to know the truth.

Mrs. Alving. How do you mean?

Oswald. He was one of the best doctors in Paris. I told him my symptoms, and then he set to work asking me a heap of questions which I thought had nothing to do with the matter. I couldn't imagine what the man was after —

Mrs. Alving. Well —

Oswald. At last he said, "From your birth you have been worm-eaten." He used that very word, *vermoulu.*

Mrs. Alving. What did he mean by that?

Oswald. I didn't understand either, and begged him to give me a clearer explanation. And then the old cynic said — (*twisting his hands*) Oh! —

Mrs. Alving. What did he say?

Oswald. He said, "The sins of the fathers are visited upon the children."

Mrs. Alving. (*Rises slowly.*) The sins of the fathers —

Oswald. I very nearly struck him in the face —

Mrs. Alving. (*Crossing the stage*) The sins of the fathers —

Oswald. (*Smiles heavily.*) Yes, what do you think of that? Of course I assured him that such a thing was out of the question. But do you think he gave in? No, he stuck to it; and it was only when I produced your letters and translated to him the passages relating to father —

Mrs. Alving. Then?

Oswald. Then he was of course bound to admit that he was on the wrong track, and so I got to know the truth — the incomprehensible truth! I ought to have held aloof from my bright and happy student life — life among my fellows. It had been too much for my strength. So I had brought it upon myself.

Mrs. Alving. Oswald! Oh, no! Don't believe it.

Oswald. No other explanation was possible, he said. That is the awful part of it. Incurably ruined for my whole life — by my own heedlessness! All that I meant to have done in the world — I never dare think of it again. Oh! If I could but live over again, and undo all I have done! (*He throws himself down and buries his face in the sofa.* Mrs. Alving *wrings her hands and paces, struggling with herself silently.*)

Oswald. (*After a moment, looks up, and remains half lying, propped on his elbow.*) If it had only been something inherited, something one wasn't responsible for! But this! To have thrown away so shamefully, thoughtlessly, one's own happiness, one's own health, everything in the world — one's future, one's very life —

Mrs. Alving. Oh, my dear, darling boy. No, no. It is impossible. (*Bending over him*) Things are not so desperate as you think.

Oswald. Oh! You don't know — . (*Jumping up*) And then, Mother, to cause you all this sorrow. Many a time have I wished and hoped that at the bottom you did not care so very much about me.

Mrs. Alving. I, Oswald; my only boy! You are all I have in the world. The only thing I care about!

Oswald. (*Seizing both her hands and kissing them*) Yes, Mother dear, I see it well enough. When I am at home I see it, of course; and that is the hardest part for me. — But you know all about it. And now we won't talk any more about it today. (*Crosses the stage.*) Get me something to drink, Mother.

Mrs. Alving. Drink? What do you want to drink now?

Oswald. Oh! Anything you like. You've got some cold punch in the house.

Mrs. Alving. Yes, but my dear —

Oswald. Don't refuse me, Mother. Do be nice now! I must have some to wash down all these gnawing thoughts. (*He goes to the Conservatory.*) And then — it is so dark here!

(Mrs. Alving *rings the servant's bell on the Right.*)

Oswald. And this ceaseless rain! It may go on week after week for months together. Never to get a glimpse of the sun! I can't recollect ever to have seen the sun shine all the times I've ever been at home.

MRS. ALVING. Oswald, you are thinking of going away from me.

OSWALD. I am not thinking of anything. I *can't* think of anything. (*Low-voiced*) I left thinking alone.

[Scene V] REGINA. (*Enters from dining room.*) Did you call, ma'am?

MRS. ALVING. Yes, let us have the lamp in.

REGINA. Right away, ma'am. It is already lighted. (*She goes out.*)

MRS. ALVING. (*Going to* OSWALD.) Oswald, don't keep anything from me.

OSWALD. I certainly haven't, Mother. I think I have told you a good deal. (REGINA *enters, crosses to the table, and places the lamp there.*)

MRS. ALVING. Regina, you might fetch us half a bottle of champagne.

REGINA. Very well, ma'am. (*She goes out again.*)

OSWALD. (*Taking his mother's face in his hands*) That's just what I wanted. I knew mother wouldn't let her son go thirsty.

MRS. ALVING. My poor darling Oswald, how could I deny you anything now?

OSWALD. (*Eagerly*) Is that true, Mother? Do you mean it?

MRS. ALVING. How? What?

OSWALD. That you couldn't deny me anything.

MRS. ALVING. My dear Oswald —

OSWALD. Hush!

(REGINA *enters with a tray containing a half bottle of champagne and two glasses. She places it on the table.*)

REGINA. Shall I open the bottle?

OSWALD. No, thanks. I'll open it. (RE-GINA *goes out.*)

[Scene VI] MRS. ALVING. (*Sits by the table.*) What was it you meant — I couldn't deny you anything?

OSWALD. (*Busy opening the bottle*) First let's have a glass — or two. (*The cork pops; he fills a glass and starts to pour the second.*)

MRS. ALVING. (*Covering the glass with her hand*) Thanks; not for me.

OSWALD. Oh! Won't you? Then I will. (*He empties glass and fills it again, empties it, and sits by the table.*)

MRS. ALVING. (*Expectantly*) Well?

OSWALD. (*Without looking at her*) Tell me — I thought you and Pastor Manders seemed strange — awfully quiet at the dinner-table today.

MRS. ALVING. Did you notice it?

OSWALD. Yes. H'm —. (*After a short pause*) Tell me, what do you think of Regina?

MRS. ALVING. What I think?

OSWALD. Yes, isn't she wonderful?

MRS. ALVING. My dear Oswald, you don't know her as well as I do.

OSWALD. Well?

MRS. ALVING. Regina, unfortunately, was allowed to stay at home too long. I ought to have taken her into my house sooner.

OSWALD. Yes, but isn't she splendid to look at, Mother? (*He fills his glass.*)

MRS. ALVING. Regina has many serious faults —

OSWALD. Yes? What of it? (*He drinks.*)

MRS. ALVING. But I'm fond of her nevertheless, and I am responsible for her. I wouldn't have any harm happen to her for anything in the world.

OSWALD. (*Rises suddenly.*) Mother! Regina is my only hope of salvation.

MRS. ALVING. (*Rising*) What do you mean by that?

OSWALD. (*Turns up.*) I can't go on bearing by myself all these tortures in my soul.

MRS. ALVING. Haven't you your mother to share them with you?

OSWALD. Yes, that's what I thought; and that's why I came home to you. But that won't do. I see that now; it won't work. I can't spend my life here.

MRS. ALVING. Oswald!

OSWALD. I must live in a different way, Mother. That's why I must go away from you. I won't have you looking on at it.

MRS. ALVING. My unhappy boy! — Ah! But, Oswald, while you are as sick as you are now —

OSWALD. If it were only the sickness, I

would stay with you, Mother; you are the best friend I have in the world.

MRS. ALVING. Yes, Oswald, I am; that's true, isn't it?

OSWALD. (*Walking restlessly*) But it is all the torment, the remorse; and besides that, the great crushing dread. Oh! That awful fear!

MRS. ALVING. (*Following him*) Dread, what dread? What do you mean?

OSWALD. Oh! You mustn't ask me any more. I don't know. I can't describe it to you. (*She crosses hurriedly down Right and rings the bell.*) What is it you want?

MRS. ALVING. I want my boy to be happy; he mustn't dwell on it. (*To* REGINA *who comes to the door*) More champagne; a whole bottle. (REGINA *goes out.*)

OSWALD. Mother!

MRS. ALVING. Do you think we don't know how to live out here in the country?

OSWALD. Isn't she wonderful to look at? What a figure! And so healthy!

MRS. ALVING. (*Sitting by the table*) Sit down, Oswald; let us talk quietly.

OSWALD. (*Sits.*) You don't know, Mother, that I owe Regina some reparation.

MRS. ALVING. You?

OSWALD. For a bit of thoughtlessness, or whatever you like to call it — very innocent anyhow. When I was home last time —

MRS. ALVING. Well?

OSWALD. She asked me so often about Paris, and I used to tell her one thing and another. Then I remember I happened to say to her one day, " Wouldn't you like to come down there yourself? "

MRS. ALVING. Well?

OSWALD. I saw her blush, and then she said, " Yes, I should like it of all things." " Ah! well," I replied, " perhaps it might be arranged," — or something like that.

MRS. ALVING. And then?

OSWALD. I had forgot the whole thing; but the day before yesterday I happened to ask her whether she was glad I was to stay at home so long —

MRS. ALVING. Yes?

OSWALD. And then she looked at me very

strangely and asked, " But what is to become of my trip to Paris? "

MRS. ALVING. Her trip?

OSWALD. And so I got out of her that she had taken the whole thing seriously; and that she had been thinking of me the whole time; and had set to work to learn French —

MRS. ALVING. So that was why —

OSWALD. Mother! When I saw that fresh, lovely splendid girl standing there before me — for I had never really paid much attention to her — standing there with open arms to receive me —

MRS. ALVING. Oswald!

OSWALD. Then it flashed upon me that she was my salvation, for I saw that she was full of the joy of life.

MRS. ALVING. (*Starting*) The joy of life? Can there be salvation in that?

[Scene VII]　　REGINA. (*Enters with champagne, and places bottle on table.*) I'm sorry to have been so long, but I had to go to the cellar.

OSWALD. And now bring another glass.

REGINA. (*She indicates the glass on table.*) There is Mrs. Alving's glass, Mr. Alving.

OSWALD. Yes, but bring one for yourself, Regina. (REGINA *looks at* MRS. ALVING.) Why do you wait?

REGINA. (*Speaks softly and hesitatingly.*) Is it Mrs. Alving's wish?

MRS. ALVING. Fetch the glass, Regina. (REGINA *exits to dining room.*)

OSWALD. (*Watching her*) Have you noticed how she walks? — so firmly and lightly!

MRS. ALVING. It can never be, Oswald.

OSWALD. It's settled. Can't you see that? (*He crosses and stands above chair.*) It is no use to say anything against it. (REGINA *enters with a glass in her hand.*) Sit down, Regina. (REGINA *looks inquiringly at* MRS. ALVING.)

MRS. ALVING. Sit down. (REGINA *sits hesitantly on the edge of a chair near the dining room.*) Oswald, what were you saying about the joy of life?

OSWALD. Ah, the joy of life, Mother;

that's a thing you don't know much about in these parts. I have never felt it here.

MRS. ALVING. Not when you are with me?

OSWALD. Not when I'm at home. But you don't understand that.

MRS. ALVING. Yes, yes; I think I almost understand it — now.

OSWALD. And then, too, the joy of work. At bottom, it's the same thing. But that too you know nothing about.

MRS. ALVING. Perhaps you are right, Oswald; tell me more about it.

OSWALD. Well, I only mean that here people are brought up to believe that work is a curse and a punishment for sin, and that life is something miserable, something we want to be done with, the sooner the better.

MRS. ALVING. " A vale of tears." Yes, and we take care to make it one.

OSWALD. But in the great world people won't hear of such things. There, you feel it's bliss and ecstasy merely to draw the breath of life. Mother, have you noticed that everything I have painted has turned upon the *joy of life?* Always, always upon the *joy of life* — light and sunshine and a holiday spirit and faces radiant with happiness? That is why I am afraid of remaining at home with you.

MRS. ALVING. Afraid? What are you afraid of here, with me?

OSWALD. I am afraid that all my sensibilities would develop into ugliness.

MRS ALVING. (*Looking at him*) Do you think *that* would happen?

OSWALD. I know it. You may live the same life here as there, and yet it won't be the same life.

MRS. ALVING. (*Having listened closely, gets up with a thoughtful expression.*) Now I see the connection.

OSWALD. What is it you see?

MRS. ALVING. I see now for the first time. And now I can speak.

OSWALD. (*Rises.*) Mother, I don't understand you.

REGINA. (*Rises.*) Perhaps I ought to go?

MRS. ALVING. No, stay here. Now, my boy you shall know the whole truth. And then you can choose. Oswald! Regina!

OSWALD. Hush! Pastor Manders —

[Scene VIII] PASTOR MANDERS. (*Enters from the hall.*) There! We've had a most edifying time down there.

OSWALD. So have we.

PASTOR MANDERS. We must help Engstrand with his Sailors' Home. Regina must go to him as an assistant —

REGINA. No, thank you, sir.

PASTOR MANDERS. (*Sees her for the first time.*) What? You here? And with a glass in your hand!

REGINA. (*Hastily puts glass on table.*) Pardon — !

OSWALD. Regina is going away with me, Mr. Manders.

PASTOR MANDERS. Going away with you!

OSWALD. Yes, as my wife — if she wishes it.

PASTOR MANDERS. But, good God — !

REGINA. It was not my idea, Pastor Manders.

OSWALD. Or she will stay here, if I stay.

REGINA. (*Involuntarily*) Here!

PASTOR MANDERS. I am amazed at you, Mrs. Alving.

MRS. ALVING. They will do neither one thing or the other; for now I can speak out plainly.

PASTOR MANDERS. You surely won't do that. No, no, no.

MRS. ALVING. Yes. I can speak and I will. And no ideal shall suffer after all.

OSWALD. Mother! What on earth are you hiding from me?

REGINA. Oh, ma'am! Listen! (*She runs up the steps to the window and looks out.*) Don't you hear shouts outside?

OSWALD. (*At the window on the Left*) What's going on? Where does that light come from?

REGINA. (*Cries out.*) The Orphanage is on fire!

MRS. ALVING. (*To the window*) On fire?

PASTOR MANDERS. On fire? Impossible! I have just come from there.

OSWALD. (*Turns.*) Where's my hat? Oh, never mind it. Father's Orphanage —

MRS. ALVING. My shawl, Regina! It is blazing.

PASTOR MANDERS. Terrible! Mrs. Alving, it is a judgment upon this abode of sin.

MRS. ALVING. Yes, of course. Come, Regina. (*She and* REGINA *hurry out.*)

PASTOR MANDERS. (*Clasping his hands*) And uninsured, too! (*Follows them out.*)

ACT THREE

[Scene I]   (*The room is as it was at the close of the second act. All doors stand open. The lamp is still burning on the table. It is dark outdoors; only a faint glow from the conflagration in the background at the Right.* MRS. ALVING, *with a shawl over her head, stands in the Conservatory looking out.* REGINA, *also with a shawl about her, stands a little behind* MRS. ALVING.)

MRS. ALVING. All burnt! Burnt to the ground!

REGINA. The basement is still burning.

MRS. ALVING. Why doesn't Oswald come home? There's nothing to be saved.

REGINA. Would you like me to take his hat to him?

MRS. ALVING. Hasn't he even got his hat on?

REGINA. (*Points to the hall.*) No, there it hangs.

MRS. ALVING. Let it hang. He must come up now. I will go and look for him myself. (*She goes out through the garden door.*)

[Scene II]   PASTOR MANDERS. (*Enters from the hall.*) Isn't Mrs. Alving here?

REGINA. She just went out through the garden door.

PASTOR MANDERS. This is the most terrible night I ever lived through.

REGINA. Yes, isn't it a terrible misfortune, Pastor?

PASTOR MANDERS. Oh! Don't talk about it! I can hardly bear to think of it.

REGINA. How *can* it have happened?

PASTOR MANDERS. Don't ask me, Miss Engstrand! How should *I* know? Are you,

too, hinting — ? Isn't it enough that your father — ?

REGINA. What about him?

PASTOR MANDERS. Oh, he has driven me clean out of my mind.

[Scene III]   ENGSTRAND. (*Enters from the hall.*) Your Reverence!

PASTOR MANDERS. (*Turning with a start*) Are you after me here, too?

ENGSTRAND. Yes. Lord strike me dead, but I must — . It's an awfully ugly business, Your Reverence.

PASTOR MANDERS. (*Walking up and down*) Oh, dear! Oh, dear!

REGINA. What do you mean?

ENGSTRAND. It happened because of our prayer-meeting, you see. (*Aside*) Now we've got the old cuckoo, my girl! (*Aloud*) And to think it's my fault that it's His Reverence's fault!

PASTOR MANDERS. But I assure you, Engstrand —

ENGSTRAND. But there wasn't another soul except Your Reverence that ever touched candles down there.

PASTOR MANDERS. (*Standing still*) Ah! So you say. But I certainly can't recollect that I ever had a candle in my hand.

ENGSTRAND. And I saw plain as day how your Reverence took the light and snuffed it with your fingers, and threw away the burned bit of wick among the shavings.

PASTOR MANDERS. You saw that?

ENGSTRAND. Yes, distinctly.

PASTOR MANDERS. It's quite beyond my comprehension. Besides it's never been a habit of mine to snuff candles with my fingers.

ENGSTRAND. And very risky it looked, that it did! But who could have guessed how much harm it would do, Your Reverence.

PASTOR MANDERS. Oh! Don't ask me.

ENGSTRAND. (*Pursuing him*) And Your Reverence hasn't insured it, neither?

PASTOR MANDERS. (*Pacing*) No, no, no; you've heard that already.

ENGSTRAND. (*Following*) Not insured! And then to go right down and set fire to the whole thing. Lord! Lord! What a misfortune!

PASTOR MANDERS. (*Wiping the sweat from his brow*) Yes, you may well say that, Engstrand.

ENGSTRAND. And to think that such a thing should happen to a benevolent institution that was to have been a blessing both to the town and country, as the saying is! The newspapers won't handle Your Reverence very gently, I expect.

PASTOR MANDERS. No, that's just what I'm thinking of. That's the worst of it. All the hateful attacks and accusations — Oh, it's terrible to think of.

[Scene IV]   MRS. ALVING. (*Enters from the garden.*) He can't be got away from the fire.

PASTOR MANDERS. Ah, there you are, Mrs. Alving.

MRS. ALVING. So you've escaped having to give the Inaugural Address, Pastor Manders.

PASTOR MANDERS. Oh! I should so gladly —

MRS. ALVING. (*Dully*) It is best that this happened as it did. That Orphanage would have done no good to anybody.

PASTOR MANDERS. Do you think not?

MRS. ALVING. Do *you* think it would?

PASTOR MANDERS. It's an immense misfortune, all the same.

MRS. ALVING. Let us speak plainly of it, as a piece of business. — Are you waiting for the Pastor, Engstrand?

ENGSTRAND. (*In the hall door*) Yes, I certainly am.

MRS. ALVING. Then sit down meanwhile.

ENGSTRAND. Thanks; I'd rather stand.

MRS. ALVING. I suppose you're going away by the steamer?

PASTOR MANDERS. Yes, it starts in an hour.

MRS. ALVING. Please take all the papers with you. I won't hear another word about that affair. I have got other things to think about —

PASTOR MANDERS. Mrs. Alving —

MRS. ALVING. (*Continues to speak.*) Later on I shall send you a power of attorney to settle everything as you please.

PASTOR MANDERS. That I shall very read-

ily take upon myself.   The original intention of the bequest must now be completely changed.

MRS. ALVING. Of course.

PASTOR MANDERS. Well, I think, first of all, I shall arrange that the Solvik property shall pass to the parish. The land is by no means without value. It can always be turned to account for some purpose or other. And the interest of the money in the bank I could, perhaps, best apply for the support of some undertaking that may prove itself a blessing to the town.

MRS. ALVING. Do exactly as you please. The whole matter is now entirely indifferent to me.

ENGSTRAND. Give a thought to my Sailors' Home, your Reverence.

PASTOR MANDERS. Yes, that's not a bad suggestion. That must be considered.

ENGSTRAND. Oh, to the devil with considering — I beg your pardon!

PASTOR MANDERS. (*Sighs.*) And I'm sorry to say I don't know how long I shall be able to retain control of these things; whether public opinion may compel me to retire. It entirely depends upon the result of the official inquiry into the fire.

MRS. ALVING. What are you talking about?

PASTOR MANDERS. And nobody can foretell what the results may be.

ENGSTRAND. (*Going closer to* MANDERS) Ah, but you can, though. For here stands Jacob Engstrand.

PASTOR MANDERS. Well, well, but — ?

ENGSTRAND. (*Lowering his voice*) And Jacob Engstrand isn't the man to desert a noble benefactor in the hour of need, as the saying goes.

PASTOR MANDERS. But my good fellow, how — ?

ENGSTRAND. Jacob Engstrand may be a sort of a guardian angel, he may, your Reverence.

PASTOR MANDERS. No, no, I can't accept that.

ENGSTRAND. Oh, you will, though, all the

same. I know a man that's taken others' sins upon himself before now, I do.

PASTOR MANDERS. Jacob! (*They shake hands.*) You are a rare character. Well, you shall be helped with your Sailors' Home. (ENGSTRAND *tries to thank him but is overcome with emotion.*) That you may rely upon. And now let's be off. We two go together.

ENGSTRAND. (*By the dining room door, aside to* REGINA) Stick with me, girl. You will be as cozy as a yolk in an egg.

REGINA. (*Tossing her head*) Merci! (*She gets* MANDERS' *things from the hall.*)

PASTOR MANDERS. Goodbye, Mrs. Alving! May the Spirit of Law and Order descend upon this house, and that quickly.

MRS. ALVING. Goodbye, Manders. (*She sees* OSWALD *coming through the garden and goes to the Conservatory to meet him.*)

ENGSTRAND. (*As he and* REGINA *are helping* MANDERS *into his clothes*) Goodbye, my child. And if any trouble should come to you, you know where Jacob Engstrand is to be found. (*Lowering his voice*) Little Harbor Street. (*To* MRS. ALVING *and* OSWALD) H'm! And the refuge for wandering mariners shall be called "Captain Alving's Home," that it shall! And if I'm spared to carry on that house in my own way, I venture to promise that it shall be worthy of his memory.

PASTOR MANDERS. (*In the door*) Ahem — h'm! Now come, my dear Engstrand. Goodbye, goodbye! (*He and* ENGSTRAND *go out by the hall door.*)

[Scene V]   OSWALD. (*Going to the table*) What house was he talking about?

MRS. ALVING. Oh, I suppose it was a kind of home he and Manders want to set up.

OSWALD. It will burn down like this one.

MRS. ALVING. What makes you think so?

OSWALD. Everything will burn. There won't remain a single thing in memory of father. Here am I, too, being burned up. (REGINA *looks at him in alarm.*)

MRS. ALVING. Oswald! You ought not to have remained so long over there, my poor boy.

OSWALD. I almost think you are right.

MRS ALVING. (*Sitting by the table*) Let me dry your face, Oswald. You are quite wet. (*Wipes his face with her handkerchief.*)

OSWALD. (*Stares in front of him.*) Thanks, Mother.

MRS. ALVING. Aren't you tired, Oswald? Would you like to go to sleep?

OSWALD. No, no — I can't sleep. I only pretend to. (*Sadly*) That will come soon enough.

MRS. ALVING. (*Is looking at him anxiously.*) Yes! You really are ill, my darling boy.

REGINA. (*Intently*) Mr. Alving ill?

OSWALD. (*Impatiently*) Shut the doors! This deadly fear —

MRS. ALVING. Shut the doors, Regina. (REGINA *closes the doors and stands by the hallway.* MRS. ALVING *removes her shawl;* REGINA *does the same.*)

MRS. ALVING. (*Draws a chair near* OSWALD *and sits beside him.*) There, now! I'm going to sit near you —

OSWALD. Yes, do. And Regina shall stay here, too. Regina shall always be with me. You'll give me a helping hand, Regina, won't you?

REGINA. I don't understand —

MRS. ALVING. A helping hand?

OSWALD. Yes, in the hour of need.

MRS. ALVING. Oswald, haven't you your mother to give you a helping hand?

OSWALD. You? (*He smiles.*) No, Mother, you can never give me the kind of helping hand I need. You! Ha! Ha! (*He looks earnestly at her.*) Though, after all, it lies nearest to you. (*Impetuously*) Why don't you call me by my Christian name, Regina? Why don't you call me Oswald?

REGINA. (*Speaks softly.*) I don't think Mrs. Alving would like it.

MRS. ALVING. You shall soon have leave to do it. And sit over here beside us, won't you? (REGINA *hesitates, then crosses to the other side of the table and sits.*) And now, my poor tortured boy, I am going to take the burden off your mind —

OSWALD. You, Mother?

MRS. ALVING. All that you call remorse and regret and self-reproach.

OSWALD. And you think you can do that.

MRS. ALVING. Yes, now I can, Oswald. You spoke of the joy of life; and at that word a new light burst for me over my life and all it has contained.

OSWALD. (*Shaking his head*) I don't understand what you are saying.

MRS. ALVING. You ought to have known your father when he was a young lieutenant. *He* was brimming over with the joy of life!

OSWALD. Yes, I know he was.

MRS. ALVING. It was like a holiday only to look at him. And what irrepressible energy and vitality there was in him!

OSWALD. Well — ?

MRS. ALVING. And then, child of joy as he was — for he *was* like a child at that time — he had to live here at home in a second-rate town which had no joys to offer him, but only dissipations. He had no work into which he could throw himself heart and soul; he had only official routine. He had not a single comrade who knew what the joy of life meant — only idlers and drunkards.

OSWALD. Mother!

MRS. ALVING. So that happened which was sure to happen.

OSWALD. And what was sure to happen?

MRS. ALVING. You said yourself this evening how it would go with you if you stayed at home.

OSWALD. Do you mean to say that father — ?

MRS. ALVING. Your poor father found no outlet for the overpowering joy of life that was in him. And I brought no brightness into his home.

OSWALD. Not even you?

MRS. ALVING. They had taught me a lot about duties and so on, which I had taken to be true. Everything was marked out into duties — into my duties and his duties, and I'm afraid I made home intolerable for your poor father, Oswald.

OSWALD. Why did you never write me anything about all this?

MRS. ALVING. I have never thought of it as a thing I could speak of to his son.

OSWALD. How did you see it then?

MRS. ALVING. (*Speaks slowly.*) I saw only this one thing. That your father was a broken man before you were born.

OSWALD. (*Choking*) Ah! (*He rises and goes to the window.*)

MRS. ALVING. And then, day after day, I dwelt on the thought that by rights Regina belonged here in the house — just like my own boy.

OSWALD. (*Turns quickly.*) Regina!

REGINA. (*Rising and speaking sharply*) I?

MRS. ALVING. Yes, now you know it, both of you.

OSWALD. Regina!

REGINA. (*To herself*) So Mother was that kind of woman after all.

MRS. ALVING. Your mother had many good qualities, Regina.

REGINA. Yes, but she was one of that sort, all the same. Oh! I've often suspected it, but — . And now, if you please, ma'am, may I be allowed to go away at once?

MRS. ALVING. Do you really wish it, Regina?

REGINA. Yes, indeed I do.

MRS. ALVING. Of course, you can do as you like, but —

OSWALD. Go away now? Now that you belong here?

REGINA. *Merci*, Mr. Alving! Or now, I suppose I may say Oswald. Though I can tell you this wasn't the way I thought it would come about.

MRS. ALVING. Regina. I have not been frank with you —

REGINA. No, that you haven't, indeed. If I'd known that Oswald was ill, why — and now, too, that it can never come to anything serious between us — No, I really can't stay out here in the country and wear myself out nursing sick people.

OSWALD. Not even one who is so near to you?

REGINA. No, that I can't. A poor girl must makes the best of her young days, or she'll be left out in the cold before she knows where she is. And I, too, have the joy of life in me, Mrs. Alving.

MRS. ALVING. I'm afraid you have. But don't throw yourself away, Regina.

REGINA. Oh! What must be must be. If Oswald takes after his father, I take after my mother, I expect. May I ask, ma'am, if Mr. Manders knows all this about me?

MRS. ALVING. Mr. Manders knows all about it.

REGINA. (*Putting on her shawl*) Well, then, I'd better hurry and get away by this steamer. Pastor Manders is so nice to deal with; and I certainly think I've as much right to a little of that money as he has — that brute of a carpenter.

MRS. ALVING. You are heartily welcome to it, Regina.

REGINA. (*Looking at her*) I think you might have brought me up as a gentleman's daughter, ma'am; it would have suited me better. (*She tosses her head.*) But it's done now — it doesn't matter! (*With a bitter glance at the unopened bottle*) All the same, I may come to drink champagne with gentle-folks yet.

MRS. ALVING. If you ever need a home, Regina, come to me.

REGINA. No, thank you, ma'am. Pastor Manders will look after me, I know. And if the worst comes to the worst, I know of one place where I belong by rights.

MRS. ALVING. Where is that?

REGINA. " Captain Alving's Home."

MRS. ALVING. Regina — now I see it — you're going to your ruin.

REGINA. Oh, stuff! *Adieu.* (*She curtsies and goes out into the hall.*)

[Scene VI]   OSWALD. (*Standing by the window and staring out*) Is she gone?

MRS. ALVING. Yes.

OSWALD. (*To himself*) I think it was wrong, all this.

MRS. ALVING. (*Going behind him and putting her hands on his shoulders*) Oswald, my dear boy, has it shaken you so very much?

OSWALD. (*Turning his face towards her*) All that about Father, do you mean?

MRS. ALVING. Yes, about your unhappy father. I'm so afraid it may have been too much for you.

OSWALD. Why should you imagine that? Of course, it came upon me as a great surprise, but after all, it can't matter much to me.

MRS. ALVING. (*Drawing back her hands*) Can't matter! That your father was so infinitely miserable!

OSWALD. Of course, I can pity him as I would anybody else, but —

MRS. ALVING. Nothing more? Your own father!

OSWALD. (*Impatiently*) Oh, there! " Father," " Father "! I never knew anything of Father. I don't remember anything about him except that he once made me throw up.

MRS. ALVING. It's dreadful to think that way. Should not a son love his father all the same?

OSWALD. When a son has nothing to thank his father for? Has never known him? Do you really cling to the old superstition — you who are so broad-minded in other ways?

MRS. ALVING. Is that only a superstition?

OSWALD. Yes. Can't you see it, Mother? It is one of those beliefs that are current in the world, and so —

MRS. ALVING. (*Speaking wildly*) Oswald — Then you don't love me, either!

OSWALD. You I know, at any rate.

MRS. ALVING. Yes, you know me, but is that all?

OSWALD. And of course I know how fond you are of me, and I ought to be grateful to you. And you can be very useful to me now that I am ill.

MRS. ALVING. Yes, can't I, Oswald? Oh, I could almost bless your illness which drove you home to me. For I can see very plainly you are not mine. I have to win you.

OSWALD. (*Impatiently*) Yes, yes, yes. All these are just so many phrases. You must remember I am a sick man, Mother. I can't be much concerned over other people; I have enough to do, thinking about myself.

MRS. ALVING. (*Gently*) I shall be easily satisfied and patient.

OSWALD. And cheerful, too, Mother.

MRS. ALVING. Yes, my dear boy, you are right. (*Goes to him.*) Now, have I relieved you of all remorse and self-reproach?

OSWALD. Yes, you have done that. But who is to relieve me of the dread?

MRS. ALVING. The dread?

OSWALD. (*Crossing the room*) Regina would have done it for one kind word.

MRS. ALVING. I don't understand you. What is all this about dread — and Regina?

OSWALD. Is it very late, Mother?

MRS. ALVING. It is early morning. (*Looking out through the conservatory windows*) The day is dawning over the hills, and the weather is fine, Oswald. In a little while you shall see the sun.

OSWALD. I'm glad of that. Oh, there may be much for me to rejoice in and live for —

MRS. ALVING. Yes, much — much, indeed!

OSWALD. Even if I can't work —

MRS. ALVING. Oh, you will soon be able to work again, my dear, now that you have no longer got all those gnawing and depressing thoughts to brood over.

OSWALD. Yes, I'm glad you were able to free me from all those fancies — And when I've got one thing more arranged — (*He sits on sofa.*) Now, we'll have a little talk, Mother.

MRS. ALVING. (*Pulls chair to the sofa.*) Yes, let us.

OSWALD. And meantime the sun will be rising. And then you will know all. And then I shan't have that dread any longer.

MRS. ALVING. What am I to know?

OSWALD. (*Without listening to his mother*) Mother, didn't you say, a little while ago, that there was nothing in the world you wouldn't do for me if I asked you?

MRS. ALVING. Yes, to be sure I said it.

OSWALD. And you'll stick to it, Mother?

MRS. ALVING. You may rely on that, my dearest boy. I have nothing in the world to live for but you.

OSWALD. All right, then; now you shall hear. Mother, you are very strong-minded, I know. You must sit quite still when you hear it.

MRS. ALVING. What dreadful thing can it be —

OSWALD. You are not to scream out. Do you hear? Do you promise me that? We'll sit and talk about it quietly. Do you promise me this, Mother?

MRS. ALVING. Yes, yes; I promise you that. Only speak!

OSWALD. Well, you must know that all this fatigue, and my not being able to think of working at all — all that is not the illness itself —

MRS. ALVING. Then what is the illness itself?

OSWALD. The disease I have as my inheritance (*He puts his hand to his head and speaks quietly.*) is seated here.

MRS. ALVING. (*Almost soundlessly*) Oswald! No, no!

OSWALD. Don't scream. I can't bear it. Yes, it is sitting here — waiting. And it may break out any day — at any moment.

MRS. ALVING. Oh, how horrible!

OSWALD. Now, do be quiet. That's how it stands with me.

MRS. ALVING. (*Rises.*) It is not true, Oswald. It is impossible. It can't be like that.

OSWALD. I have had one attack down there already. It was soon over. But when I found out what had been the matter with me, then the dread came upon me raging and tearing; and so I set off home to you as fast as I could.

MRS. ALVING. Then this is the dread?

OSWALD. Yes, for it is indescribably awful. Oh! If it had been merely an ordinary mortal disease! For I'm not afraid of death — though I should like to live as long as I can.

MRS. ALVING. Yes, yes, Oswald, you must.

OSWALD. But this is so unspeakably loathsome! To become a little baby again! To have to be fed! To have to — Oh! I can't speak of it.

MRS. ALVING. My boy has his mother to nurse him.

OSWALD. (*Rises sharply.*) No, never;

that's just what I won't have. I can't endure to think that perhaps I should lie in that state for many years — get old and gray. And in the meantime you might die and leave me. (*He sits in* Mrs. Alving's *chair.*) For the doctor said it would not necessarily prove fatal at once. He called it a sort of softening of the brain — I think that expression sounds so nice. I always think of cherry-colored velvet curtains — something soft and delicate to the touch.

Mrs. Alving. (*Screams.*) Oswald!

Oswald. (*Jumps up and walks about.*) And now you have taken Regina from me. If I'd only had her! She would have given me a helping hand, I know.

Mrs. Alving. (*Goes to him.*) What do you mean by that, my darling boy? Is there any help in the world that I wouldn't give you?

Oswald. When I got over my attack in Paris, the doctor told me that when it came again — and it will come again — there would be no more hope.

Mrs. Alving. He was heartless enough —

Oswald. I demanded it of him. I told him I had preparations to make. (*He smiles cunningly.*) And so I had. (*He draws a small box from his inner breastpocket.*) Mother, do you see these?

Mrs. Alving. What is it?

Oswald. Morphia powders.

Mrs. Alving. (*Horrified*) Oswald — my boy.

Oswald. I have scraped together twelve capsules.

Mrs. Alving. (*Snatching at it*) Give me the box, Oswald.

Oswald. (*Puts box in his pocket.*) Not yet, Mother.

Mrs. Alving. I shall never get over this.

Oswald. You must. If I had Regina here, I should have told her how it stood with me and begged her to give me a helping hand. She would have helped me. I'm certain she would.

Mrs. Alving. Never!

Oswald. When the horror had come upon me, and she saw me lying there helpless, like a little newborn baby, impotent, lost, past saving —

Mrs. Alving. Never in all the world would Regina have done this.

Oswald. Regina would have done it. Regina was so wonderfully light-hearted. And she would soon have wearied of nursing an invalid like me —

Mrs. Alving. Then Heaven be praised that Regina is not here.

Oswald. Well, then — it is you that must give me the helping hand.

Mrs. Alving. (*A loud scream*) I!

Oswald. Who is nearer to it than you?

Mrs. Alving. I? Your mother!

Oswald. For that very reason.

Mrs. Alving. I, who gave you life?

Oswald. I never asked you for life. And what sort of life is it that you have given me? I will not have it. You shall take it back again.

Mrs. Alving. Help! Help! (*Runs into the hall.*)

Oswald. (*Following*) Don't leave me. Where are you going?

Mrs. Alving. (*In the hall*) To fetch the doctor, Oswald. Let me go.

Oswald. You shall not go. And no one shall come in. (*Sound of door being locked*)

Mrs. Alving. (*Re-enters.*) Oswald — Oswald — my boy!

Oswald. (*Following her*) Have you a mother's heart for me, and yet can see me suffer from this unutterable dread?

Mrs. Alving. (*After a moment's silence, controls herself.*) Here is my hand upon it.

Oswald. Will you — ?

Mrs. Alving. If it is ever necessary. But it will never be necessary. No, no — it is impossible.

Oswald. Well, let us hope so. And let us live together as long as we can. Thank you, Mother. (*He sits in the armchair which* Mrs. Alving *had pushed to the couch. Day is breaking; the lamp on the table is still burning.*)

Mrs. Alving. (*Cautiously approaching*) Do you feel calm now?

Oswald. Yes.

MRS. ALVING. (*Bending over him*) It has been a dreadful fancy of yours. Oswald — nothing but a fancy. You have not been able to bear all this excitement. But now you shall have a long rest; at home with your own mother, my darling boy. Everything you point to you shall have, just as when you were a child. There, now! That crisis is over now. You see how easily it passed. Oh! I was sure it would — And do you see, Oswald, what a lovely day we are going to have? Brilliant sunshine! Now you will really be able to see your home. (*She goes to the table and puts out the lamp. The sun has risen. Glaciers and distant peaks are bathed in bright morning light.*)

OSWALD. (*Sits in the armchair with his back to the conservatory, motionless; suddenly he speaks.*) Mother, give me the sun.

MRS. ALVING. (*Standing by the table, looks at him in amazement.*) What do you say?

OSWALD. (*Again his voice is toneless.*) The sun. The sun.

MRS. ALVING. (*Goes to him.*) Oswald, what is the matter with you? (*He seems to shrink up in the chair; his muscles relax; his face loses its expression; his eyes stare stupidly.* MRS. ALVING *is trembling with terror.*) What is this? (*She screams.*) Oswald, what is the matter with you? (*She half kneels beside him, shaking him.*) Oswald, Oswald! Look at me! Don't you know me?

OSWALD. The sun. The sun.

MRS. ALVING. (*Jumps up in desperation, beats her head with her hands, and screams.*) I can't bear it. (*Whispers, paralyzed with fear.*) I can't bear it! Never! Where has he got them? (*Passes her hand quickly over his coat.*) Here! (*Draws back.*) No, no, no — Yes! — no, no! (*She stands a few steps from him, her hands thrust into her hair, and stares at him in speechless terror.*)

OSWALD. (*Sitting motionless.*) The sun. The sun.

After you have finished the reading of *Ghosts*, take some time to think about it before rereading. If you will ask yourself certain questions, your second reading will be a richer dramatic experience, closer to the experience of *seeing* the play in a theater.

Can you describe the setting? Check your memory by rereading the stage directions at the beginning of Act One. Are any of the details of the physical setting important for the action of the play? Or could the same action be played, *with the same effect,* in any living room? or on an empty platform?

How much time elapses in the performance of the play? What is the approximate hour when the curtain rises on Act One? when it falls on Act Three? Are there any noticeable breaks in the play, any points where you are aware that the action is not continuous? What effect does continuity of time have on the telling of the story?

Can you visualize and distinguish between the characters? What does each one look like? wear? Can you hear the speaking voice of each? Is there, for instance, a difference between Engstrand's manner of speaking and Manders'?

How many characters are there in the play? Is each one vital to the action, or could one or two be omitted without damaging the story?

What brings them all together at this particular time and place? What permits them to separate at the end of the play?

How do we find out about the situation at the beginning of the play? about the past history of each character? In your rereading check the passages that reveal the relationship between Mrs. Alving and Pastor Manders; that reveal the character of Captain Alving. Do these passages of *exposition* form a pattern with the developing *action* of the play?

After Rereading Ghosts

You should now have a point of view about *Ghosts,* some notion of what the play is about, what Ibsen meant his story to reveal. We shall have occasion to revert to the play many times in the following discussion of technique and structure, and towards the end of our discussion we shall attempt to give a complete analysis of *Ghosts* in terms of our fuller knowledge. However, the answers you have given to the questions at the end of your first reading have probably at least suggested the central idea of the play.

Ghosts, from its first production in 1881, has been a highly controversial work, attacked and defended by critics in all countries where it was performed. Since it has been, in a sense, the standard bearer of the modern drama, it has been widely produced, and widely attacked, and widely interpreted. In the light of your own present opinion of the play, you might be interested in a few indications of other critical interpretations.

At its first London performance, it was described as a " lugubrious diagnosis of sordid impropriety." Bernard Shaw saw it as an attack " on marriage as a useless sacrifice of human beings to an ideal." H. L. Mencken held that it was intended to " raise a laugh " against alarmed moralists who thought Ibsen an apostle of free love. For other critics it was a naturalistic study of heredity — this on the assumption that Oswald is the central character of the play. John Gassner, however, suggests the more generally accepted interpretation which has become possible only with the passing of the better part of a century since the original production: " Heredity . . . is conceived in a manner that suggests the Greek idea of fate and retribution rather than the dull pronunciamentos of a eugenics forum."

Many men, many opinions. And there are others, based on the premises of Freud, and Marx, and other lawgivers. It is entirely possible that the meaning of a play may change in the course of a hundred years as one historical or cultural situation gives way to another. It will be our purpose, in the following discussion, to try to arrive at certain standards for judgment which will not be dependent upon the climates of opinion or changing currents of taste — the fundamental and inherent values of an art form itself. Let us grant at once that we can never see a work of art " plain." Subjective values will enter in, since the play is addressed to human beings and human beings cannot separate themselves wholly from the society, the culture, the ideals in and by which they live. But we can at least learn to find, as it were, the evidence on which our judgment will be exercised: the materials and structure of the play by which the playwright reveals his interpretation of human experience.

II

THE PLAYHOUSE AND THE PLAY

When we use the familiar and classical term *theater* and its literal meaning of " seeing place," we are speaking from the point of view of the audience. But we have already seen that, from the point of view of the *makers* of the dramatic experience, the English term *playhouse* is more apposite. Think of its domestic analogues: the spacious Victorian mansion which demanded the acquisition of furniture and the lavish display of pictures and ornaments, and encouraged, through the privacy of many rooms, the development of individuality — a home for many, and frequently divers, activities; or, on the other hand, the modern " functional " apartment, bare of ornament, with the irreducible minimum of furnishings — little more than a headquarters for people whose interests and activities are elsewhere. Consider the tent of the nomad, the palace of the king. Each of these houses shapes to a certain extent the lives of its inhabitants, limiting or determining or encouraging their activities.

So it is with the playhouse, the home of the play and the first of the tools with which the playwright works. We will shortly see that there have been many forms of playhouses, as there have been many forms of human habitations, but they have certain things in common. Every playhouse has an area for the spectator and an area for the actor, though they may be arranged in strikingly different relationships. And each form of playhouse achieves in the course of its history a permanent state — becomes, that is, an architectural pattern to be reduplicated whenever new playhouses are constructed. It is at this point that it becomes a tool for the playwright, a fixed, conventional structure to be taken into consideration in the shaping of the drama.

The playwright, for instance, will have to consider whether his play is to be performed in the open air or in a roofed auditorium. The open-air theater, which may seat as many as ten thousand spectators, is lighted only by the sun (if the gods are propitious) and generally provides no curtain to cover the changing of scenery or the passing of time. The indoor theater, on the other hand, relies upon artificial lighting, permits the use of mechanical and scenic effects, and is generally equipped with a curtain to cover a change in scene, or a break in the action, or — very conventionally — to allow the audience to relax during an intermission.

The structure of the playhouse, as it affects the relationship between the playgoer and the play itself, will force the playwright to take into consideration such matters as audibility and visibility and will determine the broadness or the subtlety of his action, characterization, and speech, and will have much to do with the even more basic problem of the selection of a subject for dramatic treatment.

Since, according to Lord Byron, " Good workmen never quarrel with their tools," most playwrights learn to adjust their creative work to the physical and mechanical conditions of the playhouse available to them. For most, in fact, the playhouse is like the old homestead, a natural habitat, not to be questioned or changed, but to be thankfully occupied. For the more skillful and adventurous, the playhouse offers possibilities to be exploited, and for only a few, of great originality or surpassing laziness, it is too obstinate or too difficult to comply with.

The Playhouse of Realism

Most modern theater-goers are accustomed to a playhouse in which the spectators are more or less comfortably seated in rows facing a platform stage. In front of them is a picture frame, the proscenium, behind which the characters will live out their destinies in rooms with three solid walls, or exteriors which give with varying degrees of success the illusion of nature, or reality. On his first visit to such a theater, the modern spectator is apt to react much like Jonathan, the comic New Englander of one of the earliest American plays. Exploring New York, he finds himself without knowing it in a theater. " They lifted up a great green cloth," he explains with some wonder, " and let us look right into the next neighbor's house."

It was for this kind of playhouse that Ibsen wrote *Ghosts*. Because of the familiarity of this theater of realistic illusion, it will be well to pause and consider it briefly as a tool of the playwright before entering on the historical development of the playhouse and its influence on dramatic art.

Ibsen's theater was, of course, an indoor theater, and while this limited the size of his audience, it placed at his command the mechanical resources of lighting and scene painting. The stage directions in the text of *Ghosts* are plain indications of his desire to make the most of his realistic opportunities. First, the room in which the action takes place is to be carefully erected on the stage, with doors and windows and furniture and rugs and potted plants. While this is so customary in the theater of the last hundred years as to pass almost unnoticed by a spectator, it is worth pointing out that when Ibsen first began writing, it was still customary to paint furniture on a backdrop, and to make entrances onto the stage through imaginary doors between the side-scenes or wings. However, Ibsen does not stop with the creation of the scene of the action; he insists that the audience be aware of the lay-out of the unseen portion of the house, of the surrounding grounds, and even of the geographical setting. The house is remote from its little village, and even more distant from an urban center (so Manders could not have been aware of Mrs. Alving's life with her husband; so, more fundamentally, Alving's own life was destroyed by the frustration and joylessness and boredom of provincial isolation). Somewhere near the house an orphanage is being constructed (this unseen building brings all of the characters of the play together, and its burning — made visible by the reflection of the flames in the conservatory window — precipitates the climax of the action). To the left of the revealed room of the house is a dining room (here with a clink of glassware and the overturning of a chair and an almost whispered sentence is struck the blow which ultimately will complete the fall of the House of Alving).

Ibsen fills the action of his play with small domestic details: plants are watered, pipes are smoked; the characters sew, read, eat; lamps are lighted and blown out, and wet clothes drip on the carpet. Each small detail contributes, sometimes in a major way, to the dramatic experience. The evidences of Mrs. Alving's reading foreshadow the ultimate conflict between the lady and the pastor; the entrance of Oswald, smoking his father's pipe, presents to Manders an image of Captain Alving. But, aside from their organic relationship to the intention of the playwright, these small domestic details contribute to the verisimilitude of the play, to the illusion of reality. Audiences are willing to accept as tragic the adventures of kings or heroes; they have been known to reject as preposterous the efforts of playwrights to find the magnitude of tragic action in the adventures of " an average man." The basic story of *Ghosts* is not unlike the basic story of a Greek tragedy, but the Greek playwright was in a sense protected by the presence in his story of gods and legendary heroes; their violence, their catastrophic fate, was their natural reason for being. Ibsen appeals neither to legend nor divine will; the theater of realistic illusion permits him to create the appearance of a direct experience for the spectator. Because it is experienced it is true, and because it is the truth (however humble) it is worthy of understanding.

But the playhouse of realistic illusion, where the playgoer is encouraged to become a kind of licensed Peeping Tom, is only the modern end-product of a long and complex development, one in which aesthetic considerations frequently played a less important role than social or religious pressures. When in the course of its history the drama reached one of its productive peaks (in ancient Greece, or Elizabethan England, for instance), the theater building of the moment usually played an integrated organic part in the playwright's design and in the dramatic experience of the spectators.

The Focussed Playhouse

We have already noted that many of the conventions with which the playwright works are architectural: the size and shape of the playhouse, the nature of the stage and scenic devices, the physical relationship between the actor's area and the spectator's area. A knowledge of the architectural conditions of a certain theater frequently helps to explain puzzling aspects of the plays performed in that theater; some acquaintance with stage conventions frequently illuminates the whole " idea of a theater " in a given period. The attempt to study the drama of the past with only the theater of Ibsen in the mind's eye will lead inevitably to distortion and misunderstanding.

Charles Lamb, an otherwise sensitive critic with a deep love of the theater, declared at the beginning of the nineteenth century that Shakespeare's *King Lear* was really a closet drama, that it could never be realized on the stage. Now, Lamb had revealed his devotion to Shakespeare in many pious exercises, and it is strange to find him thus implying that a master craftsman did not know his business. But Lamb had never seen *Lear* on the stage. He had seen only a version that had been cut and arranged to fit vastly different mechanical and architectural conditions from those for which Shakespeare wrote. Even at the end of the nineteenth century, when knowledge of Elizabethan stage conventions was more widespread and one or two tentative experiments at reproducing the conventions had been made, Professor A. C. Bradley, in his widely influential book on *Shakespearean Tragedy*, refused to seek illumination from the theater. In Bradley's day, Shakespeare on the stage automatically meant the versions of Sir Henry Irving and other actor-managers who ruthlessly tailored the text to suit their personalities and their late-Victorian concepts of good theater. But while such vulgar errors have been corrected by the vigorous efforts of scholarly critics and directors, an equally serious and widespread misunderstanding of the nature of the Greek stage is an almost insuperable obstacle to the true appreciation of ancient drama.

It is assumed (largely on the basis of well-meant but misguided amateur productions) that a Greek dramatic performance consisted of a number of white-robed ladies wandering mournfully among white columns ranged in a row before a huge doorway reached by a long flight of steps up which the leading actress will stagger to her doom. Nothing could be farther from the dramatic conditions of fifth-century Greece, or from the dramatic experience the Greek playwrights intended for their audiences. The attempt to recover these conditions is not pedantry, but a necessary preliminary to both study and theatrical revival; the scholar and critic will acquire the controls necessary for informed judgment, and the producer will be guided to the conventions and devices of the modern theater which will evoke a dramatic experience equivalent to that contemplated by his author.

Ancient Greek drama was written to be performed in the open air in enormous circular amphitheaters. The common comparison between Greek theater and modern sports stadium is suggestive but inaccurate: the first and perhaps most controlling characteristic of the Greek theater is the circular shape of both the actor's and the spectator's areas. The theater took this shape as a response to the form of the earliest performances — the choral dances; once the circular structure had become conventional it was a strong influence in determining the structure of the drama as it continued to develop into the tragedies of Aeschylus, Sophocles, and Euripides.

While we recognize that a good deal of the early history of an art as ancient as the theater must necessarily be based on hypothesis, much patient digging, both in the actual soil of Greece and in the surviving literary texts, has established a history that in its general outline has found wide acceptance. In the preceding chapter we were present at a performance of an hypothetical dithyramb, the first formal manifestation of the drama, sung and danced by a chorus of fifty men and boys. The early natives of Greece had customarily performed round dances with a chorus circling about some central object, an altar or perhaps a chorus leader or priest. Hence the dancing area (*orchestra*) came to be circular and large enough to accommodate the free movement of the large number of performers. Since the dithyramb was originally a tribal or village rite, the spectators at first simply stood at the edge of the orchestra, making an outer circle around the dancing chorus. As dithyramb gave birth to drama, and drama became a part of the festivals of Athens, accommodations for a vast audience (as many as 14,000 spectators) were required, and these were provided in the form of tiers of wooden seats rising in concentric rings from the orchestra, but still very nearly encircling the whole performing area.

The one break in the circle of spectators was the space allowed for a scene building. This was the latest addition to the Greek theatrical structure, and during the most productive period of Greek playwrighting (490–405 B.C.) its function should be clearly distinguished from that of the acting area, the orchestra. It is not known, of course, when the great theater in Athens, the Theater of Dionysos, was begun, but it is safe to assume that it began, like the theater in Ikaria, as a dancing circle for the performers of dithyrambs. By the year 534 B.C., when Thespis won his first dramatic prize in Athens, the theater was being used regularly for the enactment of plays. It is evident that different troupes of actors, Athenian and provincial, were engaged in the dramatic festivals, and, although their plays did not require scenery, the actors did need a place to get into their costumes. At first a tent of hides (*skené*) was set up outside the orchestra. Later, as the drama became a more and more important part of the festivals, the temporary skené was replaced by a permanent scene building (*skenotheke*), a simple, one-story structure just touching the rim of the orchestra. It was not a stage in the later sense of the word; it had no elevated platform and it was not used as a major acting area. The doors (it became convenient, and therefore conventional, to have three) were used for the entrances and exits of the main actors, and the audience might be asked to assume that the building itself was a palace or a temple if it suited the playwright. Occasionally a god might make his appearance on the low roof, or a murderer dispatch his victim behind the closed doors, but the long tradition of the drama and the convenience of the spectators dictated that the main action of a play should take place at the center of the orchestra.

The earliest surviving Greek tragedy, *The Suppliant Maidens* by Aeschylus, suggests the conditions of the performance at the beginning of the recorded history of drama. Produced at the Theater of Dionysos about 492 B.C., it tells of fifty maidens who flee from an incestuous marriage with their fifty cousins. Led by their father, Danaus, they come to a sacred precinct (a place with an altar) on the shore of Argos. Here they are addressed by their father and then, hearing someone coming, they cling to the shrines. The newcomer is the King of Argos who agrees to consider their plea for succor. As he departs to put the question to his community, the maidens sing a long prayer to Zeus. Danaus returns to announce, at considerable length, that the citizens have agreed to help his daughters. They now sing a long ode of praise to the gods. However, the fifty cousins are not prepared to give up so easily. Their herald enters and tells the daughters of the pursuit which has been organized, threatens them, and even attempts to pull some of them away from the sacred spot by the hair. He is prevented by the return of the King of Argos. The play ends with the maidens temporarily safe, but with the threat of further action from their suitors hanging over them.

It will be seen that *The Suppliant Maidens* has not advanced the art of playwrighting very far beyond the first attempts of Thespis. The acting area is used mainly for reports and discussion. The actor's speeches are long, and the singing and dancing of the chorus still occupies the major portion of the play. Nothing is required in the way of setting except an altar, and around this altar the whole of the visible action of the play takes place. The scene building, permanent or temporary, served for little more than a place of entrance for the King of Argos and might — if the spectators were conscious of it — have been taken as the city wall. Certainly the maidens and Danaus and the herald, who were supposed to have arrived from the sea, would enter from some other point on the orchestra circle.

This then was the basic form of what we may conveniently call the *focussed theater*. The acting area is a large flat circle, perhaps seventy feet in diameter. In the center stands an altar or shrine, a reminder of the ritual origin of the art, and frequently the focal point of the action. Here the chief actor or actors argue and debate, quarrel and conclude. Around the chief actors, in a ring or in groups, stands or sings or dances the chorus, diminished from the fifty men of the dithyramb and *The Suppliant Maidens* to a more manageable fifteen. And around the chorus, seated on the inside of a great cone or funnel, are the spectators.

These spectators, as always, are the controlling element in dramatic art; they are the cause of its creation; the experience they are to have determines everything that the playwright does in choosing his subject, arranging his dramatic design, instructing his actors. In the focussed theater, the audience is a kind of god, both in its geographical relation to the action and in its intellectual perception. It sits, as it were, upon Mount Ida and watches the struggles of heroes and demigods. Like the gods themselves, the spectators are aware of the outcome of the story: Greek playwrights dealt always with familiar legends. If the hero is ignorant of his situation and his eventual fate, the spectator is not. The spectator, in fact, is very much like the Zeus of the *Iliad*:

But now Zeus wakened
By Hera of the golden throne on the high places of Ida,
and stood suddenly upright, and saw the Achians and Trojans,
these driven to flight, the others harrying them in confusion,
these last Argives, and saw among them the Lord Poseidon.
He saw Hector lying in the plain, his companions sitting
around him, he dazed at the heart and breathing painfully,
vomiting blood. . . .
Then the father of gods and men seeing Hector, pitied him.[1]
(Translated by Richmond Lattimore)

It was for the focussed theater with its circular orchestra, central shrine and almost completely dispensable scene building, and for an audience seated like gods around and above the actors that Aeschylus designed *Prometheus Bound*.

The audience, assembling at dawn in the vast spectator's area of the Theater of Dionysos, would know that they were about to see a play about the legendary hero, Prometheus. They would know at least the general outlines of his story: how the Titan Prometheus had assisted Zeus in overthrowing the old gods; how he had revolted against the plan of Zeus to destroy the race of man and create a new; how he had stolen fire from heaven and brought it to earth, the gift that made possible human civilization. They would know that Zeus, angry at this betrayal, had ordered the Titan to be bound to a peak in the Caucasus, and subjected to eternal torment.

[1] Quoted by permission from *The Iliad of Homer*, translated with an introduction by Richmond Lattimore, University of Chicago Press, 1951.

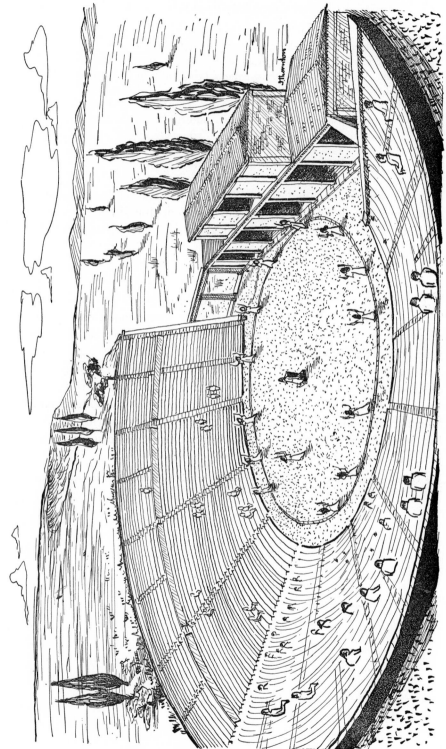

The Focussed Playhouse

PROMETHEUS BOUND

A TRAGEDY

by Aeschylus

TRANSLATED BY EDITH HAMILTON

CHARACTERS

HEPHESTUS (VULCAN)	OCEAN
FORCE	IO
VIOLENCE	HERMES (MERCURY)
PROMETHEUS	CHORUS OF OCEANIDES

SCENE: PROMETHEUS *by tradition was fastened to a peak of the Caucasus.*

FORCE

Far have we come to this far spot of earth,
this narrow Scythian land, a desert all un-
trodden.
God of the forge and fire, yours the task
the Father laid upon you.
To this high-piercing, head-long rock
in adamantine chains that none can break
bind him — him here, who dared all things.
Your flaming flower he stole to give to men,
fire, the master craftsman, through whose
power
all things are wrought, and for such error
now
he must repay the gods; be taught to yield
to Zeus' lordship and to cease
from his man-loving way.

HEPHESTUS

Force, Violence, what Zeus enjoined on you
has here an end. Your task is done.
But as for me, I am not bold to bind
a god, a kinsman, to this stormy crag.

Yet I must needs be bold.
His load is heavy who dares disobey the Father's word.
O high-souled child of Justice, the wise coun-
selor,
against my will as against yours I nail you
fast
in brazen fetters never to be loosed
to this rock peak, where no man ever comes,
where never voice or face of mortal you will
see.
The shining splendor of the sun shall wither
you.
Welcome to you will be the night
when with her mantle star-inwrought
she hides the light of day.
And welcome then in turn the sun
to melt the frost the dawn has left behind.
Forever shall the intolerable present grind
you down,
and he who will release you is not born.
Such fruit you reap for your man-loving
way.
A god yourself, you did not dread God's
anger,
but gave to mortals honor not their due,

65

and therefore you must guard this joyless
   rock —
no rest, no sleep, no moment's respite.
Groans shall your speech be, lamentation
your only words — all uselessly.
Zeus has no mind to pity. He is harsh,
like upstarts always.

FORCE

Well then, why this delay and foolish talk?
A god whom gods hate is abominable.

HEPHESTUS

The tie of blood has a strange power,
and old acquaintance too.

FORCE

And so say I—but don't you think
that disobedience to the Father's words
might have still stranger power?

HEPHESTUS

You're rough, as always. Pity is not in you.

FORCE

Much good is pity here. Why all this pother
that helps him not a whit?

HEPHESTUS

O skill of hand now hateful to me.

FORCE

Why blame your skill? These troubles here
were never caused by it. That's simple truth.

HEPHESTUS

Yet would it were another's and not mine.

FORCE

Trouble is everywhere except in heaven.
No one is free but Zeus.

HEPHESTUS

I know — I've not a word to say.

FORCE

Come then. Make haste. On with his fetters.
What if the Father sees you lingering?

HEPHESTUS

The chains are ready here if he should look.

FORCE

Seize his hands and master him.
Now to your hammer. Pin him to the rocks.

HEPHESTUS

All done, and quick work too.

FORCE

Still harder. Tighter. Never loose your hold.
For he is good at finding a way out where
   there is none.

HEPHESTUS

This arm at least he will not ever free.

FORCE

Buckle the other fast, and let him learn
with all his cunning he's a fool to Zeus.

HEPHESTUS

No one but he, poor wretch, can blame my
   work.

FORCE

Drive stoutly now your wedge straight
   through his breast,
the stubborn jaw of steel that cannot break.

HEPHESTUS

Alas, Prometheus, I grieve for your pain.

FORCE

You shirk your task and grieve for those
   Zeus hates?
Take care; you may need pity for yourself.

HEPHESTUS

You see a sight eyes should not look upon.

FORCE

I see one who has got what he deserves.
But come. The girdle now around his waist.

HEPHESTUS

What must be shall be done. No need to urge
   me.

FORCE

I will and louder too. Down with you now.
Make fast his legs in rings. Use all your
    strength.

HEPHESTUS

Done and small trouble.

FORCE

Now for his feet. Drive the nails through the
    flesh.
The judge is stern who passes on our work.

HEPHESTUS

Your tongue and face match well.

FORCE

Why, you poor weakling. Are you one to
    cast
a savage temper in another's face?

HEPHESTUS

Oh, let us go. Chains hold him, hand and
    foot.

FORCE

Run riot now, you there upon the rocks.
Go steal from gods to give their goods to
    men —
to men whose life is but a little day.
What will they do to lift these woes from
    you?
Forethought your name means, falsely
    named.
Forethought you lack and need now for your-
    self
if you would slip through fetters wrought
    like these.
    (*Exeunt* FORCE, VIOLENCE, HEPHESTUS.)

PROMETHEUS

O air of heaven and swift-winged winds,
O running river waters,
O never numbered laughter of sea waves,
Earth, mother of all, Eye of the sun, all see-
    ing,
on you I call.
Behold what I, a god, endure from gods.
See in what tortures I must struggle

through countless years of time.
This shame, these bonds, are put upon me
by the new ruler of the gods.
Sorrow enough in what is here and what is
    still to come.
It wrings groans from me.
When shall the end be, the appointed end?
And yet why ask?
All, all I knew before,
all that should be.
Nothing, no pang of pain
that I did not foresee.
Bear without struggle what must be.
Necessity is strong and ends our strife.
But silence is intolerable here.
So too is speech.
I am fast bound, I must endure.
I gave to mortals gifts.
I hunted out the secret source of fire.
I filled a reed therewith,
fire, the teacher of all arts to men,
the great way through.
These are the crimes that I must pay for,
pinned to a rock beneath the open sky.

But what is here? What comes?
What sound, what fragrance, brushed me
    with faint wings,
of deities or mortals or of both?
Has someone found a way to this far peak
to view my agony? What else?
Look at me then, in chains, a god who failed,
the enemy of Zeus, whom all gods hate,
all that go in and out of Zeus' hall.
The reason is that I loved men too well.
Oh, birds are moving near me. The air mur-
    murs
with swift and sweeping wings.
Whatever comes to me is terrible.
    (*Enter* CHORUS. *They are* SEA NYMPHS.)

LEADER

Oh, be not terrified, for friends are here,
each eager to be first,
on swift wings flying to your rock.
I prayed my father long
before he let me come.
The rushing winds have sped me on.

A noise of ringing brass went through the
    sea-caves,
and for all a maiden's fears it drove me forth,
so swift, I did not put my sandals on,
but in my winged car I came to you.

PROMETHEUS

To see this sight —
Daughters of fertile Tethys,
children of Ocean who forever flows
unresting round earth's shores,
behold me, and my bonds
that bind me fast upon the rocky height
of this cleft mountain side,
keeping my watch of pain.

SEA NYMPH

I look upon you and a mist of tears,
of grief and terror, rises as I see
your body withering upon the rocks,
in shameful fetters.
For a new helmsman steers Olympus.
By new laws Zeus is ruling without law.
He has put down the mighty ones of old.

PROMETHEUS

Oh, had I been sent deep, deep into earth,
to that black boundless place where go the
    dead,
though cruel chains should hold me fast for-
    ever,
I should be hid from sight of gods and men.
But now I am a plaything for the winds.
My enemies exult — and I endure.

ANOTHER NYMPH

What god so hard of heart to look on these
    things gladly?
Who, but Zeus only, would not suffer with
    you?
He is malignant always and his mind
unbending. All the sons of heaven
he drives beneath his yoke.
Nor will he make an end
until his heart is sated or until
someone, somehow, shall seize his sovereign-
    ty —
if that could be.

PROMETHEUS

And yet — and yet — all tortured though I
    am,
fast fettered here,
he shall have need of me, the lord of heaven,
to show to him the strange design
by which he shall be stripped of throne and
    scepter.
But he will never win me over
with honeyed spell of soft, persuading words,
nor will I ever cower beneath his threats
to tell him what he seeks.
First he must free me from this savage prison
and pay for all my pain.

ANOTHER NYMPH

Oh, you are bold. In bitter agony
you will not yield.
These are such words as only free men speak.
Piercing terror stings my heart.
I fear because of what has come to you.
Where are you fated to put in to shore
and find a haven from this troubled sea?
Prayers cannot move,
persuasions cannot turn,
the heart of Kronos' son.

PROMETHEUS

I know that he is savage.
He keeps his righteousness at home.
But yet some time he shall be mild of mood,
when he is broken.
He will smooth his stubborn temper,
and run to meet me.
Then peace will come and love between us
    two.

LEADER

Reveal the whole to us. Tell us your tale.
What guilt does Zeus impute
to torture you in shame and bitterness?
Teach us, if you may speak.

PROMETHEUS

To speak is pain, but silence too is pain,
and everywhere is wretchedness.
When first the gods began to quarrel
and faction rose among them,

some wishing to throw Kronos out of heaven,
that Zeus, Zeus, mark you, should be lord,
others opposed, pressing the opposite,
that Zeus should never rule the gods,
then I, giving wise counsel to the Titans,
children of Earth and Heaven, could not prevail.
My way out was a shrewd one, they despised
 it,
and in their arrogant minds they thought to
 conquer
with ease, by their own strength.
But Justice, she who is my mother, told
 me —
Earth she is sometimes called,
whose form is one, whose name is many —
she told me, and not once alone.
the future, how it should be brought to pass,
that neither violence nor strength of arm
but only subtle craft could win.
I made all clear to them.
They scorned to look my way.
The best then left me was to stand with Zeus
in all good will, my mother with me,
and, through my counsel, the black under-
 world
covered, and hides within its secret depths
Kronos the aged and his host.
Such good the ruler of the gods had from me,
and with such evil he has paid me back.
There is a sickness that infects all tyrants,
they cannot trust their friends.
But you have asked a question I would an-
 swer:
What is my crime that I am tortured for?
Zeus had no sooner seized his father's throne
than he was giving to each god a post
and ordering his kingdom,
but mortals in their misery
he took no thought for.
His wish was they should perish
and he would then beget another race.
And there were none to cross his will save I.
I dared it, I saved men.
Therefore I am bowed down in torment,
grievous to suffer, pitiful to see.
I pitied mortals,
I never thought to meet with this.

Ruthlessly punished here I am
an infamy to Zeus.

LEADER

Iron of heart or wrought from rock is he
who does not suffer in your misery.
Oh, that these eyes had never looked upon it.
I see it and my heart is wrung.

PROMETHEUS

A friend must feel I am a thing to pity.

LEADER

Did you perhaps go even further still?

PROMETHEUS

I made men cease to live with death in sight.

LEADER

What potion did you find to cure this sickness?

PROMETHEUS

Blind hopes I caused to dwell in them.

ANOTHER NYMPH

Great good to men that gift.

PROMETHEUS

To it I added the good gift of fire.

ANOTHER NYMPH

And now the creatures of a day
have flaming fire?

PROMETHEUS

Yes, and learn many crafts therefrom.

LEADER

For deeds like these Zeus holds you guilty,
and tortures you with never ease from pain?
Is no end to your anguish set before you?

PROMETHEUS

None other except when it pleases him.

LEADER

It pleases him? What hope there? You must
 see

you missed your mark. I tell you this with
    pain
to give you pain.
But let that pass. Seek your deliverance.

PROMETHEUS

Your feet are free.
Chains bind mine fast.
Advice is easy for the fortunate.
All that has come I knew full well.
Of my own will I shot the arrow that fell
    short,
of my own will.
Nothing do I deny.
I helped men and found trouble for myself.
I knew — and yet not all.
I did not think to waste away
hung high in air upon a lonely rock.
But now, I pray you, no more pity
for what I suffer here. Come, leave your car,
and learn the fate that steals upon me,
all, to the very end.
Hear me, oh, hear me. Share my pain. Re-
    member,
trouble may wander far and wide
but it is always near.

LEADER

You cry to willing ears, Prometheus.
Lightly I leave my swiftly speeding car
and the pure ways of air where go the birds.
I stand upon this stony ground.
I ask to hear your troubles to the end.

(*Enter* OCEAN *riding on a four-footed bird.
The* CHORUS *draws back, and he does not see
them.*)

OCEAN

Well, here at last, an end to a long journey.
I've made my way to you, Prometheus.
This bird of mine is swift of wing
but I can guide him by my will,
without a bridle.
Now you must know, I'm grieved at your
    misfortunes.
Of course I must be, I'm your kinsman.
And that apart, there's no one I think more
    of.

And you'll find out the truth of what I'm
    saying.
It isn't in me to talk flattery.
Come: tell me just what must be done to help
    you,
and never say that you've a firmer friend
than you will find in me.

PROMETHEUS

Oho! What's here? You? Come to see my
    troubles?
How did you dare to leave your ocean river,
your rock caves hollowed by the sea,
and stand upon the iron mother earth?
Was it to see what has befallen me,
because you grieve with me?
Then see this sight: here is the friend of Zeus,
who helped to make him master.
This twisted body is his handiwork.

OCEAN

I see, Prometheus. I do wish
You'd take some good advice.
I know you're very clever,
but real self-knowledge — that you haven't
    got.
New fashions have come in with this new
    ruler.
Why can't you change your own to suit?
Don't talk like that — so rude and irritating.
Zeus isn't so far off but he might hear,
and what would happen then would make
    these troubles
seem child's play.
You're miserable. Then do control your tem-
    per
and find some remedy.
Of course you think you know all that I'm
    saying.
You certainly should know the harm
that blustering has brought you.
But you're not humbled yet. You won't give
    in.
You're looking for more trouble.
Just learn one thing from me:
Don't kick against the pricks.
You see he's savage — why not? He's a
    tyrant.

He doesn't have to hand in his accounts.
Well, now I'm going straight to try
if I can free you from this wretched business.
Do you keep still. No more of this rash talk-
    ing.
Haven't you yet learned with all your wis-
    dom
the mischief that a foolish tongue can make?

PROMETHEUS

Wisdom? The praise for that is yours alone,
who shared and dared with me and yet were
    able
to shun all blame.
But — let be now. Give not a thought more
    to me.
You never would persuade him.
He is not easy to win over.
Be cautious. Keep a sharp lookout,
or on your way back you may come to harm.

OCEAN

You counsel others better than yourself,
to judge by what I hear and what I see.
But I won't let you turn me off.
I really want to serve you.
And I am proud, yes, proud to say
I know that Zeus will let you go
just as a favor done to me.

PROMETHEUS

I thank you for the good will you would
    show me.
But spare your pains. Your trouble would be
    wasted.
The effort, if indeed you wish to make it,
could never help me.
Now you are out of harm's way. Stay there.
Because I am unfortunate myself
I would not wish that others too should be.
Not so. Even here the lot of Atlas, of my
    brother,
weighs on me. In the western country
he stands, and on his shoulders is the pillar
that holds apart the earth and sky,
a load not easy to be borne.
Pity too filled my heart when once I saw

swift Typhon overpowered.
Child of the Earth was he, who lived
in caves in the Cilician land,
a flaming monster with a hundred heads,
who rose up against all the gods.
Death whistled from his fearful jaws.
His eyes flashed glaring fire.
I thought he would have wrecked God's sov-
    ereignty.
But to him came the sleepless bolt of Zeus,
down from the sky, thunder with breath of
    flame,
and all his high boasts were struck dumb.
Into his very heart the fire burned.
His strength was turned to ashes.
And now he lies a useless thing,
a sprawling body, near the narrow sea-way
by Aetna, underneath the mountain's roots.
High on the peak the god of fire sits,
welding the molten iron in his forge,
whence sometimes there will burst
rivers red hot, consuming with fierce jaws
the level fields of Sicily,
lovely with fruits.
And that is Typhon's anger boiling up,
his darts of flame none may abide,
of fire-breathing spray,
scorched to a cinder though he is
by Zeus' bolt.
But you are no man's fool; you have no need
to learn from me. Keep yourself safe,
as you well know the way.
And I will drain my cup to the last drop,
until Zeus shall abate his insolence of rage.

OCEAN

And yet you know the saying,
when anger reaches fever heat
wise words are a physician.

PROMETHEUS

Not when the heart is full to bursting.
Wait for the crisis; then the balm will soothe.

OCEAN

But if one were discreet as well as daring — ?
You don't see danger then? Advise me.

PROMETHEUS

I see your trouble wasted,
and you good-natured to the point of folly.

OCEAN

That's a complaint I don't mind catching.
Let be: I'll choose to seem a fool
if I can be a loyal friend.

PROMETHEUS

But he will lay to me all that you do.

OCEAN

There you have said what needs must send
   me home.

PROMETHEUS

Just so. All your lamenting over me
will not have got you then an enemy.

OCEAN

Meaning — the new possessor of the throne?

PROMETHEUS

Be on your guard. See that you do not vex
   him.

OCEAN

Your case, Prometheus, may well teach me —

PROMETHEUS

Off with you. Go — and keep your present
   mind.

OCEAN

You urge one who is eager to be gone.
For my four-footed bird is restless
to skim with wings the level ways of air.
He'll be well pleased to rest in his home
   stable.
(*Exit* OCEAN. *The* CHORUS *now come forward.*)

CHORUS

I mourn for you, Prometheus.
Desolation is upon you.
My face is wet with weeping.
Tears fall as waters which run continually.

The floods overflow me.
Terrible are the deeds of Zeus.
He rules by laws that are his own.
High is his spear above the others,
turned against the gods of old.
All the land now groans aloud,
mourning for the honor of the heroes of your
   race.
Stately were they, honored ever in the days
   of long ago.
Holy Asia is hard by.
Those that dwell there suffer in your trouble,
   great and sore.
In the Colchian land maidens live,
fearless in fight.
Scythia has a battle throng,
the farthest place of earth is theirs,
where marsh grass grows around Maeotis lake.
Arabia's flower is a warrior host;
high on a cliff their fortress stands,
Caucasus towers near;
men fierce as the fire, like the roar of the fire
they shout when the sharp spears clash.
All suffer with you in your trouble, great
   and sore.
Another Titan too, Earth mourns,
bound in shame and iron bonds.
I saw him, Atlas the god.
He bears on his back forever
the cruel strength of the crushing world
and the vault of the sky.
He groans beneath them.
The foaming sea-surge roars in answer,
the deep laments,
the black place of death far down in earth is
   moved exceedingly,
and the pure-flowing river waters grieve for
   him in his piteous pain.

PROMETHEUS

Neither in insolence nor yet in stubbornness
have I kept silence.
It is thought that eats my heart,
seeing myself thus outraged.
Who else but I, but I myself,
gave these new gods their honors?
Enough of that. I speak to you who know.
Hear rather all that mortals suffered.

Once they were fools. I gave them power to
  think.
Through me they won their minds.
I have no blame for them. All I would tell
  you
is my good will and my good gifts to them.
Seeing they did not see, nor hearing hear.
Like dreams they led a random life.
They had no houses built to face the sun,
of bricks or well-wrought wood,
but like the tiny ant who has her home
in sunless crannies deep down in the earth,
they lived in caverns.
The signs that speak of winter's coming,
of flower-faced spring, of summer's heat
with mellowing fruits,
were all unknown to them.
From me they learned the stars that tell the
  seasons,
their risings and their settings hard to mark.
And number, that most excellent device,
I taught to them, and letters joined in words.
I gave to them the mother of all arts,
hard-working memory.
I, too, first brought beneath the yoke
great beasts to serve the plow,
to toil in mortals' stead.
Up to the chariot I led the horse that loves
  the rein,
the glory of the rich man in his pride.
None else but I first found
the seaman's car, sail-winged, sea-driven.
Such ways to help I showed them, I who have
no wisdom now to help myself.

Leader

You suffer shame as a physician must
who cannot heal himself.
You who cured others now are all astray,
distraught of mind and faint of heart,
and find no medicine to soothe your sickness.

Prometheus

Listen, and you shall find more cause for
  wonder.
Best of all gifts I gave them was the gift of
  healing.
For if one fell into a malady

there was no drug to cure, no draught, or
  soothing ointment.
For want of these men wasted to a shadow
until I showed them how to use
the kindly herbs that keep from us disease.
The ways of divination I marked out for
  them,
and they are many; how to know
the waking vision from the idle dream;
to read the sounds hard to discern;
the signs met on the road; the flight of birds,
eagles and vultures,
those that bring good or ill luck in their
  kind,
their way of life, their loves and hates
and council meetings.
And of those inward parts that tell the future,
the smoothness and the color and fair shape
that please the gods.
And how to wrap the flesh in fat
and the long thigh bone, for the altar fire
in honor to the gods.
So did I lead them on to knowledge
of the dark and riddling art.
The fire omens, too, were dim to them
until I made them see.
Deep within the earth are hidden
precious things for men,
brass and iron, gold and silver.
Would any say he brought these forth to
  light
until I showed the way?
No one, except to make an idle boast.
All arts, all goods, have come to men from
  me.

Leader

Do not care now for mortals
but take thought for yourself, O evil-fated.
I have good hope that still loosed from your
  bonds
you shall be strong as Zeus.

Prometheus

Not thus — not yet — is fate's appointed
  end,
fate that brings all to pass.

I must be bowed by age-long pain and grief.
So only will my bonds be loosed.
All skill, all cunning, is as foolishness
before necessity.

SEA NYMPH

Who is the helmsman of necessity?

PROMETHEUS

Fate, threefold, Retribution, unforgetting.

ANOTHER NYMPH

And Zeus is not so strong?

PROMETHEUS

He cannot shun what is foredoomed.

ANOTHER NYMPH

And is he not foredoomed to rule forever?

PROMETHEUS

No word of that. Ask me no further.

ANOTHER NYMPH

Some solemn secret hides behind your silence.

PROMETHEUS

Think of another theme. It is not yet
the time to speak of this.
It must be wrapped in darkness, so alone
I shall some time be saved
from shame and grief and bondage.

CHORUS

Zeus orders all things.
May he never set his might against purpose
of mine,
like a wrestler in the match.
May I ever be found where feast the holy
gods,
and the oxen are slain,
where ceaselessly flows the pathway
of Ocean, my father.
May the words of my lips forever
be free from sin.
May this abide with me and not depart
like melting snow.
Long life is sweet when there is hope

and hope is confident.
And it is sweet when glad thoughts make the
heart grow strong,
and there is joy.
But you, crushed by a thousand griefs,
I look upon you and I shudder.
You did not tremble before Zeus.
You gave your worship where you would, to
men,
a gift too great for mortals,
a thankless favor.
What help for you there? What defense in
those
whose life is but from morning unto evening?
Have you not seen?
Their little strength is feebleness,
fast bound in darkness,
like a dream.
The will of man shall never break
the harmony of God.
This I have learned beholding your destruc-
tion.
Once I spoke different words to you
from those now on my lips.
A song flew to me.
I stood beside your bridal bed,
I sang the wedding hymn,
glad in your marriage.
And with fair gifts persuading her,
you led to share your couch,
Hesione, child of the sea.

(*Enter* Io.)

Io

What land — what creatures here?
This, that I see —
A form storm-beaten,
bound to the rock.
Did you do wrong?
Is this your punishment?
You perish here.
Where am I?
Speak to a wretched wanderer.
Oh! Oh! he stings again —
the gadfly — oh, miserable!
But you must know he's not a gadfly.
He's Argus, son of Earth, the herdsman.
He has a thousand eyes.
I see him. Off! Keep him away!

No, he comes on.
His eyes can see all ways at once.
He's dead but no grave holds him.
He comes straight up from hell.
He is the huntsman,
and I his wretched quarry.
He drives me all along the long sea strand.
I may not stop for food or drink.
He has a shepherd's pipe,
a reed with beeswax joined.
Its sound is like the locust's shrilling,
a drowsy note — that will not let me sleep.
Oh, misery. Oh, misery.
Where is it leading me,
my wandering — far wandering.
What ever did I do,
how ever did I sin,
that you have yoked me to calamity,
O son of Kronos,
that you madden a wretched woman
driven mad by the gadfly of fear?
Oh, burn me in fire or hide me in earth
or fling me as food to the beasts of the sea.
Master, grant me my prayer.
Enough — I have been tried enough —
my wandering — long wandering.
Yet I have found no place
to leave my misery.
— I am a girl who speaks to you,
but horns are on my head.

PROMETHEUS

Like one caught in an eddy, whirling round
    and round,
the gadfly drives you.
I know you, girl. You are Inachus' daughter.
You made the god's heart hot with love,
and Hera hates you. She it is
who drives you on this flight that never stops.

Io

How is it that you speak my father's name?
Who are you? Tell me for my misery.
Who are you, sufferer, that speak the truth
to one who suffers?
You know the sickness God has put upon me,
that stings and maddens me and drives me on
and wastes my life away.
I am a beast, a starving beast,

that frenzied runs with clumsy leaps and
    bounds,
oh, shame,
mastered by Hera's malice.
Who among the wretched
suffer as I do?
Give me a sign, you there.
Tell to me clearly
the pain still before me.
Is help to be found?
A medicine to cure me?
Speak, if you know.

PROMETHEUS

I will and in plain words,
as friend should talk to friend.
— You see Prometheus, who gave mortals
    fire.

Io

You, he who succored the whole race of men?
You, that Prometheus, the daring, the endur-
    ing?
Why do you suffer here?

PROMETHEUS

Just now I told the tale —

Io

But will you not still give to me a boon?

PROMETHEUS

Ask what you will. I know all you would
    learn.

Io

Then tell me who has bound you to this rock.

PROMETHEUS

Zeus was the mind that planned.
The hand that did the deed the god of fire.

Io

What was the wrong that you are punished
    for?

PROMETHEUS

No more. Enough of me.

Io

But you will tell the term set to my wandering?
My misery is great. When shall it end?

PROMETHEUS

Here not to know is best.

Io

I ask you not to hide what I must suffer.

PROMETHEUS

I do so in no grudging spirit.

Io

Why then delay to tell me all?

PROMETHEUS

Not through ill will. I would not terrify you.

Io

Spare me not more than I would spare myself.

PROMETHEUS

If you constrain me I must speak. Hear
  then —

LEADER

Not yet. Yield to my pleasure too.
For I would hear from her own lips
what is the deadly fate, the sickness
that is upon her. Let her say — then teach
  her
the trials still to come.

PROMETHEUS

If you would please these maidens, Io —
they are your father's sisters,
and when the heart is sorrowful, to speak
to those who will let fall a tear
is time well spent.

Io

I do not know how to distrust you.
You shall hear all. And yet —
I am ashamed to speak,
to tell of that god-driven storm
that struck me, changed me, ruined me.
How shall I tell you who it was?

How ever to my maiden chamber
visions came by night,
persuading me with gentle words:
" Oh happy, happy girl,
Why are you all too long a maid
when you might marry with the highest?
The arrow of desire has pierced Zeus.
For you he is on fire.
With you it is his will to capture love.
Would you, child, fly from Zeus' bed?
Go forth to Lerna, to the meadows deep in
  grass.
There is a sheep-fold there,
an ox-stall, too, that holds your father's
  oxen —
so shall Zeus find release from his desire."
Always, each night, such dreams possessed
  me.
I was unhappy and at last I dared
to tell my father of these visions.
He sent to Pytho and far Dodona
man after man to ask the oracle
what he must say or do to please the gods.
But all brought answers back of shifting
  meaning,
hard to discern, like golden coins unmarked.
At last a clear word came. It fell upon him
like lightning from the sky. It told him
to thrust me from his house and from his
  country,
to wander to the farthest bounds of earth
like some poor dumb beast set apart
for sacrifice, whom no man will restrain.
And if my father would not, Zeus would
  send
his thunderbolt with eyes of flame to end
his race, all, everyone.
He could not but obey such words
from the dark oracle. He drove me out.
He shut his doors to me — against his will
as against mine. Zeus had him bridled.
He drove him as he would.
Straightway I was distorted, mind and body.
A beast — with horns — look at me —
stung by a fly, who madly leaps and bounds.
And so I ran and found myself beside
the waters, sweet to drink, of Kerchneia
and Lerna's well-spring.
Beside me went the herdsman Argus,

the violent of heart, the earth-born,
watching my footsteps with his hundred eyes.
But death came to him, swift and unforeseen.
Plagued by a gadfly then, the scourge of God,
I am driven on from land to land.
So for what has been. But what still remains
of anguish for me, tell me.
Do not in pity soothe me with false tales.
Words strung together by a lie
are like a foul disease.

LEADER

Oh, shame. Oh, tale of shame.
Never, oh never, would I have believed that
    my ears
would hear words such as these, of strange
    meaning.
Evil to see and evil to hear,
misery, defilement, and terror.
They pierce my heart with a two-edged
    sword.
A fate like that —
I shudder to look upon Io.

PROMETHEUS

You are too ready with your tears and fears.
Wait for the end.

LEADER

Speak. Tell us, for when one lies sick,
to face with clear eyes all the pain to come
is sweet.

PROMETHEUS

What first you asked was granted easily,
to hear from her own lips her trials.
But for the rest, learn now the sufferings
she still must suffer, this young creature,
at Hera's hands. Child of Inachus,
keep in your heart my words, so you shall
    know
where the road ends. First to the sunrise,
over furrows never plowed, where wandering
    Scythians
live in huts of wattles made, raised high
on wheels smooth-rolling. Bows they have,
and they shoot far. Turn from them.
Keep to the shore washed by the moaning sea.
Off to the left live the Chalybians,

workers of iron. There be on your guard.
A rough people they, who like not strangers.
Here rolls a river called the Insolent,
true to its name. You cannot find a ford
until you reach the Caucasus itself,
highest of mountains. From beneath its brow
the mighty river rushes. You must cross
the summit, neighbor to the stars.
Then by the southward road, until you reach
the warring Amazons, men-haters, who one
    day
will found a city by the Thermodon,
where Salmydessus thrusts
a fierce jaw out into the sea that sailors hate,
stepmother of ships.
And they will bring you on your way right
    gladly
to the Cimmerian isthmus, by a shallow lake,
Maeotis, at the narrows.
Here you must cross with courage.
And men shall tell forever of your passing.
The strait shall be named for you, Bosporus,
Ford of the Cow. There leave the plains of
    Europe,
and enter Asia, the great Continent.
— Now does he seem to you, this ruler of the
    gods,
evil, to all, in all things?
A god desired a mortal — drove her forth
to wander thus.
A bitter lover you have found, O girl,
for all that I have told you is not yet
the prelude even.

Io

O, wretched, wretched.

PROMETHEUS

You cry aloud for this? What then
when you have learned the rest?

LEADER

You will not tell her of more trouble?

PROMETHEUS

A storm-swept sea of grief and ruin.

Io

What gain to me is life? Oh, now to fling my-
    self

down from this rock peak to the earth below,
and find release there from my trouble.
Better to die once than to suffer
through all the days of life.

PROMETHEUS

Hardly would you endure my trial,
whose fate it is not ever to find death
that ends all pain. For me there is no end
until Zeus falls from power.

IO

Zeus fall from power?

PROMETHEUS

You would rejoice, I think, to see that happen?

IO

How could I not, who suffer at his hands?

PROMETHEUS

Know then that it shall surely be.

IO

But who will strip the tyrant of his scepter?

PROMETHEUS

He will himself and his own empty mind.

IO

How? Tell me, if it is not wrong to ask.

PROMETHEUS

He will make a marriage that will vex him.

IO

Goddess or mortal, if it may be spoken?

PROMETHEUS

It may not be. Seek not to know.

IO

His wife shall drive him from his throne?

PROMETHEUS

Her child shall be more than his father's
match.

IO

And is there no way of escape for him?

PROMETHEUS

No way indeed, unless my bonds are loosed.

IO

But who can loose them against Zeus' will?

PROMETHEUS

A son of yours — so fate decrees.

IO

What words are these? A child of mine shall
free you?

PROMETHEUS

Ten generations first must pass and then
three more.

IO

Your prophecy grows dim through generations.

PROMETHEUS

So let it be. Seek not to know your trials.

IO

Do not hold out a boon and then withdraw it.

PROMETHEUS

One boon of two I will bestow upon you.

IO

And they are? Speak. Give me the choice.

PROMETHEUS

I give it you: the hardships still before you,
or his name who shall free me. Choose.

LEADER

Of these give one to her, but give to me
a grace as well — I am not quite unworthy.
Tell her where she must wander, and to me
tell who shall free you. It is my heart's desire.

PROMETHEUS

And to your eagerness I yield.
Hear, Io, first, of your far-driven journey.

And bear in mind my words, inscribe them
upon the tablets of your heart.
When you have crossed the stream that
    bounds
the continents, turn to the East where flame
the footsteps of the sun, and pass
along the sounding sea to Cisthene.
Here on the plain live Phorcys' children,
    three,
all maidens, very old, and shaped like swans,
who have one eye and one tooth to the three.
No ray of sun looks ever on that country,
nor ever moon by night. Here too their sisters
    dwell.
And they are three, the Gorgons, winged,
with hair of snakes, hateful to mortals,
whom no man shall behold and draw again
the breath of life. They garrison that place.
And yet another evil sight, the hounds of
    Zeus,
who never bark, griffins with beaks like birds.
The one-eyed Arimaspi too, the riders,
who live beside a stream that flows with gold,
a way of wealth. From all these turn aside.
Far off there is a land where black men live,
close to the sources of the sun, whence
    springs
a sun-scorched river. When you reach it,
go with all care along the banks up to
the great descent, where from the mountains
the holy Nile pours forth its waters
pleasant to drink from. It will be your guide
to the Nile land, the Delta. A long exile
is fated for you and your children here.
If what I speak seems dark and hard to know,
ask me again and learn all clearly.
For I have time to spare and more
than I could wish.

Leader

If in your story of her fatal journey
there is yet somewhat left to tell her,
speak now. If not, give then to us
the grace we asked. You will remember.

Prometheus

The whole term of her roaming has been told.
But I will show she has not heard in vain,
and tell her what she suffered coming hither,
in proof my words are true.
A moving multitude of sorrows were there,
too many to recount, but at the end
you came to where the levels of Molossa
surround the lofty ridge of Dodona,
seat of God's oracle.
A wonder past belief is there, oak trees that
    speak.
They spoke, not darkly but in shining words,
calling you Zeus' glorious spouse.
The frenzy seized you then. You fled
along the sea-road washed by the great inlet,
named for God's mother. Up and down you
    wandered,
storm-tossed. And in the time to come that
    sea
shall have its name from you, Ionian,
that men shall not forget your journey.
This is my proof to you my mind can see
farther than meets the eye.
From here the tale I tell is for you all,
and of the future, leaving now the past.
There is a city, Canobus, at the land's end,
where the Nile empties, on new river soil.
There Zeus at last shall make you sane again,
stroking you with a hand you will not fear.
And from this touch alone you will conceive
and bear a son, a swarthy man,
whose harvest shall be reaped on many fields,
all that are washed by the wide-watered Nile.
In the fifth generation from him, fifty sisters
will fly from marriage with their near of kin,
who, hawks in close pursuit of doves, aquiver
with passionate desire, shall find that death
waits for the hunters on the wedding night.
God will refuse to them the virgin bodies.
Argos will be the maidens' refuge, to their
    suitors
a slaughter dealt by women's hands,
bold in the watches of the night.
The wife shall kill her husband,
dipping her two-edged sword in blood.
O Cyprian goddess, thus may you come to
    my foes.
One girl, bound by love's spell, will change
her purpose, and she will not kill
the man she lay beside, but choose the name
of coward rather than be stained with blood.
In Argos she will bear a kingly child —

a story overlong if all were told.
Know this, that from that seed will spring
one glorious with the bow, bold-hearted,
and he shall set me free.
This is the oracle my mother told me,
Justice, who is of old, Earth's daughter.
But how and where would be too long a tale,
nor would you profit.

Io

Oh, misery. Oh, misery.
A frenzy tears me.
Madness strikes my mind.
I burn. A frantic sting —
an arrow never forged with fire.
My heart is beating at its walls in terror.
My eyes are whirling wheels.
Away. Away. A raging wind of fury
sweeps through me.
My tongue has lost its power.
My words are like a turbid stream,
wild waves that dash against a surging sea,
the black sea of madness.

(*Exit* Io.)

Chorus

Wise, wise was he,
who first weighed this in thought
and gave it utterance:
Marriage within one's own degree is best,
not with one whom wealth has spoiled,
nor yet with one made arrogant by birth.
Such as these he must not seek
who lives upon the labor of his hands.
Fate, dread deity,
may you never, oh, never behold me
sharing the bed of Zeus.
May none of the dwellers in heaven
draw near to me ever.
Terrors take hold of me
seeing her maidenhood
turning from love of man,
torn by Hera's hate,
driven in misery.
For me, I would not shun marriage nor fear
it,
so it were with my equal.
But the love of the greater gods,
from whose eyes none can hide,

may that never be mine.
To war with a god-lover is not war,
it is despair.
For what could I do,
or where could I fly
from the cunning of Zeus?

Prometheus

In very truth shall Zeus, for all his stubborn
pride,
be humbled, such a marriage he will make
to cast him down from throne and power.
And he shall be no more remembered.
The curse his father put on him
shall be fulfilled.
The curse that he cursed him with as he fell
from his age-long throne.
The way from such trouble no one of the
gods
can show him save I.
These things I know and how they shall come
to pass.
So let him sit enthroned in confidence,
trust to his crashing thunder high in air,
shake in his hands his fire-breathing dart.
Surely these shall be no defense,
but he will fall, in shame unbearable.
Even now he makes ready against himself
one who shall wrestle with him and prevail,
a wonder of wonders, who will find
a flame that is swifter than lightning,
a crash to silence the thunder,
who will break into pieces the sea-god's spear,
the bane of the ocean that shakes the earth.
Before this evil Zeus shall be bowed down.
He will learn how far apart are a king and a
slave.

Leader

These words of menace on your tongue
speak surely only your desire.

Prometheus

They speak that which shall surely be —
and also my desire.

Leader

And we must look to see Zeus mastered?

PROMETHEUS

Yes, and beneath a yoke more cruel than this
I bear.

LEADER

You have no fear to utter words like these?

PROMETHEUS

I am immortal — and I have no fear.

SEA NYMPH

But agony still worse he might inflict —

PROMETHEUS

So let him do. All that must come I know.

ANOTHER NYMPH

The wise bow to the inescapable.

PROMETHEUS

Be wise then. Worship power.
Cringe before each who wields it.
To me Zeus counts as less than nothing.
Let him work his will, show forth his power
for his brief day, his little moment
of lording it in heaven.
— But see. There comes a courier from Zeus,
a lackey in his new lord's livery.
Some curious news is surely on his lips.
                (*Enter* HERMES.)

HERMES

You trickster there, you biter bitten,
sinner against the gods, man-lover, thief of
    fire,
my message is to you.
The great father gives you here his orders:
Reveal this marriage that you boast of,
by which he shall be hurled from power.
And, mark you, not in riddles, each fact
    clearly.
— Don't make me take a double journey,
    Prometheus.
You can see Zeus isn't going to be made
    kinder
by this sort of thing.

PROMETHEUS

Big words and insolent. They well become
    you,

O lackey of the gods.
Young — young — your thrones just won,
you think you live in citadels grief cannot
    reach.
Two dynasties I have seen fall from heaven,
and I shall see the third fall fastest,
most shamefully of all.
Is it your thought to see me tremble
and crouch before your upstart gods?
Not so — not such a one am I.
Make your way back. You will not learn
    from me.

HERMES

Ah, so? Still stubborn? Yet this willfulness
has anchored you fast in these troubled
    waters.

PROMETHEUS

And yet I would not change my lot
with yours, O lackey.

HERMES

Better no doubt to be slave to a rock.
than be the father's trusted herald.

PROMETHEUS

I must be insolent when I must speak to
    insolence.

HERMES

You are proud, it seems, of what has come to
    you.

PROMETHEUS

I proud? May such pride be
the portion of my foes. — I count you of
    them.

HERMES

You blame me also for your sufferings?

PROMETHEUS

In one word, all gods are my enemies.
They had good from me. They return me
    evil.

HERMES

I heard you were quite mad.

PROMETHEUS

Yes, I am mad, if to abhor such foes is madness.

HERMES

You would be insufferable, Prometheus, if
you were not so wretched.

PROMETHEUS

Alas!

HERMES

Alas? That is a word Zeus does not understand.

PROMETHEUS

Time shall teach it him, gray time,
that teaches all things.

HERMES

It has not taught you wisdom yet.

PROMETHEUS

No, or I had not wrangled with a slave.

HERMES

It seems that you will tell the Father nothing.

PROMETHEUS

Paying the debt of kindness that I owe him?

HERMES

You mock at me as though I were a child.

PROMETHEUS

A child you are or what else has less sense
if you expect to learn from me.
There is no torture and no trick of skill,
there is no force, which can compel my
    speech,
until Zeus wills to loose these deadly bonds.
So let him hurl his blazing bolt,
and with the white wings of the snow,
with thunder and with earthquake,
confound the reeling world.
None of all this will bend my will
to tell him at whose hands he needs must
    fall.

HERMES

I urge you, pause and think if this will help
you.

PROMETHEUS

I thought long since of all. I planned for all.

HERMES

Submit, you fool. Submit. In agony learn
wisdom.

PROMETHEUS

Go and persuade the sea wave not to break.
You will persuade me no more easily.
I am no frightened woman, terrified
at Zeus' purpose. Do you think to see me
ape women's ways, stretch out my hands
to him I hate, and pray him for release?
A world apart am I from prayer for pity.

HERMES

Then all I say is said in vain.
Nothing will move you, no entreaty
soften your heart.
Like a young colt new-bridled,
you have the bit between your teeth,
and rear and fight against the rein.
But all this vehemence is feeble bombast.
A fool, bankrupt of all but obstinacy,
is the poorest thing on earth.
Oh, if you will not hear me, yet consider
the storm that threatens you from which
you cannot fly, a great third wave of evil.
Thunder and flame of lightning will rend
this jagged peak. You shall be buried deep,
held by a splintered rock.
After long length of time you will return
to see the light, but Zeus' winged hound,
an eagle red with blood,
shall come a guest unbidden to your banquet.
All day long he will tear to rags your body,
great rents within the flesh,
feasting in fury on the blackened liver.
Look for no ending to this agony
until a god will freely suffer for you,
will take on him your pain, and in your stead
descend to where the sun is turned to dark-
    ness,

the black depths of death.
Take thought: this is no empty boast
but utter truth. Zeus does not lie.
Each word shall be fulfilled.
Pause and consider. Never think
self-will is better than wise counsel.

LEADER

To us the words he speaks are not amiss.
He bids you let your self-will go and seek
good counsel. Yield.
For to the wise a failure is disgrace.

PROMETHEUS

These tidings that the fellow shouts at me
were known to me long since.
A foe to suffer at the hands of foes
is nothing shameful.
Then let the twisting flame of forked fire
be hurled upon me. Let the very air
be rent by thunder-crash.
Savage winds convulse the sky,
hurricanes shake the earth from its founda-
    tions,
the waves of the sea rise up and drown the
    stars,
and let me be swept down to hell,
caught in the cruel whirlpool of necessity.
He cannot kill me.

HERMES

Why, these are ravings you may hear from
    madmen.
His case is clear. Frenzy can go no further.
You maids who pity him, depart, be swift.
The thunder peals and it is merciless.
Would you too be struck down?

LEADER

Speak other words, another counsel,
if you would win me to obey.
Now, in this place, to urge
that I should be a coward is intolerable.
I choose with him to suffer what must be.
Not to stand by a friend — there is no evil
I count more hateful.
I spit it from my mouth.

HERMES

Remember well I warned you,
when you are swept away in utter ruin.
Blame then yourselves, not fate, nor ever say
that Zeus delivered you
to a hurt you had not thought to see.
With open eyes,
not suddenly, not secretly,
into the net of utter ruin
whence there is no escape,
you fall by your own folly.

(*Exit* HERMES.)

PROMETHEUS

An end to words. Deeds now.
The world is shaken.
The deep and secret way of thunder
is rent apart.
Fiery wreaths of lightning flash.
Whirlwinds toss the swirling dust.
The blasts of all the winds are battling in the
    air,
and sky and sea are one.
On me the tempest falls.
It does not make me tremble.
O holy Mother Earth, O air and sun,
behold me. I am wronged.

Prometheus Bound in the Theater of Dionysos

Prometheus Bound is in many ways the most fascinating of ancient
Greek tragedies. For the student of dramatic art it is particularly suggestive since it raises many of the basic questions about the nature and
components of the dramatic experience (see p. 141). Before we consider
such matters, however, it will be necessary to make some effort to reproduce the play, to see it as the author intended it to be seen by its original
spectators. Aeschylus was a very conscious craftsman, a skillful user of

the tools of his profession; the modern student should endeavor to share as much of the pleasure the playwright's craft gave to his original audience as imagination and understanding will permit. It is not difficult to put ourselves in the Theater of Dionysos and in our mind's eye follow the ancient players through their action.

As the first rays of the sun strike the upper tiers of the spectators' area, the play begins.[2] Through an entrance arch (called the *parados*) at the edge of the orchestra come four figures. Each is masked and wearing the long robes traditional for performers in tragedy. The masks are painted to give some suggestion of the nature or position of their wearers (see p. 134): one of noble suffering with gaping mouth turned down; two suggesting brutality and cruelty; a fourth, ruddy and lined.

The sufferer is the Titan Prometheus. Held by the two brutes, Force and Violence, he follows the red-faced Hephestus to the altar at the center of the orchestra.

At the altar, Force speaks first in a heavy chanting tone, that his words may be carried to the most distant spectator. He addresses himself to Hephestus, who stands a little apart from the other three actors, gesturing but little and making no pretence at what a modern spectator would call realistic acting. His manner is more that of a priest performing a ritual. So too is the reply of Hephestus. In the same chanting tone he speaks first to the two brutes, then, at his third line, turns away and faces the spectators. The size of the theater requires this broad, simple movement, to clarify for the spectator the meaning of what is being said. So at the seventh line of his speech he turns to Prometheus, but his manner of speaking does not alter. It must remain full and formal to be audible.

At the end of the speech, Force steps forward and begins his protests at a somewhat more rapid pace. The mute Violence remains stolidly clutching the silent Prometheus as the other two clash about duty and loyalty. When Hephestus submits, Force takes the stance of a foreman and directs the binding of the Titan. First Hephestus chains his wrists to the altar — " Still harder. Tighter," commands Force. Then Violence, the more terrible because of his silence, drives a stake through Prometheus' breast (not a difficult trick to fake, when the audience is at such a distance from the action), and Hephestus turns away with a cry of sympathy. But no sound from Prometheus.

Force reprimands the smith, directs him to fix the chain about the

---

[2] This description presupposes that *Prometheus* was the first play on the day's program. It may well have been the second. To imagine it first, however, is a useful reminder of the frequent coincidence of the rising sun and opening action of many of the surviving Greek plays. These are instances of playwrights' making a dramatic effect out of a theatrical convention.

Titan's waist, and then to kneel and make fast his legs in rings. This done, Violence silently drives nails through the feet and the three stand off to look upon their victim. There is no scene in Greek tragedy exactly comparable to this in its detailed working out of the physical horror of the hero's situation. Each step is performed and measured and commented upon before the spectators, and to crown the work, the brutal Force taunts the silent prisoner before making his exit with the other two through the parados.

Now all eyes focus on the silent, chained hero. After a further moment of silence, he begins his loud outcry upon the injustice of his fellow-god. He is still perforce motionless, but his mask is an image of noble torture and his words are a reminder to the spectators of their personal share in his sufferings.

As he finishes his lament, the sound of a flute is heard and he twists his head about to seek its source. The sea nymphs enter through the parados, fourteen boys or men, masked and wearing robes which suggest their function, and headed by a leader (in some sort of car) wearing a costume that is similar though more elaborate. With a light and wavelike motion they form a circle about Prometheus, making two arcs of seven each, while the leader's car approaches the god for the dialogue between them. The chorus, ever in delicate but restless motion, sings its speeches to the accompaniment of the flute and drum, sometimes as a unit, sometimes as a half-unit, and possibly (as the translator suggests) as individuals. At the end of their scene, invited to watch and share the pain of the god, they move back towards the spectators' area, still keeping their circular formation.

Now from the roof of the skenotheke a strange figure appears. He is a god, richly robed, and he is lowered to the orchestra on a machine shaped to look like an exotic, if not downright grotesque, bird with four legs. A cross between an ostrich and a very flat-footed goose may suggest the effect.

Ocean dismounts from his peculiar steed and makes his way somewhat hesitantly, for he is not used to dry land, to Prometheus. During the following scene his manner alternates between confidence and fear. He chants his good advice in a firm voice, and his comments on Zeus in a lower tone with an occasional look over his shoulder. As he sees that Prometheus is resolute, he becomes restless, drifting towards his bird, then returning to speak to the prisoner. Finally, as Prometheus bids him, " Off with you," his eagerness spills over; he runs to his steed, clambers on its back, and is drawn up, in ignominy, to the roof where he disappears from view.

The chorus has been standing at the outer edge of the orchestra. It now moves in, converging on Prometheus, contracting the circle, drawing the spectator's attention into sharpened focus, as it were. Their ode is again accompanied by their characteristic restless movement, emphasizing always the immobility of the hero. To them, at the end of their ode, he reveals that he possesses a secret, that even the father of gods and men is foredoomed. Their response is another choral ode and dance, a song of pity and grief and resignation. Round about the hero go the sea nymphs, by their gestures and movements evoking an image of the waves washing against a rocky shore.

Suddenly another grotesque figure bursts through the parados into the orchestra. Twitching and leaping wildly, wearing a spotted robe and mask like a heifer, Io runs from one to another of the nymphs, seeking relief. With shrieks and frantic kicks, with maddened flinging of her arms she jerks about the orchestra, " Like one caught in an eddy, whirling round and round," crying out against the injustice of Zeus. Prometheus speaks to her and she comes to a momentary rest before him. But it is only for a moment. When next she speaks, she throws herself about before the motionless Titan, until he speaks to her plainly, prophesying her future, and revealing a little more of his great secret. But at the end of his long prophecy, the fit comes upon her again. Stung by the gadfly, screaming and babbling, the heifer-maiden rushes from the orchestra through the parados and vanishes.

The violence of her scene contrasts with the calmer rhythms of the succeeding choral ode, a song of resignation and a prayer for a life without ambition or overreaching. Against this is set the further prophecy of the angered god, his open threat against the all-powerful who has subjected him to eternal torment. The leader of the nymphs counsels submission, warns of greater punishment to come; yet the helpless god is defiant. His ringing speech fills the theater, when the final character in the play makes his appearance.

This is Hermes, messenger of the gods, and his familiar costume will at once identify him to the spectators. As a god, he may descend in the machine from the roof of the skenotheke, although there is no indication in the text that this was the case. Perhaps his proud mincing walk will be better displayed if he comes from the parados where Io has just made her tormented exit.

As he approaches Prometheus with a mask thin-lipped and imperious, he speaks in a shrill and commanding voice. Prometheus continues his defiant words and Hermes, replying, moves about the prisoner lightly, pointing to his chains, and by his very freedom emphasizing the other's

helplessness. At last, goaded by Prometheus' scorn, Hermes loses his imperious dignity, rages and threatens with a screaming voice and with
small-minded triumph the greater torments in store for the hero. In his
frustration he even turns on the chorus, but they are firm in their refusal to depart. In great fury Hermes makes his exit, quite another figure
from the dapper, assured messenger of his entrance.

Prometheus, now, fixed on his altar, and the sympathetic nymphs
grouped about him are left alone in the orchestra for the final speech
of the play.

It is not certain how the play concludes. Various scholars have suggested various endings, the least satisfactory of which imagines an earthquake, with Prometheus sinking from sight. The possibility of such an
effect in the Theater of Dionysos is, to put it cautiously, remote. Greek
playwrights are usually very careful to provide for the departure of their
characters from the open and curtainless orchestra; that no such provi-
sion is included in the text of the play (or is indeed possible, given the
situation of the hero) suggests that Aeschylus intended the sequel (for
Prometheus Bound was one of a series of three plays performed on the
same morning) to begin at once, perhaps with a choral ode as a conventional indication of the passage of thousands of years.

Such matters, however, are best considered under dramatic structure.
The performance of *Prometheus Bound* is finished, with the hero at the
end as at the beginning of the play, fixed to the center of both the players' and spectators' areas, the focal point of the action of the drama and
the architecture of the playhouse.

The Panoramic Playhouse

In discussing the differences between the earliest Greek and the earliest
Christian playlets, we noticed that the playing place for the *Quem
Quaeritis* encouraged movement and change of location. How this becomes one of the distinguishing characteristics of *panoramic* drama is
best postponed until the discussion of dramatic structure (see Chapter V). First we must consider the physical conditions of the playing
place itself.

The panoramic playhouse takes several forms, but all derive from a
desire on the part of the playwright to show, and on the part of the
audience to see, multiple actions. The little Resurrection play of the
tenth century soon acquired other incidents: the Marys stop to buy spices
and unguents on their way to the tomb; having made their discovery
they run to inform the other disciples; Magdalene meets the Gardener,

and so on. The accretions were so popular that soon the cathedrals were presenting, on festival occasions, connected stories of the Nativity of Christ, or of His Passion, Death, and Resurrection. The staging of these plays was, of course, governed by the " theater " in which they were to be acted. At first, the stage and the setting consisted of a simple representation of a tomb erected at the high altar. When, however, the plays developed many scenes to be acted in rapid sequence, a custom arose of presenting all the settings to the audience simultaneously. The tomb was placed at the altar, Herod's court was at one place in the church, the manger in another. These scenes, elevated on boxes or platforms, were known by various names, the more common being Mansions or Houses.

The plays continued to grow in length and complexity as well as popularity, and were finally removed from the church buildings. Performances were then given in the open air in two different ways. On the continent it was customary to erect a long narrow stage in the public square. At the back of the stage would be displayed all the settings required for the particular incidents to be presented: Heaven at one end of the platform; Nazareth, Bethlehem, the Temple, the Sea of Galilee, and Pilate's House in the middle; and Hellmouth at the other end. In this so-called simultaneous setting, the actors would commence each play in front of the pertinent setting and then, having established the locale, move forward onto the common acting area at the front of the large platform.

In the market towns of England another method of panoramic staging was employed. Here the individual plays that made up the full drama, or cycle, were performed by the various crafts or guilds of the community. Each craft constructed a wagon, or *pageant,* on which its particular play was to be enacted. The pageants were large, with several stories, and were drawn by horses from place to place about the town. The spectators assembled at appointed locations — in front of the cathedral or the mayor's house, or in the market square — and, one by one, the plays were brought to them. This is the true beginning of the panoramic theater, with its unlimited changes of setting and free movement in time and space.

It was both an amateur and an occasional theater, but the professional players who were to give it permanence were quick to see its usefulness as well as its attraction for the public. They were vagabonds, the professional players, accustomed to acting in taverns or banqueting halls. The pageant assured them of an acting area according to their own specifications, and the structure of the English innyard enabled them to control their audiences, at least financially. It was their custom to drive their pageant through the gate of the inn (where a money-taker could

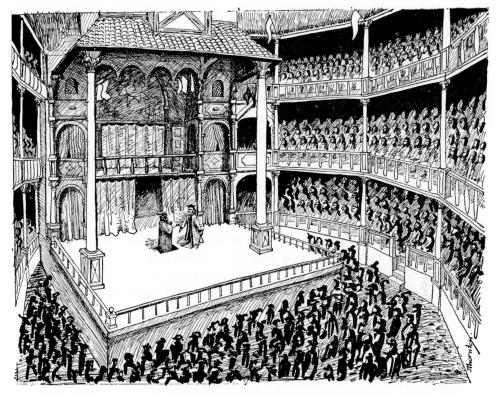

The Panoramic Theater

be posted) and to station it at the narrow end of the inner rectangular court. The spectators could then, having paid their admission fee, stand about the pageant in the courtyard or, by paying a slightly higher sum, sit at the innyard windows.

The first permanent public theater was built in London in 1576. It was circular or octagonal in shape, following the design of buildings used for the popular entertainment of bear-baiting. But the interior was clearly influenced by the temporary innyard playing places. The main audience area, called the pit, was the earthen floor which surrounded the stage on three sides. There were several galleries built into the inside walls to accommodate those who wished to sit during the performance, or to be separated for one reason or another from the common spectators (who were known as the " groundlings "). The acting area was much more elaborate than that of the Greek theater. It was, in fact, divided into four or five parts: a main stage, a huge platform five or six feet high extending from the back wall some forty feet into the spectators' area, equipped with trap doors in the floor, and reached by permanent doors on either side; an inner stage, a curtained alcove behind the main stage; a balcony or upper stage, a room above the inner stage; windows, above the stage doors; and a small room high over all in the turret that crowned the structure. The acting area was roofed over, but the spectators were exposed to the elements, and playwrights sometimes complained that their works did not get a fair hearing because of the coldness of the weather or the grey mist so customary in London.

Eventually acting companies took to using indoor theaters for winter performances, but the outdoor theaters were always preferred since they could accommodate a much larger number of paying customers. The Londoners' taste for playgoing was as great as the Athenians' and was more regularly catered to. After 1576 some ten of these public playhouses were erected, differing slightly in pattern, particularly in the number of playing areas,[3] but all conforming to the essential requirements of panoramic drama. Such a playhouse was the structure for which Christopher Marlowe planned his tragedy of the fortunes and misfortunes of *Doctor Faustus*.

[3] It has been suggested that some of the playhouses were not equipped with inner stages, but erected temporary structures (like the medieval Mansions) when the action of the drama demanded.

THE TRAGICAL HISTORY OF DOCTOR FAUSTUS

by Christopher Marlowe

CHARACTERS

JOHN FAUSTUS, doctor of theology
MEPHISTOPHILIS, a lord of devils
VALDES ⎫ magicians
CORNELIUS ⎭
Three SCHOLARS, friends to Faustus
OLD MAN

THE POPE
CARDINAL OF LORRAINE
CHARLES V, Emperor of Germany
KNIGHT
DUKE OF VANHOLT
DUCHESS OF VANHOLT

GOOD ANGEL
EVIL ANGEL

LUCIFER ⎫
BELZEBUB ⎬ Devils
SEVEN DEADLY SINS ⎭
ALEXANDER THE GREAT ⎫
PARAMOUR OF ALEXANDER ⎬ Spirits
HELEN OF TROY ⎭

WAGNER, servant to Faustus
CLOWN
ROBIN, the ostler [a stable-boy]
RALPH, a servingman [pronounced Rāfe]
VINTNER
HORSE-COURSER [horse-trader]

CHORUS

Friars, Devils, Attendants

Enter CHORUS [*covered by a long black cape*].

CHORUS

Not marching now in fields of Thrasymene
Where Mars did mate the Carthaginians,
Nor sporting in the dalliance of love
In courts of kings where state is overturned,
Nor in the pomp of proud audacious deeds
Intends our Muse to daunt his heavenly
    verse:
Only this, Gentlemen, we must perform,
The form of Faustus' fortunes good or bad.
To patient judgments we appeal our plaud

And speak for Faustus in his infancy.
Now is he born, his parents base of stock,
In Germany within a town called Rhodes;
Of riper years to Wittenberg he went
Whereas his kinsmen chiefly brought him
    up;
So soon he profits in divinity,
The fruitful plot of scholarism graced,
That shortly he was graced with Doctor's
    name,
Excelling all whose sweet delight disputes
In heavenly matters of theology,
Till swollen with cunning, of a self-conceit,

NOTE. Brackets in stage directions indicate editorial additions to the directions found in the original text.

His waxen wings did mount above his reach
And melting heavens conspired his over-
    throw.
For, falling to a devilish exercise
And glutted more with learning's golden
    gifts,
He surfeits upon cursed necromancy.
Nothing so sweet as magic is to him,
Which he prefers before his chiefest bliss —
And this the man that in his study sits.
                                    Exit.

[Scene 1]   *Enter* FAUSTUS *in his Study.*

FAUSTUS

Settle thy studies, Faustus, and begin
To sound the depth of that thou wilt pro-
    fess.
Having commenced, be a divine in show,
Yet level at the end of every art
And live and die in Aristotle's works:
Sweet Analytics, 'tis thou hast ravished me!
                                    [*Reads.*]
Bene disserere est finis logicis —
Is to dispute well logic's chiefest end?
Affords this art no greater miracle?
Then read no more; thou hast attained the
    end.
    A greater subject fitteth Faustus' wit:
Bid ON KAI MĒ ON farewell, Galen come,
Seeing *ubi desinit philosophus, ibi incipit
    medicus;* [1]
Be a physician, Faustus, heap up gold
And be eternized for some wondrous cure.
                                    [*Reads.*]
Summum bonum medicinae sanitas —
The end of physic is our bodies' health:
Why, Faustus, hast thou not attained that
    end?
Is not thy common talk sound aphorisms?
Are not thy bills hung up as monuments
Whereby whole cities have escaped the plague
And thousand desperate maladies been eased?
Yet art thou still but Faustus, and a man.
Couldst thou make men to live eternally
Or, being dead, raise them to life again,
Then this profession were to be esteemed.

Physic, farewell.
            Where is Justinian?
                                    [*Reads.*]
*Si una eademque res legatur duobus,
Alter rem, alter valorem rei, etc.* — [2]
A pretty case of paltry legacies!
Exhaereditare filium non potest pater nisi — [3]
Such is the subject of the Institute
And universal body of the law.
His study fits a mercenary drudge
Who aims at nothing but external trash,
Too servile and illiberal for me.
    When all is done, divinity is best.
Jerome's Bible, Faustus, view it well:
                                    [*Reads.*]
Stipendium peccati mors est — Ha! *Stipen-
    dium, etc.*
The reward of sin is death. That's hard.
*Si pecasse negamus, fallimur, et nulla est in
    nobis veritas* —
If we say that we have no sin
We deceive ourselves, and there's no truth in
    us.
Why then belike
We must sin and so consequently die,
Ay, we must die an everlasting death.
What doctrine call you this, *Che sera, sera:*
What will be, shall be? Divinity, adieu!
    These metaphysics of magicians
And necromantic books are heavenly:
Lines, circles, signs, letters and characters —
Ay, these are those that Faustus most desires.
O what a world of profit and delight,
Of power, of honor, of omnipotence,
Is promised to the studious artisan!
All things that move between the quiet poles
Shall be at my command. Emperors and
    kings
Are but obeyed in their several provinces,
Nor can they raise the wind or rend the
    clouds;
But his dominion that exceeds in this
Stretcheth as far as doth the mind of man.
A sound magician is a mighty god:
Here, Faustus, try thy brains to gain a deity!

---

[1] Where the philosopher stops, there the physician
begins.

[2] If one and the same thing be bequeathed to two
persons, the one shall have the thing itself, the other
something of equal value, and so on.

[3] The father may not disinherit the son unless —

Enter WAGNER.

Wagner, commend me to my dearest friends,
The German Valdes and Cornelius;
Request them earnestly to visit me.

WAGNER

I will, sir.   *Exit.*

FAUSTUS

Their conference will be a greater help to me
Than all my labors, plod I ne'er so fast.
Enter the GOOD ANGEL *and the* EVIL ANGEL.

GOOD ANGEL

O Faustus, lay that damned book aside
And gaze not on it, lest it tempt thy soul
And heap God's heavy wrath upon thy head.
Read, read the Scriptures! That is blasphemy.

EVIL ANGEL

Go forward, Faustus, in that famous art
Wherein all nature's treasury is contained:
Be thou on earth, as Jove is in the sky,
Lord and commander of these elements.
                              Exeunt ANGELS.

FAUSTUS

How am I glutted with conceit of this!
Shall I make spirits fetch me what I please,
Resolve me of all ambiguities,
Perform what desperate enterprise I will?
I'll have them fly to India for gold,
Ransack the ocean for orient pearl,
And search all corners of the new-found
  world
For pleasant fruits and princely delicates;
I'll have them read me strange philosophy
And tell the secrets of all foreign kings;
I'll have them wall all Germany with brass
And make swift Rhine circle fair Witten-
  berg;
I'll have them fill the public schools [4] with
  silk
Wherewith the students shall be bravely
  clad;
I'll levy soldiers with the coin they bring,
And chase the Prince of Parma from our
  land
And reign sole king of all our provinces;

[4] universities

Yea, stranger engines for the brunt of war
Than was the fiery keel at Antwerp's bridge
I'll make my servile spirits to invent!
          Enter VALDES *and* CORNELIUS.

Come, German Valdes and Cornelius,
And make me blest with your sage confer-
  ence.
Valdes, sweet Valdes and Cornelius,
Know that your words have won me at the
  last
To practise magic and concealed arts;
Yet not your words only, but mine own fan-
  tasy
That will receive no object for my head
But ruminates on necromantic skill.
Philosophy is odious and obscure,
Both law and physic are for petty wits,
Divinity is basest of the three,
Unpleasant, harsh, contemptible and vile;
'Tis magic, magic, that hath ravished me!
Then, gentle friends, aid me in this attempt,
And I that have with concise syllogisms
Gravelled [5]   the pastors of the German
  church,
And made the flowering pride of Wittenberg
Swarm to my problems as the infernal spirits
On sweet Musaeus when he came to hell,
Will be as cunning as Agrippa [6] was
Whose shadows made all Europe honor him.

VALDES

Faustus, these books, thy wit and our experi-
  ence
Shall make all nations to canonize us.
As Indian Moors [7] obey their Spanish lords
So shall the subjects of every element
Be always serviceable to us three:
Like lions shall they guard us when we
  please,
Like Almain rutters [8] with their horsemen's
  staves,
Or Lapland giants trotting by our sides;
Sometimes like women, or unwedded maids,
Shadowing more beauty in their airy brows

[5] silenced
[6] Cornelius Agrippa, a sixteenth-century scholar-
magician
[7] American Indians
[8] German horsemen

Than has the white breasts of the queen of
love;
From Venice shall they drag huge argosies
And from America the golden fleece
That yearly stuffs old Philip's treasury,
If learned Faustus will be resolute.

FAUSTUS

Valdes, as resolute am I in this
As thou to live; therefore object it not.

CORNELIUS

The miracles that magic will perform
Will make thee vow to study nothing else.
He that is grounded in astrology,
Enriched with tongues, well seen in minerals,
Hath all the principles magic doth require.
Then doubt not, Faustus, but to be renowned
And more frequented for this mystery
Than heretofore the Delphian oracle.
The spirits tell me they can dry the sea
And fetch the treasure of all foreign
wrecks —
Ay, all the wealth that our forefathers hid
Within the massy entrails of the earth.
Then tell me, Faustus, what shall we three
want? [9]

FAUSTUS

Nothing, Cornelius. O this cheers my soul!
Come, show me some demonstrations magi-
cal
That I may conjure in some lusty grove
And have these joys in full possession.

VALDES

Then haste thee to some solitary grove
And bear wise Bacon's [10] and Albanus' [11]
works,
The Hebrew Psalter and New Testament;
And whatsoever else is requisite
We will inform thee ere our conference
cease.

CORNELIUS

Valdes, first let him know the words of art,
And then, all other ceremonies learned,
Faustus may try his cunning by himself.

9 lack
10 Roger Bacon, English scientist and magician
11 an alchemist

VALDES

First I'll instruct thee in the rudiments,
And then wilt thou be perfecter than I.

FAUSTUS

Then come and dine with me, and after meat
We'll canvas every quiddity thereof;
For ere I sleep I'll try what I can do:
This night I'll conjure though I die there-
fore.   *Exeunt.*
[Scene 2]   *Enter two* SCHOLARS.

1 SCHOLAR

I wonder what's become of Faustus, that
was wont to make our schools ring with
sic probo? [1]

2 SCHOLAR

That shall we know, for see here comes his
boy.
Enter WAGNER [*carrying wine*].

1 SCHOLAR

How now, sirrah; where's thy master?

WAGNER

God in heaven knows.

2 SCHOLAR

Why, dost not thou know?

WAGNER

Yes, I know; but that follows not.

1 SCHOLAR

Go to, sirrah; leave your jesting and tell us
where he is.

WAGNER

That follows not necessary by force of argument that you, being licentiate,[2] should
stand upon it; therefore acknowledge
your error and be attentive.

1 " thus I prove," a formula used by scholarly de-
baters
2 candidate for a degree (Wagner is parodying
academic jargon.)

2 SCHOLAR

Why, didst thou not say thou knewest?

1 SCHOLAR

Yes, sirrah, I heard you.

WAGNER

Ask my fellow if I be a thief.

2 SCHOLAR

Well, you will not tell us?

WAGNER

Yes, sir, I will tell you. Yet if you were not dunces you would never ask me such a question, for is not he *corpus naturale*,[3] and is not that *mobile*?[4] Then wherefore should you ask me such a question? But that I am by nature phlegmatic, slow to wrath and prone to lechery (to love, I would say), it were not for you to come within forty foot of the place of execution, although I do not doubt to see you both hanged the next sessions. Thus having triumphed over you, I will set my countenance like a precisian,[5] and begin to speak thus: Truly, my dear brethren, my master is within at dinner with Valdes and Cornelius, as this wine, if it could speak, would inform your worships; and so the Lord bless you, preserve you, and keep you, my dear brethren, my dear brethren.

Exit.

1 SCHOLAR

Nay, then I fear he is fallen into that damned art for which they two are infamous through the world.

2 SCHOLAR

Were he a stranger and not allied to me, yet should I grieve for him. But come, let us go and inform the Rector, and see if he by his grave counsel can reclaim him.

3 natural body
4 movable
5 Puritan. Wagner now parodies the solemn face, the nasal whine, and the foolish speech of the sect.

1 SCHOLAR

O but I fear me nothing can reclaim him.

2 SCHOLAR

Yet let us try what we can do.   *Exeunt.*

[Scene 3]   *Enter* FAUSTUS *to conjure.*

FAUSTUS

Now that the gloomy shadow of the earth,
Longing to view Orion's drizzling look,
Leaps from the antarctic world unto the sky
And dims the welkin with her pitchy breath,
Faustus, begin thine incantations
And try if devils will obey thy hest,
Seeing thou hast prayed and sacrificed to
    them.
Within this circle is Jehovah's name
    [*He draws the circle on the ground.*]
Forward and backward anagrammatized,
The breviated names of holy saints,
Figures of every adjunct to the heavens
And characters of signs and erring stars,
By which the spirits are enforced to rise.
Then fear not, Faustus, but be resolute
And try the uttermost magic can perform.
    [*Thunder.*]
Sint mihi dei Acherontis propitii! Valeat nu-
    men triplex Iehovae!
Ignei aerii aquatici spiritus, salvete! Orientis
    princeps
Belzebub, inferni ardentis monarcha, et
    Demogorgon, propitiamus vos, ut ap-
    pareat et surgat Mephistophilis!
    [FAUSTUS *pauses. Thunder.*]
Quid tu moraris? Per Iehovam, Gehennam
    et consecratam aquam quam nunc
    spargo, signumque crucis quod nunc
    facio, et per vota nostra, ipse nunc sur-
    gat nobis dicatus Mephistophilis![1]

1 Favor me, you gods of Acheron! Yield to the triune power of Jehovah! Hail, likewise, you spirits of fire, air, and water! Belzebub, prince of the east, monarch of blazing hell, and Demogorgon, we invoke your favor that Mephistophilis may appear and ascend. . . . Why do you delay? By Jehovah, by Gehenna, and by the holy water which now I sprinkle, by the sign of the cross which now I make, and by the prayers I have offered you, at my command let Mephistophilis arise.

[MEPHISTOPHILIS *in the shape of a dragon
rises from the earth outside the circle.*]
I charge thee to return and change thy
    shape;
Thou art too ugly to attend on me.
Go, and return an old Franciscan friar;
That holy shape becomes a devil best.
                              Exit MEPHISTOPHILIS.
I see there's virtue in my heavenly words:
Who would not be proficient in this art?
How pliant is this Mephistophilis,
Full of obedience and humility!
Such is the force of magic and my spells.
Now, Faustus, thou art conjuror laureate
That canst command great Mephistophilis:
Quin redis, Mephistophilis, fratris imagine! [2]
    Re-enter MEPHISTOPHILIS *like a Friar.*

MEPHISTOPHILIS

Now, Faustus, what wouldst thou have me
    do?

FAUSTUS

I charge thee wait upon me whilst I live
To do whatever Faustus shall command,
Be it to make the moon drop from her sphere
Or the ocean to overwhelm the world.

MEPHISTOPHILIS

I am a servant to great Lucifer
And may not follow thee without his leave:
No more than he commands must we per-
    form.

FAUSTUS

Did not he charge thee to appear to me?

MEPHISTOPHILIS

No, I came now hither of my own accord.

FAUSTUS

Did not my conjuring speeches raise thee?
    Speak!

MEPHISTOPHILIS

That was the cause, but yet *per accidens,*[3]
For when we hear one rack the name of God,

Abjure the Scriptures and his Savior Christ,
We fly in hope to get his glorious soul;
Nor will we come unless he use such means
Whereby he is in danger to be damned;
Therefore the shortest cut for conjuring
Is stoutly to abjure the Trinity
And pray devoutly to the prince of hell.

FAUSTUS

So Faustus hath
Already done, and holds this principle,
There is no chief but only Belzebub
To whom Faustus doth dedicate himself.
This word damnation terrifies not him
For he confounds hell in Elisium; [4]
His ghost be with the old philosophers!
But leaving these vain trifles of men's
    souls —
Tell me what is that Lucifer thy lord?

MEPHISTOPHILIS

Arch-regent and commander of all spirits.

FAUSTUS

Was not that Lucifer an angel once?

MEPHISTOPHILIS

Yes, Faustus, and most dearly loved of God.

FAUSTUS

How comes it, then, that he is prince of
    devils?

MEPHISTOPHILIS

O by aspiring pride and insolence
For which God threw him from the face of
    heaven.

FAUSTUS

And what are you that live with Lucifer?

MEPHISTOPHILIS

Unhappy spirits that fell with Lucifer,
Conspired against our God with Lucifer,
And are forever damned with Lucifer.

FAUSTUS

Where are you damned?

---

2 Return, Mephistophilis, in the image of a Friar.
3 indirectly

4 the pagan world of the dead

MEPHISTOPHILIS

In hell.

FAUSTUS

How comes it, then, that thou art out of
   hell?

MEPHISTOPHILIS

Why, this is hell, nor am I out of it:
Thinkst thou that I who saw the face of God
And tasted the eternal joys of heaven
Am not tormented with ten thousand hells
In being deprived of everlasting bliss?
O Faustus, leave these frivolous demands
Which strike a terror to my fainting soul!

FAUSTUS

What, is great Mephistophilis so passionate
For being deprived of the joys of heaven?
Learn thou of Faustus manly fortitude
And scorn those joys thou never shalt pos-
   sess.
Go, bear these tidings to great Lucifer:
Seeing Faustus hath incurred eternal death
By desperate thoughts against Jove's deity,
Say he surrenders up to him his soul
So he will spare him four-and-twenty years,
Letting him live in all voluptuousness,
Having thee ever to attend on me:
To give me whatsoever I shall ask,
To tell me whatsoever I demand,
To slay mine enemies and aid my friends,
And always be obedient to my will.
Go, and return to mighty Lucifer,
And meet me in my study at midnight
And then resolve me of thy master's mind.

MEPHISTOPHILIS

I will, Faustus.   *Exit.*

FAUSTUS

Had I as many souls as there be stars
I'd give them all for Mephistophilis!
By him I'll be great Emperor of the world,
And make a bridge thorough the moving air
To pass the ocean with a band of men;
I'll join the hills that bind the Afric shore
And make that country continent to Spain,
And both contributory to my crown;

The Emperor shall not live but by my leave,
Nor any potentate of Germany.
Now that I have obtained what I desire
I'll live in speculation of this art
Till Mephistophilis return again.   *Exit.*
   [Scene 4]   *Enter* WAGNER *and the*
CLOWN.[1]

WAGNER

Sirrah boy, come hither.

CLOWN

How, boy? Swowns, boy! I hope you have
   seen many boys with such pickade-
   vaunts [2] as I have. Boy, quotha!

WAGNER

Tell me, sirrah, hast thou any comings in? [3]

CLOWN

Ay, and goings out [4] too; you may see else.

WAGNER

Alas, poor slave. See how poverty jesteth in
   his nakedness: the villain is bare and out
   of service, and so hungry that I know
   he would give his soul to the Devil for
   a shoulder of mutton, though it were
   blood-raw.

CLOWN

How, my soul to the Devil for a shoulder of
   mutton though it were blood raw? Not
   so, good friend: by'r Lady, I had need
   have it well roasted, and good sauce to
   it, if I pay so dear.

WAGNER

Well, wilt thou serve me, and I'll make thee
   go like *Qui mihi discipulus?* [5]

CLOWN

How, in verse?

[1] a rustic
[2] pointed beards
[3] income
[4] (pointing to the holes in his tattered clothing)
[5] one who is my pupil

WAGNER

No, sirrah, in beaten silk and stavesacre.[6]

CLOWN

How, how: knave's acre? Ay, I thought that was all the land his father left him.[7] Do ye hear, I would be sorry to rob you of your living.

WAGNER

Sirrah, I say in stavesacre.

CLOWN

Oho, oho: stavesacre! When then, belike, if I were your man I should be full of vermin.

WAGNER

So thou shalt, whether thou beest with me or no. But sirrah, leave your jesting, and bind yourself presently unto me for seven years, or I'll turn all the lice about thee into familiars,[8] and they shall tear thee in pieces.

CLOWN

Do you hear, sir? You may save that labor; they are too familiar with me already. Swowns, they are as bold with my flesh, as if they had paid for my meat and drink.

WAGNER

Well, do you hear, sirrah: hold, take these guilders.   [*Gives money.*]

CLOWN

Gridirons — what be they?

WAGNER

Why, French crowns.[9]

CLOWN

Mass, but for the name of French crowns a man were as good have as many English counters.[10] And what should I do with these?

WAGNER

Why now, sirrah, thou art at an hour's warning whensoever or wheresoever the devil shall fetch thee.

CLOWN

No, no! Here, take your gridirons again.

WAGNER

Truly, I'll none of them.

CLOWN

Truly, but you shall.

WAGNER

Bear witness, I gave them him.

CLOWN

Bear witness, I give them you again.

WAGNER

Well, I will cause two devils presently to fetch thee away. Baliol [11] and Belcher!
                              [*Conjures.*]

CLOWN

Let your Belly-oh and your Belcher come here, and I'll knock them, they were never so knocked since they were devils. Say I should kill one of them, what would folks say: do ye see yonder tall fellow in the round slop? [12] He has killed the devil! So I should be called kill-devil all the parish over.

Enter two DEVILS, *and the* CLOWN *runs up and down crying.*

WAGNER

Baliol and Belcher! Spirits away!
                         Exeunt [DEVILS].

---

6 a kind of cloth; also a lice-killer
7 (This sentence is addressed to the audience, in confidence.)
8 demons
9 a coin often counterfeited
10 " slugs," toy money; also, a prison
11 i.e., Belial
12 wide breeches

CLOWN

What, are they gone? A vengeance on them,
   they have vile long nails! There was a
   he-devil, and a she-devil. I'll tell you
   how you may know them: all he-devils
   has horns, and all she-devils has clifts
   and cloven feet.

WAGNER

Well, sirrah, follow me.

CLOWN

But do you hear, if I should serve you, would
   you teach me to raise up Banios and
   Belcheos?

WAGNER

I will teach thee to turn thyself to anything
   — to a dog, or a cat, or a mouse, or a
   rat, or any thing.

CLOWN

How? a Christian fellow to a dog or a cat,
   a mouse or a rat? No, no, sir! If you
   turn me into any thing, let it be in the
   likeness of a little pretty frisking flea,
   that I may be here and there and everywhere. O I'll tickle the pretty wenches'
   plackets, I'll be amongst them, i'faith!

WAGNER

Well, sirrah, come.

CLOWN

But do you hear, Wagner?

WAGNER

How? Baliol and Belcher!

CLOWN

O Lord, I pray sir, let Banio and Belcher go
   sleep.

WAGNER

Villain, call me Master Wagner, and let thy
   left eye be diametarily fixt upon my
   right heel with *quasi vestigias nostras
   insistere.*[13]   *Exit.*

13 as if to walk in our footsteps

CLOWN

God forgive me, he speaks Dutch fustian.
   Well, I'll follow him, I'll serve him;
   that's flat.   *Exit.*

[Scene 5]   *Enter* FAUSTUS *in his Study.*

FAUSTUS

Now, Faustus, must thou needs be damned
And canst thou not be saved.
What boots it, then, to think of God or
   heaven?
Away with such vain fancies, and despair —
Despair in God and trust in Belzebub.
Now go not backward, no!
Faustus, be resolute: why waverest thou?
O something soundeth in mine ears:
" Abjure this magic, turn to God again! "
Ay, and Faustus will turn to God again.
To God? He loves thee not;
The God thou servest is thine own appetite,
Wherein is fixed the love of Belzebub.
To him I'll build an altar and a church
And offer lukewarm blood of newborn babes.
   Enter GOOD ANGEL *and* EVIL ANGEL.

GOOD ANGEL

Sweet Faustus, leave that execrable art.

EVIL ANGEL

Go forward, Faustus, in that famous art.

FAUSTUS

Contrition, prayer, repentance — what of
   them?

GOOD ANGEL

O they are means to bring thee unto heaven!

EVIL ANGEL

Rather illusions, fruits of lunacy,
That makes men foolish that do trust them
   most.

GOOD ANGEL

Sweet Faustus, think of heaven and heavenly
   things.

EVIL ANGEL

No, Faustus, think of honor and of wealth.
                          [*Exeunt* ANGELS.]

FAUSTUS

Of wealth!
Why, the signiory of Emden shall be mine.
When Mephistophilis shall stand by me
What God can hurt me? Faustus, thou art safe;
Cast no more doubts. Come, Mephistophilis,
And bring glad tidings from great Lucifer.
Is't not midnight? Come, Mephistophilis!
Veni, veni, Mephistophile! [1]
  Enter MEPHISTOPHILIS.
Now tell me what says Lucifer, thy lord?

MEPHISTOPHILIS

That I shall wait on Faustus whilst I live,
So he will buy my service with his soul.

FAUSTUS

Already Faustus hath hazarded that for thee.

MEPHISTOPHILIS

But, Faustus, thou must bequeath it solemnly
And write a deed of gift with thine own blood,
For that security craves great Lucifer.
If thou deny it, I will back to hell.

FAUSTUS

Stay, Mephistophilis, and tell me what good
Will my soul do thy lord?

MEPHISTOPHILIS

    Enlarge his kingdom.

FAUSTUS

Is that the reason why he tempts us thus?

MEPHISTOPHILIS

Solamen miseris socios habuisse doloris. [2]

FAUSTUS

Why, have you any pain that tortures others?

MEPHISTOPHILIS

As great as have the human souls of men.
But tell me, Faustus, shall I have thy soul?

---

1 Come! come! Mephistophilis!
2 " Misery loves company."

And I will be thy slave, and wait on thee,
And tell thee more than thou hast wit to ask.

FAUSTUS

Ay, Mephistophilis, I give it thee.

MEPHISTOPHILIS

Then, Faustus, stab thine arm courageously,
And bind thy soul that at some certain day
Great Lucifer may claim it as his own,
And then be thou as great as Lucifer.

FAUSTUS

Lo, Mephistophilis, for love of thee
    [*Stabbing his arm.*]
I cut mine arm, and with my proper blood
Assure my soul to be great Lucifer's.
Chief lord and regent of perpetual night,
View here the blood that trickles from mine arm
And let it be propitious for my wish!

MEPHISTOPHILIS

But, Faustus, thou must
Write it in manner of a deed of gift.

FAUSTUS

Ay, so I will. [*Writes.*] But, Mephistophilis,
My blood congeals and I can write no more.

MEPHISTOPHILIS

I'll fetch thee fire to dissolve it straight.
    Exit.

FAUSTUS

What might the staying of my blood portend?
Is it unwilling I should write this bill?
Why streams it not, that I may write afresh?
" Faustus gives to thee his soul " — ah, there it stayed.
Why shouldst thou not? Is not thy soul thine own?
Then write again: " Faustus gives to thee his soul."
Re-enter MEPHISTOPHILIS *with a chafer* [3] *of coals.*

---

3 chafing dish

MEPHISTOPHILIS

Here's fire; come, Faustus, set it on.

FAUSTUS

So: now the blood begins to clear again;
Now will I make an end immediately.

[Writes.]

MEPHISTOPHILIS

[Aside.] O what will not I do to obtain his
    soul!

FAUSTUS

Consummatum est [4] — this bill is ended;
And Faustus hath bequeathed his soul to
    Lucifer.
But what is this inscription on mine arm?
" *Homo, fuge!* " [5] Whither should I fly?
If unto God, he'll throw me down to hell.
My senses are deceived; here's nothing writ.
I see it plain: here in this place is writ
" *Homo, fuge!* " Yet shall not Faustus fly.

MEPHISTOPHILIS

I'll fetch him somewhat to delight his mind.

Exit.

Re-enter MEPHISTOPHILIS *with* DEVILS, *giving crowns and rich apparel to* FAUSTUS, *and dance, and then depart.*

FAUSTUS

Speak, Mephistophilis, what means this show?

MEPHISTOPHILIS

Nothing, Faustus, but to delight thy mind
    withal
And to show thee what magic can perform.

FAUSTUS

But may I raise up spirits when I please?

MEPHISTOPHILIS

Ay, Faustus, and do greater things than
    these.

FAUSTUS

Then there's enough for a thousand souls.
Here, Mephistophilis, receive this scroll,

4 It is completed.
5 " Man, flee! "

A deed of gifts of body and of soul;
But yet conditionally that thou perform
All articles prescribed between us both.

MEPHISTOPHILIS

Faustus, I swear by hell and Lucifer
To effect all promises between us made.

FAUSTUS

Then hear me read them: *[Reads.]*
" On these conditions following:
First, that Faustus may be a spirit in form
    and substance.
Secondly, that Mephistophilis shall be his
    servant and at his command.
Thirdly, that Mephistophilis shall do for him,
    and bring him whatsoever.
Fourthly, that he shall be in his chamber or
    house invisible.
Lastly, that he shall appear to the said John
    Faustus at all times, in what form or
    shape soever he please.
I, John Faustus of Wittenberg, Doctor, by
    these presents do give both body and
    soul to Lucifer, Prince of the East, and
    his minister Mephistophilis, and further-
    more grant unto them, that 24 years
    being expired, the articles above written
    inviolate, full power to fetch or carry
    the said John Faustus body and soul,
    flesh, blood, or goods, into their habita-
    tion wheresoever.
        By me John Faustus."

MEPHISTOPHILIS

Speak, Faustus, do you deliver this as your
    deed?

FAUSTUS

Ay, take it, and the devil give thee good
    on't.

MEPHISTOPHILIS

Now, Faustus, ask what thou wilt.

FAUSTUS

First will I question with thee about hell.
Tell me, where is the place that men call
    hell?

MEPHISTOPHILIS

Under the heavens.

FAUSTUS

Ay, but whereabout?

MEPHISTOPHILIS

Within the bowels of these elements,
Where we are tortured and remain forever.
Hell hath no limits, nor is circumscribed
In one self place, for where we are is hell
And where hell is there must we ever be;
And, to conclude, when all the world dis-
solves
And every creature shall be purified,
All places shall be hell that is not heaven.

FAUSTUS

Come, I think hell's a fable.

MEPHISTOPHILIS

Ay, think so, till experience change thy
mind.

FAUSTUS

Why, thinkst thou then that Faustus shall
be damned?

MEPHISTOPHILIS

Ay, of necessity, for here's the scroll
Wherein thou hast given thy soul to Lucifer.

FAUSTUS

Ay, and body too; but what of that?
Thinkst thou that Faustus is so fond to im-
agine
That after this life there is any pain?
Tush, these are trifles and mere old wives'
tales.

MEPHISTOPHILIS

But, Faustus, I am an instance to prove the
contrary,
For I am damned, and am now in hell.

FAUSTUS

How, now in hell?
Nay, and this be hell I'll willingly be damned.
What, walking, disputing, etcetera?

But leaving off this, let me have a wife,
The fairest maid in Germany,
For I am wanton and lascivious
And cannot live without a wife.

MEPHISTOPHILIS

How, a wife?
I prithee, Faustus, talk not of a wife.

FAUSTUS

Nay, sweet Mephistophilis, fetch me one, for
I will have one.

MEPHISTOPHILIS

Well, thou will have one. Sit there till I
come;
I'll fetch thee a wife in the devil's name.
                                        [*Exit.*]
Re-enter MEPHISTOPHILIS *with a* DEVIL
dressed like a woman, with fireworks.

MEPHISTOPHILIS

Tell me, Faustus, how dost thou like thy
wife?

FAUSTUS

A plague on her for a hot whore!

MEPHISTOPHILIS

Tut, Faustus,
Marriage is but a ceremonial toy.
If thou lovest me, think no more of it.
I'll cull thee out the fairest courtesans
And bring them every morning to thy bed;
She whom thine eye shall like thy heart shall
have,
Be she as chaste as was Penelope,[6]
As wise as Saba,[7] or as beautiful
As was bright Lucifer before his fall.
                                      [*Exeunt.*]
[Scene 6]   *Enter again* FAUSTUS *and*
MEPHISTOPHILIS.

MEPHISTOPHILIS

Hold, take this book: peruse it thoroughly.
The iterating of these lines brings gold,

---

[6] the faithful wife of Ulysses
[7] Queen of Sheba

The framing of this circle on the ground
Brings whirlwinds, tempests, thunder and
 lightning;
Pronounce this thrice devoutly to thyself
And men in armor shall appear to thee,
Ready to execute what thou desirest.

FAUSTUS

Thanks, Mephistophilis, yet fain would I
have a book wherein I might behold all
spells and incantations, that I might
raise up spirits when I please.

MEPHISTOPHILIS

Here they are in this book.
     There turn to them.

FAUSTUS

Now would I have a book where I might see
all characters and planets of the heavens, that I might know their motions
and dispositions.

MEPHISTOPHILIS

Here they are too. *Turn to them.*

FAUSTUS

Nay, let me have one book more, and then
I have done, wherein I might see all
plants, herbs, and trees that grow upon
the earth.

MEPHISTOPHILIS

Here they be.

FAUSTUS

O thou art deceived!

MEPHISTOPHILIS

Tut, I warrant thee. *Turn to them.*

FAUSTUS

When I behold the heavens then I repent
And curse thee, wicked Mephistophilis,
Because thou hast deprived me of those joys.

MEPHISTOPHILIS

Why, thinkest thou heaven is such a glorious
 thing?

I tell thee, Faustus, 'tis not half so fair
As thou or any man that breathes on earth.

FAUSTUS

How provest thou that?

MEPHISTOPHILIS

It was made for man; therefore is man more
 excellent.

FAUSTUS

If it were made for man 'twas made for me.
I will renounce this magic and repent.
 Enter GOOD ANGEL *and* EVIL ANGEL.

GOOD ANGEL

Faustus, repent; yet God will pity thee.

EVIL ANGEL

Thou art a spirit; God cannot pity thee.

FAUSTUS

Who buzzeth in mine ears I am a spirit?
Be I a devil yet God may pity me.
Ay, God will pity me, if I repent.

EVIL ANGEL

Ay, but Faustus never shall repent.
     [*Exeunt* ANGELS.]

FAUSTUS

My heart's so hardened I cannot repent.
Scarce can I name salvation, faith, or heaven,
But fearful echoes thunder in mine ears:
" Faustus, thou art damned! " Then swords
 and knives,
Poison, guns, halters, and envenomed steel
Are laid before me to despatch myself,
And long ere this I should have slain myself
Had not sweet pleasure conquered deep de-
 spair.
Have I not made blind Homer sing to me
Of Alexander's love and Oenon's death,
And hath not he that built the walls of
 Thebes
With ravishing sound of his melodious harp
Made music with my Mephistophilis?
Why should I die, then, or basely despair?
I am resolved Faustus shall ne'er repent.

Come, Mephistophilis, let us dispute again
And argue of divine astrology.
Tell me, are there many heavens above the
    moon?
Are all celestial bodies but one globe
As is the substance of this centric earth?

MEPHISTOPHILIS

As are the elements, such are the spheres,
Mutually folded in each other's orb;
And jointly move upon one axletree
Whose terminine is termed the world's wide
    pole;
Nor are the names of Saturn, Mars, or Ju-
piter
Feigned, but are erring [1] stars.

FAUSTUS

But tell me, have they all one motion, both
situ et tempore? [2]

MEPHISTOPHILIS

All jointly move from East to West in 24
    hours upon the poles of the world, but
    differ in their motion upon the poles of
    the zodiac.

FAUSTUS

Tush,
These slender trifles Wagner can decide.
Hath Mephistophilis no greater skill?
Who knows not the double motion of the
    planets?
The first is finished in a natural day;
The second thus, as Saturn in 30 years, Ju-
    piter in 12, Mars in 4, the Sun, Venus,
    and Mercury in a year, the Moon in 28
    days. Tush, these are freshmen's sup-
    positions. But tell me, hath every sphere
    a dominion or *Intelligentia?* [3]

MEPHISTOPHILIS

Ay.

FAUSTUS

How many heavens or spheres are there?

MEPHISTOPHILIS

Nine: the seven planets, the firmament, and
    the empyreal heaven.

FAUSTUS

But is there not *coelum igneum, et crystal-
linum?* [4]

MEPHISTOPHILIS

No, Faustus, they be but fables.

FAUSTUS

Well, resolve me in this question: why have
    we not conjunctions, oppositions, as-
    pects, eclipses, all at one time, but in
    some years we have more, in some less?

MEPHISTOPHILIS

Per inequalem motum respectu totius. [5]

FAUSTUS

Well, I am answered. Tell me, who made the
    world?

MEPHISTOPHILIS

I will not.

FAUSTUS

Sweet Mephistophilis, tell me.

MEPHISTOPHILIS

Move me not, for I will not tell thee.

FAUSTUS

Villain, have I not bound thee to tell me
    anything?

MEPHISTOPHILIS

Ay, that is not against our kingdom; but
    this is.
Think thou on hell, Faustus, for thou art
    damned.

FAUSTUS

Think, Faustus, upon God that made the
    world!

---

[1] wandering
[2] in direction and time of revolution
[3] governing spirit

[4] a sphere of fire, and one of crystal
[5] because of unequal rates of motion in respect to
the whole [universe]

MEPHISTOPHILIS

Remember this!   *Exit.*

FAUSTUS

Ay, go, accursed spirit, to ugly hell;
'Tis thou hast damned distressed Faustus'
  soul.
Is't not too late?
  Enter GOOD ANGEL *and* EVIL ANGEL.

EVIL ANGEL

Too late.

GOOD ANGEL

Never too late, if Faustus can repent.

EVIL ANGEL

If thou repent, devils shall tear thee in
  pieces.

GOOD ANGEL

Repent, and they shall never raze [6] thy skin.

                              Exeunt ANGELS.

FAUSTUS

Ah Christ, my Savior!
Seek to save distressed Faustus' soul.
  Enter LUCIFER, BELZEBUB, *and* MEPHI-
STOPHILIS.

LUCIFER

Christ cannot save thy soul, for he is just;
There's none but I have interest in the same.

FAUSTUS

O who art thou that look'st so terrible?

LUCIFER

I am Lucifer,
And this is my companion prince in hell.

FAUSTUS

O Faustus, they are come to fetch away thy
  soul!

LUCIFER

We come to tell thee thou dost injure us:
Thou call'st on Christ, contrary to thy
  promise.

  6 scratch

Thou shouldst not think of God; think of
  the devil, —
And of his dam too.

FAUSTUS

Nor will I henceforth. Pardon me in this,
And Faustus vows never to look to heaven,
Never to name God or to pray to him,
To burn his Scripture, slay his ministers,
And make my spirits pull his churches down.

LUCIFER

Do so, and we will highly gratify thee.
Faustus, we are come from hell to show thee
  some pastime: sit down, and thou shalt
  see all the Seven Deadly Sins appear in
  their proper shapes.

FAUSTUS

That sight will be as pleasing unto me as
  paradise was to Adam, the first day of
  his creation.

LUCIFER

Talk not of paradise nor creation, but mark
  this show; talk of the devil and nothing
  else. Come, away!
  Enter the SEVEN DEADLY SINS.
Now, Faustus, examine them of their several
  names and dispositions.

FAUSTUS

That shall I soon. What art thou, the first?

PRIDE

I am Pride. I disdain to have any parents. I
  am like to Ovid's flea: I can creep into
  every corner of a wench; sometimes like
  a periwig I sit upon her brow; next like
  a necklace I hang about her neck, or
  like a fan of feathers I kiss her lips;
  and then turning myself to a wrought
  smock do what I list. But fie, what a
  scent is here! I'll not speak another
  word except the ground were perfumed
  and covered with cloth of arras.

FAUSTUS

Thou art a proud knave indeed. What art
  thou, the second?

COVETOUSNESS

I am Covetousness, begotten of an old churl in an old leathern bag; and, might I have my wish, I would desire that this house and all the people in it were turned to gold, that I might lock you up in my chest. O my sweet gold!

FAUSTUS

What art thou, the third?

WRATH

I am Wrath. I had neither father nor mother; I leaped out of a lion's mouth when I was scarce half an hour old, and ever since I have run up and down the world with this case of rapiers, wounding myself when I had nobody to fight withal. I was born in hell; and look to it, for some of you shall be my father.

FAUSTUS

What art thou, the fourth?

ENVY

I am Envy, begotten of a chimney-sweeper and an oyster-wife. I cannot read, and therefore wish all books were burned. I am lean with seeing others eat. O that there would come a famine through all the world, that all might die, and I live alone; then thou shouldst see how fat I would be! But must thou sit and I stand? Come down, with a vengeance!

FAUSTUS

Away, envious rascal! What art thou, the fifth?

GLUTTONY

Who, I, sir? I am Gluttony. My parents are all dead, and the devil a penny they have left me but a bare pension, and that is 30 meals a day and ten bevers [7] — a small trifle to suffice nature. O I come of a royal parentage: my grandfather was a gammon of bacon, my grandmother a hogshead of claret wine. My godfathers were these: Peter Pickle-herring and Martin Martlemas-beef. O but my godmother — she was a jolly gentlewoman, and well beloved in every good town and city: her name was mistress Margery March-beer. Now, Faustus, thou hast heard all my progeny; wilt thou bid me to supper?

FAUSTUS

No, I'll see thee hanged! Thou wilt eat up all my victuals.

GLUTTONY

Then the devil choke thee.

FAUSTUS

Choke thyself, glutton. What art thou, the sixth?

SLOTH

I am Sloth. I was begotten on a sunny bank, where I have lain ever since, and you have done me great injury to bring me from thence; let me be carried thither again by Gluttony and Lechery. I'll not speak another word for a king's ransom.

FAUSTUS

What are you, mistress minx, the seventh and last?

LECHERY

Who, I, sir? I am one that loves an inch of raw mutton better than an ell of fried stockfish, and the first letter of my name begins with L — .

LUCIFER

Away, to hell, to hell!   *Exeunt the* SINS.
Now, Faustus, how dost thou like this?

FAUSTUS

O this feeds my soul!

LUCIFER

Tut, Faustus, in hell is all manner of delight.

---

[7] light lunches

FAUSTUS

O that I might see hell and return again,
how happy were I then!

LUCIFER

Thou shalt. I will send for thee at midnight.
In meantime take this book, peruse it
thoroughly, and thou shalt turn thyself
into what shape thou wilt.

FAUSTUS

Great thanks, mighty Lucifer;
This will I keep as chary as my life.

LUCIFER

Farewell, Faustus, and think on the devil.

FAUSTUS

Farewell, great Lucifer. Come, Mephistoph-
ilis.   *Exeunt omnes.*
   [Scene 7]   *Enter* WAGNER *solus, as
Chorus.*[1]

WAGNER

Learned Faustus,
To know the secrets of astronomy
Graven in the book of Jove's high firma-
ment,
Did mount himself to scale Olympus' top,
Being seated in a chariot burning bright
Drawn by the strength of yoked dragons'
necks,
He views the clouds, the planets, and the
stars,
The tropic zones and quarters of the sky
From the bright circle of the horned moon
Even to the height of *Primum Mobile;* [2]
And whirling round with this circumference
Within the concave compass of the pole,
From east to west his dragons swiftly glide
And in eight days did bring him home again.
Not long he stayed within his quiet house
To rest his bones after his weary toil
But new exploits do hale him out again;

And mounted then upon a dragon's back
That with his wings did part the subtle air,
He now is gone to prove cosmography
That measures coasts and kingdoms of the
earth:
And, as I guess, will first arrive at Rome
To see the Pope and manner of his court
And take some part of holy Peter's feast,
The which this day is highly solemnized.
                              Exit WAGNER.
   Enter FAUSTUS *and* MEPHISTOPHILIS.

FAUSTUS

Having now, my good Mephistophilis,
Passed with delight the stately town of Trier
Environed round with airy mountain tops,
With walls of flint and deep-entrenched
lakes,
Not to be won by any conquering prince;
From Paris next coasting the realm of
France,
We saw the river Maine fall into Rhine,
Whose banks are set with groves of fruitful
vines;
Then up to Naples, rich Campania,
Whose buildings fair and gorgeous to the eye,
The streets straight forth and paved with
finest brick
Quarter the town in four equivalents.
There saw we learned Maro's [3] golden tomb,
The way he cut, an English mile in length,
Thorough a rock of stone in one night's
space.
From thence to Venice, Padua, and the rest,
In midst of which a sumptuous temple stands
That threats the stars with her aspiring top,
Whose frame is paved with sundry colored
stones
And roofed aloft with curious work in gold.
Thus hitherto hath Faustus spent his time.
But tell me now, what resting place is this?
Hast thou, as erst I did command,
Conducted me within the walls of Rome?

MEPHISTOPHILIS

Faustus, I have; and because we will not be
unprovided,

_____

[1] alone, dressed in the black cape of a chorus-
speaker
[2] the outermost heaven

[3] the Roman poet, Virgil

I have taken up his Holiness' privy chamber
for our use.

FAUSTUS

I hope his Holiness will bid us welcome.

MEPHISTOPHILIS

Tut, 'tis no matter, man; we'll be bold with
his good cheer.
And now, my Faustus, that thou may'st per-
ceive
What Rome containeth to delight thee with,
Know that this city stands upon seven hills
That underprop the groundwork of the
same;
Just through the midst runs flowing Tiber's
stream,
With winding banks that cut it in two parts,
Over the which four stately bridges lean
That makes safe passage to each part of
Rome.
Upon the bridge called Ponto Angelo
Erected is a castle passing strong,
Within whose walls such store of ordnance
are,
And double cannons framed of carved brass,
As match the days within one complete
year —
Besides the gates and high pyramides [4]
Which Julius Caesar brought from Africa.

FAUSTUS

Now by the kingdoms of infernal rule,
Of Styx, Acheron, and the fiery lake
Of ever-burning Phlegethon, I swear
That I do long to see the monuments
And situation of bright-splendent Rome.
Come, therefore, let's away.

MEPHISTOPHILIS

Nay, Faustus, stay; I know you'd fain see
the Pope
And take some part of holy Peter's feast,
Where thou shalt see a troop of bald-pate
friars
Whose *summum bonum* [5] is in belly-cheer.

FAUSTUS

Well, I am content to compass then some
sport
And by their folly make us merriment.
Then charm me that I may be invisible,
To do what I please
Unseen of any whilst I stay in Rome.
                    [MEPHISTOPHILIS *charms him.*]

MEPHISTOPHILIS

So, Faustus; now
Do what thou wilt thou shalt not be dis-
cerned.
Sound a sennet. [6] *Enter the* POPE *and the*
CARDINAL OF LORRAINE *to the banquet,*
with FRIARS *attending.*

POPE

My Lord of Lorraine, will't please you draw
near?

FAUSTUS

Fall to, and the devil choke you and [7] you
spare.

POPE

How now, who's that which spake? Friars
look about.

FRIAR

Here's nobody, if it like your Holiness.

POPE

My lord, here is a dainty dish was sent me
from the Bishop of Milan.

FAUSTUS

I thank you, sir.   *Snatch it.*

POPE

How now, who's that which snatched the
meat from me? Will no man look? My
lord, this dish was sent me from the
Cardinal of Florence.

FAUSTUS

You say true; I'll ha't.   [*Snatch it.*]

---

4 obelisks
5 greatest good

6 trumpet fanfare
7 if

POPE

What, again! My lord, I'll drink to your
grace.

FAUSTUS

I'll pledge [8] your grace.   [*Snatch it.*]

LORRAINE

My Lord, it may be some ghost newly crept
out of Purgatory come to beg a pardon
of your Holiness.

POPE

It may be so. Friars, prepare a dirge to lay
the fury of this ghost. Once again, my
lord, fall to.

The POPE *crosseth himself.*

FAUSTUS

What, are you crossing of yourself?
Well, use that trick no more, I would advise
you.   *Cross again.*
Well, that's the second time. Aware the third,
I give you fair warning.
Cross again, and FAUSTUS *hits him a box of
the ear, and they all run away.*

FAUSTUS

Come on, Mephistophilis, what shall we do?

MEPHISTOPHILIS

Nay, I know not; we shall be cursed with
bell, book, and candle.[9]

FAUSTUS

How! bell, book, and candle, candle, book,
and bell,
Forward and backward to curse Faustus to
hell.
Anon you shall hear a hog grunt, a calf
bleat, and an ass bray,
Because it is Saint Peter's holy day.
Enter all the FRIARS *to sing the dirge.*

FRIAR

Come, brethren, let's about our business with
good devotion.
All sing this:

8 toast
9 i.e., excommunicated

Cursed be he that stole away his Holiness'
meat from the table — *maledicat dominus!* [10]
Cursed be he that struck his Holiness a blow
on the face — *maledicat dominus!*
Cursed be he that took Friar Sandelo a blow
on the face — *maledicat dominus!*
Cursed be he that disturbeth our holy dirge
— *maledicat dominus!*
Cursed be he that took away his Holiness'
wine — *maledicat dominus! Et omnes
sancti!* [11] *Amen.*
Beat the FRIARS, *and fling fireworks among
them, and so exeunt.*

[Scene 8]   *Enter* ROBIN *the Ostler
with a book in his hand.*

ROBIN

O this is admirable! Here I ha' stolen one of
Doctor Faustus' conjuring books, and,
i'faith, I mean to search some circles for
my own use: now will I make all the
maidens in our parish dance at my pleasure stark naked before me, and so by
that means I shall see more than e'er I
felt or saw yet.
Enter RALPH *calling* ROBIN.

RALPH

Robin, prithee come away; there's a gentleman tarries to have his horse, and he
would have his things rubbed and made
clean. He keeps such a chafing with my
mistress about it, and she has sent me
to look thee out; prithee, come away.

ROBIN

Keep out, keep out, or else you are blown up,
you are dismembered, Ralph; keep out,
for I am about a roaring piece of work.

RALPH

Come, what dost thou with that same book?
Thou canst not read.

10 May God damn him!
11 May God, together with all the Saints, damn
him!

ROBIN

Yes, my master and mistress shall find that I can read — he for his forehead,[1] she for her private study. She's born to bear with me, or else my art fails.

RALPH

Why, Robin, what book is that?

ROBIN

What book? Why the most intolerable book for conjuring that e'er was invented by any brimstone devil.

RALPH

Canst thou conjure with it?

ROBIN

I can do all these things easily with it: first, I can make thee drunk with ippocras[2] at any tavern in Europe for nothing; that's one of my conjuring works.

RALPH

Our master Parson says that's nothing.

ROBIN

True, Ralph; and more, Ralph, if thou hast any mind to Nan Spit our kitchen maid, then turn her and wind her to thy own use as often as thou wilt, and at midnight.

RALPH

O brave, Robin! Shall I have Nan Spit, and to mine own use? On that condition I'll feed thy devil with horse-bread as long as he lives, of free cost.

ROBIN

No more, sweet Ralph. Let's go and make clean our boots which lie foul upon our hands, and then to our conjuring in the devil's name.   *Exeunt.*

[Scene 9]   *Enter* ROBIN *and* RALPH *with a silver goblet.*

ROBIN

Come, Ralph, did I not tell thee we were forever made by this Doctor Faustus' book? *Ecce signum:*[1] here's a simple purchase for horse-keepers! Our horses shall eat no hay as long as this lasts.
               Enter the VINTNER.

RALPH

But Robin, here comes the vintner.

ROBIN

Hush, I'll gull him supernaturally. Drawer, I hope all is paid; God be with you. Come, Ralph.

VINTNER

Soft, sir, a word with you: I must yet have a goblet paid from you ere you go.

ROBIN

I a goblet? Ralph — I a goblet? I scorn you, and you are but a etc.[2] I a goblet? Search me.[3]

VINTNER

I mean so, sir, with your favor.
                    [*Searches* ROBIN.]

ROBIN

How say you now?

VINTNER

I must say somewhat to your fellow: you sir.
                    [*Searches* RALPH.]

RALPH

Me, sir? Search your fill. Now, sir, you may be ashamed to burden honest men with a matter of truth.

VINTNER

Well, t'one of you hath this goblet about you.

---

[1] Behold, the proof.
[2] [Robin is directed to *ad lib* abuse at this point.]
[3] [At this point, Robin and Ralph hand the cup back and forth, out of sight of the Vintner, but in full view of the audience.]

---

[1] the place where a cuckold's horns grew
[2] a spiced wine

ROBIN

[*Aside.*] You lie, drawer, 'tis afore me. —
Sirrah you, I'll teach ye to impeach honest men! Stand by: I'll scour you for a
goblet; stand aside, you had best, I
charge you in the name of Belzebub.
[*Aside.*] Look to the goblet, Ralph.

VINTNER

What mean you, sirrah?

ROBIN

I'll tell you what I mean: *Reads.*
*Sanctobulorum Periphrasticon*⁴ — nay, I'll
tickle you, vintner. [*Aside.*] Look to the
goblet, Ralph.
*Polypragmos Belseborams framanto pacos-
tiphos tostu Mephistophilis etc.*⁴
Enter MEPHISTOPHILIS, *sets squibs at their
backs* [*and withdraws*]. *They run about.*

VINTNER

O *nomine Domine!*⁵ what meanest thou,
Robin? Thou hast no goblet.

RALPH

*Peccatum peccatorum!*⁶ here's thy goblet,
good vintner.

ROBIN

*Misericordia pro nobis!*⁷ what shall I do?
Good devil, forgive me now and I'll
never rob thy library more.
Re-enter to them MEPHISTOPHILIS.

MEPHISTOPHILIS

Vanish, villains! th' one like an ape, another
like a bear, the third an ass, for doing
this enterprise.   [*Exit* VINTNER.]
Monarch of hell, under whose black survey
Great potentates do kneel with awful fear,
Upon whose altars thousand souls do lie,
How am I vexed with these villains' charms!

⁴ solemn sounding gibberish
⁵ In God's name!
⁶ Sinner of sinners!
⁷ Pity us!

From Constantinople am I hither come
Only for pleasure of these damned slaves.

ROBIN

How, from Constantinople? You have had a
great journey: will you take sixpence in
your purse to pay for your supper, and
be gone?

MEPHISTOPHILIS

Well, villains, for your presumption I transform thee into an ape, and thee into a
dog; and so be gone.   *Exit.*

ROBIN

How, into an ape? That's brave: I'll have fine
sport with the boys; I'll get nuts and
apples enow.

RALPH

And I must be a dog.

ROBIN

I'faith, thy head will never be out of the
pottage-pot.   *Exeunt.*
[Scene 10]   *Enter* CHORUS.

CHORUS

When Faustus had with pleasure ta'en the
view
Of rarest things and royal courts of kings,
He stayed his course and so returned home,
Where such as bear his absence but with
grief,
I mean his friends and nearest companions,
Did gratulate his safety with kind words,
And in their conference of what befell
Touching his journey through the world and
air,
They put forth questions of astrology
Which Faustus answered with such learned
skill
As they admired and wondered at his wit.
Now is his fame spread forth in every land:
Amongst the rest the Emperor is one,
Carolus the Fifth, at whose palace now
Faustus is feasted 'mongst his noblemen.
What there he did in trial of his art

I leave untold, your eyes shall see performed.
Enter EMPEROR, FAUSTUS, MEPHISTOPHILIS,
and a KNIGHT, *with* ATTENDANTS.

EMPEROR

Master Doctor Faustus, I have heard strange
report of thy knowledge in the black
art, how that none in my empire nor in
the whole world can compare with thee
for the rare effects of magic. They say
thou hast a familiar spirit, by whom
thou canst accomplish what thou list.
This, therefore, is my request, that thou
let me see some proof of thy skill, that
mine eyes may be witnesses to confirm
what mine ears have heard reported;
and here I swear to thee, by the honor
of mine imperial crown, that whatever
thou doest thou shalt be no ways prej-
udiced or endamaged.

KNIGHT

I'faith, he looks much like a conjuror.[1]

FAUSTUS

My gracious Sovereign, though I must confess myself far inferior to the report
men have published, and nothing an-
swerable to the honor of your imperial
Majesty, yet for that love and duty
binds me thereunto, I am content to do
whatsoever your majesty shall command
me.

EMPEROR

Then, Doctor Faustus, mark what I shall say:
As I was sometime solitary set
Within my closet, sundry thoughts arose
About the honor of mine ancestors —
How they had won by prowess such exploits,
Got such riches, subdued so many kingdoms,
As we that do succeed or they that shall
Hereafter possess our throne shall,
I fear me, never attain to that degree
Of high renown and great authority.
Amongst which kings is Alexander the great,
Chief spectacle of the world's pre-eminence,[2]

[1] common trickster
[2] pre-eminent men

The bright shining of whose glorious acts
Lightens the world with his reflecting beams,
As when I hear but motion made of him
It grieves my soul I never saw the man.
If, therefore, thou by cunning of thine art
Canst raise this man from hollow vaults be-
    low
Where lies entombed this famous conqueror,
And bring him with his beauteous paramour,
Both in their right shapes, gesture, and at-
    tire
They used to wear during their time of life,
Thou shalt both satisfy my just desire
And give me cause to praise thee whilst I live.

FAUSTUS

My gracious Lord, I am ready to accomplish
    your request, so far forth as by art and
    power of my spirit I am able to perform.

KNIGHT

I'faith, that's just nothing at all.

FAUSTUS

But if it like your Grace, it is not in my
    ability to present before your eyes the
    true substantial bodies of those two
    deceased princes which long since are
    consumed to dust.

KNIGHT

Ay marry, Master Doctor, now there's a
    sign of grace in you, when you will con-
    fess the truth.

FAUSTUS

But such spirits as can lively [3] resemble Alex-
    ander and his paramour shall appear be-
    fore your Grace, in that manner that
    they best lived in in their most flourish-
    ing estate, which I doubt not shall suffi-
    ciently content your imperial Majesty.

EMPEROR

Go to, Master Doctor; let me see them pres-
    ently.

[3] in a lifelike way

KNIGHT

Do you hear, Master Doctor, you bring Alexander and his paramour before the Emperor?

FAUSTUS

How then, sir?

KNIGHT

I'faith, that's true as Diana turned me to a
stag.[4]

FAUSTUS

No, sir, but when Actaeon died he left the
horns for you. Mephistophilis, be gone!
Exit MEPHISTOPHILIS.

KNIGHT

Nay, and you go to conjuring I'll be gone.
Exit KNIGHT.

FAUSTUS

I'll meet with you anon for interrupting me
so. —
Here they are, my gracious Lord.
Enter MEPHISTOPHELIS *with* [*spirits as*]
ALEXANDER *and his paramour.*

EMPEROR

Master Doctor, I heard this lady while she
lived had a wart or mole in her neck.
How shall I know whether it be so or
no?

FAUSTUS

Your Highness may boldly go and see.
[EMPEROR *sees the mole; then spirits exeunt.*]

EMPEROR

Sure these are no spirits but the true substantial bodies of those two deceased princes.

FAUSTUS

Will't please your Highness now to send for
the knight that was so pleasant with me
here of late?

EMPEROR

One of you call him forth.
Enter the KNIGHT *with a pair of horns on his
head.*

EMPEROR

How now, sir knight! Why, I had thought
thou hadst been a bachelor, but now I
see thou hast a wife that not only gives
thee horns but makes thee wear them.
Feel on thy head.

KNIGHT

Thou damned wretch and execrable dog
Bred in the concave of some monstrous rock,
How dar'st thou thus abuse a gentleman?
Villain, I say, undo what thou hast done!

FAUSTUS

O not so fast, sir; there's no haste but good.[5]
Are you remembered how you crossed
me in my conference with the Emperor?
I think I have met with you for it.

EMPEROR

Good Master Doctor, at my entreaty release
him; he hath done penance sufficient.

FAUSTUS

My gracious Lord, not so much for the injury
he offered me here in your presence, as
to delight you with some mirth hath
Faustus worthily requited this injurious
knight, which being all I desire, I am
content to release him of his horns. And,
sir knight, hereafter speak well of scholars. Mephistophilis, transform him
straight. Now, good my Lord, having
done my duty I humbly take my leave.

EMPEROR

Farewell, Master Doctor; yet ere you go expect from me a bounteous reward.
[*Exeunt.*]

---

4 The goddess Diana turned her lover Actaeon
into a stag.

5 i.e., haste makes waste.

[Scene 11]   *Enter* FAUSTUS *and* MEPH-
ISTOPHELIS.

FAUSTUS

Now, Mephistophilis, the restless course
That time doth run with calm and silent
    foot,
Short'ning my days and thread of vital life,
Calls for the payment of my latest years.
Therefore, sweet Mephistophilis, let us
Make haste to Wittenberg.

MEPHISTOPHILIS

What, will you go on horseback or on foot?

FAUSTUS

Nay, till I am past this fair and pleasant
green I'll walk on foot.
    Enter a HORSE-COURSER.

HORSE-COURSER

I have been all this day seeking one Master
Fustian: mass, see where he is! — God
save you, Master Doctor.

FAUSTUS

What, horse-courser, you are well met.

HORSE-COURSER

Do you hear, sir, I have brought you forty
dollars for your horse.[1]

FAUSTUS

I cannot sell him so; if thou lik'st him for
fifty, take him.

HORSE-COURSER

Alas, sir, I have no more. [*To* MEPHISTOPH-
ILIS.] I pray you speak for me.

MEPHISTOPHILIS

I pray you, let him have him: he is an honest
fellow, and he has a great charge[2]
[*Aside.*] neither wife nor child.

FAUSTUS

Well, come, give me your money. My boy
will deliver him to you; but I must tell

¹ Horse-traders are proverbial cheaters.
² family responsibility

you one thing before you have him: ride
him not into the water at any hand.

HORSE-COURSER

Why, sir, will he not drink of all waters?

FAUSTUS

O yes, he will drink of all waters, but ride
him not into the water. Ride him over
hedge or ditch, or where thou wilt, but
not into the water.

HORSE-COURSER

Well, sir, now am I made man forever: I'll
not leave[3] my horse for forty. If he had
but the quality of hey ding, hey ding
ding,[4] I'd make a brave living on him:
he has a buttock as slick as an eel. Well,
God b'wi'ye, sir, your boy will deliver
him me — but hark ye, sir, if my horse
be sick or ill at ease, if I bring his water
to you you'll tell me what it is?

FAUSTUS

Away, you villain! What, dost think I am a
horse-doctor?   *Exit* HORSE-COURSER.
What art thou, Faustus, but a man con-
demned to die?
Thy fatal time doth draw to final end,
Despair doth drive distrust unto my
    thoughts.
Confound these passions with a quiet sleep:
Tush, Christ did call the thief upon the cross;
Then rest thee, Faustus, quiet in conceit.
        Sleep in his chair.
    Enter HORSE-COURSER *all wet, crying.*

HORSE-COURSER

Alas, alas, Doctor Fustian quotha! Mass,
Doctor Lopus[5] was never such a doctor; he has given me a purgation, has
purged me of forty dollars; I shall never
see them more. But yet, like an ass as I
was, I would not be ruled by him, for
he bade me I should ride him into no
water. Now I, thinking my horse had
had some rare quality that he would not

³ sell
⁴ nonsense refrain of popular songs, usually covering a suggestion of obscenity, as here
⁵ Lopez, a physician hanged for treason in 1597

have had me know of, I, like a venturous youth, rid him into the deep pond at the town's end. I was no sooner in the middle of the pond but my horse vanished away, and I sat upon a bottle [6] of hay, never so near drowning in my life. But I'll seek out my Doctor and have my forty dollars again, or I'll make it the dearest horse! — O, yonder is his snipper-snapper.[7] [*To* MEPHISTOPHILIS.] Do you hear, you hey-pass, where's your master?

MEPHISTOPHILIS

Why, sir, what would you? You cannot speak with him.

HORSE-COURSER

But I will speak with him.

MEPHISTOPHILIS

Why, he's fast asleep; come some other time.

HORSE-COURSER

I'll speak with him now, or I'll break his glass-windows [8] about his ears.

MEPHISTOPHILIS

I tell thee, he has not slept this eight nights.

HORSE-COURSER

And he have not slept this eight weeks I'll speak with him.

MEPHISTOPHILIS

See where he is, fast asleep.

HORSE-COURSER

Ay, this is he. God save ye, Master Doctor. Master Doctor! Master Doctor Fustian! Forty dollars, forty dollars for a bottle of hay!

MEPHISTOPHILIS

Why, thou seest he hears thee not.

6 bundle
7 conjuror's assistant
8 eyeglasses

HORSE-COURSER

So ho ho! So ho ho!   *Hallow in his ear.*
No, will you not wake? I'll make you wake ere I go.
        Pull him by the leg, and pull it away.[9]
Alas, I am undone! What shall I do?

FAUSTUS

O my leg, my leg! Help, Mephistophilis: call the officers! My leg, my leg!

MEPHISTOPHILIS

Come, villain, to the Constable.

HORSE-COURSER

O Lord, sir, let me go, and I'll give you forty dollars more.

MEPHISTOPHILIS

Where be they?

HORSE-COURSER

I have none about me; come to my ostry [10] and I'll give them to you.

MEPHISTOPHILIS

Be gone quickly.
        HORSE-COURSER *runs away.*

FAUSTUS

What, is he gone? Farewell he! Faustus has his leg again, and the Horse-Courser, I take it, a bottle of hay for his labor. Well, this trick shall cost him forty dollars more.
        Enter WAGNER.
How now, Wagner, what's the news with thee?

WAGNER

Sir, the Duke of Vanholt doth earnestly entreat your company.

FAUSTUS

The Duke of Vanholt! — an honorable gentleman, to whom I must be no niggard of my cunning. Come, Mephistophilis, let's away to him.   *Exeunt.*

9 [a simple trick of low comedy]
10 hostelry, inn

[Scene 12]   *Re-enter* FAUSTUS *and*
MEPHISTOPHELIS *with the* DUKE *and* DUCH-
ESS OF VANHOLT.

DUKE

Believe me, Master Doctor, this merriment
hath much pleased me.

FAUSTUS

My gracious Lord, I am glad it contents you
so well. But it may be, Madam, you take
no delight in this. I have heard that
great-bellied [1] women do long for some
dainties or other: what is it, Madam?
Tell me, and you shall have it.

DUCHESS

Thanks, good Master Doctor; and for I see
your courteous intent to pleasure me, I
will not hide from you the thing my
heart desires, and were it now summer,
as it is January and the dead time of the
winter, I would desire no better meat
than a dish of ripe grapes.

FAUSTUS

Alas, Madam, that's nothing. Mephistophilis,
be gone!   [*Exit* MEPHISTOPHILIS.]
Were it a greater thing than this, so it would
content you you should have it.
Re-enter MEPHISTOPHILIS *with the grapes.*
Here they be, Madam: will't please you taste
on them?

DUCHESS

Believe me, Master Doctor, this makes me
wonder above the rest, that being in the
dead time of winter and in the month of
January, how you should come by these
grapes.

FAUSTUS

If it like your Grace, the year is divided
into two circles over the whole world,
that when it is here winter with us in
the contrary circle it is summer with
them, as in India, Saba, and farther

¹ pregnant

countries in the East, and, by means of
a swift spirit that I have, I had them
brought hither as ye see. How do you
like them, Madam? be they good?

DUCHESS

Believe me, Master Doctor, they be the best
grapes that e'er I tasted in my life before.

FAUSTUS

I am glad they content you so, Madam.

DUKE

Come, Madam, let us in,
Where you must well reward this learned
man
For the great kindness he hath showed to
you.

DUCHESS

And so I will, my Lord, and whilst I live
Rest beholding for this courtesy.

FAUSTUS

I humbly thank your Grace.

DUCHESS

Come, Master Doctor, follow us and receive your reward.   *Exeunt*
[Scene 13]   *Enter* WAGNER *solus.*

WAGNER

I think my master means to die shortly
For he hath given to me all his goods;
And yet methinks if that death were near
He would not banquet, and carouse, and swill
Amongst the students, as even now he doth,
Who are at supper with such belly-cheer
As Wagner ne'er beheld in all his life.
See where they come: belike the feast is
ended.   [*Exit.*]
Enter FAUSTUS *and* MEPHISTOPHILIS *with
two or three* SCHOLARS.

1 SCHOLAR

Master Doctor Faustus, since our conference
about fair ladies, which was the beauti-
fullest in all the world, we have determined with ourselves that Helen of

Greece was the admirablest lady that
ever lived. Therefore, Master Doctor, if
you will do us that favor as to let us see
that peerless dame of Greece whom all
the world admires for majesty, we
should think ourselves much beholding
unto you.

FAUSTUS

Gentlemen,
For that I know your friendship is unfeigned,
And Faustus' custom is not to deny
The just requests of those that wish him well,
You shall behold that peerless dame of
    Greece,
No otherways for pomp and majesty
Than when Sir Paris crossed the seas with
    her
And brought the spoils to rich Dardania.
Be silent, then, for danger is in words.
Music sounds, and HELEN *passeth over the
stage.*

2 SCHOLAR

Too simple is my wit to tell her praise
Whom all the world admires for majesty.

3 SCHOLAR

No marvel though the angry Greeks pursued
With ten years' war the rape of such a queen
Whose heavenly beauty passeth all compare.

1 SCHOLAR

Since we have seen the pride of Nature's
    works
And only paragon of excellence,
Let us depart, and for this glorious deed
Happy and blessed be Faustus evermore.

FAUSTUS

Gentlemen, farewell; the same I wish to you.
                    [*Exeunt* SCHOLARS.]
            Enter an OLD MAN.

OLD MAN

Ah, Doctor Faustus, that I might prevail
To guide thy steps unto the way of life,
By which sweet path thou may'st attain the
    goal
That shall conduct thee to celestial rest!

Break, heart, drop blood, and mingle it with
    tears —
Tears falling from repentant heaviness,
Of thy most vile and loathsome filthiness,
The stench whereof corrupts the inward soul
With such flagitious crimes of heinous sins
As no commiseration may expel
But mercy, Faustus, of thy Savior sweet,
Whose blood alone must wash away thy guilt.

FAUSTUS

Where art thou, Faustus? Wretch, what hast
    thou done?
Damned art thou, Faustus, damned! Despair
    and die.
Hell calls for right, and with a roaring voice
Says, "Faustus, come; thine hour is come!"
And Faustus will come to do thee right.
            MEPHISTOPHILIS *gives him a dagger.*

OLD MAN

Ah stay, good Faustus, stay thy desperate
    steps!
I see an angel hovers o'er thy head
And with a vial full of precious grace
Offers to pour the same into thy soul:
Then call for mercy and avoid despair.

FAUSTUS

Ah my sweet friend, I feel thy words
To comfort my distressed soul.
Leave me awhile to ponder on my sins.

OLD MAN

I go, sweet Faustus, but with heavy cheer,
Fearing the ruin of thy hopeless soul.
                            [*Exit.*]

FAUSTUS

Accursed Faustus, where is mercy now?
I do repent and yet I do despair:
Hell strives with grace for conquest in my
    breast.
What shall I do to shun the snares of death?

MEPHISTOPHILIS

Thou traitor, Faustus, I arrest thy soul
For disobedience to my sovereign lord.
Revolt, or I'll in piecemeal tear thy flesh.

FAUSTUS

I do repent I e'er offended him.
Sweet Mephistophilis, entreat thy lord
To pardon my unjust presumption,
And with my blood again I will confirm
My former vow I made to Lucifer.

MEPHISTOPHILIS

Do it then quickly with unfeigned heart
Lest greater danger do attend thy drift.

FAUSTUS

Torment, sweet friend, that base and crooked
    age
That durst dissuade me from thy Lucifer,
With greatest torments that our hell affords.

MEPHISTOPHILIS

His faith is great: I cannot touch his soul;
But what I may afflict his body with
I will attempt, which is but little worth.

FAUSTUS

One thing, good servant, let me crave of
    thee
To glut the longing of my heart's desire:
That I might have unto my paramour
That heavenly Helen which I saw of late,
Whose sweet embracings may extinguish
    clean
These thoughts that do dissuade me from my
    vow,
And keep mine oath I made to Lucifer.

MEPHISTOPHILIS

This, or what else my Faustus shall desire
Shall be performed in twinkling of an eye.
    Enter HELEN.

FAUSTUS

Was this the face that launched a thousand
    ships
And burnt the topless towers of Ilium?
Sweet Helen, make me immortal with a kiss.
Her lips suck forth my soul — see where it
    flies!
Come, Helen, come, give me my soul again.
Here will I dwell, for heaven is in these lips

And all is dross that is not Helena.
Enter OLD MAN [*and stands watching* FAUS-
TUS.]
I will be Paris, and for love of thee
Instead of Troy shall Wittenberg be sacked,
And I will combat with weak Menelaus
And wear thy colors on my plumed crest;
Yea, I will wound Achilles in the heel
And then return to Helen for a kiss.
O thou art fairer than the evening air
Clad in the beauty of a thousand stars!
Brighter art thou than flaming Jupiter
When he appeared to hapless Semele,
More lovely than the monarch of the sky
In wanton Arethusa's azured arms,
And none but thou shalt be my paramour!
    Exeunt all except the OLD MAN.

OLD MAN

Accursed Faustus, miserable man,
That from thy soul exclud'st the grace of
    heaven
And fliest the throne of his tribunal seat.
    Enter the DEVILS *to torment him.*
Satan begins to sift me with his pride.
As in this furnace God shall try my faith,
My faith, vile hell, shall triumph over thee!
Ambitious fiends, see how the heavens smile
At your repulse, and laugh your state to
    scorn.
Hence, hell! for hence I fly unto my God.
    Exeunt.
[Scene 14]   *Enter* FAUSTUS *with the*
SCHOLARS.

FAUSTUS

Ah, gentlemen!

1 SCHOLAR

What ails Faustus?

FAUSTUS

Ah, my sweet chamber-fellow, had I lived
    with thee then had I lived still, but now
    I die eternally. Look! comes he not?
    comes he not?

2 SCHOLAR

What means Faustus?

3 SCHOLAR

Belike he is grown into some sickness by being over-solitary.

1 SCHOLAR

If it be so, we'll have physicians cure him;
'tis but a surfeit, never fear, man.

FAUSTUS

A surfeit of deadly sin that hath damned
both body and soul.

2 SCHOLAR

Yet, Faustus, look up to heaven: remember
God's mercies are infinite.

FAUSTUS

But Faustus' offence can ne'er be pardoned;
the Serpent that tempted Eve may be
saved, but not Faustus. Ah, gentlemen,
hear me with patience, and tremble not
at my speeches. Though my heart pants
and quivers to remember that I have
been a student here these thirty years,
O would I had never seen Wittenberg,
never read book! And what wonders I
have done all Germany can witness, yea
all the world, for which Faustus hath
lost both Germany and the world, yea
heaven itself — heaven the seat of God,
the throne of the blessed, the kingdom
of joy, and must remain in hell forever,
hell, ah hell, forever! Sweet friends,
what shall become of Faustus, being in
hell forever?

3 SCHOLAR

Yet, Faustus, call on God.

FAUSTUS

On God, whom Faustus hath abjured? On
God, whom Faustus hath blasphemed?
Ah, my God, I would weep, but the
devil draws in my tears! Gush forth,
blood, instead of tears, yea life and soul.
O he stays my tongue; I would lift up
my hands but, see, they hold them, they
hold them!

ALL

Who, Faustus?

FAUSTUS

Lucifer and Mephistophilis.
Ah, gentlemen, I gave them my soul for my
cunning.

ALL

God forbid!

FAUSTUS

God forbade it indeed, but Faustus hath done
it: for vain pleasure of 24 years hath
Faustus lost eternal joy and felicity. I
writ them a bill with mine own blood,
the date is expired, the time will come,
and he will fetch me.

1 SCHOLAR

Why did not Faustus tell us of this before,
that divines might have prayed for thee?

FAUSTUS

Oft have I thought to have done so, but the
devil threatened to tear me in pieces if
I named God, to fetch both body and
soul if I once gave ear to divinity; and
now 'tis too late. Gentlemen, away, lest
you perish with me.

2 SCHOLAR

O what shall we do to save Faustus?

FAUSTUS

Talk not of me, but save yourselves and depart.

3 SCHOLAR

God will strengthen me: I will stay with
Faustus.

1 SCHOLAR

Tempt not God, sweet friend, but let us into
the next room, and there pray for him.

FAUSTUS

Ay, pray for me, pray for me! And what
noise soever ye hear, come not unto me,
for nothing can rescue me.

2 SCHOLAR

Pray thou, and we will pray that God may
have mercy upon thee.

FAUSTUS

Gentlemen, farewell. If I live till morning
I'll visit you; if not, Faustus is gone to
hell.

ALL

Faustus, farewell.   *Exeunt* SCHOLARS.
                    The clock strikes eleven.

FAUSTUS

Ah, Faustus,
Now hast thou but one bare hour to live
And then thou must be damned perpetually!
Stand still, you ever-moving spheres of
heaven,
That time may cease and midnight never
come;
Fair Nature's eye, rise, rise again, and make
Perpetual day; or let this hour be but
A year, a month, a week, a natural day,
That Faustus may repent and save his soul!
O *lente lente currite noctis equi.*[1]
The stars move still, time runs, the clock will
strike,
The devil will come, and Faustus must be
damned.
O I'll leap up to my God! Who pulls me
down?
See, see, where Christ's blood streams in the
firmament! —
One drop would save my soul — half a drop!
ah, my Christ!
Ah, rend not my heart for naming of my
Christ;
Yet will I call on him — Oh, spare me, Lu-
cifer!
Where is it now? 'Tis gone; and see where
God
Stretcheth out his arm and bends his ireful
brows.
Mountains and hills, come, come and fall on
me

And hide me from the heavy wrath of God,
That when you vomit forth into the air
My limbs may issue from your smoky
mouths,
So that my soul may but ascend to heaven.
No, no —
Then will I headlong run into the earth:
Earth, gape! O no, it will not harbor me.
You stars that reigned at my nativity,
Whose influence hath allotted death and hell,
Now draw up Faustus like a foggy mist
Into the entrails of yon laboring cloud
So that my soul may but ascend to heaven.
                    The watch strikes.[2]
Ah, half the hour is past;
'Twill all be past anon.
O God,
If thou wilt not have mercy on my soul,
Yet for Christ's sake whose blood hath ran-
somed me
Impose some end to my incessant pain:
Let Faustus live in hell a thousand years,
A hundred thousand, and at last be saved!
O, no end is limited to damned souls.
Why wert thou not a creature wanting
soul?
Or why is this immortal that thou hast?
Ah,   Pythagoras'   *metempsychosis* — were
that true,
This soul should fly from me, and I be
changed
Unto some brutish beast. All beasts are
happy,
For when they die
Their souls are soon dissolved in elements,
But mine must live still to be plagued in hell.
Cursed be the parents that engendered me!
No, Faustus, curse thyself, curse Lucifer
That hath deprived thee of the joys of
heaven.
                    The clock strikes twelve.
O it strikes, it strikes! Now, body, turn to air
Or Lucifer will bear thee quick to hell.
                    Thunder and lightning.
O soul, be changed into little water drops
And fall into the ocean, ne'er be found.
My God, my God, look not so fierce on me!

---

[1] Oh slowly, slowly run, ye horses of the night.

[2] clock strikes the half-hour

Enter DEVILS.

Adders and serpents, let me breathe awhile!
Ugly hell, gape not — come not, Lucifer —
I'll burn my books — ah, Mephistophilis!

Exeunt with him.

Enter CHORUS.

CHORUS

Cut is the branch that might have grown full
    straight,
And burned is Apollo's [3] laurel bough
That sometime grew within this learned man.
Faustus is gone: regard his hellish fall,
Whose fiendful fortune may exhort the wise
Only to wonder at unlawful things
Whose deepness doth entice such forward
    wits
To practise more than heavenly power per-
    mits.   [*Exit.*]

[3] the god of learning

Doctor Faustus in the Panoramic Theater

A spectator at one of the original performances of *Doctor Faustus*, presumably at the Rose Theater in London, would find himself in mid-
afternoon crowded with several thousand of his fellows from all walks
and ranks of life, into the open space about the front platform. If he
had come early enough, he would be one of the lucky hundred who
might be able to lean their elbows on the stage itself, although the structure of the auditorium was such that no spectator could be very distant
from the acting area. These panoramic plays were performed in the
very laps (or jaws) of the audience, and Olympian detachment was not
sought, expected, or encouraged.

The audience, in the afternoon sunshine, is noisy and restless, cracking nuts and gossiping about the small affairs of their daily lives. The
stage platform is empty, strewn with the rushes which were the Elizabethan substitutes for carpeting, but without furniture or scenery of
any sort. The stage doors on either side of the back are shut, and the curtains across the inner stage drawn tight. A blare of trumpets announces
that the performance is at last to begin, and some of the spectators try
to quiet their neighbors.

Through one of the stage doors comes an actor robed in black. He is
the speaker of the Chorus and he walks majestically to the very front
of the platform, waits for something approaching complete silence, and
then commences in a solemn voice to speak the introduction to the play.
From this speech the audience learns, perhaps for the first time for some
of them, what it is to see — " The Form of Faustus' Fortunes Good and
Bad " — the name of the hero, and the scene of the action, Wittenberg.
After 28 lines of orientation, the Chorus opens the curtain which has
masked the inner stage: " And this the man that in his study sits "; and
departs through the stage door.

The inner stage is revealed as an ordinary small room, with plain
wooden walls and with a window and door at the back. For this particu-

lar scene a table and chair have been placed in the center of the room, helping further to establish the place as the " study " announced by the Chorus. On the table are half a dozen heavy books which Faustus, in the robes of an Elizabethan scholar or doctor, picks up one after another as he proceeds through his opening speech. The actor does not, however, remain in the " study " for the whole speech. The inner stage is located too far at the back of the acting area; the actor feels remote from his audience. After staying there just long enough to establish place, Faustus sweeps up an armful of books and moves out onto the main stage where he can be seen by all spectators without difficulty, where he can maintain the intimacy which is characteristic of the structure of the Elizabethan playhouse.

The staging, that is, is basically formal (an unchanging, generalized setting) but with a touch of " realism," derived perhaps from the tradition of the simultaneous scene. The actor himself performs in a similar way a certain set of stylized, basic gestures and movements forming the groundwork of a style that could at moments shift into precise, not to say horrifying, and graphic realistic detail. For the present speech Faustus is at his most formal, most commanding. At its end, his servant Wagner, dressed in the common clothing of his contemporaries in the audience, enters through the stage door and is sent to summon his master's dearest friends.

The door is scarcely shut behind Wagner when Faustus is joined by two other figures, on his right a winged man robed in white, on his left a black-robed, thin-faced imp with a tail. These, the Good and Evil Angels, are familiar characters to the spectators, who have seen them in the religious plays performed on holy days. There is no attempt to make them anything more or less than they are, solid dimensional figures, more natural than supernatural. Each strikes a pose and cries his message into Faustus' ear; then, in unison, they make their exits through the stage doors. Faustus, who has not moved during their scene, breaks suddenly into his wild imaginings, at the climax of which he sees his fellow scholars, robed and solemn, approaching through one of the stage doors. The three learned men confer, and Faustus convinces them of his determination to learn the mystery. They agree to share their knowledge with him and then exit through the stage door on the left, one after the other, Faustus pausing in the doorway to speak his final line of resolution.

As the three scholars make their exits on the left of the stage, two other scholars enter from the right door in search of Faustus. There is no break in the action of the play, although the opening words of the First Scholar make it apparent that some time has elapsed. Through the left door comes Wagner with a pitcher of wine. He meets them, mocks them with a parody of scholarly jargon and academic quibbling. At the end of his long speech, he finally answers their question: Faustus is " within," dining with his brother magicians. He goes between the curtains onto the inner stage; the scholars grieve for their master and go out, stage door right.

Again there is no break in the action as Faustus enters through the stage door left with a heavy book and a wand. Nothing but the words of his speech indicate that the scene is now supposed to be the " lusty grove " in which he purposed to try his skill. With the wand he makes magic figures on the floor of the stage. Thunder rumbles from the dressing room. Faustus opens the great book and launches into his Latin charm, rolling out the pompous sounds with orotund satisfaction, rising to a roar at the command to Mephistophilis. At the name, a trap in the floor of the stage flies open, a cloud of red and evil-smelling smoke belches out, and Mephistophilis in a tight black suit, with a forked tail and an ugly mask, stands before him. Faustus turns away his face, appalled, and orders the devil to change his shape. Mephistophilis disappears into the trap, and Faustus looks with wonder and pleasure at the success of his experiment. Once again he summons the devil, and the trap spews him forth with more smoke and smell, completely covered with the robe and cowl of a Friar.

Next comes the questioning of the devil as Faustus seeks to satisfy his thirst for all knowledge, leading to Faustus' offer to follow Lucifer forever if he may be granted the power to live as he wills for twenty-four years. Mephistophilis agrees to consult with his superior and exits through the trap. Faustus, ecstatic at his prospects, leaves through the right-hand door.

Enter at once, through the opposite door, the now familiar servant Wagner followed by a country youth. Again there is no indication that the setting has been changed, or that there is a lapse of time after the scene of conjuring. The scene is comic, full of the verbal puns in which the audience takes such delight, and proceeds much like a variety-show act with remarks directed to the surrounding spectators and a burlesque of the solemn conjuring of the preceding scene. As Wagner says the magic words, the trap door opens once again and two devils equipped with fireworks and pitchforks jump out on the stage. They chase the countryman up and down, and doubtless make several jabs at the spectators who are laughing at his roars of fright. Then, on command, the devils jump back into the trap and disappear. The countryman rubs himself where the pitchforks had stuck him and then agrees to become

Wagner's indentured servant for seven years. As the two comic figures make their exit, the curtains across the inner stage are once again opened.

Faustus is seated at his table considering the position he has committed himself to. As he speaks of the pros and cons of his agreement with the devil, the two Angels enter through the stage doors, Good on the left and Evil on the right. Standing in fixed positions, they assume the debate, while Faustus listens enrapt. With the last words of the Evil Angel they go off as they had entered, and Faustus rises and comes forward to summon Mephistophilis again.

The devil appears through the trap and reports Lucifer's decision. Faustus is eager to sign the deed of gift and produces a knife with which he seems to stab his arm. (The Elizabethan actors had a trick for producing " real " blood whenever the situation demanded by stabbing a small container of wine or sheep's blood attached to their costume.) Returning to the table he takes up a quill pen and prepares to sign the paper produced by Mephistophilis, but the blood " congeals." Once again Mephistophilis disappears into the trap, to return with a small pan of hot coals to melt the blood and permit the closing of the agreement. Yet Faustus is not at ease in his mind and the devil summons up assistants who dance grotesquely about the Doctor, placing a crown on his head and draping rich clothing over his scholar's robes. This diversion is followed by the reading of the agreement and Faustus' questioning of Mephistophilis, and concluded with the comic introduction of a devil-wife with fireworks.

As Faustus resolves to have a better woman than this, he and Mephistophilis make a slow circuit of the front stage, the conventional way of indicating a change of place or a lapse of time. The devil gives him a book of magic spells, and yet his mind is troubled. The Good and Evil Angels make another appearance, in their conventional fashion, but Faustus feels himself to be lost. Mephistophilis tries to distract him by answering his questions, but refuses to answer the most material of them. Once again the Good and Evil Angels appear and speak, but before Faustus can repent Lucifer and Belzebub come to the aid of Mephistophilis. They bring with them a kind of pageant of the Seven Deadly Sins, each of which crosses the stage in a symbolic costume and identifies himself in a characteristic speech. It is a spectacular and glittering show and achieves its purpose. But to crown the effect, Lucifer gives Faustus yet another book of more advanced magic. The learned man is delighted, promises to study it with care. The devils bid farewell, Lucifer and Belzebub descending into the trap as Faustus and Mephistophilis go out through the stage door.

The stage is now empty for the first time since the performance began.

Thus ends the first part of " The Form of Faustus' Fortunes," and since the remainder of the play was represented in the same manner, the reader will be able to complete the commentary for himself. We have, however, " visualized " enough of the play to suggest the nature of a panoramic drama in performance: the emphasis upon movement, upon doing things before the eyes of the spectators; the freedom of movement in time and space — in the remainder of the play Faustus will journey over most of Europe, and will live through twenty-four years in less than an hour's acting time; the variety of movement, ritual, burlesque, comic, serious — involving symbolic characters, real blood, supernatural figures from the netherworld and types (like Wagner and the Clown) from everyday life. The term panoramic suggests a sweeping survey that takes in everything, and this the panoramic theater was designed to present. There was room on its stage for every aspect of physical and spiritual life, often presented side by side; the panoramic playhouse is a bustling, a living picture of the whole world, known or imagined.

III

THE PLAYER

Any discussion of the actor and his art must be carefully limited at the beginning, for the subject is as complex as the dramatic experience itself. For most playgoers, as we have seen, the actor *is* the play, and for most actors, too. Actors become public figures, interesting in themselves apart from their contribution to the playwright's work. Actors are human and arouse all the emotional and diversionary appeals that cannot be alien to any human.

Such aspects of playing are not by any means mere distractions, for in one sense the actor is the play. It has been pointed out that in ancient Greece the first playmaker was certainly the first actor also, and it is quite probable that this was the case with the early playlets of the Christian church. Aeschylus was an actor, and Shakespeare, and Molière, and it would be difficult to determine in their cases, or those of hundreds of other actor-playwrights, where the act of creation ceased and the act of recreation began.

However it is as a recreator that the actor must be considered in a preliminary discussion of the nature of drama. Granted all the special characteristics that his humanity bestows on him, the actor is, like the theater, another of the playwright's tools. And like the theater he is a very demanding tool to be used for a very special purpose, both liberating and confining the poetic process.

In terms of narrative art generally, the actor corresponds to the " character " in fiction or epic poetry. If we observe carefully this correspondence we will have gone far towards defining the nature of the player's art and towards an understanding of dramatic characterization. For it is at this point that criticism has most often erred in the analysis of dramatic art. Misled by the humanity of the tool or the similarity to

126

fiction, critics have permitted themselves to romance endlessly and to lose sight of the purpose of the playwright and his work.

The novelist commands an unlimited number of words and the attention of his reader is limited solely by his skill as a writer. The novelist is thus able to refine and qualify at length and at will, and to make any demands upon his characters that his art requires or his ingenuity pleases. It is not just that Gulliver can wade through the harbor tugging the entire navy behind him, or that Alice can nibble a cake and shoot up to an enormous size; trickery and hocus-pocus have always been a part of the theater, also. But less spectacular feats of characterization in the novel are completely impossible for the playwright.

Perhaps a very simple comparison will clarify the point. Here is a novelist, as creator, inventing a man, characterizing him at his first appearance.

. . . I went on my way, trembling, to Mr. Creakle's presence: which so abashed me, when I was ushered into it, that I hardly saw Mrs. Creakle or Miss Creakle (who were both there in the parlor), or anything but Mr. Creakle, a stout gentleman with a bunch of watch-chain and seals, in an armchair, with a tumbler and bottle beside him. . . .
Mr. Creakle's face was fiery, and his eyes were small and deep in his head; he had thick veins in his forehead, a little nose, and a large chin. He was bald on the top of his head; and had some thin wet-looking hair that was just turning grey, brushed across each temple, so that the two sides interlaced on his forehead. But the circumstance about him which impressed me most, was, that he had no voice, but spoke in a whisper. The exertion this cost him, or the consciousness of talking in that feeble way, made his angry face so much more angry, and his thick veins so much thicker, when he spoke, that I am not surprised, on looking back, at this peculiarity striking me as his chief one.
— Charles Dickens, *David Copperfield*, Ch. VI

Now compare this with the playwright's introduction of an equally " stout gentleman ": *Enter Falstaff*.

To be sure, Shakespeare conventionally does not describe his characters in stage directions; but it should be apparent that no playwright can describe his characters in stage directions with any confidence. The spectators need not be told that Falstaff is fat and jovial; his entrance on stage will indicate that. The true nature of Falstaff — his " character " — will be revealed by what he says and does in the following two hours of the action of his play.

The dramatist must never permit himself to trust, as the novelist can with complete confidence, in the appearance of his characters. For example, on page 128 is a series of portraits of famous actors interpreting the role of Falstaff. One is bald, one is grey-haired, one is spruce, one is

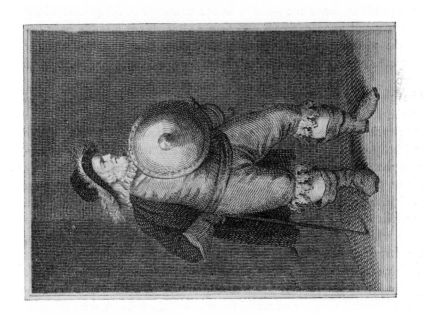

Four Interpretations of Falstaff. Upper left, James H. Hackett, American, 19th Century. Upper right, Maurice Evans. Lower left, John Henderson, English, 18th Century. Lower right, Stephen Kemble, English, 18th–19th Centuries.

unkempt, one is quaint, one is grotesque; they have one quality only to indicate their community of interest as actors: they are all fat.

The playwright can get what he sees in his mind's eye only by employing puppets or some kind of animated drawings. Yet the effect of his art demands human interpreters, and he must therefore surrender one aspect of the creator's power which the novelist finds indispensable. The actor must be permitted his own " conformation." To be sure the art of make-up is effective to a degree, but it can seldom hide the familiar features of the familiar actor without resort to trickery that calls attention to itself. The master of make-up, like Lon Chaney of the silent movies, ceases to be an actor, to have any part in the creation of a play. He becomes a freak, an exhibit in and for himself, the " man of a thousand faces," a magician.

Many of the great actors of the past have been cited as masters of make-up, among them Sir Henry Irving. But however skilled they were, they never succeeded in effacing their own persons. And it is worth noting that Sir John Gielgud, the present leader of the English theater, reading King Lear in a business suit and with no make-up at all, can produce the same effect on his hearers as when, in the theater, he was disguised in crêpe hair and a hoary wig.

That is to say, by his art as an actor, Sir John was able to extract and present to his audience the element in the character of King Lear which did not depend upon external appearance. But this is possible only because the playwright had constructed Lear as a *dramatic* character; Shakespeare is concerned with the inner nature, the active essence of his hero.

The playwright may, of course, control or direct the costume and what the Elizabethans used to call the " excrements " of a character: Lear's flowing white beard, Hamlet's suit of mourning, Falstaff's fair round belly. But the playwright of the modern world, with its addiction to the subtleties of psychological motivation, must be particularly aware of the restrictions his art places upon him. One of the actors in the original production of Chekhov's *The Cherry Orchard* asked the playwright for an interpretation of his character. Chekhov replied: " He wears a white waistcoat, yellow shoes; when walking, swings his arms, a broad stride, thinks deeply while walking, walks as if on a straight line. Hair not short, therefore often throws back head; while in thought he passes his hand through his beard, combing it from the back forward." Costume, manner of walking, gesture, these items were selected to indicate to the audience the direct and forthright nature which was the dramatic essence of the character of Lopakhin. The color of his eyes, the sound of his voice, his stature and build, such things as would be a customary part of the novelist's portrait are left to chance; they may appear in the stage directions, but no playwright places any dependence upon them. He can control only the inner nature, the active essence, of his characters, and the external symbols of that nature or essence.

Consider, for example, Parson Manders in *Ghosts*. Ibsen says almost nothing of his personal appearance: he may be tall or short, plump or lean, high-voiced or low. Presumably he is an attractive man, or Mrs. Alving would not have fallen in love with him; but such matters may be left to the actor who is to give flesh and blood to the dramatic essence. Manders as the tool of the playwright is required and permitted to talk of one subject only, duty, and to exemplify the meaning of the word in the actions he performs. For him duty is obedience to outmoded standards of conduct and willing blindness to the facts of a given situation. Many years before the play commences, this motivating essence had forced him to send Mrs. Alving back to her husband; now he tries to force Regina to obey the will of 'her " father." His characteristic argument with Oswald over life in Paris enables Mrs. Alving to see clearly her own position; his objection on principle to insurance leads to the irreplaceable loss of the orphanage. Even his entrance in the second act, which prevents Mrs. Alving from revealing the truth to Regina and Oswald is a typical, almost symbolic, action. True, it serves the purposes of the plot in preventing a disclosure that might have ended the play prematurely, but it is Manders' dramatic function, and hence his character, to avoid reality, to prevent the truth from being known and faced frankly. And he is never shown in any situation in which this essence is not a decisive element. It might be amusing, it might reveal some other aspect of the man, to see Manders at dinner, or consulting with his parishioners, or discussing art; but the theater demands economy and the playwright must practise selection and arrangement at every step.

The modern play, surrounded as it is with the modern preoccupation with scientific realism, presents difficulties to the playwright and actor alike. The principle of the active essence, however, is clearly present in the origin of both of the major forms of drama; it is exemplified in the mask of the Greek focussed theater and in the allegorical or symbolic figures of the Christian panoramic theater.

The Greek Mask

We have already considered something of the origin of the drama and the conditions under which dramatic character emerged. The fifty-man chorus of celebrants was singing a song of Dionysos. Their inspired, or intoxicated, leader was struck with the idea that he was Dionysos and, stepping into their midst, he recounted a moment of his autobiography: this is how I avenged myself on Lycurgus, or this is how I rescued the abandoned Ariadne — a single incident, displaying the hero in a single mood or frame of mind, revengeful or loving. Obviously, Dionysos was more complex than either of those emotions alone, and when his story came to be told by the epic writers (who correspond to modern novelists) he must have been displayed in the full panoply of his emotions, winsome, lustful, imperious, one after the other. But in the dithyramb — the proto-drama — it was one emotion per play, so to speak. This does not mean that a play could not have been written in which the various moods of Dionysos or some other hero were displayed, episode by episode — it could have been, but it was not.

That is, in its origin the play conventionally was confined to a single situation which displayed the hero in a single temper. For a further explanation of why this dramatic convention was not abandoned, we must turn to the conventions of the focussed theater.

It is important to remember that from the very beginning Greek plays were performed in the open air as a part of a ritual of worship or celebration. Originally the audiences must have assembled as spontaneously as the performers, and perhaps on occasion the fifty-man chorus outnumbered the spectators (a condition that is still to be met with in the theater). But as the ritual became formalized, as it became the established thing to do — a part of the social and cultural life of the community as well as a religious act — the audience increased in numbers.

When Thespis took his little troupe of travelling players to Athens in 534 B.C., he chose as the occasion for his first public performance the City Dionysia, a festival for the entire population of Athens, attended by some fifteen or twenty thousand people. The obvious problem that confronted the actors and their manager was not one which could be met merely by the Greek method of acting with the body; the face must be made visible to the most distant spectator. First Thespis tried to solve the problem by coating the actors' faces with white lead. This, for unstated but easily guessed reasons, proved unsatisfactory. He then covered the actors' heads with linen before applying the paint, and this was the origin of the mask. In the huge open-air theaters the mask was indispensable and hence became a conventional part of theatrical equipment.

But a mask, solving one problem, creates another. All the masks in a play cannot be painted alike, and something has to be done with the gaping mouth (gaping to permit the clear projection of the speeches), to make it somehow a part of the theatrical face. It is easy enough to draw a few significant lines on a piece of linen to indicate old age, or imperial pride, or rosy-cheeked youth; it is easy enough to make the open mouth a laughing or a grieving one. But once it has been made, it is fixed. As long as the actor is, in the modern sense, " on stage," his expression is frozen. He cannot run through the gamut of emotions as modern actors are fond of pretending they can do, he cannot weep and laugh in succession. For at least an episode, his expression is set. True he could shift between episodes, but that was rarely done.

Each play was conventionally confined to a maximum of three speaking actors who must fill all the roles. In *Prometheus Bound,* the first actor (*protagonist*) played Prometheus, who is present throughout the action. The other roles would be distributed between the two other speaking actors who make their first appearance in the prologue as Hephestus and Force. When he had left the orchestra, that is, and during the first choral passage, Hephestus would shift his mask and his costume to reappear as Ocean, while his fellow actor prepared to assume the role of Io. The changing of the mask thus became one of the ways of indicating a change of *person.*

The protagonist, then, would be unlikely to shift his mask during the performance. For Prometheus this presents no problem. A tortured face would be quite appropriate for all the situations which arise during his play. But consider the case of Sophocles' Electra. In the course of her play she seems to go from despair, through fear, to eager plotting, to exultation: an emotional gamut, not a single emotion. Since the mask may not be changed, it must be painted with some single expression which will convey — perhaps by a further convention — the essential character of the heroine. The " further convention " would be a pattern of lines and colors which the audience would recognize as standing for an emotion or mood. The most extreme examples of this technique are to be found in the Chinese and Japanese theaters, so closely related to the early theaters of Greece and medieval England in so many ways.

What essence would do for all the scenes in which Electra appears? Clearly the answer to that question is one of the important steps in the analysis of any drama. A design must be found which would convey the idea of resentment carried to the extreme of obsession: a gaping mouth half turned down, thin cheeks, pallid complexion, and a shaping of the eye openings to give the impression of a wild fixed stare.

If the character, like Klytemnaestra in *Agamemnon,* could leave the orchestra, there would be opportunity to shift the mask, but little reason; rather there would be reason against the shift, since it might cause confusion among the spectators because of the convention of doubling.

It would be simpler to design a mask for Klytemnaestra that would be
an emblem of female duplicity, and wear it throughout — and indeed
it is recorded that Aeschylus had special masks made for special roles.

This Aeschylean practice has an interesting implication. It would seem
to suggest that the usual mask was designed to be worn in a number of
plays: that is, it was designed as a symbol of a particular mood or attitude, and might be worn by any character to which that mood was appropriate or essential. The mask revealed the inner nature, the active essence of the character; it did not generally simply display the particular
features of the person.

Mask of Electra

Thus both dramatic convention and theatrical convenience have had
a dominant effect on what is peculiarly dramatic in the characterization
of the persons of the play. In any given play the character of any given
person rarely changes or develops as it might in a novel. The playwright
is not concerned with fully realizing his characters, and indeed the old
classical term for " Cast of Characters " was *dramatis personae,* the Masks
of the Play. In focussed drama it can be observed that the mask of Oedipus is rashness, of Antigone fanaticism, of Kassandra madness, of Aegis-
thos petty tyranny. And each of these masks, or essences, is an organic
part of the over-all plan of the play.

Aristotle in his famous analysis of tragedy defines the hero as a worthy
man fallen into adversity through his own error. Error, sometime rendered as " tragic flaw," is the active essence of the character, depicted
symbolically on his mask. The hero is a normal man brought low by
some characteristic which dominates, controls, his actions. And that
characteristic, painted on his mask, would be a visual indication of his
place in the author's scheme of drama.

Christian Allegory

It is probable that some of the characters in the medieval panoramic plays were regularly masked. Entries in the account books of the producing guilds indicate that " faces " were provided for the actors who played God and occasionally the devils. But for the most part the actors appeared without masks, and quite probably without make-up. So, where the masked Greek actor was required to make his effects by posture and bodily attitudes, the medieval actor was able to establish the convention of expression through facial grimace, a convention which endured well into the time of Shakespeare. It is the hypercritical Hamlet who orders the player to stop making his " damnable faces " and get on with the business of the action.

In place of the Greek mask as a simplifying or organizing device, the panoramic playwright turned to the Christian church and the habit of thinking it had imposed on the whole culture. The Middle Ages was incorrigibly addicted to allegory, to the personification of the abstract and to the discovery of the abstract in the particular. History, the events of the past whether recorded in the Bible or by pagan historians, was considered at one and the same time as fact and as fable. But the readers of history were not concerned with the fact so much as with discovering how it might be fitted into a scheme of morality, a kind of dogmatic spectrum on which the whole of human behavior was assessed. Handbooks were issued for the use of preachers, enabling them to discover at a glance the established meaning of classical myth, ancient history, or sacred story. And since these men were the first playwrights in the panoramic theater, and since they had been responsible for the habit of mind of the congregations who formed the first audiences, it is not surprising that moral allegory takes control of the drama almost from the start.

One of the favorite subjects for the medieval playwright was the story of Noah and the Ark. Each of the several versions is constructed in true panoramic fashion, beginning with God's commands, the building of the ark, the forty days at sea, the disembarkation, and the covenant. All this material, of course, is drawn from the Biblical narrative, which is literally followed. But in addition to the derived material the playwrights add material of their own, generally dealing with a character only mentioned in passing in the Old Testament. In several versions of the play, Noah's Wife emerges as a character almost as important as her husband.

Mrs. Noah introduces the element of conflict missing in the historical narrative; she does not want to go on board the ark, she does not want to leave her friends, her " good gossips," she does not want to give up their daily chat over a pottle of malmsey. Noah argues with her — in one version he wrestles with her — but to no effect. In the play performed in Chester, England, he finally sends his sons to rescue her from the flood against her will.

Shrewish wives were no novelty to the medieval audience, but their preachers had taught them to see in the stereotype something more than low comedy. Unquestioning obedience and maintainance of the proper relationships between the orders of society were capstones of medieval social thinking: tenants obeyed landlords, landlords obeyed overlords, overlords obeyed the king; children obeyed parents, wives obeyed husbands, men obeyed God. The Chester play begins with a scene between God and Noah in which God expresses his will and Noah obeys without question. This is followed by a scene in which Noah expresses his will and Mrs. Noah expresses her contrary will.

Mrs. Noah represents disobedience, revolt. Her very human affection for her friends, her home, her comforts, is moralized as the vanity of the flesh, seeking the things of this world rather than the world of the spirit. And while it is difficult for us to observe with our changed frame of reference, the medieval spectator would doubtless have recognized in Noah's very pointed sending of his sons to rescue the " sinner " an anticipation of things to come in the New Testament portion of the cycle.

In such moral interpretations of history, the panoramic drama discovered the character essences which are equivalent to the Greek mask. So strong was the allegorizing habit of mind, however, that a special dramatic type, the *morality play*, developed side by side with the Craft Cycles in England.

Morality plays began as dramatized sermons, with no pretense of historicity. They quickly became very popular and were performed not so much by religious amateurs as by the strolling professional players who were after the spectator's pennies. The most famous of these plays, *Everyman* (1475), tells the story of a youth who is summoned to court to give an account of his stewardship. Since he has spent his time in riotous living he looks about for some character witnesses to accompany him. His boon companion, Fellowship, begs off, as does Cousin, but Beauty, Five Wits, Strength, Knowledge, and Good Deeds (very small and weak, but willing) agree to bear him company. However, as they approach the door of the courthouse — that is, the grave — one by one they fall away, until only Good Deeds and Knowledge are left. Even Knowledge must abandon him at the tomb, but Good Deeds goes bravely on to face the trial.

The allegorical nature of the action will be considered in a later chapter (p. 148); for the moment we are concerned with the special quality of the characterization. Each person in the play has a single characteristic, one aspect of the total character of Everyman clothed in flesh. The play itself is too brief to allow the moral characters to do much more than declare themselves, but their construction and their function is plain. Each is an essence, a passion, a vice, a virtue, an attribute; and each speaks and acts in the manner of his essence.

Allegorical Characterization: Jealousy. Note the design on her costume and her symbolic properties.

In the next century, with the gradual secularization of the drama, the convention of morality characterization is continued. Though the characters are now given historical or fictional names, they continue to personify qualities. In Bale's *King John* (1538), which may be taken as the beginning of the great panoramic tradition of historical drama, the characters are even given double names, at one moment appearing as Pope Innocent III and at another as Usurped Power; but the essence is constant however the name may change. The Pope, in Bale's play, is permitted to demonstrate " usurped power " and nothing else in the historical as well as the moral action.

Marlowe's *Doctor Faustus*, written a half-century later, shows the continuing force of this idea of dramatic characterization. Ostensibly a " true history " based on the life of a real, and famous, scholar, it is in fact a morality play. It is not a coincidence that the playwright introduces the pageant of the Seven Deadly Sins to distract Faustus from his inner debate. These allegorical figures, so familiar to the audience, appear just as they might have in *Everyman* or any of the pure moralities; they dress, move, and speak their characteristics. But Faustus himself, for all his appearance of historicity, for all his costume of the Renaissance scholar, for all his great speeches about manifesting pride or ambition or the infinite possibilities of the imagination, is in effect the Eighth and Deadliest Sin in the pageant.

Each of the Deadly Sins represents an aspect of willfulness, a human failing which sets itself against the commands of God. Faustus, in signing his pact with the devil, recommits the sin of Adam, desiring to possess the knowledge forbidden by divine command. This leads him repeatedly to deny the strictest of Christian principles, belief in the grace of God. The Deadliest Sin is Despair, and it is this sin that Faustus commits over and over as he rejects the advice of the Good Angel to repent and of the Old Man to turn his back on the devil and seek forgiveness. Everything in the play is designed to illustrate this aspect, this single aspect, of his character.

The text of the play as it has come down to us is in a very corrupt state. It is evident from the speeches of the Chorus, as well as from entries in the expense book of the theater, that many of Faustus' adventures have been lost. But those which have been retained suggest the original design of the playwright. " The Form of Faustus' Fortunes " was illustrated in a series of scenes much like the ones in which Faustus desires a wife and is supplied with a pyrotechnic devil, demonstrating, that is, his indulgence in the sin of lust. Even the scene with Helen of Troy, filled as it is with the full orchestra of Marlowe's verse, points to the damnation that follows such self-indulgence: " Her lips suck forth my soul." The original play may have contained similar scenes in which Faustus demonstrated his pride (cf. Scene 1), his greed (cf. Scene 3), his gluttony. The little scene of revenge on the doubting knight (Scene 10) may be taken as a demonstration of jealousy. But each action, each sin demonstrated, only forces the hero towards the greatest sin, the despair that eventually drives him into the waiting arms of the troops of Hell.

Marlowe is, of course, early in the great period of panoramic playwrighting, and closer to the morality conventions than were Shakespeare and Jonson and Webster. But the convention of allegorical characterization, so plain in his work, underlies the technique of all his successors. It is perhaps most clear in the systematic writings of Ben Jonson, who elaborated a theory of characterization commonly called the " humours," but which is little more than medieval morality characterization dressed up as the Elizabethan equivalent of psychology. The plots of such brilliant comedies as *Volpone* and *Bartholomew Fair* are essentially the interplay of various aspects of the Deadly Sins leading to a final scene of Judgment (secular, but standing for divine). Nor was this principle of playwrighting limited to the Elizabethan panoramic dramatists. A reading of *Tartuffe* will suggest the pervasiveness of the technique in a world united by Christian morality if disunited by national politics.

It is perhaps more difficult to discover this principle of characterization in the plays of Shakespeare, since his technique has been hidden by the pervasive obscurantism of hundreds of idolatrous and romantic critics. However, if we turn our backs upon the rhapsodies of nineteenth-century enthusiasts and look steadily at the plays themselves, we will discover that Shakespeare was not a workman to quarrel with his tools.

Take the tragedy of *King Lear*. Shakespeare adapted to his purposes the story of a legendary British king who, growing whimsical with age, chose to divide his kingdom among his daughters, giving each a portion determined by her declaration of love for him. Two, Regan and Goneril, hypocritically make elaborate professions; the third, Cordelia, refuses to speak. In anger he drives her from his kingdom and divides it between the deceitful ones. Regan and Goneril, once they are in power, betray their motives by treating their father most shamefully until, in the original legend, he is rescued by the return of Cordelia with a continental army.

Post-Elizabethan critics have often claimed that the power of the tragedy was weakened by the triviality of its opening situation. It has seemed to them silly that audiences should be asked to sympathize deeply with a king of quirks and fancies. Yet, unquestionably audiences do sympathize with Lear, and Shakespeare intended that they should. To discover the secret of the play's power we must look behind history or legend, must ignore the temptation to think of Lear as a man or a king, and see him as a tool in the hands of a consummate and hard-headed craftsman. Lear, seen in the convention of Christian dramatic characterization, is (like Faustus) an Everyman coming to judgment. His self-will, his pride, readily places him in the hands of the power of Evil (Regan and Goneril) and drives him to reject Cordelia, who may be taken as Reason or Knowledge and who certainly exercises the divine function of forgiveness. Considering the play even more closely in the morality convention, the daughters may stand for projections of Lear's inner nature: Regan and Goneril as the old Adam predominant, Cordelia as the small bit of good that saves his soul from despair, though not his body from death.

This, of course, is only the innermost, conventional pattern of the tragedy. Upon it Shakepeare has built a vast and complicated structure to which the attention of audiences and the judgment of critics must be turned. Yet an awareness of the convention of characterization, of the morality essence, may keep both critics and audiences from going astray in their evaluations.

The Active Essence

Both allegory and the mask were discarded by the theater of modern realism, but the common principle which they reflect continues in force. Dramatic characterization is still based on the single essence, vice, passion, emotion, humour, or " psychological drive," which dominates the character and his action.

Two things must, however, be kept constantly in mind: the essence must be active and it must be organic.

Action, movement, becoming, revealing are distinctive characteristics of dramatic art. The essence of the dramatic character must be such that it contributes to (or hinders) the forward progress of the action. So Parson Manders with his continual interfering " on principle " is an essential cog in the moving machine that destroys not only the material fortunes of the Alving family but the spiritual life of the heroine. A lesser playwright might have been content to allow Manders to mumble pious comments; the able craftsman, with a full sense of dramatic economy, sees to it that the attitude Manders represents is expressed in action as well as in words.

And it is action which is central to the play as a whole. There is neither room nor time in the economy of the drama for mere fancy or eccentricity or preaching. Whatever is said or done must be directly related to the purpose of the playwright. Constantin Stanislavsky, one of the founders of the Moscow Art Theater, once remarked that if a play were thought of as a living body, the playwright's purpose might be called the spine of the body, and each character a kind of rib. But, he went on, the relation of the rib to the spine, or each character to the purpose of the playwright, must be formulated as a verb or a verbal noun, must convey the sense of action. The drama, that is, while it presents an image of life, has also the concentration and selection of a game, where every player has his assigned active function in getting a ball across a goal line. The dramatic character is a means to an end, to the progress of the action. It is never an end in itself.

IV

ACTION

The dramatist must work with many tools in the making of his play: words, scenery, the acting area, lighting, sound, and music. But his unique tool, one shared by no other creative artist, is the actor. It is not illogical to assume, then, that the unique characteristic of the total play will be its action, the element inseparable from the actor.

Action, however, is a very general term which has acquired far too many meanings. Loosely it may stand for the whole narrative, the beginning, the middle, and the end of the plot. It may stand for the physical coming and going and conflicting on the stage, the small movement within a given situation, or the sequence of movements which fills the time between the rising and falling of the curtain. It may mean the development or revelation of the play's theme, its informing idea. Of these several meanings, it is apparent that only one is essentially and specifically dramatic: dramatic action is the complex of physical movements performed by actors on the stage. It can be great or small — it can be the assassination of a king or the smoking of a pipe; it can be chaining the hero to a rock or signing a paper, girding on a sword or straightening a necktie. In the economy of the theater no movement is trivial or without significance in the dramatic experience.

Action is the one element of a play that cannot be represented in any other way than by itself. Dialogue, words, can be conveyed in print; setting, costuming, and lighting can all be reproduced by painting or photography. Action can be described only by approximations and it can be recorded only as a *moving* picture, that is, as itself.

The modern playwright, of course, tries to suggest the physical action in his stage directions, and an especially stage-conscious author like Eugene O'Neill will sometimes describe the action in detail and define the impression it is intended to convey. In the older theater, however, where the playwright and the protagonist were frequently the same person, or where the author worked closely with the performing group, there is no attempt in the text to indicate the dramatic action. As a consequence the plays of Sophocles or Shakespeare are commonly read as poems or narratives, and the dramatic experience which they were designed to provide is completely lost.

Since there can be no substitute for dramatic action, illustrations of this point must necessarily be approximations, but it is possible to suggest the *affective* quality of stage movement, the dramatic aspect of an action which insists not upon the end of the action (*" Kills him."*), but upon the way it is done.

In Shakespeare's *Richard the Third*, the central figure, a king who is determined to prove a villain, having fought his way through the play in a series of completely ruthless actions, is confronted in the final scene by his nemesis, Richmond.

(*Scene: The Field of Battle*)

CATESBY. (*To Norfolk*) Rescue, my Lord of Norfolk, rescue, rescue!
  The King enacts more wonders than a man,
  Daring an opposite to every danger.
  His horse is slain, and all on foot he fights,
  Seeking for Richmond in the throat of death.
  Rescue, fair lord, or else the day is lost!
       (*Enter* RICHARD.)
RICHARD. A horse! a horse! my kingdom for a horse!
CATESBY. Withdraw, my lord. I'll help you to a horse.
RICHARD. Slave, I have set my life upon a cast
  And I will stand the hazard of the die.
  I think there be six Richmonds in the field;
  Five have I slain today instead of him.
  A horse! a horse! my kingdom for a horse!

                                                      (*Exeunt*)

(*Scene: Another part of the Field of Battle*)

Alarum. Enter RICHARD *and* RICHMOND; *they fight;* RICHARD *is slain.*

                                                  [V. 4, 5]

Here is a description of the way the final combat was performed by Edmund Kean, perhaps the greatest interpreter of the role of Richard:

His death-scene was the grandest conception, and executed in the most impressive manner; it was a piece of noble poetry, expressed by action instead of language. He fights desperately; . . . like one drunk with wounds. He is disarmed, and the attitude in which he stands with his hands stretched out, after his sword is taken from him, has a preternatural and terrific grandeur, as if his will could not be disarmed, and the very phantoms of his despair had a withering power.

Exhausted of all bodily strength, he disdains to fall and his strong volition keeps him standing. He fixes that head, full of intellectual and heroic power, directly on his enemy. He bears up his chest with an expansion which seems swelling with more than human spirit. He holds his uplifted arm in calm but dreadful defiance of his conqueror. But he is but a man, and he falls after his sublime effort senseless to the ground.

This description has been pieced together from the writings of two contemporary admirers of Kean, Thomas Barnes and William Hazlitt. There is nothing in Shakespeare's stage directions to indicate how Richard was to die beyond the fact that Richmond was to kill him in combat, and there are certainly a thousand several ways of effecting this. What determined Kean's choice, and what was its effect on the audience? To be sure, any actor will welcome the opportunity to stage a good fight, if only for the excitement it gives the audience. But there is more to Kean's death than just excitement.

Barnes called it a piece of noble poetry and declared that the " novel sublimity of this catastrophe " kindled the emotions of the spectators as a passage of exquisite poetry or a noble picture might. The action that Kean invented for his combat and death grew out of his speech to Catesby in the preceding scene; he had freely entered the game and would play it out to the end. A kind of Satan, the personification of evil, there was a romantic grandeur in his fall which enraptured audiences who were equally thrilled with the Byronic heroes, fated also to a life of evil but without the vitality of Kean's " destroying demon." Dramatic action, then, is not just a fact but an interpretation of a fact; it is a kind of running commentary on itself.

In such matters as death in combat, the actor has frequently to determine for himself how the author visualized the action. His understanding of his character and the intention of the play will be his trustworthy guides. But very often the playwright is most specific about the effect he intends, even though he may not employ explanatory stage directions.

In the third act of Shakespeare's *Richard the Second,* the weak king has been overtaken by his greatest enemy, Bolingbroke. Bolingbroke's eventual purpose, as Richard foresees, is the deposition of the king, but his immediate pretense is to seek nothing more than an understanding about some disputed property. Richard is standing on the top of the castle wall (that is, on the upper stage) as Bolingbroke's messenger speaks to him from the main stage.

NORTHUMBERLAND. My lord, in the base court he doth attend
    To speak with you; may it please you to come down.

RICHARD. Down, down I come; like glistering Phaeton,
  Wanting the manage of unruly jades.
  In the base court? Base court, where kings grow base,
  To come at traitors' calls and do them grace.
  In the base court? Come down? Down, court! down, king!
  For night-owls shriek where mounting larks should sing.
                                        (*Exeunt from above*)
BOLINGBROKE. What says his majesty?
NORTHUMBERLAND.   Sorrow and grief of heart
  Makes him speak fondly, like a frantic man;
  Yet he is come.
        (*Enter* KING RICHARD *and his* ATTENDANTS *below.*)
BOLINGBROKE. Stand all apart,
  And show fair duty to his Majesty. (*He kneels down.*)
  My gracious lord —
RICHARD. Fair cousin, you debase your princely knee
  To make the base earth proud with kissing it.
  Me rather had my heart might feel your love
  Than my unpleased eye see your courtesy.
  Up, cousin, up; your heart is up, I know,
  Thus high at least (*touching his own head*), although your knee be low.
                                                  [III. 3]

It is true that the words convey some of the meaning of the situation
to our bookish intellect. Such an allusion as " glistering Phaeton " should
remind us of the classical myth of the youth who attempted to drive the
chariot of the sun without the requisite knowledge or ability. But the
human tragedy of the situation, that which we can share rather than
analyze, is conveyed by the king's quick march down the back stairs.

The Language of Action

These comments on the various aspects of action in the drama may have
suggested that action does not exist to give characters an opportunity
to talk, but that it is, in itself, a kind of language that speaks with its
own vocabulary and syntax. The parallel can be extended: there is both
a prose action and a poetic action. The action which merely reports,
merely imitates, as in melodrama, as in the play whose sole interest lies
in the story it tells, may be called prose action. Poetic action is both
imitative and creative, its function is something more than narration.

If it is safe to judge from the dramatic dances of primitive tribes,
action was originally demonstration: it was used to show *how* some historical or contemporary event took place, and *what* was done on that
occasion, and by *whom*; it was, in fact, primitive journalism. When it
attached itself to religious ritual, however, it acquired another dimen-

sion; it became a kind of magic. The original war dance may have been a report of a victory. The ritual war dance is performed in anticipation of victory. Since the lives of many individuals, perhaps the very survival of the tribe, may depend upon the success of the ritual, great care will be taken that the pattern of movement, the action, assure its greatest effectiveness. The action becomes not simply reportorial, but *affective,* poetic; it is created as an organic, functional part of the whole ritual, the drama.

Dramatic action, then, is not something done, but something done in a special way, with a purpose, with art.

We may look back for a moment at the most ancient of the plays in this collection, *Prometheus Bound.* Let us assume that one of the members of the original audience was a deaf man; what kind of dramatic experience would the performance yield for him? Granted that he will miss much, for the dialogue and words of the songs are not expendable, yet Aeschylus can still speak to him with this most mysterious organ of dramatic action.

The spectator would, of course, know something of the action in advance. He would know the story of Prometheus and his defiance of the gods and his punishment. But the playwright would be the first to admit that the legend was only the starting point for his play, and that familiarity with the story would not assure comprehension of his purpose. The theater is no place for mere reiteration. What then of the inner purpose of *Prometheus Bound* could the deaf man discover? [1]

As the first rays of the sun strike the upper tiers of the theater, the play begins. Through an entrance arch at the edge of the orchestra come four figures. All are masked and wearing the long robes conventional for the performers in tragedy. Each mask is painted to give some suggestion of the nature or position of its wearer: one of noble suffering, two suggesting brutality and cruelty, a fourth ruddy and lined.

The sufferer is the Titan Prometheus. Tightly held by the two brutes, he is dragged behind the red-faced god (carrying the hammer of the smith, which identifies him as Hephestus) to the altar at the center of the orchestra.

Once the group has taken up its positions about the altar, the deaf man would see one of the brutes step apart, gesture with his arm to indicate the path they had just followed, and then turn to Hephestus. The words of his speech would be lost, but its purpose as he points first

---

[1] Much of the material in the following nine paragraphs necessarily repeats the description beginning on page 84. A comparison will help to establish the basic point: what is repeated here is *action;* what is to be found only in the earlier description is *narration,* dialogue.

to the chains and then to the altar would be clear. Hephestus, replying, addressing each of the brutes in turn and then Prometheus, indicates his unwillingness to follow the suggestions of Force by his gestures, the attitude of his body, the very length of time he spends in talking. The reaction of Force to Hephestus' speech helps to establish the fact of the smith's reluctance. He interrupts, impatiently. Ten brief speeches, whose content can only be guessed, and Force once again gestures towards Prometheus, and points to the chains in Hephestus' hands. Force dominates the scene, giving instructions to the silent Violence and the reluctant god.

Even to the deaf man the essential fact of the opening situation will be apparent: there is conflict over the punishment of Prometheus between a shame-and-pity filled immortal and the ruthless brute. Aeschylus presents not just a situation, but an attitude towards a situation; not just an experience but the meaning of that experience is made clear through the planning of the dramatic action.

The following scene, the binding of the Titan, speaks directly in the language of action. The words of the dialogue are only cues to tell the actor what he should do and how he should do it. Violence and Hephestus, directed by Force, press Prometheus against the altar and commence to bind him and fasten the chains with great spikes. The action is not perfunctory. When the chains are made fast, a gesture from Force insists upon a tightening of the bonds. A stake is driven through the heart of the victim, and other bonds placed about his body and feet. But always the action is dominated by the brute, and performed with reluctance by Hephestus. Always the action, horrible enough in the telling, is enacted in detail, with precisely directed intensifications for emphasis. And always the hero remains silent, unprotesting.

The subject of the action of the first scene, its prose meaning, is the binding of Prometheus. But its poetic purpose, its organic function in the play as a whole, is conveyed by the silent suffering of the hero, the contrasting brutality and reluctance of Force and Hephestus, the emphasis on the physical torment of the binding. All these things would be apparent to the deaf spectator, who would perhaps be more aware than some of his fellows of the contribution to the horror of the scene made by the industrious brutality of Violence, who speaks not a word either of protest or shame.

The key to the dramatic action of this scene, unyielding determination in the face of unjust punishment, becomes the keynote of the whole play. Prometheus, by his legendary action, had increased the potential power of mankind — had in a sense freed man for greater action. Yet he is fixed for all eternity, incapable of movement on his Caucasian peak. By the dramatic actions he has selected for the rest of his play, Aeschylus emphasizes and points up this image of the denial of life. Although the hero cannot move, there are few serious dramas in the whole repertory that are so full of motion. The constant coming and going of the Oceanides, the landing and bird-borne departure of Ocean, the maddened leaping of Io, and the introduction of wing-footed Hermes; all these, quite apart from anything spoken, are images of movement by land and sea and air.

The selection of characters for the action following the prologue has been further determined by another demand of the particular dramatic situation. Conflict demands the presence of at least two characters, a protagonist and an antagonist. In *Prometheus Bound* the protagonist is unable to move and the antagonist, Zeus, never appears. Yet the conflict is strong and sensed actively in the dramatic experience. With the exception of the Chorus all the characters who seek out Prometheus are representatives of Zeus: in the prologue they carry out his commands (with the secondary conflict already discussed); Ocean recommends compromise (his action is shifty, nervous, and made altogether grotesque by his mode of transportation); Io, introduced into the story without " historical " warrant, is a familiar example of the unjust rewards of those who become entangled with the ambitions of Zeus; Hermes, personal messenger of Zeus, is offensive, mincing, supercilious.

Throughout the play the audiences' admiration and sympathy is directed towards the chained Titan. For the deaf man, his noble words of defiance would be lost; but the essential idea, the unyielding determination of the hero in the most hopeless of situations, is available as a dramatic experience through the carefully selected actions of the play.

Thus early in the history of dramatic art, Aeschylus conceives his story in terms of actors, their movements and relations to each other. And thus early, symbolism becomes a fully developed and functional part of the drama. What the deaf man saw at the performance of *Prometheus Bound* was a series of visual symbols that conveyed their meaning to him instantaneously, without the interpretative power of words. Symbolism is an inevitable and conventional element in any visual art, but it appears in different degrees of complexity. It may be the actor shaking his fist at an enemy, or Hephestus shrugging his shoulders before chaining Prometheus: a gesture intended to reveal an inner state of mind. It may be Everyman pleading with Death for more time to straighten out his accounts: a direct allegory. It may be Richard the Second coming down from the walls at the command of his enemy: an

action which is the exact equivalent of a poetic metaphor. In understanding the contribution of action to the dramatic experience it is necessary to distinguish among the degrees of symbolic complexity.

Allegoric Action

The development of dramatic action into that special kind of symbolism
that may be called visual metaphor is most easily traced in the panoramic theater of the Christian world. Documentary evidence is abun-
dant and complete in the texts of plays ranging from the *Quem Quaeritis* to the works of Shakespeare, and there is little need to resort to
hypothesis or to the evidence of archaeology or anthropology as with
the focussed theater. Through the texts of surviving plays we can watch
the language of action shifting from simple denotation, the equivalent
of prose statement, to denotation plus connotation, the equivalent of
poetic metaphor, communicating on several levels at once.

A rereading of the description of the performance of the *Quem Quaeritis* will show that the earliest author of panoramic drama was concerned primarily, if not exclusively, with denotative action. The Three
Marys, though dressed in non-representational costumes, are directed to
approach the altar " stepping delicately as those who seek something."
And the recorder of the performance continues, " These things are done
in imitation of . . . the women with spices coming to anoint the body
of Jesus." *Done in imitation* — that is, acted in imitation, according to
the behavior of. And since the purpose of the early drama was not to
entertain but to instruct those who could not understand the Latin
words in which the story was customarily related (and Latin remained
the language of the dialogue of the little play), the imitation must have
been very explicit indeed. It is of course, a simple enough action to imi-
tate. A certain amount of finger-pointing, peering, and consulting
among the three should make the idea of a search apparent to the most
unlearned.

The medieval successors of the *Quem Quaeritis*, though elaborated,
continue its function and method. The Craft Cycles, drawing their materials from all the available stories of the Old and New Testaments,
moving freely not only through the " middle earth," but into Heaven
above and Hell below, are action-crammed. And the characteristic nature of the action in each play and in every Cycle is the imitation of
life, of the manners and customs of men. Such a play as the *Crucifixion*,
found in the Cycle performed at York, clearly recalls the opening of
Prometheus Bound. The simple words of the Biblical narrative, " and
crucified Him," are expanded to three hundred lines of dramatic nar-

rative with an almost unparalleled emphasis on physical horror. The stretching of the sinews of Christ's arms, the piercing of His hands, the jarring of the Cross into a hole bring home to the spectators the full meaning of *crucifixion*, a word remote from their experience. The action is a demonstration or definition, but it is also an interpretation of the word; it gives the audience a " feeling " about it. So the Slaughter of the Innocents becomes a tangible atrocity rather than a shadowy legend as the author introduces a mother singing a lullaby to her baby before it is snatched from her arms to be brutally murdered. Noah, outfitted with a shrewish wife, is translated from a name in a history book into a contemporary Englishman, into the man next door, and his exemplary act of obedience becomes something that touches directly every man in the audience.

The most famous of the English Cycle plays, *The Second Shepherds' Play*, shows the direction in which the panoramic playwrights began to move very early in the history of the form. Here the Biblical incident of the Nativity is almost swamped by a fully developed non-Biblical farce: three cold, oppressed, unhappy shepherds are victimized by Mac, who steals one of their sheep and hides it in a cradle, pretending that it is his new-born son. Yet, because they are men of good will, when they discover his knavery they toss him in a blanket, an act of justice which causes them more pain than it does the criminal, instead of hanging him as the law allowed.

For this gesture of tempering justice with mercy they are immediately rewarded. An angel directs them to go to Bethlehem to behold the Messiah; they obey, circling the stage to arrive at the manger, kneeling before the Child and presenting their gifts; and they make their final exit in high spirits, *singing*. The physical action was designed by the playwright first, denotatively, to tell his story in the clearest possible way and second, connotatively, to show either the happy reward of an act of charity, or the tremendous significance of the revelation of the birth of Christ to the common man, or perhaps both. In such a play, the author is using his chief tools — the actors and their movements on the stage — to present more than the literal record of events as the poet uses images for more than their representational value.

The Cycles were pedagogic devices, intended first to make plain their stories as a kind of historical documentary, and next to suggest the meaning of their stories by the selection and arrangement of events within their structure. The morality plays, developing independently and concurrently, were even more insistent on the meaning of the actions imitated by their players; they were frankly allegorical and fictional.

The use of allegory in the total action of a play has already been indicated in the synopsis of *Everyman* (p. 136). But allegory, the obvious use of action for a double purpose, is to be found also in the particular action within the whole. For instance, *The Castle of Perseverance* includes a full-scale battle scene of the sort beloved of the popular audience. Here the angels and the devils are contesting over the posssssion of the body of Humanum Genus, the hero, and the angels defeat the devils temporarily with a broadside of roses. The rose was the familiar symbol of Christ's sacrifice for man, and the narrative or denotative meaning of the action is obscure until the connotative, or symbolic, meaning has been understood.

The two levels of action, the denotative and the connotative, existing more or less independently in the Cycle and Morality plays of the fourteenth and fifteenth centuries, begin to mingle in the popular professional plays, the so-called " secular moralities," of the fifteenth century, and finally merge into metaphorical action in the great repertory of the Elizabethan and Jacobean age.

It is significant that the secular moralities were performed by professional players, not by amateurs or priests on some religious occasion. The professional player, whatever his standing or purpose as an artist, must always be concerned with the commercial possibilities of his play; he must, in the famous words of Samuel Johnson, " please to live." If his plays in the fifteenth century were filled with allegorical action, it must be because allegory was attractive to his public; because it represented a popular habit of mind, a way of evaluating human experience.

Although these are plays of almost no enduring artistic or dramatic merit, they deserve brief consideration because they demonstrate so plainly, even crudely, the kind of action that will become conventional for the subtler and greater playwrights to come. Of the large number of these plays, varying — to our taste — from dull to intolerable, one is of particular interest historically because it reproduces in its dramatic structure the whole history of the morality form: sermon, allegorical discussion, allegorical action. Further, the date of its printing is 1578, only a decade before the first masterpieces of Elizabethan panoramic drama.

The play is *All for Money* by the otherwise unknown playwright, T. Lupton. The theme, *omni pecunia effici possunt,* is stated at once in Latin, is remarked upon in the dialogue over and over, and is illustrated in the pattern of action of the play. That the action was not an afterthought, but the major intention of the play, is indicated by its subtitle:

" A moral and pitiful comedy . . . plainly representing the manners of men and the fashion of the world nowadays."

All for Money begins with a prologue, a 98-line detachable sermon, completely anonymous, and with no reference to the fact that it is to be illustrated in action. This graceless and unpromising beginning is followed by a rather primitive attempt at dramatization, an allegorical discussion. " Theology cometh in a long ancient garment like a prophet," and in a speech of 28 lines identifies himself to the audience as " knowledge of God's law " and comments that far too many study theology for wealth and easy living. Next " cometh in Science, clothed like a Philosopher "; he explains that he represents all good secular knowledge, but that he is often studied for " great living and also for money." Finally Art enters, " with certain tools about him of divers occupations." He too laments that while good arts are of highest value, all men seek money.

When the three allegorical figures are gathered together and have completed their introductions, Science points out that no good order can exist without the presence of all three. Theology, commenting that the others have confirmed his original point, mentions Judas as an example of those who sought consolation in money and found instead damnation. " *Dives vix bonus*," agrees Science, and adds that money makes pleasures. Art develops the idea:

> If money bring pleasure, pleasure brings forth sin,
> And sin brings damnation, unless God's grace we win.

The round table is concluded and the three figures stalk off. The scene is both brief and tedious, consisting for the most part of direct interpretation by the characters of their meaning for the audience, with a minimum of physical action.

It is followed by the main body of the play, an allegorical action that is at least recognizable as drama. This consists of three situations, each of which turns upon some commonly experienced action. In each situation something is done which is so much an everyday occurrence that any man in the audience will recognize its truth to life as he knows it. But to each of these situations the author has added an allegorical meaning which the very commonplaceness of the events makes readily acceptable. The situations are birth, job-hunting, and the administration of justice, and the first and last are sufficiently interesting to be worth description and comment.

The first situation begins with the entrance of Money, wearing a typi-

Covetousness

cal allegorical costume, " the one-half his gown yellow and the other white, having the coin of silver and gold painted on it." He sings a jolly song of self-praise, relating how all men seek him and bow down before him, and sits in a chair placed beside a trap door in the platform. To him enters a character named Adulation, bowing and whinnying and declaring that he would refuse to do anything at all, he would neither flatter nor pretend, were it not for Money. Whereupon Money falls sick, clutching his belly, and Adulation summons Mischievous Help to hold Money's head. Through the trap door Pleasure steps onto the stage, and it is explained to the audience that Money has vomited up Pleasure. Actually this seems to be the normal way of giving birth in the Pecunius family, for Money hails Pleasure as his offspring and leaves the stage. Pleasure enumerates all the fine things that money can get (that is, *beg*et) and in turn falls sick. While he " fries in his fits " Prest-for-Pleasure is summoned to act as midwife, and up comes Sin. After a few allegorical comments, Sin falls into labor, and Swift-to-Sin is employed as midwife. This time the offspring is Damnation, with a " terrible vizard [mask]," and a garment painted with flames of fire.

It would be difficult to find a clearer demonstration of the principle that action can exist on two levels at once. The action is realistic (people do give birth), and symbolic (they do not give birth to allegorical figures), and the total meaning is moral, not reportorial. However crude the scene may be, in it the author has made a statement *in visual language* of his moral idea, that money leads to pleasure, pleasure leads to sin, and sin to damnation.

The third situation, dealing with the administration of justice, is closer to the kind of drama that was to develop in the Elizabethan period. Money returns to the stage, out of breath and puffing. He com-

plains that he does not have a minute's peace. As the best criminal lawyer in regular practice — he has only to speak in his client's defense and
the criminal, no matter what his crime, goes free — he has so many
clients and suitors that he requires an assistant. Sin enters, and there is
a mock recognition scene between grandfather and grandson. After discussing family matters, Sin says he has just the man to help Money in
his profession, a fellow who will do anything for him — and his name,
of course, is All-for-Money.

All-for-Money enters, " in great haste, apparelled like a ruler or mag-
istrate." He takes over from his master to hear pleas and decide which
cases are worth his attention. The suitors are Gregory Graceless, a cut-
purse (" like a ruffian "), Moneyless-and-Friendless, who is to be hanged
for petit larceny, William-with-the-Two-Wives (" like a countryman "),
Nichol-never-out-of-Law (" like a rich franklin, with a long bag of
books at his side "), Sir Lawrence Livingless (" like a foolish priest "),
Mother Croote (" dressed evil-favored like an old woman: she shall be
muffled and have a staff in her hand and go stooping," and she speaks
dialect and makes feeble malapropisms). Each client, except Moneyless-
and-Friendless, who is sent packing, gives All-for-Money something to
put in his purse, and at the end of the day's business his bags are full.
The judge exits and Sin remains to comment to the audience. All-for-
Money, he points out unnecessarily, cares not what happens to him so
long as his bags are full:

> money brings him to pleasure, and pleasure sends him to me,
> And I send him to Damnation, and he sends him to Hell quickly.

After offering his son, Damnation, to any member of the audience as a
husband and finding no takers, he goes off to drown his disappointment
in drink with Sir Lawrence Livingless.

From the standpoint of action this scene is the most interesting patch
in Master Lupton's patchwork. The theme and the moral idea, that
money is the rooter for all evil, is made transparently clear by the action
itself as the lawyer takes fees from a series of particularly revolting
criminals. But the actors in the scene are not the usual figures of a morality who enter, speak their allegorical minds, and exit. They have been
given personalities. Money puffs and mops his brow and collapses in a
chair like a harried tycoon; Mother Croote limps and mumbles in dialect; Gregory Graceless alternates between the furtiveness and assurance
of those who are " the minions of the moon." Out of such materials a

later playwright would make a complete " realistic " comedy; and indeed the situation seems made to order for Ben Jonson.

Master Lupton, of course, follows his own method. The next scene discards realism and the familiar situation. Judas, whose appearance was anticipated when Theology cited him in Part I as a bad example, enters " like a damned soul, in black painted with flames of fire and with a fearful vizard," his costume duplicating that of Damnation, Sin's son, in Part II. Judas curses the money that led him to evil. He is joined by Dives, who was also announced in the earlier scene, wearing a similar costume, regretting his lack of charity. Then Damnation himself appears to taunt them and drive them off to Hell, howling pitifully. The effectiveness of the scene depends almost entirely on its visual language, the successive appearance of two characters in exactly similar costumes, followed by a third dressed in the same manner, but whom the audience has seen before and the significance of whose costume is established.

Dramatically, *All for Money* is a very bad play indeed and it richly deserves the obscurity it has achieved. But it is not closet drama; it has all the marks of a work intended for stage production, and the Tudor appetite for this sort of thing was enormous. Quite likely it was intended for production by strolling companies in country towns. Whatever its stage history, however, the play remains a particularly apt illustration of a point reached in the development of dramatic action in the panoramic tradition. It is the point where action not merely *may* be understood upon several levels, it *must* be. The symbolic meaning cannot be understood apart from the realistic. And the literal action is meaningless without a recognition of its connotation.

Dramatic Metaphor

The full and obvious allegory, as in such plays as *Everyman* and *All for Money*, is rarely employed in the drama after 1580. Recognition of its existence, its all-pervasiveness, and its influence, however, is a key to the planning of dramatic action in the more complex and sophisticated plays which follow it. It is simple to demonstrate that symbolic action was the stock-in-trade of the great Elizabethan playwrights; symbolic action is, less obviously but no less certainly, a major tool of the playwrights of the modern realistic theater.

We have already noticed that Christopher Marlowe was chronologically close to the flourishing period of the allegorical drama. A rereading of *Doctor Faustus* will show that he was close to it in dramatic theory also. The devils, the Good and Evil Angels, the pageant of the Seven Deadly Sins as employed in that tragedy, would appear as familiar materials to the popular audience trained on the secular moralities. The basic action, too, of a hero's quest for salvation or damnation might awaken memories of *The Castle of Perseverance* or *Everyman*.

True, the hero was a particularized hero, John Faustus, rather than a generalized type, Humanum Genus. True, the learned doctor had a history, a personal biography, a career recorded in the medieval equivalent of *Who's Who*. The dramatization of that career, which was Marlowe's ostensible purpose, would have resulted in an interesting case history. But case histories do not make successful dramas, however valuable they may be in the scientific study of mankind. Since the play is intended to speak to a mass audience, it must generalize upon its particular material, and the dramatic action must constantly be a commentary upon itself.

The case history of John Faustus would tell of his birth and background, his academic progress through the four faculties of Law, Medicine, Philosophy, and Theology at his university, and his resort to Magic, the outlawed faculty. It would record his pact with Satan, the various achievements of his magic powers, and the fulfillment of the pact with the final surrender of his person to the nether world. This is in part the story that Marlowe tells, and it makes an entertaining and startling two hours in the theater. But as a case history it presents Faustus as a kind of freak, a man apart from other men, and the spectator's reaction would be comparable to that of the sight-seer at a country fair who has just looked into a tent occupied by a sword swallower, a bearded lady, a giant, and a midget.

If the dramatic experience of *Doctor Faustus* is something different, something more lasting, than that of a side-show, it is because Marlowe has managed to create in his hero not just a unique and remarkable individual, but a generalized type, a Humanum Genus in whom every man in the audience may see his own image. Admittedly there were few men in Marlowe's audience, or in any later audience, who could see themselves in the person of the great Renaissance scholar. How could the playwright make clear to the average, general spectator that what he was seeing was more than an entertainment, was in fact a dramatic experience with significance for his own average and general life?

The simplest way, of course, was by preaching, by treating his action as if it were the illustration for a sermon. The contemporary spectator of a documentary film or listener to a radio or television play is familiar with the commentator who, with carefully anonymous voice, underlines the issues and makes the points for the playwright. There is a suggestion of this commentator in the figure of the Chorus, which Marlowe had

inherited from the morality play, the priest who comes on at the end
to draw conclusions for the congregation: " Cut is the branch that might
have grown full straight." But this is the way of the sermon, the lecture,
the narrative; it is only in part the way of the drama.

The way of the drama is the employment of symbolic action, either
in the fully developed allegory or in the suggestive dramatic metaphor.
This is the method which Marlowe exploits and passes on to his successors, to Shakespeare and Jonson and Webster, who in turn use it so successfully and perhaps unconsciously that it becomes a convention of
panoramic drama.

The term *dramatic metaphor* explains the presence in *Doctor Faustus*
of the low comedy characters — Wagner, the Clown, the Horse Courser,
Robin, and Ralph. For some centuries after the play was written they
were taken to be excrescences, " comic relief," imposed upon the serious
plot to amuse the light-minded groundlings. Indeed, since the text has
survived in a very corrupt state, it was thought that they were the late
additions of a miserable hack-writer or some over-weening comedians.
Yet, paradoxical though it may seem, if they are eliminated from the
text the play loses much of its serious import, becomes in fact a diabolic
spectacle, a melodrama, like a Hollywood version of the Old Testament.

The footnotes to the second scene of *Doctor Faustus* (pp. 94, 95)
have pointed out the instances where Wagner parodies first the learned
jargon of the academies and then the manner and cant of the Puritans.
Wagner's function throughout the play is to parody his master as well
as to serve him. In this instance, however, parody means much more
than making sport of or mocking the serious incidents: parody (mis-
called comic relief) means clarifying and universalizing.

Scene 4, beginning on page 97, provides the first fully developed
instance of the parallel action, or dramatic metaphor. Wagner and the
Clown, the ignorant countryman, exchange jokes that are nearly without meaning to the modern audience and perform a comic action that
seems more at home in a burlesque show than a tragedy. The center of
this action, expressed by a verbal noun, is *contracting* — that is, *signing
a contract*. It is a particular kind of contract, and one that most members of the audience would have had actual experience with. For certain
considerations, monetary and otherwise, the Clown agrees to become
Wagner's apprentice for seven years. This was an agreement of the most
solemn sort, the apprentice becoming in effect the slave of his master;
and any attempt to escape from apprenticeship resulted in strict and
severe punishment. In itself this scene has nothing to do with the main
action of the play; the Clown is never seen again. The next scene, how-

ever, contains the first major incident of the main action, the detailed
and sensational signing of the bond between Faustus and the Devil. The
parallel between Faustus' diabolic contract and the domestic contract
between Wagner and the Clown is inescapable for an audience familiar
with the system of apprenticeship. Older plays had suggested to the
audience that at the end of his life a man must render an account of his
good and evil actions *just as* a steward must render an account of his
stewardship before a court of law (*Everyman*), or that possession of
money leads to the pursuit of pleasure which in turn leads to acts of sin
and finally to damnation (*All for Money*). In Doctor *Faustus* Marlowe
suggests that Faustus' bargain was as final and inescapable as the contract of apprenticeship. By reference or parallel to familiar things,
something remote and fantastical is brought home to the audience and
made a part of their own experience.

Note that the parallel is suggested, not stated. No commentator points
out that Faustus' bond is *like* the apprentice's bond. The scenes are presented side by side and the audience is left to make the comparison for
itself. But the playwright leaves little to chance. Wagner conjures up
devils to help the Clown come to a decision; Mephistophilis fetches
" somewhat to delight [Faustus'] mind." Faustus and the Clown both
seek supernatural powers, that is, powers beyond their normal capacity.
The Clown tries to return to Wagner the coins that were to bind the
bargain between them, Faustus' blood congeals as he attempts to sign
the contract. And the legal phraseology of Faustus' oath, " I . . . by
these presents do give both body and soul to Lucifer . . ." is but an
echo of the Clown's " Well, I'll follow him and I'll serve him: that's
flat." By suggestion rather than by statement, the parallel is drawn, a
dramatic metaphor to bring home to the audience in terms of their own
daily living the meaning of Faustus' absolute deliverance of himself to
the powers of darkness.

The later scenes of apparently idle fooling with Robin the Ostler,
Ralph, and the Vintner serve a similar purpose. In Scenes 6 and 7 the
audience has been shown something of Faustus' magic powers, particularly as he has snatched food from the banquet table of the Pope.
While this incident would doubtless have been gratifying to the anti-
Catholic sentiments of an Elizabethan audience, Marlowe makes it clear
that his purpose is something more than mockery of the Pope. In the
following scene, Robin has stolen one of Faustus' books and uses it to
snatch a goblet from the Vintner and to conjure up Mephistophilis,
whom he is unable to control, and who turns him into an ape and his
companion into a dog. The main action of the play in this central por-

tion shows Faustus using his magic powers for equally trivial feats, and the comic scenes remind the audience of their triviality, of their devilish origin, and of the price that Faustus must pay.

This interpretation of Faustus' experience made plain for the audience by the comic action, is of course present in the main action of the play. Conjuring up Alexander and his paramour (Scene 10), he must admit that he cannot produce the " true substantial bodies " but only spirits, that is, evil spirits in their semblance. When the Duchess of Vanholt desires grapes in the dead of winter, he provides them, with the rueful comment, " Alas, Madam, that's nothing." At the end of his career, with repentance and forgiveness still within his grasp, he surrenders his soul to the kisses of that " peerless dame," Helen of Troy, who is, like all the other apparitions, a devil in disguise.

Thus " The Form of Faustus' Fortunes " ceases to be a dramatic biography or case history and becomes a play of generalized truth. The symbolism of the main action, such as the appearance and function of Helen of Troy, is available to the more learned members of the audience. But for those on whom literary allusion or theological argument is lost, there is the dramatic metaphor of the parallel actions to translate a spectacular legendary entertainment into a dramatic experience in which they too may participate.

The employment of the dramatic metaphor is characteristic of the action designed by the dramatists of the Elizabethan and Jacobean theater. As poets they were accustomed to thinking in images, verbal metaphors; as playwrights they were accustomed to thinking in symbols, visual metaphors. Manifestations of this double-meaning action are to be found everywhere, in specific situations, in character business, in the over-all pattern. They are to be found at both ends of the seventy-year period, and there are few plays constructed about a serious idea within the period which could not contribute illustrative examples. But instead of burdening the text with many later examples, it may be more instructive to confine ourselves to one example, seen in more detail — an example chosen from the most familiar of the works of the most familiar of playwrights.

Macbeth

To what extent symbolic action has become the major tool of the Elizabethan playwright is revealed by a brief comparison of the action of a typical Elizabethan play, like Shakespeare's Macbeth, with a typical Greek tragedy, like Sophocles' Oedipus Rex. Both are " historical " in subject, dealing with a situation accepted as having occurred at some past period in the history of the respective countries. For both, a king is the hero, and for both, fate is, in a sense, the villain, or the chief opponent of the hero. King Oedipus tries to defy the oracle's prediction that he will murder his father and marry his own mother; King Macbeth tries to nullify the witches' prophecies that, although he possesses the throne of Scotland, the children of Banquo will succeed him, and that he will die by the hand of one not born of woman.

Sophocles constructs his action in the conventional manner of the focussed theater, writing for an audience that watched, like gods, a story whose outcome was well known to them, in a performance that was part of a festival, still associated with the sacred origin of the drama.

Shakespeare's audience, while predominantly Christian and members of what might be called a state church, did not attend the theater with any sense that it was an aspect of religious ritual; they were in this more like the audiences in the modern theater than like those in the theaters of ancient Greece. Furthermore, since the idea of ritual — the prescribed reiteration of conventional material — was lost for the Elizabethans as for the modern spectators, the story was unfamiliar or " original," its outcome and its events essentially unknown to the audience. In such a theater and for such an audience Olympian detachment could give no satisfaction; their dramatic experience should be direct and immediate, an action felt and vivid from beginning to end.

The Elizabethan playwright went about providing his audience with this dramatic experience partly in the structure of his play (which will be discussed in Chapter V) and partly by the use of symbolic action.

The problem for Shakespeare was to make his audience feel the full horror of Macbeth's actions and yet retain a certain respect for Macbeth as a hero, as a man. There is always a danger that the monstrous actions of a ruthless tyrant may seem bold, daring, even admirable (see, for instance, the impressions of *Richard the Third* quoted from Thomas Barnes on page 142); on the other hand, it is far too easy a satisfaction for an audience to watch the destruction of a wholly evil villain. Shakespeare avoids the first danger by following the example of Marlowe, and the second by using a device conventional in the oldest moralities.

Macbeth's first evil action is the assassination of King Duncan while a guest in his castle. From this moment he wades in gore, murdering his closest friend, slaughtering women and children to attain his ends. That the audience may judge the later acts with a moral eye, and not merely accept them as political expediency, the playwright introduces a much-disputed scene of " comic relief."

Macbeth and his Lady have completed the murder of the old king when, in the dead of night, they hear a thunderous knocking at the castle gates. They hasten to their chambers to establish an alibi, and their place on the stage is taken by a drunken porter.

PORTER. Here's a knocking indeed! If a man were porter of hell gate, he should have old turning the key. Knock, knock, knock! Who's there, i' th' name of Belzebub? Here's a farmer that hanged himself on th' expectation of plenty. Come in time! Have napkins enow about you; here you'll sweat for it. Knock, knock! who's there, in the other devil's name? Faith, here's an equivocator, that could swear in both the scales against either scale; who committed treason enough for God's sake, yet could not equivocate to heaven. O, come in, equivocator! Knock, knock, knock! Who's there? Faith, here's an English tailor come hither for stealing out of a French hose. Come in tailor. Here you may roast your goose. Knock, knock! Never at quiet! What are you? But this place is too cold for hell. I'll devil-porter it no further. I had thought to let in some of all professions that go the primrose way to th' everlasting bonfire. (*Knock*) Anon, anon! (*Opens the gate.*) I pray you remember the porter.

For many years critics have described this scene as a comic passage, thrown into the play to appease the tastes of the lower-class members of the audience. But the assumption that this segment of the audience could not be held enthralled by the blood and violence of the main action is not borne out by the great popularity of melodrama and primitive sports like wrestling and boxing throughout the ages. Other critics have professed to find in the scene a skillful employment of a delaying action to increase the suspense.

Neither of these explanations, however, explains why the character should be a porter or gate-keeper, and why he should pretend to be the gate-keeper of hell. Remember that the Elizabethan stage was without realistic scenery, that the Elizabethan audience was accustomed to imagine the setting to be whatever and wherever the character on stage declared it to be. Earlier in this same play, King Duncan had " set the stage " of Macbeth's castle:

> This castle hath a pleasant seat. The air
> Nimbly and sweetly recommends itself
> Unto our gentle senses.
> BANQUO.   This guest of summer,
> The temple-haunting martlet, does approve
> By his loved mansionry that the heaven's breath
> Smells wooingly here. No jutty, frieze,
> Buttress, nor coign of vantage, but this bird
> Hath made his pendant bed and procreant cradle.
> [I. 6, 1–8]

In similar and conventional fashion, the porter in his words and actions constructs a vivid image of hellmouth (which was, of course, a familiar property in the medieval plays) and the applicants for admission. For a moment, for as long as the porter speaks of it, the stage is hell, and the imaginary characters of his monologue are walking through the gates into hell, into the place of damnation. And when the knocking becomes so persistent that he cannot ignore it, the porter goes to one of the stage doors and opens it. Because of the porter's insistent development of the image, it will seem to the audience that Macduff and Lennox are stepping into hell, as well as into Macbeth's castle. By a dramatic metaphor, Shakespeare has impressed on his audience a judgment of the enormity of Macbeth's actions and an awareness of the destination towards which he is moving.

Yet the play is to be a tragedy, not a melodrama or a morality. Macbeth must emerge as a man, not a convenient stereotype or conventional villain. Otherwise the play will be merely a time-passer, with no more meaning than the average western movie or detective story. The audience must recognize that Macbeth is a good man, in his proper place and function, become evil only when he subjects himself to " ill-weaved ambition."

On his first entrance, from the field of battle, he presumably wears his soldier's uniform. While he is in this costume, the audience is told of his prowess and of the rewards that are rightfully his. After the murder of Duncan, Macbeth and his wife, who have not put on their bed garments, wrap themselves in flowing dressing gowns to disguise, to cover up, the truth about themselves and their actions. Later the assassin assumes the royal costume as he embarks upon his career of misrule. (" Adieu," says Macduff, with fervor, " Lest our old robes sit easier than our new! ") During this part of the play Macbeth falls to his lowest depth. The porter scene has established that his actions are those of one damned to hell; the audience sees the murder of Banquo, and especially the revolting slaughter of young Macduff. During these scenes Macbeth appears little other than a madman or the ogre of a fairytale, unbelievable because of his inhumanity.

Yet the audience craves humanity, and the dramatic experience is never satisfying unless it is in some way related to human experience. Having reached his lowest point, Macbeth is permitted to regain enough of his former virtue to remind the audience that this bloody, political, prideful action casts illumination into the dark corners of the smaller world in which they live.

After his ill-fated attempts to govern the kingdom he has usurped, after all his immoral and ill-judged actions committed in the name of political expediency, each of which only leads him deeper into chaos, Macbeth is suddenly confronted by a challenge with which he is familiar. A messenger informs him that an army headed by his political opponents is moving against him. There is an instant change in his manner and his actions; a kind of joy comes over him, replacing the depression that accompanied his actions as assassin, usurper, and butcher. He sends for his armor and dons it with the greatest impatience, hurls defiance at his enemies, and otherwise comports himself as the heroic soldier should. True, the audience is never permitted to forget that he is *not* the heroic soldier, but his reappearance in the costume in which he began the play is a visual reminder, a dramatic symbol, of the essential goodness destroyed while he was dressed in borrowed and stolen robes. Thus the audience will applaud his death as a just punishment for his evil deeds, but they will regret it, too, recognizing that all men are but " indifferent honest " and that the line between good and evil action, or good and evil motivation, is visible only to those with the longest and steadiest vision.

The partial rehabilitation of Macbeth, his restoration to the status of hero, is accomplished by dramatic metaphor. The several changes of his costume speak as eloquently as any commentator and more dramatically. This is a dramatic device that is almost second nature in Shakespeare and his contemporaries, a convention deeply rooted in the origins and early development of panoramic drama. That it has not ceased to be effective in the drama after the Elizabethans may be suggested by the quotation from Anton Chekhov (page 130), and its pervasiveness may be estimated by the commonness of the proverb that " the apparel oft proclaims the man."

Symbolism in Realistic Drama

We must consider finally what part symbolism plays in the action of the drama of the modern realistic theater.

Realism, of course, represents a break with the older concepts of dramatic action. As it developed in the nineteenth century, realistic drama attempted to find some kind of theatrical equivalent for the scientific and pragmatic spirit manifested in all other intellectual pursuits. The realistic, and later the naturalistic, writers were determined to show life as it is, with an appearance of cold and objective detachment. Émile Zola, one of the founders of the movement, declared that the naturalistic drama should have no " plot," no artificially planned action; the dramatist should place his characters in a room together and let them work out their own conflicts and destinies on the basis of their inherited characteristics. The notion of the author as play*wright* was to be completely abandoned in favor of dispassionate truth to life.

Without the hand of the craftsman — the artificer, the play*wright* — allegory, symbolic action, dramatic metaphor are impossible. The action of the drama of complete naturalism can have meaning only as it reveals the motivation of some particular individual or group of individuals; it is case history. A single case history must not be generalized upon, therefore the completely naturalistic drama is lacking in the universality necessary for communication with a mass audience. The plays of Émile Zola, for example, were totally unsuccessful except with the minute audiences of a specialized private theater in Paris.

But there have been very few plays in the modern theater which might be described as completely naturalistic. Both the instinct of the playmaker and the nature of dramatic art assert themselves on the side of artifice and intention, even in the most commonplace settings and dealing with the most domestic situations. For the drama of realism and naturalism purports to be a close reflection of character and society.

Perhaps it is superfluous to remind ourselves that the daily life of modern man is filled with symbolic actions. Yet most of them are so conventional as to be unconsciously performed. A friendly encounter begins with a handshake, a less friendly one with a shaking of fists. Gentlemen of the old school instinctively lift their hats when passing one another, or rise when a lady enters the room. District attorneys, cross-examining lawyers, and teachers stand; criminals, witnesses, and students are seated before them. When the red light flashes, the driver's foot automatically goes to the brake pedal.

In a modern play these casual symbolic acts can assume an emphasis and an importance completely lost in the informal traffic of modern daily life. Consider some of the actions Ibsen devises for his players in *Ghosts*. Just before the entrance of Pastor Manders, " Regina glances at herself, hastily, in the mirror, fans herself with a handkerchief, adjusts the collar of her uniform. Then she resumes watering the flowers." Since the audience already knows that the watering pot is empty and that Regina is merely a serving maid in Mrs. Alving's house, the action indicates clearly her pretension and her ambition: she assumes the pose of a lady.

After the discussion with Oswald about artistic society in Paris, Manders " paces up and down." Mrs. Alving, however, remains still, looking at him steadily. The conflict in their attitudes, which becomes the central conflict of the play, is revealed by the contrast between their reactions, nervous pacing against calm acceptance. Later, Manders' action of " groping for a chair " when Mrs. Alving confesses that her husband died as dissolute as he had lived is an outward and visible sign of his inward and mental distress. The total action of *Ghosts* is built up on dozens of such small, revealing actions, each of which makes its contribution to the dramatic experience of the audience.

There are, of course, other kinds or degrees of symbolism in the play, larger, less casual, more important actions. The stolen kiss in the dining room, for instance, which gives rise to the whole thematic idea of " ghosts," first as the repeated actions which establish the inevitable relationship between the past and the present, then as the persistent ideals or conventional beliefs which dominate and control present actions. When Oswald makes his first entrance, he is smoking his father's pipe: Manders is immediately struck by his physical resemblance to his father. As the action and the dialogue proceed it becomes apparent that the resemblance is something more than physical, and that the pipe is, in fact, a symbol of Oswald's heritage. On page 43, Mrs. Alving orders Regina to serve champagne. A bottle of champagne has its commonplace symbolism for the modern audience; it stands for a feast, a celebration. It is introduced into the play at this point practically because Oswald has asked for something to drink, but symbolically because his mother is trying to promise him life, renewed through his return to her. And the symbol is equally applicable to Oswald himself, since it is Regina who brings the bottle of champagne, Regina who, for him, stands for the *joy of living*.

Although these are symbolic actions, as in the older drama, they frequently involve the presence or handling of inanimate objects to a greater degree than did symbolic action in the theater of the Elizabethans or the Greeks. One reason for this is, quite simply, the nature of the realistic theater, requiring the detailed reproduction on the stage of the locale of the action: a room with furniture and windows and doors and rugs and books and lamps, as opposed to the bare orchestra of Aeschylus or the formal platform of Marlowe or Shakespeare. The other reason is more organic, a result of the development of the art of playwrighting.

The theater of the early years of the nineteenth century, before the advent of Ibsen, was preoccupied with the kind of entertainment loosely described as melodrama. That is, the actions were commonly conflicts of absolutely good characters against absolutely bad characters, generally over the possession of some object of material value. There is a bewildering variety of these disputed objects — a list of conspirators, a mortgage, a coal mine, a ship, buried treasure, company funds, a horse, a diary, a

throne, a diamond necklace; everything from an old chair to the Suez
Canal — yet they have one thing in common. All disputed objects are
inanimate, and inanimate in a double sense: they are without life, and
they are without spiritual value for the audience. When, in Douglas
Jerrold's *The Rent Day,* the dispossessed tenant struggles with the bailiff
to retain possession of an old chair, the chair is, as it were, a chair only
by accident. It might as well be a washtub, a bed, a bookcase. The
spectator is expected to be interested in who will *win* the struggle; the
struggle itself has no significance. In Bulwer-Lytton's *Richelieu,* the
contest is for the possession of a secret roster of conspirators, ownership
of which carries with it power to influence the king. Only narrative
convenience determines that the disputed object must be such a list; it
would alter the plot only slightly (and the action not at all) if the
object had been a family Bible, the report of a secret agent, or a time
bomb. To permit the audience to become emotionally concerned over the
whereabouts of a scrap of paper or a capsule of poison is to allow only
the experience of melodrama, which is about equal to solving crossword
puzzles or reading detective fiction.

But an inanimate object, the orphanage, plays a decisive role in the
action of *Ghosts.* Constructed under the direction of Mrs. Alving as a
memorial to her husband, its dedication is the excuse to bring all the
characters together at the beginning of the play; each is somehow connected with its erection and dedication. The burning of the orphanage
is the climax of the action and precipitates the denouement: because of
the burning, Engstrand gets Manders into his power, Oswald is excited
to an early collapse, and Mrs. Alving is forced to face the truth about
herself.

An orphanage, however, though an inanimate object, belongs to a
different class from the mortgage, " the papers," the poison. As a charitable institution it has an inherent symbolic value; it is " for the sake
of others," as Ibsen wrote in his working notes for the play. And at the
beginning of *Ghosts* it is presented as a dutiful wife's suitable memorial
in honor of her dead husband. And so it remains to the end for Pastor
Manders, as he takes refuge in conventional ideas to escape from ugly
reality. For Mrs. Alving and, as the action progresses, for the audience
the meaning of the orphanage takes an ironic turnabout: it is intended
to disguise the memory of Captain Alving, an ironic mask to cover the
rottenness of the old way of life.

Manders accepts the mask, as it were, at face value; Mrs. Alving tries
desperately to ignore the face. But the action in which she is involved
drives her to recognition. The burning of the orphanage shows her the

impossibility of living with a disguise; the mask is destroyed and she has no choice but to live with the face. She must even understand that the face is not quite what she thought it was when she designed its mask.

For Oswald, too, the orphanage becomes a symbol; it is his father, whom he scarcely knew. And as the orphanage is destroyed, he cries out, " Everything will burn. There won't remain a single thing in memory of father. Here am I, too, being burned up." Everything in memory of father will be burned except, of course, Engstrand's " Snug Harbor for Seamen." Regina now has no excuse to stay away from her " father's " home, and Manders is trapped into supporting it. Engstrand's combination saloon and brothel remains at the end of the play a fitting tribute to the honor of the Alving name.

Thus in *Ghosts* an inanimate object which is functional in the development of the action becomes also a dramatic symbol essential to the generalizing of the action into a dramatic experience for a mass audience. It has often been a source of wonder that Norway, a small country and one not in the direct line of cultural transmission from ancient Greece to modern times, should suddenly give to the world a playwright like Ibsen, whose works have held the international stage successfully for more than a century. Of what concern can the customs and beliefs of the inhabitants of provincial towns in a remote country be to audiences half a world and more than half a century away? The answer cannot lie in the average spectator's passionate search for sociological information: the modern theater is no classroom. The answer must lie in the generalizing power of the symbol, whether in object or action, whereby the fate of Mrs. Alving illuminates the fate of all men.

Ibsen used to be thought of as a reformer, in particular as an exponent of women's rights. To this description he once publicly objected. He was not so much, he declared, the social thinker as the poet; he was not interested in answering questions but in asking them. He was, of course, interested in " the woman question," but principally as it was an aspect of the larger question of Man in general. " My task," he said, " is the description of Man." Symbolism is an indispensable tool for the playwright who directs his efforts to so great an end.

PART TWO

THE DRAMATIC UNIT

V

DRAMATIC STRUCTURE

During the first part of this book we have been, as it were, on stage, observing the actor as he moves and speaks, the director as he goes about his business, the designer as he responds to the demands upon his art. It is necessary to remember that, however interesting the individual parts may be, our final concern is with the play as a whole. Having observed the members and their separate articulation, we must draw back, step away from the stage, the scenery, the footlights, to our proper place in the auditorium and see the playwright's work as he meant it to be seen: the play as a whole. The discovery and analysis of a symbol, the underlining of a particular action, the definition of the active essence of a character are but contributory steps to the total dramatic experience.

It is obvious, of course, even to the uninstructed spectator in the playhouse that the whole play is the result of construction, that many parts have been joined into an artistic whole. For the Greeks, the interruptions of the chorus; for the Elizabethans, the clearing of the platform; for the moderns, the fall of the curtain: these mark the divisions of a play as periods mark the ends of sentences, or half-blank pages the ends of chapters in a novel. The total action of a play is subdivided into major units (the *episodes* of Greek tragedy, the *acts* of the modern theater), and every major unit is made up of smaller units, called scenes, as chapters are made up of paragraphs. Yet the joining of scenes to form acts, and of acts to form plays, must not be thought of as an architectural process: a playmaker is not a bricklayer; a play is a living work, not an inorganic structure.

The basic unit in the dramatic structure is properly called the *scene;* but it is necessary to be aware constantly that the term has several meanings in theatrical usage. It may be the notation on the program indicating the place of the action: " *Scene, Elsinore. A platform before the*

castle." It may designate the actual setting, or some part of it, as
" Painted scenery," " side-scene . . . back scene, etc." It may designate
a formal division of the act-structure (Act One, Scene Two) as in the
plays of Shakespeare. As the basic unit of play construction, however,
it means simply a portion of the total play in which the stage is occupied
by an unchanging group of players. When anything happens to change
the constitution of the group (i.e., the exit or entrance of a player) a
new scene commences.

It is not difficult to discover the scene-divisions that make up the
units of the dramatic structure of Greek tragedy or of the panoramic
Christian plays. In modern drama, particularly in the realistic drama,
every effort is made to disguise the structure and to keep the audience
from an awareness of the divisions. The discovery of the component
units remains, however, the first step in the analysis of the total structure
of a play.

If we select a painstakingly realistic play, *Ghosts,* as a working example, we may divide the first act into six scenes as follows:

1. Regina and Engstrand
2. Regina and Manders
3. Manders and Mrs. Alving
4. Manders, Mrs. Alving, and Oswald
5. Manders and Mrs. Alving
6. Manders and Mrs. Alving (Regina and Oswald off stage)

You will notice that, although the exit of Engstrand marks the end
of the first scene, and the entrance of Manders the beginning of the
second, Regina remains on stage to serve as a link between the two
scenes, to give the impression of a continuous flow rather than a succession of episodes. So Manders serves as a link between scenes Two and
Three, Manders and Mrs. Alving between scenes Three and Four and
scenes Four and Five. The final scene is distinguished from scene Five by
the enlargement of the action to include the characters off stage in the
dining room.

Each of the scenes in the act is made up of varying amounts of
three elements: exposition, action, and preparation. Exposition is the
recounting of the past, action is the forward movement of the scene,
and preparation is the hint of things to come, the unanswered questions.
Let us analyze the contents of the opening scenes of the first act of
Ghosts, measuring each element against the others, to determine the
structure of the basic unit.

Scene One. Time: Before dinner. Characters: Regina and Engstrand. Action, or business of the scene: Engstrand invites Regina to come " home "; Regina has other ideas. Exposition: (Silent) The rain-misted landscape, Regina's healthy good looks, Engstrand's limp; (Narrated) The building of the orphanage, the return of Oswald, the revelation of Engstrand's hypocrisy and Regina's elegance, the mystery of Regina's mother. Preparation: Pastor Manders is coming; Engstrand plans to build a sailors' home. The scene is a brief one and heavily loaded with exposition, as you might expect in the opening of a play. Yet, since the exposition comes out of a conflict between the two characters in the scene, the spectator is never aware that he is being told the things he must know to understand the situation and the advancing action.

Scene Two. Regina and Manders. Action: Regina works on Manders (whose pliability is a major factor in the action of the play); Manders speaks for the first time about " duty," which is a controlling idea and motivating force in the play. Exposition: Oswald is physically worn out; Regina, flirting with Manders, shows herself to be full of the joy of living. Preparation: Manders hints at his reaction to the proposal to establish a sailors' home. In this scene the exposition and action are more nearly in balance, the relationship between the elements being determined by what the scene is designed to accomplish: to establish the character of Pastor Manders, his *active essence,* as a motive force for future use.

Scene Three. Characters: Manders and Mrs. Alving. Action: The Orphanage is not to be insured; Regina must stay at the Alving home. Exposition: Oswald has been to Paris, Mrs. Alving has been reading " questionable " literature, Manders worries about the public reaction to his decisions, and there has been a small fire at the Orphanage. Here the exposition, in quantity, outweighs the action once more, but by now it has become so functional that it is equally preparation for future action. The small fire is an instance of this. It occurred in the past and is duly reported to us, but it also looks forward and prepares us for the great fire to come. The relationship between the elements, the structure of the scene, is determined by what the scene is designed to accomplish: to show Mrs. Alving's irrational submission to Manders' code of conduct (irrational since she knows that the Orphanage is far from fireproof). This irrational submission, as the later exposition of the play will reveal, has been the *active essence* of the character of Mrs. Alving.

Scene Four. Characters: Mrs. Alving, Manders, Oswald. Action: Oswald presents the case for the freedom of the individual. Exposition:

Oswald's memory of his father, his impression of his father's character, life among the artists in Paris and its corruption by tourists. Again, the exposition heavily outweighs the action, but it becomes increasingly difficult to determine the line between exposition and action. The past is, paradoxically, too active, too vital a part of the argument to be wholly a narrative of things gone by.

Scene Five. Characters: Manders, Mrs. Alving. Action: Manders lays down the law of duty. Exposition: The truth about Regina's parentage; Mrs. Alving describes the horrors of life with father, and her attempts to cover up the truth out of her sense of family honor and wifely duty. This long scene is almost completely made up of exposition, of things past; but the exposition is preparation for the final scene of the act.

Scene Six. Characters: Manders, Mrs. Alving (Regina and Oswald off stage). Action: The ode to be sung in Captain Alving's honor is unwrapped as Mrs. Alving sees her ghost. This is the shortest scene in the play. It has been so carefully prepared that only one brief tap is sufficient to explode it. In the earlier scenes some attempt has been made to keep past and present at their proper distances, but here all time becomes one: past and future are united in the present, and in this very pattern of arrangement, in the structure of the scene, the play's central idea is made explicit. "Ghosts," says Mrs. Alving. "When I heard Regina and Oswald in there, it was as though I saw ghosts before me. But I almost think we are all of us ghosts, Pastor Manders. It is not only what we have inherited from our father and mother that walks again in us. It is all sorts of dead ideas, and lifeless old beliefs. They have no vitality, but they cling to us all the same. . . ." The ideals and codes of conduct of past generations determine the ideals and codes of conduct of the present; past actions control present decisions. And in the structure of the scene, exposition outweighs, dominates, and even replaces action.

We will consider presently the larger structure, the total play of *Ghosts.* But this consideration of the smaller structure, of the design of the individual scenes, conveniently illustrates in little the larger pattern. Within the small unit of the scene, structure involves the arrangement of exposition and action. In the larger unity of the entire play, structure means the selection and arrangement of incidents, or scenes. Controlling in part the playwright's selection and arrangement are two other elements involved in any action, dramatic or otherwise — *time* and *place.* We may say that the playwright's concept of time and place, plus the structure of his action, determine the form of his play. And as the discussion of the theater building itself has suggested, there are two basic dramatic forms, the focussed and the panoramic.

Focussed Structure

The conventional structure of focussed drama was in part decided by the nature of the playhouse and the relationship between the spectator and the players. The auditorium was built around an orchestra, the orchestra was centered on the altar, and at the altar stood the leading actor. Perhaps the altar represented itself, a place of sacrifice, as in *Electra* or *Agamemnon;* perhaps it represented a rock, as in *Prometheus,* or a tomb as in the *Choephoroe.* Once its identity had been established it could be changed only with a certain awkwardness, which the playwrights were happy to avoid. To this center, the protagonist would be fixed, literally as in *Prometheus,* or by function or intent: Klytemnaestra comes to the altar to sacrifice in *Agamemnon,* the suppliant maidens seek sanctuary at the altar in their play. And around the protagonist and the altar stood the chorus: the elders of Thebes, the women of the household, the sea-nymphs. Once the chorus was, so to speak, " on stage," the locale of the action was fixed; only by changing the chorus could the locale be changed. In one or two of the surviving plays such a change does occur; but, conventionally and generally, the chorus and the " scene," once established, remained fixed throughout the action of the play; once set, the focus is never altered.

The principle of *fixed focus* in staging determines to a considerable extent the principle of focus in dramatic structure. The plot of any play, as distinguished from its action, is the whole story of the play. It begins, let us say, with the conspiracy of Zeus to overthrow the Old Gods; Prometheus joins in the conspiracy, and yet, after the victory of the rebels, he sets himself against Zeus to give to Mankind certain benefits which the Father of the Gods would deny them. As a result of his disobedience, he is arrested by the order of Zeus and doomed to eternal torment. Aeschylus begins his action at the point where Prometheus' punishment is put into effect. The earlier portion of the story must be presented as exposition, and the action will be confined to a brief succession of incidents taken from the concluding portion of the history.

Stated as a rule of dramaturgy, focussed structure may be said to confine itself to the few hours at the very end of a plot when the action comes to its climax and resolution, concentrating on a minimum of characters and a single locale. From the analysis of a number of Greek plays, it will be seen that this rule is perhaps more hypothetical than actual: *Agamemnon* begins with the announcement that signal fires lighted one after another between Asia Minor and Greece have conveyed the news of the fall of Troy to the Greek armies; almost immediately Agamemnon, leader of the Greeks, returns to his palace with the spoils of war. It is hardly to be assumed that the visitors to Prometheus arrive one after another within the hour and a half that it requires to act his play. Frequently, that is to say, focussed drama achieves its unity by ignoring the ticking of the clock or the turning of the pages of a calendar. For the duration of the action, time stands still, and its very stillness adds an intensity and concentration to the action.

Panoramic Structure

Panoramic drama, growing out of the playlets of the Christian church, handles the elements of time and place and focus in an entirely different manner. Beginning with a playing area which encouraged freedom of movement and with a conventional narrative every scene of which was a kind of commentary or exegesis of every other scene, it developed a structure which permitted the playwright to employ dozens of characters, to shift his focus from one central figure to another, and to move his action without hesitation from city to city, from country to country, and even from earth to heaven.

The Craft Cycles, or Biblical plays, generally began with the story of creation and ended with the Last Judgment, encompassing the whole history of mankind, past, present, and future, and as much of the geography of the earth, the heavens, and hell as the story demanded, with the action centering now on God, now on Lucifer, now on the Virgin Mary, now on Christ. This same freedom of movement in time and space was bequeathed to the playwrights of the age of Elizabeth, who willingly seized the opportunity to present to the eyes of their spectators the whole story of a man's life, from his matriculation at the university to his death twenty-four years after the beginning of the play and half-a-continent away. In several of Shakespeare's plays (*The Winter's Tale,* for instance, and *Pericles*) a child born in the first half of the action is ready for marriage at its conclusion, and some of the playwrights' more classical- (or literal-) minded contemporaries used to object that it was absurd to pretend to believe that such things could happen in the two hours required for the performance of a play.

It is, however, stupid to become involved in arguments as to which form is better. Each has its special function in fulfilling the author's intention and in meeting the expectations of the audience. It is convenient to speak of the concentration and economy of the focussed form, and the looseness and diffusion of the panoramic; but the focussed form can, on occasion, include as much of the whole story of its hero as the panoramic (*Oedipus Rex,* for example, manages to work into its action

by expository narration the whole of its hero's childhood and adoles-
cence); and panoramic tragedy can achieve the same tension and magnitude as its more compact counterpart. Both structures have been
designed for the same purpose — to provide a dramatic experience for
the playgoer; and as a means of achieving that experience, they create
through structure, through selection and arrangement of incidents, a
unity that will catch the consciousness of king and priest, tired business-
man and housewife, visiting fireman and lover, sighing like a furnace.

Unity

The unity of a drama, or indeed of any work of art, is the special selection and arrangement of materials within its structure which emphasize
its singleness of purpose and the clarity of the artist's vision. Much has
been said, both before and after Prince Hamlet, about the drama as a
mirror of life. There is truth in the description, but it is only half the
truth; if the drama is a mirror of life it is a magic mirror with the
power to accept and reject details as it chooses.

For most of us, the experience of living is mysterious and chaotic.
We are always in the middle of an action whose end is unknown and
whose beginning may not be apparent. Bernard Shaw once declared that
the function of the playwright was to select incidents from the chaos of
everyday living and arrange them in a pattern so that the spectator
might leave the theater an enlightened man. Erich Auerbach suggests
that the purpose of this selection and arrangement, this design for unity,
is to turn the intellectual and spiritual powers of the audience in one
direction; the assembled mass is enabled to share the perception of the
single author. Both Shaw and Auerbach are tendentious writers, Shaw
insisting on the social and Auerbach on the moral function of art. But
unity is a necessary element of " pure " art also, as is suggested by a
casual remark of Alfred North Whitehead: " Art is the imposing of a
pattern on experience," he said, " and our esthetic enjoyment [arises
from our] recognition of the pattern."

Although it was formerly believed that only one kind of unity was
possible in the theater, it should be apparent that each of the basic dramatic forms finds its own pattern. In each case, as we have seen, this
will be determined partly by the physical conditions of the playhouse,
by the relation between actor and spectator, by the nature of the audience and the society it represents, and by the particular ritual origin
of the form.

For the Greek playwright working in the focussed form, the attain-
ment of unity was a simple matter. Analysts of the classical playwrights

point out that they tended to divide the total unity into three tributary
unities, of time, of place, of action. They suggest that the classical
playwright undertook to observe a *rule* that his play should concern itself with a single action performed with an unbroken time scheme in a
single place. Actually, as we have seen, the Greek playwright was more
apt to ignore place and time completely, or rather, to give these elements
no importance in his dramatic scheme. It is true that it is possible to
say that the action of *Agamemnon* takes place before his palace, as does
the action of *Oedipus Rex,* and that the action of *Prometheus* is set on
a peak in the Caucasus. Yet much of the action of the plays would be
incongruous if the playwright insisted on maintaining the actuality
of the chosen locale. In Sophocles' tragedy, Electra and her sister
Chrysosthemis steal into what is apparently the public square to conspire; in the *Eumenides* of Aeschylus the " setting " is first a shrine,
then a temple, then a vaguely defined public place, but without any
clearly proclaimed shift. As for the unity of time, the playwrights tend
to concentrate their action on the last hour or two of the hero's story,
automatically achieving a chronological realism: yet we have seen that
Aeschylus was quite capable of telescoping many days into the performing time of a single chorus: at the beginning of *Agamemnon* it is announced that Troy has just fallen; in the third episode of the play the
victors parade into the orchestra after a voyage that, in Homer's account, took many months. Much ingenuity has been employed by
classical scholars in adjusting this disunity of time to the supposed rule;
it seems more in accordance with our understanding of the nature of the
Greek dramatic experience to reconsider the rule. The Greek playwright
was not a clock-watcher at all; he ignored the clock as he ignored
geography. His attention, like the attention of his audience, was focussed
always upon his characters. The real unity of Greek drama is the unity
which comes from the architectural and structural focus on the central
figure.

At this point it is necessary to recall the spectator, both in his physical
relation to the actor and in his intellectual perception of the play. In
the theater, nothing stood between him and the actors, and everything
was arranged to direct his attention to the chief actor in the center of
the orchestra. No scenery or mechanical effects distracted his eye, and
the not infrequent moments of spectacle were always provided by the
performers. A part of the unity of the Greek dramatic experience then
was achieved by the direct and unbroken focus of the spectator on the
protagonist.

We must recall also that the playwright chose to deal without exception with familiar materials, with gods and heroes whose names and biographies were the common heritage of the spectators. Attending a tragedy whose announced subject was the story of Oedipus, the spectator would know that the hero was to be punished for incest and patricide; at an Agamemnon play he would anticipate the assassination of the hero by his wife. When the public heralds proclaimed a new tragedy on the subject of Prometheus, the audience was prepared in advance for the story of a rebellion and an eventual reconciliation. That is, the audience was as informed as the mysterious force known as Fate about the resolution of the action, about what would happen finally to the hero. Always, while the play was in progress, they would have as a fixed point in their minds the catastrophe, and with the end always in focus they would inevitably judge the events of the play against it.

Although only a small body of Greek playwrighting survives, it is fortunately possible to test this principle of focal unity in several ways. Each of the great masters, Aeschylus, Sophocles, and Euripides, wrote a play about the familiar story of Electra, the daughter of Agamemnon who avenged his death by conspiring to bring about the murder of her own mother. Each play utilizes common materials: in the beginning her brother returns to assist her, in the middle the scheme of assassination is developed, and in the end a double murder is accomplished. Yet each of the plays is utterly different as a dramatic experience from the other two. Aeschylus, keeping his eye always on the expected conclusion, selects and arranges his materials so that the spectator is made aware of the moral or judicial issue involved; his *Choephoroe* is almost a problem play. Sophocles, keeping his eye on the expected conclusion, selects and arranges his materials so that the spectator is made progressively aware of the inner nature of the heroine, of the psychology of an avenger. Euripides, keeping his eye on the expected conclusion, arranges his materials in such a way as to create a stunning theatrical effect, a kind of melodrama emphasizing pathos and sensation for their own sakes.

If the Greek playwright was bound by certain rules, which we may reduce if we like to the rule of unity of focus, and was further restricted by the known facts of his story, he was permitted great freedom in his arrangement of the known facts, and never hesitated to introduce into the story inventions of his own to clarify his purpose and direct the interest or attention of the audience to his interpretation of myth or history.

We may use Aeschylus' treatment of the story of Prometheus as a test of the intention of the Greek playwright and the experience of the Greek audience. The outlines of the story were, we have seen, commonly known; Prometheus sinned against the authority of Zeus and was punished with horrible torture, and finally won forgiveness or at least an end of his torture. The legend apparently furnished the plot of the complete trilogy of which we have only the play of *Prometheus Bound*. (Fragments of the missing plays suggest that Aeschylus followed the myth for his total plot.) The chaining of the hero and the increasing severity of his punishment would meet the expectations of the audience (as would his eventual liberation in the missing plays). But for the rest of his matter, Aeschylus was free to choose what he would. Among other things, he chose the restless Oceanides to be his chorus, the free spirits of water whose constant movement and whose pity for anyone unable to move as freely emphasizes the plight of the hero. He chose Ocean, Io, and Hermes for his secondary actors, each of whom moved in a way that called attention to the very act of movement. He chose Ocean as a symbol of craven fear, or of ignoble compromise with the tyrannic power of Zeus; he chose Io as a representative of the numberless victims of the tyrant's whims and injustices; he chose Hermes as the bearer of the god's commands and characterized him as vain, supercilious, petty, and unstable. As the spectator sees the consecutive episodes in which each of these characters appears, he will inevitably (and perhaps unconsciously) judge them in terms of the *known conclusion*. He will, in a sense, be constantly focussing the episodes against the conclusion of the action.

We have already noticed that *Prometheus Bound* is an imperfect play: it has no antagonist to conflict actively with the protagonist. Zeus is always " off stage." Yet, by the selection and arrangement of incidents, and by the maintenance of focus, Aeschylus has given him a reality and presence which his actual appearance might weaken. The revengeful, lustful, whimsical tyrant, whose absence emphasizes his impalpable supremacy, strengthens the sympathy of the audience for Prometheus, and strengthens as well their admiration and sense of his heroic stature.

If, as we have said, one of the characteristics of dramatic action is to provide a kind of commentary on itself, one of the most important functions of structure is to give the spectator a point of view about the action he is seeing. In the focussed drama, the freedom of the playwright to select and arrange incidents on the unchanging outline of his received story determines the reaction of the spectator to his dramatic experience. If he were not aware of the eventual reconciliation of Zeus and Prometheus, the heroic determination of the Titan to resist the tyrant might seem mere willfulness, might seem the result of a martyr complex, might seem melodramatic. As it is, the *irony* of the situation controls his reaction: however great the sufferings of the hero may be, however determined the pressures applied by Zeus, in the end the victim will emerge triumphant over his persecutor — his actions, his rebellion, and his stubbornness justified.

If the spectator did not know at the beginning of *Oedipus Rex* that the hero was to blame for the plague that had overtaken the city, the hero's quest for a scapegoat would take on the aspects of a detective story. As it is, the irony of the situation, with the audience in possession of knowledge denied the hero, keeps the focus clearly on the character of the hero as it is revealed by his actions scene by scene, but always set against the known conclusion.

The unity of focussed drama is achieved by a structural pattern which insists on concentration: a few brief hours at the end of a long and complex story are performed with as little reference to time and place as possible. Episode by episode the action moves to its conventional conclusion, each episode bringing into clearer focus the central concern of the play, whether it be an abstraction like the nature of justice or a concrete study of human character. And with this structure and by this unity the playwright sets forth the particular human or superhuman experience which will illuminate human experience in general.

It is obvious that, if the panoramic drama achieves unity, it does so in a very different manner from the focussed drama. Staged in a theater which from the very beginning encouraged freedom of movement, it grew into a conventional form which did not hesitate to shift the locale of its action, insisting upon the change, and to permit the action to cover a day, a year, or many years in the hero's life, calling attention to the swift or slow passage of time when it seemed useful. Indeed, an older contemporary of Shakespeare, one whose educated taste preferred the focussed form of drama, parodied the performance of a panoramic play. He complains first of the stage " where you shall have Asia on one side and Africa on the other, and so many under-kingdoms, that the player when he cometh in, must ever begin by telling where he is, or else the tale will not be conceived. Now ye shall have three ladies walk to gather flowers, and then we must believe the stage to be a garden. By and by we hear news of a shipwreck in the same place, and then we are to blame if we accept it not for a rock. . . . Now of time they are much more liberal. For ordinary is it that two young princes fall in love; after many traverses she is got with child, delivered of a fair boy, he is lost, groweth a man, falleth in love, and is ready to get another child, — and all this in two hours' space."

Such a description suggests that the conventional panoramic play is a patchwork of incidents strung together without focus (in the Greek sense), a dizzying sight to follow in the theater. Yet our experience tells us that this is not so; it is as easy to follow the complicated wanderings of a Shakespearean hero as the static passion of Prometheus. The treatment of the clock and the calendar in *Faustus* — skimming over twenty-four years in an hour's playing time, and then counting the last scene in portions of an hour — may cause distress to the literal-minded or the classically-trained: but for its audience, as a reflection of a particular way of looking at and judging human experience, it constituted a model dramatic structure.

The focussed form, concentrating as it does on the last hours of a long story, must rely heavily on narrated exposition to explain the relationship between past events and present action; its present action is concerned with bringing about the inevitable, foredoomed ending. For the Christian theater, however, the fated misstep, the great decision, the happy choice was but one moment of concern. *Any* action, any decision, any choice was of equal importance in determining the fate of the hero. For in a sense the hero had no fate, or at least he created his own fate as the result of a series of actions. At no moment in his life, save the very last, could any action be decisive, any choice final. So the hero's life is spread before us panoramically, from the beginning of his important actions, if not from his birth, to the concluding moment when further decision or choice is impossible.

The panoramic playwright, then, selects a series of incidents from the whole of his hero's story and displays them in such a pattern that the meaning of the hero's experiences will remain in the spectator's consciousness. The subjects available to him, as far as we can tell, are much more varied than those available to his classical predecessor. He may draw upon familiar historical or religious stories, but these he will treat with the greatest freedom, changing the emphasis or the ending if it suits his purpose. He will frequently employ original plots, or dramatizations of prose fiction or narrative poems whose subjects can hardly be said to occupy the same predominant place in the public domain as the adventures of kings or mythical heroes. He does not, therefore, play on the spectator's knowledge of the basic story and indeed will sometimes deliberately twist a familiar story to an unexpected conclusion, as Shakespeare did with *King Lear*. The playwright intends the spectator to be interested in the events of and for themselves as they unfold, and then to perceive the cumulative weight of the events as the play moves to its end.

This theory of playwrighting yields such a work as " The Form of

Faustus' Fortunes Good and Bad " — a more accurate statement of the contents of Marlowe's play than its usual title of *Doctor Faustus*. It produces *Macbeth*, which begins with the act of temptation and demonstrates the consequences of yielding. Demonstration is perhaps the distinguishing characteristic of panoramic drama. We might say that in this form a hero is considered innocent until he *shows* himself to be guilty. In the focussed drama, the hero's doom is decreed before he is permitted to assume the role. A Roman poet wrote that the path leading down into hell was easy to find and to descend, and for the classical heroes this is true. But the tragic heroes of Christian panoramic drama had to fight every inch of the way to reach their infernal goal. Thus Faustus must move from Germany to Italy and apparently up into the heavens before slipping into hellmouth; thus Mark Antony will quarter the Mediterranean world before meeting his doom in Egypt.

But the panoramic playwright is often not contented to follow the wideranging fortunes of a single hero. He will shift his focus from one character, say Faustus, to another, say Wagner. He will weave together two stories, either of which might have made a play by itself, as Shakespeare combines the two plots of King Lear and his daughters and the Duke of Gloucester and his sons. Not infrequently three plots will find their way into one drama, as in *A Midsummer Night's Dream, Fuente Ovejuna*, or *Hamlet*. Clearly, if panoramic drama is to have any unity at all, the unifying principle must be sought elsewhere than in the conventional unities of time, place, and action.

We may find the clue in the eminent patchwork by Master Lupton, *All for Money*. Lupton brought together on his stage personifications of the branches of knowledge, caricatures of contemporary types, historical figures; he directed his actors through a kind of debate, a farce comedy, a bit of moral tragedy, several allegorical actions, and a concluding sermon. We recognize at once that *All for Money* is a bad play, but its badness does not proceed from its lack of unity. For in spite of its strange collection of characters and its incongruous juxtaposition of scenes, *All for Money* has a unity so firm that it is almost oppressive. That is, if nothing else is clear in this indifferent hodgepodge, the central idea that controls and dominates all else is inescapable. Early in the play the debating abstractions, who appear to us poor but self-satisfied, announce that money leads to pleasure, and pleasure leads to sin, and sin leads to damnation. Once established by the authority of the speakers as a principle of human experience, the money-pleasure-sin-damnation formula is tested in different ways and on different levels and demonstrated to be accurate. The focus of the play is not determined by the place, or the time, or the singleness of the action, but by the idea which the action is designed to illustrate.

At first glance *Doctor Faustus* is a less disorderly play than *All for Money*. At least Marlowe has designed the main part of his action around a single figure. But the focus has hardly become fixed on the great scholar when it slips, perhaps to Wagner and the clown, perhaps to Robin and Ralph, perhaps to the Horse Courser. True, it returns to Faustus again eventually; but, as we have seen, critics have been so distressed by these passages of low comedy that most of them have taken refuge in the hypothesis that they are post-Marlovian " improvements " or revisions. But we have pointed out that even if these particular passages are not by Marlowe, they must be present to replace similar passages of his work. The nature of the play demands the shifting focus.

In the earlier discussion of these scenes we observed that, far from being reliefs or diversions for the audience, they have tended to underline or comment on the main action. When Faustus signs his pact with Devil, the Clown signs a pact of apprenticeship whose strictness was common knowledge. When Faustus uses his magic powers to conjure, he is parodied by Robin and Ralph, who are carried off to hellmouth by the Devil. The comic commentary always emphasizes the finality and infernal nature of the agreement: the threat of damnation constantly hangs over the hero. And yet he is not damned; the Good Angel pleads with him, the Old Man exhorts him, salvation is always within his reach. The panoramic structure of the play, with its long series of demonstrations on the part of Faustus and its explicit commentary by the lower characters, permits the audience to watch a man deliberately damning himself by a kind of presumption.

The Good Angel and the Old Man repeatedly point out that God is merciful, that forgiveness awaits the repentant sinner. But Faustus cannot bring himself to believe this promise. He himself is jealous and vengeful against those who question his magic powers: behold the fate of the Horse Courser and the doubting Knight. It is the final act of the perversion of the reason in him to assume that God is made in his image, that because Faustus cannot forgive, God will not. And for this presumption, for this despair of God's mercy, he is borne screaming to hell by the assembled devils.

The unity of panoramic drama is achieved by a structural pattern of maximum diffuseness controlled by constant reference to the central idea. Always the selection and arrangement of incidents is made with the intention of demonstrating the idea in detail and in depth, sometimes in terms of a single hero, sometimes by balancing or contrasting one hero against another. The effect is a full and lively picture of a bustling world from which no class is barred as a participant, where comedy mingles with tragedy and the grotesque with the pathetic, and where every man in the audience will sooner or later see his own image.

The History of the Basic Dramatic Forms

Focussed drama, as it is known to us, originated and developed in ancient Greece and dominated the theater of the Greeks and their successors the Romans. In fact, the form is sometimes called *classical drama,* a term of limited usefulness. The classical drama as a form did not die with the Roman Empire. Although the theaters of the ancient world were effectively closed in the fourth century, A.D., a large part of the repertory managed to endure in the libraries of monasteries and private collectors. During the great Renaissance of the fifteenth century, critics in search of a master turned to Aristotle on the drama, and scholars and authors began to read the classical plays with a view to imitation. In Italy, in France, and in England, plays were produced in the classical mode, using the heroic or mythical subject matter of Greco-Roman legend, or reasonable native facsimiles. In England the revival had almost no effect except among academics, for the momentum of the panoramic drama was too great. In France, however, under the patronage of the court and the inspired playwrighting of Corneille and Racine, among others, the focussed form experienced a genuine rebirth. Through the seventeenth and eighteenth centuries it controlled the French serious drama and was only temporarily shaken by the assault of the romantics at the beginning of the nineteenth century.

Panoramic drama, on the other hand, although it had a general birth all over the medieval world, had its greatest success in England. Both serious and comic drama of the age of Elizabeth and James, with one or two notable exceptions, is constructed in this pattern, even by playwrights whose education had been distinctly classical. It is interesting to see, for example, a university-trained poet like Thomas Kyd deliberately adapting the subject matter and techniques of Seneca, the most academic of ancient tragic writers, to the uses of the panoramic revenge play. The revenge play, of which *Hamlet* is the most famous example, with its visible butchery and widely ranging violent action, is the complete antithesis of classical tragedy, with its focus firmly fixed on question and answer.

It is quite possible that the conventions of the playhouse had something to do with the continuing success of the panoramic drama in England and the resurrection of the focussed drama on the continent.

The Elizabethan theater, with its unique arrangement of multiple play-ing areas and freedom from the restrictions imposed by illusionistic scenery, encouraged the preservation of medieval conventions of dra-matic structure. The continental theater, on the other hand, began to use scenery about the time that it rediscovered the classical playwrights. At first, scenery seems to have been employed for spectacular effects and for decoration, but soon the possibilities of *illusion* suggested them-selves. Since the theaters were roofed, with the audience in fixed seats before the platform, and since the focussed form generally permitted only one locale for the entire play, it was possible to erect on the stage a setting, painted in perspective to suggest the place and time of the action. Ingenious stage managers soon devised machines for shifting the settings, but their employment in any given play was necessarily restricted. How-ever skillful, a change of scene interrupts the action, and part of the success of panoramic drama depends upon the unimpeded progress of the story. Consequently the theater of illusion, the representational stage, encouraged the development of focussed drama, while it presented obstacles to panoramic playwrights that were never really surmounted until the invention of the motion picture camera. So, although both of the basic structures of the drama continue to be employed in modern times, in general the focussed form has become conventional for the realistic, representational stage, and the panoramic has found its greatest usefulness in the movies.

Such in very general terms and brief compass is the history of the basic forms of the drama. There will be an opportunity to consider their modern counterparts at greater length in the next chapter. But now it is time to demonstrate the use of the structural analysis in detail and at length by reverting to the play which has served us as an example of many specific aspects of technique.

Ghosts: An Analysis and Synthesis

Ibsen was the most meticulous of craftsmen. In an art whose transitory nature often encourages haste, expediency, and compromise, he worked slowly and painstakingly. *Ghosts* was two years in the writing, and it is as nearly perfect technically as a play in its form can be. Surviving among Ibsen's papers at his death was a small collection of notes made while his plays were being planned; they were made available in a volume accurately titled *From Ibsen's Workshop*. Among the notes on *Ghosts* are three which may serve as an indication of the playwright's intentions.

1) "The play is to be like a picture of life. Belief undermined. But it does not do to say so. The Orphanage — 'for the sake of others.' "

These jottings are a kind of shorthand which it is not difficult to interpret. It is Ibsen's intention to write a play which shall carry conviction
in part because of its verisimilitude. He will use the stage of realistic
illusion, he will create characters and design their actions so that the
audience will react as to actual experience. " The play is to be like a
picture of life."

It is important to note, however, that before Ibsen indicates who his
characters are to be, or what action they will be involved in, he determines on the theme, the central idea, of his play. " Belief undermined."
This theme, he reminds himself, must not be explicitly stated. If the
play is to be like a picture of life, the central idea must emerge from
the action and the characters, not from the comment of an observer or
chorus character. Everything the play is to accomplish must be accomplished within the framework of daily, domestic experience.

The reference to the orphanage indicates that Ibsen had chosen, along
with his central idea, a controlling symbol. The central position of this
object in the action and the thematic pattern of the finished play was
planned from the author's earliest thinking about the work. *The playwright commences with an idea.*

2) " A leading point: she has been a believer and a romantic — this
is not entirely obliterated by the standpoint reached later." The phrasing
of this note is, at least, awkward, but its meaning is not difficult to
decipher. This is the first reference to Mrs. Alving, but we must observe
that she is not yet given a name, or a biography, or an action. She is
conceived as an active essence, to be clothed in flesh as work on the play
proceeds. The central figure is designed to illustrate the theme already
determined, and the action will be constructed afterwards as a vehicle
for the revelation of character.

3) " Marriage for external reasons, even when these are religious or
moral, brings a Nemesis upon the offspring." Without reading the play
it would be difficult to see how this secondary theme is united with
" Belief undermined " to serve as a basis for the action of *Ghosts*. The
clue lies in the curious phrase " external reasons," which, with the reference to religion and morality, seems to suggest conventional ideals and
hence the " belief " which is to be undermined by the action. However,
as with the major theme, " it will not do to say so ": the idea must be
stated by the action, not by the actor, except incidentally or by way
of summary. Verbal statement may not replace dramatic action, though
it may reinforce it.

These Workshop Notes indicate how much *Ghosts* was the result of
careful planning. The nature of the artistic unit was determined before

any writing was done: the design, the action, situations, chief character, and major symbol always controlled by the central idea, the theme. Partly as a result of this careful planning, partly because of the dramatic form he chose, Ibsen was able to create a work of the greatest economy and compression. A single setting, five characters and about twelve hours of elapsed time serve to project the tragedy of Mrs. Alving.

Such compression and economy almost inevitably indicate that the playwright is working with the focussed form of the drama, and it is instructive to compare the structure of *Ghosts* with the structure of *Oedipus Rex,* where the same careful balance of exposition and action throughout the play creates a similar tension, a sense of swift and inevitable doom. But Ibsen is also writing for the representational stage (see Chapter VI), which gave him at once more devices for making his point than were available to Sophocles and greater temptations to digress. The spareness of *Ghosts,* never apparent until the play is carefully analyzed, is one of the characteristics which makes it a model of the revitalized focussed form in the modern theater.

In spite of this spareness, this compression and economy, the plot of *Ghosts* is the complex working out of a series of human desires, all in conflict. Stated simply, they are: REGINA's attempt to hang on to her blessings, and get more; ENGSTRAND's attempt to get Regina for his house; OSWALD's attempt to get Regina for his nurse; MANDERS' attempt to keep everybody in a moral line: and MRS. ALVING's attempt to preserve the honor of the family name. These strangely assorted characters are brought together and their conflicting desires united into a single action by the building and dedication of the orphanage; the focus and the three climaxes of the action are related to the Captain Alving Home. In spite of the singleness of focus, then, and the compression of the story, there is plenty of excitement, horror, even melodramatic incident in the play — incest, arson, madness, murder, are seen or suggested — but each event exists not for itself or its attendant thrill, but for its relationship to the central idea: the revelation of Mrs. Alving's character and the forces responsible for it, her awakening to the realization that the free development of the individual is more important than obedience to ghosts.

The incidents that Ibsen selected from the whole story to present in action and the arrangement of these incidents in the play determine the play's structure. From this selection we can in part discover the point that Ibsen intends to make. The plot of the play, the *whole story,* might be narrated as follows: In a small, dull, provincial town, narrow-minded, out of the stream of the times and of progressive thought, Helene is persuaded by her aunts to marry Captain Alving; the marriage is advantageous, as a large sum of money is settled on her, but no love, no companionship, no mutual respect is involved. Learning of her husband's infidelity, Helene flies to Manders, the family parson, with whom she is deeply in love. He rejects her, reminding her of her duty. She allows herself to be persuaded and returns to Alving. She tries to make the best of her aunts' bargain and preserve the honor of the family in the public eye. She keeps Alving at home by sharing his excesses, buys off the maid who had become his mistress, sends Oswald to Paris, takes in her husband's bastard daughter as maid-companion, and after his death resolves to build an orphanage to maintain the fiction of his greatness and the good name of the family. At this point the play begins, and the forward action completes the story.

But it is necessary to observe not only the chronological order of events in the plot, the whole story, but the arrangement of these events in the structure of the dramatic unit, the play. Ibsen does not choose to narrate the story from the beginning, though that is a possible way to do it. Rather, he begins almost at the end, twelve hours before the conclusion of a plot that covers some thirty years in the unravelling. Within those twelve hours he arranges his incidents so that we may know the whole story, though not in the direct order of its happening. Some of the incidents he chooses to show us in the action of the play, some to have narrated in the exposition. And the precise way that he puts together or balances exposition and action, past and present, expresses and emphasizes the theme for which *Ghosts* is the vehicle.

Ibsen's handling of exposition is particularly noteworthy, since he makes it (as we have seen from the analysis of the first act) a functioning part of the forward movement of the play. Thus the spectator is never aware that he is being given information for information's sake; each scene " is like a picture of life "; there are no heralds, messengers, or First and Second Gentlemen. Exposition is revealed incidentally, in the course of the action, and a past incident may require many scenes for its complete narration. For instance, a major controlling factor in the present is the past relationship between Helen and Pastor Manders. Yet this is never explained directly in a connected discourse. Instead (p. 23) Helene greets Manders' refusal to stay in the house by " making fun " of him. The joke is not explained, and we credit the remark to Manders' embarrassment. Two scenes later, Mrs. Alving's defense of Oswald forces Manders to read her a moral lesson, just as he had " in the moment of [her] life when [she] needed counsel most." He reminds her that she had once left her husband and sought refuge with her priest, her (apparently disinterested) friend and guide. It is not until the second act, however, that the full truth about their relationship becomes known to us: that she had come to her " disinterested " friend in the fullness of love for him, crying, " Here I am, take me! "

The revelation is of something more than the past acquaintance of Manders and Mrs. Alving. That she was passionately in love with him and disgusted with her husband is another demonstration of how the " ghost " of old ideas — here of a wife's duty, even though she be a wife in legal title only — could dominate the most powerful and natural emotion, could, in fact, kill it.

And each bit of the story of the past is provoked by some action in the present, increasing the dramatic effect of the present action. One of the stunning theatrical moments in the play is the juxtaposition at the end of the first act of Oswald's love-making to Regina and the revelation of his father's love affair with her mother. The idea, explicitly stated in the title of the play, is here dramatized, brought to vivid life on the stage in an example of dramatic structure at its most artificial, economical, and effective.

A corollary to exposition is preparation, a device of great importance if the play is to be a picture of life, to appear realistic. Although the events of the plot cannot always be anticipated by the spectator, they never come as a total surprise to him — unawares, he has been prepared for them by what a French playwright called " the logic of events." There is, in *Ghosts*, always a logical reason for every entrance and exit; no one enters unannounced at the moment of greatest dramatic convenience. For instance, the necessary scene of the first act, in which Manders and Oswald argue over the codes by which men live, precipitates the more important revelations of the past and the subsequent actions of the present in Mrs. Alving's house. Yet, notice how carefully Ibsen leads up to it. He first establishes Oswald as resting in his room in the opening scene of the play. At frequent intervals thereafter we are reminded of him, that he is refreshing himself, and that he will be coming down for a walk shortly. Thus his entrance in the fourth scene seems to take place in the normal course of daily living; the spectator is never aware that a debate is being deliberately set up on which the action of the play is to turn.

Likewise there is a logical reason for every climax. The burning of the orphanage is a sensational incident and it brings the curtain of Act Two down at an exciting moment. But early in the first act Mrs. Alving has revealed that Engstrand's carelessness with matches has already caused one small fire — and he has been sent off to light the lamps in

preparation for a prayer meeting. Even the suspense devices, the most
" theatrical " effects in the play, follow a logical pattern. When Manders
interrupts Mrs. Alving in the final scene of the second act, she is about to
disclose the whole story of Regina's parentage and straighten matters
out for the young people. Manders prevents the revelation, and the
orphanage fire which follows is thus able to work its catastrophic effect on
Oswald. But Manders' interruption is more than just a theatrical suspense device. In the discussion of the active essence of his character we
have seen that it is a kind of symbolic action: his is the way of life that
prevents the truth in general from being known. His intrusion at this
point is thus not only a structural necessity, but is closely related to the
central idea of the play.

Logical preparation and disguised exposition are necessities for the
play that is to be like a picture of life. But the playwright must also
arouse the interest of the audience, must keep his spectators guessing
about what will happen next, must somehow create suspense. The author
must be continually raising questions, the answers to which are postponed. Sometimes Ibsen does this openly. In the first scene between
Regina and Engstrand, the " father " asks whether she is prepared to
throw herself away on a houseful of orphans. She replies, mysteriously,
" If things were to go as I want them to, then — Well, there's no telling." Engstrand asks, not unnaturally, what may happen, but she merely
replies, " Never you mind." The device is hardly subtle, yet it is not
inappropriate to the characters and the situation: Regina feels herself
superior to Engstrand and is determined not to reveal her plans to him.

In a larger sense every scene in the play is a suspense device; every
scene stops, but is not finished. The audience is always left with the
feeling that there is more to be revealed. At the end of the scene between
Regina and Engstrand, for instance, all the questions that have been
raised between them are as unanswered as when they were posed, but
Manders is coming and Engstrand must leave. Suspense is an even greater
issue at the end of an act. The curtain always descends on a major
question which not only will serve to bridge the intermission but will
underline and emphasize the issue of the play as it reaches a climactic
statement.

We have seen that much of the exposition of the past arises out of
a conflict between characters in the present situation, and that much
of the preparation, the suspense, is achieved by the same device. Conflict, of course, is one of the basic dramatic patterns, whether it be the
struggle of the good and evil angels for the soul of Humanum Genus in
the medieval morality or the more direct contest for supremacy between

the protagonist and the antagonist, say between Dionysos and Pentheus. Conflict is the basis even of *Prometheus Bound,* where the hero cannot move and the " villain " is seen only through the parade of his representatives. *Ghosts,* although it is a character play and a play of ideas, is also a play of conflicts. The major conflict is not a simple one; it is not Mrs. Alving *versus* Manders. To state the whole plot of the play in terms of conflict it is necessary to return for an analogue to the medieval morality: *Ghosts* is the conflict between ways of life for the soul of Mrs. Alving.

That is, the conflict is essentially moral or spiritual, external to the central character. Yet there is plenty of concrete human opposition in the play. Ibsen opens with a disagreement between Engstrand and Regina over her future, through which he is able to establish much of the basic exposition of the play. The relationship of Manders and Mrs. Alving is revealed during a series of agreements and disagreements over literature and various matters connected with the dedication of the orphanage. The fourth scene of the first act turns on a conflict of creeds between Manders and Oswald which sets up the major theme of the play.

In general, the total structure of *Ghosts* exemplifies the careful selection and arrangement of materials to provide constant conflict out of which exposition of the past, present action, and preparation for the future (suspense) can arise with the appearance of complete naturalness, preserving the effect of a picture of life.

As a kind of prologue to this chapter we have analyzed in some detail the first act of *Ghosts.* Before moving on to the details of later acts it will be useful to review that analysis, to see how the careful balance of exposition and action throughout the act builds up the idea of the close connection between past and present, and how the great amount of exposition emphasizes the *influence* of the past on the present, one of the play's major ideas. The logic of Ibsen's technique never allows the spectator to question the reality of what is happening; everything is prepared for and explained, and the suspense device of asking but not answering questions keeps the audience constantly alert and interested in the outcome.

The second act of *Ghosts* comes to a point, a climax, just as the first act did. In the penultimate scene, Mrs. Alving declares, " Now I see the connection. . . . I see it now for the first time. And now I can speak." The whole act is a gradual revelation to the protagonist of the meaning of her past experience. She understands now what forced her to marry Alving, what forced her to obey Manders, what forced her to lies and hypocrisy for the family honor. That thing was the way of her world, the code of her society.

It will not be necessary to analyze Act Two in as great detail as Act One, since it continues the structural principles established by its predecessor, but certain scene-by-scene observations will demonstrate how the structure builds towards the climactic moment of self-awareness. In the first scene we learn that Mrs. Alving's wide reading in " liberal " publications has opened her eyes to the facts of life, of nature. Although these publications are not named, we may assume that they are popular philosophical treatises inspired by the discoveries of Darwin and the progressive social thinkers whose English counterparts might have been Spencer or Ruskin or John Stuart Mill. In addition we learn of the depth of her love for Manders and how coldly he turned her away, and how Engstrand was persuaded to marry Johanna for a sum of money. In the second scene we are given Engstrand's version of the story of his marriage, complete with pious clichés. We in the audience know how hypocritical they are, since at the very start of the play we were permitted to see into Engstrand's evil intentions towards Regina and his scheming to get the better of Manders. As a passage of dramatic irony, the scene makes us intensely aware of Manders' essential folly; we can assume that Mrs. Alving can hardly shut her eyes to this exposure of the weakness of the man on whom she has relied for moral instruction. In the following scene Oswald tells his mother something of his illness and discloses that he believes himself responsible for the destruction of his future. Mrs. Alving is horrified that her endeavor to keep the father's sins a secret has resulted in this despair in her son. The brief appearance of Regina in Scene Four, however, prepares us for Oswald's suggestion in Scene Five that she may be his salvation, that she can restore the " joy of life " for him. This is the final blow to Mrs. Alving's security; she had forgotten about the " joy of life " and acted, thanks to Manders and the code he represents, as if life were a " vale of tears."

These events are placed in order of increasing impact within the structure of the whole unit: her liberated mind, Manders' essential folly as he is taken in by meaningless clichés, the terrible effect of her behavior on Oswald, whom she loved and wished to protect, and the forgotten idea that life might be a thing of joy. These events and ideas add up to her conclusion in the final scene: " I see it now for the first time. And now I can speak." The whole act has been a careful preparation for this moment, yet she cannot speak even now because of Manders' symbolic entrance and the ensuing catastrophe. And the final lines of the act are a summary of the play's action up to this point. To Manders' exclama-

tion that the fire " is a judgment on this abode of sin," Mrs. Alving
replies, " Yes, of course." But this it not an automatic acceptance of
Manders' judgment as in the first act. Her apparent assent is really a dis-
sent; she understands much more than Manders is capable of meaning.

The third act reaches its climax as Mrs. Alving stands undecided over
her insane son. As in the preceding acts, the situations have been selected
and arranged, the action and exposition balanced, to lead inexorably to
this conclusion. One by one her supports are taken away: first Manders,
forever and humiliatingly enslaved by the triumphant Engstrand; then
Regina, impelled by the ambition Mrs. Alving has implanted in her and
her own reluctance to wear herself out nursing sick people — " I, too,
have the joy of life in me," she points out. Mrs. Alving is left alone with
her son, on whom her ambitions and hopes have been settled. But even
the small comfort of his return to her side is snatched away as he tells her
the full truth about his disease and its inevitable end. The final conflict
of the play, whether she will agree to give him " a helping hand," brings
her face to face with the final realization. " I who gave you life? " she
protests, and Oswald replies, mercilessly, " I never asked you for life.
And what sort of life is it you have given me? " Although they are
speaking, as it were, biologically, the echoes of the discussion in the
second act are inescapable. The rising sun which is to enable Oswald to
see his home for the first time finds him shrunk into his chair, relaxed,
expressionless, staring stupidly before him. And at this moment Mrs.
Alving is finally forced to see with absolute clarity the tragedy for which
she is responsible.

The rising sun is, of course, an ironic symbol of the meaning of the
play. In Chapter IV we have considered the function of several of the
symbolic objects and actions in *Ghosts,* most importantly the orphanage
and the champagne bottle. We should by now be aware that in so tightly
constructed a play there is hardly an object or action which, important
to the development of the plot, is not equally important in the revelation
of the theme. Before moving on to a synthesis of the elements we have
been discussing, we may pause for a paragraph or two over another
aspect of symbolism.

When Oswald makes his first appearance in Act One he is smoking
a pipe and Parson Manders is at once struck by his resemblance to his
father. By the end of the play, of course, we know how deep that
resemblance really goes; for the moment it seems only a superficial one
largely created by the pipe. Actually, the situation is designed to reveal
not only the surface resemblance, but Oswald's heritage. He remembers
how he had smoked the same pipe as a small boy and was overcome

with nausea. In this narrated action there is a symbol of pollution spreading and infecting the young son. We should recall, perhaps, how the nineteenth century regarded tobacco smoking in the house (and Mrs. Alving will not have the pipe smoked in her sitting room). Later Mrs. Alving will explain to Manders that she sent Oswald to Paris that he might not be " poisoned by merely breathing the air in this polluted home." But since the scene with Oswald has preceded this statement, it should be clear to the spectator that Oswald has been polluted, that he has inherited far more from Captain Alving than his name.

Such a situation, involving a symbolic action and a symbolic object, involves far more. It creates a symbolic pattern of ideas available for reference and extension and closely related to the theme of the play. A more important and more obvious example of the same device is in Mrs. Alving's use of the word *ghosts*. At first it refers simply to a repeated action, as, at the end of the first act, Oswald and Regina repeat the behavior of Alving and Johanna. But out of this image, Mrs. Alving makes a symbolic idea of the widest general application; it is here that Ibsen relates his specific human experience to human experience in general.

The final step in the discussion of a work of art is to see it whole, to step back from the close analysis of the parts and, with fuller knowledge, experience the play as a dramatic unit. From the examination of the structure, characterization, action, and symbols of *Ghosts* we may decide that the whole play is really two things — a characterization of Mrs. Alving and an interpretation of her character, a statement of her meaning in relation to the daily life of those who watch from the auditorium.

In conclusion, then, we must *synthesize* Mrs. Alving by restating her story in terms of what we now know to be the function of every element in the dramatic structure.

She began life as a dutiful member of a tradition-bound society, perhaps in love with Pastor Manders. Captain Alving came to town, obviously fascinating, wealthy, " full of the joy of living " — to a " second-rate town which had none of the joy of living to offer him, but only dissipations." Since he had nothing but routine work to do, boredom and tippling resulted. Helene had been taught duty; " everything seemed to turn upon duty, my duty or his duty." Even before Oswald was born, Captain Alving was philandering. So Mrs. Alving fled to Manders and refused to return to Alving despite his pleas. But Manders told her that " it is not a wife's part to be her husband's judge. . . .

[It was her] bounden duty to [bear] the cross that a Higher Will had laid upon her." She did not question his authority, or remind him that the Higher Will was the will of her aunts. Manders turned her back to Alving, although she had come to him half-mad, crying, " Here I am, take me! "

Mrs. Alving, that is, denied her nature, her rights as an individual, and assumed her " duties." Examined in the cold light of the Norwegian sun at the end of Act Three, these duties assume particularly horrible shapes. Alving went from bad to worse, seducing the maid and begetting Regina. To the maid Mrs. Alving gave money and sent her off to Engstrand, to prevent gossip. To keep Alving at home and prevent gossip, she drank with him and listened to his ribaldry — all to obey the social code which decreed that unhappy family affairs must be borne in secret. Her duty led her to compound a felony in connection with Regina's birth, and to debase herself in keeping her husband company. Oswald was sent to the country at seven and later to Paris to get him away from the " polluted " atmosphere and shield him from the truth; yet it is on this shield that he is ironically returned, dying. On Mrs. Alving fell all the care of the property which she struggled to preserve and improve for the " honor and glory " of the Alving name.

In the course of the action of the play she is led to realize that there is no escape from the inexorable process of nature; Oswald cannot escape his heritage by living in Paris. She recognizes that certain of the ideals she has been taught to cling to are ghosts, old worn-out beliefs; these are presented largely in terms of marriage, as a convenient symbol of all relationships between men. And as exemplified by the inexorable process of nature, she cannot escape the consequences of belief in these ghosts. Her final tragic discovery is that clinging to her ideals in the face of reason and nature has kept her, Alving, perhaps Manders, and certainly Oswald from living a full individual life of happiness and self-realization.

The responsibility, Ibsen makes clear, lies both within her and without her. She is the cause of the tragedy insofar as she accepts the duty imposed on her. But part of the responsibility must be borne by the social order, as represented by Manders, the dead way of thinking, the denial of life. The final dramatic symbol, summing up the action and theme of the play, comes at the awful moment when she must take the life of her son, her victim, as he cries idiotically for the symbol of life, of light, of truth — the sun, which, for the first time in the play, bathes the peaks and glaciers in the distance with bright morning light.

ANTONY AND CLEOPATRA

by William Shakespeare

ᴵᴵᵗᵗᵗ

CHARACTERS

ANTONY, 〗
OCTAVIUS CÆSAR, 〗 *triumvirs*
LEPIDUS, 〗

SEXTUS POMPEIUS.

DOMITIUS ENOBARBUS, 〗
VENTIDIUS, 〗
EROS, 〗
SCARUS, 〗 *friends to Antony*
DERCETAS, 〗
DEMETRIUS, 〗
PHILO, 〗

MÆCENAS, 〗
AGRIPPA, 〗
DOLABELLA, 〗 *friends to Cæsar*
PROCULEIUS, 〗
THYREUS, 〗
GALLUS, 〗

MENAS, 〗
MENECRATES, 〗 *friends to Sextus Pompeius*
VARRIUS, 〗

TAURUS, *lieutenant-general to Cæsar*

CANIDIUS, *lieutenant-general to Antony*

SILIUS, *an officer in Ventidius's army*

EUPHRONIUS, *a schoolmaster*

ALEXAS, 〗
MARDIAN, *a eunuch,* 〗 *attendants on*
SELEUCUS, 〗 *Cleopatra*
DIOMEDES, 〗

LAMPRIUS, *a soothsayer*

CLEOPATRA, *queen of Egypt*

OCTAVIA, *sister to Cæsar, and wife to Antony*

CHARMIAN, 〗 *attendants on Cleopatra*
IRAS, 〗

A Clown.

Officers, Soldiers, Messengers, and other Attendants.

SCENE: *In several parts of the Roman Empire.*

ACT ONE

[Alexandria]   *Enter* DEMETRIUS *and* PHILO.

PHILO

Nay, but this dotage of our general's
O'erflows the measure: those his goodly eyes,
That o'er the files and musters of the war
Have glow'd like plated Mars, now bend, now turn
The office and devotion of their view
Upon a tawny front. His captain's heart,
Which in the scuffles of great fights hath burst
The buckles on his breast, reneges all temper,[1]
And is become the bellows and the fan
To cool a gipsy's lust.
                        Look where they come:
Take but good note, and you shall see in him
The triple pillar of the world transform'd
Into a strumpet's fool. Behold and see.
(*Flourish. Enter* ANTONY, CLEOPATRA, *her Ladies, the train, with Eunuchs fanning her.*)

---

[1] rejects all restraint

CLEOPATRA

If it be love indeed, tell me how much.

ANTONY

There's beggary in the love that can be
reckon'd.

CLEOPATRA

I'll set a bourn [2] how far to be belov'd.

ANTONY

Then must thou needs find out new heaven,
new earth.

(*Enter a Messenger.*)

MESSENGER

News, my good lord, from Rome.

ANTONY

           Grates me — the sum.

CLEOPATRA

Nay, hear them, Antony:
Fulvia [3] perchance is angry; or who knows
If the scarce-bearded Cæsar have not sent
His powerful mandate to you, " Do this, or
this;
Take in that kingdom, and enfranchise that;
Perform 't, or else we damn thee."

ANTONY

           How, my love?

CLEOPATRA

Perchance? nay, and most like:
You must not stay here longer, your dismis-
sion
Is come from Cæsar, therefore hear it, Antony.
Where 's Fulvia's process? (Cæsar's I would
say.) Both?
Call in the messengers. As I am Egypt's
queen,
Thou blushest, Antony, and that blood of
thine
Is Cæsar's homager: else so thy cheek pays
shame

   [2] limit
   [3] Antony's wife

When shrill-tongu'd Fulvia scolds. The messengers!

ANTONY

Let Rome in Tiber melt, and the wide arch
Of the rang'd empire fall! Here is my space;
Kingdoms are clay: our dungy earth alike
Feeds beast as man; the nobleness of life
Is to do thus: [*Embracing*] when such a mu-
tual pair
And such a twain can do 't, in which I bind,
On pain of punishment, the world to weet [4]
We stand up peerless.

CLEOPATRA

         Excellent falsehood!
Why did he marry Fulvia, and not love her?
I 'll seem the fool I am not; Antony
Will be himself.

ANTONY

         But stirr'd by Cleopatra.
Now for the love of Love, and her soft hours,
Let 's not confound the time with conference
harsh:
There 's not a minute of our lives should
stretch
Without some pleasure now. What sport to-
night?

CLEOPATRA

Hear the ambassadors.

ANTONY

         Fie, wrangling queen;
Whom everything becomes, to chide, to
laugh,
To weep; whose every passion fully strives
To make itself, in thee, fair, and admir'd!
No messenger but thine, and all alone
Tonight we'll wander through the streets,
and note
The qualities of people. Come, my queen,
Last night you did desire it. Speak not to us.
(*Exeunt* ANTONY *and* CLEOPATRA *with
their train.*)

DEMETRIUS

Is Cæsar with Antonius priz'd so slight?

   [4] know

PHILO

Sir, sometimes, when he is not Antony,
He comes too short of that great property
Which still should go with Antony.

DEMETRIUS

          I am full sorry
That he approves [5] the common liar, who
Thus speaks of him at Rome; but I will hope
Of better deeds tomorrow. Rest you happy!
                         (*Exeunt.*)

Enter ENOBARBUS, LAMPRIUS, *a Soothsayer,*
CHARMIAN, IRAS, MARDIAN, *and* ALEXAS.

CHARMIAN

Lord Alexas, sweet Alexas, most anything
Alexas, almost most absolute Alexas,
where's the soothsayer that you prais'd
so to the queen? O, that I knew this
husband, which, you say, must change
his horns [6] with garlands!

ALEXAS

Soothsayer!

LAMPRIUS

Your will?

CHARMIAN

Is this the man? Is 't you sir, that know
things?

LAMPRIUS

In nature's infinite book of secrecy
A little I can read.

ALEXAS

        Show him your hand.

ENOBARBUS

Bring in the banquet quickly; wine enough
Cleopatra's health to drink.

CHARMIAN

Good sir, give me good fortune.

    [5] confirms
    [6] i.e., the cuckold's horns

LAMPRIUS

I make not, but foresee.

CHARMIAN

Pray then, foresee me one.

LAMPRIUS

You shall be yet far fairer than you are.

CHARMIAN

He means in flesh.

IRAS

No, you shall paint when you are old.

CHARMIAN

Wrinkles forbid!

ALEXAS

Vex not his prescience, be attentive.

CHARMIAN

Hush!

LAMPRIUS

You shall be more beloving than belov'd.

CHARMIAN

I had rather heat my liver with drinking.

ALEXAS

Nay, hear him.

CHARMIAN

Good now, some excellent fortune! Let me be
married to three kings in a forenoon,
and widow them all: let me have a child
at fifty, to whom Herod of Jewry may
do homage: find me to marry me with
Octavius Cæsar, and companion me
with my mistress.

LAMPRIUS

You shall outlive the lady whom you serve.

CHARMIAN

O excellent! I love long life better than figs.

LAMPRIUS

You have seen and prov'd a fairer former fortune
Than that which is to approach.

CHARMIAN

Then belike my children shall have no names: prithee, how many boys and wenches must I have?

LAMPRIUS

If every of your wishes had a womb,
And fertile every wish, a million.

CHARMIAN

Out, fool! I forgive thee for a witch.

ALEXAS

You think none but your sheets are privy to your wishes.

CHARMIAN

Nay, come, tell Iras hers.

ALEXAS

We'll know all our fortunes.

ENOBARBUS

Mine, and most of our fortunes tonight, shall be, drunk to bed.

IRAS

There's a palm presages chastity, if nothing else.

CHARMIAN

E'en as the o'erflowing Nilus presageth famine.

IRAS

Go, you wild bedfellow, you cannot soothsay.

CHARMIAN

Nay, if an oily palm be not a fruitful prognostication, I cannot scratch mine ear. Prithee, tell her but a workaday fortune.

LAMPRIUS

Your fortunes are alike —

IRAS

But how, but how? give me particulars.

LAMPRIUS

I have said.

IRAS

Am I not an inch of fortune better than she?

CHARMIAN

Well, if you were but an inch of fortune better than I, where would you choose it?

IRAS

Not in my husband's nose.

CHARMIAN

Our worser thoughts heavens mend! Alexas, — come, his fortune, his fortune! O, let him marry a woman that cannot go, sweet Isis, I beseech thee, and let her die too, and give him a worse, and let worse follow worse, till the worst of all follow him laughing to his grave, fifty-fold a cuckold! Good Isis, hear me this prayer, though thou deny me a matter of more weight; good Isis, I beseech thee!

IRAS

Amen, dear goddess, hear that prayer of the people! for, as it is a heart-breaking to see a handsome man loose-wiv'd, so it is a deadly sorrow to behold a foul knave uncuckolded: therefore, dear Isis, keep decorum, and fortune him accordingly!

CHARMIAN

Amen.

ALEXAS

Lo, now, if it lay in their hands to make me a cuckold, they would make themselves whores, but they'd do 't!

ENOBARBUS

Hush! here comes Antony.

CHARMIAN

    Not he, the queen.
(*Enter* CLEOPATRA.)

CLEOPATRA

Saw you my lord?

ENOBARBUS

No, lady.

CLEOPATRA

Was he not here?

CHARMIAN

No, madam.

CLEOPATRA

He was dispos'd to mirth, but on the sudden
A Roman thought hath struck him. Enobarbus!

ENOBARBUS

Madam?

CLEOPATRA

Seek him, and bring him hither. Where's
Alexas?

ALEXAS

Here at your service. My lord approaches.

CLEOPATRA

We will not look upon him: go with us.

(*Exeunt.*)

(*Enter* ANTONY *with a Messenger and Attendants.*)

MESSENGER

Fulvia thy wife first came into the field.

ANTONY

Against my brother Lucius?

MESSENGER

Ay:
But soon that war had end, and the time's
state
Made friends of them, jointing their force
'gainst Cæsar,
Whose better issue in the war from Italy
Upon the first encounter drave them.

ANTONY

Well, what worst?

MESSENGER

The nature of bad news infects the teller.

ANTONY

When it concerns the fool or coward. On:
Things that are past are done, with me. 'Tis
thus;
Who tells me true, though in his tale lie
death,
I hear him as he flatter'd.

MESSENGER

Labienus
(This is stiff news) hath with his Parthian
force
Extended Asia: from Euphrates
His conquering banner shook, from Syria
To Lydia and to Ionia,
Whilst —

ANTONY

Antony, thou wouldst say —

MESSENGER

O, my lord!

ANTONY

Speak to me home, mince not the general
tongue,[7]
Name Cleopatra as she is call'd in Rome;
Rail thou in Fulvia's phrase, and taunt my
faults
With such full license, as both truth and
malice
Have power to utter. O, then we bring forth
weeds
When our quick minds lie still, and our ills
told us
Is as our earing.[8] Fare thee well awhile.

MESSENGER

At your noble pleasure.

ANTONY

From Sicyon, ho, the news! Speak there!

1st ATTENDANT

The man from Sicyon, is there such an one?

---

[7] common report
[8] ploughing

2nd ATTENDANT

He stays upon your will.

ANTONY

       Let him appear.
These strong Egyptian fetters I must break,
Or lose myself in dotage.
    (*Enter another Messenger.*)
          What are you?

2nd MESSENGER

Fulvia thy wife is dead.

ANTONY

       Where died she?

2nd MESSENGER

In Sicyon:
Her length of sickness, with what else more
   serious
Importeth thee to know, this bears.
       (*Gives a letter.*)

ANTONY

         Forbear me.
    (*Exit 2nd Messenger.*)
There's a great spirit gone! Thus did I desire
   it:
What our contempts doth often hurl from
   us,
We wish it ours again; the present pleasure,
By revolution lowering, doth become
The opposite of itself: she's good, being
   gone;
The hand could pluck her back that shov'd
   her on.
I must from this enchanting queen break off,
Ten thousand harms, more than the ills I
   know,
My idleness doth hatch. How now! Enobar-
   bus!
    (*Re-enter ENOBARBUS.*)

ENOBARBUS

What's your pleasure, sir?

ANTONY

I must with haste from hence.

ENOBARBUS

Why then we kill all our women. We see how
   mortal an unkindness is to them; if they
   suffer our departure, death's the word.

ANTONY

I must be gone.

ENOBARBUS

Under a compelling occasion, let women die:
   it were pity to cast them away for nothing, though, between them and a great
   cause, they should be esteemed nothing.
   Cleopatra, catching but the least noise
   of this, dies instantly; I have seen her
   die twenty times upon far poorer moment: I do think there is mettle in
   death, which commits some loving act
   upon her, she hath such a celerity in dying.

ANTONY

She is cunning past man's thought.

ENOBARBUS

Alack, sir, no, her passions are made of nothing but the finest part of pure love: we
   cannot call her winds and waters sighs
   and tears; they are greater storms and
   tempests than almanacs can report: this
   cannot be cunning in her; if it be, she
   makes a shower of rain as well as Jove.

ANTONY

Would I had never seen her!

ENOBARBUS

O, sir, you had then left unseen a wonderful
   piece of work, which not to have been
   blest withal would have discredited your
   travel.

ANTONY

Fulvia is dead.

ENOBARBUS

Sir?

ANTONY

Fulvia is dead.

ENOBARBUS

Fulvia?

ANTONY

Dead.

ENOBARBUS

Why, sir, give the gods a thankful sacrifice. When it pleaseth their deities to take the wife of a man from him, it shows the man the tailors of the earth, comforting therein, that when old robes are worn out, there are members to make new. If there were no more women but Fulvia, then had you indeed a cut, and the case to be lamented: this grief is crown'd with consolation; your old smock brings forth a new petticoat, and indeed the tears live in an onion that should water this sorrow.

ANTONY

The business she hath broached in the state
Cannot endure my absence.

ENOBARBUS

And the business you have broach'd here cannot be without you, especially that of Cleopatra's, which wholly depends on your abode.

ANTONY

No more light answers. Let our officers
Have notice what we purpose. I shall break
The cause of our expedience [9] to the queen,
And get her leave to part. For not alone
The death of Fulvia, with more urgent
    touches,
Do strongly speak to us, but the letters too
Of many our contriving friends in Rome
Petition us at home: Sextus Pompeius
Hath given the dare to Cæsar, and commands
The empire of the sea: our slippery people,
Whose love is never link'd to the deserver,
Till his deserts are past, begin to throw
Pompey the Great, and all his dignities,
Upon his son, who high in name and power,

Higher than both in blood and life, stands up
For the main soldier: whose quality, going on,
The sides o' the world may danger. Much is
    breeding,
Which, like the courser's hair, hath yet but
    life,[10]
And not a serpent's poison. Say our pleasure,
To such whose places under us require,
Our quick remove from hence.

ENOBARBUS

I shall do 't.   (Exeunt.)

Enter CLEOPATRA, CHARMIAN, IRAS, and ALEXAS.

CLEOPATRA

Where is he?

CHARMIAN

I did not see him since.

CLEOPATRA

See where he is, who 's with him, what he
    does:
I did not send you: if you find him sad,
Say I am dancing; if in mirth, report
That I am sudden sick: quick, and return.
                    (Exit ALEXAS.)

CHARMIAN

Madam, methinks, if you did love him dearly,
You do not hold the method to enforce
The like from him.

CLEOPATRA

    What should I do, I do not?

CHARMIAN

In each thing give him way, cross him in
    nothing.

CLEOPATRA

Thou teachest like a fool: the way to lose
    him.

[9] haste

[10] A horsehair in water is supposed to become a snake.

CHARMIAN

Tempt him not so too far; I wish, forbear,
In time we hate that which we often fear.
But here comes Antony.

(*Enter* ANTONY.)

CLEOPATRA

         I am sick, and sullen.

ANTONY

I am sorry to give breathing to my purpose, —

CLEOPATRA

Help me away, dear Charmian, I shall fall,
It cannot be thus long, the sides of nature
Will not sustain it.

ANTONY

      Now, my dearest queen, —

CLEOPATRA

Pray you, stand farther from me.

ANTONY

         What 's the matter?

CLEOPATRA

I know, by that same eye, there 's some good
   news.
What says the married woman; you may go?
Would she had never given you leave to
   come!
Let her not say 'tis I that keep you here,
I have no power upon you; hers you are.

ANTONY

The gods best know —

CLEOPATRA

      O, never was there queen
So mightily betray'd! yet at the first
I saw the treasons planted.

ANTONY

      Cleopatra —

CLEOPATRA

Why should I think you can be mine, and
   true,

(Though you in swearing shake the throned
   gods)
Who have been false to Fulvia? Riotous madness,
To be entangled with those mouth-made
   vows,
Which break themselves in swearing!

ANTONY

      Most sweet queen —

CLEOPATRA

Nay, pray you, seek no color for your go-
   ing,
But bid farewell, and go: when you sued
   staying,
Then was the time for words: no going then;
Eternity was in our lips, and eyes,
Bliss in our brows' bent; none our parts so
   poor
But was a race [11] of heaven: they are so still,
Or thou, the greatest soldier of the world,
Art turn'd the greatest liar.

ANTONY

      How, now, lady?

CLEOPATRA

I would I had thy inches; thou shouldst know
There were a heart in Egypt.

ANTONY

        Hear me, queen:
The strong necessity of time commands
Our services awhile; but my full heart
Remains in use with you. Our Italy
Shines o'er with civil swords: Sextus Pom-
   peius
Makes his approaches to the port of Rome:
Equality of two domestic powers
Breed scrupulous faction: the hated, grown
   to strength,
Are newly grown to love: the condemn'd
   Pompey,
Rich in his father's honor, creeps apace
Into the hearts of such as have not thriv'd
Upon the present state, whose numbers
   threaten,

[11] taste

And quietness, grown sick of rest, would
  purge
By any desperate change. My more particular,
And that which most with you should safe
  my going,
Is Fulvia's death.

CLEOPATRA

Though age from folly could not give me
  freedom,
It does from childishness: can Fulvia die?

ANTONY

She 's dead, my queen:
Look here, and at thy sovereign leisure read
The garboils [12] she awak'd: at the last, best,
See when and where she died.

CLEOPATRA

                O most false love!
Where be the sacred vials thou shouldst fill
With sorrowful water? Now I see, I see,
In Fulvia's death, how mine receiv'd shall be.

ANTONY

Quarrel no more, but be prepar'd to know
The purposes I bear; which are, or cease,
As you shall give the advice. By the fire
That quickens Nilus' slime, I go from hence
Thy soldier, servant, making peace or war
As thou affect'st.

CLEOPATRA

                Cut my lace,[13] Charmian, come,
But let it be, I am quickly ill, and well,
So Antony loves.

ANTONY

                My precious queen, forbear,
And give true evidence to his love, which
  stands
An honorable trial.

CLEOPATRA

                So Fulvia told me.
I prithee, turn aside, and weep for her,
Then bid adieu to me, and say the tears

12 disturbances
13 corset-string

Belong to Egypt: good now, play one scene
Of excellent dissembling, and let it look
Like perfect honor.

ANTONY

You 'll heat my blood; no more!

CLEOPATRA

You can do better yet; but this is meetly.

ANTONY

Now, by my sword, —

CLEOPATRA

                And target. Still he mends,
But this is not the best. Look, prithee, Char-
  mian,
How this Herculean Roman does become
The carriage of his chafe.[14]

ANTONY

I 'll leave you, lady.

CLEOPATRA

                Courteous lord, one word.
Sir, you and I must part, but that 's not it:
Sir, you and I have lov'd, but there 's not it:
That you know well, something it is I
  would, —
O, my oblivion is a very Antony,
And I am all forgotten.

ANTONY

                But that your royalty
Holds idleness your subject, I should take
  you
For idleness itself.

CLEOPATRA

                'Tis sweating labor
To bear such idleness so near the heart
As Cleopatra this. But, sir, forgive me,
Since my becomings kill me, when they do
  not
Eye well to you. Your honor calls you
  hence,
Therefore be deaf to my unpitied folly,

14 anger

And all the gods go with you! Upon your
   sword
Sit laurel victory, and smooth success
Be strew'd before your feet!

ANTONY

            Let us go. Come;
Our separation so abides and flies,
That thou, residing here, go'st yet with me;
And I, hence fleeting, here remain with thee.
Away!   (*Exeunt.*)

[Rome]   *Enter* OCTAVIUS CÆSAR,
reading a letter, LEPIDUS, *and their train.*

CÆSAR

You may see, Lepidus, and henceforth know,
It is not Cæsar's natural vice to hate
Our great competitor: [15] from Alexandria
This is the news: he fishes, drinks, and wastes
The lamps of night in revel: is not more man-
   like
Than Cleopatra; nor the queen of Ptolemy
More womanly than he: hardy gave audience,
   or
Vouchsaf'd to think he had partners: you
   shall find there
A man who is the abstract of all faults
That all men follow.

LEPIDUS

           I must not think there are
Evils enow [16] to darken all his goodness:
His faults in him seem as the spots of heaven,
More fiery by night's blackness; hereditary
Rather than purchas'd; what he cannot
   change
Than what he chooses.

CÆSAR

You are too indulgent. Let us grant it is not
Amiss to tumble on the bed of Ptolemy,
To give a kingdom for a mirth, to sit
And keep the turn of tippling with a slave,
To reel the streets at noon, and stand the
   buffet [17]

With knaves that smell of sweat: say this be-
   comes him —
(As his composure must be rare indeed
Whom these things cannot blemish) yet
   must Antony
No way excuse his soils, when we do bear
So great weight in his lightness. If he fill'd
His vacancy with his voluptuousness,
Full surfeits, and the dryness of his bones,
Call on him for 't: but to confound such
   time,
That drums him from his sport, and speaks
   as loud
As his own state, and ours, 'tis to be chid;
As we rate boys, who, being mature in
   knowledge,
Pawn their experience to their present pleas-
   ure,
And so rebel to judgment. [18]

LEPIDUS

             Here 's more news.
(*Enter a Messenger.*)

MESSENGER

Thy biddings have been done, and every hour,
Most noble Cæsar, shalt thou have report
How 'tis abroad. Pompey is strong at sea,
And it appears he is belov'd of those
That only have fear'd Cæsar: to the ports
The discontents repair, and men's reports
Give him much wrong'd.

CÆSAR

         I should have known no less:
It had been taught us from the primal state,
That he which is was wish'd until he were;
And the ebb'd man, ne'er lov'd till ne'er
   worth love,
Comes dear'd by being lack'd. This common
   body,
Like to a vagabond flag [19] upon the stream,
Goes to and back, lackeying the varying tide,
To rot itself with motion.

MESSENGER

          Cæsar, I bring thee word,
Menecrates and Menas, famous pirates,

---

15 partner
16 sufficient
17 spar, box

18 i.e., good judgment
19 water plant

Make the sea serve them, which they ear and
      wound
With keels of every kind; many hot inroads
They make in Italy; the borders maritime
Lack blood to think on 't, and flush youth
      revolt:
No vessel can peep forth, but 'tis as soon
Taken as seen; for Pompey's name strikes
      more
Than could his war resisted.

CÆSAR

                    Antony,
Leave thy lascivious wassails. When thou
      once
Wast beaten from Modena, where thou
      slew'st
Hirtius and Pansa, consuls, at thy heel
Did famine follow, whom thou fought'st
      against,
(Though daintily brought up) with patience
      more
Than savages could suffer. Thou didst drink
The stale of horses, and the gilded puddle
Which beasts would cough at: thy palate
      then did deign
The roughest berry on the rudest hedge;
Yet, like the stag when snow the pasture
      sheets,
The barks of trees thou browsedst. On the
      Alps
It is reported thou didst eat strange flesh,
Which some did die to look on: and all this
(It wounds thine honor that I speak it now)
Was borne so like a soldier that thy cheek
So much as lank'd [20] not.

LEPIDUS
            'Tis pity of him.

CÆSAR

Let his shames quickly
Drive him to Rome; 'tis time we twain
Did show ourselves i' the field, and to that
      end
Assemble we immediate council: Pompey
Thrives in our idleness.

[20] grew thin

LEPIDUS

                    Tomorrow, Cæsar,
I shall be furnish'd to inform you rightly
Both what by sea and land I can be able
To front this present time.

CÆSAR

                    Till which encounter,
It is my business too. Farewell.

LEPIDUS

Farewell, my lord; what you shall know
      meantime
Of stirs abroad, I shall beseech you, sir,
To let me be partaker.

CÆSAR

                    Doubt not, sir,
I know it for my bond.   (Exeunt.)

[Alexandria]   Enter   CLEOPATRA,
CHARMIAN, IRAS, and MARDIAN.

CLEOPATRA

Charmian!

CHARMIAN

Madam?

CLEOPATRA

Ha, ha!
Give me to drink mandragora.[21]

CHARMIAN

                              Why, madam?

CLEOPATRA

That I might sleep out this great gap of time,
My Antony is away.

CHARMIAN
      You think of him too much.

CLEOPATRA

O, 'tis treason!

CHARMIAN
      Madam, I trust, not so.

[21] an opiate

CLEOPATRA

Thou, eunuch Mardian!

MARDIAN

What 's your highness' pleasure?

CLEOPATRA

Not now to hear thee sing; I take no pleasure
In aught a eunuch has: 'tis well for thee,
That, being unseminar'd,[22] thy freer
    thoughts
May not fly north of Egypt. Hast thou affec-
    tions?

MARDIAN

Yes, gracious madam.

CLEOPATRA

Indeed?

MARDIAN

Not in deed, madam, for I can do nothing
But what indeed is honest to be done:
Yet I have fierce affections, and think
What Venus did with Mars.

CLEOPATRA

                    O Charmian,
Where think'st thou he is now? Stands he,
    or sits he?
Or does he walk? or is he on his horse?
O happy horse, to bear the weight of Antony!
Do bravely, horse! for wot'st thou whom
    thou mov'st?
The demi-Atlas of this earth, the arm
And burgonet [23] of men. He 's speaking now,
Or murmuring, " Where 's my serpent of old
    Nile? "
(For so he calls me:) now I feed myself
With most delicious poison. Think on me,
That am with Phœbus' armorous pinches
    black
And wrinkled deep in time. Broad-fronted
    Cæsar,[24]
When thou wast here above the ground, I
    was

22 castrated
23 helmet
24 i.e., Julius Caesar

A morsel for a monarch: and great Pompey
Would stand and make his eyes grow in my
    brow,
There would he anchor his aspect, and die
With looking on his life.
            (*Enter* ALEXAS.)

ALEXAS

            Sovereign of Egypt, hail!

CLEOPATRA

How much unlike art thou Mark Antony!
Yet, coming from him, that great medicine
    hath
With his tinct gilded thee. How goes it with
My brave Mark Antony?

ALEXAS

            Last thing he did, dear queen,
He kiss'd — the last of many doubled kiss-
    es —
This orient pearl. His speech sticks in my
    heart.

CLEOPATRA

Mine ear must pluck it thence.

ALEXAS

            " Good friend," quoth he,
" Say, the firm Roman to great Egypt sends
This treasure of an oyster; at whose foot,
To mend the pretty present, I will piece [25]
Her opulent throne with kingdoms; all the
    east,
(Say thou) shall call her mistress." So he
    nodded,
And soberly did mount an arm-gaunt steed,
Who neigh'd so high, that what I would have
    spoke
Was beastly dumb'd by him.

CLEOPATRA

            What, was he sad, or merry?

ALEXAS

Like to the time o' the year between the ex-
    tremes
Of hot and cold, he was nor sad nor merry.

25 add to

CLEOPATRA

O well divided disposition! Note him,
Note him, good Charmian, 'tis the man; but
   note him:
He was not sad, for he would shine on those
That make their looks by his; he was not
   merry,
Which seem'd to tell them his remembrance
   lay
In Egypt with his joy; but between both.
O heavenly mingle! Be'st thou sad, or merry,
The violence of either thee becomes,
So does it no man else. Met'st thou my posts?

ALEXAS

Ay, madam, twenty several messengers:
Why do you send so thick?

CLEOPATRA

         Who 's born that day
When I forget to send to Antony,
Shall die a beggar. Ink and paper, Charmian.
Welcome, my good Alexas. Did I, Charmian,
Ever love Cæsar so?

CHARMIAN

       O that brave Cæsar!

CLEOPATRA

Be chok'd with such another emphasis!
Say, the brave Antony.

CHARMIAN

       The valiant Cæsar!

CLEOPATRA

By Isis, I will give thee bloody teeth,
If thou with Cæsar paragon again
My man of men.

CHARMIAN

      By your most gracious pardon,
I sing but after you.

CLEOPATRA

      My salad days,
When I was green in judgment, cold in blood,
To say as I said then! But come, away,

Get me ink and paper; he shall have every
   day
A several greeting, or I'll unpeople Egypt.
              (*Exeunt.*)

ACT TWO

[Messina]   *Enter* POMPEY, MENECRA-
TES, *and* MENAS, *in warlike manner.*

POMPEY

If the great gods be just, they shall assist
The deeds of justest men.

MENECRATES

        Know, worthy Pompey,
That what they do delay, they not deny.

POMPEY

Whiles we are suitors to their throne, decays
The thing we sue for.

MENECRATES

        We, ignorant of ourselves,
Beg often our own harms, which the wise
   powers
Deny us for our good; so find we profit
By losing of our prayers.

POMPEY

        I shall do well:
The people love me, and the sea is mine;
My powers are crescent, and my auguring
   hope
Says it will come to the full. Mark Antony
In Egypt sits at dinner, and will make
No wars without doors: Cæsar gets money
   where
He loses hearts: Lepidus flatters both,
Of both is flatter'd; but he neither loves,
Nor either cares for him.

MENAS

        Cæsar and Lepidus
Are in the field, a mighty strength they
   carry.

POMPEY

Where have you this? 'tis false.

MENAS

From Silvius, sir.

POMPEY

He dreams: I know they are in Rome together,
Looking for Antony. But all the charms of love,
Salt [1] Cleopatra, soften thy wann'd lip!
Let witchcraft join with beauty, lust with both,
Tie up the libertine in a field of feasts,
Keep his brain fuming; Epicurean cooks
Sharpen with cloyless sauce his appetite,
That sleep and feeding may prorogue [2] his honor,
Even till a Lethe'd [3] dullness —
(*Enter* VARRIUS.)
How now, Varrius!

VARRIUS

This is most certain that I shall deliver:
Mark Antony is every hour in Rome
Expected: since he went from Egypt 'tis
A space for further travel.

POMPEY

I could have given less matter
A better ear. Menas, I did not think
This amorous surfeiter would have donn'd his helm
For such a petty war: his soldiership
Is twice the other twain: but let us rear
The higher our opinion, that our stirring
Can from the lap of Egypt's widow pluck
The ne'er-lust-wearied Antony.

MENAS

I cannot hope
Cæsar and Antony shall well greet together:
His wife that's dead did trespasses to Cæsar,
His brother warr'd upon him, although, I think,
Not mov'd [4] by Antony.

POMPEY

I know not, Menas,
How lesser enmities may give way to greater.
Were 't not that we stand up against them all,
'Twere pregnant they should square [5] between themselves,
For they have entertained cause enough
To draw their swords: but how the fear of us
May cement their divisions, and bind up
The petty difference, we yet not know.
Be 't as our gods will have 't! It only stands
Our lives upon to use our strongest hands.
Come, Menas.   (*Exeunt.*)

[**Rome**]   *Enter* ENOBARBUS *and* LEPIDUS.

LEPIDUS

Good Enobarbus, 'tis a worthy deed,
And shall become you well, to entreat your captain
To soft and gentle speech.

ENOBARBUS

I shall entreat him
To answer like himself: if Cæsar move him,
Let Antony look over Cæsar's head,
And speak as loud as Mars. By Jupiter,
Were I the wearer of Antonius' beard,
I would not shave 't to-day.

LEPIDUS

'Tis not a time
For private stomaching. [6]

ENOBARBUS

Every time
Serves for the matter that is then born in 't.

LEPIDUS

But small to greater matters must give way.

ENOBARBUS

Not if the small come first.

---

1 lecherous
2 put off the consideration of
3 immersed in the river of forgetfulness (*Lethe*)
4 inspired

5 quarrel
6 grumbling

LEPIDUS

Your speech is passion:
But, pray you, sir, stir no embers up. Here
   comes
The noble Antony.
   (*Enter* ANTONY *and* VENTIDIUS.)

ENOBARBUS

And yonder, Cæsar.
(*Enter* CÆSAR, MÆCENAS, *and* AGRIPPA.)

ANTONY

If we compose well here, to Parthia:
Hark, Ventidius.

CÆSAR

I do not know,
Mæcenas; ask Agrippa.

LEPIDUS

Noble friends,
That which combin'd us was most great,
   and let not
A leaner action rend us. What 's amiss,
May it be gently heard. When we debate
Our trivial difference loud, we do commit
Murder in healing wounds. Then, noble part-
   ners,
The rather for I earnestly beseech,
Touch you the sourest points with sweetest
   terms,
Nor curstness ⁷ grow to the matter.

ANTONY

'Tis spoken well.
Were we before our armies, and to fight,
I should do thus.   (*Flourish of trumpets.*)

CÆSAR

Welcome to Rome.

ANTONY

Thank you.

CÆSAR

Sit.

ANTONY

Sit, sir.

CÆSAR

Nay, then.

ANTONY

I learn, you take things ill which are not so:
Or being, concern you not.

CÆSAR

I must be laugh'd at,
If, or ⁸ for nothing, or a little, I
Should say myself offended, and with you
Chiefly i' the world; more laugh'd at, that I
   should
Once name you derogately, when to sound
Your name it not concern'd me.

ANTONY

My being in Egypt,
Cæsar, what was 't to you?

CÆSAR

No more than my residing here in Rome
Might be to you in Egypt: yet, if you there
Did practise on my state, your being in Egypt
Might be my question.

ANTONY

How intend you, practis'd?

CÆSAR

You may be pleas'd to catch at mine intent
By what did here befall me. Your wife and
   brother
Made wars upon me, and their contestation
Was theme for you, you were the word of
   war.

ANTONY

You do mistake your business, my brother
   never
Did urge ⁹ me in his act: I did inquire it,
And have my learning from some true re-
   ports
That drew their swords with you. Did he not
   rather
Discredit my authority with yours,

⁷ short temper

⁸ either
⁹ associate

And make the wars alike against my stomach,
Having alike your cause? of this, my letters
Before did satisfy you. If you 'll patch a
    quarrel,
As matter whole you have not to make it
    with,
It must not be with this.

CÆSAR

You praise yourself
By laying defects of judgment to me, but
You patch'd up your excuses.

ANTONY

Not so, not so;
I know you could not lack, I am certain
    on 't,
Very necessity of this thought, that I,
Your partner in the cause 'gainst which he
    fought,
Could not with graceful eyes attend those
    wars
Which fronted mine own peace. As for my
    wife,
I would you had her spirit in such another:
The third o' the world is yours, which with a
    snaffle
You may pace easy, but not such a wife.

ENOBARBUS

Would we had all such wives, that the men
    might go to wars with the women!

ANTONY

So much uncurbable, her garboils, Cæsar,
Made out of her impatience (which not
    wanted
Shrewdness of policy too) I grieving grant
Did you too much disquiet: for that you
    must
But say, I could not help it.

CÆSAR

I wrote to you,
When rioting in Alexandria you
Did pocket up my letters; and with taunts
Did gibe my missive out of audience.

ANTONY

Sir,
He fell upon me ere admitted: then
Three kings I had newly feasted, and did
    want
Of what I was i' the morning: but next day
I told him of myself, which was as much
As to have ask'd him pardon. Let this fellow
Be nothing of our strife; if we contend,
Out of our question wipe him.

CÆSAR

You have broken
The article of your oath, which you shall
    never
Have tongue to charge me with.

LEPIDUS

Soft, Cæsar!

ANTONY

No, Lepidus, let him speak:
The honor is sacred which he talks on now,
Supposing that I lack'd it. But on, Cæsar:
The article of my oath.

CÆSAR

To lend me arms, and aid when I requir'd
    them;
The which you both denied.

ANTONY

Neglected rather;
And then when poison'd hours had bound me
    up
From mine own knowledge. As nearly as I
    may,
I 'll play the penitent to you: but mine hon-
    esty
Shall not make poor my greatness, nor my
    power
Work without it. Truth is, that Fulvia,
To have me out of Egypt, made wars here;
For which myself, the ignorant motive, do
So far ask pardon as befits mine honor
To stoop in such a case.

LEPIDUS

'Tis noble spoken.

MÆCENAS

If it might please you, to enforce no further
The griefs between ye: to forget them quite
Were to remember that the present need
Speaks to atone [10] you.

LEPIDUS

Worthily spoken, Mæcenas.

ENOBARBUS

Or, if you borrow one another's love for the
instant, you may, when you hear no
more words of Pompey, return it again:
you shall have time to wrangle in, when
you have nothing else to do.

ANTONY

Thou art a soldier only: speak no more.

ENOBARBUS

That truth should be silent I had almost forgot.

ANTONY

You wrong this presence; therefore speak no
more.

ENOBARBUS

Go to, then; your considerate stone.

CÆSAR

I do not much dislike the matter, but
The manner of his speech; for 't cannot be
We shall remain in friendship, our conditions
So differing in their acts. Yet, if I knew
What hoop should hold us stanch, from edge
to edge
O' the world I would pursue it.

AGRIPPA

Give me leave, Cæsar.

CÆSAR

Speak, Agrippa.

AGRIPPA

Thou hast a sister by the mother's side,
Admir'd Octavia: great Mark Antony
Is now a widower.

CÆSAR

Say not so, Agrippa:
If Cleopatra heard you, your reproof
Were well deserv'd of rashness.

ANTONY

I am not married, Cæsar: let me hear
Agrippa further speak.

AGRIPPA

To hold you in perpetual amity,
To make you brothers, and to knit your
hearts
With an unslipping knot, take Antony
Octavia to his wife; whose beauty claims
No worse a husband than the best of men,
Whose virtue, and whose general graces,
speak
That which none else can utter. By this mar-
riage
All little jealousies which now seem great,
And all great fears, which now import [11]
their dangers,
Would then be nothing: truths would be
tales,
Where now half tales be truths: her love to
both
Would each to other, and all loves to both,
Draw after her. Pardon what I have spoke,
For 'tis a studied, not a present thought,
By duty ruminated.

ANTONY

Will Cæsar speak?

CÆSAR

Not till he hears how Antony is touch'd
With what is spoke already.

ANTONY

What power is in Agrippa,
If I would say, " Agrippa, be it so,"
To make this good?

CÆSAR

The power of Cæsar, and
His power unto Octavia.

[10] reconcile

[11] foreshadow

ANTONY

May I never
To this good purpose, that so fairly shows,
Dream of impediment! Let me have thy
    hand:
Further this act of grace; and from this hour
The heart of brothers govern in our loves,
And sway our great designs!

CÆSAR

There is my hand.
A sister I bequeath you, whom no brother
Did ever love so dearly. Let her live
To join our kingdoms, and our hearts; and
    never
Fly off our loves again!

LEPIDUS

Happily, amen!

ANTONY

I did not think to draw my sword 'gainst
    Pompey,
For he hath laid strange courtesies and great
Of late upon me: I must thank him only,
Lest my remembrance suffer ill report;
At heel of that, defy him.

LEPIDUS

Time calls upon 's:
Of us must Pompey presently be sought,
Or else he seeks out us.

ANTONY

Where lies he?

CÆSAR

About the Mount Misenum.

ANTONY

What 's his strength
By land?

CÆSAR

Great and increasing: but by sea
He is an absolute master.

ANTONY

So is the fame.[12]
Would we had spoke together! Haste we for
    it:
Yet, ere we put ourselves in arms, dispatch
    we
The business we have talk'd of.

CÆSAR

With most gladness,
And do invite you to my sister's view,
Whither straight I 'll lead you.

ANTONY

Let us, Lepidus,
Not lack your company.

LEPIDUS

Noble Antony,
Not sickness should detain me.
            (Flourish. Exeunt CÆSAR, ANTONY, and
                                LEPIDUS.)

MÆCENAS

Welcome from Egypt, sir.

ENOBARBUS

Half the heart of Cæsar, worthy Mæcenas!
My honorable friend, Agrippa!

AGRIPPA

Good Enobarbus!

MÆCENAS

We have cause to be glad that matters are so
    well digested. You stayed well by 't in
    Egypt.

ENOBARBUS

Ay, sir, we did sleep day out of countenance,
    and made the night light with drinking.

MÆCENAS

Eight wild-boars roasted whole at a break-
    fast, and but twelve persons there; is
    this true?

12 report

ENOBARBUS

This was but as a fly by an eagle; we had
much more monstrous matter of feast,
which worthily deserved noting.

MÆCENAS

She's a most triumphant lady, if report be
square to her.

ENOBARBUS

When she first met Mark Antony, she purs'd
up his heart upon the river of Cydnus.

AGRIPPA

There she appear'd indeed, or my reporter
devis'd well for her.

ENOBARBUS

I will tell you.
The barge she sat in, like a burnish'd throne,
Burn'd on the water: the poop was beaten
gold,
Purple the sails, and so perfumed that
The winds were love-sick with them; the
oars were silver,
Which to the tune of flutes kept stroke, and
made
The water which they beat to follow faster,
As amorous of their strokes. For her own
person,
It beggar'd all description: she did lie
In her pavilion, cloth-of-gold of tissue,
O'er-picturing that Venus where we see
The fancy outwork nature; on each side her
Stood pretty dimpled boys, like smiling Cu-
pids,
With divers-color'd fans, whose wind did
seem
To glow the delicate cheeks which they did
cool,
And what they undid did.

AGRIPPA

O, rare for Antony!

ENOBARBUS

Her gentlewomen, like the Nereides,
So many mermaids, tended her i' the eyes,[13]

[13] closely

And made their bends adornings: at the helm
A seeming mermaid steers: the silken tackle
Swell with the touches of those flower-soft
hands,
That yarely frame [14] the office. From the
barge
A strange invisible perfume hits the sense
Of the adjacent wharfs. The city cast
Her people out upon her; and Antony,
Enthron'd i' the market-place, did sit alone,
Whistling to the air; which, but for vacancy,
Had gone to gaze on Cleopatra too,
And made a gap in nature.

AGRIPPA

Rare Egyptian!

ENOBARBUS

Upon her landing, Antony sent to her,
Invited her to supper: she replied,
It should be better he became her guest,
Which she entreated: our courteous Antony,
Whom ne'er the word of "No" woman
heard speak,
Being barber'd ten times o'er, goes to the
feast,
And, for his ordinary,[15] pays his heart,
For what his eyes eat only.

AGRIPPA

Royal wench!
She made great Cæsar lay his sword to bed,
He plough'd her, and she cropp'd.[16]

ENOBARBUS

I saw her once
Hop forty paces through the public street,
And having lost her breath, she spoke, and
panted,
That she did make defect perfection,
And, breathless, power breathe forth.

MÆCENAS

Now Antony must leave her utterly.

ENOBARBUS

Never, he will not:
Age cannot wither her, nor custom stale

[14] properly perform
[15] supper bill
[16] bore fruit

Her infinite variety: other women cloy
The appetites they feed, but she makes hun-
gry
Where most she satisfies: for vilest things
Become themselves in her, that the holy
priests
Bless her, when she is riggish.[17]

MÆCENAS

If beauty, wisdom, modesty, can settle
The heart of Antony, Octavia is
A blessed lottery to him.

AGRIPPA

Let us go.
Good Enobarbus, make yourself my guest,
Whilst you abide here.

ENOBARBUS

Humbly, sir, I thank you.   (*Exeunt.*)

Enter ANTONY, CÆSAR, OCTAVIA *between
them, and Attendants.*

ANTONY

The world and my great office will sometimes
Divide me from your bosom.

OCTAVIA

All which time
Before the gods my knee shall bow my
prayers
To them for you.

ANTONY

Good night, sir. My Octavia,
Read not my blemishes in the world's report:
I have not kept my square, but that to come
Shall all be done by the rule. Good night, dear
lady.
Good night, sir.

CÆSAR

Good night.   (*Exeunt all but* ANTONY.)
(*Enter* LAMPRIUS.)

ANTONY

Now, sirrah; you do wish yourself in Egypt?

LAMPRIUS

Would I had never come from thence, nor
you
Thither!

ANTONY

If you can, your reason?

LAMPRIUS

I see it in
My motion,[18] have it not in my tongue: but
yet
Hie you to Egypt again.

ANTONY

Say to me,
Whose fortunes shall rise higher, Cæsar's or
mine?

LAMPRIUS

Cæsar's.
Therefore, O Antony, stay not by his side:
Thy demon, that thy spirit which keeps thee,
is
Noble, courageous, high, unmatchable,
Where Cæsar's is not; but near him thy angel
Becomes afeard, as being o'erpower'd: there-
fore
Make space enough between you.

ANTONY

Speak this no more.

LAMPRIUS

To none but thee; no more but when to thee.
If thou dost play with him at any game,
Thou art sure to lose; and, of that natural
luck,
He beats thee 'gainst the odds: thy luster
thickens,
When he shines by: I say again, thy spirit
Is all afraid to govern thee near him,
But he away, 'tis noble.

ANTONY

Get thee gone:
Say to Ventidius I would speak with him.
(*Exit* LAMPRIUS.)

---

[17] wanton

[18] intuition

He shall to Parthia. Be it art or hap,
He hath spoken true: the very dice obey him,
And in our sports my better cunning faints
Under his chance: if we draw lots, he speeds;
His cocks do win the battle still of mine
When it is all to nought; and his quails ever
Beat mine, inhoop'd, at odds. I will to Egypt:
And though I make this marriage for my
    peace,
I' the east my pleasure lies.
            (*Enter* VENTIDIUS.)
                    O, come, Ventidius,
You must to Parthia: your commission 's
    ready;
Follow me, and receive 't.   (*Exeunt.*)

Enter LEPIDUS, MÆCENAS, *and* AGRIPPA.

LEPIDUS

Trouble yourselves no further: pray you,
    hasten
Your generals after.

AGRIPPA

            Sir, Mark Antony
Will e'en but kiss Octavia, and we'll follow.

LEPIDUS

Till I shall see you in your soldier's dress,
Which will become you both, farewell.

MÆCENAS

                    We shall,
As I conceive the journey, be at Mount
Before you, Lepidus.

LEPIDUS

            Your way is shorter,
My purposes do draw me much about,
You 'll win two days upon me.

MÆCENAS, AGRIPPA

            Sir, good success!

LEPIDUS

Farewell.   (*Exeunt.*)

[Alexandria]   *Enter*   CLEOPATRA,
CHARMIAN, IRAS, *and* ALEXAS.

CLEOPATRA

Give me some music; music, moody food
Of us that trade in love.

ALL

            The music, ho!
        (*Enter* MARDIAN.)

CLEOPATRA

Let it alone, let 's to billiards: come, Charmian.

CHARMIAN

My arm is sore, best play with Mardian.

CLEOPATRA

As well a woman with an eunuch play'd
As with a woman. Come, you'll play with me,
    sir?

MARDIAN

As well as I can, madam.

CLEOPATRA

And when good will is show'd, though 't
    come too short,
The actor may plead pardon. I'll none now;
Give me mine angle,[19] we 'll to the river
    there,
My music playing far off; I will betray
Tawny-finn'd fishes, my bended hook shall
    pierce
Their slimy jaws; and as I draw them up,
I 'll think them every one an Antony,
And say " Ah, ha! you 're caught."

CHARMIAN

                    'Twas merry when
You wager'd on your angling, when your
    diver
Did hang a salt-fish on his hook, which he
With fervency drew up.

CLEOPATRA

                    That time? O times!
I laugh'd him out of patience, and that night
I laugh'd him into patience, and next morn,
Ere the ninth hour, I drunk him to his bed;

19 fishing-rod

Then put my tires and mantles [20] on him, whilst
I wore his sword Philippan.
             (*Enter a Messenger.*)
                    O, from Italy!
Ram thou thy fruitful tidings in mine ears,
That long time have been barren.

        MESSENGER
        Madam, madam, —

        CLEOPATRA
Antonius dead! If thou say so, villain,
Thou kill'st thy mistress: but well and free,
If thou so yield him, there is gold, and here
My bluest veins to kiss: a hand that kings
Have lipp'd, and trembled kissing.

        MESSENGER
First, madam, he is well.

        CLEOPATRA
           Why, there's more gold.
But, sirrah, mark, we use
To say the dead are well: bring it to that,
The gold I give thee will I melt and pour
Down thy ill-uttering throat.

        MESSENGER
Good madam, hear me.

        CLEOPATRA
           Well, go to, I will;
But there's no goodness in thy face, if Antony
Be free and healthful, — so tart a favor [21]
To trumpet such good tidings! If not well,
Thou shouldst come like a Fury crown'd with snakes,
Not like a formal man.

        MESSENGER
        Will 't please you hear me?

        CLEOPATRA
I have a mind to strike thee ere thou speak'st:
Yet, if thou say Antony lives, is well,

[20] woman's clothing
[21] face

Or friends with Cæsar, or not captive to him,
I 'll set thee in a shower of gold, and hail
Rich pearls upon thee.

        MESSENGER
        Madam, he 's well.

        CLEOPATRA
              Well said.

        MESSENGER
And friends with Cæsar.

        CLEOPATRA
        Thou 'rt an honest man.

        MESSENGER
Cæsar and he are greater friends than ever.

        CLEOPATRA
Make thee a fortune from me.

        MESSENGER
        But yet, madam —

        CLEOPATRA
I do not like " But yet," it does allay
The good precedence, fie upon " But yet "!
" But yet " is a jailer to bring forth
Some monstrous malefactor. Prithee, friend,
Pour out the pack of matter to mine ear,
The good and bad together: he 's friends with Cæsar,
In state of health, thou say'st, and, thou say'st, free.

        MESSENGER
Free, madam! no; I made no such report,
He 's bound unto Octavia.

        CLEOPATRA
        For what good turn?

        MESSENGER
For the best turn i' the bed.

        CLEOPATRA
        I am pale, Charmian.

MESSENGER
Madam, he 's married to Octavia.

CLEOPATRA
The most infectious pestilence upon thee!
(*Strikes him down.*)

MESSENGER
Good madam, patience.

CLEOPATRA
        What say you? Hence,
        (*Strikes him again.*)
Horrible villain, or I 'll spurn [22] thine eyes
Like balls before me; I'll unhair thy head,
        (*She hales him up and down.*)
Thou shalt be whipp'd with wire, and stew'd
    in brine,
Smarting in lingering pickle.

MESSENGER
        Gracious madam,
I that do bring the news made not the match.

CLEOPATRA
Say 'tis not so, a province I will give thee,
And make thy fortunes proud: the blow thou
    hadst
Shall make thy peace, for moving me to rage,
And I will boot [23] thee with what gift beside
Thy modesty can beg.

MESSENGER
        He 's married, madam.

CLEOPATRA
Rogue, thou hast liv'd too long.
        (*Draws a knife.*)

MESSENGER
        Nay, then I'll run.
What mean you, madam? I have made no
    fault.   (*Exit.*)

CHARMIAN
Good madam, keep yourself within yourself,
The man is innocent.

22 kick
23 favor

CLEOPATRA
Some innocents 'scape not the thunderbolt.
Melt Egypt into Nile! and kindly creatures
Turn all to serpents! Call the slave again,
Though I am mad, I will not bite him: call.

CHARMIAN
He is afeard to come.

CLEOPATRA
        I will not hurt him,
        (*Exit* CHARMIAN.)
These hands do lack nobility, that they strike
A meaner than myself; since I myself
Have given myself the cause.
        (*Re-enter* CHARMIAN *and Messenger.*)
        Come hither, sir.
Though it be honest, it is never good
To bring bad news: give to a gracious mes-
    sage
An host of tongues, but let ill tidings tell
Themselves when they be felt.

MESSENGER
        I have done my duty.

CLEOPATRA
Is he married?
I cannot hate thee worser than I do,
If thou again say " Yes."

MESSENGER
        He 's married, madam.

CLEOPATRA
The gods confound thee! dost thou hold there
    still?

MESSENGER
Should I lie, madam?

CLEOPATRA
        O, I would thou didst,
So half my Egypt were submerg'd and made
A cistern for scal'd snakes! Go get thee
    hence,
Hadst thou Narcissus [24] in thy face, to me

24 a legendary youth of great beauty

Thou wouldst appear most ugly. He is married?

MESSENGER

I crave your highness' pardon.

CLEOPATRA

He is married?

MESSENGER

Take no offence that I would not offend you:
To punish me for what you make me do
Seems much unequal: he 's married to Octavia.

CLEOPATRA

O, that his fault should make a knave of thee,
That art not what thou 'rt sure of! Get thee hence:
The merchandise which thou hast brought from Rome
Are all too dear for me; lie they upon thy hand,
And be undone by 'em!   (*Exit Messenger.*)

CHARMIAN

Good your highness, patience.

CLEOPATRA

In praising Antony, I have disprais'd Cæsar.

CHARMIAN

Many times, madam.

CLEOPATRA

I am paid for 't now.
Lead me from hence,
I faint: O Iras, Charmian! 'tis no matter.
Go to the fellow, good Alexas; bid him
Report the feature of Octavia; her years,
Her inclination, let him not leave out
The color of her hair: bring me word
quickly.   (*Exit* ALEXAS.)
Let him forever go, let him not, Charmian,
Though he be painted one way like a Gorgon,[25]
The other way 's a Mars.[26] (*to* MARDIAN)
Bid you Alexas

25 Medusa, the supreme ugliness
26 god of war

Bring me word how tall she is. Pity me, Charmian,
But do not speak to me. Lead me to my chamber.   (*Exeunt.*)

[**Mount Misenum**]   *Flourish. Enter*
POMPEY *and* MENAS *from one side, with drum and trumpet: at another,* CÆSAR, ANTONY, LEPIDUS, ENOBARBUS, MÆCENAS, AGRIPPA, *with Soldiers marching.*

POMPEY

Your hostages I have, so have you mine;
And we shall talk before we fight.

CÆSAR

Most meet
The first we come to words, and therefore have we
Our written purposes [27] before us sent,
Which, if thou hast consider'd, let us know
If 'twill tie up thy discontented sword,
And carry back to Sicily much tall [28] youth,
That else must perish here.

POMPEY

To you all three,
The senators alone of this great world,
Chief factors [29] for the gods, I do not know
Wherefore my father should revengers want,
Having a son and friends, since Julius Cæsar,
Who at Philippi the good Brutus ghosted,
There saw you laboring for him. What was 't
That mov'd pale Cassius to conspire? and what
Made the all-honor'd honest Roman, Brutus,
With the arm'd rest, courtiers of beauteous freedom,
To drench the Capitol, but that they would
Have one man but a man? And that is it
Hath made me rig my navy, at whose burthen
The anger'd ocean foams, with which I meant

27 propositions
28 brave
29 agents

To scourge the ingratitude that despiteful
    Rome
Cast on my noble father.

CÆSAR
                Take your time.

ANTONY

Thou canst not fear [30] us, Pompey, with thy
    sails;
We 'll speak with thee at sea: at land, thou
    know'st
How much we do o'ercount thee.

POMPEY
                At land indeed
Thou dost o'ercount [31] me of my father's
    house:
But since the cuckoo builds not for himself,
Remain in 't as thou mayst.

LEPIDUS
             Be pleas'd to tell us
(For this is from the present) how you take
The offers we have sent you.

CÆSAR
             There 's the point.

ANTONY

Which do not be entreated to, but weigh
What it is worth embrac'd.

CÆSAR
            And what may follow,
To try a larger fortune.

POMPEY
           You have made me offer
Of Sicily, Sardinia; and I must
Rid all the sea of pirates; then, to send
Measures of wheat to Rome; this 'greed upon,
To part with unhack'd edges,[32] and bear back
Our targes [33] undinted.

[30] frighten
[31] deprive
[32] swords
[33] shields

CÆSAR, ANTONY, LEPIDUS
           That's our offer.

POMPEY
                Know then,
I came before you here a man prepar'd
To take this offer: but Mark Antony
Put me to some impatience: though I lose
The praise of it by telling: you must know,
When Cæsar and your brother were at blows,
Your mother came to Sicily and did find
Her welcome friendly.

ANTONY
           I have heard it, Pompey,
And am well studied for a liberal thanks,
Which I do owe you.

POMPEY
           Let me have your hand:
I did not think, sir, to have met you here.

ANTONY

The beds i' the east are soft, and thanks to
    you,
That call'd me timelier than my purpose
    hither;
For I have gain'd by 't.

CÆSAR
           Since I saw you last,
There is a change upon you.

POMPEY
           Well, I know not
What counts harsh fortune casts upon my
    face;
But in my bosom shall she never come,
To make my heart her vassal.

LEPIDUS
           Well met here.

POMPEY

I hope so, Lepidus. Thus we are agreed:
I crave our composition [34] may be written
And seal'd between us.

[34] agreement

CÆSAR
    That 's the next to do.

POMPEY
We 'll feast each other ere we part, and let 's
Draw lots who shall begin.

ANTONY
    That will I, Pompey.

POMPEY
No, Antony, take the lot:
But, first or last, your fine Egyptian cookery
Shall have the fame. I have heard that Julius
    Cæsar
Grew fat with feasting there.

ANTONY
    You have heard much.

POMPEY
I have fair meaning, sir.

ANTONY
    And fair words to them.

POMPEY
Then so much have I heard:
And I have heard, Apollodorus carried —

ENOBARBUS
No more of that: he did so.

POMPEY
    What, I pray you?

ENOBARBUS
A certain queen to Cæsar in a mattress.

POMPEY
I know thee now, how far'st thou, soldier?

ENOBARBUS
    Well;
And well am like to do, for I perceive
Four feasts are toward.

POMPEY
    Let me shake thy hand,
I never hated thee: I have seen thee fight,
When I have envied thy behavior.

ENOBARBUS
    Sir,
I never lov'd you much, but I ha' prais'd ye,
When you have well deserv'd ten times as
    much
As I have said you did.

POMPEY
    Enjoy thy plainness,
It nothing ill becomes thee.
Aboard my galley I invite you all:
Will you lead, lords?

CÆSAR, ANTONY, LEPIDUS
    Show us the way, sir.

POMPEY
    Come.
(*Exeunt all but* MENAS *and* ENOBARBUS.)

MENAS
(*Aside.*) Thy father, Pompey, would ne'er
    have made this treaty — You and I
    have known, sir.

ENOBARBUS
At sea, I think.

MENAS
We have, sir.

ENOBARBUS
You have done well by water.

MENAS
And you by land.

ENOBARBUS
I will praise any man that will praise me;
    though it cannot be denied what I have
    done by land.

MENAS
Nor what I have done by water.

ENOBARBUS

Yes, something you can deny for your own safety: you have been a great thief by sea.

MENAS

And you by land.

ENOBARBUS

There I deny my land service: but give me your hand, Menas, if our eyes had authority, here they might take [35] two thieves kissing.

MENAS

All men's faces are true, whatsoe'er their hands are.

ENOBARBUS

But there is never a fair woman has a true face.

MENAS

No slander, they steal hearts.

ENOBARBUS

We came hither to fight with you.

MENAS

For my part, I am sorry it is turn'd to a drinking. Pompey doth this day laugh away his fortune.

ENOBARBUS

If he do, sure he cannot weep 't back again.

MENAS

You 've said, sir; we looked not for Mark Antony here: pray you, is he married to Cleopatra?

ENOBARBUS

Cæsar's sister is called Octavia.

MENAS

True, sir; she was the wife of Caius Marcellus.

[35] arrest

ENOBARBUS

But she is now the wife of Marcus Antonius.

MENAS

Pray ye, sir?

ENOBARBUS

'Tis true.

MENAS

Then is Cæsar and he forever knit together.

ENOBARBUS

If I were bound to divine [36] of this unity, I would not prophesy so.

MENAS

I think the policy of that purpose made more in the marriage than the love of the parties.

ENOBARBUS

I think so too. But you shall find, the band that seems to tie their friendship together will be the very strangler of their amity: Octavia is of a holy, cold, and still conversation. [37]

MENAS

Who would not have his wife so?

ENOBARBUS

Not he that himself is not so; which is Mark Antony. He will to his Egyptian dish again: then shall the sighs of Octavia blow the fire up in Cæsar; and (as I said before) that which is the strength of their amity shall prove the immediate author of their variance. Antony will use his affection where it is: he married but his occasion here.

MENAS

And thus it may be. Come, sir, will you aboard? I have a health for you.

[36] read (the omens)
[37] manner

ENOBARBUS

I shall take it, sir: we have us'd our throats in Egypt.

MENAS

Come, let 's away.   (*Exeunt.*)

[Pompey's Galley.]   *Music plays. Enter two or three Servants, with a banquet.*

1st SERVANT

Here they'll be, man. Some o' their plants are ill-rooted already; the least wind i' the world will blow them down.

2nd SERVANT

Lepidus is high-colored.

1st SERVANT

They have made him drink alms-drink.[38]

2nd SERVANT

As they pinch one another by the disposition, he cries out "No more"; reconciles them to his entreaty, and himself to the drink.

1st SERVANT

But it raises the greater war between him and his discretion.

2nd SERVANT

Why, this it is to have a name in great men's fellowship: I had as lief have a reed that will do me no service as a partisan [39] I could not heave.

1st SERVANT

To be call'd into a huge sphere, and not to be seen to move in 't, are the holes where eyes should be, which pitifully disaster the cheeks.
(*A sennet* [40] *sounded. Enter* CÆSAR, ANTONY, POMPEY, LEPIDUS, AGRIPPA, MÆCENAS, ENOBARBUS, MENAS, *with other captains.*)

38 the dregs, the poorest wine
39 weapon
40 trumpet-flourish

ANTONY

(*To* CÆSAR) Thus do they, sir: they take the flow o' the Nile
By certain scales i' the pyramid; they know
By the height, the lowness, or the mean, if dearth
Or foison [41] follow: the higher Nilus swells,
The more it promises: as it ebbs, the seedsman
Upon the slime and ooze scatters his grain,
And shortly comes to harvest.

LEPIDUS

You 've strange serpents there?

ANTONY

Ay, Lepidus.

LEPIDUS

Your serpent of Egypt is bred now of your mud by the operation of your sun: so is your crocodile.

ANTONY

They are so.

POMPEY

Sit, and some wine! A health to Lepidus!

LEPIDUS

I am not so well as I should be, but I 'll ne'er out.

ENOBARBUS

Not till you have slept; I fear me you 'll be in till then.

LEPIDUS

Nay, certainly, I have heard the Ptolemies pyramises are very goodly things; without contradiction, I have heard that.

MENAS

(*Aside to* POMPEY) Pompey, a word.

POMPEY

(*Aside to* MENAS) Say in mine ear, what is 't?

41 bumper crops

MENAS

(*Aside to* POMPEY) Forsake thy seat, I do
    beseech thee, captain.
And hear me speak a word.

POMPEY

(*Aside to* MENAS) Forbear me till anon. —
This wine for Lepidus.

LEPIDUS

What manner o' thing is your crocodile?

ANTONY

It is shap'd, sir, like itself, and it is as broad
    as it hath breadth; it is just so high as
    it is, and moves with its own organs: it
    lives by that which nourisheth it, and
    the elements once out of it, it transmi-
    grates.

LEPIDUS

What color is it of?

ANTONY

Of its own color too.

LEPIDUS

'Tis a strange serpent.

ANTONY

'Tis so, and the tears of it are wet.

CÆSAR

Will this description satisfy him?

ANTONY

With the health that Pompey gives him, else
    he is a very epicure.

POMPEY

Go hang, sir, hang! Tell me of that? Away!
Do as I bid you. Where 's this cup I call'd
    for?

MENAS

(*Aside to* POMPEY) If for the sake of merit
    thou wilt hear me,
Rise from thy stool.

POMPEY

(*Aside to* MENAS) I think thou 'rt mad. The
    matter?   (*Rises, and walks aside.*)

MENAS

I have ever held my cap off to thy fortunes.

POMPEY

Thou hast serv'd me with much faith.
    What 's else to say?
Be jolly, lords.

ANTONY

        These quick-sands, Lepidus,
Keep off them, for you sink.

MENAS

Wilt thou be lord of all the world?

POMPEY

                    What say'st thou?

MENAS

Wilt thou be lord of the whole world?
    That 's twice.

POMPEY

How should that be?

MENAS

                    But entertain it,
And, though thou think me poor, I am the
    man
Will give thee all the world.

POMPEY

                    Hast thou drunk well?

MENAS

No, Pompey, I have kept me from the cup.
Thou art, if thou dar'st be, the earthly Jove:
Whate'er the ocean pales, or sky inclips,[42]
Is thine, if thou wilt ha 't.

POMPEY

                    Show me which way.

[42] encloses

MENAS

These three world-sharers, these competitors,
Are in thy vessel: let me cut the cable,
And, when we are put off, fall to their
    throats:
All there is thine.

POMPEY

            Ah, this thou shouldst have done,
And not have spoke on 't! In me 'tis villainy;
In thee 't had been good service. Thou must
    know,
'Tis not my profit that does lead mine
    honor;
Mine honor, it. Repent that e'er thy tongue
Hath so betray'd thine act; being done un-
    known,
I should have found it afterwards well done,
But must condemn it now. Desist, and drink.

MENAS

(Aside) For this,
I 'll never follow thy pall'd fortunes more;
Who seeks, and will not take when once 'tis
    offer'd,
Shall never find it more.

POMPEY

            This health to Lepidus!

ANTONY

Bear him ashore, I 'll pledge it for him, Pompey.

ENOBARBUS

Here 's to thee, Menas!

MENAS

            Enobarbus, welcome!

POMPEY

Fill till the cup be hid.

ENOBARBUS

There 's a strong fellow, Menas.
            (Pointing to the Attendant who
                carries off LEPIDUS.)

MENAS

Why?

ENOBARBUS

A' bears the third part of the world, man;
    see'st not?

MENAS

The third part then he is drunk: would it
    were all,
That it might go on wheels! [43]

ENOBARBUS

Drink thou; increase the reels.

MENAS

Come.

POMPEY

This is not yet an Alexandrian feast.

ANTONY

It ripens towards it. Strike the vessels, ho!
Here 's to Cæsar!

CÆSAR

            I could well forbear 't;
It 's monstrous labor, when I wash my brain
And it grows fouler.

ANTONY

            Be a child o' the time.

CÆSAR

Possess it, I 'll make answer:
But I had rather fast from all four days
Than drink so much in one.

ENOBARBUS

            (To ANTONY) Ha, my brave emperor,
Shall we dance now the Egyptian Bacchanals,
And celebrate our drink?

POMPEY

Let 's ha 't, good soldier.

ANTONY

Come, let 's all take hands,
Till that conquering wine hath steep'd our
    sense
In soft and delicate Lethe.

[43] faster

ENOBARBUS

All take hands.
Make battery to our ears with the loud mu-
sic,
The while I 'll place you, then the boy shall
sing;
The holding [44] every man shall bear as loud
As his strong sides can volley.
(*Music plays.* ENOBARBUS *places
them hand in hand.*)

THE SONG

Come, thou monarch of the vine,
Plumpy Bacchus, with pink eyne!
In thy fats our cares be drown'd,
With thy grapes our hairs be crown'd:
Cup us till the world go round,
Cup us till the world go round!

CÆSAR

What would you more? Pompey, good night.
Good brother,
Let me request you off: our graver business
Frowns at this levity. Gentle lords, let 's
part;
You see we have burnt our cheeks: strong
Enobarb
Is weaker than the wine, and mine own
tongue
Splits what it speaks: the wild disguise [45]
hath almost
Antick'd us all. What needs more words?
Good night.
Good Antony, your hand.

POMPEY

I 'll try [46] you on the shore.

ANTONY

And shall, sir: give 's your hand.

POMPEY

O Antony,
You have my father's house — But, what?
we are friends.
Come, down into the boat.

44 refrain, chorus
45 intoxication
46 test

ENOBARBUS

Take heed you fall not.
(*Exeunt all but* ENOBARBUS *and* MENAS.)
Menas, I 'll not on shore.

MENAS

No, to my cabin.
These drums! these trumpets, flutes! what!
Let Neptune hear we bid a loud farewell
To these great fellows: sound and be hang'd,
sound out!
(*Sound a flourish, with drums.*)

ENOBARBUS

Hoo! says a'. There 's my cap. [47]

MENAS

Ho! Noble captain, come.   (*Exeunt.*)

ACT THREE

[Syria]   *Enter* VENTIDIUS *as it were in
triumph, with* SILIUS, *and other Romans,
Officers, and Soldiers; the dead body of* PA-
CORUS *borne before him.*

VENTIDIUS

Now, darting Parthia,[1] art thou struck and
now
Pleas'd fortune does of Marcus Crassus' death
Make me revenger. Bear the king's son's body
Before our army. Thy Pacorus, Orodes,
Pays this for Marcus Crassus.

SILIUS

Noble Ventidius,
Whilst yet with Parthian blood thy sword is
warm
The fugitive Parthians follow; spur through
Media,
Mesopotamia, and the shelters whither
The routed fly: so thy grand captain Antony
Shall set thee on triumphant chariots, and
Put garlands on thy head.

VENTIDIUS

O Silius, Silius,
I have done enough: a lower place, note well,

47 i.e., a salute
1 leader of the arrow-shooting Parthians

May make too great an act; for learn this,
   Silius,
Better to leave undone than by our deed
Acquire too high a fame when him we
   serve 's away.
Cæsar and Antony have ever won
More in their officer than person: Sossius,
One of my place in Syria, his lieutenant,
For quick accumulation of renown,
Which he achiev'd by the minute, lost his
   favor.
Who does i' the wars more than his captain
   can
Becomes his captain's captain: and ambition
(The soldier's virtue) rather makes choice of
   loss
Than gain which darkens him.
I could do more to do Antonius good,
But 'twould offend him; and in his offence
Should my performance perish.

SILIUS

          Thou hast, Ventidius, that
Without the which a soldier and his sword
Grants scarce distinction. Thou wilt write to
   Antony?

VENTIDIUS

I 'll humbly signify what in his name,
That magical word of war, we have effected,
How, with his banners and his well-paid
   ranks,
The ne'er-yet-beaten horse of Parthia
We have jaded out o' the field.

SILIUS

          Where is he now?

VENTIDIUS

He purposeth to Athens, whither, with what
   haste
The weight we must convey with 's will permit,
We shall appear before him. On, there, pass
   along!   (*Exeunt.*)

[Rome]   *Enter* AGRIPPA *at one door,
and* ENOBARBUS *at another.*

AGRIPPA

What, are the brothers parted?

ENOBARBUS

They have dispatch'd with Pompey; he is
   gone;
The other three are sealing. Octavia weeps
To part from Rome; Cæsar is sad, and Lepi-
   dus
Since Pompey's feast, as Menas says, is trou-
   bled
With the green sickness.

AGRIPPA

          'Tis a noble Lepidus.

ENOBARBUS

A very fine one: O, how he loves Cæsar!

AGRIPPA

Nay, but how dearly he adores Mark Antony!

ENOBARBUS

Cæsar? Why, he 's the Jupiter of men.

AGRIPPA

What 's Antony? The god of Jupiter.

ENOBARBUS

Spake you of Cæsar? How! the nonpareil!

AGRIPPA

O Antony, O thou Arabian bird! [2]

ENOBARBUS

Would you praise Cæsar, say " Cæsar ": go
   no further.

AGRIPPA

Indeed, he plied them both with excellent
   praises.

ENOBARBUS

But he loves Cæsar best, yet he loves Antony:
Ho! hearts, tongues, figures, scribes, bards,
   poets, cannot

   [2] the phoenix

Think, speak, cast, write, sing, number —
  hoo! —
His love to Antony. But as for Cæsar,
Kneel down, kneel down, and wonder.

AGRIPPA
           Both he loves.

ENOBARBUS
They are his shards,[3] and he their beetle.
  (*Trumpet within.*) So;
This is to horse. Adieu, noble Agrippa.

AGRIPPA
Good fortune, worthy soldier, and farewell.
  (*Enter* CÆSAR, ANTONY, LEPIDUS, *and* OC-
TAVIA.)

ANTONY
No further, sir.

CÆSAR
You take from me a great part of myself;
Use me well in 't. Sister, prove such a wife
As my thoughts make thee, and as my far-
  thest band
Shall pass on thy approof. Most noble An-
  tony,
Let not the piece of virtue which is set
Betwixt us, as the cement of our love,
To keep it builded, be the ram to batter
The fortress of it; for better might we
Have lov'd without this mean, if on both
  parts
This be not cherish'd.

ANTONY
         Make me not offended
In your distrust.

CÆSAR
I have said.

ANTONY
         You shall not find,
Though you be therein curious, the least
  cause
For what you seem to fear: so, the gods keep
  you,

[3] wings

And make the hearts of Romans serve your
  ends!
We will here part.

CÆSAR
Farewell, my dearest sister, fare thee well,
The elements be kind to thee, and make
Thy spirits all of comfort! fare thee well.

OCTAVIA
My noble brother!

ANTONY
The April 's in her eyes, it is love's spring,
And these the showers to bring it on. Be
  cheerful.

OCTAVIA
Sir, look well to my husband's house, and —

CÆSAR
            What,
Octavia?

OCTAVIA
I 'll tell you in your ear.

ANTONY
Her tongue will not obey her heart, nor can
Her heart inform her tongue, the swan's-
  down feather,
That stands upon the swell at full of tide
And neither way inclines.

ENOBARBUS
(*Aside to* AGRIPPA) Will Cæsar weep?

AGRIPPA
(*Aside to* ENOBARBUS) He has a cloud in 's
  face.

ENOBARBUS
(*Aside to* AGRIPPA) He were the worse for
  that, were he a horse;
So is he, being a man.

AGRIPPA
(*Aside to* ENOBARBUS) Why, Enobarbus,
When Antony found Julius Cæsar dead,

He cried almost to roaring; and he wept
When at Philippi he found Brutus slain.

ENOBARBUS

(*Aside to* AGRIPPA) That year indeed he was
    troubled with a rheum; [4]
What willingly he did confound he wail'd,
Believe 't, till I wept too.

CÆSAR

                        No, sweet Octavia,
You shall hear from me still; the time shall
    not
Out-go my thinking on you.

ANTONY

                        Come, sir, come;
I 'll wrestle with you in my strength of love:
Look, here I have you, thus I let you go,
And give you to the gods.

CÆSAR

                        Adieu, be happy!

LEPIDUS

Let all the number of the stars give light
To thy fair way!

CÆSAR

Farewell, farewell!   (*Kisses* OCTAVIA.)

ANTONY

                Farewell!
            (*Trumpets sound. Exeunt.*)

[Alexandria]   *Enter*   CLEOPATRA,
CHARMIAN, IRAS, *and* ALEXAS.

CLEOPATRA

Where is the fellow?

ALEXAS

                Half afeard to come.

CLEOPATRA

Go to, go to.
        (*Enter the Messenger as before.*)
            Come hither, sir.

    [4] head-cold

ALEXAS

                        Good majesty,
Herod of Jewry dare not look upon you
But when you are well pleas'd.

CLEOPATRA

                    That Herod's head
I 'll have: but how? When Antony is gone
Through whom I might command it? Come
    thou near.

MESSENGER

Most gracious majesty —

CLEOPATRA

                    Didst thou behold
Octavia?

MESSENGER

    Ay, dread queen.

CLEOPATRA

                    Where?

MESSENGER

                Madam, in Rome:
I look'd her m the face, and saw her led
Between her brother and Mark Antony.

CLEOPATRA

Is she as tall as me?

MESSENGER

                She is not, madam.

CLEOPATRA

Didst hear her speak? is she shrill-tongu'd or
    low?

MESSENGER

Madam, I heard her speak; she is low-voic'd.

CLEOPATRA

That 's not so good; he cannot like her long.

CHARMIAN

Like her! O Isis! 'tis impossible.

CLEOPATRA

I think so, Charmian: dull of tongue, and
dwarfish.
What majesty is in her gait? Remember,
If e'er thou look'dst on majesty.

MESSENGER

She creeps:
Her motion and her station [5] are as one;
She shows a body, rather than a life,
A statue than a breather.

CLEOPATRA

Is this certain?

MESSENGER

Or I have no observance.

CHARMIAN

Three in Egypt
Cannot make better note.

CLEOPATRA

He's very knowing,
I do perceive 't: there's nothing in her yet:
The fellow has good judgment.

CHARMIAN

Excellent.

CLEOPATRA

Guess at her years, I prithee.

MESSENGER

Madam,
She was a widow —

CLEOPATRA

Widow? Charmian, hark.

MESSENGER

And I do think she's thirty.

CLEOPATRA

Bear'st thou her face in mind? is 't long or
round?

[5] standing still

MESSENGER

Round, even to faultiness.

CLEOPATRA

For the most part, too, they are foolish that
are so.
Her hair what color?

MESSENGER

Brown, madam: and her forehead
As low as she would wish it.

CLEOPATRA

There's gold for thee.
Thou must not take my former sharpness ill:
I will employ thee back again; I find thee
Most fit for business: go make thee ready;
Our letters are prepar'd. (*Exit Messenger.*)

CHARMIAN

A proper man.

CLEOPATRA

Indeed, he is so: I repent me much
That so I harried him. Why, methinks, by
him,
This creature's no such thing.

CHARMIAN

Nothing, madam.

CLEOPATRA

The man hath seen some majesty, and should
know.

CHARMIAN

Hath he seen majesty? Isis else defend;
And serving you so long!

CLEOPATRA

I have one thing more to ask him yet, good
Charmian:
But 'tis no matter, thou shalt bring him to
me
Where I will write; all may be well enough.

CHARMIAN

I warrant you, madam. (*Exeunt.*)

[Athens]   *Enter* ANTONY *and* OCTA-
VIA.

ANTONY

Nay, nay, Octavia, not only that,
That were excusable, that and thousands
    more
Of semblable [6] import, but he hath wag'd
New wars 'gainst Pompey; made his will,
    and read it
To public ear,
Spoke scantly [7] of me: when perforce he
    could not
But pay me terms of honor, cold and sickly
He vented them; most narrow measure lent
    me;
When the best hint was given him, he not
    took 't,
Or did it from his teeth.

OCTAVIA

                    O my good lord,
Believe not all, or, if you must believe,
Stomach not all. A more unhappy lady,
If this division chance, ne'er stood between,
Praying for both parts:
The good gods will mock me presently,
When I shall pray, " O, bless my lord and
    husband! "
Undo that prayer, by crying out as loud,
" O, bless my brother! " Husband win, win
    brother,
Prays, and destroys the prayer; no midway
'Twixt these extremes at all.

ANTONY

                    Gentle Octavia,
Let your best love draw to that point, which
    seeks
Best to preserve it; if I lose mine honor,
I lose myself: better I were not yours
Than yours so branchless. But, as you re-
    quested,
Yourself shall go between 's: the meantime,
    lady,
I 'll raise the preparation of a war

6 similar
7 slightingly

Shall stain [8] your brother: make your soonest
    haste;
So your desires are yours.

OCTAVIA

                    Thanks to my lord.
The Jove of power make me, most weak,
    most weak,
Your reconciler! Wars 'twixt you twain
    would be
As if the world should cleave, and that slain
    men
Should solder up the rift.

ANTONY

When it appears to you where this begins,
Turn your displeasure that way, for our
    faults
Can never be so equal, that your love
Can equally move with them. Provide your
    going,
Choose your own company, and command
    what cost
Your heart has mind to.   (*Exeunt.*)

Enter ENOBARBUS *and* EROS, *meeting.*

ENOBARBUS

How now, friend Eros?

EROS

There 's strange news come, sir.

ENOBARBUS

What, man?

EROS

Cæsar and Lepidus have made wars upon
    Pompey.

ENOBARBUS

This is old: what is the success?

EROS

Cæsar, having made use of him in the wars
    'gainst Pompey, presently denied him
    rivality,[9] would not let him partake in

8 over-shadow
9 equal share

the glory of the action, and not resting here, accuses him of letters he had formerly wrote to Pompey; upon his own appeal, seizes him: so the poor third is up,[10] till death enlarge his confine.

ENOBARBUS

Then, world, thou hast a pair of chaps,[11] no
  more;
And throw between them all the food thou
  hast,
They 'll grind the one the other. Where 's
  Antony?

EROS

He 's walking in the garden — thus; and
  spurns [12]
The rush that lies before him; cries " Fool
  Lepidus! "
And threats the throat of that his officer
That murder'd Pompey.

ENOBARBUS

Our great navy 's rigg'd —

EROS

For Italy and Cæsar. More, Domitius,
My lord desires you presently: my news
I might have told hereafter.

ENOBARBUS

'Twill be nought,
But let it be. Bring me to Antony.

EROS

Come, sir.   (Exeunt.)

[Rome]   Enter CÆSAR, AGRIPPA, and
MÆCENAS.

CÆSAR

Contemning Rome, he has done all this, and
  more,
In Alexandria: here 's the matter of 't:
I' the market-place, on a tribunal silver'd,
Cleopatra and himself in chairs of gold

---

10 imprisoned
11 jaws
12 kicks

Were publicly enthron'd: at the feet sat
Cæsarion, whom they call my father's son,
And all the unlawful issue that their lust
Since then hath made between them. Unto
  her
He gave the stablishment of Egypt, made her
Of lower Syria, Cyprus, Lydia,
Absolute queen.

MÆCENAS

This in the public eye?

CÆSAR

I' the common show-place, where they exer-
  cise.
His sons he there proclaim'd the kings of
  kings:
Great Media, Parthia, and Armenia,
He gave to Alexander; to Ptolemy he as-
  sign'd
Syria, Cilicia and Phœnicia. She
In the habiliments of the goddess Isis
That day appear'd, and oft before gave audi-
  ence,
As 'tis reported, so.

MÆCENAS

Let Rome be thus
Inform'd.

AGRIPPA

Who, queasy with his insolence
Already, will their good thoughts call from
  him.

CÆSAR

The people knows it, and have now receiv'd
His accusations.

AGRIPPA

Who does he accuse?

CÆSAR

Cæsar, and that, having in Sicily
Sextus Pompeius spoil'd, we had not rated
  him [13]
His part o' the isle: then does he say, he lent
  me

---

13 allotted

Some shipping unrestor'd; lastly, he frets
That Lepidus of the triumvirate
Should be depos'd; and, being, that we de-
 tain
All his revenue.

AGRIPPA

Sir, this should be answer'd.

CÆSAR

'Tis done already, and the messenger gone.
I have told him, Lepidus was grown too
 cruel,
That he his high authority abus'd
And did deserve his change: for what I have
 conquer'd,
I grant him part; but then, in his Armenia
And other of his conquer'd kingdoms, I
Demand the like.

MÆCENAS

He 'll never yield to that.

CÆSAR

Nor must not then be yielded to in this.
 (*Enter* OCTAVIA, *with her train.*)

OCTAVIA

Hail, Cæsar, and my lord! hail, most dear
 Cæsar!

CÆSAR

That ever I should call thee castaway!

OCTAVIA

You have not call'd me so, nor have you
 cause.

CÆSAR

Why have you stol'n upon us thus? You
 come not
Like Cæsar's sister: the wife of Antony
Should have an army for an usher, and
The neighs of horse to tell of her approach,
Long ere she did appear; the trees by the way
Should have borne men, and expectation
 fainted,
Longing for what it had not; nay, the dust
Should have ascended to the roof of heaven,

Rais'd by your populous troops: but you are
 come
A market-maid to Rome, and have prevented
The ostentation [14] of our love; which, left
 unshown,
Is often left unlov'd: we should have met
 you
By sea and land, supplying every stage
With an augmented greeting.

OCTAVIA

                        Good, my lord,
To come thus I was not constrain'd, but did
 it
On my free will. My lord, Mark Antony,
Hearing that you prepar'd for war, ac-
 quainted
My grieved ear withal; whereon, I begg'd
His pardon for return.

CÆSAR

                    Which soon he granted,
Being an obstruct 'tween his lust and him.

OCTAVIA

Do not say so, my lord.

CÆSAR

                    I have eyes upon him.
And his affairs come to me on the wind.
Where is he now?

OCTAVIA

                My lord, in Athens.

CÆSAR

No, my most wronged sister, Cleopatra
Hath nodded him to her. He hath given his
 empire
Up to a whore, who now are levying
The kings o' the earth for war: he hath as-
 sembled
Bocchus, the king of Libya, Archelaus
Of Cappadocia, Philadelphos king
Of Paphlagonia, the Thracian king Adallas,
King Malchus of Arabia, King of Pont,
Herod of Jewry, Mithridates king
Of Comagene, Polemon and Amyntas,

[14] demonstration

The kings of Mede and Lycaonia,
With a more larger list of scepters.

OCTAVIA

             Ay me most wretched,
That have my heart parted betwixt two
    friends
That does afflict each other!

CÆSAR

              Welcome hither:
Your letters did withhold our breaking forth,
Till we perceiv'd both how you were wrong
    led
And we in negligent danger. Cheer your
    heart,
Be you not troubled with the time, which
    drives
O'er your content these strong necessities,
But let determin'd things to destiny
Hold unbewail'd their way. Welcome to
    Rome,
Nothing more dear to me. You are abus'd
Beyond the mark of thought: and the high
    gods,
To do you justice, make their ministers
Of us, and those that love you. Best of com-
    fort,
And ever welcome to us.

AGRIPPA

            Welcome, lady.

MÆCENAS

Welcome, dear madam,
Each heart in Rome does love and pity you,
Only the adulterous Antony, most large
In his abominations, turns you off;
And gives his potent regiment to a trull,
That noises it against us.

OCTAVIA

           Is it so, sir?

CÆSAR

Most certain. Sister, welcome: pray you,
Be ever known to patience: my dear'st sis-
    ter!   (*Exeunt.*)

[Near Actium]   *Enter* CLEOPATRA
and ENOBARBUS.

CLEOPATRA

I will be even with thee, doubt it not.

ENOBARBUS

But why, why, why?

CLEOPATRA

Thou hast forspoke my being in these wars,
And say'st it is not fit.

ENOBARBUS

           Well, is it, is it?

CLEOPATRA

If not denounc'd against [15] us, why should
    not we
Be there in person?

ENOBARBUS

    (*Aside*) Well, I could reply:
If we should serve with horse and mares to-
    gether,
The horse were merely lost; the mares would
    bear
A soldier and his horse.

CLEOPATRA

          What is 't you say?

ENOBARBUS

Your presence needs must puzzle Antony;
Take from his heart, take from his brain,
    from 's time,
What should not then be spar'd. He is al-
    ready
Traduc'd [16] for levity, and 'tis said in Rome
That Photinus, an eunuch, and your maids
Manage this war.

CLEOPATRA

        Sink Rome, and their tongues rot
That speak against us! A charge we bear i'
    the war,
And, as the president of my kingdom, will

15 i.e., forbidden to
16 criticized

Appear there for a man. Speak not against it,
I will not stay behind.

ENOBARBUS
                    Nay, I have done;
Here comes the emperor.
               (*Enter* ANTONY *and* CANIDIUS.)

ANTONY
                    Is it not strange, Canidius,
That from Tarentum and Brundusium
He could so quickly cut the Ionian sea,
And take in Toryne? You have heard on 't,
     sweet?

CLEOPATRA
Celerity is never more admir'd
Than by the negligent.

ANTONY
                    A good rebuke,
Which might have well become the best of
     men,
To taunt at slackness. Canidius, we
Will fight with him by sea.

CLEOPATRA
                    By sea: what else?

CANIDIUS
Why will my lord do so?

ANTONY
                    For that he dares us to 't.

ENOBARBUS
So hath my lord dar'd him to single fight.

CANIDIUS
Ay, and to wage this battle at Pharsalia,
Where Cæsar fought with Pompey: but these
     offers,
Which serve not for his vantage, he shakes
     off,
And so should you.

ENOBARBUS
                    Your ships are not well mann'd,
Your mariners are muleters, reapers, people

Ingross'd by swift impress; [17] in Cæsar's fleet
Are those that often have 'gainst Pompey
     fought,
Their ships are yare,[18] yours heavy: no dis-
     grace
Shall fall you for refusing him at sea,
Being prepar'd for land.

ANTONY
                    By sea, by sea.

ENOBARBUS
Most worthy sir, you therein throw away
The absolute soldiership you have by land,
Distract your army, which doth most consist
Of war-mark'd footmen, leaving unexecuted
Your own renowned knowledge, quite forgo
The way which promises assurance, and
Give up yourself merely to chance and haz-
     ard
From firm security.

ANTONY
                    I 'll fight at sea.

CLEOPATRA
I have sixty sails, Cæsar none better.

ANTONY
Our overplus of shipping will we burn;
And, with the rest full-mann'd, from the
     head of Actium
Beat the approaching Cæsar. But if we fail,
We then can do 't at land.
               (*Enter a Messenger.*)
                    Thy business?

MESSENGER
The news is true, my lord; he is descried;
Cæsar has taken Toryne.

ANTONY
Can he be there in person? 'Tis impossible;
Strange, that his power should be. Canidius,
Our nineteen legions thou shalt hold by land,
And our twelve thousand horse. We 'll to our
     ship:

17 collected by hasty draft
18 ready

Away, my Thetis! [19]

> (*Enter a Soldier.*)
>
> How now, worthy soldier?

SOLDIER

O noble emperor, do not fight by sea,
Trust not to rotten planks. Do you misdoubt
This sword, and these my wounds? Let the
    Egyptians
And the Phœnicians go a-ducking: we
Have us'd to conquer, standing on the earth,
And fighting foot to foot.

ANTONY

> Well, well, away!
> (*Exeunt* ANTONY, CLEOPATRA,
>   *and* ENOBARBUS.)

SOLDIER

By Hercules, I think I am i' the right.

CANIDIUS

Soldier, thou art: but his whole action grows
Not in the power on 't: so our leader 's led,
And we are women's men.

SOLDIER

> You keep by land
The legions and the horse whole, do you not?

CANIDIUS

Marcus Octavius, Marcus Justeius,
Publicola and Cælius, are for sea:
But we keep whole by land. This speed of
    Cæsar's
Carries beyond belief.

SOLDIER

> While he was yet in Rome,
His power went out in such distractions [20] as
Beguil'd all spies.

CANIDIUS

Who 's his lieutenant, hear you?

SOLDIER

They say, one Taurus.

[19] sea goddess
[20] detachments

CANIDIUS

> Well I know the man.
> (*Enter a Messenger.*)

MESSENGER

The emperor calls Canidius.

CANIDIUS

With news the time 's with labor, and
    throes [21] forth
Each minute some.   (*Exeunt.*)

Enter CÆSAR, *and* TAURUS, *with his army,
marching.*

CÆSAR

Taurus!

TAURUS

My lord?

CÆSAR

Strike not by land, keep whole, provoke not
    battle
Till we have done at sea. Do not exceed
The prescript [22] of this scroll: our fortune lies
Upon this jump.   (*Exeunt.*)

Enter ANTONY *and* ENOBARBUS.

ANTONY

Set we our squadrons on yond side o' the hill,
In eye of Cæsar's battle, from which place
We may the number of the ships behold,
And so proceed accordingly.   (*Exeunt.*)

Enter CANIDIUS, *marching with his land
army one way over the stage; and* TAURUS,
the lieutenant of CÆSAR, *with his army, the
other way. After their going in, is heard the
noise of a sea-fight.*

Alarum. Enter ENOBARBUS.

ENOBARBUS

Nought, nought, all nought, I can behold no
    longer!
The Antoniad, the Egyptian admiral,

[21] gives birth
[22] limits

With all their sixty, fly and turn the rudder:
To see 't, mine eyes are blasted.
(*Enter* Scarus.)

SCARUS

Gods and goddesses,
All the whole synod [23] of them!

ENOBARBUS

What 's thy passion?

SCARUS

The greater cantle [24] of the world is lost.
With very ignorance, we have kiss'd away
Kingdoms and provinces.

ENOBARBUS

How appears the fight?

SCARUS

On our side, like the token'd pestilence,
Where death is sure. Yon ribaudred nag [25] of
    Egypt
(Whom leprosy o'ertake!) i' the midst o' the
    fight,
When vantage like a pair of twins appear'd,
Both as the same, or rather ours the elder,
The breese [26] upon her, like a cow in June,
Hoist sails and flies.

ENOBARBUS

That I beheld:
Mine eyes did sicken at the sight, and could
    not
Endure a further view.

SCARUS

She once being loof'd,
The noble ruin of her magic, Antony,
Claps on his sea-wing, and (like a doting mal-
    lard)
Leaving the fight in height, flies after her:
I never saw an action of such shame;
Experience, manhood, honor, ne'er before
Did violate so itself.

---
[23] fleet of vessels
[24] section
[25] unbridled horse
[26] gadfly

ENOBARBUS

Alack, alack!
(*Enter* Canidius.)

CANIDIUS

Our fortune on the sea is out of breath,
And sinks most lamentably. Had our general
Been what he knew himself, it had gone well:
O, he has given example for our flight
Most grossly by his own!

ENOBARBUS

Ay, are you thereabouts? Why then good
    night
Indeed.

CANIDIUS

Toward Peloponnesus are they fled.

SCARUS

'Tis easy to 't; and there I will attend
What further comes.

CANIDIUS

To Cæsar will I render
My legions and my horse: six kings already
Show me the way of yielding.

ENOBARBUS

I 'll yet follow
The wounded chance of Antony, though my
    reason
Sits in the wind against me.   (*Exeunt.*)

[Alexandria]   *Enter* ANTONY *with
Attendants.*

ANTONY

Hark! the land bids me tread no more up-
    on 't,
It is ashamed to bear me. Friends, come
    hither.
I am so lated [27] in the world that I
Have lost my way for ever. I have a ship
Laden with gold, take that, divide it; fly,
And make your peace with Cæsar.

ALL

Fly! not we.

---
[27] overtaken by darkness

ANTONY

I have fled myself, and have instructed cow-
   ards
To run, and show their shoulders. Friends, be
   gone;
I have myself resolv'd upon a course
Which has no need of you; be gone,
My treasure 's in the harbor; take it. O,
I follow'd that I blush to look upon,
My very hairs do mutiny, for the white
Reprove the brown for rashness, and they
   them
For fear and doting. Friends, be gone; you
   shall
Have letters from me to some friends that
   will
Sweep your way for you. Pray you, look not
   sad,
Nor make replies of loathness, take the hint
Which my despair proclaims; let that be left
Which leaves itself: to the sea-side straight-
   way:
I will possess you of that ship and treasure.
Leave me, I pray, a little: pray you now,
Nay, do so; for indeed I have lost command,
Therefore I pray you: I 'll see you by and by.
                            (*Sits down.*)
(*Enter* CLEOPATRA *led by* CHARMIAN *and*
IRAS; EROS *following.*)

EROS

Nay, gentle madam, to him, comfort him.

IRAS

Do, most dear queen.

CHARMIAN

Do! why, what else.

CLEOPATRA

Let me sit down. O Juno!

ANTONY

No, no, no, no, no.

EROS

See you here, sir?

ANTONY

O fie, fie, fie!

CHARMIAN

Madam!

IRAS

Madam, O good empress!

EROS

Sir, sir!

ANTONY

Yes, my lord, yes; he at Philippi kept
His sword e'en like a dancer, while I struck
The lean and wrinkled Cassius, and 'twas I
That the mad Brutus ended: he alone
Dealt on lieutenantry,[28] and no practice had
In the brave squares [29] of war: yet now —
   No matter.

CLEOPATRA

Ah! stand by.

EROS

The queen, my lord, the queen.

IRAS

Go to him, madam, speak to him,
He is unqualitied [30] with very shame.

CLEOPATRA

Well then, sustain me: O!

EROS

Most noble sir, arise, the queen approaches,
Her head 's declin'd, and death will seize her,
   but
Your comfort makes the rescue.

ANTONY

I have offended reputation,
A most unnoble swerving.

EROS
                            Sir, the queen,

---

[28] sat in the command-post
[29] formations
[30] unmanned

ANTONY

O, whither hast thou led me, Egypt? See,
How I convey my shame out of thine eyes
By looking back what I have left behind
'Stroy'd in dishonor.

CLEOPATRA

                    O my lord, my lord,
Forgive my fearful sails! I little thought
You would have follow'd.

ANTONY

                    Egypt, thou knew'st too well
My heart was to thy rudder tied by the
    strings,
And thou shouldst tow me after: o'er my
    spirit
Thy full supremacy thou knew'st, and that
Thy beck might from the bidding of the
    gods
Command me.

CLEOPATRA

O, my pardon!

ANTONY

                            Now I must
To the young man send humble treaties,
    dodge
And palter [31] in the shifts of lowness,[32] who
With half the bulk o' the world play'd as I
    pleas'd,
Making and marring fortunes. You did know
How much you were my conqueror, and that
My sword, made weak by my affection,
    would
Obey it on all cause.

CLEOPATRA

                    Pardon, pardon!

ANTONY

Fall not a tear, I say, one of them rates
All that is won and lost: give me a kiss,
Even this repays me. We sent our school-
    master,
Is he come back? Love, I am full of lead.

[31] bargain
[32] beggary

Some wine, within there, and our viands!
    Fortune knows
We scorn her most, when most she offers
    blows.   (*Exeunt.*)

[The Roman Camp]   *Enter* CÆSAR,
DOLABELLA, THYREUS, *with others.*

CÆSAR

Let him appear that 's come from Antony.
Know you him?

DOLABELLA

                    Cæsar, 'tis his schoolmaster,
An argument that he is pluck'd, when hither
He sends so poor a pinion of his wing,
Which had superfluous kings for messengers,
Not many moons gone by.
(*Enter* EUPHRONIUS, *ambassador from* AN-
TONY.)

CÆSAR

                    Approach, and speak.

EUPHRONIUS

Such as I am, I come from Antony:
I was of late as petty to his ends
As is the morn-dew on the myrtle-leaf
To his grand sea.

CÆSAR

                    Be 't so: declare thine office.

EUPHRONIUS

Lord of his fortunes he salutes thee, and
Requires to live in Egypt, which not granted,
He lessens his requests, and to thee sues
To let him breathe between the heavens and
    earth,
A private man in Athens: this for him.
Next, Cleopatra does confess thy greatness,
Submits her to thy might, and of thee craves
The circle [33] of the Ptolomies for her heirs,
Now hazarded to thy grace.

CÆSAR

                            For Antony,
I have no ears to his request. The queen

[33] crown

Of audience nor desire shall fail, so she
From Egypt drive her all-disgraced friend,
Or take his life there. This if she perform,
She shall not sue unheard. So to them both.

EUPHRONIUS

Fortune pursue thee!

CÆSAR

      Bring him through the bands.[34]
             (*Exit* EUPHRONIUS.)
(*To* THYREUS) To try thy eloquence, now
  'tis time, dispatch;
From Antony win Cleopatra: promise,
And in our name, what she requires, add
  more,
From thine invention, offers: women are not
In their best fortunes strong; but want will
  perjure
The ne'er-touch'd vestal: try thy cunning,
  Thyreus;
Make thine own edicts for thy pains, which
  we
Will answer as a law.

THYREUS

      Cæsar, I go.

CÆSAR

Observe how Antony becomes [35] his flaw,
And what thou think'st his very action
  speaks
In every power that moves.

THYREUS

      Cæsar, I shall.   (*Exeunt.*)

[Alexandria]   *Enter* CLEOPATRA,
ENOBARBUS, CHARMIAN, *and* IRAS.

CLEOPATRA

What shall we do, Enobarbus?

ENOBARBUS

          Think, and die.

CLEOPATRA

Is Antony or we in fault for this?

34 soldiers
35 reacts to

ENOBARBUS

Antony only, that would make his will
Lord of his reason. What though you fled
From that great face of war, whose several
  ranges
Frighted each other? Why should he follow?
The itch of his affection should not then
Have nick'd his captainship, at such a point,
When half to half the world oppos'd, he
  being
The mered [36] question: 'twas a shame no less
Than was his loss, to course [37] your flying
  flags,
And leave his navy gazing.

CLEOPATRA

         Prithee, peace.
(*Enter* ANTONY, *with* EUPHRONIUS *the
ambassador.*)

ANTONY

Is that his answer?

EUPHRONIUS

Ay, my lord.

ANTONY

The queen shall then have courtesy, so she
Will yield us up.

EUPHRONIUS

      He says so.

ANTONY

         Let her know 't.
To the boy Cæsar send this grizzled head,
And he will fill thy wishes to the brim
With principalities.

CLEOPATRA

      That head, my lord?

ANTONY

To him again, tell him he wears the rose
Of youth upon him, from which the world
  should note
Something particular: his coin, ships, legions,

36 only
37 follow

May be a coward's, whose ministers would
prevail
Under the service of a child as soon
As i' the command of Cæsar: I dare him
therefore
To lay his gay comparisons apart
And answer me declin'd, sword against
sword,
Ourselves alone. I 'll write it: follow me.
(*Exeunt* ANTONY *and* EUPHRONIUS.)

ENOBARBUS

(*Aside*) Yes, like enough; high-battled Cæ-
sar will
Unstate his happiness, and be stag'd to the
show
Against a sworder! I see men's judgments are
A parcel of their fortunes, and things out-
ward
Do draw the inward quality after them,
To suffer all alike; that he should dream,
Knowing all measures, the full Cæsar will
Answer his emptiness; Cæsar, thou hast sub-
du'd
His judgment too.
(*Enter a Servant.*)

SERVANT

A messenger from Cæsar.

CLEOPATRA

What, no more ceremony? See, my women,
Against the blown rose may they stop their
nose
That kneel'd unto the buds. Admit him, sir.
(*Exit Servant.*)

ENOBARBUS

(*Aside*) Mine honesty and I begin to
square.[38]
The loyalty well held to fools does make
Our faith mere folly: yet he that can endure
To follow with allegiance a fall'n lord
Does conquer him that did his master con-
quer,
And earn a place i' the story.
(*Enter* THYREUS.)

[38] quarrel

CLEOPATRA

Cæsar's will!

THYREUS

Hear it apart.

CLEOPATRA

None but friends: say boldly.

THYREUS

So, haply, are they friends to Antony.

ENOBARBUS

He needs as many, sir, as Cæsar has,
Or needs not us. If Cæsar please, our master
Will leap to be his friend: for us, you know,
Whose he is we are, and that is Cæsar's.

THYREUS

So.
Thus then, thou most renown'd, Cæsar en-
treats
Not to consider in what case thou stand'st
Further than he is Cæsar.

CLEOPATRA

Go on: right royal.

THYREUS

He knows that you embrace not Antony
As you did love him, but as you fear'd him.

CLEOPATRA

O!

THYREUS

The scars upon your honor therefore he
Does pity, as constrained blemishes,
Not as deserv'd.

CLEOPATRA

He is a god and knows
What is most right: mine honor was not
yielded,
But conquer'd merely.

ENOBARBUS

(*Aside*) To be sure of that,
I will ask Antony. Sir, sir, thou art so leaky

That we must leave thee to thy sinking, for
Thy dearest quit thee.   (*Exit.*)

THYREUS
            Shall I say to Cæsar
What you require of him? for he partly begs
To be desir'd to give. It much would please
    him,
That of his fortunes you should make a staff
To lean upon: but it would warm his spirits,
To hear from me you had left Antony,
And put yourself under his shroud,
The universal landlord.

CLEOPATRA
            What 's your name?

THYREUS
My name is Thyreus.

CLEOPATRA
            Most kind messenger,
Say to great Cæsar this in deputation;
I kiss his conquering hand: tell him, I am
    prompt
To lay my crown at 's feet, and there to
    kneel:
Tell him, from his all-obeying breath I hear
The doom of Egypt.

THYREUS
            'Tis your noblest course.
Wisdom and fortune combating together,
If that the former dare but what it can,
No chance may shake it. Give me grace to
    lay
My duty on your hand.

CLEOPATRA
            Your Cæsar's father oft,
(When he hath mus'd of taking kingdoms
    in)
Bestow'd his lips on that unworthy place,
As it rain'd kisses.
    (*Re-enter* ANTONY *and* ENOBARBUS.)

ANTONY
            Favors? By Jove that thunders! —
What art thou, fellow?

THYREUS
            One that but performs
The bidding of the fullest man, and wor-
    thiest
To have command obey'd.

ENOBARBUS
    (*Aside*) You will be whipp'd.

ANTONY
Approach, there! Ah, you kite! [39] Now, gods
    and devils!
Authority melts from me of late. When I
    cried " Ho! "
Like boys unto a muss, kings would start
    forth,
And cry, " Your will? " Have you no ears?
I am Antony yet.
            (*Enter Attendants.*)
    Take hence this Jack, [40] and whip him.

ENOBARBUS
(*Aside*) 'Tis better playing with a lion's
    whelp,
Than with an old one dying.

ANTONY
            Moon and stars,
Whip him! Were 't twenty of the greatest
    tributaries
That do acknowledge Cæsar, should I find
    them
So saucy with the hand of she here — what 's
    her name,
Since she was Cleopatra? Whip him, fellows,
Till, like a boy, you see him cringe his face,
And whine aloud for mercy. Take him hence.

THYREUS
Mark Antony —

ANTONY
            Tug him away: being whipp'd,
Bring him again, the Jack of Cæsar's shall
Bear us an errand to him.
            (*Exeunt Attendants, with* THYREUS.)
You were half blasted ere I knew you: ha!

[39] bird of prey
[40] fellow

Have I my pillow left unpress'd in Rome,
Forborne the getting of a lawful race,
And by a gem of women, to be abus'd
By one that looks on feeders? [41]

CLEOPATRA

Good my lord —

ANTONY

You have been a boggler ever,
But when we in our viciousness grow hard
(O misery on 't!) the wise gods seel [42] our
    eyes;
In our own filth drop our clear judgments,
    make us
Adore our errors, laugh at 's while we strut
To our confusion.

CLEOPATRA

O, is 't come to this?

ANTONY

I found you as a morsel, cold upon
Dead Cæsar's trencher; nay, you were a frag-
    ment
Of Cneius Pompey's, besides what hotter
    hours,
Unregister'd in vulgar fame, you have
Luxuriously pick'd out: for I am sure,
Though you can guess what temperance
    should be,
You know not what it is.

CLEOPATRA

Wherefore is this?

ANTONY

To let a fellow that will take rewards,
And say " God quit you! " be familiar with
My playfellow, your hand; this kingly seal
And plighter of high hearts! O, that I were
Upon the hill of Basan, to outroar
The horned herd! for I have savage cause,
And to proclaim it civilly, were like
A halter'd neck which does the hangman
    thank
For being yare about him.
    (*Re-enter Attendants, with* THYREUS.)
        Is he whipp'd?

1st ATTENDANT

Soundly, my lord.

ANTONY

Cried he? and begg'd a pardon?

1st ATTENDANT

He did ask favor.

ANTONY

If that thy father live, let him repent
Thou wast not made his daughter, and be
    thou sorry
To follow Cæsar in his triumph, since
Thou hast been whipp'd for following him:
    henceforth
The white hand of a lady fever thee,
Shake thou to look on 't. Get thee back to
    Cæsar,
Tell him thy entertainment: look thou say
He makes me angry with him; for he seems
Proud and disdainful, harping on what I am,
Not what he knew I was: he makes me angry,
And at this time most easy 'tis to do 't;
When my good stars, that were my former
    guides,
Have empty left their orbs, and shot their
    fires
Into the abysm of hell. If he mislike
My speech, and what is done, tell him he has
Hipparchus, my enfranched [43] bondman,
    whom
He may at pleasure whip, or hang, or torture,
As he shall like to quit me: urge it thou:
Hence with thy stripes, begone!
                    (*Exit* THYREUS.)

CLEOPATRA

Have you done yet?

ANTONY

Alack, our terrene [44] moon
Is now eclips'd, and it portends alone
The fall of Antony.

CLEOPATRA

I must stay his time?

[41] servants
[42] sew up

[43] freed
[44] earthly

ANTONY

To flatter Cæsar, would you mingle eyes
With one that ties his points? [45]

CLEOPATRA

Not know me yet?

ANTONY

Cold-hearted towards me?

CLEOPATRA

Ah, dear, if I be so,
From my cold heart let heaven engender hail,
And poison it in the source, and the first
stone
Drop in my neck: as it determines, so
Dissolve my life; the next Cæsarion smite,
Till by degrees the memory of my womb,
Together with my brave Egyptians all,
By the discandying [46] of this pelleted storm
Lie graveless, till the flies and gnats of Nile
Have buried them for prey!

ANTONY

I am satisfied.
Cæsar sits down in Alexandria, where
I will oppose his fate. Our force by land
Hath nobly held, our sever'd navy too
Have knit again, and fleet, threatening most
sea-like.
Where hast thou been, my heart? Dost thou
hear, lady?
If from the field I shall return once more
To kiss these lips, I will appear in blood,
I, and my sword, will earn our chronicle;
There 's hope in 't yet.

CLEOPATRA

That 's my brave lord!

ANTONY

I will be treble-sinew'd, hearted, breath'd,
And fight maliciously: for when mine hours
Were nice and lucky, men did ransom lives
Of me for jests; but now I 'll set my teeth,
And send to darkness all that stop me.
Come,

45 i.e., is his groom
46 melting

Let 's have one other gaudy [47] night: call to
me
All my sad captains, fill our bowls once more:
Let 's mock the midnight bell.

CLEOPATRA

It is my birthday,
I had thought to have held it poor, but since
my lord
Is Antony again, I will be Cleopatra.

ANTONY

We will yet do well.

CLEOPATRA

Call all his noble captains to my lord.

ANTONY

Do so, we 'll speak to them, and tonight I 'll
force
The wine peep through their scars. Come on,
my queen,
There 's sap in 't yet. The next time I do
fight
I 'll make death love me; for I will contend
Even with his pestilent scythe.
(*Exeunt all but* ENOBARBUS.)

ENOBARBUS

Now he 'll outstare the lightning. To be
furious
Is to be frighted out of fear, and in that
mood
The dove will peck the estridge; [48] and I see
still,
A diminution in our captain's brain
Restores his heart: when valor preys on rea-
son,
It eats the sword it fights with. I will seek
Some way to leave him. (*Exit.*)

ACT FOUR

[The Roman Camp] *Enter* CÆSAR,
AGRIPPA, *and* MÆCENAS, *with his army:*
CÆSAR *reading a letter.*

CÆSAR

He calls me boy, and chides as he had power
To beat me out of Egypt; my messenger

47 festival
48 hawk

He hath whipp'd with rods, dares me to per-
    sonal combat:
Cæsar to Antony; let the old ruffian know
I have many other ways to die; meantime
Laugh at his challenge.

MÆCENAS

            Cæsar must think,
When one so great begins to rage, he's
    hunted
Even to falling. Give him no breath, but now
Make boot [1] of his distraction; never anger
Make good guard for itself.

CÆSAR

           Let our best heads
Know that tomorrow that last of many
    battles
We mean to fight. Within our files there are,
Of those that serv'd Mark Antony but late,
Enough to fetch him in. See it done:
And feast the army; we have store to do 't,
And they have earned the waste. Poor An-
    tony!   (*Exeunt.*)

[**Alexandria**]   *Enter* ANTONY, CLEO-
PATRA, ENOBARBUS, CHARMIAN, IRAS,
ALEXAS, *with others.*

ANTONY

He will not fight with me, Domitius?

ENOBARBUS

              No.

ANTONY

Why should he not?

ENOBARBUS

He thinks, being twenty times of better for-
    tune,
He is twenty men to one.

ANTONY

          Tomorrow, soldier,
By sea and land I'll fight: or [2] I will live,
Or bathe my dying honor in the blood

    [1] profit
    [2] either

Shall make it live again. Woo't thou fight
    well?

ENOBARBUS

I'll strike, and cry " Take all."

ANTONY

          Well said, come on.
Call forth my household servants, let's to-
    night
Be bounteous at our meal.
    (*Enter three or four Servitors.*)
          Give me thy hand,
Thou hast been rightly honest; — so hast
    thou; —
Thou — and thou — and thou: you have
    serv'd me well,
And kings have been your fellows.

CLEOPATRA

(*Aside to* ENOBARBUS) What means this?

ENOBARBUS

(*Aside to* CLEOPATRA) 'Tis one of those odd
    tricks which sorrow shoots [3]
Out of the mind.

ANTONY

          And thou art honest too:
I wish I could be made so many men,
And all of you clapp'd up together in
An Antony; that I might do you service,
So good as you have done.

SERVANT

          The gods forbid!

ANTONY

Well, my good fellows, wait on me tonight:
Scant not my cups, and make as much of me
As when mine empire was your fellow too,
And suffer'd my command.

CLEOPATRA

(*Aside to* ENOBARBUS) What does he mean?

ENOBARBUS

(*Aside to* CLEOPATRA) To make his follow-
    ers weep.

    [3] produces

ANTONY

                              Tend me, tonight;
May be it is the period [4] of your duty,
Haply you shall not see me more, or if,
A mangled shadow: perchance tomorrow
You 'll serve another master. I look on you,
As one that takes his leave. Mine honest
          friends,
I turn you not away, but, like a master
Married to your good service, stay till death:
Tend me tonight two hours, I ask no more,
And the gods yield [5] you for 't!

ENOBARBUS

                              What mean you, sir,
To give them this discomfort? Look, they
          weep,
And I, an ass, am onion-eyed: for shame,
Transform us not to women.

ANTONY

                              Ho, ho, ho!
Now the witch take me, if I meant it thus!
Grace grow where those drops fall! My hearty
          friends,
You take me in too dolorous a sense,
For I spake to you for your comfort, did de-
          sire you
To burn this night with torches: know, my
          hearts,
I hope well of tomorrow, and will lead you
Where rather I 'll expect victorious life,
Than death, and honor. Let 's to supper,
          come,
And drown consideration.   (*Exeunt.*)

Enter two Soldiers to their guard.

1st SOLDIER
Brother, good night: tomorrow is the day.

2nd SOLDIER
It will determine one way: fare you well.
Heard you of nothing strange about the
          steets?

4 end
5 reward

1st SOLDIER
Nothing. What news?

2nd SOLDIER
Belike 'tis but a rumor; good night to you.

1st SOLDIER
Well, sir, good night.
                    (*Enter other Soldiers.*)

2nd SOLDIER
Soldiers, have careful watch.

3rd SOLDIER
And you. Good night, good night.
(*They place themselves in every corner of
the stage.*)

4th SOLDIER
Here we: and if tomorrow
Our navy thrive, I have an absolute hope
Our landmen will stand up.

3rd SOLDIER
                              'Tis a brave army,
And full of purpose.
(*Music of the hautboys [6] is under the stage.*)

4th SOLDIER
          Peace, what noise?

1st SOLDIER
                              List, list!

2nd SOLDIER
Hark!

1st SOLDIER
Music i' the air.

3rd SOLDIER
          Under the earth.

4th SOLDIER
It signs well, does it not?

3rd SOLDIER
          No.

6 oboes

1st SOLDIER

Peace, I say!
What should this mean?

2nd SOLDIER

'Tis the god Hercules, whom Antony lov'd,
Now leaves him.

1st SOLDIER

Walk, let 's see if other watchmen
Do hear what we do.

2nd SOLDIER

How now, masters!

ALL

(*Speaking together*) How now? How now?
Do you hear this?

1st SOLDIER

Ay, is 't not strange?

3rd SOLDIER

Do you hear, masters? do you hear?

1st SOLDIER

Follow the noise so far as we have quarter;
Let 's see how it will give off.

ALL

Content. 'Tis strange.   (*Exeunt.*)

Enter ANTONY *and* CLEOPATRA, CHAR-
MIAN *and others attending.*

ANTONY

Eros! mine armor, Eros!

CLEOPATRA

Sleep a little.

ANTONY

No, my chuck. Eros, come, mine armor,
Eros!
     (*Enter* EROS *with armor.*)
Come, good fellow, put thine iron on:
If fortune be not ours today, it is
Because we brave her: come.

CLEOPATRA

Nay, I 'll help too.
What 's this for?

ANTONY

Ah, let be, let be! thou art
The armorer of my heart: false, false; this,
     this.

CLEOPATRA

Sooth, la, I 'll help: thus it must be.

ANTONY

Well, well,
We shall thrive now. Seest thou, my good
     fellow?
Go put on thy defences.

EROS

Briefly, sir.

CLEOPATRA

Is not this buckled well?

ANTONY

Rarely, rarely:
He that unbuckles this, till we do please
To doff 't for our repose, shall hear a storm.
Thou fumblest, Eros, and my queen 's a
     squire
More tight [7] at this than thou: dispatch. O
     love,
That thou couldst see my wars today, and
     knew'st
The royal occupation! thou shouldst see
A workman in 't.
     (*Enter an armed Soldier.*)
Good morrow to thee; welcome:
Thou look'st like him that knows a warlike
     charge:
To business that we love we rise betime,
And go to 't with delight.

SOLDIER

A thousand, sir, early though 't be, have on
Their riveted trim, and at the port expect
     you.   (*Shout. Trumpets flourish.*)
     (*Enter Captains and Soldiers.*)

[7] skilled

CAPTAIN

The morn is fair. Good morrow, general.

ALL

Good morrow, general.

ANTONY

'Tis well blown, lads:
This morning, like the spirit of a youth
That means to be of note, begins betimes.[8]
So, so; come, give me that: this way; well
said.
Fare thee well, dame, whate'er becomes of
me,
This is a soldier's kiss: rebukeable
And worthy shameful check it were, to stand
On more mechanic [9] compliment; I'll leave
thee
Now like a man of steel. You that will fight,
Follow me close, I'll bring you to 't. Adieu.
(*Exeunt,* ANTONY, EROS, *Captains and Sol-
diers.*)

CHARMIAN

Please you retire to your chamber?

CLEOPATRA

Lead me.

He goes forth gallantly. That he and Cæsar
might
Determine this great war in single fight!
Then Antony — but now — Well, on.
(*Exeunt.*)

Trumpets sound. Enter ANTONY *and* EROS;
a Soldier meeting them.

SOLDIER

The gods make this a happy day to Antony!

ANTONY

Would thou, and those thy scars, had once
prevail'd
To make me fight at land!

SOLDIER

Hadst thou done so,
The kings that have revolted, and the soldier

That has this morning left thee, would have
still
Follow'd thy heels.

ANTONY

Who's gone this morning?

SOLDIER

Who?

One ever near thee: call for Enobarbus,
He shall not hear thee, or from Cæsar's camp
Say " I am none of thine."

ANTONY

What say'st thou?

SOLDIER

Sir,

He is with Cæsar.

EROS

Sir, his chests and treasure
He has not with him.

ANTONY

Is he gone?

SOLDIER

Most certain.

ANTONY

Go, Eros, send his treasure after, do it,
Detain no jot, I charge thee: write to him
(I will subscribe) [10] gentle adieus, and greet-
ings;
Say, that I wish he never find more cause
To change a master. O, my fortunes have
Corrupted honest men! Dispatch. Enobarbus!
(*Exeunt.*)

Flourish. Enter CÆSAR *with* AGRIPPA, ENO-
BARBUS, *and others.*

CÆSAR

Go forth, Agrippa, and begin the fight:
Our will is Antony be took alive;
Make it so known.

8 early
9 according to etiquette

10 countersign

AGRIPPA

Cæsar, I shall.   (*Exit.*)

CÆSAR

The time of universal peace is near:
Prove this is a prosperous day, the three-
     nook'd world
Shall bear the olive freely.
          (*Enter a Messenger.*)

MESSENGER

                    Antony
Is come into the field.

CÆSAR

              Go charge Agrippa,
Plant those that have revolted in the van,
That Antony may seem to spend his fury
Upon himself.
          (*Exeunt all but* ENOBARBUS.)

ENOBARBUS

Alexas did revolt, and went to Jewry
On affairs of Antony, there did dissuade [11]
Great Herod to incline himself to Cæsar,
And leave his master Antony: for this pains,
Cæsar hath hang'd him. Canidius and the rest
That fell away have entertainment, but
No honorable trust. I have done ill,
Of which I do accuse myself so sorely
That I will joy no more.
          (*Enter a Soldier of* CÆSAR's.)

SOLDIER

              Enobarbus, Antony
Hath after thee sent all thy treasure, with
His bounty overplus: the messenger
Came on my guard, and at thy tent is now
Unloading of his mules.

ENOBARBUS

              I give it you.

SOLDIER

Mock not, Enobarbus,
I tell you true: best you saf'd [12] the bringer

---

[11] persuade
[12] gave safe conduct to

Out of the host; I must attend mine office,
Or would have done 't myself. Your emperor
Continues still a Jove.   (*Exit.*)

ENOBARBUS

I am alone the villain of the earth,
And feel I am so most. O Antony,
Thou mine of bounty, how would'st thou
     have paid
My better service, when my turpitude
Thou dost so crown with gold! This blows [13]
     my heart:
If swift thought break it not, a swifter mean
Shall outstrike thought: but thought will
     do 't, I feel.
I fight against thee? No: I will go seek
Some ditch, wherein to die; the foul'st best
     fits
My latter part of life.   (*Exit.*)

Alarum. Drums and trumpets. Enter AGRIP-
PA *and others.*

AGRIPPA

Retire, we have engag'd ourselves too far:
Cæsar himself has work,[14] and our oppression
Exceeds what we expected.   (*Exeunt.*)

Alarums. Enter ANTONY, *and* SCARUS
wounded.

SCARUS

O my brave emperor, this is fought indeed!
Had we done so at first, we had droven them
     home
With clouts about their heads.

ANTONY

              Thou bleed'st apace.

SCARUS

I had a wound here that was like a T,
But now 'tis made an H. (*Retreat afar off.*)

ANTONY

              They do retire.

---

[13] strikes
[14] hard work

SCARUS

We 'll beat 'em into bench-holes,[15] I have yet
Room for six scotches [16] more.

(*Enter* EROS.)

EROS

They are beaten, sir, and our advantage serves
For a fair victory.

SCARUS

Let us score their backs,
And snatch 'em up, as we take hares, behind:
'Tis sport to maul a runner.

ANTONY

I will reward thee
Once for thy spritely comfort, and ten-fold
For thy good valor. Come thee on.

SCARUS

I 'll halt after.   (*Exeunt.*)

Alarum, Enter ANTONY, *in a march;*
SCARUS, *with others.*

ANTONY

We have beat him to his camp: run one be-
fore,
And let the queen know of our gests.[17]
Tomorrow,
Before the sun shall see 's, we 'll spill the
blood
That has today escap'd. I thank you all;
For doughty-handed are you, and have
fought
Not as you serv'd the cause, but as 't had
been
Each man's like mine; you have shown all
Hectors.[18]
Enter the city, clip [19] your wives, your
friends,
Tell them your feats, whilst they with joyful
tears
Wash the congealment from your wounds
and kiss

15 latrines
16 wounds
17 deeds
18 i.e., heroic fighters
19 embrace

The honor'd gashes whole. (*To* SCARUS)
Give me thy hand;
(*Enter* CLEOPATRA, *attended.*)
To this great fairy I 'll commend thy acts,
Make her thanks bless thee. O thou day o' the
world,
Chain mine arm'd neck, leap thou, attire and
all,
Through proof of harness to my heart, and
there
Ride on the pants triumphing!

CLEOPATRA

Lord of lords!
O infinite virtue, com'st thou smiling from
The world's great snare uncaught?

ANTONY

My nightingale,
We have beat them to their beds. What, girl!
though grey
Do something mingle with our younger
brown, yet ha' we
A brain that nourishes our nerves, and can
Get goal for goal of youth. Behold this man,
Commend unto his lips thy favoring hand:
Kiss it, my warrior: he hath fought today
As if a god in hate of mankind had
Destroy'd in such a shape.

CLEOPATRA

I 'll give thee, friend,
An armor all of gold; it was a king's.

ANTONY

He has deserv'd it, were it carbuncled [20]
Like Holy Phœbus' car. Give me thy hand,
Through Alexandria make a jolly march,
Bear our back'd targets [21] like the men that
owe them:
Had our great palace the capacity
To camp this host, we all would sup together,
And drink carouses to the next day's fate,
Which promises royal peril. Trumpeters,
With brazen din blast you the city's ear,
Make mingle with our rattling tabourines,

20 bejewelled
21 shields

That heaven and earth may strike their
    sounds together,
Applauding our approach.   (*Exeunt.*)

Enter Sentinels.

1st SENTINEL

If we be not reliev'd within this hour,
We must return to the court of guard: the
    night
Is shiny, and they say we shall embattle
By the second hour i' the morn.

2nd SENTINEL

                This last day was
A shrewd one to 's.
    (*Enter* ENOBARBUS.)

ENOBARBUS

      O bear me witness, night —

3rd SENTINEL

What man is this?

2nd SENTINEL

      Stand close, and list him.

ENOBARBUS

Be witness, O thou blessed moon,
When men revolted shall upon record
Bear hateful memory, poor Enobarbus did
Before thy face repent!

1st SENTINEL

      Enobarbus!

3rd SENTINEL

             Peace!
Hark further.

ENOBARBUS

O sovereign mistress of true melancholy,
The poisonous damp of night disponge upon
    me,
That life, a very rebel to my will,
May hang no longer on me: throw my heart
Against the flint and hardness of my fault,
Which, being dried with grief, will break to
    powder,

And finish all foul thoughts. O Antony,
Nobler than my revolt is infamous,
Forgive me in thine own particular,
But let the world rank me in register
A master-leaver and a fugitive:
O Antony! O Antony!   (*Dies.*)

2nd SENTINEL

      Let 's speak to him.

1st SENTINEL

Let 's hear him, for the things he speaks
May concern Cæsar.

3rd SENTINEL

      Let 's do so. But he sleeps.

1st SENTINEL

Swoons rather, for so bad a prayer as his
Was never yet for sleep.

2nd SENTINEL

      Go we to him.

3rd SENTINEL

Awake, sir, awake, speak to us.

2nd SENTINEL

           Hear you, sir?

1st SENTINEL

The hand of death hath raught him. (*Drums
    afar off.*) Hark! the drums
Demurely wake the sleepers. Let us bear him
To the court of guard; he is of note: our
    hour
Is fully out.

3rd SENTINEL

Come on, then; he may recover yet.
    (*Exeunt with the body.*)

Enter ANTONY *and* SCARUS, *with their army.*

ANTONY

Their preparation is today by sea,
We please them not by land.

SCARUS

      For both, my lord.

ANTONY

I would they 'd fight i' the fire, or i' the air;
We 'd fight there too. But this it is; our foot
Upon the hills adjoining to the city
Shall stay with us: order for sea is given;
They have put forth the haven
Where their appointment we may best dis-
cover
And look on their endeavor.   (*Exeunt.*)

Enter CÆSAR, *and his army.*

CÆSAR

But [22] being charg'd, we will be still by land,
Which, as I take 't, we shall; for his best
force
Is forth to man his galleys. To the vales,
And hold our best advantage.   (*Exeunt.*)

Enter ANTONY *and* SCARUS.

ANTONY

Yet they are not join'd: where yond pine does
stand,
I shall discover all: I 'll bring thee word
Straight, how 'tis like to go.   (*Exit.*)
          (*Alarum afar off, as at a sea-fight.*)

SCARUS

                    Swallows have built
In Cleopatra's sails their nests: the augurers
Say they know not, they cannot tell, look
grimly,
And dare not speak their knowledge. Antony
Is valiant, and dejected, and by starts
His fretted fortunes give him hope and fear
Of what he has, and has not.
          (*Re-enter* ANTONY.)

ANTONY

                    All is lost;
This foul Egyptian hath betrayed me:
My fleet hath yielded to the foe, and yonder
They cast their caps up, and carouse together
Like friends long lost. Triple-turn'd whore,
'tis thou
Hast sold me to this novice, and my heart
Makes only wars on thee. Bid them fly;

For when I am reveng'd upon my charm,[23]
I have done all. Bid them all fly; begone.
          (*Exit* SCARUS.)
O sun, thy uprise shall I see no more,
Fortune and Antony part here, even here
Do we shake hands. All come to this? The
hearts
That spaniel'd me at heels, to whom I gave
Their wishes, do discandy,[24] melt their sweets
On blossoming Cæsar; and this pine is bark'd,
That overtopp'd them all. Betray'd I am.
O this false soul of Egypt! this grave charm,
Whose eye beck'd forth my wars, and call'd
them home;
Whose bosom was my crownet, my chief end,
Like a right gipsy, hath at fast and loose
Beguil'd me, to the very heart of loss.
What, Eros, Eros!
          (*Enter* CLEOPATRA.)
                    Ah, thou spell! Avaunt!

CLEOPATRA

Why is my lord enrag'd against his love?

ANTONY

Vanish, or I shall give thee thy deserving,
And blemish Cæsar's triumph. Let him take
thee,
And hoist thee up to the shouting plebeians,
Follow his chariots, like the greatest spot
Of all thy sex. Most monster-like be shown
For poor'st diminutives, for dolts; and let
Patient Octavia plough thy visage up
With her prepared nails.
          (*Exit* CLEOPATRA.)
                    'Tis well thou 'rt gone,
If it be well to live; but better 'twere
Thou fell'st into my fury, for one death
Might have prevented many. Eros, ho!
The shirt of Nessus [25] is upon me: teach me,
Alcides, thou mine ancestor, thy rage:
Let me lodge Lichas on the horns o' the
moon,
And with those hands that grasp'd the
heaviest club

---

[22] unless

[23] charmer, witch
[24] dissolve
[25] a poisoned shirt given to Hercules (Alcides) to
drive him mad

Subdue my worthiest self. The witch shall
    die:
To the young Roman boy she hath sold me,
    and I fall
Under this plot: she dies for 't. Eros, ho!
                                    (*Exit.*)

[Alexandria]   *Enter* CLEOPATRA, CHAR-
MIAN, IRAS, *and* MARDIAN.

CLEOPATRA

Help me, my women! O, he is more mad
Than Telamon for his shield; the boar of
    Thessaly
Was never so emboss'd.[26]

CHARMIAN

                        To the monument,
There lock yourself, and send him word you
    are dead.
The soul and body rive not more in parting
Than greatness going off.

CLEOPATRA

                        To the monument!
Mardian, go tell him I have slain myself;
Say that the last I spoke was " Antony,"
And word it, prithee, piteously: hence,
    Mardian,
And bring me how he takes my death. To the
    monument!   (*Exeunt.*)

Enter ANTONY *and* EROS.

ANTONY

Eros, thou yet behold'st me?

EROS

                        Ay, noble lord.

ANTONY

Sometime we see a cloud that 's dragonish,
A vapor sometime, like a bear, or lion,
A tower'd citadel, a pendent rock,
A forked mountain, or blue promontory
With trees upon 't, that nod unto the world,
And mock our eyes with air: thou hast seen
    these signs,
They are black vesper's pageants.

26 foaming

EROS

                        Ay, my lord.

ANTONY

That which is now a horse, even with a
    thought
The rack dislimns, and makes it indistinct
As water is in water.

EROS

                        It does, my lord.

ANTONY

My good knave Eros, now thy captain is
Even such a body: here I am Antony,
Yet cannot hold this visible shape, my knave.
I made these wars for Egypt, and the queen,
Whose heart I thought I had, for she had
    mine,
(Which, whilst it was mine, had annex'd
    unto 't
A million more, now lost) she, Eros, has
Pack'd cards [27] with Cæsar, and false-play'd
    my glory
Unto an enemy's triumph.
Nay, weep not, gentle Eros, there is left us
Ourselves to end ourselves.
                (*Enter* MARDIAN.)
                        O, thy vile lady!
She has robb'd me of my sword.

MARDIAN

                        No, Antony;
My mistress lov'd thee, and her fortunes
    mingled
With thine entirely.

ANTONY

                Hence, saucy eunuch; peace!
She hath betray'd me, and shall die the death.

MARDIAN

Death of one person can be paid but once,
And that she has discharg'd: what thou
    wouldst do
Is done unto thy hand: the last she spake
Was " Antony! most noble Antony! "
Then in the midst a tearing groan did break

27 cheated

The name of Antony; it was divided
Between her heart and lips: she render'd life,
Thy name so buried in her.

ANTONY

Dead then?

MARDIAN

Dead.

ANTONY

Unarm, Eros, the long day's task is done,
And we must sleep. (*To* MARDIAN.) That
thou depart'st hence safe
Does pay thy labor richly; go.
(*Exit* MARDIAN.)
Off, pluck off,
The seven-fold shield of Ajax cannot keep
The battery [28] from my heart. O, cleave, my
sides!
Heart, once be stronger than thy conti-
nent,[29]
Crack thy frail case! Apace, Eros, apace!
No more a soldier: bruised pieces, go,
You have been nobly borne. From me awhile.
(*Exit* EROS.)
I will o'ertake thee, Cleopatra, and
Weep for my pardon. So it must be, for now
All length is torture: since the torch is out,
Lie down and stray no farther. Now all la-
bor
Mars what it does; yea, very force entangles
Itself with strength: seal [30] then, and all is
done.
Eros! — I come, my queen. Eros! — Stay for
me:
Where souls do couch on flowers, we 'll hand
in hand,
And with our sprightly port make the ghosts
gaze:
Dido and her Æneas shall want troops,
And all the haunt be ours. Come, Eros, Eros!
(*Re-enter* EROS.)

EROS

What would my lord?

28 blow
29 casing
30 finish

ANTONY

Since Cleopatra died
I have liv'd in such dishonor, that the gods
Detest my baseness. I, that with my sword
Quarter'd the world, and o'er green Nep-
tune's back
With ships made cities, condemn myself to
lack
The courage of a woman, less noble mind
Than she which by her death our Cæsar tells
" I am conqueror of myself." Thou art
sworn, Eros,
That, when the exigent should come —
which now
Is come indeed — when I should see behind
me
The inevitable prosecution of
Disgrace and horror, that, on my command,
Thou then wouldst kill me: do 't; the time
is come:
Thou strikest not me, 'tis Cæsar thou de-
feat'st.
Put color in thy cheek.

EROS

The gods withhold me!
Shall I do that which all the Parthian darts,
(Though enemy) lost aim and could not?

ANTONY

Eros,
Wouldst thou be window'd in great Rome,
and see
Thy master thus with pleach'd [31] arms,
bending down
His corrigible neck, his face subdu'd
To penetrative shame, whilst the wheel'd
seat
Of fortunate Cæsar, drawn before him,
branded
His baseness that ensued?

EROS

I would not see 't.

ANTONY

Come, then; for with a wound I must be
cur'd.

31 folded

Draw that thy honest sword, which thou
  hast worn
Most useful for thy country.

 EROS

O, sir, pardon me!

ANTONY

When I did make thee free, swor'st thou not
  then
To do this when I bade thee? Do it at once,
Or thy precedent services are all
But accidents unpurpos'd. Draw, and come.

EROS

Turn from me then that noble countenance,
Wherein the worship of the whole world lies.

ANTONY

Lo thee!   (*Turning from him.*)

EROS

My sword is drawn.

ANTONY

Then let it do at once
The thing why thou hast drawn it.

EROS

My dear master,
My captain, and my emperor; let me say,
Before I strike this bloody stroke, farewell.

ANTONY

'Tis said, man, and farewell.

EROS

Farewell, great chief. Shall I strike now?

ANTONY

Now, Eros.

EROS

Why, there then: thus I do escape the sorrow
Of Antony's death.   (*Kills himself.*)

ANTONY

Thrice-nobler than myself!
Thou teachest me, O valiant Eros, what

I should, and thou couldst not. My queen
  and Eros
Have by their brave instruction got upon me
A nobleness in record: but I will be
A bridegroom in my death, and run into 't
As to a lover's bed. Come then, and, Eros,
Thy master dies thy scholar: to do thus
I learn'd of thee.   (*Falling on his sword.*)

How! not dead? not dead?
The guard, ho! O, dispatch me!
          (*Enter* DERCETAS *and Guard.*)

1st GUARD

What 's the noise?

ANTONY

I have done my work ill, friends: O, make an
  end
Of what I have begun.

2nd GUARD

The star is fall'n.

1st GUARD

And time is at his period.

ALL

Alas, and woe!

ANTONY

Let him that loves me strike me dead.

1st GUARD

Not I.

2nd GUARD

Nor I.

3rd GUARD

Nor any one.   (*Exeunt Guard.*)

DERCETAS

Thy death and fortunes bid thy followers fly.
This sword but shown to Cæsar, with this
  tidings,
Shall enter me with him.
          (*Enter* DIOMEDES.)

DIOMEDES

Where 's Antony?

DERCETAS
There, Diomed, there.

DIOMEDES
Lives he?
Wilt thou not answer, man?
(*Exit* DERCETAS.)

ANTONY
Art thou there, Diomed? Draw thy sword,
and give me
Sufficing strokes for death.

DIOMEDES
Most absolute lord,
My mistress Cleopatra sent me to thee.

ANTONY
When did she send thee?

DIOMEDES
Now, my lord.

ANTONY
Where is she?

DIOMEDES
Lock'd in her monument. She had a prophe-
sying fear
Of what hath come to pass: for when she
saw
(Which never shall be found) you did sus-
pect
She had dispos'd with Cæsar, and that your
rage
Would not be purg'd, she sent you word she
was dead;
But, fearing since how it might work, hath
sent
Me to proclaim the truth; and I am come,
I dread, too late.

ANTONY
Too late, good Diomed: call my guard, I
prithee.

DIOMEDES
What, ho, the emperor's guard! The guard,
what, ho!

Come, your lord calls.
(*Enter four or five of the Guard of* AN-
TONY.)

ANTONY
Bear me, good friends, where Cleopatra bides;
'Tis the last service that I shall command
you.

1st GUARD
Woe, woe are we, sir, you may not live to
wear
All your true followers out.

ALL
Most heavy day!

ANTONY
Nay, good my fellows, do not please sharp
fate
To grace it with your sorrows: bid that wel-
come
Which comes to punish us, and we punish it
Seeming to bear it lightly. Take me up,
I have led you oft, carry me now, good
friends,
And have my thanks for all.
(*Exeunt, bearing* ANTONY.)

Enter CLEOPATRA *and her maids, aloft,
with* CHARMIAN *and* IRAS.

CLEOPATRA
O Charmian, I will never go from hence.

CHARMIAN
Be comforted, dear madam.

CLEOPATRA
No, I will not:
All strange and terrible events are welcome,
But comforts we despise; our size of sorrow,
Proportion'd to our cause, must be as great
As that which makes it.
(*Enter, below,* DIOMEDES.)
How now? is he dead?

DIOMEDES
His death 's upon him, but not dead.
Look out o' the other side your monument:

His guard have brought him thither.
(*Enter, below,* ANTONY, *borne by the Guard.*)

CLEOPATRA

O sun,
Burn the great sphere thou mov'st in! darkling [32] stand
The varying shore o' the world. O Antony,
Antony, Antony! Help, Charmian, help,
Iras, help;
Help, friends below; let 's draw him hither.

ANTONY

Peace!
Not Cæsar's valor hath o'erthrown Antony,
But Antony's hath triumph'd on itself.

CLEOPATRA

So it should be, that none but Antony
Should conquer Antony; but woe 'tis so!

ANTONY

I am dying, Egypt, dying; only
I here importune death awhile, until
Of many thousand kisses the poor last
I lay upon thy lips.

CLEOPATRA

I dare not, dear,
Dear my lord, pardon, I dare not,
Lest I be taken: not the imperious show
Of the full-fortun'd Cæsar ever shall
Be brooch'd with me, if knife, drugs, serpents, have
Edge, sting, or operation: I am safe:
Your wife Octavia, with her modest eyes,
And still conclusion, shall acquire no honor
Demurring upon me. But come, come, Antony, —
Help me, my women, — we must draw thee up;
Assist, good friends.

ANTONY

O, quick, or I am gone.

CLEOPATRA

Here 's sport indeed! How heavy weighs my lord!

[32] in the dark

Our strength is all gone into heaviness;
That makes the weight. Had I great Juno's power,
The strong-wing'd Mercury should fetch thee up,
And set thee by Jove's side. Yet come a little —
Wishers were ever fools — O, come, come, come;

(*They heave* ANTONY *aloft to* CLEOPATRA.)

And welcome, welcome! die where thou hast liv'd,
Quicken with kissing: had my lips that power,
Thus would I wear them out.

ALL

A heavy sight!

ANTONY

I am dying, Egypt, dying:
Give me some wine, and let me speak a little.

CLEOPATRA

No, let me speak, and let me rail so high,
That the false housewife Fortune break her wheel,
Provok'd by my offence.

ANTONY

One word, sweet queen:
Of Cæsar seek your honor, with your safety. O!

CLEOPATRA

They do not go together.

ANTONY

Gentle, hear me:
None about Cæsar trust but Proculeius.

CLEOPATRA

My resolution, and my hands, I 'll trust;
None about Cæsar.

ANTONY

The miserable change now at my end
Lament nor sorrow at; but please your thoughts

In feeding them with those my former for-
tunes
Wherein I liv'd; the greatest prince o' the
world,
The noblest; and do now not basely die,
Not cowardly put off my helmet to
My countryman; a Roman by a Roman
Valiantly vanquish'd. Now my spirit is go-
ing,
I can no more.

CLEOPATRA
    Noblest of men, woo't die?
Hast thou no care of me? shall I abide
In this dull world, which in thy absence is
No better than a sty? O, see, my women,
                            (ANTONY dies.)
The crown o' the earth doth melt. My lord?
O, wither'd is the garland of the war,
The soldier's pole is fall'n: young boys and
girls
Are level now with men; the odds is gone,
And there is nothing left remarkable
Beneath the visiting moon.   (Faints.)

CHARMIAN
            O, quietness, lady!

IRAS
She's dead, too, our sovereign.

CHARMIAN
                    Lady!

IRAS
                        Madam!
CHARMIAN
O madam, madam, madam!

IRAS
                Royal Egypt,
Empress!
CHARMIAN
    Peace, peace, Iras!

CLEOPATRA
No more but e'en a woman, and commanded
By such poor passion as the maid that milks,
And does the meanest chares.[33] It were for
    me

33 chores

To throw my scepter at the injurious gods,
To tell them that this world did equal theirs
Till they had stol'n our jewel. All's but
    naught;
Patience is sottish, and impatience does
Become [34] a dog that's mad; then is it sin
To rush into the secret house of death,
Ere death dare come to us? How do you,
    women?
What, what? good cheer! Why, how now,
    Charmian?
My noble girls? Ah, women, women! look,
Our lamp is spent, it's out. Good sirs, take
    heart,
We'll bury him; and then, what's brave,
    what's noble,
Let's do it after the high Roman fashion,
And make death proud to take us. Come,
    away,
This case of that huge spirit now is cold:
Ah, women, women! Come, we have no
    friend
But resolution, and the briefest end.
            (Exeunt: those above bearing
                off ANTONY's body.)

ACT FIVE

Enter CÆSAR, AGRIPPA, DOLABELLA, MÆ-
CENAS, GALLUS, PROCULEIUS, and others, his
council of war.

CÆSAR
Go to him, Dolabella, bid him yield;
Being so frustrate, tell him he mocks [1]
The pauses that he makes.

DOLABELLA
            Cæsar, I shall.   (Exit.)
(Enter DERCETAS, with the sword of AN-
TONY.)

CÆSAR
Wherefore is that? and what art thou that
    dar'st
Appear thus to us?

34 suit
1 behaves foolishly in

DERCETAS

I am call'd Dercetas,
Mark Antony I serv'd, who best was worthy
Best to be serv'd: whilst he stood up and
    spoke,
He was my master, and I wore my life
To spend upon his haters. If thou please
To take me to thee, as I was to him
I 'll be to Cæsar; if thou pleasest not,
I yield thee up my life.

CÆSAR

What is 't thou say'st?

DERCETAS

I say, O Cæsar, Antony is dead.

CÆSAR

The breaking of so great a thing should make
A greater crack: the round world
Should have shook lions into civil streets,
And citizens to their dens. The death of An-
    tony
Is not a single doom; in the name lay
A moiety ² of the world.

DERCETAS

He is dead, Cæsar,
Not by a public minister of justice,
Nor by a hired knife; but that self hand,
Which writ his honor in the acts it did,
Hath, with the courage which the heart did
    lend it,
Splitted the heart. This is his sword,
I robb'd his wound of it; behold it stain'd
With his most noble blood.

CÆSAR

Look you sad, friends?
The gods rebuke me, but it is tidings
To wash the eyes of kings.

AGRIPPA

And strange it is
That nature must compel us to lament
Our most persisted deeds.

MÆCENAS

His taints and honors
Wag'd equal ³ with him.

AGRIPPA

A rarer spirit never
Did steer humanity: but you, gods, will give
    us
Some faults to make us men. Cæsar is
    touch'd.

MÆCENAS

When such a spacious mirror 's set before
    him,
He needs must see himself.

CÆSAR

O Antony!
I have follow'd thee to this. But we do lance
Diseases in our bodies: I must perforce
Have shown to thee such a declining day,
Or look'd on thine; we could not stall to-
    gether,
In the whole world: but yet let me lament,
With tears as sovereign as the blood of hearts,
Thou thou, my brother, my competitor
In top of all design; my mate in empire,
Friend and companion in the front of war,
The arm of mine own body, and the heart
Where mine his thoughts did kindle; that our
    stars
Unreconciliable should divide
Our equalness to this. Hear me, good
    friends, —
        (*Enter an* EGYPTIAN.)
But I will tell you at some meeter season,
The business of this man looks out of him,
We 'll hear him what he says. Whence are
    you?

EGYPTIAN

A poor Egyptian yet. The queen my mis-
    tress,
Confin'd in all she has, her monument,
Of thy intents desires instruction,
That she preparedly may frame herself
To the way she 's forc'd to.

---

² half

³ i.e., were evenly balanced

CÆSAR

   Bid her have good heart,
She soon shall know of us, by some of ours,
How honorable and how kindly we
Determine for her; for Cæsar cannot live
To be ungentle.

EGYPTIAN

 So the gods preserve thee! (*Exit.*)

CÆSAR

Come hither, Proculeius. Go and say,
We purpose her no shame: give her what
  comforts
The quality of her passion shall require;
Lest in her greatness, by some mortal stroke,
She do defeat us; for her life in Rome
Would be eternal in our triumph: go,
And with your speediest bring us what she
  says,
And how you find of her.

PROCULEIUS

   Cæsar, I shall. (*Exit.*)

CÆSAR

Gallus, go you along. (*Exit* GALLUS.)
  Where 's Dolabella,
To second Proculeius?

ALL

  Dolabella!

CÆSAR

Let him alone, for I remember now
How he 's employ'd; he shall in time be
  ready.
Go with him to my tent, where you shall see
How hardly [4] I was drawn into this war;
How calm and gentle I proceeded still
In all my writings: go with me, and see
What I can show in this. (*Exeunt.*)

Enter CLEOPATRA, CHARMIAN, *and* IRAS,
aloft.

CLEOPATRA

My desolation does begin to make
A better life. 'Tis paltry to be Cæsar;

 ⁴ reluctantly

Not being Fortune, he 's but Fortune's
  knave,
A minister of her will: and it is great
To do that thing that ends all other deeds,
Which shackles accidents and bolts up
  change;
Which sleeps, and never palates more the
  dung,
The beggar's nurse and Cæsar's.
(*Enter, to the gates of the monument,* PRO-
CULEIUS, GALLUS, *and Soldiers.*)

PROCULEIUS

Cæsar sends greeting to the Queen of Egypt,
And bids thee study on what fair demands
Thou mean'st to have him grant thee.

CLEOPATRA

   What 's thy name?

PROCULEIUS

My name is Proculeius.

CLEOPATRA

  Antony
Did tell me of you, bade me trust you, but
I do not greatly care to be deceiv'd,
That have no use for trusting. If your mas-
  ter
Would have a queen his beggar, you must
  tell him,
That majesty, to keep decorum, must
No less beg than a kingdom: if he please
To give me conquer'd Egypt for my son,
He gives me so much of mine own as I
Will kneel to him with thanks.

PROCULEIUS

   Be of good cheer;
You 're fall'n into a princely hand, fear
  nothing,
Make your full reference freely to my lord,
Who is so full of grace that it flows over
On all that need. Let me report to him
Your sweet dependency, and you shall find
A conquerer that will pray in aid for kind-
  ness,
Where he for grace is kneel'd to.

CLEOPATRA

Pray you, tell him
I am his fortune's vassal and I send him
The greatness he has got. I hourly learn
A doctrine of obedience, and would gladly
Look him i' the face

PROCULEIUS

This I 'll report, dear lady.
Have comfort, for I know your plight is
 pitied
Of him that caus'd it.
(*Here* PROCULEIUS *and two of the Guard
exeunt below and re-enter aloft, behind*
CLEOPATRA.)

GALLUS

You see how easily she may be surpris'd.
Guard her till Cæsar come.   (*Exit.*)

IRAS

Royal queen!

CHARMIAN

O Cleopatra! thou art taken, queen!

CLEOPATRA

Quick, quick, good hands.
           (*Drawing a dagger.*)

PROCULEIUS

Hold, worthy lady, hold:
           (*Seizes and disarms her.*)
Do not yourself such wrong, who are in this
Reliev'd, but not betray'd.

CLEOPATRA

What, of death too,
That rids our dogs of languish?

PROCULEIUS

Cleopatra,
Do not abuse my master's bounty by
The undoing of yourself: let the world see
His nobleness well acted, which your death
Will never let come forth.

CLEOPATRA

Where art thou, death?
Come hither, come! come, come, and take a
 queen
Worth many babes and beggars!

PROCULEIUS

O, temperance, lady!

CLEOPATRA

Sir, I will eat no meat, I 'll not drink, sir,
If idle talk will once be necessary,
I 'll not sleep neither: this mortal house [5] I 'll
 ruin,
Do Cæsar what he can. Know, sir, that I
Will not wait pinion'd at your master's court,
Nor once be chastis'd with the sober eye
Of dull Octavia. Shall they hoist me up,
And show me to the shouting varletry
Of censuring Rome? Rather a ditch in Egypt
Be gentle grave unto me, rather on Nilus'
 mud
Lay me stark naked, and let the water-flies
Blow me into abhorring; rather make
My country's high pyramides my gibbet,
And hang me up in chains!

PROCULEIUS

You do extend
These thoughts of horror further than you
 shall
Find cause in Cæsar.
           (*Enter* DOLABELLA.)

DOLABELLA

Proculeius,
What thou hast done thy master Cæsar
 knows,
And he hath sent for thee: for the queen,
I 'll take her to my guard.

PROCULEIUS

So, Dolabella,
It shall content me best: be gentle to her.
(*To* CLEOPATRA.) To Cæsar I will speak
 what you shall please,
If you 'll employ me to him.

    [5] body

CLEOPATRA

Say, I would die.
(*Exeunt* PROCULEIUS *and Soldiers.*)

DOLABELLA

Most noble empress, you have heard of me?

CLEOPATRA

I cannot tell.

DOLABELLA

Assuredly you know me.

CLEOPATRA

No matter, sir, what I have heard or known.
You laugh when boys or women tell their
dreams;
Is 't not your trick?

DOLABELLA

I understand not, madam.

CLEOPATRA

I dreamt there was an emperor Antony:
O, such another sleep, that I might see
But such another man!

DOLABELLA

If it might please ye, —

CLEOPATRA

His face was as the heavens, and therein
stuck
A sun and moon, which kept their course,
and lighted
The little O, the earth.

DOLABELLA

Most sovereign creature, —

CLEOPATRA

His legs bestrid the ocean, his rear'd arm
Crested the world: his voice was propertied
As all the tuned spheres, and that to friends:
But when he meant to quail, and shake the
orb,
He was as rattling thunder. For his bounty,
There was no winter in 't; an autumn 'twas

That grew the more by reaping: his delights
Were dolphin-like, they show'd his back
above
The element they liv'd in: in his livery [6]
Walk'd crowns and crownets; realms and
islands were
As plates [7] dropp'd from his pocket.

DOLABELLA

Cleopatra —

CLEOPATRA

Think you there was, or might be, such a
man
As this I dreamt of?

DOLABELLA

Gentle madam, no.

CLEOPATRA

You lie up to the hearing of the gods.
But if there be, or ever were, one such,
It 's past the size of dreaming: nature wants
stuff
To vie strange forms with fancy, yet to im-
agine
An Antony, were nature's piece 'gainst
fancy,
Condemning shadows quite.

DOLABELLA

Hear me, good madam.
Your loss is as yourself, great; and you bear
it
As answering to the weight: would I might
never
O'ertake pursued success, but I do feel,
By the rebound of yours, a grief that smites
My very heart at root.

CLEOPATRA

I thank you, sir.
Know you what Cæsar means to do with me?

DOLABELLA

I am loath to tell you what I would you
knew.

[6] service
[7] coins

CLEOPATRA

Nay, pray you, sir —

DOLABELLA

Though he be honorable —

CLEOPATRA

He 'll lead me then in triumph?

DOLABELLA

Madam, he will, I know 't.
(*Flourish and shout within:* " Make way there: Cæsar! ")
(*Enter* CÆSAR, GALLUS, PROCULEIUS, MÆCENAS, SELEUCUS, *and others of his Train.*)

CÆSAR

Which is the Queen of Egypt?

DOLABELLA

It is the emperor, madam.
                    (CLEOPATRA *kneels.*)

CÆSAR

Arise, you shall not kneel:
I pray you, rise, rise, Egypt.

CLEOPATRA

                    Sir, the gods
Will have it thus, my master and my lord
I must obey.

CÆSAR

                    Take to you no hard thoughts:
The record of what injuries you did us,
Though written in our flesh, we shall remember
As things but done by chance.

CLEOPATRA

                    Sole sir o' the world,
I cannot project mine own cause so well
To make it clear, but do confess I have
Been laden with like frailties, which before
Have often sham'd our sex.

CÆSAR

                    Cleopatra, know,
We will extenuate rather than enforce:
If you apply yourself to our intents,

Which towards you are most gentle, you shall find
A benefit in this change; but if you seek
To lay on me a cruelty, by taking
Antony's course, you shall bereave yourself
Of my good purposes, and put your children
To that destruction which I 'll guard them from,
If thereon you rely. I 'll take my leave.

CLEOPATRA

And may, through all the world: 'tis yours; and we,
Your scutcheons and your signs of conquest, shall
Hang in what place you please. Here, my good lord.

CÆSAR

You shall advise me in all for Cleopatra.

CLEOPATRA

This is the brief of money, plate and jewels,
I am possess'd of: 'tis exactly valued,
Not petty things admitted. Where 's Seleucus?

SELEUCUS

Here, madam.

CLEOPATRA

This is my treasurer: let him speak, my lord,
Upon his peril, that I have reserv'd
To myself nothing. Speak the truth, Seleucus.

SELEUCUS

Madam,
I had rather seal my lips, than to my peril
Speak that which is not.

CLEOPATRA

                    What have I kept back?

SELEUCUS

Enough to purchase what you have made known.

CÆSAR

Nay, blush not, Cleopatra, I approve
Your wisdom in the deed.

CLEOPATRA

          See, Cæsar! O, behold,
How pomp is follow'd! mine will now be
    yours,
And, should we shift estates, yours would be
    mine.
The ingratitude of this Seleucus does
Even make me wild. O slave, of no more
    trust
Than love that's hir'd! What, goest thou
    back? thou shalt
Go back, I warrant thee; but I'll catch thine
    eyes,
Though they had wings: slave, soulless vil-
    lain, dog!
O rarely base!

CÆSAR

    Good queen, let us entreat you.

CLEOPATRA

O Cæsar, what a wounding shame is this,
That thou vouchsafing here to visit me,
Doing the honor of thy lordliness
To one so meek, that mine own servant
    should
Parcel the sum of my disgraces by
Addition of his envy! Say, good Cæsar,
That I some lady trifles have reserv'd,
Immoment toys, things of such dignity
As we greet modern [8] friends withal, and
    say,
Some nobler token I have kept apart
For Livia and Octavia, to induce
Their mediation, must I be unfolded
With one that I have bred? The gods! it
    smites me
Beneath the fall I have. (*To* SELEUCUS.)
    Prithee, go hence,
Or I shall show the cinders of my spirits
Through the ashes of my chance: wert thou
    a man,
Thou wouldst have mercy on me.

CÆSAR

          Forbear, Seleucus.
          (*Exit* SELEUCUS.)

8 common

CLEOPATRA

Be it known, that we, the greatest, are mis-
    thought
For things that others do; and when we fall,
We answer others' merits in our name,
Are therefore to be pitied.

CÆSAR

          Cleopatra,
Not what you have reserv'd, nor what ac-
    knowledg'd,
Put we i' the roll of conquest: still be 't
    yours,
Bestow it at your pleasure, and believe
Cæsar's no merchant, to make price with you
Of things that merchants sold. Therefore be
    cheer'd,
Make not your thoughts your prisons; no,
    dear queen,
For we intend so to dispose you, as
Yourself shall give us counsel. Feed, and
    sleep:
Our care and pity is so much upon you,
That we remain your friend, and so adieu.

CLEOPATRA

My master, and my lord!

CÆSAR

          Not so. Adieu.
    (*Flourish. Exeunt* CÆSAR
           and his train.)

CLEOPATRA

He words me, girls, he words me, that I
    should not
Be noble to myself: but, hark thee, Char-
    mian.   (*Whispers* CHARMIAN.)

IRAS

Finish, good lady, the bright day is done,
And we are for the dark.

CLEOPATRA

          Hie thee again,
I have spoke already, and it is provided,
Go put it to the haste.

CHARMIAN

Madam, I will.

(*Re-enter* DOLABELLA.)

DOLABELLA

Where is the queen?

CHARMIAN

Behold, sir.   (*Exit.*)

CLEOPATRA

Dolabella!

DOLABELLA

Madam, as thereto sworn by your command.
(Which my love makes religion to obey)
I tell you this: Cæsar through Syria
Intends his journey, and within three days,
You with your children will he send before:
Make your best use of this: I have perform'd
Your pleasure, and my promise.

CLEOPATRA

Dolabella,
I shall remain your debtor.

DOLABELLA

I your servant.
Adieu, good queen, I must attend on Cæsar.

CLEOPATRA

Farewell, and thanks.   (*Exit* DOLABELLA.)
Now, Iras, what think'st thou?
Thou, an Egyptian puppet, shalt be shown
In Rome as well as I: mechanic slaves
With greasy aprons, rules, and hammers, shall
Uplift us to the view: in their thick breaths,
Rank of gross diet, shall we be encluded
And forc'd to drink their vapor.

IRAS

That gods forbid!

CLEOPATRA

Nay, 'tis most certain, Iras: saucy lictors
Will catch at us like strumpets, and scald [9]
rhymers

[9] inferior

Ballad us out o' tune: the quick comedians
Extemporally will stage us, and present
Our Alexandrian revels; Antony
Shall be brought drunken forth, and I shall see
Some squeaking Cleopatra boy [10] my greatness
I' the posture of a whore.

IRAS

O the good gods!

CLEOPATRA

Nay, that 's certain.

IRAS

I 'll never see 't; for I am sure my nails
Are stronger than mine eyes.

CLEOPATRA

Why, that 's the way
To fool their preparation, and to conquer
Their most absurd intents.
(*Re-enter* CHARMIAN.)
Now, Charmian!
Show me, my women, like a queen: go fetch
My best attires: I am again for Cydnus,
To meet Mark Antony: sirrah Iras, go.
Now, noble Charmian, we 'll dispatch indeed,
And when thou hast done this chare I 'll give thee leave
To play till doomsday. Bring our crown and all.   (*Exit* IRAS. *A noise within.*)
Wherefore 's this noise?
(*Enter a* GUARDSMAN.)

GUARDSMAN

Here is a rural fellow,
That will not be denied your highness' presence:
He brings you figs.

CLEOPATRA

Let him come in.   (*Exit* GUARDSMAN.)
What poor an instrument
May do a noble deed! he brings me liberty.
My resolution 's plac'd, and I have nothing

[10] i.e., the boy acting a woman's role

Of woman in me: now from head to foot
I am marble-constant; now the fleeting moon
No planet is of mine.
(*Re-enter* GUARDSMAN, *with* CLOWN *bringing in a basket.*)

GUARDSMAN

This is the man.

CLEOPATRA

Avoid, and leave him. (*Exit* GUARDSMAN.)
Hast thou the pretty worm of Nilus there,
That kills and pains not?

CLOWN

Truly I have him: but I would not be the
party that should desire you to touch
him, for his biting is immortal; those
that do die of it do seldom or never recover.

CLEOPATRA

Rememberest thou any that have died on 't?

CLOWN

Very many, men and women too. I heard of
one of them no longer than yesterday,
a very honest woman, but something
given to lie, as a woman should not do,
but in the way of honesty, how she died
of the biting of it, what pain she felt:
truly, she makes a very good report o'
the worm; but he that will believe all
that they say, shall never be saved by
half that they do: but this is most fallible, the worm 's an odd worm.

CLEOPATRA

Get thee hence, farewell.

CLOWN

I wish you all joy of the worm.
                (*Setting down his basket.*)

CLEOPATRA

Farewell.

CLOWN

You must think this, look you, that the
worm will do his kind.

CLEOPATRA

Ay, ay, farewell.

CLOWN

Look you, the worm is not to be trusted but
in the keeping of wise people; for indeed there is no goodness in the worm.

CLEOPATRA

Take thou no care, it shall be heeded.

CLOWN

Very good. Give it nothing, I pray you, for
it is not worth the feeding.

CLEOPATRA

Will it eat me?

CLOWN

You must not think I am so simple but I
know the devil himself will not eat a
woman: I know that a woman is a dish
for the gods, if the devil dress her not.
But, truly, these same whoreson devils
do the gods great harm in their women;
for in every ten that they make, the
devils mar five.

CLEOPATRA

Well, get thee gone, farewell.

CLOWN

Yes, forsooth: I wish you joy o' the worm.
                            (*Exit.*)
(*Re-enter* IRAS *with a robe, crown, &c.*)

CLEOPATRA

Give me my robe, put on my crown, I have
Immortal longings in me. Now no more
The juice of Egypt's grape shall moist this
    lip:
Yare, yare, good Iras; quick! Methinks I hear
Antony call; I see him rouse himself
To praise my noble act; I hear him mock
The luck of Cæsar, which the gods give men
To excuse their after wrath. Husband, I
    come:
Now to that name my courage prove my
    title!

I am fire, and air; my other elements
I give to baser life. So, have you done?
Come then, and take the last warmth of my
 lips.
Farewell, kind Charmian, Iras, long farewell.
 (*Kisses them.* IRAS *falls and dies.*)
Have I the aspic in my lips? Dost fall?
If thou and nature can so gently part,
The stroke of death is as a lover's pinch,
Which hurts, and is desir'd. Dost thou lie
 still?
If thus thou vanishest, thou tell'st the world
It is not worth leave-taking.

CHARMIAN

Dissolve, thick cloud, and rain, that I may
 say
The gods themselves do weep!

CLEOPATRA

                    This proves me base:
If she first meet the curled [11] Antony
He 'll make demand of her, and spend that
 kiss
Which is my heaven to have. Come, thou
 mortal wretch,
              (*To an asp, which she applies
                    to her breast.*)
With thy sharp teeth this knot intrinsicate
Of life at once untie; poor venomous fool,
Be angry, and dispatch. O, couldst thou
 speak,
That I might hear thee call great Cæsar ass,
Unpolicied! [12]

CHARMIAN

O eastern star!

CLEOPATRA

                    Peace, peace!
Dost thou not see my baby at my breast,
That sucks the nurse asleep?

CHARMIAN

                    O, break! O, break!

[11] curly-haired
[12] out-smarted

CLEOPATRA

As sweet as balm, as soft as air, as gentle.
O Antony! Nay, I will take thee too:
 (*Applying another asp to her arm.*)
What, should I stay —   (*Dies.*)

CHARMIAN

In this vile world? So, fare thee well.
Now boast thee, death, in thy possession lies
A lass unparallel'd. Downy windows, close;
And golden Phœbus [13] never be beheld
Of eyes again so royal! Your crown 's awry;
I 'll mend it, and then play.
 (*Enter the Guard, rushing in.*)

1st GUARD

Where is the queen?

CHARMIAN

                    Speak softly, wake her not.

1st GUARD

Cæsar hath sent —

CHARMIAN

                    Too slow a messenger.
                    (*Applies an asp.*)
O, come apace, dispatch: I partly feel thee.

1st GUARD

Approach, ho! All 's not well: Cæsar's beguil'd.

2nd GUARD

There 's Dolabella sent from Cæsar; call him.

1st GUARD

What work is here, Charmian? Is this well
 done?

CHARMIAN

It is well done, and fitting for a princess
Descended of so many royal kings.
Ah, soldier!   (*Dies.*)
 (*Re-enter* DOLABELLA.)

DOLABELLA

How goes it here?

[13] the sun

2nd GUARD

All dead.

DOLABELLA

　　　　　Cæsar, thy thoughts
Touch their effects in this: thyself art coming
To see perform'd the dreaded act which thou
So sought'st to hinder.
(*Within:* " A way there, a way for Cæsar! ")
(*Re-enter* CÆSAR *and his train.*)

DOLABELLA

O sir, you are too sure an augurer;
That you did fear is done.

CÆSAR

　　　　　Bravest at the last,
She levell'd [14] at our purposes, and being royal
Took her own way. The manner of their deaths?
I do not see them bleed.

DOLABELLA

　　　　Who was last with them?

1st GUARD

A simple countryman, that brought her figs:
This was his basket.

CÆSAR

　　　Poison'd then.

1st GUARD

　　　　　　　O Cæsar,
This Charmian liv'd but now, she stood and spake:

[14] guessed

I found her trimming up the diadem
On her dead mistress; tremblingly she stood,
And on the sudden dropp'd.

CÆSAR

　　　　　O noble weakness!
If they had swallow'd poison, 'twould appear
By external swelling: but she looks like sleep,
As she would catch another Antony
In her strong toil of grace.

DOLABELLA

　　　　　Here, on her breast,
There is a vent of blood, and something blown:
The like is on her arm.

1st GUARD

This is an aspic's trail, and these fig-leaves
Have slime upon them, such as the aspic leaves
Upon the caves of Nile.

CÆSAR

　　　　　Most probable
That so she died; for her physician tells me
She hath pursued conclusions infinite
Of easy ways to die. Take up her bed,
And bear her women from the monument:
She shall be buried by her Antony:
No grave upon the earth shall clip in it
A pair so famous. High events as these
Strike those that make them; and their story is
No less in pity than his glory which
Brought them to be lamented. Our army shall
In solemn show attend this funeral,
And then to Rome. Come, Dolabella, see
High order in this great solemnity.

　　　　　　　　　　(*Exeunt.*)

A Note on Structure

After a first reading, *Antony and Cleopatra* may seem somewhat haphazard in its structure, as if it followed the techniques of history or narrative rather than drama. Its excursions into the far corners of the Roman world, its parade of major and minor characters, its consumption of weeks and months may seem extravagant, even within the panoramic

Antony and Cleopatra, Act V. See page 267. Katherine Cornell as Cleopatra. Photo by Vandamm.

form. We must recognize at once that Shakespeare is retelling one of the most familiar of the world's love stories, and that he is following the historical account in Plutarch's *Life of Antony*. Is the complexity of structure an attempt to follow his source faithfully? Or does the structure, the selection and arrangement of incidents, serve as a vehicle for the central idea of the play?

In regular editions of the text, not only act divisions but scene divisions are painstakingly indicated. In the present version, however, act divisions are kept and scene divisions, if not eliminated, are minimized. It has been pointed out that the stage action of an Elizabethan play was practically continuous. Scenes flowing into one another without pause yield a vastly different dramatic experience from scenes divided by the drawing of a curtain. The present arrangement of the text should suggest to the reader the *continuity of the action*. The sense of continuous action, de-emphasizing the " shifts " in locale, directs the attention of the spectator to the action itself, away from chronology or geography. The spectator, or reader, is first of all aware of the alterations in the grouping of the characters brought about by the shifting of Antony from one side to the other. But geography in a more general sense must not be ignored.

On rereading the play it will become apparent that the opening scenes, set in Egypt, are intended to establish the quality of the Egyptian way of life — a world of indulgence, luxury, mirth — and to present the character of Cleopatra as the crystallization of that way of life. Contrasted with this is the Roman world of duty, policy, and hard-headed reason characterized by Octavius and his sister. Neither world is presented in black and white; the virtues and shortcomings of each are revealed. The action of the play thus acquires more than narrative significance as Antony is drawn from one geographical and ethical extreme to the other.

Visualization is essential if the play is to be experienced to the full. The reader must be constantly aware of the costuming of the characters, and thus to measure the effect of the " parenthetical " appearance of two Roman soldiers in the opening Egyptian scene, or the intrusion of the Oriental soothsayer in Rome. The minor figures, Pompey and his scheming lieutenant, or the victorious and single-minded Ventidius, either cumulatively or by contrast contribute indirectly to the spectator's understanding of the central concern of the action.

TARTUFFE

or

The Impostor

A COMEDY IN FIVE ACTS

by Molière

TRANSLATED BY ROBERT HARTLE

CHARACTERS

MADAME PERNELLE, mother of Orgon
ORGON, Elmire's husband
ELMIRE, Orgon's wife
MARIANE, Orgon's daughter
DAMIS, Orgon's son
VALÈRE, Mariane's sweetheart

CLÉANTE, Orgon's brother-in-law
TARTUFFE, religious hypocrite
DORINE, lady's maid to Mariane
MONSIEUR LOYAL, Justice of the Peace
An Officer of the Crown
FLIPOTE, Mme. Pernelle's servant

SCENE: *Paris; a room in the house of* ORGON.
*A door at each side and a raised entrance at
the back. Down Right a small door leading
into a tiny room. A table covered with a great
cloth; chairs.*

ACT ONE

Enter Right, MME. PERNELLE, *pushing* FLI-
POTE *ahead of her with her cane.* ELMIRE,
MARIANE, DORINE, DAMIS, *and* CLÉANTE
follow. MME. PERNELLE *limps badly but
moves along with determination and speed.*

MME. PERNELLE. Come on, Flipote. Come
on, let me get away from them.

ELMIRE. It's hard to follow you at such a
pace.

MME. PERNELLE. Never mind, my dear
daughter-in-law, never mind; don't come any
farther; those are airs you don't need for me.

ELMIRE. What you deserve you shall receive in full. But why are you leaving so
quickly, Mother?

MME. PERNELLE. Because I can't look at
such a household and, as for pleasing me, no
one takes any thought. Yes, I leave your
house not very highly edified; all my advice
is contradicted; nothing is sacred, everyone
shouts, and it is a perfect Court of Fools.

DORINE. If. . . .

MME. PERNELLE. You, dearie, are a serv-
ing-girl who's a little too strong in the tongue
and very impertinent; you butt in to give
your advice about everything.

DAMIS. But. . . .

MME. PERNELLE. You are a fool, my boy,
— *f-o-o-l;* I'm the one who's telling you so
and I'm your grandmother. I have warned my
son, your father, a hundred times that you

270

were turning out to be a good-for-nothing, and would always give him nothing but trouble.

MARIANE. I think. . . .

MME. PERNELLE. And his sister — heavens! you play the quiet one, and you're so innocent and sweetie-sweet, but, just like they say, there's no water worse than still water, and on the sly you carry on in a way I detest.

ELMIRE. But, Mother. . . .

MME. PERNELLE. If you please, my dear daughter-in-law, your behavior is altogether bad; you ought to set a good example for them, and their late mother led a much better life. You're loose with your money and it offends me to see you decked out like a princess. Whoever wants to please her husband only, my dear daughter-in-law, does not need so much finery.

CLÉANTE. But Madame, after all. . . .

MME. PERNELLE. As for her brother, sir, I respect you greatly, love and revere you; but if I were my son, her husband, I would strongly beg you not to enter our house. You are forever preaching maxims to live by which decent people should not follow. I'm speaking a little frankly to you, but that's the way I am, I don't mince words when I have something to say.

DAMIS. Your Monsieur Tartuffe is perfect, I suppose.

MME. PERNELLE. He is a good man who must be listened to, and I can't help getting angry to see a fool like you dispute him.

DAMIS. What! I am supposed to allow a sanctimonious critic to come into this house and usurp tyrannical power, so that we can't amuse ourselves in any way if *that* (*points to* TARTUFFE's *door center stage, at the back*) fine gentleman does not deign to consent?

DORINE. If you're supposed to listen to him and believe his maxims, you can't do anything without committing a crime, because that fanatical critic condemns everything.

MME. PERNELLE. And everything he condemns is very well condemned. It's the way

to heaven he wants to lead you on, and my son's example ought to bring you all to love him.

DAMIS. Now look, Mother, there's no father, or anything else, that can force me to wish him well. I would betray my heart if I said anything else; his way of acting makes me lose my temper every time; I can see the end of it: that lout and I will have some kind of fine explosion.

DORINE. Yes, and it's a scandalous thing to see a stranger set himself up in this house — a beggar, who didn't have any shoes when he came and whose whole suit wasn't worth six cents, should go so far as to forget himself, to interfere with everything and play the master.

MME. PERNELLE. Oh! Lord love me! Everything would be much better off if it were all governed by his pious commands.

DORINE. He passes for a saint in your fancy; his whole conduct — believe me — is nothing but hypocrisy.

MME. PERNELLE. Listen at her chatter!

DORINE. I wouldn't trust him any more than I would his servant, Laurent, without a good guarantee.

MME. PERNELLE. I don't know what the servant may be underneath, but I guarantee the master for a good man. The only reason you wish him ill and snub him is that he tells you all the truth about yourselves,

His heart is stirred to anger against *sin*
And heaven's cause is all that stirs *him*.

DORINE. Yes; but why, especially lately, can't he stand for anyone to hang around the house? How does a decent visit offend heaven so that he has to kick up a row about it that'd drive you crazy? Do you want me to tell you my opinion — just among ourselves? I think it's over Madame (*indicating* ELMIRE), and that he's just plain jealous.

MME. PERNELLE. Hush up and think what you're saying. He's not the only one who blames those visits: all that hullabaloo that follows the people you associate with, those carriages always parked at the door and the noisy crowd of so many lackeys make an unpleasant uproar in the whole neighborhood. I'm willing to believe that there's really nothing to it, but people *are* talking about it and that isn't good.

CLÉANTE. Come, come, Madame, do you want to stop people from talking? It would be an unfortunate thing in life if, on account of the stupid way people can talk, one had to give up one's best friends; and, even if you could bring yourself to do it, would you expect to impose silence on everyone? Against slander there are no ramparts. So let us pay no attention to all the silly cackle; let us make every effort to live in all innocence and let the gossips go their way.

DORINE. Daphne, our neighbor, and her little husband, aren't they the ones who talk about us?

Those whose behavior is most open to laughter
Are always the first ones to pile on the slander.

They never fail to leap on the slightest glimmer of an inclination and joyfully publish the news, giving it the twist they want it to take. By tinting other people's actions with *their* colors they think they can justify their own in the eyes of the world, and, with the false hope of some similarity, lend an innocence to their *real* intrigues, or scatter elsewhere some of the arrows of public disapproval which overwhelm them.

MME. PERNELLE. All those arguments have nothing to do with the case. It is well known that Orante leads an exemplary life; all her thoughts are directed towards heaven; and I have learned through some people that she highly disapproves of the crowd which comes to this house.

DORINE. That's a wonderful example! She is a good lady! It is true that she leads an austere life, but age has put that burning zeal in her soul and everyone knows that she is a prude through physical necessity. As long as she could attract amorous attentions she made full use of her advantages; but, seeing the lights dim in her eyes, now that the world is passing her by she wants to renounce it, and with the high and mighty veil of a lofty virtue disguise the weakness of her outworn charms. Those are the tricks of yesterday's coquettes. It's hard on them to be deserted by their gentlemen-in-waiting. In such neglect their anxious gloom sees no other way out but to trade on prudery. The severity of these upright ladies censures everything and pardons nothing. Loudly they criticize everyone's life — not for charity's sake but because their barbed envy won't permit anyone else to enjoy the pleasures from which declining age has severed their desires.

MME. PERNELLE. That's the kind of bedtime stories it takes to please you. My dear daughter-in-law, one is forced to keep silence in your house, for Madame (*indicating* DORINE) holds the floor all day long with her chattering; but just the same I intend to take my turn at airing my opinion. — I tell you that my son never did anything wiser than taking in that devout person; that heaven sent him to this house in time of need to put all your souls back on the right track; that you must listen to him for your own salvation, and that he doesn't reprimand anything which doesn't need reprimanding. These visits, these fancy balls, these little chats are all inventions of the Evil One. Here a pious word is never heard; it's all idle tales, nonsense and foolishness; very often one's neighbor gets his, and you know how to slander first one and then the other. Anyway, the uproar from such gatherings makes sensible people's heads spin; a thousand cacklings start up in a flash, and, like a preacher said very well the other day, it's a real tower of Babylon, where all the people babble on; and the story he went on to tell — (*Pointing to* CLÉANTE) Isn't that Monsieur snickering already? Go find somebody else to laugh at, and without. . . . Farewell, daughter-in-law, I won't say another word, but let me tell you that my opinion of this place has gone down fifty percent, and it'll be a long time before I set foot in here again. (*Giving* FLIPOTE *a slap*)

Come on, you, quit dreaming there with your mouth hanging open. You'll see if I don't give your ears a rubbing. Forward, slut, forward!

(*Exeunt Left all but* CLÉANTE *and* DORINE.)

CLÉANTE. I don't want to go along for fear she might scold me again. How that dear old lady. . . .

DORINE. Ah! Goodness! It's too bad she didn't hear you say that; she'd tell you right enough that you're very kind but she isn't that old.

CLÉANTE. How excited she got over nothing! She seems to be completely silly over her Tartuffe.

DORINE. Oh, really all that is nothing compared with her son; and if you had seen him you would say, "It's even worse." The civil wars had set him up as a sensible man, and he showed courage in serving his king, but he's been like a man out of his senses ever since he's been infatuated with Tartuffe. He calls him his brother and loves him in spirit a hundred times more than he does mother, son, wife, and daughter. He makes him sole confidant of all his secrets and the prudent director of his actions. He pets him and embraces him; I don't think you could have more affection for a mistress; at table he wants him to sit in the place of honor and joyously sees him eat enough for six; he makes everyone give him the choicest morsels; and, if Tartuffe should happen to belch, he says, "God bless you!" All in all, he is crazy about him; Tartuffe is his all, his hero, he admires him all the time, quotes him on every occasion, thinks his slightest actions are miracles and everything he says, an oracle.

Tartuffe, of course, who knows his dupe well and wants to make the best of it, artfully dazzles him with a thousand false colors; his false devotion draws money out of Monsieur all the time, and assumes the right to find fault with every one of us. It's gone so far that even the stupid ass who acts as his servant takes a hand at lecturing us, and comes to sermonize us with ferocious looks and throw out our ribbons, our rouge and our beauty spots. The other day the wretch tore up a handkerchief which he found in a copy of the *Flower of the Saints,* saying that we were mixing, by a frightful crime, holiness with the snares of the devil.

(*Re-enter* ELMIRE *and* DAMIS.)

ELMIRE. You're lucky you weren't present for the harangue she gave us at the door. But I saw my husband; since he didn't see me, I shall go upstairs to wait for his arrival.

CLÉANTE. I'll wait for him here to save time: I just want to say good-day to him.
(*Exit* ELMIRE.)

DAMIS. Mention my sister's wedding to him. I suspect that Tartuffe is opposed to it and is forcing my father to these great delays. You know of course why I'm interested in it. If like passion kindles both my sister and Valère, the sister of that friend, you know, is dear to me; and if we had to —

DORINE. He's coming. (*Exit* DAMIS.)
(*Enter* ORGON.)

ORGON. Ah, my brother, good-day.

CLÉANTE. I was leaving, but I am very pleased to see you back; the countryside is not much in flower just now.

ORGON. Dorine. . . . (*To* CLÉANTE) My brother-in-law, wait a moment, I beg you. Would you allow me to ease my mind — to inquire a bit about the news here? (*To* DORINE) Has everything gone well these past two days? What have you been doing? How is everyone?

DORINE. Madame, day before yesterday, had a fever all day with a headache that was hard to understand.

ORGON. And Tartuffe?

DORINE. Tartuffe? He's fat and sleek, Rosy lipped and pink of cheek.

ORGON. The poor fellow!

DORINE. In the evening she was quite upset and her headache was so painful that at supper she could touch nothing at all.

ORGON. And Tartuffe?

DORINE. He supped alone in front of her And consumed with great devotion Two partridges and half a leg of mutton.

ORGON. The poor fellow!

DORINE. The whole night long she couldn't close her eyes because of a fever

which prevented sleep, and we had to watch
over her till daybreak.

ORGON. And Tartuffe?

DORINE. Urged on by a drowsiness quite
  agreeable
He went to his room upon rising from table;
Then into his nice warm bed he leapt,
Where, completely untroubled, till daylight
  he slept.

ORGON. The poor fellow!

DORINE. Finally, she let herself be persuaded to undergo a blood-letting and relief
followed immediately.

ORGON. And Tartuffe?

DORINE. He plucked up his courage as
  best he could,
And, fortifying his soul against all ills,
To make up for the price of the blood Madame lost,
At breakfast four large swigs of wine down
  he tossed.

ORGON. The poor fellow!

DORINE. They are *both* well at last;
And I shall go and inform Madame of your
  presence,
And the interest you take in her convalescence.   (*Exit.*)

CLÉANTE. She's laughing right in your
face, brother, and, without meaning to make
you angry, I must say that she's quite right.
Has anyone ever heard of such a caprice?
Can a man cast such a spell these days as to
make you forget everything for him? When
you brought him into your house a wretched
pauper, that you should go so far as to —

ORGON. Stop right there, my dear brother-
in-law; you don't know the man you are
speaking of.

CLÉANTE. All right, I don't know him,
but, after all, to know what kind of man he
may be —

ORGON. My brother, he would enchant
  you, and your delights would never end.
He is a man . . . who . . . ah . . . a man
  . . . well, anyway, a man.
Who follows well his lessons enjoys a peace
  profound
And looks upon the world as so much dung.

Yes, I am becoming another man from my
  talks with him;
He teaches me to love nothing,
From all affection he detaches my soul,
And I could see my brother, children, moth-
  er, wife all die
Without caring any more than that.
                        (*He snaps his fingers.*)

CLÉANTE. Such humane feelings, dear
brother!

ORGON. Ah! if you had seen how I met
  him
You would have felt for him the same
  friendship.
Each day to the church he came with an air
  so sweet
And right opposite me went down on his
  knees.
He drew the attention of the whole congre-
  gation
By the warmth with which he uttered his
  prayer;
He sighed, he bent way down,
He moaned, and over and over he kissed the
  ground;
And when I was leaving he would run ahead
  quickly
To offer me holy water in the entry.
His servant, who imitated him in every way,
Told me who he was and how poor he was,
So I would give him gifts; but, with his
  modesty,
He always wanted to give some back to me.
" It's too much," he would say. " It's twice
  too much.
I am not worthy that you should have pity
  on me."
And, when I refused to take it back,
He would pass it to beggars right in front of
  my eyes.
Finally, Heaven chose for me to take him
  into my household,
And since that time everything in it seems to
  prosper.
He finds fault with everything; and even in
  my wife
I see him take — for the sake of my honor
  — an extreme interest;

He warns me about people who make eyes at
her,
And he's six times more jealous of her than
I am.
You wouldn't believe the extent of his zeal;
He counts the least little thing he does as a
sin;
A trifle is enough to shock him;
To the point where he came the other day to
denounce himself
For having caught a flea, while in prayer,
And killed it with excessive wrath.

CLÉANTE. Good heavens! I think you must
be crazy. Are you trying to make fun of me
with your talk? And what do you think that
all this farcical —

ORGON. Brother, such talk smells of free-
thinking. Your soul is slightly tainted with it,
and I have preached to you a dozen times
that you will get yourself into hot water.

CLÉANTE. That's the way your kind always talk. They want everyone to be blind
as they are; to have a good pair of eyes is
to be a free-thinker, and anyone who doesn't
worship empty posturing has neither respect
nor belief in holiness.

Go on, all your speeches don't frighten me;
I know how I speak, and Heaven sees my
heart. We aren't all the slaves of affectation;
there is false piety just as there is false bravery; and, just as on the field of honor the
truly brave ones make the least noise, the
good and truly pious, in whose footsteps we
should follow, are likewise those who posture
least.

What! will you make no distinction between hypocrisy and piety? You want to
treat them on the same terms and render the
same honor to the mask as to the face: to
treat fraud and sincerity on the same foot-
ing; confuse appearance with reality, esteem
the wraith as much as the person and the
counterfeit as much as the real?

Men, for the most part, are strangely
made! They never find natural rightness; the
limits of good sense are too narrow for them;
in each respect they go beyond its limits, and
the noblest thing they often spoil by trying

to overdo it and exceed all measure. This is
just a passing remark, brother.

ORGON. Yes, you are, doubtless, a revered
scholar; all the knowledge in the world has
found its last refuge in you; you alone are
wise, you alone are enlightened, an oracle, a
Cato in our own times, and next to you all
men are fools.

CLÉANTE. I am not, my brother, a revered
scholar, and all of knowledge has not taken
refuge in me; but, in a word, I *do*, for my
knowledge, know how to distinguish between
the true and the false. And, just as I see no
kind of heroism more to be valued than perfect piety — nothing nobler or more beautiful in the world than the holy fire of true
zeal — likewise I consider nothing more
odious than the cardboard façade of specious
zeal. I find nothing more odious than those
out-and-out charlatans, those pray-ers in the
market-place. With sacrilegious and deceitful
grimace they misuse at their pleasure everything that men hold most sacred and holy,
and get off scot-free with making sport of it.
Having sold out their soul for gain, those
people make of their devotions both trade and
merchandise, and want to buy authority and
honors with false looks and affected trans-
ports. I'm talking about those people whom
one sees take the road to heaven with uncom-
mon fervor in order to speed to their fortune.
With ardent prayers they go begging every
day, and preach retreat from the world while
they stay on in court.

They're hasty, vindictive, faithless, full of
tricks, and to destroy someone they insolently
cloak their savage spite with the best interests of heaven. Their bitter wrath is all
the more dangerous because they take up
against us arms which people respect, so that
people look on with approval when that passion sets out to assassinate us with a holy
sword.

We see too many appear who are of that
false nature, but the pious in heart are easy
to recognize. Our own day, my brother, sets
before our eyes some who can serve us as
glorious examples. Look at Ariston, Polydore,
Clitandre, look at Oronte, Alcidamas, Péri-

andro — no one denies them that title. They aren't all braggarts of virtue, you don't see in them that insufferable display, and their piety is human and gentle. They don't criticize all our actions — they feel there's too much arrogance in those corrections. And leaving the pride of words to others it is by their actions that they reprove ours. The appearance of evil has little influence on them, and their soul is disposed to judge well of their neighbor. They have no cliques, no intrigues. The only business they mind is to lead a good life. They never go after a sinner tooth and nail; they attach their hatred to the sin alone, and don't try, with an excessive zeal, to outdo heaven in taking care of its own interests.

Those are my people, that's the way to act, there is the example we must set before us. Your man — to speak the truth — is not of that model. It's in all good faith that you glorify his zeal, but I think you are dazzled by a false luster.

ORGON. My dear sir, brother-in-law, are you quite finished?

CLÉANTE. Yes.

ORGON. (*Ironically*) I am your humble servant. (*He starts to leave.*)

CLÉANTE. Please, one word, brother. Let's drop that subject. You know that Valère has your word to become your son-in-law.

ORGON. Yes.

CLÉANTE. You had set a date for that tender union.

ORGON. That is true.

CLÉANTE. Then why put off its celebration?

ORGON. I don't know.

CLÉANTE. Could you have some other thought in mind?

ORGON. Perhaps.

CLÉANTE. Would you want to go back on your word?

ORGON. I don't say that.

CLÉANTE. No obstacle, I think, can be in the way of accomplishing your promises.

ORGON. That's according. (*Shrugs.*)

CLÉANTE. Do you need so many subleties

to say one word? I have come to you at Valère's request.

ORGON. Heaven be praised.

CLÉANTE. But what shall I tell him?

ORGON. Anything you please.

CLÉANTE. But it's necessary to know your plans. What are they?

ORGON. To do . . . what heaven wishes.

CLÉANTE. Come, come, let's speak straight out. Valère has your word. Will you keep it or not?

ORGON. Farewell.   (*Exit.*)

CLÉANTE. I fear some misfortune for his love; I must warn him of all that goes on.

(*Exit.*)

ACT TWO

Enter MARIANE. *To her,* ORGON.

ORGON. Mariane.

MARIANE. Yes, Father.

ORGON. Come here. I want to speak with you in secret.

MARIANE. What are you looking for? (ORGON *looks in a small room on the Right towards the front.*)

ORGON. I'm looking to see if there isn't someone there who might hear us, for that little place is just right for catching someone unawares. Now then, we're all set. Mariane, I have always recognized in you a quite docile spirit and you have always been dear to me.

MARIANE. I am very grateful for my father's love.

ORGON. That's very well said, my dear, and, to deserve it, you must have no other care than to please me.

MARIANE. It is in so doing that I take my highest pride.

ORGON. Very good. What do you say about Tartuffe, our guest?

MARIANE. Who, me?

ORGON. You. Watch carefully how you answer.

MARIANE. Alas, I shall say whatever you please.

(DORINE *enters from behind and listens.*)

ORGON. That's the proper way to speak. Say then, my dear, that in his whole character great worth shines forth, that he has touched your heart, and that it would make you content if by my choice he were to become your husband. (MARIANE *suddenly shrinks backward in surprise.*) Eh?

MARIANE. Eh?

ORGON. What is it?

MARIANE. I beg your pardon?

ORGON. What?

MARIANE. Was I mistaken?

ORGON. What?

MARIANE. Who, father, do you want me to say has touched my heart and who would make me content if by your choice he were to become my husband?

ORGON. Tartuffe.

MARIANE. It's nothing of the kind, father, I swear it. Why make me tell such a lie?

ORGON. But I want it to be a truth; and it's enough for you that I have decided it.

MARIANE. What! Father, you want —

ORGON. Yes, I intend, my dear, to unite, by your marriage, Tartuffe to my family. He will be your husband, I have settled it; and since, concerning your wishes, I — (*He sees* DORINE.) What are you doing there? Curiosity must be pushing you pretty hard, dearie, to come listen to us that way.

DORINE. Really, I don't know if the rumor was based on guess-work or chance, but I had heard talk about this marriage and I treated it as pure nonsense.

ORGON. What? is it unbelievable?

DORINE. So much so, sir, that I don't believe even you.

ORGON. I know the way to make you believe it.

DORINE. Yes, yes, you're telling us a funny story.

ORGON. I'm telling what you will shortly see.

DORINE. Fairy tales!

ORGON. (*To* MARIANE) What I am saying, my dear, is not a game.

DORINE. Come on, don't believe your father. He's joking.

ORGON. I tell you. . . .

DORINE. No, no matter what, we won't believe you.

ORGON. Pretty soon my wrath. . . .

DORINE. All right, we believe you, so much the worse for you. How, sir, can it be that with the look of a man of sense and that big beard in the middle of your face you would be crazy enough to want to. . . .

ORGON. Listen, you have taken certain liberties in this household which don't please me at all, I'm telling you, dearie.

DORINE. Let's speak without growing angry, sir, I beg you. Are you trying to make fun of people with this plot? Your daughter is not the dish for a fanatic — he has other affairs he has to think about; and besides, what does such a match bring you? Why go out with all your wealth and pick a son-in-law in rags. . . .

ORGON. Be quiet. If he has nothing,
Know that that's exactly why we should revere him.
His wretched shape is no doubt an honest wretchedness.
It should exalt him far above all kinds of greatness
Since after all he was deprived of all his riches
By his lack of care for all that is temporal
And his powerful ties with all that is eternal.
But my help will be able to give him the means to come out of his difficulties and get back possession of his properties. They are fields which with good reason are renowned in his province, and, just as you see him, he is of the real nobility.

DORINE. Yes, and he's the one who says so; that vanity,
Sir, doesn't go well with true piety.
He who takes on the pure and holy life
Should not exalt his name and birth so high,
And the humble conduct of devotion
Does not fit well with loud bursts of ambition.
Why all that pride? . . . But you find this subject bothersome;
Let's skip his nobility and speak of his person.
Will you give in possession without some pain
A girl like her to a man like him?

Hadn't you better think about the proper-
ness
Of this marriage and foresee its consequence?
Know that a girl's virtue is at stake
When in her marriage you frustrate her
taste.
The resolve to live as an honest woman
Depends on the kind of a husband she's
given,
And often those whom we point at in fun
Themselves make their wives into what they
become.
In short, it is hard to be faithful
To husbands built on a certain model,
And he who gives to his daughter a man that
she hates
Will answer to heaven for the slips that she
makes.
Think to what perils your plan gives you
over.

ORGON. I tell you I have to learn how to
live from her!

DORINE. You couldn't do better than to
follow my lessons.

ORGON. Let's not waste time, my dear, on
these tales: I know what you need and I am
your father. I had pledged you to Valère,
but, besides the fact that they say he's inclined to gambling, I suspect him also of being somewhat of a free-thinker — I haven't
noticed him frequenting the churches.

DORINE. Do you want him to race there at
exactly your hours, like those who go only to
be seen?

ORGON. I didn't ask your opinion about it.
Whatever, the other is on the best terms with
heaven,
And that is a treasure to none other second.
In all good things this marriage will exceed
your desires;
It will be all candied in sweetness and pleas-
ures.
Together you'll live, in your faithful fervor,
Like two little children, like two turtledoves.
To unhappy disputes you never will come,
And you will make of him whatever you
want.

DORINE. Her? She'll just make an ass of
him, I can assure you.

ORGON. Ay! What talk!

DORINE. I'm telling you he's got the mak-
ings of one,
And his inborn talent, sir, will carry the day,
Over all the virtue your daughter will have.

ORGON. Stop interrupting me and see that
you keep quiet without putting your nose in
where you have no business.

DORINE. I'm only speaking, sir, in your
own best interests. (*She continually interrupts him at the moment when he turns
around to speak to his daughter.*)

ORGON. You take too much trouble;
please be quiet.

DORINE. If we didn't love you. . . .

ORGON. I *don't want* to be loved.

DORINE. But, sir, I want to love you in
spite of yourself.

ORGON. Ohhh!

DORINE. Your honor is dear to me and I
can't allow you to lay yourself open to everyone's mockery.

ORGON. Will you not be quiet?

DORINE. It's a matter of conscience to
keep you from making such an alliance.

ORGON. Will you shut up, serpent, whose
shameless barbs. . . .

DORINE. Ah! you are religious and you get
angry!

ORGON. Yes, I get all worked up hearing
that twaddle and I positively want you to
shut up.

DORINE. All right. But even if I don't
speak, I'll go on thinking just the same.

ORGON. Think if you want to, but make
every effort not to tell me about it, or. . . .
Enough. (*Turning back to his daughter*) In
my wisdom I have weighed everything with
mature deliberation.

DORINE. I get furious at not being able to
talk. (*She becomes silent as soon as he turns
his head.*)

ORGON. Without being a dandy, Tartuffe
is made in such a way. . . .

DORINE. Yes, a fine snout!

ORGON. That even if you should have no
sympathy for all the other gifts. . . . (*He
turns in front of* DORINE *and looks at her
with his arms crossed.*)

DORINE. Now she's well provided for!
If I were in her place, a man, certainly
Would not force me in marriage with impunity,
And I'd make him see, right after the wedding,
That a woman has always one vengeance ready.

ORGON. So, no attention is going to be paid to what I say?

DORINE. What are you complaining about? I'm not talking to you.

ORGON. What are you doing then?

DORINE. I'm talking to myself.

ORGON. Very well. (*Aside*) To punish her extreme insolence I'm going to have to give her the back of my hand. (*He gets in position to slap her face; and* DORINE, *every time he looks back at her, stands stiffly without speaking.*) . . . My dear, you must approve my plan. . . . Believe that the husband . . . I have chosen for you. . . . (*To* DORINE) Why don't you talk to yourself?

DORINE. I have nothing to say to myself.

ORGON. Just one more little word.

DORINE. I don't feel like it.

ORGON. (*Aside*) Of course, I was watching for you.

DORINE. I'm not *that* stupid!

ORGON. In short, my dear, you must respond with obedience and show for my choice absolute deference.

DORINE. (*Running away*) I'd go to the devil before I'd take such a husband.

ORGON. (*He tries to slap her and misses.*) My dear, that girl of yours is an absolute plague. I simply can't stay in the same house with her without sinning. I feel completely out of shape to continue . . . her impudent talk has set my mind on fire and I'm going out for a walk to settle my spirits a little. (*Exit.*)

(*Re-enter* DORINE.)

DORINE. Tell me, have you lost your tongue, and do I have to play your part for you in this? Allow someone to propose such a mad project without the slightest word of resistance!

MARIANE. Against a father's absolute power what do you want me to do?

DORINE. Whatever's necessary to ward off such a threat.

MARIANE. What?

DORINE. Tell him the heart doesn't love through somebody else;
That you're not getting married for him but for yourself;
That since you're the one for whom the business is done,
It's you — not him — should be pleased with the husband.
And that if he finds his Tartuffe so delicious
He can marry him without any hindrance.

MARIANE. I admit, a father has so much power over us that I have never had the strength to speak up for myself.

DORINE. Let's think this out. Valère has taken steps to marry you. Do you love him, please, or do you not?

MARIANE. Ah! how great is your injustice towards my love,
Dorine! Need you ask me such a question?
Have I not a hundred times disclosed to you my heart?
And don't you know the full extent of my tender passion?

DORINE. How do I know whether your mouth was speaking for your heart or if this suitor has *really* stirred your affection?

MARIANE. You do me great wrong, Dorine, to doubt it — my true feelings have shone forth only too clearly.

DORINE. In short, you do love him?

MARIANE. Yes, with an extremity of passion.

DORINE. And, at least in appearance, he loves you the same?

MARIANE. I believe so.

DORINE. And likewise both of you are dying to be married to each other.

MARIANE. Certainly.

DORINE. About this other match, then, what do you have in mind?

MARIANE. To put myself to death if I am forced.

DORINE. Very good! That's a resource I hadn't thought of. To get out of trouble all you have to do is die. The cure is certainly wonderful. I get furious when I hear people talk like that.

MARIANE. My goodness, Dorine, what a pet you're getting into! You don't sympathize with people in distress.

DORINE. I don't sympathize with people who talk twaddle and who, at the moment of decision, go limp like you do.

MARIANE. But can I help it if I'm timid?

DORINE. *But* love demands firmness of heart.

MARIANE. But haven't I been firm in my love for Valère? And isn't it up to him to obtain my father's permission?

DORINE. *But* look, if your father is an absolute wild man, who is completely infatuated with his Tartuffe and calls off the match he had decided on, can you blame that on your sweetheart?

MARIANE. But, by a great refusal and signal scorn, shall I reveal a heart too smitten with its choice? Shall I put aside for him — however splendid his worth — womanly modesty and filial duty? And do you want my tender ardor displayed to all the world. . . .

DORINE. No, no, I don't want a thing, I see you want to

Belong to Monsieur Tartuffe, and, now that I think of it, I'd

Be wrong to turn you away from such an alliance.

What reason would I have to combat your wishes?

In itself it is quite a superior match.

Monsieur Tartuffe! Oh-ho! Is this any-old-body being proposed?

Certainly Monsieur Tartuffe, when properly considered,

Is not a man — no sir! — to be sneezed at,

And it's no small fortune to be his better half.

Already everyone crowns him with glory;

He's a nobleman back home, a fine figure of a man.

He has a ruddy ear and florid complexion;

You'll live only too happily with such a husband.

MARIANE. My goodness. . . .

DORINE. What joy you will have in your heart when you see yourself the wife of so handsome a husband!

MARIANE. Oh, please stop such talk and find me some way out of this marriage. I'm done for, I give in — I'm ready to do anything.

DORINE. No, even if he'd wed her to a monkey,

A girl her father must obey.

Your lot is very fine, why should you complain?

You'll go by public coach to his little town,

Which in uncles and cousins you'll find quite fruitful,

And you'll enjoy *so much* your conversations with them.

Right off you'll be taken out in high society;

You will go to visit, for your welcome,

Miladies the wives of the bailiff and the first assessor,

Who will honor you with a camp stool in some corner.

There, at carnival time, you may hope for

A ball and the royal violins, namely two bagpipers,

And sometimes Punch and Judy and the organ-grinder.

However, if your husband. . . .

MARIANE.   Ah! you're making me die! Try to think of a plan to save my life.

DORINE. I am your humble servant.

MARIANE.   Oh, Dorine, have pity.

DORINE. For your own punishment this thing will be.

MARIANE. My dear girl!

DORINE.   No!

MARIANE. If the avowals I have made . . .

DORINE. None of that. Tartuffe is your man, and you're going to get a taste.

MARIANE. You know that I have always confided only in you. Please do. . . .

DORINE. No. You will just be tartuffi-fied.

MARIANE. All right! since you cannot be moved by my fate,

Leave me alone henceforth to my despair.

From desperation my heart will find its help,
And I know the infallible cure for all my
ills.   (*She starts to leave.*)

DORINE. Oh, there, there now, come back,
I'll stop being angry. A person has to have
pity on you in spite of everything.

MARIANE. You see, if I am exposed to this
cruel martyrdom, I tell you Dorine, I shall
simply expire.

DORINE. Don't torment yourself — with
a little skill we can prevent. . . . But here
is Valère, your sweetheart.

(*Enter* VALÈRE.)

VALÈRE. People have begun to spread,
Madame, a piece of news which I did not
know, and which is doubtless quite fine.

MARIANE. What!

VALÈRE. That you are marrying Tartuffe.

MARIANE. It is true that my father has
got this idea into his head.

VALÈRE. Your father, Madame. . . .

MARIANE. Has changed his plan. He has
just finished proposing it to me.

VALÈRE. What! Seriously?

MARIANE. Yes, seriously; he has declared
himself for this match in no uncertain tones.

VALÈRE. And what is the plan which you
have settled on, Madame?

MARIANE. I don't know.

VALÈRE. That's an honest answer. You
don't know?

MARIANE. No.

VALÈRE. No?

MARIANE. What do you advise me?

VALÈRE. *I* advise you to take this husband.

MARIANE. You advise me to?

VALÈRE. Yes.

MARIANE. Really?

VALÈRE. Certainly. The choice is illustrious and well worth listening to.

MARIANE. All right, that is advice, sir,
which I accept.

VALÈRE. You won't have much trouble in
following it, I think.

MARIANE. No more than your heart suffered in giving it.

VALÈRE. *I* gave it to please *you*, Madame.

MARIANE. And *I* shall follow it to please
you.

DORINE. (*Aside*) Let's see what will come
out of all this.

VALÈRE. Is that the way to love? And it
was deceit when you. . . .

MARIANE. Let's not speak of that, please.
You told me straight out that I should accept for a husband the one they want to give
me, and *I* declare that I intend to do so, since
you give me the salutary advice.

VALÈRE. Don't excuse yourself with my
intentions — you had already made up your
mind, and are seizing upon a frivolous pre-
text for authority to break your word.

MARIANE. It's true; that is well said.

VALÈRE. Of course, and your heart never
had any real flame for me.

MARIANE. Alas! You may think so if you
like.

VALÈRE. Yes, yes, if I like; but my offended heart will anticipate you perhaps, in
a similar plan, and I know where to take the
offer of my hand.

MARIANE. Ah, I don't doubt it; and the
passions which merit arouses. . . .

VALÈRE. Heavens, let's leave merit out of
this; I have very little, no doubt, and you are
giving me the proof; but I have hope in the
kindness another will have for me, and I
know someone whose heart will give me refuge and consent, without pride, to make up
for my loss.

MARIANE. The loss is not great, and with
this change you will console yourself quite
easily. . . .

VALÈRE. I shall do my best, and you may
believe so.
A heart which forgets us puts our honor at
stake;
To forget it we, too, must apply all of our
care.
If one does not succeed, one must feign it at
least;
And this weakness is never forgiven
Of showing love when we are abandoned.

MARIANE. Doubtless this sentiment is noble and lofty.

VALÈRE. Quite right, and should be approved by all.

After all! Would you want me to keep forever in my soul the ardors of my love for you, and see you pass, before my eyes, into another's arms without taking elsewhere a heart which you will have none of?

MARIANE. On the contrary, that is what I hope, and I wish it were already done.

VALÈRE. You wish it?

MARIANE. Yes.

VALÈRE. I have been insulted enough, madame; I shall straightway make you content. (*He takes a step to go away.*)

MARIANE. Very well.

VALÈRE. (*Returning*) Just remember that you're the one forcing my heart to this extreme effort. (*Departs.*)

MARIANE. Yes.

VALÈRE. (*Returning*) And that the plan I have conceived in my breast is nothing but following your example. (*Departs.*)

MARIANE. My example — so be it.

VALÈRE. (*Returning*) Enough; you will be punctually served.

MARIANE. That's fine.

VALÈRE. You will never see me again as long as I live.

MARIANE. How delightful!

VALÈRE. (*Goes away, and, when he is near the door, turns around.*) Huh?

MARIANE. What?

VALÈRE. Didn't you call me?

MARIANE. I! You're dreaming.

VALÈRE. Well, then, I shall proceed on my way. Farewell, madame.

MARIANE. Farewell, monsieur.

DORINE. Well, *I* think you're losing your minds with this absurd nonsense. I let you quarrel yourselves out just to see how far it would go. Hey there! Monsieur Valère. (*She goes to stop him by the arm, and* VALÈRE *puts up a show of great resistance.*)

· VALÈRE. Hey, what do you want, Dorine?

DORINE. Come here. (*Drags him into the room.*)

VALÈRE. No, no, resentment holds me in sway. Do not turn me aside from what *she* desired.

DORINE. Stop.

VALÈRE. No, you see, it's all settled.

DORINE. Ah!

MARIANE. He suffers at the sight of me, my presence drives him away — I shall do much better to give him free room. (*Starts for the door opposite.*)

DORINE. (*Leaves* VALÈRE *and runs to* MARIANE.) Now the other one! Where are you running off to?

MARIANE. Let me go.

DORINE. You must come back.

MARIANE. No, no, Dorine, it's useless to try to hold me back.

VALÈRE. It's clear that seeing me is torture to her, so it's probably better for me to free her from it (*Going to the door*).

DORINE. (*Leaves* MARIANE *and runs to* VALÈRE.) Again? Devil take you if I'll allow it! Stop this playing around and come here, both of you. (*She pulls them together.*)

VALÈRE. But what is your plan?

MARIANE. What are you trying to do?

DORINE. Bring you back together and get you out of trouble. (*To* VALÈRE) Are you out of your head to make such a fuss?

VALÈRE. Didn't you hear how she talked to me?

DORINE. (*To* MARIANE) Are *you* out of your head to have lost your temper?

MARIANE. Didn't you see the whole thing, how he treated me?

DORINE. (*To* VALÈRE) Stupidity on both sides. She has no other thought but to keep herself for you — I am a witness. (*To* MARIANE) He loves only you, and has no other desire than to be your husband — I'll swear it on my life.

MARIANE. Then why give me such advice?

VALÈRE. Why ask it on such a subject?

DORINE. You're both out of your heads. Here, give me your hands, both of you. (*To* VALÈRE) Come on, you.

VALÈRE. (*Giving his hand to* DORINE) What good's my hand?

DORINE. (*To* MARIANE) Oh, come on! Yours.

MARIANE. (*Also giving her hand to* DORINE) What good's all that?

DORINE. Good heavens! Quick, come forward. You both love each other more than you think.

VALÈRE. (*To* MARIANE) Then don't be so distressed at doing things, and look at people a little without hatred. (MARIANE *turns her eye towards* VALÈRE *and makes a little smile.*)

DORINE. To tell you the truth, lovers are really mad!

VALÈRE. Now! don't I have a right to complain about you? And, truthfully, aren't you mean to enjoy telling me something hurtful?

MARIANE. But you, aren't you the most ungrateful man. . . .

DORINE. Let's leave this whole debate for another time, and let's think about avoiding this vexatious marriage.

MARIANE. Tell us what means we should put to use.

DORINE. We'll pull every string there is. This is all foolishness — your father is talking sheer nonsense. But, for your part, it's best for you to give the appearance of gentle consent to his folly, so that in case of emergency it will be easier to postpone this proposed marriage. By gaining time you can find a cure for anything. One time you'll put him off with some sudden sickness which requires a delay, another time you'll put him off with bad omens: you're upset because you passed a funeral on the street, broke a mirror, or dreamed of muddy water. Anyway, the main thing is that you cannot be united to anyone but him (*points to* VALÈRE) unless you say yes. But, in order to win out, I think it's a good idea for you two not to be seen talking together. (*To* VALÈRE) Go away and without delay employ your friends to obtain what you've been promised. We are going to stir up her brother's efforts and get her stepmother on our side. Farewell.

VALÈRE. (*To* MARIANE) Whatever efforts we may all prepare, truly my greatest hope is in you.

MARIANE. (*To* VALÈRE) I cannot answer for my father's will, but I will belong to none but Valère.

VALÈRE. You overwhelm me with joy! And whoever may dare. . . .

DORINE. Ah! Lovers are never tired of babbling. Go away, I tell you.

VALÈRE. (*Takes a step and returns.*) Anyway. . . .

DORINE. What a chatterbox! (*Pushing each one by the shoulder*) You go that way and you go the other way.

ACT THREE

Enter DAMIS *and* DORINE.

DAMIS. May lightning strike me dead on the spot,

May I be called the greatest cad who ever lived

If by any respect or power I can be stopped,

And if I don't strike some blow on my own.

DORINE. Please, calm your storm;

Your father merely talked about it;

One does not carry out all one's ideas,

And the way is long from the thought to the deed.

DAMIS. I've got to stop that ass's plot and talk to him the only way I know.

DORINE. Ah! gently! As for him and for your father, leave it up to your step-mother. She has some influence with Tartuffe; he's agreeable to everything she says and might well have some sweet feeling for her. Would to heaven it were true! Wouldn't that be fun! Anyway, for your sake she has sent for him; she wants to sound him out on the marriage which bothers you, to find out his feelings and to let him know what an upset might arise if he should encourage this plan. His valet said he is praying and I couldn't see him, but the valet said he was going to come down. So go away, please, and let me wait for him.

DAMIS. I can be present for the whole interview.

DORINE. Not at all: they must be alone.

DAMIS. I won't say a thing to him.

DORINE. You're joking — everyone knows about you and your temper — that's the real way to spoil things. Go away.

DAMIS. No, I want to see without getting angry.

DORINE. What a bother you are! He's coming — go away. (DAMIS *hides in the little room, unnoticed by* DORINE.)

(*Enter* TARTUFFE *from the center door at the back of the stage.*)

TARTUFFE. (*Perceiving* DORINE, *speaks to his servant, off stage.*) Laurent, hang up my hair shirt along with my lash,
And at all times pray to heaven for guidance.
I'm going out; if I should have any visitors,
I have gone to share my poor alms with the prisoners.

DORINE. What affectation and swaggering!

TARTUFFE. What do you wish?

DORINE. To tell you. . . .

TARTUFFE. (*Takes out a handkerchief.*) Ah! good heavens, please! Before speaking take this handkerchief.

DORINE. What?

TARTUFFE. Cover that breast which I must not see.
By sights such as those souls are wounded,
And it makes guilty thoughts come into one's head.

DORINE. Are you, then, quite an easy mark for temptation?
Does the flesh on your senses make such an impression?
I'm sure I don't know how *your* fever goes up,
But *I* am not so quick and ready to lust,
And I could see you naked from head to feet,
And your whole skin wouldn't tempt me a bit.

TARTUFFE. Put a little modesty in your speech,
Or this very minute I shall leave.

DORINE. No, no, it is I who shall leave you in peace;
I have only one thing to tell you. Madame is coming down to this parlor and asks the favor of a word with you.

TARTUFFE. Alas! with pleasure.

DORINE. (*To herself*) Look at him soften up! I'll certainly stick to what I said before.

TARTUFFE. Is she coming soon?

DORINE. I think I hear her. Yes, it's she. I'll leave you together. (*Exit.*)

(*Enter* ELMIRE.)

TARTUFFE. May you be given by the infinite goodness of heaven
Health in both body and soul forever,
And may your days be blessed as much as desires
The humblest of those whom its love inspires.

ELMIRE. I am much obliged for this pious wish; but let us sit down and be more comfortable.

TARTUFFE. Do you feel quite recovered from your illness?

ELMIRE. Quite well — the fever soon lost hold.

TARTUFFE. My prayers are not worthy enough
To have drawn down this grace from above,
But I have made to heaven no pious instance
For causes other than your convalescence.

ELMIRE. Your zeal went to too much trouble for me.

TARTUFFE. One cannot cherish too much your dearest health, and to bring it back I would have given my own.

ELMIRE. That's pushing Christian charity pretty far — I am much indebted for all your kindness.

TARTUFFE. I do much less than you deserve.

ELMIRE. I wanted to speak to you about something in secret — I'm very glad no one is listening.

TARTUFFE. I, too, am delighted, and it is certainly sweet for me, Madame, to find myself alone with you. It is an opportunity which I have begged from heaven without its being granted until this moment.

ELMIRE. For my part, I desire a moment of conversation in which you open your whole heart, hiding nothing.

TARTUFFE. And, as a unique blessing, my only desire
Is to bare my soul before your eyes,
And to swear to you that the rows I have raised
About the visitors whom your beauty fascinates
Are not the result of hatred for you,

But rather a flight of zeal by which I am moved

And a pure transport. . . .

ELMIRE. I don't take it amiss; I feel that the health of my soul worried you.

TARTUFFE. (*He squeezes the tips of her fingers.*) Yes, Madame, of course, and my fervor is such. . . .

ELMIRE. Ooh! you're squeezing too hard.

TARTUFFE. From excessive zeal. To do you harm was never my intention and I would far rather. . . . (*He puts his hand on her knee.*)

ELMIRE. What is your hand doing there?

TARTUFFE. I'm feeling your dress; the material is silken.

ELMIRE. Oh! please, stop; I'm very ticklish.

(*She pushes her chair back, and* TARTUFFE *brings his nearer.*)

TARTUFFE. My goodness! The workmanship of this lace (*around her neck and bosom*) is marvelous; never have such things been done in every way.

ELMIRE. That's true. But let's get down to business for a moment. I have heard that my husband wants to take back his word and give his daughter to you; tell me, is that true?

TARTUFFE. To tell the truth — though he has mentioned something like —
Madame, *that* is not the bliss for which I sigh,
And elsewhere I see the marvelous grace
Of that felicity which is my sole aspiration.

ELMIRE. That's because you can love nothing here below.

TARTUFFE. My breast does not enclose a heart of stone.

ELMIRE. Oh, *I* am sure that all your sighs are directed towards heaven, and that nothing earthly stays your desires.

TARTUFFE. The love which binds us to the things eternal
Does not quench in us all love of the temporal.
And easily our senses may be charmed
By the perfect works which heaven has formed.

Its loveliness reflected shines in those of your nature,
But in you it displays its rarest treasures.
Its beauties, on your face poured forth,
Catch eyes unawares and hearts are transported;
And I could not look on you, O perfect creature,
Without admiring in you the Author of nature,
And with a fervent love I felt my heart stricken
By the fairest portrait in which He is depicted
At first I feared that this secret ardor
Was an ambush of the Prince of Darkness,
And my heart resolved to flee from your sight,
Believing you an obstruction on the road to paradise.
But at last I knew, O adorable beauty,
That this passion can be not guilty —
That I can fit it in with modest behavior,
And so, therefore, I let my heart surrender.
It is, I confess, an act of great boldness,
This offering of love, to you addressed;
But I expect, in my vows, all from your mercy,
Presuming naught from my infirmity.
In you is my hope, my weal, my rest;
On you depends my torment or my blessedness;
And I shall be at last, by your sole decree,
Blessed, if you will it, cursed, if you please.

ELMIRE. The declaration is quite gallant, but, to tell the truth, it's somewhat surprising. It seems to me you should have steeled your heart a little more and thought sensibly about such a notion. Pious as you are, whom everyone calls. . . .

TARTUFFE. Ah! Though I am pious, I am none the less a man;
And when a person sees your divine attractions,
One's heart lets itself be ensnared and doesn't reason.
I know that such talk from me seems strange;
But, Madame, after all, I am not an angel,

And, if you condemn this confession I make,
The blame must be placed on your own fascinations.
As soon as I saw their suprahuman splendor
You became queen of my spiritual nature.
The unspeakable sweetness of your divine regard
Broke down the resistance of my obdurate heart;
Fasting, tears, prayers — all — it swept aside,
And towards your charms all my vows inclined.
My looks and sighs have told you this a thousand times,
And now, to tell it more clearly, my tongue I employ.
If your soul looks down with any compassion
On your unworthy slave and his tribulations,
If your mercy should vouchsafe to give me solace
And stoop as low as my utter insignificance,
For you I shall have, O vessel of fragrance,
Forever a matchless allegiance.
Your reputation runs no risk with me,
Where I'm concerned has no ill luck to fear.
All the courtly fops that women are mad for
Are noisy in their deeds and vain in their words;
Constantly their progress they boast,
And they get no favor which they do not disclose;
Their tongue, indiscreet, in which women confide,
Besmirches the altar of their heart's sacrifice.
But people like us burn with a flame that is quiet,
With us one is always assured of one's secret.
The care which we take of our reputation
Is a firm guarantee to the person beloved,
And in us can be found, by accepting our heart,
Love without scandal and pleasure without fear.

ELMIRE. I have been listening to your oration, and you have made me a declaration in rather strong terms. Aren't you afraid I might feel like telling my husband about this amorous fervor, and that the sudden news of such a love might very well alter his friendship for you?

TARTUFFE. I know that you have too much clemency,
And that you will pardon my temerity;
That you will forgive the all too human weakness,
The violent raptures, of a love which offends;
And that you will consider, as you look at yourself,
That one cannot be blind, and a man is but flesh.

ELMIRE. Perhaps others would react differently, but I wish to show my discretion. I shall not repeat this to my husband, but in return I want something from you: that you urge straight out, and with no double-dealing, the union of Valère with Mariane; that you yourself renounce this unjust use of power which would enrich you at another's expense, and. . . .

DAMIS. (*Coming out of the room in which he had hidden*) No, Madame, no, this news must be spread far and wide. I was in this place where I could hear everything; divine bounty seems to have led me there to confound the pride of my treacherous enemy, to open up to me a path of vengeance on his hypocrisy and insolence, to undeceive my father and to expose to him in broad daylight the soul of a scoundrel who speaks to you of love.

ELMIRE. No, Damis, it's enough if he behaves himself and tries to deserve the forgiveness which I pledge. Since I have promised, don't contradict me. It's not my nature to create a row; a woman laughs at that kind of nonsense and never troubles her husband's ears with it.

DAMIS. You have your reasons for behaving that way, and I have mine for acting otherwise. It would seem mockery to spare him; the impudent pride of his bigotry has triumphed only too much over my righteous anger and fomented only too much disorder in our household. The swindler has governed my father too long and done an ill turn to my passion and Valère's too. Father must have his eyes opened to this traitor, and heaven has offered me an easy way to do it. I am grateful for this chance — it is too good to neglect; I would deserve to have it snatched away from me if I had it in my hands and didn't use it.

ELMIRE. Damis. . . .

DAMIS. No, if you please, I must have it my own way. My heart is bursting with joy, and all your talk is in vain, trying to make me give up the pleasure of vengeance: without going any farther I'm going to settle this thing, and here is just what I need.

(*Enter* ORGON.)

We are going to treat your arrival, Father, to a piece of fresh news which will greatly surprise you. You are well paid back for your marks of affection, and Monsieur makes you a nice return on your fondness. His great zeal for you has just declared itself. It falls nothing short of dishonoring you; I caught him here making the outrageous confession to Madame of a guilty passion. She has a sweet nature and a discreet heart — she was determined to keep it quiet, but I can't indulge such shamelessness. I think that keeping it from you is to do you offense.

ELMIRE. Yes, I maintain that we should never disturb a husband's peace of mind with all this foolish gossip; honor cannot depend on such trifles, and it's enough for us to know how to defend ourselves. Those are my feelings, and you would have said nothing, Damis, if I had had any influence on you.

(*Exit.*)

ORGON. What do I hear, O Lord, can it be true?

TARTUFFE. Yes, dear brother, I am a wicked, guilty,
Wretched sinner, full of all iniquities,
The greatest villain who ever lived.
My life is soiled and stained at every minute;
It's nothing but a mass of crimes and filth,
And I see that heaven, to chastise me,
Seeks at this time to mortify me.
However gross a crime may be alleged,
I refrain from the pride of self-defense.

Believe what you are told, arm your wrath,
And like a thief drive me from your home.
The measure of my shame could not fail
To be much less than I deserve.

ORGON. (*To his son*) Ah, traitor! do you dare, with falsehood, try to tarnish the pureness of his virtue?

DAMIS. What! The sham meekness of that hypocrite soul will make you impugn. . . .

ORGON. Shut up, cursed plague!

TARTUFFE. Ah! let him speak; you accuse him wrongly, and you would do much better to believe his account. Why should you favor me so much in such a matter? After all, do you know what I am capable of? Do you trust, dear brother, in my looks? And do you think I'm any better than what you can see? No, no, you let yourself be deceived by appearance, and I am nothing less — alas! — than what they think. Everyone takes me for a good man, but the pure truth is that I have no worth. (*Speaking to* DAMIS) Yes, my dear son, speak, call me traitor, vile, debauched, thief, murderer; heap on me names more hateful still; I don't deny it — I have deserved them, and I will suffer the shame on my knees (*He kneels.*) as a disgrace earned by the crimes of my life.

ORGON. (*To* TARTUFFE) Dear brother, this is too much. (*To his son*) Doesn't your heart surrender, traitor?

DAMIS. What! His talk can lead you so far astray as. . . .

ORGON. Shut up, villain! (*To* TARTUFFE) Dear brother, oh! get up, please! (TARTUFFE *rises.*) (*To his son*) Vile . . . !

DAMIS. He can. . . .

ORGON. Shut up.

DAMIS. This infuriates me! What! I pass. . . .

ORGON. If you say a single word, I'll break both your arms.

TARTUFFE. Dear brother, in heaven's name, don't get angry. I would rather suffer the severest torture than for him to receive the slightest scratch for my sake.

ORGON. (*To his son*) Ungrateful . . . !

TARTUFFE. Leave him in peace. If I must

intercede for him on both knees. . . . (*Kneels.*)

ORGON. (*Overcome by emotion, also kneels, embraces* TARTUFFE *and tries to get him to rise.*) Alas! You don't mean it? (*Arises rapidly;* TARTUFFE, *more leisurely.*) (*To his son*) Wretch, behold his goodness.

DAMIS. So. . . .

ORGON. Peace!

DAMIS. What, I. . . .

ORGON. Peace, I tell you! I'm well aware of the motive for your attack. You all hate him, and today I see wife, children, and valets in a rage against him. You shamelessly put everything to work to get this pious person out of my house; but the more efforts you make to banish him, the more I will use to keep him, and I shall hasten to give him my daughter to confound the pride of my whole family.

DAMIS. You plan to make her accept his hand?

ORGON. Yes, traitor, this very evening, to drive you all into fury. Ah! I will stand up to all of you and make you realize that I *will* be obeyed and that I am the master. Come on, take it back this instant, rascal; throw yourself at his feet and ask for pardon.

DAMIS. Who, me? from this wretch, who by his imposture. . . .

ORGON. Ah! you resist, beggar, and insult him? A stick, a stick! (*To* TARTUFFE) Don't hold me back. (TARTUFFE *has made no move to do so.*) (*To his son*) Now then, leave my house at once, and never dare to come back again.

DAMIS. Yes, I shall leave, but. . . .

ORGON. Quick, get out. (*Exit* DAMIS.) I cut you off, villain, from your inheritance and give you my curse besides. (ORGON *returns.*) Offend a saintly person like that!

TARTUFFE. O heaven! Forgive him the pain he does unto me. (*To* ORGON) If you only knew how unhappy it makes me to see them try to degrade me in the eyes of my dear brother. . . .

ORGON. Alas!

TARTUFFE. Just the thought of that ingratitude makes my soul suffer such harsh torment. The horror it makes me feel. . . . My heart is so heavy I cannot talk and I shall probably die.

ORGON. (*Runs all in tears to the door through which he has driven his son.*) Wretch! I repent that my hand spared you, and didn't strike you dead on the spot. Calm yourself, dear brother, and don't be sad.

TARTUFFE. Let us break, let us break off this painful discussion.

I look about me and see that I bring great dissension,

And I feel I must leave here, dear brother.

ORGON. What? You don't mean it?

TARTUFFE. I am despised, and I see they are trying to make you suspect my good faith.

ORGON. What is the difference! Do you see my heart pay any attention to them?

TARTUFFE. They cannot fail to pursue it; and these same accounts which now you reject. . . . Perhaps another time you will listen.

ORGON. No, dear brother, never.

TARTUFFE. Ah, dear brother, a wife can easily catch a husband's soul unawares.

ORGON. No, no.

TARTUFFE. By going far away from here let me quickly take away all their grounds for attacking me so.

ORGON. No, you will stay; it's a matter of life and death to me.

TARTUFFE. All right then, I shall have to mortify myself. However, if you would. . . .

ORGON. Ah!

TARTUFFE. So be it, let's speak of it no more. But I know how one must behave in this matter. Honor is a delicate thing, and friendship obliges me to forestall rumors and grounds for suspicion: I shall run from your wife and you won't see me. . . .

ORGON. No, in spite of everyone, you will keep her company. To drive people to fury is my greatest joy, and I want you to be seen with her constantly. That's still not all: to defy them all even better, I want to have no other heir but you, and I am going right away to make over to you in proper form a gift of my entire fortune. A good and true friend whom I take as my son-in-law is far dearer to me than son, wife, or kin. Won't you accept my proposal?

TARTUFFE. May heaven's will be done in all things.

ORGON. (*Aside*) The poor fellow! (*To* TARTUFFE) Let's quickly go and draw it up in writing, and may the envious die of spite!

(*Exeunt.*)

ACT FOUR

Enter CLÉANTE *and* TARTUFFE.

CLÉANTE. Yes, everybody's talking about it, and — you may take my word — the scandal is not to your credit; I'm glad I ran across you, sir, so I can tell you my thoughts straight out in a couple of words. I shan't delve into the details, I shall pass over that and accept things at their worst. Let us suppose that Damis acted improperly and accused you wrongly, is it not up to a Christian to pardon the offense and to smother in his heart all desire for vengeance? And should you allow a son to be banished from his father's house on account of your dispute? I tell you again — and I'm speaking frankly — there's no one, high or low, who isn't scandalized by the situation. If you take my advice, you will smooth everything over and not push things to their bitter end. Sacrifice your wrath to God, and bring the son back into the father's good graces.

TARTUFFE. Alas, I would be glad to, for myself; I harbor no bitterness against him, sir; I forgive him all — I blame him for nothing, and would like to serve him with the greatest good will; but it would be incompatible with the best interests of heaven, and if he comes back here, it will be up to me to leave. After his action — the like of which has never been seen — any relations between us would cause a scandal: Lord knows what people would think of it; they'd impute it to sheer politics on my part, and everyone would say that, knowing myself guilty, I was feigning a charitable zeal for my accuser, that I fear him in my heart and want to handle him with care so I can pledge him to silence on the sly.

CLÉANTE. You are paying us now with counterfeit excuses, and all your reasons, sir, are too tenuous; why do you take on your shoulders the interests of heaven? Does it need us to punish the guilty? Leave it to heaven to avenge itself, and take thought only of the forgiveness it prescribes for offenses: pay no attention to human judgments when you are following the sovereign commands of heaven. What! the insipid care for what people may think will prevent the glorious doing of a good action? No, no; let us always do what heaven prescribes, and with no other care trouble our minds.

TARTUFFE. I have already told you that I forgive him in my heart, and that, sir, is doing what heaven ordains: but after the scandal of today's affront, heaven does not ordain that I live with him.

CLÉANTE. And does it ordain, sir, that you should open your ears to his father's counsel of caprice and accept the gift of a fortune to which you have no rightful claim?

TARTUFFE. Those who know me will not think it a result of self-interest in my soul. All the goods of this world have little appeal for me; by their deceitful splendor I am not dazzled; and if I have come to the decision to receive from the father this gift which he has chosen to make, it is solely — to tell the truth — because I fear that that great fortune might fall into wicked hands; that it might find its way by inheritance to people who would, in the world, put it to criminal use and not employ it — as I plan to — to the glory of Heaven and the good of their neighbor.

CLÉANTE. Ah, Monsieur, do not hold such exquisite fears, which could cause the complaints of a rightful heir. Don't trouble yourself about a thing, and just allow him to possess his fortune at his own risk, and remember that it is much better for him to misuse it than for you to be accused of defrauding him. I am simply amazed that you could submit to the proposal without embarrassment; for, after all, does true religion have some maxim which teaches us to despoil the legitimate heir? And if it is true that heaven has placed some insuperable barrier in the way of your living with Damis, wouldn't it be better for you, as a gentleman, to make a prudent exit than to allow — against all reason — a son to be driven out of his house on your account? Believe me, on the score of your *decency*, sir. . . .

TARTUFFE. It is, sir, three-thirty; certain religious duties call me (*points to his room*) and you will forgive me for leaving you so soon. (*Exit.*)

CLÉANTE. Ah!

(*Enter* ELMIRE, MARIANE, DORINE.)

DORINE. Please, sir, help us on her behalf; her soul is in mortal pain: at every moment she falls into despair when she thinks of the betrothal her father has set for this evening. He's on his way here; let's unite our efforts, please, and try, by force or by wit, to unhinge this wretched plan which has us all upset.

(*Enter* ORGON, *with a legal document.*)

ORGON. Ah! I'm delighted to find you all gathered together. (*To* MARIANE) I have here in this contract something that will make you laugh, and you know already what that means.

MARIANE. (*On her knees*) Dear Father, in the name of heaven, which knows my grief,
By all that in your own heart may plead,
Of your paternal rights so much release
That from such obedience my love may be free.
Do not reduce me, by such harsh rule,
To complain to heaven of what I owe to you;
And this life, dear Father, of which you were the maker —
Do not, alas, render it totally hateful.
If you forbid me, against my sweetest hopes,
To belong to the one I make bold to love,
At least, by your mercy, which at your knees I implore,
Save me from belonging to one whom I loathe,
And do not push me to some act of despair
By using on me all of your power.

ORGON. (*Aside, feeling himself soften-*

ing) Come, come, steady, my heart; no human weakness!

MARIANE. Your favors to him do not distress me;
Make them shine forth, give him your fortune,
And, if that isn't enough, give him mine too;
I consent cheerfully and give it up forever;
But at least don't carry this as far as my person;
And permit me, amidst a convent's austerities,
To wear out the sad days which heaven has allotted me.

ORGON. Ah! so there's one of those sudden nuns as soon as a father goes counter to her sweet passion! Stand up! The more your heart shrinks from accepting him, the more meritorious for you will be the act. Mortify your senses with this marriage, and don't give me any more headaches.

DORINE. What! . . .

ORGON. Shut up, you. Mind your own business; I forbid you straight out to dare say a single word.

CLÉANTE. If you would permit a word of advice in answer to. . . .

ORGON. My dear brother, your advice is the best in the world; it is very logical, and I value it highly, but you will permit me not to take it.

ELMIRE. (*To her husband*) I am dumfounded at what I see — your blindness amazes me. You are being biased — a proper mule — for him, to give us the lie about what happened today.

ORGON. I am your humble servant, and I believe in the appearance; I know about your sympathy for my rascally son — you were afraid to contradict him in the trick he tried to play on that poor fellow. Besides, you were too calm to be believed; you would have appeared quite differently upset.

ELMIRE. Does our honor have to fly up in arms at a simple declaration of amorous fancy? Can't we answer it any way except with flaming eyes and abusive tongue? For my part I don't like any uproar about it, so I content myself with laughing at such remarks. I like women to be modest without harshness; I don't agree at all with those savage prudes whose honor is armed with claws and teeth, who want to commit mayhem on people at the slightest word. May heaven preserve me from such goodness! I want a virtue which isn't shrewish; and I think that discreet chill in refusal is no less strong to rebuff a heart.

ORGON. Well, I know the whole business and am not thrown off the track.

ELMIRE. I'm still amazed at this bizarre weakness. But what would your disbelief answer if I made you see that we're telling you the truth?

ORGON. See?

ELMIRE. Yes.

ORGON. Nonsense!

ELMIRE. What! Suppose I found a way to make you see it in broad daylight?

ORGON. Idle tales!

ELMIRE. What a man! At least give me an answer. I'm not asking you to have faith in us, but let's suppose now that from a certain well-chosen spot you were made to see and hear everything clearly, then what would you say about your good gentleman?

ORGON. In that case I would say. . . . I wouldn't say anything, because it can't be.

ELMIRE. The error has endured too long, and my lips have been charged too much with imposture. I must have the pleasure right now of making you a witness to everything you've been told.

ORGON. Agreed — I'll take you up on that. We shall see your skill in fulfilling that promise.

ELMIRE. (*To* DORINE) Send him to me.

DORINE. His wits are sharp — it may not be so easy to trap him.

ELMIRE. No, one is easily duped by what one loves, and self-esteem undertakes to deceive itself. Send him down to me. (*Speaking to* CLÉANTE *and* MARIANE) You, withdraw. (*They go out.*) (*To* ORGON) Let's pull up this table. . . . Get under it.

ORGON. What!

ELMIRE. You must be well hidden.

ORGON. Why under this table?

ELMIRE. Ah, my heavens! Leave it to me: I have my plan in mind and you will judge it. Get in there, I say, and when you're in there don't let yourself be seen or heard.

ORGON. I must admit my indulgence is going pretty far, but I have to see how you are going to get out of this business.

ELMIRE. I don't think you'll have a thing to answer back. (*To her husband who is under the table*) Remember, I'm going to bring up a strange topic — don't be at all scandalized. Whatever I may say must be permitted me, since it's to convince you, as I promised. Since I am reduced to this, I am going to use sweetness; to make that hypocrite soul lay aside his mask, I shall encourage his shameless desires and leave a clear field to his temerity. Inasmuch as it's for you alone — the better to confound him — that my heart is going to sham responsiveness to his declarations, I shall be ready to stop as soon as you give in, and things will go only as far as you wish. It's up to you to stop his blind passion when you think the thing has been carried far enough, and spare your wife from being exposed to any more than is necessary to open your eyes. It's in your own interests — you will be the master, and . . . someone's coming; be still and don't show yourself.

(*Enter* TARTUFFE.)

TARTUFFE. I was told that you wished to speak to me in here.

ELMIRE. Yes, there are secrets to be revealed to you. But pull that door shut first and look around everywhere for fear of being caught; an affair like the one a little while ago is certainly not what we need right now. I've never been so startled in my life; Damis gave me quite a fright on your account, and you must have seen how I did all I could to break off his plan and calm his fits of temper. However, I was so upset that it didn't occur to me to contradict him; but, thank heavens, everything turned out for the best, and, as a result of it all, things are more secure than ever. The esteem in which you are held dissipated the storm — my husband

Tartuffe. Sketched from the eighteenth-century stage.

is unable to suspect you of anything. And, the better to defy rumors of scandal, he wants us to be together all the time; that is how — without fear of being blamed — I can be closeted here with you, and that is what permits me to reveal to you a heart perhaps a trifle too prompt in submitting to your ardor.

TARTUFFE. This language is rather difficult to understand, Madame; a while ago you spoke in a different style.

ELMIRE. Ah! if you are angry over such a
    refusal,
How little a woman's heart is known to you!
And how little you know what it wants to
    express
When it struggles so weakly in self-defense.
Our modesty always opposes, at such a mo-
    ment,
Any proffer of tender sentiment.
However fit we think the love which wins,
One always finds it somewhat shameful to
    admit.
At first we put up some resistance, but in our
    manner
We can make it clear our heart surrenders,
That our lips oppose our desires for the sake
    of honor,
And that such refusals promise everything.
No doubt this is a rather free admission I am
    making,
And modesty would call for more restraint;
But, since the word has now escaped me,
Would I have tried so hard to stop Damis?
Would I, if you please, have listened quite so
    sweetly,
And heard to the end the offer of your heart?
Would I have taken the whole thing as I did,
If the offer of that heart were in no way
    pleasing?
And when I tried, myself, to make you turn
    down
The wedding plans which had just been an-
    nounced,
What should this request have made you un-
    derstand,
If not the care for you which we have taken
    on,

And the pain which would ensue if the union
    that's proposed
Should come to share a heart we'd rather keep
    whole?
    TARTUFFE. To be sure, Madame, it is
    sweetness extreme
From lips one loves to hear words such as
    these;
Their honey flows through all my senses,
As they drink in this novel fragrance.
The joy of pleasing you is my supreme en-
    deavor;
In your desires my heart finds blessedness.
But this heart now asks the liberty
To question its felicity.
I might think those words an honest strata-
    gem
To make me break off an approaching mar-
    riage;
And, if I may speak plainly with you,
I will not put my trust in such sweet dis-
    course,
Until some sample of your favors, which I
    sigh for,
Bestowed on me, confirms what has been
    stated,
And implants in my soul a steadfast faith
In the enchanting kindness you have for me.
    ELMIRE. (Coughs to warn her husband.)
What! You want to move with such haste
And drain a heart of its sweetness straight-
    way?
A person kills herself making the tenderest
    declaration,
But that's still not enough for you;
Can't you be satisfied until things
Are pushed to the ultimate kind of favors?
    TARTUFFE. The more unworthy of bless-
    ing, the less one dares to hope.
Our vows are not made firm by talk alone.
One easily doubts such a glorious fate,
And one wants to possess it before one be-
    lieves it.
And I — who feel myself so unworthy of
    your goodness,
I distrust the good fortune of my boldness;
I shall believe in nothing until you have,
    Madame,
By something real convinced my passion.

ELMIRE. Heavens! your love is acting like a tyrant,
And stirs up strange disorder in my mind!
Our hearts are taken in such fierce command,
And with what violence it wants what it desires!
What! is there no way to ward off your pursuit —
Don't you even give one time to breathe?
Is it proper of you to be so adamant,
To give no quarter in the things that you demand,
And by your urgent efforts to take advantage
Of the weakness people have for you?
TARTUFFE. But if with compassionate eye you view my worship,
Then why refuse me certain proof of it?
ELMIRE. But how can one consent to what you want
Without offending heaven, of which you always talk?
TARTUFFE. If heaven is all that's opposed to my wishes,
To remove such hindrance is for me very little,
And that should not restrain your heart.
ELMIRE. But they frighten us so with heaven's decrees.
TARTUFFE. I can dispel for you such ridiculous fears
Madame — I know the art of removing scruples.
Heaven forbids, it's true, certain satisfactions; [1]
But one can arrange a give-and-take settlement.
According to differing needs there is a science
Of stretching the fetters of our conscience,
And of rectifying the evil of the action
With the purity of our intention.
Concerning those secrets, madame, I can instruct you —
You have only to let yourself be guided.
Satisfy my desire and have no fear;
I'll answer to you for it and I take the wrong on myself.
                    (ELMIRE coughs again loudly.)

[1] This is a scoundrel speaking. [Molière's note.]

You are coughing hard, Madame.
ELMIRE. Yes, I'm in terrible pain.
TARTUFFE. Would you like one of these licorice drops?
ELMIRE. It must be an obstinate cold — I can see that
All the drops in the world won't help now.
TARTUFFE. This is certainly trying.
ELMIRE. Yes, more than one can say.
TARTUFFE. Well, your scruple is easy to destroy;
You are assured of complete secrecy here,
And the evil lies in the stir created.
Scandal in the world is what makes the offense,
And it's not sinning to sin in silence.
ELMIRE. (After having coughed some more) Well, I see I shall have to make up my mind to yield,
That I must agree to grant you all,
And that with anything short of that I cannot expect
You to be satisfied or willing to give in.
Of course it is unfortunate to come to this,
And it is in spite of myself that I cross this line;
But since you stubbornly want to reduce me to it,
Since you don't want to believe anything you're told,
And you have to have more convincing proof,
I must make up my mind to it and give satisfaction.
If this consent bears some offense in itself,
All the worse for the one who forces me to this violent act —
The fault surely cannot be mine.
TARTUFFE. Yes, Madame, I take all this on my shoulders, and the thing in itself. . . .
ELMIRE. Open the door, please, and see if my husband is not in that hallway.
TARTUFFE. Why do you need to take any care for him? Between you and me, he is a man to lead about by the nose. He takes pride in all our tête-à-têtes, and I have got him to the point where he could see all and believe nothing.

ELMIRE. Never mind. Please go out a minute and look carefully everywhere.

(*Exit* TARTUFFE.)

ORGON. (*Coming out from under the table*) There, I admit, is an abominable man! I can't get over it; this stuns me.

ELMIRE. What! coming out so soon? You're joking. Go back under the cloth; it isn't time yet; wait until the end to see positive proof, and don't trust in plain conjecture.

ORGON. No, nothing more wicked has come out of hell.

ELMIRE. My heavens, you mustn't jump to conclusions; let yourself be properly convinced before you give in, and don't do it hastily, for fear of being mistaken. (*She puts her husband behind her.*)

TARTUFFE. (*Entering*) Everything is in accord, madame, for my satisfaction; I have looked through this whole suite — no one is here, and my soul, delighted. . . .

ORGON. (*Stopping him*) Not so fast! you're following your amorous desire too far — you shouldn't let yourself be such a prey to passion. Ah-ha! Mister Man-of-good-will, you want to play one on me! How your soul gives way to temptation! Marrying my daughter and lusting for my wife! For a long time I couldn't believe my ears, and I kept thinking you'd change your style; but the proof has been pushed far enough; I'm satisfied and for my part want no more.

ELMIRE. (*To* TARTUFFE) It was against my will that I did all this, but I was forced to the point of treating you that way.

TARTUFFE. What! you think. . . .

ORGON. Come on, no trouble, please let's clear out of here with no more ado.

TARTUFFE. My plan. . . .

ORGON. That talk is out of date; you must leave the house this very minute.

(TARTUFFE *starts to leave, crestfallen, then turns around and straightens up.*)

TARTUFFE. It's up to you to leave, you who speak like the master. The house belongs to me; I shall make it known, and I will show you clearly that recourse to that cheap deviousness in order to pick a quarrel with me is all in vain. You may think you can do me harm but I have just what I need to upset and punish imposture, avenge the offense to heaven, and force repentance on those who are now talking of making me leave.

(*Exit* TARTUFFE.)

ELMIRE. What kind of talk is that? What does he mean?

ORGON. My word, I am upset and have no reason to laugh.

ELMIRE. What?

ORGON. I see my mistake from the things he said; the deed of gift disturbs my mind.

ELMIRE. The deed of gift? . . .

ORGON. Yes, it's all done. But I have something else besides which worries me.

ELMIRE. What?

ORGON. You'll soon find out, but first let's see if a certain strong-box is still upstairs.

ACT FIVE

Enter ORGON *and* CLÉANTE.

CLÉANTE. Where are you off to?

ORGON. Alas, how do I know?

CLÉANTE. It seems to me that we should begin by consulting together over what can be done in this case.

ORGON. That strong-box keeps me in an uproar; more than all the rest it puts me in despair.

CLÉANTE. That box, then, is some important mystery?

ORGON. It's a trust which Argas, that friend I feel sorry for, put into my hands himself in great secret. He chose me for that when he fled; and they are papers — from what he told me — in which his life and his fortune are wrapped up.

CLÉANTE. Then why did you let them get into another's hands?

ORGON. The cause was a case of conscience. I went straight to my traitor and confided in him, and his logic managed to persuade me that it would be better to give the strong-box to him to keep, so that in case of some inquiry I could make a denial and have the help of a subterfuge at hand, by which my conscience in all safety could swear oaths contrary to the truth.

CLÉANTE. You are in a bad way, at least it appears so to me; both the deed of gift and the custody of this trust were, to tell you my own feelings, steps you took too rashly. With pledges like those in his possession he can lead you a merry chase; and, seeing he had these holds over you, it was even more imprudent of you to put pressure on him — you should have tried to find some gentler, more round-about way.

ORGON. Oh! Under such a fine appearance of touching fervor to hide a heart so deceitful, a soul so wicked! And I, who took him in a beggar, with nothing. . . . That does it, I renounce all pious men. From now on I'll have a frightful horror of them — I'm going to treat them worse than a demon.

CLÉANTE. Well, now! Isn't that one of your fine fits of anger! You don't keep a calm temperament in anything; your reason never finds the right path, and you always rush from one excess to the other. You have seen your mistake, and you have recognized that you were led astray by a sham zeal; but what reason requires you to mend your ways by falling into a greater error, confusing the hearts of all pious people with the heart of a treacherous blackguard? What? Because one rascal tricks you boldly with a high and mighty disguise of austerity, you think that everyone is made like him, and that no truly pious person is alive today? Leave such stupid conclusions to the free-thinkers; discriminate between virtue and its appearance; never risk your esteem too quickly, and in that respect find the proper mean. Keep, if you can, from honoring imposture, but just the same do no harm to true zeal, and, if you have to fall into some extreme, it's better still to sin on the other side.

(*Enter* DAMIS.)

DAMIS. What, Father! is it true that a wretch threatens you, that he blots all of your kindness from his soul, and that his base pride, only too worthy of wrath, arms himself against you with your own gifts?

ORGON. Yes, my son, and it gives me untold pain.

DAMIS. Leave it to me, I'll cut off both his ears. Against his insolence we must not waver; it's up to me to set you free at one stroke, and, to settle this, I must strike him dead.

CLÉANTE. Isn't it just like a young man to talk that way? Please calm these noisy outbursts; we live under a reign and at a time when violence is a poor way to conduct one's affairs.

(*Enter* MME. PERNELLE, MARIANE, ELMIRE, DORINE.)

MME. PERNELLE. What is this? I hear terrible mysteries here.

ORGON. These are innovations which my own eyes have witnessed, and you see the reward of my pains. I fervently take in a man in his wretchedness; I house him and treat him like my own brother; every day he is loaded down with gifts from me; I give him my daughter and all of my fortune; and at the same time the vile traitor makes the foul attempt to seduce my wife; and, still not satisfied with these base efforts, he dares to threaten me with my own gifts and sets out to ruin me by using advantages which my own imprudent kindness has just armed him with; he wants to drive me from the fortune which I have deeded to him and reduce me to the level where he was when I rescued him.

DORINE. The poor fellow!

MME. PERNELLE. My son, I simply cannot believe that he tried to commit so foul an act.

ORGON. What?

MME. PERNELLE. Pious people are always the objects of envy.

ORGON. What do you mean by that talk, Mother?

MME. PERNELLE. People behave in your household in an outlandish way, and the hatred they bear him is only too well known.

ORGON. What does that hatred have to do with what's been said?

MME. PERNELLE. I told you a hundred times when you were little:

Virtue in this world is hunted forever;
The envious die, but envy, never.

ORGON. But what does this talk have to do with what happened today?

MME. PERNELLE. They've probably made up a hundred foolish tales about him.

ORGON. I've already told you that I saw everything myself.

MME. PERNELLE. Nothing is stronger than slanderers' malice.

ORGON. You'll make me damn myself, Mother. I tell you I saw with my own eyes this brazen crime.

MME. PERNELLE. Gossips always have poison to spread,
And nothing is safe, living or dead.

ORGON. That's talking sheer nonsense. I *saw* it, I say, *saw*, with my own eyes *saw*, what you call *saw*. Do I have to scream it in your ears a hundred times at the top of my lungs?

MME. PERNELLE. Appearance almost always deceives;
One must not judge by what one sees.

ORGON. This is driving me wild.

MME. PERNELLE. False doubt is a weakness of all kinds of people,
And a good act is often construed to be evil.

ORGON. So I should construe as charity the desire to kiss my wife?

MME. PERNELLE. Before you accuse people you need to have just causes, and you should have waited until you were sure of things.

ORGON. What the devil, Mother! What better assurance could I have? Should I have waited until, right before my eyes, he'd . . . You'll make me say something stupid.

MME. PERNELLE. After all, his soul is smitten with too pure a zeal — I cannot bring myself to think that he tried to do the things they say.

ORGON. Really, I'm so mad, if you weren't my mother, I don't know *what* I might say to you.

DORINE. A fitting repayment, sir, of earthly things: you didn't want to believe and now you're not believed.

CLÉANTE. We are losing time in sheer trifling which we ought to use in taking some steps. In the face of that swindler's threats we shouldn't be napping.

DAMIS. What! his effrontery would go that far?

ELMIRE. For my part, I don't think that action is possible because his ingratitude would show up too clearly.

CLÉANTE. Don't count on it; he will have ways and means of making his efforts against you seem right; with less than that a strong cabal can tangle people up in a maze of trouble. I tell you again; armed with what he has, you should never have put that much pressure on him.

ORGON. That's true, but what could I do? I couldn't master my indignation at that traitor's pride.

CLÉANTE. I really wish we could arrange some pretence of peace again between you two.

ELMIRE. If I had known he had such arms in his hands, I would never have given any basis for so much alarm, and my. . . .

(MONSIEUR LOYAL *appears at the door.*)

ORGON. (*To* DORINE) What does that man want? Go find out right away. I'm in fine shape to have people come to see me!

M. LOYAL. Good day, dear sister. Allow me, I pray, to speak to Monsieur.

DORINE. He has company and I doubt if he can see anyone now.

M. LOYAL. I have no intention of making an intrusion.
My arrival, I think, will in no way displease him,
And I come for something which he will find pleasing.

DORINE. Your name?

M. LOYAL. Just tell him that I have come on behalf of Monsieur Tartuffe, for his good fortune.

DORINE. (*To* ORGON) It's a man with a mild manner who has come on behalf of Monsieur Tartuffe on some business which he says you will find pleasing.

CLÉANTE. You must see who this man is and what he wants.

ORGON. Perhaps he has come to reconcile us. How shall I act towards him?

CLÉANTE. Your resentment must not
break out, and if he speaks of agreement you
must listen.

M. LOYAL. Greetings, Monsieur.
May your enemies burn in eternal fire,
And may heaven favor you as I would desire.

ORGON. This mild beginning agrees with
my judgment,
And already foreshadows some kind of settlement.

M. LOYAL. Your whole house has always
been dear to me,
And your good father was often served by
me.

ORGON. Monsieur, I am very ashamed and
beg your pardon for not recognizing you or
knowing your name.

M. LOYAL. My name is Loyal, native of
Normandy,
Justice of the Peace, in spite of all envy.
For forty years, thanks be to heaven,
I have in all honor practiced that function
And I have come, with your kind permission,
To serve on you a certain writ.

ORGON. What! you are here. . . .

M. LOYAL. Monsieur, no anger:
It's nothing but a little court order,
A notice of eviction of you and yours,
To move your goods and chattels, and make
way for others,
Without delay or hindrance, as it requires
here.

ORGON. I! Leave this house?

M. LOYAL.   Yes, sir, if you please.
The house, as you know, belongs at present
To good Monsieur Tartuffe without question.
Of your fortune he is henceforth lord and
master
By virtue of a contract of which I am the
bearer.
It is in good form and cannot be contested.

DAMIS. This is surely great impudence — I
am amazed.

M. LOYAL. Sir, I have no business to do
with you — It's with Monsieur; he is both
reasonable and gentle, and knows too well the
duty of a good man to wish to oppose the
law in any way.

ORGON. But. . . .

M. LOYAL. Yes, Monsieur, I know that you
will not
Want at any price to try rebellion,
And that you will allow me as an honest
person
To carry out here the orders I am given.

DAMIS. You might very well get yourself
a piece of cane on your black apron, Mister
Justice of the Peace.

M. LOYAL. Make your son be silent or retire, Monsieur; I should be sorry to be forced
to couch you in a bill of particulars.

DORINE. (Aside) This Monsieur Loyal has
a quite disloyal air.

M. LOYAL. For all respectable people I have
great affection, and I only took these papers
upon myself, sir, to do you service and pleasure, so that no one would be chosen who —
not having for you the same zeal as I do —
might have proceeded in less gentle a fashion.

ORGON. And what worse could a person
do than to order people to leave their own
house?

M. LOYAL. You have some time,
And until tomorrow I will defer
The execution, sir, of the order.
I shall just come here and spend the night,
With ten of my men, in peace and quiet,
You must bring me, please, for the sake of
form,
Before going to bed, the keys to your door.
I shall take care not to trouble your rest
Or permit anything not entirely correct.
But tomorrow, early, you must be agile
To empty this house to its least utensil.
My men will help you — I chose them pretty
stout
To be at your service in the carrying-out.
I think no one could have treated you with
any more kindness;
And, since I have acted with such great in-
dulgence,
I entreat you also, Monsieur, to behave with
propriety,
That I may be nowise disturbed in my per-
formance of duty.

ORGON. (Aside to CLÉANTE) Right now
I would gladly give a hundred of the finest
gold crowns I have left to be able to plant

the hardest blow I could right square on that snout.

CLÉANTE. (*Aside to* ORGON) Hold on, let's not spoil anything.

DAMIS. His brazen nerve makes it hard to hold back — my fist itches.

DORINE. With such a fine back — I say! Monsieur Loyal,
A few blows with the stick would suit you quite well.

M. LOYAL. Those disgraceful words might be punished quite easily;
Warrants are issued for women too, dearie.

CLÉANTE. Let's finish all that, Monsieur; that's enough.
Give us that paper quickly, please, and leave us.

M. LOYAL. Until we meet again may heaven continue to bless you!

ORGON. May it confound you and the one who sent you! Now you see, Mother, whether I'm right — you can judge the rest by this writ. Do you admit his treachery now?

MME. PERNELLE. I am flabbergasted and dumfounded.

DORINE. You are complaining and blaming him without right or reason — his pious designs are confirmed by all this. His virtue reaches its peak in love of his neighbor; he knows that worldly goods often corrupt man, and, out of pure charity, he wants to remove anything that might be a hindrance to your salvation.

ORGON. Shut up; that's the word to say to you every time.

CLÉANTE. Come, let's see what plan you ought to choose.

ELMIRE. Go and make known his brazen ingratitude. That form of action will make the contract null and void; his unfairness will appear too foul for them to allow him to have the success you think.

(*Enter* VALÈRE.)

VALÈRE. Regretfully, sir, I come to add to your burdens, but urgent danger forces me to. A very dear friend of mine who knows the grounds of my concern for you, violated for me, with great thoughtfulness and tact, the secrecy which ought to be given affairs of state; he has just sent me information, the consequences of which are that you must take immediate flight. The scoundrel who has long deceived you denounced you to the king an hour ago and, among his attacks, put into his hands a strong-box belonging to an important political fugitive, which, he says, you have been guilty of keeping secret in spite of your duty as a subject. I don't know the particulars of what they call your crime, but an order is out for your person and — the better to execute it — he himself is charged with accompanying the one who is to arrest you.

CLÉANTE. Now his claims are armed; that's how the traitor hopes to get possession of your fortune.

ORGON. Man, I admit, is a wicked beast.

VALÈRE. The slightest delay may be fatal. I have my carriage at the door to take you away and a thousand crowns which I have brought you. Let's not lose any time; this is a crushing blow — one of those you can ward off only by fleeing. I will arrange to put you in a safe place and will go with you the whole way myself.

ORGON. Alas, how indebted I am to you for your kind trouble! To thank you for it another occasion is needed, and I ask heaven to favor me enough that one day I may reward this generous service. Farewell, take care, the rest of you. . . .

CLÉANTE. Go quickly, dear brother, we will think over what has to be done.

(*Enter* TARTUFFE *and the* OFFICER OF THE CROWN.)

TARTUFFE. Gently sir, gently, don't run so fast; you won't have far to go to find your resting-place — you are arrested in the name of the king.

ORGON. Traitor, you kept this stroke for the last! Scoundrel, that's the blow you finish me off with — that's how you crown your treachery.

TARTUFFE. Your insults have no power to provoke me — I am schooled to suffer all for the sake of heaven.

CLÉANTE. Great moderation, I agree.

DAMIS. With what insolence the cad makes sport of heaven.

TARTUFFE. All your rages cannot move me — I am thinking of nothing but doing my duty.

MARIANE. You have a great claim to glory from this — your undertaking is very honest.

TARTUFFE. An undertaking cannot help being glorious when it stems from the power which has sent me here.

ORGON. But did you remember, ungrateful soul, that my hand rescued you from squalor?

TARTUFFE. Yes, I know what help I have received from you, but the king's best interest is my first duty; the righteous violence of that sacred duty stifles in my heart all gratitude, and to such powerful bonds I would sacrifice friends, wife, relations, and myself with them.

ELMIRE. The impostor!

DORINE. How well he knows the treacherous means of throwing about himself a fine cloak of everything we revere!

CLÉANTE. But if it's as perfect as you declare, this zeal which impels you and which you deck yourself out in, how does it happen that it decides to put off its appearance until he has caught you chasing his wife, and that you didn't think of going to denounce him until his honor forced him to drive you away? I don't mention the gift of all his fortune, which he had just made you, as something which should have changed your mind; but if you wanted to treat him as a criminal today, why did you consent to accept anything from him?

TARTUFFE. (To the OFFICER OF THE CROWN) Deliver me, sir, from this shrilling, and kindly accomplish your order, please.

OFFICER OF THE CROWN. Yes, I have stayed too long in the accomplishment,
Your timely invitation asks me to fulfill it —
To carry it out, follow me at once
To the prison which is appointed for your keep.

TARTUFFE. Who? I, sir?

OFFICER. Yes, you.

TARTUFFE. Why to prison, then?

OFFICER. To you I have no account to render.

(To ORGON) Sir, be at peace once more: the alarm is past.
We live under a prince hostile to fraud,
A prince who sees clearly into every heart,
Who is not deceived by the impostor's art.
With fine discernment his great soul provided
On all things gazes with clearest sight;
There no stealth finds furtive entrance,
And his steady reason falls into no excess.
To pious men he gives immortal glory,
But without blindness his zeal shines forth,
And his love for the true does not close his heart
To a just horror of those who are false.
Here was not a one to catch him unawares —
From finer snares than this he can defend himself.
Straight off, his brilliance pierced
To the dark folds of his base heart.
Come to accuse you, he betrayed himself,
And, by an act of divine justice,
Was revealed to the Prince as a renowned swindler
About whom he had information under another name;
It is a long list of actions, every one foul,
Which would form many a volume of accounts.
This monarch, in a word, detested
His base ingratitude and disloyalty to you;
He has added these items to his other crimes,
And allowed him to lead me here only
To see his impudence go to the bitter end
And make total satisfaction to you.
Yes, all your papers, of which he says he is master,
Are returned to you from the hands of this traitor.
With sovereign power the prince breaks the bonds
Of the deed which made him a gift of your fortune,
And, finally, he forgives you that secret offense
Into which a friend's exile caused you to fall;
That is the prize he gives to the zeal which formerly
You publicly proved in upholding his rights,

To show that his heart knows, when least
we expect it,
To pour forth the reward for a good action,
That with him no merit is ever lost,
And, that, better than evil, he remembers
the good.

DORINE. Heaven be praised!

MME. PERNELLE. Now I can breathe again.

ELMIRE. What a fortunate outcome!

MARIANE. Who would have dared believe?

ORGON. (*To* TARTUFFE) Ha-ha, there you are, traitor. . . .

CLÉANTE. Ah! dear brother, stop — do not descend to indignities. Leave a wretch to his bad fate and don't add to the remorse which overwhelms him. Wish, rather, that his heart this day may make a blessed return to the arms of virtue, that he may mend his ways, detest his viciousness, and that he may soften the justice of our great prince; meanwhile you will go down on your knees before his graciousness and offer the thanks due for such gentle treatment.

ORGON. Well said. Now let us go before
his feet with praise,
Rejoicing in the kindness that his heart dis-
plays;
And with that primal debt discharged in
part,
Then must we grant the claims of a noble
heart,
And in sweet wedlock crown Valère,
Whose tender passion is true and fair.

VI

DRAMATIC ILLUSION AND POINT OF VIEW

Since we have been looking at the art of playwrighting in terms of the tools of the playwright and the forces and influences that determine the structure of his work, we have had little occasion to mention the long line of critics and estheticians who, since Aristotle, have set up, demolished, and re-erected theories of drama. Many of these theories are beguiling; some of them may even be true; and it will be surprising if, as a consequence of exercises in play analysis, we should not indulge ourselves in a little theorizing also.

Theorizing can lead to illumination, but it ought to be the result of illumination, too. The critic must have looked long and coolly at the work before him, must be more familiar with it than with his own mind, before he will be able to produce a light that will shine an adequate distance in a confusing world of critical opinion. When Samuel Butler defined life as the art of drawing sufficient conclusions from insufficient evidence, he was also making the distinction between life and *art*. In drama the evidence is never insufficient; it is all there and it is the function of the critic to discover and appraise it.

Before moving on to the temptations of theory, then, let us look back over the chapters behind us and summarize the method of exploration suggested. It is, to put it briefly, to stimulate the development of a dramatic imagination in the rereader. An *active* imagination alone leads to aberration, to seeing things out of proportion to their place in the dramatist's scheme and in proportion to your own romantic or social interests. A trained, scholarly imagination is the first requirement for a serious critic — an imagination that can maintain the proper balance among a sense of fact, a sense of history, a sense of proportion and, not least, a sense of humor. A certain amount of humility would not be amiss in the recipe; it is a rare and expensive ingredient enabling us to separate the scholarly critic from the critic who reacts only with his nerve endings, abandoning any sense of the past for a kind of impertinent modern pride of place.

Here, in tabular form, are the steps in the functioning of the dramatic imagination:

1) Erect in your mind the theater, or the essential setting for which the play was intended. Perhaps because this is the simplest, the most mechanical, of all the steps, it is the most often neglected. The necessary information is readily available in histories of the theater, or can be derived from a careful reading of the stage directions of the play itself (see Chapter II).

2) Discover the pattern of the action, how the selection and arrangement of incidents determines the structure (see Chapter V).

3) Discover the "active essences" of the characters and determine their relation to the pattern of action. How do they direct and control the events revealed by the playwright? (See Chapter III.)

4) Consider the symbolic functions of action, setting, properties, and characters in relation to the central idea of the play (see Chapters II through IV).

5) Synthesize. If the discovery of the essential theater is the easiest step in the functioning of the dramatic imagination, synthesis is the most difficult. Analysis is an act possible for any industrious hack; synthesis calls for more than perseverance. Synthesis is an act calling for sympathy, judgment, imagination — and a foreknowledge that it is never going to be completely finished, that it can always be revised.

You can put a jigsaw puzzle together, or reconstruct a demolished building, and dust your hands together and say, "That's that." But a surgeon who has reconstructed a human interior knows that his work is tentative and may have to be done over. A play, as previous chapters have reiterated, is a living body. Until the words of *Hamlet* are propelled by breath from a living lung, *Hamlet* is only a poem, not a dramatic experience. To arrive at an approximation of the dramatic experience is the purpose of analyzing and synthesizing the printed text of a play. For the playwright's purpose is not necessarily the discovery of an idea or the presentation of character or the interpretation of history. We must continually remind ourselves that the purpose of any serious playwright is to treat his selected matter in such a fashion that the spectator may find in his dramatic experience an ordering of the chaos, or an illumination of the mystery, of his day-to-day existence.

The Aristotelian Pigeonholes

Aristotle, a Greek schoolmaster of the fourth century, B.C., was apparently the first esthetician to attempt to define and describe drama as an art. Not content with distinguishing it from epic and other forms of poetry, he surveyed the plays in the repertory of the Greek theater and established the principles governing the comic and tragic modes of dramatic expression. His conclusions, which survive only in the form of the lecture notes of one of his students, are sufficiently dogmatic to be easily transmitted and sufficiently ambiguous to be adjusted (not quite so easily) to the dogmas of later critics.

As a guide to Greek drama, to the original focussed form of playwrighting, Aristotle is without peer. He had available to him a vast number of plays which have since been lost, but many of his illustrations are taken from *Oedipus Rex,* which still survives. The modern student thus has the benefit of his survey and a check against his conclusions. Further, since Aristotle seems to have had no predecessor, he was driven to working from the evidence of the texts themselves, from the dramatic experience; he was not rearguing, or refining upon, the critical judgments of others. His practice is exemplary, even if his conclusions have blinded some of his successors to his method and intention.

He distinguishes between tragedy and comedy chiefly in terms of subject matter. Comedy he finds to be the imitation of characters of low virtue, involving error unattended by pain and not destructive. Tragedy, on the other hand, concerns itself with characters superior to average men and is " an imitation of an action that is serious, complete, and of a certain magnitude . . . through pity and fear effecting the proper purgation of those emotions." Aristotle discusses the deliberate arrangement of the parts within the whole (" structure ") and defines both magnitude and tragic action: ". . . the time of [the play's] duration is such as to render it probable that there can be a transition from prosperous to adverse or from adverse to prosperous fortune, according to the necessity or probable order of things as they take place."

This is an excellent description of the structure and action, and perhaps of the purpose, of *Oedipus Rex* as a focussed tragedy. Without too much twisting it can be made to fit certain other tragedies of Sophocles, *Antigone,* for instance, and *Electra.* But it can hardly be said to describe *Prometheus Bound.* Perhaps *Prometheus* is a special case, since it is the only surviving member of a three-part play. Yet in *The Orestaeia,* the trilogy of Aeschylus which has come down to us, the action is quite other than that of a Sophoclean tragedy, investigating an ethical problem rather than the fate of man in conflict with the forces of super-nature. It is worth noting that the plays which most nearly approximate Aristotle's description of tragedy are those written long after his day by Roman, Italian, and French playwrights instructed in their dramatic method by the critical disciples of Aristotle propounding with dogmatic assurance the " rules " of the art.

There is little point in quarreling with Aristotle or the neo-Aristotelians at this date. Critics who seek refuge in rules or take comfort from authority could find a worse guide, philosopher, and dictator, though Aristotle himself never aspired to this last post. But it should be apparent to us that the drama, having been born in many eras and many places in response to different attitudes and visions, must of necessity seek different forms of expression and encompass more than one kind of serious or comic action.

For the older drama, however, the recognition of tragic and comic modes is useful as a preliminary to analysis. But the distinction must be based upon the plays themselves rather than upon statements about the plays; it will be determined primarily by the particular nature of the *action* in any given text and its effect upon the *characters* involved in it.

According to Aristotle, tragic action encompassed the reversal of the hero's fortunes from bad to good or good to bad brought about by the interplay of circumstances (perhaps fate) and the peculiar characteristics of the central figure. Several plays do survive in which the reversal is from bad to good fortune, suggesting that such action was reasonably common, yet the accepted notion of tragic action, based on the majority of the available texts, involves the downfall or death of the hero. Death and tragedy are inseparable in the popular mind.

The fact of death, however, is not in itself tragic. King Lear, betrayed by his daughters, driven to insanity, lies dying beside the corpse of the child who loved him and tried to rescue him. One of his followers attempts to revive him, but is stopped by a wise old man who says:

> Vex not his ghost. O, let him pass! He hates him
> That would upon the rack of this tough world
> Stretch him out longer.

It is not death that causes the emotions of pity and terror, but the action that leads to death. Death is the end of the story; the falling curtain cannot rise again, for there is nothing more to be revealed. One of the characteristics of tragic action, then, is its finality.

The action of comedy comes to a rest, but not to the absolute stop of death. One of the favorite subjects of classical comedy was disagree-

ment between a father and his son, generally over a marriage which the
older man thought unsuitable, since the woman involved was frequently
a slave or courtesan. The machinations of a clever servant or parasite on
the side of the young man bring about a compromise and domestic peace
is assured, *on the issue.* Sophocles' tragedy *Antigone* is in part concerned
with the same kind of disagreement between father and son. The son
will marry a princess whom his father, King Creon, bitterly opposes
for reasons of state. When Antigone is condemned to living burial the
young man kills himself in her tomb. The final moment of the play
finds the king bearing the dead body of his son into the palace, the
perfect symbol of a tragic action. Tragedy comes to a full stop; comedy
ends with a promise for the future, not necessarily untroubled, but
possible because of the compromise between the conflicting parties.

Compromise presupposes illumination. Although the characters in a
comic action may take strong positions, may hold firmly to their points
of view, the playwright so arranges his structure as to demonstrate to
one, or to both, of his conflicting actors the folly of such behavior.
Menander, Plautus, and Terence — the chief comic writers of Greek and
Roman drama — delight in revealing to the stubborn old man that the
heroine he is condemning as a slave is really the long-lost daughter of a
fellow merchant and consequently a woman of unquestionable respecta-
bility and eligibility as a daughter-in-law. Their object is always matri-
mony, which is as much a symbol of future developments as death is a
symbol of finality. Later comedians rejoice to follow in their path.
Molière exhibits the stubborn Orgon driven to acts of the utmost folly
and inhumanity by his addiction to the pious impostor, Tartuffe. He designs his structure so that one potentially disastrous scene exposes to
Orgon the hypocrisy of his idol; the hero reverses his position and the action ends with the prophecy of the future in a double wedding. Comic
action might be described as recognition leading to compromise.

Recognition is also an essential part of tragic action. The tragic hero,
like the comic hero, is often a man blinded by his own delusions about
himself. The playwright confronts him with a series of situations which
force him to see the truth about himself. Unlike the comic hero, however, the tragic hero arrives at his recognition only after his actions
have taken him too far for compromise. King Creon, in *Antigone,* has
committed himself so completely to the idea of the supremacy of the
written letter of the law and to the infallibility of his own authority that
he will tolerate opposition from no one, whether the grounds be human
sympathy or religious principles. He thus condemns his niece, his son,
and his wife to death, and himself to damnation. A similar confidence

in his own infallibility brings doom upon King Lear. Both Creon and
Lear arrive at the moment of recognition. The Theban King, looking
upon the corpse of his son; cries:

> I have been rash and foolish.
> I have killed my son and wife.
> I look for comfort; my comfort lies here dead.
> Whatever my hands have touched has come to nothing.
> Fate has brought all my pride to a thought of dust.
> (Translated by Dudley Fitts and Robert Fitzgerald)

The old King of Britain, awakened after his mad wanderings on the
heath, kneels before his daughter and begs:

> Pray do not mock me.
> I am a very foolish, fond old man,
> Fourscore and upward, not an hour more nor less;
> And, to deal plainly,
> I fear I am not in my perfect mind.

But what is done cannot be undone; the self-recognition has come too
late.

One way of describing the difference between tragic and comic action
and tragic and comic recognition might be in terms of seriousness —
high seriousness or lesser seriousness. Aristotle limits tragedy to characters of great stature or worth and says that comedy concerns itself
with lesser men. And it is true that Greek tragedy and its imitators in
Rome and Renaissance Europe restrict themselves pretty much to kings
and the heroes of myth and legend whose activities affect the fate of
nations. Even Christian tragedy tends to center on royalty or on heroes
of mighty aspiration, like Faustus. Comedy, on the other hand, chooses
to work at the lower level of domestic complication with merchants
and laborers, " middle class " fathers and sons and lovers. Comedy, as
a more precise mirror of the larger audience, must reflect what that
audience knows to be true: that the life of the average man is a series
of compromises and that the great compromiser is perhaps the most
exemplary comic hero. For Oedipus, for Prometheus (insofar as we have
his story), for Faustus, for Lear, the action takes place on such a level
of high consequence that their cases but echo the grim admission of
Macbeth:

> I am in blood
> Stepp'd in so far that, should I wade no more,
> Returning were as tedious as go o'er.

Unlike the comic hero, the tragic hero must always pass beyond the point of no return.

These essential distinctions between tragic action and comic action are true and meaningful and may be widely applied. They are equally pertinent to a discussion of Sophocles and Shakespeare, of Molière and Plautus, of Lope de Vega and Aeschylus. They can be invoked whether the play be focussed or panoramic in structure, pagan or Christian in attitude.

To be sure not all plays written before modern times can be classified as comic or tragic. There are plays of high seriousness which end without recognition or death for the hero, and there are those of a lesser seriousness where the compromises are forced upon the characters by fortuitous circumstance. The first sort of play is generally described as *melodrama,* which may be taken to mean a serious action imitated for its own sake, for the sake of the action and its attendant thrill, rather than to bring the hero to the point of self-discovery; indeed the action may very well conclude with the compromise impossible to pure tragedy (in this case the play is often described as *tragicomedy,* an evasive term appropriate to such ambiguous action). The *Electra* and *Medea* of Euripides may stand as classical examples of melodrama; more familiar, of course, is the great mass of popular serious drama of the nineteenth century of which the *Richelieu* of Bulwer-Lytton is representative.

The comic equivalent of melodrama is known as *farce* and may be defined in analogous terms. The main interest of the play lies in the action, in what happens, in the ingenuity of the playwright in inventing complications, turns, and counterturns — a kind of structural prestidigitation. *The Comedy of Errors* and *The Taming of the Shrew* are frequently cited as examples of Shakespearean farce as distinguished from the true comedies of *Twelfth Night* and *As You Like It.* So, in the French theater, it is customary to distinguish between Molière's comedy of *Tartuffe* and his farce of *The Doctor in Spite of Himself.* But the lines between farce and comedy, between melodrama and tragedy are not so sharply drawn as those between comedy and tragedy, and the distinction may be more dependent upon subjective reactions and the taste of the times than upon absolute criteria.

The Classification of Modern Drama

The terms *comic* and *tragic* describe ways of looking at life; we speak of the tragic vision of Shakespeare, the tragic irony of Sophocles, and we recall the epitaph of a famous writer of comic drama:

Life is a joke and all things show it;
I thought so once, and now I know it.
(John Gay)

Comedy and *tragedy*, then, will apply to dramatic actions based on a firmly established set of values, of standards. What happens to Oedipus will be judged in the light of the generally accepted moral code of fifth-century Athens; what happens to Orgon will be judged in the light of the code of the French court of the seventeenth century. And the audience for Aeschylus, for Shakespeare, for Molière, while a cross section of the populace, was generally united in at least the recognition, if not the practice, of the code of its day. When both audience and playwright share a set of values, classification of a dramatic action as comic or tragic becomes possible.

With the modern drama such classification is no longer simple or automatic. The nineteenth century, during which modern drama came to maturity, was a period of questioning. Pioneering expeditions into unmapped territory in the sciences, in social studies, in the human personality, created doubts about many of the hitherto accepted standards. First playwrights and then, very gradually, mass audiences found themselves unsure of the interpretation to be put upon a given action. In erecting new edifices, Darwin, Marx, and Freud, the revolutionary architects, must needs undermine a good many structures of impressive antiquity. The action of *Oedipus*, to take an example, was found to be not a tragedy of fate but a case history of an eponymous " complex." To replace the oracle at Delphi with the psychiatrist's couch is to shift the emphasis, effect, and meaning of tragedy.

Yet it might be shown that the " revolutionary architects " were as much the products as the makers of the new codes. Change, doubt, revolution were in the air long before these men made their defining contributions. Consider the writings of Frederich Hebbel (1813–1863), a German poet and playwright who for the most part devoted his theatrical efforts to a series of romantic historical dramas in the standard pattern of panoramic tragedy. In 1844, however, he wrote *Maria Magdalene*, a domestic drama about village life. It tells a grim little story of a cabinetmaker whose uncompromising observance of the letter of moral law leads to the estrangement and ruin of his son and the suicide of his daughter. The final curtain finds him shaking his head sadly and remarking, " I don't understand the world any more." For Creon, King of Thebes, Hebbel has substituted Anton, father of a middle-class family. And for Sophocles' tragic symbol of Creon bearing his own damnation in his arms and recognizing his own responsibility for the catastrophe, Hebbel substitutes the picture of a bewildered old man, bereft and lonely, but utterly without consciousness of personal responsibility. If this is tragedy, it is tragedy with a new accent; it seems to say the fate of man is determined, not by the code he chooses to follow, but by the conflict between the inevitable evolution of society and the equally inevitable conservatism of an inherited code of behavior.

Hebbel, in this one play, and the men who followed him — Ibsen, Zola, Chekhov, Gorki — thought of themselves as realists or naturalists, looking upon the world objectively, as scientists look upon the world, and reporting what they found. Their creed is stated in its purest form by Émile Zola, an effective lawgiver even though a total failure as a playwright. " There should no longer be any school," he wrote, " no more formulas, no standard of any sort; there is only life itself . . . the human problem studied in the framework of reality."

The new realism was made possible not only by the intellectual climate of the century but by advances in the method of play production which preceded by some decades the development of realistic playwrighting. The English theater had always lagged behind the continental theater in the use of illusionistic scenery. In the period between 1830–1840 it suddenly stepped into leadership in a movement to employ settings for something more than decoration or spectacle. Macready, a leading producer and actor of the day, was made to recognize the gap that existed between the great advances in every aspect of the cultural and social life of man in the nineteenth century and the stereotyped conventionality of theatrical procedures. Macready's radical innovations — specially designed settings and costumes reproducing accurately the milieu of the play — made possible the later experiments of English and continental producers, culminating in the realistic theory of staging. Truth to life, naturalism, became the theatrical as well as the dramatic creed. André Antoine, founder of the Paris Théâtre Libre, equipped a stage butcher shop with real quarters of beef and furnished the dining room of a play with tables and chairs borrowed from his mother's home. Stanislavsky, director of the Moscow Art Theater, sent the players of *The Lower Depths* to live for several weeks among thieves and prostitutes that they might know whereof they were acting. David Belasco, the most famous American apostle of stage naturalism, constructed a complete Childs restaurant for a scene in *The Governor's Lady*, and for another play spent thousands of dollars and many hours arranging a series of small spotlights to give the exact effect of the glow of a hand lantern being carried across the stage. The audience must feel that it is witnessing a " slice of life."

Such demonstrations of naturalistic staging, extravagant though they may seem, were a necessary auxiliary to the development of the drama of the modern world, a drama which is basically naturalistic or realistic in style and domestic in its concerns. The heroes and kings made their departure during the various revolutions, political, philosophical, economic, and scientific, that marked the nineteenth century, and were replaced by more or less common men and women. Husbands and wives, merchants and sailors, farmers and farmers' daughters, hitherto the actors of comedy or melodrama, now became the central figures in serious actions, even tragedies. While the older theater had based its characters on and motivated their actions by Fate and a conventional code of morality, the theater of naturalism substituted forces derived from the newer scientific code: a man's character and his actions were determined by his environment and heredity.

The physical setting, the scenery, of a play thus becomes an organic part of the dramatic experience. We may remember Chekhov's concern with the dress and mannerisms of a character as revealing his inner nature; he was equally concerned with the precise reproduction of environmental details. One of the climactic scenes in *The Three Sisters* is played against the background of a fire in a provincial town. As the naturalist Belasco had spent hours achieving the effect of a glowing lantern, so the naturalist Chekhov worked indefatigably to discover the exact combination of sounds suggesting a fire. But there is an interesting difference between Chekhov and Belasco.

The moving lantern is merely a part of the stage business in Belasco's play; it is carried by one of the actors as he crosses the stage. It is a realistic detail, nothing more. The burning house, on the other hand, has nothing to do with the immediate action of *The Three Sisters*; it is never seen. Yet the hollow tolling of the fire bell is a contributory element to the dramatic effect of the scene in which it is heard: the sense of terror, of helplessness that is the inevitable accompaniment of such an event in a community unequipped to meet it. Chekhov has reproduced the realistic detail, that is, but he has first selected it with a definite view of its usefulness in increasing the spectator's understanding of the situation. Instead of realism for its own sake, the slice of life, he is employing what has been called *selective realism,* details which give the impression of real life while serving the ends of the dramatist.

The modern drama, then, begins in a theater prepared to give its audiences the illusion of reality in setting, costumes, lighting, sound effects, and properties. Playwrights, responding to the new theater and to the demands of the age, directed their attention less and less to the action that went on in palaces and great houses and more and more to the action that took place around middle-class dining-room tables and peasant hearths. Aristotle felt that the tragic hero should be an illustrious man from one of the great families; a Victorian critic, however, recognized that " a drama to come home to the hearts and bosoms of men must be of a domestic nature."

Ibsen, who may be thought of as the father of the modern drama, illustrates the shift in subject matter. At the beginning of his career, he was writing of Vikings and royal heroes and villains. But as we come to the plays for which he is remembered today, *A Doll's House, Ghosts, Hedda Gabler,* he is writing of middle-class husbands and wives and mothers and sons. It is true that in *Ghosts* and *Hedda Gabler* he is still using an action that can be classified as tragic according to the definition of Aristotle, even if his characters are nonheroic. But the effectiveness of his work, its power to move an audience, depends less on the catastrophe than on its domesticity. In fact, Bernard Shaw, in an essay otherwise devoted to pointing out the greatness of the Norwegian playwright's achievement, criticizes him for clinging to an outmoded convention by resolving his action in a violent ending after the old-school convention. And Chekhov, after seeing one of Ibsen's plays in Moscow, commented that " Ibsen does not know life. In life it does not happen like that."

Although *Ghosts* ends in tragedy, Ibsen labelled it a " domestic drama." Although many of the plays of Chekhov involve death, defeat, or frustration, he describes them as comedies. Shaw classifies his own work as " tragicomedy " and interprets the term as meaning " that kind of comedy which is so true to life that it is not only an entertainment but a history and criticism of contemporary morals." The drama of selective realism may concern itself with all classes of men, or any class of men; it may mingle comedy and tragedy, buffoonery and pathos, satire and sentiment. In its subject matter, characters and action, selective realism may be as unselective as life itself. For this reason, and to avoid the ambiguity and confusion that accompany such terms as *realism, selective realism,* and *naturalism,* it may best be called *representational drama.*

The Sea Gull

Chekhov was a medical man and a scientist before he became a writer, and this to a certain extent governed his choice of subjects and the treatment of his themes. " To a chemist," he pointed out, " nothing on earth is unclean. A writer must be as objective as a chemist." So, as Ibsen shocked his audiences with a more or less open discussion of venereal disease in *Ghosts*, Chekhov shocked or at least disturbed his audiences with the behavior and open-speaking of his characters. The first audience at *The Sea Gull* was made so uneasy by the performance that as the first act neared its conclusion the actors were depressed with a sense of failure. It is certainly true that there is much in the play to bewilder spectators accustomed to romantic behavior and heroic action: a young woman addicted to the snuffbox, a schoolmaster whose drawling, dismal, hopeless talk creates neither a comic stereotype nor a figure of pathos, a hero who accuses his mother of being jealous of his sweetheart, a long and seemingly pointless monologue demonstrating the nature of the " new drama," and unanswered questions, speeches ignored by the other characters, emotions and situations hinted at but not developed. An audience accustomed to the clear development of action and conflict in the focussed or panoramic tradition or to the logical precision of the well-made play must have been bewildered by the structure, or lack of structure, of the new representational drama.

Yet if the acts of *The Sea Gull* are broken up into their component scenes, the structural principle becomes clear enough. For the carefully balanced exposition and action, the logical succession of events, the action rising towards climaxes or turning points — for these characteristics of Ibsen's plays, Chekhov substitutes a series of juxtapositions or contrasts, giving a surface impression of the inconsequence of life, but actually through repetition serving as a vehicle for the author's interpretation of life.

The materials of *The Sea Gull* are not very different from the materials of dozens of well-made plays. At the heart of the " plot " are two triangles: Trepleff, Nina, and Trigorin; Nina, Trepleff, and Madame Arcadina. Yet Chekhov is not concerned, as the usual dramatist of the eternal triangle is, with which boy gets which girl. His triangles are only an excuse for holding his characters together until they can exemplify his larger theme. Romantic love is not the end of the play, but only one of the ways that the true facts of life reveal themselves. The conflicts between the conventional form of theater (Madame Arcadina) and the new (Nina), and the older style of writing (Trigorin) and the new (Trepleff) are also not themselves the central concern of the play but a way of revealing its theme; they are symbolic of the universal conflict.

The key to the method and purpose of the playwright is to be found in the scene in the last act, a scene typical of his work, where the attention of the audience is divided between the pathetic interplay between Nina and Trepleff, and their elders, who are amusing themselves in the dining room, and made more pointed as Trepleff commits suicide off stage while the other characters engage in a game of cards. Chekhov's theme is the unbridgeable gap between the old and the new, the old drama and the new, the old writing and the new, the older generation and the younger. By repetition and demonstration it becomes for the audience a fact of nature, an interpretation of human experience; tragic because of the blindness of the participants to the meaning of their experience, comic because the refusal to see the future will not prevent its arrival, representational because of the illusion that life is displayed objectively, without interference from the artist.

Point of View

Representational drama involves the concept of point of view for the first time in dramatic art. The audience for both the focussed and panoramic theaters had accepted without question that a play was, in the Aristotelian phrase, the imitation of an action. It did not occur to them that they might be anything save onlookers at an event.

To be sure, playwrights were frequently conscious that their characters might be motivated by a thoroughly distorted notion of the world through which they moved. Although Creon in *Oedipus Rex* is the most normal of honorable men, Oedipus sees him as a warped, envious opportunist; but it is part of the dramatic pattern that the spectator must see with true vision what the actor sees falsely. There is clearly a difference between the " reality " of the action of an allegorical play like *Everyman* and a chronicle history like *King Henry the Fifth,* between the projection of inner and outer experience. However, the concept of the dramatic metaphor, so central to panoramic drama, permits the entire action in both cases to be presented objectively; all human and historical action was an allegory related to a moral code which represented the ultimate reality, the final truth, for spectator, actor, and playwright.

The attack on conventionally accepted moral and ethical codes and evaluations of human experience which accompanied the accelerated advances in scientific method in the nineteenth century led to a new awareness for playgoer and dramatist of the necessity for objectivity. Ibsen, you will remember, said that the task of the playwright was the description of man, and Zola felt that living drama was to be made of the " two-fold life of the character and its environment . . . the human problem studied in the framework of reality." Chekhov believed his scientific training and his experiences as a physician were responsible for his success as a creative writer.

One of the often-quoted comic moments from Molière's *Le Bourgeois*

Gentilhomme is the discovery by the hero that he has been speaking prose all his life. So, in the theater of the nineteenth century, all the participants in the dramatic experience were slowly awakened to the fact that, whereas the novelist or poet might write in the first person, the dramatist in effect wrote always in the third person; that he had to pretend to be a nonparticipant and that the spectators were bystanders at the passing show. The objective *point of view* thus becomes an additional tool for the modern playwright.

Once the idea of point of view becomes established, once it becomes a tool, the playwright will experiment with its possibilities. The objectivity of the scientist, however highly touted as an ideal by Ibsen, Zola, and Chekhov, places unnatural restrictions upon the creative artist. The scientist will generalize only upon the greatest number of case histories available to him; the playwright endeavors to find in each " case " a general truth. Zola, the complete naturalist, failed to find a place in the theater; Ibsen and Chekhov, while maintaining the objective point of view, by conscious and deliberate selection and arrangement of materials and by the employment of symbols achieved the universality which is the ultimate aim of the creative artist.

It was their intention, however, in such plays as *Ghosts* and *The Sea Gull*, to write " third person " drama, to capitalize on the appearance of objectivity. But Ibsen's practice, particularly in the development of dramatic symbolism in his later plays (*The Master Builder, John Gabriel Borkman*), suggested to some of his successors the possibility of another kind of dramatic illusion.

Non-Representational Drama

The development of non-representational drama was anything but an orderly process, and the following account must not be taken as the history of a movement. It is rather an attempt to select certain contributions and contributors and to comment on their significance, with the intention of explicating the nature of the dramatic illusion they created.

We may begin with the symbolic dramas of Maurice Maeterlinck, the Belgian poet, philosopher, and playwright. For him the great achievement of Ibsen was not the appearance of objectivity but the " symbolic dialogue " which enabled the playwright to present characters " living in the atmosphere of the soul." That is, the real action and conflict are beneath the carefully represented surface. Ibsen, like Chekhov, felt that the surface was important as the outward sign of the inner truth. For the authors of non-representational drama the surface was often a mask, a deliberate disguise placed over the truth; instead of finding accord between outer and inner reality, they found conflict. In this conflict they chose to side with the inner reality and began to develop methods of presenting it, at first indirectly, then directly to the audience.

The most famous of Maeterlinck's " dramas of signs and silences " is *Pelléas and Mélisande* (1893), whose basic plot is the conventional triangular love affair involving two brothers, Pelléas and Golaud, and Mélisande, the wife of Golaud. But as always it is not the plot but the treatment of the plot that determines the play's effect. Pelléas and Mélisande are both very young, both very inexperienced; they fall in love without knowing they are in love; when awareness comes they are afraid to be alone together.

As an indication of the direction in which the playwright is moving it is instructive to compare a romantic passage in this play with what is quite possibly the most famous love scene in the dramatic repertory, the " balcony scene " in *Romeo and Juliet*. The Shakespearean situation was undoubtedly in Maeterlinck's mind as he wrote, and the inevitable recollection of it by the modern playgoer is certain to color his reaction to *Pelléas*. In Shakespeare the two young people have met briefly at a ball and fallen in love. Their second meeting takes place later that night in the moonlit garden of Juliet's house; the lovers are separated, Juliet at her window, Romeo in the garden beneath her. They declare their love in fervent and memorable lines until the impatient summons of Juliet's nurse forces them to part.

> *Juliet.* I would have thee gone —
> Yet no farther than a wanton's bird,
> That lets it hop a little from her hands,
> Like a poor prisoner in his twisted gyves,
> And with a silk thread plucks it back again,
> So loving-jealous of his liberty.
> *Romeo.* I would I were thy bird.
> *Juliet.*   Sweet, so would I
> Yet I should kill thee with much cherishing.
> Good night, good night. Parting is such sweet sorrow
> That I shall say good night till it be morrow.
> *Romeo.* Sleep dwell upon thine eyes, peace in thy breast —
> Would I were sleep and peace, so sweet to rest.

While it is true that the melody of Shakespeare's language sometimes tends to lull our sense of reality, the highly sensual imagery presents a direct and inescapable impression of two young people deeply and impatiently in love: an impression that will be reinforced in later speeches of passionate longing.

In Maeterlinck's play, Mélisande sits in the window of a tower combing her hair. Pelléas comes through the darkened garden and speaks to her.

Pelléas. Oh! oh! Mélisande! . . . oh, thou art beautiful! . . . thou art beautiful so! Lean out! lean out! . . . Let me come nearer thee. . .

Mélisande. I cannot come nearer thee. . . . I am leaning out as far as I can. . .

Pelléas. I cannot come up higher . . . give me at least thy hand tonight . . . before I go away. . . . I leave tomorrow. . .

Mélisande. No, no, no!

Pelléas. Yes, yes, yes; I leave, I shall leave tomorrow . . . Give me thy hand, thy hand, thy little hand upon my lips. . .

Mélisande. I give thee not my hand if thou wilt leave. . . .

Pelléas. Give, give, give!

Mélisande. Thou wilt not leave?

Pelléas. I will wait; I will wait. . . .

Mélisande. I see a rose in the shadows.

Pelléas. Where? . . . I see only the boughs of the willow hanging over the wall. . . .

Mélisande. Farther down, farther down, in the garden; farther down in the somber green.

Pelléas. It is not a rose. . . . I will go see by and by, but give me thy hand first; first thy hand. . . .

Mélisande. There, there. . . . I cannot lean out farther. . . .

Pelléas. I cannot reach thy hand with my lips. . . .

Mélisande. I cannot lean out farther. . . . I am on the point of falling — Oh! Oh! my hair is falling down the tower! (*Her tresses fall suddenly over her head, as she is leaning out so, and stream over* PELLÉAS.)

Pelléas. Oh! oh! what is it? . . . Thy hair, thy hair is falling down to me! All thy locks, Mélisande, all thy locks have fallen down the tower! . . . I hold them in my hands; I hold them in my mouth. . . I hold them in my arms; I put them about my neck. . . . I will not open my hands again tonight. . . .

Mélisande. Let me go! let me go! . . . Thou wilt make me fall! . . .

Pelléas. No, no, no. . . . I have never seen such hair as thine, Mélisande! . . . See, see, see; it comes from so high and yet it floods me to the heart! . . . And yet it floods me to the knees! . . . And it is sweet, sweet as if it fell from heaven! . . . I see the sky no longer through thy locks. Thou seest, thou seest? . . . I can no longer hold them with both hands; there are some on the boughs of the willow. . . . They are alive like birds in my hands, . . . and they love me, they love me more than thou! . . .

Mélisande. Let me go; let me go! . . . Someone might come. . . .

Pelléas. No, no, no; I shall not set thee free tonight. . . . Thou art my prisoner tonight; all night, all night! . . .

Mélisande. Pelléas, Pelléas! . . .

Pelléas. I tie them, I tie them to the willow boughs. . . . Thou shalt not go away now. . . . Thou shalt not go away now. . . . Look, look, I am kissing thy hair. . . . I suffer no more in the midst of thy hair. . . . Hearest thou my kisses along thy hair? . . . They mount along thy hair. . . . Each hair must bring thee some. . . . Thou seest, thou seest, I can open my hands. . . . My hands are free, and thou canst not leave me now. . . .

Mélisande. Oh! oh! thou hurtest me. . . . (*Doves come out of the tower and fly about them in the night.*) — What is that, Pelléas? — What is flying about me?

Pelléas. It is the doves coming out of the tower. . . . I have frightened them; they are flying away. . . .

Mélisande. It is my doves, Pelléas. — Let us go away, let me go; they will not come back again. . . .

Pelléas. Why will they not come back again?

Mélisande. They will be lost in the dark. . . . Let me go; let me raise my head. . . . I hear a noise of footsteps. . . . Let me go! — It is Golaud! . . . I believe it is Golaud! . . . He has heard us!

Pelléas. Wait! Wait! . . . Thy hair is about the boughs. . . . It is caught there in the darkness. . . . Wait, wait! . . . It is dark.

Although the passage is in prose, the language is poetic, rich in sensual images. Shakespeare's lovers were separated by a family feud and by the height of a balcony; Maeterlinck's by a moral code and the height of a tower. Yet the mysterious force of love overrides law and custom and, in the latter play, the architectural obstacle also. We in the audience can see the surface reality: the lovers are kept physically apart. But from the imagery of the language and the dramatic symbols (tower, hair, rose, doves) we can sense the inner truth, that spiritually they have consummated their union. Golaud experiences something like this double vision too. Interrupting them, he says merely: " Mélisande, do not lean out so at the window; you will fall. . . . Do you not know it is late? It is nearly midnight. — Do not play so in the darkness. — You are children," but in the following scene he attempts to murder his brother.

The non-representational playwrights soon discovered that the modern theater, with all its apparatus designed to create the illusion demanded by naturalism and representationalism, was a tool of great value for the artist who was not governed by a passion for the appearance of scientific objectivity. The manipulation of artificial lighting, which became progressively simpler as gas replaced oil, limelight replaced gas, and electricity replaced limelight, is an expressive device whose limits have yet to be reached. If the stage carpenters can construct on demand the world in which Mrs. Alving lives, a detailed and recognizable facsimile of an appropriate Norwegian parlor, there is every reason to believe them able to construct a world of fantasy, a dream world for which there is no convenient model in the middle-class suburbs.

Indeed it is in a play subtitled " A Dream Poem " that we may find a clear demonstration of how the point of view can shift from objective to subjective, from the external world of naturalism to the inner world of the ego and its vision. *The Assumption of Hannele* was written in the same year as *Pelléas* by Gerhart Hauptmann, one of the founders of naturalistic drama in Germany. It is only in part fantasy, the dream vision being used to reinforce the naturalistic purpose, to arouse the audience to the necessity of reforming the conditions depicted in the action.

Hannele begins as a conventional naturalistic drama. The setting is an almshouse, bare, cold, dirty, ill-lighted, ill-furnished; and the occupants are dirty, quarrelsome, profane, given to picking one another's pockets of their squalid contents. The action begins with the entrance of the handsome young village schoolmaster, Gottwald, carrying the limp wet body of Hannele, a young girl who has tried to drown herself in an icy pond. While a doctor is being summoned we are told something of the girl and her past. She is the daughter of a cruel stone mason who abuses her and drove her mother to death; according to rumor, she is illegitimate, her real father being one of the village officials. Hannele is a dreamy, romantic, pathetic child, frightened of her father, adoring her schoolmaster, and in her speeches confusing Christian stories and fairy tales. She is left alone in the almshouse with a Nun who talks to her of sin and redemption, and of Judas, the traitor who hanged himself. Hannele declares her affection for the beautiful things of religion: pictures and hymns.

While the Nun leaves the room momentarily, there is a preparatory shift of the lights and one of Hannele's dreams and fears is materialized. On the darkened stage her father suddenly appears and threatens her for lying about when she should be working. In terror, Hannele crawls from the bed and collapses in the ashes of the fireplace. The father vanishes as the Nun returns and helps her back to her bed, but Hannele continues to rave feverishly, begging Jesus to take her and declaring that he has promised to take her:

> *Nun.* Who has promised?
> *Hannele.* The dear Lord — Gottwald.

The Nun tries to make her sleep by singing a lullaby, putting out the light as she does so. As the room is darkened, she is suddenly replaced by " the pale and ghostly form of a woman." This is Hannele's dead mother, now confused in her mind with Mary Magdalene, the prostitute who won forgiveness for her sins. Mother describes the pleasures of heaven to her daughter, a kind of child's version of the afterlife, while a group of " beautiful winged youths," holding music in their hands, and not unlike the angels of popular religious art, sing to her.

The second act is almost entirely fantasy, although it begins naturally enough with Hannele's awakening from her visions. But her own feverish elation sends her into delirium again as she takes the attendant Nun for the Angel of Death. The Nun is bewildered by speeches apparently addressed to her, but since we have been prepared by the first act for the experience of sharing Hannele's visions directly, of seeing the world as she sees it, the Nun is forced off the stage and replaced by the Angel. (The stage direction reads: *During this incident, Sister Martha has stood looking on, perplexed and thoughtful, with folded hands. She slowly passes out of the room.*) Hannele now receives a series of visitors: the Village Tailor brings her a bridal dress and a pair of glass slippers, sent at the order of her father, " The Count "; the schoolmaster and his pupils arrive to pay their respects, and the children apologize for calling her Princess Rag-Tag now that they see how beautiful death has made her; other characters bring a crystal coffin in which she is placed. The schoolmaster is metamorphosed into Christ and in a scene with Hannele's father denounces him as a traitor; the father goes off to hang himself. Gottwald-Christ then enacts the raising of Lazarus with Hannele and a song is sung of the wonders of heaven: marble mansions with golden roofs, rivers of wine, iridescent butterflies and snowy swans — but also clean clothes, warm houses, and comfortable beds. At the end of the vision the angels sing, not the conventional alleluiah, but the lullaby begun by the Nun in the first act.

Once again the lights change. " *The interior of the almshouse is seen, exactly as before the first apparition. Hannele — a poor, sick child, once more lies on the bed. Doctor Wachler bends over her with a stethoscope. . . .*"

> Doctor *Wachler.* You are right!
> *Deaconess.* Is she dead?
> Doctor *Wachler.* She is dead.

The play is neither pure fantasy nor pure realism, but a kind of naturalistic fantasy, since the situations, characters, and ideas of the dream-vision are completely conditioned by the nature of Hannele herself, her surroundings, and her upbringing, which Hauptmann emphasizes by returning us to harsh reality at the end. This treatment of imaginative materials is in key with the purposes of the naturalistic playwright. The wretchedness of Hannele's life is made more touching by contrast with her pathetic little dream of the Rich, Full Afterlife. And if the audience comforts itself with the thought that Hannele is escaping into happiness, the playwright points out in the last scene that the conditions that made

Hannele the wretched child she was still exist, and other Hanneles will continue to suffer from them.

The structure of the well-made play was based on a concept of the logic of events; the naturalistic play based its structure on a logic of character and emotion. The structure of *Hannele* might be described as a kind of dream-logic. Once the playwright has made us understand that we are seeing the events of the vision from Hannele's point of view we share her experiences and thought processes directly. Instead of looking at the action objectively through the fourth wall as in representational drama, we look at it subjectively through the eyes of the central character.

Hauptmann, as we have pointed out, uses his fantasy only to reinforce his naturalism. Other playwrights who began in the naturalistic tradition were more definite in cutting themselves free. Of these, none was more uncompromising, successful, or fecund than the bewildering Swedish genius, August Strindberg. Several of his early plays are among the classics of naturalistic theater, and the preface to *Miss Julie* (1888) is a definitive statement of the aims of the whole school as well as an illuminating analysis of his own work. He was by avocation, but only by avocation, an experimental scientist; his nondramatic writings show him to have been essentially romantic, delighted with soul-searching and self-analysis, aware of the gap between illusion and reality but puzzled as to which of the worlds, outer or inner, was illusory.

In *The Spook Sonata* (1907), one of a number of symbolic dramas, Strindberg sets out to investigate the inner nature of life, the springs of sin which provide the motive force for action, the difficulty of escape from this force save through blind faith. It is completely subjective in its point of view, with no representational framework as a control for the spectator's understanding. It is a violent, obscure, and completely enthralling play; once the spectator has been drawn into the playwright's point of view, *The Spook Sonata* is a dramatic experience of almost unparalleled intensity.

Up to a point, the story is extremely simple. A young, impoverished Student has set his heart on a Young Lady whose wealth and family position set her quite out of his reach. By chance he meets an invalided old man who, recognizing him as the son of a man he had ruined financially, promises to help him attain his desires, hoping thus to expiate the injury he had done him. The old man goes directly to the Young Lady's family and in the ruthless manner that had characterized the actions of his whole lifetime commences to expose them as impostors, cheats, and hypocrites. In his blind determination to effect his promise he turns on the Young Lady's mother, but she recognizes him as the man who had seduced her, the man who was actually the Young Lady's father. The family having been thoroughly exposed, it is now possible for the Student to approach his sweetheart, and the young couple try to find happiness and innocence where the older generation had found only corruption and evil. But the Young Lady is inescapably a product of evil forces; she is being consumed by a disease, and she dies as the Student discovers the only possible way of life in an ancient hymn recommending religious resignation.

This does not perhaps sound like a plot promising tension or significance or any interest save of the most commonplace sort. The ingredients also include two triangles, ghosts, the walking dead, a mummy, and a parrot. As the old man remarks, " It certainly is complicated . . . both inside and out." However, this is only the plot, and the study of dramatic art emphasizes, if nothing else, that structure and technique (rather than plot) are the measure of a play's effectiveness. In *The Spook Sonata*, the commonplace is seen with fresh vision, yielding greater effect and clearer significance, and with added impressiveness for the audience.

The play begins in a deceptively realistic manner. The curtain rises on the exterior of a solid brick house. A maid is cleaning the steps, bed clothes are being aired from a second-floor balcony, an old man is sunning himself in a wheel chair beside an advertising pillar, and opposite him is a public pump where a milkmaid draws water and a young man pauses to refresh himself. Despite the representational solidity of the setting and the disposition of the characters, Strindberg permits the spectator to see everything that happens from two subjective viewpoints. The first of these is that of the Student. A Sunday child, he is blessed with second sight. He sees and talks to the milkmaid, much to the confusion of the old man, who can neither see nor hear her — though he had murdered her many years before. The Student is also able to see the corpse of a more recently deceased man going to count the mourners at his coffin. A strange experience has brought the young man to the pump: walking along the street he heard a cracking noise; looking up he saw a house crashing to the ground; he dashed into the crumbling ruin, caught up a baby who was lying there and returned to the street in the nick of time. Only, on regaining the street, he found no baby in his arms. It was a dream of a romantic impossibility, like his forlorn pursuit of the Young Lady.

The old man, Jacob Hummel, will have no truck with romantic dreams. He has made his way in the world without second sight, idealism, or doubts. Without hesitation, he has done the expedient thing, whether it involved murder, financial ruin, or seduction. Ruthlessness has brought him to the top, but success has left him crippled and old age has found him uneasy, and with no understanding of his own uneasiness. He has arrived at a position analogous to that of the hero of classical tragedy: he has blinded himself to his own nature.

The second act of the play takes place in the interior of the house, a " Round Room " of which we have had glimpses from the street in the first act. The family is about to gather for evening tea, but as the butler points out, it is like a ghost tea: " They look like ghosts . . . and they have kept this up for twenty years, always the same people saying the same things, or saying nothing at all for fear of being found out." The lady of the house, Hummel's cast mistress and the Young Lady's mother, is a startling victim of the chain of evil. Her husband had seduced Hummel's fiancée; in revenge, Hummel had seduced the wife, and in shame and fear she had shut herself up until at the end of twenty years she looks like a mummy and sounds like a parrot.

Mummy. Are you invited here tonight?
Hummel. No, but I mean to get an invitation for this Ghost supper.
Mummy. Do you know who are coming?
Hummel. Not exactly.
Mummy. The Baron . . . who lives above here and whose father-in-law was buried this afternoon. . . .
Hummel. The man who is getting a divorce to marry the daughter of the cleaning woman . . . the man who once was — your lover.
Mummy. Another guest will be your former fiancée who was seduced by my husband. . . .
Hummel. A pretty collection. . . .
Mummy. Oh God, if we might die! *If* we might die.
Hummel. But why do you keep together then?
Mummy. Crime and guilt bind us together! — We have broken our chains and separated over and over, but we are always irresistibly drawn back together again.

In the Mummy's final speech there is a second echo of the Greek idea of tragedy. But if the audience, under the influence of the Round Room and the carefully distributed types of the human family who dwell in it, is beginning to see the action as a symbol of humanity in general, it must also observe that Strindberg has substituted crime and guilt — the sin of Adam and the sin of Cain — for the mysterious but not always malignant force known to the Greeks as Fate. At any rate the central figure of this part of the play, Hummel, is being forced to look upon certain things he had willfully ignored throughout his life.

Before the Ghost supper, Hummel undertakes the exposure of the

Young Lady's supposed father. At first he reasonably points out that his military title of Colonel was a temporary one which has been abolished, that his title of nobility has been extinct for a century. The Colonel, resentful, demands, " What right have you to sit there stripping me naked in this fashion? " The suggestion is seized by Hummel:

Take off that wig, and have a look at yourself in the mirror. And take out your false teeth at the same time and shave off your mustache. Let your valet remove your stays, and perhaps a certain lackey will recognize himself once more. . . .

One by one Hummel " strips " the other participants at the Ghost supper until with a kind of self-righteousness that is almost Oedipodean he can declare that his " mission " in the house was to pull out the weeds and let in fresh air, so that the house may become a happy home for the young couple. But now the Mummy takes the stage. As a repentant sinner she feels that she too can face the naked truth. She reminds Hummel of his own crimes and deceptions, and of one particular black spot in his life at which she can only guess. At this point, the Milkmaid of the first act suddenly appears in the doorway, and now only Hummel can see her. Having started a chain of recognition, he can no longer refuse to look upon his own nature. Driven mad by self-realization, he rushes off stage to destroy himself.

The action now shifts back to the point of view of the Student. We have moved still deeper into the interior of the house, into the Hyacinth Room where the Young Lady lives. Hyacinths, the playwright tells us, are the Oriental symbol of faith, hope, and the future, and it is thus that the Student views the room and his union with the Young Lady. But to reach the room he has had to pass through the Round Room, whose interlocking chain of evil is but an emblem of the seeming-virtue that covers the corruption of the great world outside the house. Recognition comes to the Student, too; knowledge replaces innocence:

By keeping still too long water stagnates and becomes rotten, and so it is in this house, for there is something very rotten here. And yet I thought it Eden itself when I saw you enter the first time. . . . It was a Sunday morning and I stood looking into these rooms. I saw a Colonel who was no Colonel. I saw a generous benefactor who was a criminal and had to hang himself. I saw a Mummy who was not a mummy, and a virgin — what about the virginity, by the way? . . . Where is beauty to be found? In nature, in my mind when it is in its Sunday dress. Where honor and faith? In fairy tales and children's stories. Where can I find anything that fulfills its promise? In my imagination. . . . Why would you not be my bride? Because the well-spring of life in you is sick. . . . Jesus Christ descended into hell. That meant his pilgrimage on earth, to this madhouse, this jail, this morgue — this earth. And the madmen killed him when he wished to liberate them, but the robber was set free. The robber always gets sympathy! Woe, woe, to all of us! Savior of the world, save us, we perish!

The audience has seen the incidents of the play from two subjective points of view, those of old Hummel and the Young Student. But ultimately the entire action is seen from only one point of view, the Student's, since Hummel's self-realization is a part of the younger man's illumination. As Hummel remarks: " Though the stories are separate, they hang together on a common thread, and the dominant theme recurs regularly." The theme is the search of a baffled and thwarted soul for the meaning of life and the agony of his final discovery: Evil *is,* and furnishes the chief motivation for human actions; the bonds of sin and crime once assumed are inescapable, man can only repent and die. The Student sings:

> I saw the Sun; then lo! methought
> Mine eyes beheld the Hidden Power.
> All men's actions have their recompense;
> Blest is he that doeth good.
> No deed that we have wrought in anger
> Can find in evil its atonement.

[Hummel's exposure of the Colonel's family cannot atone for his own evil acts.]

> Comfort him whom thou hast grieved
> With goodness: this alone availeth.
> He feareth not who doth no evil:
> Good is to be innocent.

Expressionism

Strindberg, in his symbolic plays, is often credited with originating the dramatic form known as expressionism. He does not, however, in his own writings systematically establish the principles of dramatic expressionism as he had those of dramatic naturalism; that function was reserved for the German playwrights of the first quarter of this century. For them, expressionism became a philosophical theory as well as a way of writing, bearing the same relation to the non-representational drama in general that naturalism bears to representational drama in general.

Expression denotes the attempt on the part of the artist to give the spectator a direct experience of the essence of life rather than a representation of its surface. As one of the playwrights of this school roundly declared: " The world is *there;* it would be foolish to reproduce it." Instead the artist reproduces the spirit, the inner reality of an object, a situation, a character, or an idea; he reproduces it from a subjective point of view by means of a significant distortion of observed reality.

The distortion had been prepared for in such plays as *Hannele* and

The Spook Sonata, where the action is seen from a personal point of view: Hannele's schoolmaster is transmuted into Christ; because Hummel tells the Student that the Young Lady's mother is like a mummy, she appears as The Mummy.

The action of expressionistic drama tends to de-emphasize the situations that had been the main concern of naturalism: success or failure in society, domestic problems, psychological determinism. The naturalistic ending of *Hannele* would be impossible in pure expressionism, and even Strindberg uses his interwoven love affairs as symbols of a larger evil; they are not of concern in themselves.

Symbols are highly developed and are meant to be directly perceived and interpreted as such; they are not used for their suggestive power, as in representational drama. Settings, distorted or fragmented, are always to be considered as aspects of the theme rather than as indicating the locale of the action. Characters are frequently masked or symbolically costumed (the Mummy) to isolate the single aspect of the personality which is of concern to the playwright; the " active essence " is presented as directly as possible. While these are devices of representational drama also, in expressionism they are sharpened and intensified so that the *design* of the play is insistently brought to the spectator's attention.

Expressionistic symbolism in general is intellectual; the symbols are not inanimate actors, they are not intended to stir the senses. The object is only an excuse for revealing a subjective impression and has no meaning other than that assigned to it in the play. In *Ghosts* Ibsen was not under the necessity of explaining the orphanage; it is a widely recognized symbol of charity. Strindberg, in *The Spook Sonata,* associates the Young Lady with a hyacinth; he is forced to supply a detailed exposition of the legend of the flower as an image of the Cosmos. Expressionism is almost as personal a form of drama as the lyric is in verse, and it often demands the same kind of historical and biographical commentary.

In its pure form, expressionism achieved wide popular success only in Germany in the period between the two World Wars. In such plays as *Transfiguration* by Ernst Toller (the hero, artist and dreamer, undergoes a series of experiences which turn him into a man of action and the new Messiah) and *Gas* by Georg Kaiser (the death of humanity at the hands of its own machines), the subjectively-viewed action, the distortion and symbolism are applied to themes that are both comprehensible and universal. Here, and in a few other examples, pure expressionism achieves the ultimate purpose of all great playwrighting, to provide a dramatic experience for the general audience.

But for the most part the success of pure expressionism is restricted by geography and time: it speaks to a limited audience which has shared certain experiences and beliefs. Its chief contribution to dramatic art is the liberation of the playwright from the bonds of strict representationalism. Expressionism demonstrated the possibility of the direct presentation of inner reality, showing that the viewpoint of the drama need not be unvarying objectivity. As the novelist can shift from third person narrative to stream-of-consciousness, so the playwright may mingle his points of view, writing now with the objective detachment of the scientific observer and now with the agonized perception of a participant.

The Emperor Jones

The curtain had hardly fallen on the first performance of *The Emperor Jones* by the Provincetown Players in 1920 when critics began talking of the play as an example of expressionism. Eugene O'Neill, never much interested in labels, once denied that he knew much about expressionism when he wrote the play, referring to it merely as " a new piece of drama." Judged in terms of pure expressionism as either a dramatic technique or a philosophical theory, *The Emperor Jones* might more properly be described as expression*istic;* it pushes the expressive powers of various tools of the playwright to their limit, but, largely because of the nature and situation of the central figure, it never achieves (or attempts) a complete shift in point of view from objective to subjective. In structure and technique it is a unique play, exemplifying the fact that in the modern theater a play is free to find its own form, restricted or governed only by the purpose of the playwright.

O'Neill centers his action on the mythic-historic figure of Brutus Jones, a Pullman porter who had murdered a co-worker, escaped from a chain gang, and made himself the Emperor of a small island in the West Indies. The action itself is Jones' flight from the natives who rise in rebellion against him, though it proves ironically to be a flight backwards, into the past, instead of the escape into the future he had planned.

The play is divided into eight scenes, but it employs only two locales: the audience chamber of the palace and the Great Forest. In the audience chamber all is as naturalistic and objective as can be; once in the Great Forest we are in the realm of symbolism, if not of expressionism — the very name of the place carries echoes of disturbing allegories.

Jones, seen plain in the throne room, is part Oedipus, part " Empire-builder." He is proud of his mind, which has enabled him not only to attain his present status of dictator over the " common bush niggers " and to outsmart the white trader, but to make careful plans for escape from the revolt which he knows is bound to come. He is proud too of the silver bullet, the symbol he has himself invented to maintain his authority over his subjects. He is proud, finally, of his uniform, with its brass buttons and gold braid, laced boots with totally useless spurs, and expensive Panama hat. It is this uniform which establishes him as the Emperor Brutus Jones, and it is in this pride of place that he makes his unhurried exit through the front door of his palace.

During the rest of the brief play the hero tries to follow his path through the Great Forest to safety. But he finds himself in an unfamiliar world, menaced by the ever-approaching jungle drum of his enemies; he is soon lost, and frightened. As his terror increases, his imagination becomes more active. The point of view is very nearly subjective in the third, fourth, and fifth scenes as Jones is confronted with episodes from his past, but the remaining scenes present situations which Jones himself never experienced, part of the past of his race: the slave auction, the slave ship, the Witch Doctor.

The hero undergoes a similar change from the particular to the general. We see first an objective portrait of the Emperor Brutus Jones. One by one the trappings of his state are torn from him — his canned goods, his hat, coat, spurs, boots, breeches — until he is only Brutus Jones, common man and criminal. But O'Neill goes beyond this situation, the removal of the mask, to a removal of the personality. In the sixth scene, Jones is absorbed into the rhythmic movement and chant of the ghostly figures on the slave ship. In the seventh scene, " The expression of his face is fixed and stony, his eyes have an obsessed glare, he moves with a strange deliberation like a sleepwalker or one in a trance " — nothing remains but the primitive human animal, not the Emperor, not Brutus with its fine classical intonation, but only Jones swaying helplessly under the spell of the Witch Doctor.

The point of view shifts in the play from objective to subjective to objective as O'Neill undertakes to expose the ultimate motive force in Jones. It is the playwright's purpose that gives unity to the play: from the first our attention is directed to a hero enacting a chosen role in a chosen theater, a role he cannot maintain when the theater is changed. Precarious is his grasp of what he identifies with reality, for it is a reality he has invented for himself as he has invented the charm of the silver bullet.

The Emperor Jones is a remarkable demonstration of the power of the playwright using all the tools at his command — actors, setting, properties, lights, sound and silence — to create a dramatic unit precisely adjusted to his purposes. In this freedom to experiment, to confront the spectator with new and unexpected patterns, the contemporary theater

has found a dramatic method adjusted to the complex and unhomo-
geneous audience for which it exists. True tragedy, true comedy demand
a generally accepted moral code. For a world of conflicting and shifting
codes, the vital dramatic experience comes only with the freedom for
form to follow function, to mingle tragedy and comedy, to move from
the objective to the subjective point of view, and to shift on necessity
from representational to non-representational illusion.

THE SEA GULL

A COMEDY IN FOUR ACTS

by Anton Chekhov

TRANSLATED BY STARK YOUNG

CHARACTERS

IRINA NICOLAYEVNA ARCADINA, MADAME TREPLEFF, *an actress*

CONSTANTINE GAVRILOVITCH TREPLEFF, *her son*

PETER NICOLAYEVITCH SORIN, *her brother*

NINA MIKHAILOVNA ZARYETCHNY, *a young girl, the daughter of a wealthy landowner*

ILYA AFANASYEVITCH SHAMREYEFF, *a retired lieutenant, Sorin's steward*

PAULINE ANDREYEVNA, *his wife*

MASHA (MARYA ILYINISHNA), *his daughter*

BORIS ALEXEYEVITCH TRIGORIN, *a literary man*

EUGENE SERGEYEVITCH DORN, *a doctor*

SEMYON SEMYONOVITCH MEDVEDENKO, *a schoolmaster*

YACOV, *a laborer*

COOK

TWO HOUSEMAIDS

ACT ONE

A section of the park on SORIN's *estate. The wide avenue leading away from the spectators into the depths of the park towards the lake is closed by a platform hurriedly put together for private theatricals, so that the lake is not seen at all. To Left and Right of the platform there are bushes. A few chairs, a small table.*

The sun has just set. On the platform behind the curtain are YACOV *and other workmen; sounds of coughing and hammering are heard.* MASHA *and* MEDVEDENKO *enter on the Left, returning from a walk.*

MEDVEDENKO. Why do you always wear black?

MASHA. I am in mourning for my life. I'm unhappy.

MEDVEDENKO. You unhappy? I can't understand it. Your health is good, and your father is not rich but he's well enough off. My life is much harder to bear than yours. I get twenty-three rubles a month, and that's all, and then out of that the pension fund has to be deducted, but I don't wear mourning.

(They sit down.)

MASHA. It isn't a question of money. Even a beggar can be happy.

MEDVEDENKO. Yes, theoretically he can, but not when you come right down to it. Look at me, with my mother, my two sisters, and my little brother, and my salary twenty-three rubles in all. Well, people have

330

to eat and drink, don't they? Have to have tea and sugar? have tobacco? So it just goes round and round.

MASHA. (*Glancing towards the stage*) The play will begin soon.

MEDVEDENKO. Yes. The acting will be done by Nina Zaretchny and the play was written by Constantine Gavrilovitch. They are in love with each other, and today their souls are mingled in a longing to create some image both can share and true to both. But my soul and your soul can't find any ground to meet on. You see how it is. I love you; I can't stay at home because I keep wishing so for you; and so every day I walk four miles here and four miles back and meet with nothing but indifference on your side. That's only natural. I've got nothing; we're a big family. Who wants to marry a man who can't even feed himself?

MASHA. Fiddlesticks! (*She takes snuff.*) Your love touches me, but I can't return it, that's all. (*Offers him snuff.*) Help yourself.

MEDVEDENKO. I'd as soon not.

(*A pause.*)

MASHA. My, how close it is! It must be going to storm tonight. All you do is philosophize or talk about money. You think the worst misery we can have is poverty. But I think it's a thousand times easier to go ragged and beg for bread than — But you'd never understand that —

(*Enter* SORIN, *leaning on his walking stick, and* TREPLEFF.)

SORIN. For some reason, who knows, my dear boy, the country's not my style. Naturally. You can't teach an old horse new tricks. Last night I went to bed at ten o'clock, and at nine this morning I awoke feeling as if my brain stuck to my skull, and so on. (*Laughing*) And then on top of all that I fell asleep after dinner just the same. And so now I'm a wreck, I'm still lost in a nightmare, and all the rest of it.

TREPLEFF. That's true, Uncle, you really ought to live in town. (*Sees* MASHA *and* MEDVEDENKO.) Look, my friends, we'll call you when the play starts, but don't stay here now. I'll have to ask you to go.

SORIN. (*To* MASHA) Marya Ilyinishna, won't you kindly ask your father to leave that dog unchained, to stop that howling? All last night again my sister couldn't sleep.

MASHA. You'll have to tell my father yourself. I shan't do it, so please don't ask me to. (*To* MEDVEDENKO) Let's go.

MEDVEDENKO. Then you'll let us know before the play starts.

(MASHA *and* MEDVEDENKO *go out.*)

SORIN. That just means the dog will howl all night again. You see how 'tis; in the country I have never had what I wanted. It used to be I'd get leave for twenty-eight days, say, and come down here to recoup, and so on; but they plagued me so with one silly piece of nonsense after another that the very first day I wanted to be out of it. (*Laughs.*) I've always left here with relish. Well, now that I'm retired, I have nowhere to go and all the rest of it. Like it — like it not, I live —

YAKOV. We're going for a swim, Constantine Gavrilovitch.

TREPLEFF. So long as you are back in ten minutes. (*Looks at his watch.*) We're about to begin.

YAKOV. Yes, sir.

TREPLEFF. Here's your theater. The curtain, then the first wing, then the second wing, and still farther open space. No scenery at all. You see what the background is — it stretches to the lake and on to the horizon. And the curtain will go up at 8:30, just when the moon's rising.

SORIN. Magnificent!

TREPLEFF. If Nina's late, then, of course, the whole effect will be spoilt. It's time she were here now. But her father and stepmother watch her so she can hardly get out of the house; it's like escaping from prison. (*Straightening his uncle's tie*) Uncle, your hair and beard are rumpled up — oughtn't you to have them trimmed?

SORIN. (*Combing his beard*) It's the tragedy of my life. I always look as if I'd been drunk, even when I was young I did — and so on. Women never have loved me. (*Sits down.*) Why is my sister in such bad humor?

TREPLEFF. Why? Bored. (*Sits down by* SORIN.) Jealous. She's set against me, against the performance, and against my play, because Nina's going to act in it and she's not. She's never read my play but she hates it.

SORIN. You (*Laughing*) imagine things, really.

TREPLEFF. Yes, she's furious because even on this little stage it's Nina will have a success and not she. (*Looks at his watch.*) A psychological case, my mother: She's undeniably talented, intelligent, capable of sobbing over a novel; she recites all of Nekrassov's poetry [1] by heart; she nurses the sick like an angel; but you just try praising Duse [2] to her; Oh, ho! You praise nobody but her, write about her, rave about her, go into ecstasies over her marvelous performance in " La Dame Aux Camélias " [3] or in " The Fumes of Life." [4] But all that is a drug she can't get in the country, so she's bored and cross. We are all her enemies — it's all our fault. And then she's superstitious — afraid of three candles or number thirteen. She's stingy. She's got seventy thousand rubles in an Odessa bank, I know that for a fact. But ask her for a loan, she'll burst into tears.

SORIN. You've got it into your head your play annoys your mother, and that upsets you, and so forth. Don't worry, your mother worships the ground you walk on.

TREPLEFF. (*Picking petals from a flower*) Loves me — loves me not, loves me — loves me not, loves me — loves me not. (*Laughing*) You see, my mother doesn't love me, of course not. I should say not! What she wants is to live, and love, and wear pretty clothes; and here I am twenty-five years old and a perpetual reminder that she's no longer young. You see when I'm not there she's only thirty-two, and when I am she's forty-three — and for that she hates me. She

---

[1] Nekrassov was a romantic poet, dedicated to the production of pure art, without " ideas."

[2] Eleanora Duse, Italian tragedian of international repute

[3] i.e., *Camille*, by Alexandre Dumas *fils*

[4] by the Russian author, B. Markevitch

---

knows too that I refuse to admit the theater. She loves the theater; it seems to her that she's working for humanity, for holy art. But to my thinking her theater today is nothing but routine, convention. When the curtain goes up, and by artifical light in a room with three walls, these great geniuses, these priests of holy art, show how people eat, drink, make love, move about and wear their jackets; when they try to fish a moral out of these flat pictures and phrases, some sweet little bit anybody could understand and any fool take home; when in a thousand different dishes they serve me the same thing over and over, over and over, over and over — well, it's then I run and run like Maupassant from the Eiffel Tower and all that vulgarity about to bury him.

SORIN. But we can't do without the theater.

TREPLEFF. We must have new forms. New forms we must have, and if we can't get them we'd better have nothing at all. (*He looks at his watch.*) I love my mother — I love her very much — but she leads a senseless life, always making a fuss over this novelist, her name forever chucked about in the papers — it disgusts me. It's just the simple egotism of an ordinary mortal, I suppose, stirring me up sometimes that makes me wish I had somebody besides a famous actress for a mother, and fancy if she had been an ordinary woman I'd have been happier. Uncle, can you imagine anything more hopeless than my position is in her house? It used to be she'd entertain, all famous people — actors and authors — and among them all I was the only one who was nothing, and they put up with me only because I was her son. Who am I? What am I? I left the university in my third year, owing to circumstances, as they say, for which the editors are not responsible; I've no talent at all, not a kopeck on me; and according to my passport I am — a burgher of Kiev. My father, as you know, was a burgher of Kiev, though he was also a famous actor. So when these actors and writers of hers bestowed on me their gracious attentions, it seemed to me their eyes were measuring my insignificance. I guessed their thoughts and felt humiliated.

SORIN. By the bye, listen, can you please tell me what sort of man this novelist is. You see I can't make him out. He never opens his mouth.

TREPLEFF. He's an intelligent man, he's simple, apt to be melancholy. Quite decent. He's well under forty yet but he's already celebrated, he's had more than enough of everything. As for his writings — well, we'll say charming, full of talent, but after Tolstoy or Zola, of course, a little of Trigorin goes a long way.

SORIN. My boy, I'm fond of writers, you know. Once there were two things I wanted passionately. To marry and to be an author. I never succeeded in doing either. It must be pleasant being a minor writer even, and all the rest of it.

TREPLEFF. I hear footsteps. (*Embraces his uncle.*) I can't live without her. Just the sound of her footsteps is lovely. (*Going to meet* NINA ZARETCHNY *as she enters*) I'm insanely happy! My enchantress! My dream!

NINA. I'm not late, surely I'm not late.

TREPLEFF. (*Kissing her hands*) No, no, no.

NINA. All day I worried, was so frightened — I was so afraid father wouldn't let me come. But at last he's gone out. He went out just now with my stepmother. The sky has turned red, the moon will soon be up, and I raced the horse, raced him. (*Laughs.*) But I'm so happy. (*Warmly shaking* SORIN's *hand.*)

SORIN. (*Laughing*) You've been crying, I see by your little eyes. That's not fair.

NINA. That's so. You can see how out of breath I am. Do let's hurry. I've got to go in half an hour. I must. Don't ask me to stay, my father doesn't know I'm here.

TREPLEFF. It's time to begin anyhow — I'll go call them.

SORIN. I'll go. I'll go this minute. (*Begins to sing "The Two Grenadiers," then stops.*) Once I started singing like that and a deputy who was standing by said, "Your Ex-

cellency has a very strong voice" — then he thought awhile and said, "Strong but unpleasant." (*Exits, laughing.*)

NINA. My father and his wife won't let me come here; they say it's Bohemia. They are afraid I'll go on the stage. But I am drawn here to this lake like a sea gull. My heart is full of you.

TREPLEFF. We're alone.

NINA. Isn't that someone over there?

TREPLEFF. No, nobody. (*Kisses her.*)

NINA. What kind of tree is that?

TREPLEFF. It's an elm.

NINA. Why does it look so dark?

TREPLEFF. Because it's evening and everything looks darker. Don't go away early, please don't.

NINA. I must.

TREPLEFF. But if I should follow you, Nina? I'll stand all night in the garden, looking up at your window.

NINA. Oh, no! You mustn't. The watchman would see you and Treasure doesn't know you yet, he'd bark.

TREPLEFF. I love you.

NINA. Ssh — !

TREPLEFF. Who's that? — You, Yakov?

YAKOV. (*From behind stage*) Yes, sir.

TREPLEFF. You must get to your seats, it's time to begin. The moon's coming up.

YAKOV. Yes, sir.

TREPLEFF. Have you got that methylated spirit? Is the sulphur ready? (*To* NINA) You see when the red eyes appear there must be a smell of sulphur around. You'd better go now, everything's ready. Do you feel nervous?

NINA. Yes, awfully. It's not that I'm afraid of your mother so much, it's Boris Trigorin terrifies me, acting before him, a famous author like him. Tell me, is he young?

TREPLEFF. Yes.

NINA. What marvelous stories he writes!

TREPLEFF. (*Coldly*) I don't know. I don't read them.

NINA. It's hard to act in your play. There are no living characters in it.

TREPLEFF. Living characters! I must rep-

resent life not as it is and not as it should
be, but as it appears in my dreams.

NINA. In your play there's no action; it's
all recitation. It seems to me a play must
have some love in it.

(*They go out by way of the stage. Enter*
PAULINE ANDREYEVNA *and* DORN.)

PAULINE. It's getting damp, go back and
put on your galoshes.

DORN. I'm hot.

PAULINE. You don't take any care of
yourself and it's just contrariness. You're a
doctor and know very well how bad damp
air is for you, but you like to make me miserable. You sat out on that terrace all last
evening on purpose.

DORN. (*Sings low.*) " Oh, never say that
I — "

PAULINE. You were so enchanted by Madame Arcadina's conversation you didn't even
notice the cold. You may as well own up —
she charms you.

DORN. I'm fifty-five.

PAULINE. Fiddlesticks! What's that for a
man, it's not old. You're still young enough
looking — women still like you.

DORN. (*Gently*) Tell me, what is it you
want?

PAULINE. Before an actress you are all
ready to kiss the ground. All of you!

DORN. (*Sings low.*) " Once more I stand
before thee — " (*Speaking*) If society does
make a fuss over actors, treats them differently from, say shopkeepers — it's only
right and natural. That's the pursuit of the
ideal.

PAULINE. Women have always fallen in
love with you and hung on your neck. Is
that the pursuit of the ideal too?

DORN. (*Shrugs his shoulders.*) Why? In
the relations women have had with me there
has been a great deal that was fine. What
they chiefly loved in me was the fact that I
was a first-class doctor for childbirths. Ten
or fifteen years ago, you remember, I was
the only decent accoucheur they had in all
this part of the country. Besides, I've always
been an honorable man.

PAULINE. (*Clasping his hand*) My dear!

DORN. Ssh — here they come!

(*Enter* MADAME ARCADINA *on* SORIN's *arm,*
TRIGORIN, SHAMREYEFF, MEDVEDENKO, *and*
MASHA.)

SHAMREYEFF. In '73 at the Poltava Fair
— pure delight — I can assure you she was
magnificent, ah, magnificent! Pure delight!
But tell me if you know where Chadin,
Paul Semyonovitch, the comedian, is now?
Take his Raspluyef [5] — 'twas better than
Sadovsky's,[6] I can assure you, most esteemed
lady. But what's become of him?

ARCADINA. You keep asking me about
someone before the flood — how should I
know? (*Sits down.*)

SHAMREYEFF. Ah (*sighs*) Paulie Chadin!
Nobody like that now. The stage is not what
it was, Irina Nicolayevna, ah no! In those
days there were mighty oaks, now we have
nothing but stumps.

DORN. There are not many brilliant talents nowadays, it's true, but the general
average of the acting is much higher.

SHAMREYEFF. I can't agree with you
there. However, that's a matter of taste, *De
gustibus aut bene, aut nihil.*[7]

(TREPLEFF *comes out from behind the
stage.*)

ARCADINA. My dear son, when does it
begin?

TREPLEFF. Please be patient. It's only a
moment.

ARCADINA. (*Reciting from Hamlet*) My
son!

" Thou turnst mine eyes into my very soul,
    And there I see such black and grained
        spots
As will not leave their tinct."

TREPLEFF. (*Paraphrasing from Hamlet*)
Nay, but to live in wickedness, seek love in
the depths of sin — (*Behind the stage a
horn blows.*) Ladies and gentlemen, we begin! I beg your attention. (*A pause.*) I begin. (*Tapping the floor with a stick. In a
loud voice.*) Harken ye mists, out of ancient

---

[5] a low-comedy character in *Kretchinsky's Wedding* by Kobylin

[6] Moscow actor

[7] i.e., " Speak nothing but good about taste."

time, that drift by night over the bosom of this lake, darken our eyes with sleep and in our dream show us what will be in 200,000 years.

SORIN. In 200,000 years nothing will be.

TREPLEFF. Then let them present to us that nothing.

ARCADINA. Let them. We are asleep.

(*The curtain rises. Vista opens across the lake. Low on the horizon the moon hangs, reflected in the water.* NINA ZARETCHNY, *all in white, seated on a rock.*)

NINA. Men and beasts, lions, eagles and partridges, antlered deer, mute fishes dwelling in the water, starfish and small creatures invisible to the eye — these and all life have run their sad course and are no more. Thousands of creatures have come and gone since there was life on the earth. Vainly now the pallid moon doth light her lamp. In the meadows the cranes wake and cry no longer; and the beetles' hum is silent in the linden groves. Cold, cold, cold. Empty, empty, empty! Terrible, terrible, terrible. (*A pause.*) Living bodies have crumbled to dust, and Eternal Matter has changed them into stones and water and clouds and there is one soul of many souls. I am that soul of the world. — In me the soul of Alexander the Great, of Cæsar, of Shakespeare, of Napoleon and of the lowest worm. The mind of man and the brute's instinct mingle in me. I remember all, all, and in me lives each several life again.

(*The will-o'-the-wisps appear.*)

ARCADINA. (*In a stage whisper*) We're in for something decadent.

TREPLEFF. (*Imploring and reproaching*) Mother!

NINA. I am alone. Once in a hundred years I open my lips to speak, and in this void my sad echo is unheard. And you, pale fires, you do not hear me. . . . Before daybreak the putrid marsh begets you, and you wander until sunrise, but without thought, without will, without the throb of life. For fear life should spring in you the father of Eternal Matter, the Devil, causes every instant in you, as in stones and in water, an interchange of the atoms, and you are changing endlessly. I, only, the world's soul, remain unchanged and am eternal. (*A pause.*) I am like a prisoner cast into a deep, empty well, and know not where I am nor what awaits me. One thing only is not hidden from me: in the stubborn, savage fight with the Devil, the principle of material forces, I am destined to conquer; and when that has been, matter and spirit shall be made one in the shadow of my soul forever. And lo, the kingdom of universal will is at hand. But that cannot be before long centuries of the moon, the shining dog star, and the earth, have run to dust. And till that time horror shall be, horror, horror, horror! (*A pause; upon the background of the lake appear two red spots.*) Behold, my mighty adversary, the Devil, approaches. I see his awful, blood-red eyes.

ARCADINA. I smell sulphur, is that necessary?

TREPLEFF. Yes, it is.

ARCADINA. Oh, I see (*Laughing*) — it's a stage effect!

TREPLEFF. Mother!

NINA. But without man he is lost —

PAULINE. (*To* DORN) You're taking your hat off. Put it on, you'll catch cold.

ARCADINA. The doctor has taken off his hat to the Devil, the father of Eternal Matter?

TREPLEFF. (*Blazing up, in a loud voice*) The play's over! That's enough! Curtain!

ARCADINA. Why are you angry?

TREPLEFF. That's enough. Curtain! Drop the curtain! (*Stamping his foot*) Curtain! (*The curtain falls.*) You must excuse me! I don't know how it was but I forgot somehow that only a chosen few can write plays and act them. I was infringing on a monopoly — My — I — (*Instead of saying more he makes a gesture of having done with it and goes out to the Left.*)

ARCADINA. What's the matter with him?

SORIN. Irina, my dear, you mustn't treat a young man's pride like that.

ARCADINA. Now what have I said?

SORIN. You've hurt his feelings.

ARCADINA. But he told us beforehand it was all in fun, that's the way I took it — of course.

SORIN. Just the same —

ARCADINA. And now it appears he's produced a masterpiece. Well, I declare! Evidently he had no intention of amusing us, not at all; he got up this performance and fumigated us with sulphur to demonstrate to us how plays should be written and what's worth acting in. I'm sick of him. Nobody could stand his everlasting digs and outbursts. He's an unruly, conceited boy.

SORIN. He was only hoping to give you some pleasure.

ARCADINA. Yes? I notice he didn't choose some familiar sort of play, but forced his own decadent raving on us. I can listen to raving. I don't mind listening to it, so long as I'm not asked to take it seriously; but this of his is not like that. Not at all, it's introducing us to a new epoch in art, inaugurating a new era in art. But to my mind it's not new forms or epochs, it's simply bad temper.

TRIGORIN. Everyone writes as he wants to and as he can.

ARCADINA. Well, let him write as he wants to and as he can, so long as he leaves me out of it.

DORN. Great Jove angry is no longer Jove.

ARCADINA. I'm not Jove, I'm a woman. (*Lighting a cigarette*) I'm not angry — I'm merely vexed to see a young man wasting his time so. I didn't mean to hurt him.

MEDVEDENKO. Nobody has any grounds for separating matter from spirit, for it may be this very spirit itself is a union of material atoms. (*Excitedly, to* TRIGORIN) You know, somebody ought to put in a play, and then act on the stage, how we poor schoolmasters live. It's a hard, hard life.

ARCADINA. That's so, but we shan't talk of plays or atoms. The evening is so lovely. Listen — they're singing! (*Pausing to listen*) How good it is!

PAULINE. It's on the other side of the lake.

(*A pause.*)

ARCADINA. Sit down by me here. (*To* TRIGORIN) You know, ten or fifteen years ago we had music on this lake every night almost. There were six big country houses then around the shore; and it was all laughter, noise, shooting and lovemaking — making love without end. The *jeune premier* [8] and the idol of all six houses was our friend here, I must present (*Nods toward* DORN.) Doctor Eugene Sergeyevitch. He's charming now, but then he was irresistible. Why did I hurt my poor boy's feelings? I'm worried about him. (*Calls.*) Kostya! Son! Kostya!

MASHA. I'll go look for him.

ARCADINA. Would you, my dear?

MASHA. (*Calling*) Ah-oo! Constantine. Ah-oo! (*She goes out.*)

NINA. (*Coming from behind the stage*) Evidently we're not going on, so I may as well come out. Good evening! (*Kisses* MADAME ARCADINA *and* PAULINE ANDREYEVNA.)

SORIN. Bravo! Bravo!

ARCADINA. Bravo! Bravo! We were all enchanted. With such looks and such a lovely voice, it's a sin for you to stay here in the country. You have talent indeed. Do you hear? You owe it to yourself to go on the stage.

NINA. Oh, that's my dream. (*Sighing*) But it will never come true.

ARCADINA. Who can tell? Let me present Boris Alexeyevitch Trigorin.

NINA. Oh, I'm so glad — (*Much embarrassed*) I'm always reading your —

ARCADINA. (*Drawing* NINA *down beside her*) Don't be shy, dear. He may be a famous author, but his heart's quite simple. Look, he's embarrassed too.

DORN. I suppose we may raise the curtain now. This way it's frightening.

SHAMREYEFF. (*Loudly*) Yakov, my man, raise the curtain!

(*The curtain is raised.*)

NINA. (*To* TRIGORIN) It's a strange play, isn't it?

8 " romantic lead," a theatrical term

TRIGORIN. I didn't understand a word of it. However, I enjoyed watching it. You acted with so much sincerity, and the scenery was so lovely. (*A pause.*) I dare say there are quantities of fish in this lake.

NINA. Yes.

TRIGORIN. I love fishing. I can think of no greater pleasure than to sit along towards evening by the water and watch a float.

NINA. But, I'd have thought that for anyone who had tasted the joy of creation, no other pleasures could exist.

ARCADINA. (*Laughing*) Don't talk like that. When people make him pretty speeches he simply crumples up.

SHAMREYEFF. I remember one evening at the Opera in Moscow when the celebrated Silva was singing, how delighted we were when he took low C. Imagine our surprise — it so happened the bass from our church choir was there and all at once we heard "Bravo Silva" from the gallery a whole octave lower — like this — "Bravo Silva." The audience was thunderstruck.

(*A pause.*)

DORN. The angel of silence is flying over us.

NINA. Oh, I must go. Goodbye.

ARCADINA. Where to? Where so early? We won't allow it.

NINA. Papa is waiting for me.

ARCADINA. What a man, really! (*Kissing her*) Well, there's no help for it. It's too sad losing you.

NINA. If you only knew how I don't want to go.

ARCADINA. Somebody must see you home, child.

NINA. (*Frightened*) Oh, no, no.

SORIN. (*Imploring her*) Don't go.

NINA. I must, Peter Nicolayevitch.

SORIN. Stay an hour more, and so on. Come now, really!

NINA. (*Hesitating with tears in her eyes*) I can't. (*She shakes hands and hurries out.*)

ARCADINA. Now there's a really poor, unfortunate girl. They say her mother when she died willed the husband all her immense fortune, everything to the very last kopeck, and now this little girl is left with nothing, since her father has already willed everything he has to the second wife. That's shocking.

DORN. Yes, her papa is rather a beast, I must grant him that.

SORIN. (*Rubbing his hands to warm them*) What do you say, we'd better go in too, it's getting damp. My legs ache.

ARCADINA. It's like having wooden legs, you can hardly walk on them. Come on, you poor old patriarch. (*She takes his arm.*)

SHAMREYEFF. (*Offering his arm to his wife*) Madame?

SORIN. There's that dog howling again. (*To* SHAMREYEFF) Be good enough, Ilya Afanasyevitch, to tell them to let that dog off the chain.

SHAMREYEFF. It can't be done, Peter Nicolayevitch, or we'll be having thieves in the barn, and the millet's there. (*To* MEDVEDENKO *walking beside him*) Yes, a whole octave lower "Bravo Silva"! And not your concert singer, mind you, just ordinary church choir.

MEDVEDENKO. And what salary does a church singer get?

(*All except* DORN *go out.*)

DORN. (*Alone*) I don't know — maybe I'm no judge, I may be going off my head, but I liked that play. There's something in it. When the girl spoke of the vast solitude, and afterward when the Devil's eyes appeared, I could feel my hands trembling. It was all so fresh and naïve. But here he comes. I want to say all the nice things I can to him.

(*Enter* TREPLEFF.)

TREPLEFF. They've all gone.

DORN. I'm here.

TREPLEFF. Masha's been hunting for me all over the park. Unbearable creature!

DORN. Constantine Gavrilovitch, I admired your play extremely. It's a curious kind of thing and I haven't heard the end, but still it made a deep impression on me. You've got great talent. You must keep on! (CONSTANTINE *presses his hand and embraces him impulsively.*) Phew, what a nervous fellow! Tears in his eyes! What I wanted to say is you chose your subject from the realm of abstract ideas, and that's right — a work of art should express a great idea. There is no beauty without seriousness. My, you are pale!

TREPLEFF. So you think — I ought to go on?

DORN. Yes. But write only of what is profound and eternal. You know how I have lived my life, I have lived it with variety and choiceness; and I have enjoyed it; and I am content. But if ever I had felt the elevation of spirit that comes to artists in their creative moments I believe I should have despised this body and all its usages, and tried to soar above all earthly things.

TREPLEFF. Forgive me, where's Nina?

DORN. And another thing. In a work of art there must be a clear, definite idea. You must know what your object is in writing, for if you follow that picturesque road without a definite aim, you will go astray and your talent will be your ruin.

TREPLEFF. (*Impatiently*) Where is Nina?

DORN. She's gone home.

TREPLEFF. (*In despair*) What shall I do? I want to see her. I must see her. I'm going —

(MASHA *enters.*)

DORN. Calm yourself, my friend!

TREPLEFF. But all the same I'm going. I must go.

MASHA. Constantine Gavrilovitch, come indoors. Your mother wants you. She's anxious.

TREPLEFF. Tell her I've gone — and please — all of you let me alone! Don't follow me around.

DORN. Come, come, come, boy, you mustn't act like this — it won't do.

TREPLEFF. (*In tears*) Goodbye, Doctor — and thank you — (*Exits.*)

DORN. (*Sighing*) Ah, youth, youth —

MASHA. When there is nothing else left to say, people always say, " Ah, youth, youth." (*Takes a pinch of snuff.*)

DORN. (*Takes snuffbox out of her hand and flings it into the bushes.*) It's disgust-

ing. (*A pause*) There in the house they seem to be playing. We'd better go in.

MASHA. No, no, wait a minute.

DORN. What is it?

MASHA. Let me talk to you — I don't love my father, I can't talk to him, but I feel with all my heart that you are near me — Help me — help me — (*Starts to sob.*) or I shall do something silly, I'll make my life a mockery, ruin it — I can't keep on —

DORN. How? Help you how?

MASHA. I'm tortured. No one, no one knows what I'm suffering — (*Laying her head on his breast, softly*) I love Constantine.

DORN. How nervous they all are! How nervous they all are! And so much love! O magic lake! (*Tenderly*) What can I do for you, child? What, what?

ACT TWO

A croquet lawn. In the background on the Right is the house with a large terrace; on the Left is seen the lake, in which the blazing sun is reflected. Flower beds. Noon. Hot. On one side of the croquet lawn, in the shade of an old linden tree, MADAME ARCADINA, DORN, *and* MASHA *are sitting on a garden bench.* DORN *has an open book on his knees.*

ARCADINA. (*To* MASHA) Here, let's stand up. (*They both stand up.*) Side by side. You are twenty-two and I am nearly twice that. Doctor Dorn, tell us, which one of us looks the younger?

DORN. You, of course.

ARCADINA. There you are — you see? — And why is it? Because I work, I feel I'm always on the go, but you sit in the same spot all the time; you're not living. I make it a rule never to look ahead into the future. I let myself think neither of old age nor of death. What will be will be.

MASHA. But I feel as if I were a thousand; I trail my life along after me like an endless train. — Often I have no wish to be living at all. (*Sits down.*) Of course that's all nonsense. I ought to shake myself and throw it all off.

DORN. (*Sings softly.*) " Tell her, pretty flowers — "

ARCADINA. Then I'm correct as an Englishman. I'm always dressed and my hair always *comme il faut.* Would I permit myself to leave the house, even to come out here in the garden, in a dressing-gown or with my hair blousy? Never, I should say not! The reason I have kept my looks is because I've never been a frump, never let myself go, as some do. (*Arms akimbo, she walks up and down the croquet green.*) Here I am, light as a bird. Ready to play a girl of fifteen any day.

DORN. Well, at any rate, I'll go on with my reading. (*Takes up the book.*) We stopped at the corn merchants and the rats.

ARCADINA. And the rats. Go on. (*Sits.*) Let me have it, I'll read. It's my turn anyhow. (*She takes the book and looks for the place.*) And the rats — here we are — (*Reads.*) " And certainly, for people of the world to pamper the romantics and make them at home in their houses is as dangerous as for corn merchants to raise rats in their granaries. And yet they are beloved. And so when a woman has picked out the author she wants to entrap, she besieges him with compliments, amenities, and favors." Well, among the French that may be, but certainly here with us there's nothing of the kind, we've no set program. Here with us a woman before she ever sets out to capture an author is usually head over heels in love with him herself. To go no further, take me and Trigorin —

(*Enter* SORIN, *leaning on a stick, with* NINA *at his side.* MEDVEDENKO *follows him, pushing a wheel chair.*)

SORIN. (*Caressingly, as if to a child*) Yes? We're all joy, eh? We're happy today after all. (*To his sister*) We're all joy. Father and stepmother are gone to Tver, and we are free now for three whole days.

NINA. (*Sits down beside* ARCADINA *and embraces her.*) I am so happy! I belong now to you.

SORIN. (*Sitting down in the wheel chair*) She looks lovely today.

ARCADINA. Beautifully dressed, intriguing — that's a clever girl. (*She kisses* NINA.) We mustn't praise her too much. It's bad luck. Where's Boris Alexeyevitch?

NINA. He's at the bathhouse fishing.

ARCADINA. You'd think he'd be sick of it. (*She begins reading again.*)

NINA. What is that you have?

ARCADINA. Maupassant's " On the Water," darling. (*Reads a few lines to herself.*) Well, the rest is uninteresting and untrue. (*Shutting the book*) I'm troubled in my soul. Tell me, what's the matter with my son? Why is he so sad and morose? He spends day after day on the lake and I hardly ever see him any more.

MASHA. His heart's troubled. (*To* NINA, *timidly*) Please, Nina, read something out of his play, won't you?

NINA. (*Shrugging her shoulders*) You really want me to? It's so uninteresting.

MASHA. (*With restrained eagerness*) When he recites anything his eyes shine and his face grows pale. He has a beautiful sad voice, and a manner like a poet's.

(*Sound of* SORIN's *snoring.*)

DORN. Pleasant dreams.

ARCADINA. (*To* SORIN) Petrusha!

SORIN. Eh?

ARCADINA. Are you asleep?

SORIN. Not at all.

(*A pause.*)

ARCADINA. You are not following any treatment for yourself, that's not right, brother.

SORIN. I'd be glad to follow a treatment, but the doctor won't give me any.

DORN. Take care of yourself at sixty!

SORIN. Even at sixty a man wants to live.

DORN. (*Impatiently*) Bah! Take your valerian drops.

ARCADINA. I'd think it would do him good to take a cure at some springs.

DORN. Well — he might take it. He might not take it.

ARCADINA. Try and understand that!

DORN. Nothing to understand. It's all clear.

(*A pause.*)

MEDVEDENKO. Peter Nicolayevitch ought to give up smoking.

SORIN. Fiddlesticks!

DORN. No, it's not fiddlesticks! Wine and tobacco rob us of our personality. After a cigar or a vodka, you're not Peter Nicolayevitch, you're Peter Nicolayevitch plus somebody else; your ego splits up, and you begin to see yourself as a third person.

SORIN. Fine (*laughs*) for you to argue! You've lived your life, but what about me? I've served the Department of Justice twenty-eight years, but I've never lived, never seen anything, and all the rest of it, so naturally I want to have my life. You've had your fill and that's why you turn to philosophy. I want to live, and that's why I turn to sherry after dinner and smoking cigars, and so on. And that's that.

DORN. One must look seriously at life, but to go in for cures at sixty and regret the pleasures you missed in your youth, is, if you'll forgive me, frivolous.

MASHA. (*Gets up.*) It must be time for lunch. (*Walking slow and hobbling*) My foot's gone to sleep. (*Exits.*)

DORN. She'll down a couple of glasses before lunch.

SORIN. The poor thing gets no happiness of her own.

DORN. Fiddlesticks, your Excellency.

SORIN. You argue like a man who's had his fill.

ARCADINA. Oh, what can be duller than this darling country dullness is! Hot, quiet, nobody ever does anything, everybody philosophizes. It's good to be here with you, my friends, delightful listening to you, but — sitting in my hotel room, all by myself, studying my part — how much better!

NINA. (*Ecstatically*) Good! I understand you.

SORIN. Of course, in town's better. You sit in your study, the footman lets nobody in without announcing them, there's the telephone — on the street cabs and so on —

DORN. (*Singing sotto voce*) " Tell her, my flowers — "

(*Enter* SHAMREYEFF, *behind him* PAULINE.)

SHAMREYEFF. Here they are. Good morning! (*Kisses* MADAME ARCADINA's *hand, then* NINA's.) Very glad to see you looking so well. (*To* MADAME ARCADINA) My wife tells me you are thinking of driving into town with her today. Is that so?

ARCADINA. Yes, we are thinking of it.

SHAMREYEFF. Hm! That's magnificent, but what will you travel on, my most esteemed lady? Today around here we are hauling rye, all the hands are busy. And what horses would you take, may I ask?

ARCADINA. What horses? How should I know — what horses!

SORIN. There are carriage horses here!

SHAMREYEFF. (*Flaring up*) Carriage horses? But where do I get the harness? Where do I get the harness? It's amazing. It's incomprehensible! Most esteemed lady! Excuse me, I am on my knees before your talent; I'd gladly give ten years of my life for you, but I cannot let you have the horses!

ARCADINA. But what if I have to go? It's a fine business!

SHAMREYEFF. Most esteemed lady! You don't know what a farm means.

ARCADINA. (*Flaring up*) The same old story! In that case I'll start for Moscow today. Order me horses from the village, or I'll walk to the station.

SHAMREYEFF. (*Flaring up*) In that case I resign my position! Find yourself another steward! (*Exits.*)

ARCADINA. Every summer it's like this, every summer here they insult me! I'll never put my foot here again! (*Goes out in the direction of the bathhouse.*)

(*Presently she is seen going into the house.* TRIGORIN *follows, with fishing rods and a pail.*)

SORIN. (*Flaring up*) This is insolent! The devil knows what it is! I'm sick of it, and so on. Bring all the horses here this very minute!

NINA. (*To* PAULINE) To refuse Irina

Nicolayevna, the famous actress! Any little wish of hers, the least whim, is worth more than all your farm. It's simply unbelievable!

PAULINE. (*In despair*) What can I do? Put yourself in my shoes, what can I do?

SORIN. (*To* NINA) Let's go find my sister. We'll all beg her not to leave us. Isn't that so? (*Looking in the direction* SHAMREYEFF *went*) You insufferable man! Tyrant!

NINA. (*Prevents his getting up.*) Sit still, sit still. We'll wheel you. (*She and* MEDVEDENKO *push the wheel chair.*) Oh, how awful it is!

SORIN. Yes, yes, it's awful. But he won't leave; I'll speak to him right off.

(*They go out.* DORN *and* PAULINE *remain.*)

DORN. People are certainly tiresome. Really the thing to do, of course, is throw that husband of yours out by the neck; but it will all end by this old woman, Peter Nicolayevitch, and his sister begging him to pardon them. See if they don't.

PAULINE. He has put the carriage horses in the fields, too. And these misunderstandings happen every day. If you only knew how it all upsets me. It's making me ill; you see how I'm trembling. I can't bear his coarseness. (*Entreating*) Eugene, my darling, light of my eyes — take me with you. Our time is passing, we're not young any longer; if — if only we could — for the rest of our lives at least — stop hiding, stop pretending.

(*A pause.*)

DORN. I am fifty-five, it's too late to change now.

PAULINE. I know, you refuse me because there are other women close to you. It's impossible for you to take them all with you. I understand. I apologize! Forgive me, you are tired of me.

(NINA *appears before the house picking a bunch of flowers.*)

DORN. No, not all that.

PAULINE. I am miserable with jealousy. Of course you are a doctor. You can't escape women. I understand.

DORN. (*To* NINA, *as she joins them*) What's happening?

NINA. Irina Nicolayevna is crying and Peter Nicolayevitch having his asthma.

DORN. (*Rising*) I must go and give them both some valerian drops.

NINA. (*Giving him the flowers*) Won't you?

DORN. *Merci bien.* (*Goes toward the house.*)

PAULINE. What pretty flowers! (*Nearing the house, in a low voice*) Give me those flowers! Give me those flowers!

(*He hands her the flowers, she tears them to pieces and flings them away. They go into the house.*)

NINA. (*Alone*) How strange it is seeing a famous actress cry, and about such a little nothing! And isn't it strange that a famous author should sit all day long fishing? The darling of the public, his name in the papers every day, his photograph for sale in shop windows, his book translated into foreign languages, and he's delighted because he's caught two chub. I imagined famous people were proud and distant, and that they despised the crowd, and used their fame and the glamor of their names to revenge themselves on the world for putting birth and money first. But here I see them crying or fishing, playing cards, laughing or losing their tempers, like everybody else.

(TREPLEFF *enters, without a hat, carrying a gun and a dead sea gull.*)

TREPLEFF. Are you here alone?

NINA. Alone. (TREPLEFF *lays the sea gull at her feet.*) What does that mean?

TREPLEFF. I was low enough today to kill this sea gull. I lay it at your feet.

NINA. What's the matter with you? (*Picks up sea gull and looks at it.*)

TREPLEFF. (*Pause.*) It's the way I'll soon end my own life.

NINA. I don't recognize you.

TREPLEFF. Yes, ever since I stopped recognizing you. You've changed toward me. Your eyes are cold. You hate to have me near you.

NINA. You are so irritable lately, and you

talk — it's as if you were talking in symbols. And this sea gull, I suppose that's a symbol, too. Forgive me, but I don't understand it. (*Lays the sea gull on the seat.*) I'm too simple to understand you.

TREPLEFF. This began that evening when my play failed so stupidly. Women will never forgive failure. I've burnt it all, every scrap of it. If you only knew what I'm going through! Your growing cold to me is terrible, unbelievable; it's as if I had suddenly waked and found this lake dried up and sunk in the ground. You say you are too simple to understand me. Oh, what is there to understand? My play didn't catch your fancy, you despise my kind of imagination, you already consider me commonplace, insignificant, like so many others. (*Stamping his foot*) How well I understand it all, how I understand it. It's like a spike in my brain, may it be damned along with my pride, which is sucking my blood, sucking it like a snake. (*He sees* TRIGORIN, *who enters reading a book.*) Here comes the real genius, he walks like Hamlet, and with a book too. (*Mimicking*) " Words, words, words." This sun has hardly reached you, and you are already smiling, your glance is melting in his rays. I won't stand in your way. (*He goes out.*)

TRIGORIN. (*Making notes in a book*) Takes snuff and drinks vodka, always wears black. The schoolmaster in love with her.

NINA. Good morning, Boris Alexeyevitch!

TRIGORIN. Good morning. It seems that things have taken a turn we hadn't expected, so we are leaving today. You and I aren't likely to meet again. I'm sorry. I don't often meet young women, young and charming. I've forgotten how one feels at eighteen or nineteen, I can't picture it very clearly, and so the girls I draw in my stories and novels are mostly wrong. I'd like to be in your shoes for just one hour, to see things through your eyes, and find out just what sort of a little person you are.

NINA. And how I'd like to be in your shoes!

TRIGORIN. Why?

NINA. To know how it feels being a famous genius. What's it like being famous? How does it make you feel?

TRIGORIN. How? Nohow, I should think. I'd never thought about it. (*Reflecting*) One of two things: either you exaggerate my fame, or else my fame hasn't made me feel it.

NINA. But if you read about yourself in the papers?

TRIGORIN. When they praise me I'm pleased; when they abuse me, I feel whipped for a day or so.

NINA. It's a marvelous world! If you only knew how I envy you! Look how different different people's lots are! Some have all they can do to drag through their dull, obscure lives; they are all just alike, all miserable; others — well, you for instance — have a bright, interesting life that means something. You are happy.

TRIGORIN. I? (*Shrugging his shoulders*) H'm — I hear you speak of fame and happiness, of a bright, interesting life, but for me that's all words, pretty words that — if you'll forgive my saying so — mean about the same to me as candied fruits, which I never eat. You are very young and very kind.

NINA. Your life is beautiful.

TRIGORIN. I don't see anything so very beautiful about it. (*Looks at his watch.*) I must get to my writing. Excuse me, I'm busy — (*Laughs.*) You've stepped on my pet corn, as they say, and here I am, beginning to get excited and a little cross. At any rate let's talk. Let's talk about my beautiful, bright life. Well, where shall we begin? (*After reflecting a moment*) You know, sometimes violent obsessions take hold of a man, some fixed idea pursues him, the moon, for example, day and night he thinks of nothing but the moon. Well, I have just such a moon. Day and night one thought obsesses me: I must be writing, I must be writing, I must be — I've scarcely finished one novel when somehow I'm driven on to write another, then a third, and after the third a fourth. I write incessantly, and always at a breakneck speed, and that's the only way I can write. What's beautiful and bright about that, I ask you? Oh, what a wild life! Why now even, I'm here talking to you, I'm excited, but every minute I remember that the story I haven't finished is there waiting for me. I see that cloud up there, it's shaped like a grand piano — instantly a mental note — I must remember to put that in my story — a cloud sailing by — grand piano. A whiff of heliotrope. Quickly I make note of it: cloying smell, widow's color — put that in next time I describe a summer evening. Every sentence, every word I say and you say, I lie in wait for it, snap it up for my literary storeroom — it might come in handy — As soon as I put my work down, I race off to the theater or go fishing, hoping to find a rest, but not at all — a new idea for a story comes rolling around in my head like a cannon ball, and I'm back at my desk, and writing and writing and writing. And it's always like that, everlastingly. I have no rest from myself, and I feel that I am consuming my own life, that for the honey I'm giving to someone in the void, I rob my best flowers of their pollen, I tear up those flowers and trample on their roots. Do I seem mad? Do my friends seem to talk with me as they would to a sane man? " What are you writing at now? What shall we have next? " Over and over it's like that, till I think all this attention and praise is said only out of kindness to a sick man — deceive him, soothe him, and then any minute come stealing up behind and pack him off to the madhouse. And in those years, my young best years, when I was beginning, why then writing made my life a torment. A minor writer, especially when he's not successful, feels clumsy, he's all thumbs, the world has no need for him; his nerves are about to go; he can't resist hanging around people in the arts, where nobody knows him, or take any notice of him, and he's afraid to look them straight in the eyes, like a man with a passion for gambling who hasn't any money to play with. I'd never seen my readers but for some reason or other I pictured them as hating me and mistrusting me, I had a deathly fear of the public, and when my first play was produced it seemed to me all the dark eyes in the audience were looking at it with hostility and all the light eyes with frigid indifference. Oh how awful that was! What torment it was!

NINA. But surely the inspiration you feel and the creation itself of something must give you a moment of high, sweet happiness, don't they?

TRIGORIN. Yes. When I'm writing I enjoy it and I enjoy reading my proofs, but the minute it comes out I detest it; I see it's not what I meant it to be; I was wrong to write it at all, and I'm vexed and sick at heart about it. (*Laughs.*) Then the public reads it. " Yes, charming, clever — Charming but nothing like Tolstoy: A very fine thing, but Turgenev's *Fathers and Sons* is finer." To my dying day that's what it will be, clever and charming, charming and clever — nothing more. And when I'm dead they'll be saying at my grave, " Here lies Trigorin, a delightful writer but not so good as Turgenev."

NINA. Excuse me, but I refuse to understand you. You are simply spoiled by success.

TRIGORIN. What success? I have never pleased myself. I don't like myself as a writer. The worst of it is that I am in a sort of daze and often don't understand what I write — I love this water here, the trees, the sky, I feel nature, it stirs in me a passion, an irresistible desire to write. But I am not only a landscape painter, I am a citizen too, I love my country, the people, I feel that if I am a writer I ought to speak also of the people, of their sufferings, of their future, speak of science, of the rights of man, and so forth, and I speak of everything, I hurry up, on all sides they are after me, are annoyed at me, I dash from side to side like a fox the hounds are baiting, I see life and science getting always farther and farther ahead as I fall always more and more behind, like a peasant, missing his train, and the upshot is I feel that I can write only landscape, and in all the rest I am false and false to the marrow of my bones.

NINA. You work too hard, and have no time and no wish to feel your own importance. You may be dissatisfied with yourself, of course, but other people think you are great and excellent. If I were such a writer as you are I'd give my whole life to the people, but I should feel that the only happiness for them would be in rising to me; and they should draw my chariot.

TRIGORIN. Well, in a chariot — Agamemnon am I, or what?

(*They both smile.*)

NINA. For the happiness of being an author or an actress I would bear any poverty, disillusionment, I'd have people hate me. I'd live in a garret and eat black bread, I'd endure my own dissatisfaction with myself and all my faults, but in return I should ask for fame — real resounding fame. (*Covers her face with her hands.*) My head's swimming — Ouf!

ARCADINA. (*From within the house*) Boris Alexeyevitch!

TRIGORIN. She's calling me. I dare say, to come and pack. But I don't feel like going away. (*He glances at the lake.*) Look, how beautiful it is! Marvelous!

NINA. Do you see over there that house and garden?

TRIGORIN. Yes.

NINA. It used to belong to my dear mother. I was born there. I've spent all my life by this lake and I know every little island on it.

TRIGORIN. It's all very charming. (*Seeing the sea gull*) What is that?

NINA. A sea gull. Constantine shot it.

TRIGORIN. It's a lovely bird. Really, I don't want to leave here. Do try and persuade Irina Nicolayevna to stay. (*Makes a note in his book.*)

NINA. What is it you're writing?

TRIGORIN. Only a note. An idea struck me. (*Putting the notebook away*) An idea for a short story: a young girl, one like you, has lived all her life beside a lake; she loves the lake like a sea gull and is happy and free

like a sea gull. But by chance a man comes, sees her, and out of nothing better to do, destroys her, like this sea gull here. (*A pause.* MADAME ARCADINA *appears at the window.*)

ARCADINA. Boris Alexeyevitch, where are you?

TRIGORIN. Right away! (*Goes toward the house, looking back at* NINA. MADAME ARCADINA *remains at the window.*) What is it?

ARCADINA. We're staying.

(TRIGORIN *enters the house.*)

NINA. (*Coming forward, standing lost in thought*) It's a dream!

ACT THREE

The dining room in SORIN's *house. On the Right and Left are doors. A sideboard. A medicine cupboard. In the middle of the room a table. A small trunk and hatboxes, signs of preparations for leaving.*

TRIGORIN *is at lunch,* MASHA *standing by the table.*

MASHA. I tell you this because you're a writer. You might use it. I tell you the truth: if he had died when he shot himself I wouldn't live another minute. Just the same I'm getting braver; I've just made up my mind to tear this love out of my heart by the roots.

TRIGORIN. How will you do it?

MASHA. I'm going to get married. To Medvedenko.

TRIGORIN. Is that the schoolmaster?

MASHA. Yes.

TRIGORIN. I don't see why you must do that.

MASHA. Loving without hope, waiting the whole year long for something — but when I'm married I won't have any time for love, there'll be plenty of new things I'll have to do to make me forget the past. Anyhow it will be a change, you know. Shall we have another?

TRIGORIN. Haven't you had about enough?

MASHA. Ah! (*Pours two glasses.*) Here! Don't look at me like that! Women drink oftener than you imagine. Not so many of them drink openly like me. Most of them hide it. Yes. And it's always vodka or cognac. (*Clinks glasses.*) Your health. You're a decent sort, I'm sorry to be parting from you. (*They drink.*)

TRIGORIN. I don't want to leave here myself.

MASHA. You should beg her to stay.

TRIGORIN. She'd never do that now. Her son is behaving himself very tactlessly. First he tries shooting himself and now, they say, he's going to challenge me to a duel. But what for? He sulks, he snorts, he preaches new art forms — but there's room for all, the new and the old — why elbow?

MASHA. Well, and there's jealousy. However, that's not my business.

(*Pause.* YAKOV *crosses Right to Left with a piece of luggage.* NINA *enters, stops near window.*)

MASHA. That schoolmaster of mine is none too clever, but he's a good man and he's poor, and he loves me dearly. I'm sorry for him, and I'm sorry for his old mother. Well, let me wish you every happiness. Think kindly of me. (*Warmly shakes his hand.*) Let me thank you for your friendly interest. Send me your books, be sure to write in them. Only don't put " esteemed lady," but simply this: " To Marya, who not remembering her origin, does not know why she is living in this world." Goodbye. (*Goes out.*)

NINA. (*Holding out her hand closed to* TRIGORIN) Even or odd?

TRIGORIN. Even.

NINA. (*Sighing*) No. I had only one pea in my hand. I was trying my fortune: To be an actress or not. I wish somebody would advise me.

TRIGORIN. There's no advice in this sort of thing.

(*A pause.*)

NINA. We are going to part — I may never see you again. Won't you take this little medal to remember me? I've had it engraved with your initials and on the other side the title of your book: *Days and Nights.*

TRIGORIN. What a graceful thing to do! (*Kisses the medal.*) It's a charming present.

NINA. Sometimes think of me.

TRIGORIN. I'll think of you. I'll think of you as I saw you that sunny day — do you remember — a week ago when you had on your white dress — we were talking — a white sea gull was lying on the bench beside us.

NINA. (*Pensive*) Yes, the sea gull. (*A pause.*) Someone's coming — let me see you two minutes before you go, won't you? (*Goes out on the Left as* MADAME ARCADINA *and* SORIN, *in full dress, with a decoration, enter, then* YAKOV, *busy with the packing.*)

ARCADINA. Stay at home, old man. How could you be running about with your rheumatism? (*To* TRIGORIN) Who was it just went out? Nina?

TRIGORIN. Yes.

ARCADINA. *Pardon!* We intruded. (*Sits down.*) I believe everything's packed. I'm exhausted.

TRIGORIN. (*Reading the medal*) " *Days and Nights,* page 121, lines eleven and twelve."

YAKOV. (*Clearing the table*) Shall I pack your fishing rods as well?

TRIGORIN. Yes, I'll want them again. But the books you can give away.

YAKOV. Yes, sir.

TRIGORIN. (*To himself*) " Page 121, lines eleven and twelve." What's in those lines? (*To* ARCADINA) Have you my works here in the house?

ARCADINA. Yes, in my brother's study, the corner bookcase.

TRIGORIN. Page 121. (*Exits.*)

ARCADINA. Really, Petrusha, you'd better stay at home.

SORIN. You're going away. It's dreary for me here at home without you.

ARCADINA. But what's there in town?

SORIN. Nothing in particular, but all the same. (*Laughs.*) There's the laying of the foundation stone for the town hall, and all that sort of thing. A man longs if only for an hour or so to get out of this gudgeon existence, and it's much too long I've been lying around like an old cigarette holder. I've ordered the horses around at one o'clock; we'll set off at the same time.

ARCADINA. (*After a pause*) Oh, stay here, don't be lonesome, don't take cold. Look after my son. Take care of him. Advise him. (*A pause*) Here I am leaving and so shall never know why Constantine tried to kill himself. I have a notion the main reason was jealousy, and the sooner I take Trigorin away from here the better.

SORIN. How should I explain it to you? There were other reasons besides jealousy. Here we have a man who is young, intelligent, living in the country in solitude, without money, without position, without a future. He has nothing to do. He is ashamed and afraid of his idleness. I love him very much and he's attached to me, but he feels just the same that he's superfluous in this house, and a sort of dependent here, a poor relation. That's something we can understand; it's pride of course.

ARCADINA. I'm worried about him. (*Reflecting*) He might go into the service, perhaps.

SORIN. (*Whistling, then hesitatingly*) It seems to me the best thing you could do would be to let him have a little money. In the first place he ought to be able to dress himself like other people, and so on. Look how he's worn that same old jacket these past three years; he runs around without an overcoat. (*Laughs.*) Yes, and it wouldn't harm him to have a little fun — he might go abroad, perhaps — it wouldn't cost much.

ARCADINA. Perhaps I could manage a suit, but as for going abroad — no. Just at this moment I can't even manage the suit. (*Firmly*) I haven't any money! (SORIN *laughs.*) I haven't. No.

SORIN. (*Whistling*) Very well. Forgive me, my dear, don't be angry. You're a generous, noble woman.

ARCADINA. (*Weeping*) I haven't any money.

SORIN. Of course if I had any money, I'd give him some myself, but I haven't anything, not a kopeck. (*Laughs.*) My manager takes all my pension and spends it on agriculture, cattle-raising, bee-keeping, and my money goes for nothing. The bees die, the cows die, horses they never let me have.

ARCADINA. Yes, I have some money, but I'm an actress, my costumes alone are enough to ruin me.

SORIN. You are very good, my dear. I respect you. Yes — But there again something's coming over me — (*Staggers.*) My head's swimming. (*Leans on table.*) I feel faint, and so on.

ARCADINA. (*Alarmed*) Petrusha! (*Trying to support him*) Petrusha, my darling! (*Calls.*) Help me! Help!

(*Enter* TREPLEFF, *his head bandaged, and* MEDVEDENKO.)

ARCADINA. He feels faint.

SORIN. It's nothing, it's nothing — (*Smiles and drinks water.*) It's gone already — and so on.

TREPLEFF. (*To his mother*) Don't be alarmed, Mother, it's not serious. It often happens now to my uncle. Uncle, you must lie down a little.

SORIN. A little, yes. All the same I'm going to town — I'm lying down a little and I'm going to town — that's clear. (*He goes, leaning on his stick.*)

MEDVEDENKO. (*Gives him his arm.*) There's a riddle: in the morning it's on four legs, at noon on two, in the evening on three.

SORIN. (*Laughs.*) That's it. And on the back at night. Thank you, I can manage alone.

MEDVEDENKO. My, what ceremony! (*He and* SORIN *go out.*)

ARCADINA. How he frightened me!

TREPLEFF. It's not good for him to live in the country. He's low in his mind. Now, Mother, if you'd only have a burst of sudden generosity and lend him a thousand or fifteen hundred, he could spend a whole year in town.

ARCADINA. I haven't any money. I'm an actress, not a banker.

(*A pause.*)

TREPLEFF. Mother, change my bandage. You do it so well.

ARCADINA. (*Takes bottle of iodoform and*

a box of bandages from cupboard.) And the doctor's late.

TREPLEFF. He promised to be here at ten, but it's already noon.

ARCADINA. Sit down. (*Takes off bandage.*) You look as if you were in a turban. Some man who came by the kitchen yesterday asked what nationality you were. But it's almost entirely healed. What's left is nothing. (*Kisses him on the head.*) While I'm away, you won't do any more click-click?

TREPLEFF. No, Mother. That was a moment when I was out of my head with despair, and couldn't control myself. It won't happen again. (*Kisses her fingers.*) You have clever fingers. I remember long, long ago when you were still playing at the Imperial Theatre — there was a fight one day in our court, and a washerwoman who was one of the tenants got beaten almost to death. Do you remember? She was picked up unconscious — you nursed her, took medicines to her, bathed her children in the washtub. Don't you remember?

ARCADINA. No. (*Puts on fresh bandage.*)

TREPLEFF. Two ballet dancers were living then in the same house we did, they used to come and drink coffee with you.

ARCADINA. That I remember.

TREPLEFF. They were very pious. (*A pause.*) Lately, these last days, I have loved you as tenderly and fully as when I was a child. Except for you, there's nobody left me now. Only why, why do you subject yourself to the influence of that man?

ARCADINA. You don't understand him, Constantine. He's a very noble character.

TREPLEFF. Nevertheless, when he was told I was going to challenge him to a duel, nobility didn't keep him from playing the coward. He's leaving. Ignominious retreat!

ARCADINA. Such tosh! I myself begged him to leave here.

TREPLEFF. Noble character! Here we both are nearly quarreling over him, and right now very likely he's in the drawing room or in the garden laughing at us — developing Nina, trying once and for all to convince her he's a genius.

ARCADINA. For you it's a pleasure — saying disagreeable things to me. I respect that man and must ask you not to speak ill of him in my presence.

TREPLEFF. And I don't respect him. You want me too to think he's a genius, but, forgive me, I can't tell lies — his creations make me sick.

ARCADINA. That's envy. People who are not talented but pretend to be have nothing better to do than to disparage real talents. It must be a fine consolation!

TREPLEFF. (*Sarcastically*) Real talents! (*Angrily*) I'm more talented than both of you put together, if it comes to that! (*Tears off the bandage.*) You two, with your stale routine, have grabbed first place in art and think that only what you do is real or legitimate; the rest you'd like to stifle and keep down. I don't believe in you two. I don't believe in you or in him.

ARCADINA. Decadent!

TREPLEFF. Go back to your darling theater and act there in trashy, stupid plays!

ARCADINA. Never did I act in such plays. Leave me alone! You are not fit to write even wretched vaudeville.[1] Kiev burgher! Sponge!

TREPLEFF. Miser!

ARCADINA. Beggar! (*He sits down, cries softly.*) Nonentity! (*Walks up and down.*) Don't cry! You mustn't cry! (*Weeps. Kisses him on his forehead, his cheeks, his head.*) My dear child, forgive me! Forgive me, your wicked mother! Forgive miserable me!

TREPLEFF. (*Embracing her*) If you only knew! I've lost everything. She doesn't love me; now I can't write. All my hopes are gone.

ARCADINA. Don't despair. It will all pass. He's leaving right away. She'll love you again. (*Dries his tears.*) That's enough. We've made it up now.

TREPLEFF. (*Kissing her hands*) Yes, Mother.

ARCADINA. (*Tenderly*) Make it up with him, too. You don't want a duel. You don't, do you?

[1] a low form of musical comedy

TREPLEFF. Very well, only, Mother, don't let me see him. It's painful to me. It's beyond me. (TRIGORIN *comes in.*) There he is. I'm going. (*Quickly puts dressings away in cupboard.*) The doctor will do my bandage later.

TRIGORIN. (*Looking through a book*) Page 121 — lines eleven and twelve. Here it is. (*Reads.*) " If you ever, ever need my life, come and take it."

(TREPLEFF *picks up the bandage from the floor and goes out.*)

ARCADINA. (*Looking at her watch*) The horses will be here soon.

TRIGORIN. (*To himself*) " If you ever, ever need my life, come and take it."

ARCADINA. I hope you are all packed.

TRIGORIN. (*Impatiently*) Yes, yes — (*In deep thought*) Why is it I thought I felt sadness in that call from a pure soul, and my heart aches so with pity? " If you ever, ever need my life, come and take it." (*To* MADAME ARCADINA) Let's stay just one more day. (*She shakes her head.*)

TRIGORIN. Let's stay!

ARCADINA. Darling, I know what keeps you here. But have some self-control. You're a little drunk, be sober.

TRIGORIN. You be sober, too, be understanding, reasonable, I beg you; look at all this like a true friend — (*Presses her hand.*) You are capable of sacrificing. Be my friend, let me be free.

ARCADINA. (*Excited*) Are you so infatuated?

TRIGORIN. I am drawn to her! Perhaps this is just what I need.

ARCADINA. The love of some provincial girl? Oh, how little you know yourself!

TRIGORIN. Sometimes people talk but are asleep. That's how it is now — I'm talking to you but in my dream see her. I'm possessed by sweet, marvelous dreams. Let me go —

ARCADINA. (*Trembling*) No, no, I'm an ordinary woman like any other woman, you shouldn't talk to me like this. Don't torture me, Boris. It frightens me.

TRIGORIN. If you wanted to, you could be far from ordinary. There is a kind of love that's young, and beautiful, and is all poetry, and carries us away into a world of dreams; on earth it alone can ever give us happiness. Such a love I still have never known. In my youth there wasn't time, I was always around some editor's office, fighting off starvation. Now it's here, that love, it's come, it beckons me. What sense, then, is there in running away from it?

ARCADINA. (*Angry*) You've gone mad.

TRIGORIN. Well, let me!

ARCADINA. You've all conspired today just to torment me. (*Weeps.*)

TRIGORIN. (*Clutching at his breast*) She doesn't understand. She doesn't want to understand.

ARCADINA. Am I so old or ugly that you don't mind talking to me about other women? (*Embracing and kissing him*) Oh, you madman! My beautiful, my marvel — you are the last chapter of my life. (*Falls on knees.*) My joy, my pride, my blessedness! (*Embracing his knees*) If you forsake me for one hour even, I'll never survive it, I'll go out of my mind, my wonderful, magnificent one, my master.

TRIGORIN. Somebody might come in. (*Helps her to rise.*)

ARCADINA. Let them, I am not ashamed of my love for you. (*Kisses his hands.*) My treasure! You reckless boy, you want to be mad, but I won't have it, I won't let you. (*Laughs.*) You are mine — you are mine. This brow is mine, and the eyes mine, and this beautiful silky hair, too, is mine. You are all mine. You are so talented, so intelligent, the best of all modern writers; you are the one and only hope of Russia — you have such sincerity, simplicity, healthy humor. In one stroke you go to the very heart of a character or a scene; your people are like life itself. Oh, it's impossible to read you without rapture! Do you think this is only incense? I'm flattering you? Come, look me in the eyes — Do I look like a liar? There you see, only I can appreciate you; only I tell you the truth, my lovely darling. — You are coming? Yes? You won't leave me?

TRIGORIN. I have no will of my own — I've never had a will of my own. Flabby, weak, always submitting! Is it possible that might please women? Take me, carry me away, only never let me be one step away from you.

ARCADINA. (*To herself*) Now he's mine. (*Casually, as if nothing had happened*) However, if you like you may stay. I'll go by myself, and you come later, in a week. After all, where would you hurry to?

TRIGORIN. No, let's go together.

ARCADINA. As you like. Together, together then. (*A pause.* TRIGORIN *writes in notebook.*) What are you writing?

TRIGORIN. This morning I heard a happy expression: " Virgin forest." It might be useful in a story. (*Yawns.*) So, we're off. Once more the cars, stations, station buffets, stews, and conversations!

(SHAMREYEFF *enters.*)

SHAMREYEFF. I have the honor with deep regret to announce that the horses are ready. It's time, most esteemed lady, to be off to the station; the train arrives at five minutes after two. So will you do me the favor, Irina Nicolayevna, not to forget to inquire about this: Where's the actor Suzdaltsev [2] now? Is he alive? Is he well? We used to drink together once upon a time. In " The Stolen Mail " he was inimitable. In the same company with him at Elisavetgrad, I remember, was the tragedian Izmailov, also a remarkable personality. Don't hurry, most esteemed lady, there are five minutes still. Once in some melodrama they were playing conspirators, and when they were suddenly discovered, he had to say " We are caught in a trap," but Izmailov said, " We are traught in a clap." (*Laughs.*) Clap!

(YAKOV *is busy with luggage.* MAID *brings* ARCADINA's *hat, coat, parasol, gloves. All help her put them on. The* COOK *peers through door on Left, as if hesitating, then he comes in. Enter* PAULINE, SORIN, *and* MEDVEDENKO.)

PAULINE. (*With basket*) Here are some plums for the journey. They are sweet ones. In case you'd like some little thing.

[2] an actor of popular melodrama, like the " tragedian " Izmailov

ARCADINA. You are very kind, Pauline Andreyevna.

PAULINE. Goodbye, my dear: If anything has been not quite so, forgive it. (*Cries.*)

ARCADINA. (*Embracing her*) Everything has been charming, everything's been charming. Only you mustn't cry.

PAULINE. Time goes so.

ARCADINA. There's nothing we can do about that.

SORIN. (*In a greatcoat with a cape, his hat on and his stick in his hand, crossing the stage*) Sister, you'd better start if you don't want to be late. I'll go get in the carriage. (*Exits.*)

MEDVEDENKO. And I'll walk to the station — to see you off. I'll step lively.

ARCADINA. Goodbye, my friends. If we are alive and well next summer we'll meet again. (*The* MAID, COOK *and* YAKOV *kiss her hand.*) Don't forget me. (*Gives* COOK *a ruble.*) Here's a ruble for the three of you.

COOK. We humbly thank you, Madame. Pleasant journey to you. Many thanks to you.

YAKOV. God bless you!

SHAMREYEFF. Make us happy with a letter. Goodbye, Boris Alexeyevitch.

ARCADINA. Where's Constantine? Tell him I'm off now. I must say goodbye to him. Well, remember me kindly. (*To* YAKOV) I gave the cook a ruble. It's for the three of you.

(*All go out. The stage is empty. Off stage are heard the usual sounds when people are going away. The* MAID *comes back for the basket of plums from the table and goes out again.*)

TRIGORIN. (*Returning*) I forgot my stick. It's out there on the terrace, I think. (*As he starts to go out by the door on the Left, he meets* NINA *coming in.*) Is it you? We are just going —

NINA. I felt we should meet again. (*Excited*) Boris Alexeyevitch, I've come to a decision, the die is cast. I am going on the stage. Tomorrow I shall not be here. I am leaving my father, deserting everything, beginning a new life. I'm off like you — for Moscow — we shall meet there.

TRIGORIN. (*Glancing around him*) Stay at Hotel Slavyansky Bazaar. Let me know at once. Molchanovka, Groholsky House. I must hurry.

(*A pause.*)

NINA. One minute yet.

TRIGORIN. (*In a low voice*) You are so beautiful — Oh, how happy to think we'll be meeting soon. (*She puts her head on his breast.*) I shall see those lovely eyes again, that ineffably beautiful, tender smile — those gentle features, their pure, angelic expression — my darling —

(*A long kiss.*)

(*Two years pass between the Third and Fourth Acts.*)

ACT FOUR

One of the drawing rooms in SORIN'S *house, turned by* CONSTANTINE TREPLEFF *into a study. On the Right and Left, doors leading into other parts of the house. Facing us, glass doors on to the terrace. Besides the usual furniture of a drawing room, there is a writing table in the corner to the Right; near the door on the Left, a sofa, a bookcase full of books, and books in the windows and on the chairs.*

Evening. A single lamp with a shade is lighted. Semidarkness. The sound from outside of trees rustling and the wind howling in the chimney. The night watchman is knocking. MEDVEDENKO *and* MASHA *come in.*

MASHA. Constantine Gavrilovitch! Constantine Gavrilovitch! (*Looking around*) Nobody here. Every other minute all day long the old man keeps asking where's Kostya, where's Kostya? He can't live without him.

MEDVEDENKO. He's afraid to be alone. (*Listening*) What terrible weather! It's two days now.

MASHA. (*Turning up the lamp*) Out on the lake there are waves. Tremendous.

MEDVEDENKO. The garden's black. We ought to have told them to pull down that stage. It stands all bare and hideous, like a skeleton, and the curtain flaps in the wind. When I passed there last night it seemed to me that in the wind I heard someone crying.

MASHA. Well, here — (*Pause.*)

MEDVEDENKO. Masha, let's go home.

MASHA. (*Shakes her head.*) I'm going to stay here tonight.

MEDVEDENKO. (*Imploring*) Masha, let's go. Our baby must be hungry.

MASHA. Nonsense. Matriona will feed it.

(*A pause.*)

MEDVEDENKO. It's hard on him. He's been three nights now without his mother.

MASHA. You're getting just too tiresome. In the old days you'd at least philosophize a little, but now it's all baby, home, baby, home — and that's all I can get out of you.

MEDVEDENKO. Let's go, Masha.

MASHA. Go yourself.

MEDVEDENKO. Your father won't let me have a horse.

MASHA. He will if you just ask him.

MEDVEDENKO. Very well, I'll try. Then you'll come tomorrow.

MASHA. (*Taking snuff*) Well, tomorrow. Stop bothering me.

(*Enter* TREPLEFF *and* PAULINE; TREPLEFF *carries pillows and a blanket,* PAULINE *sheets and pillowcases. They lay them on the sofa, then* TREPLEFF *goes and sits down at his desk.*)

MASHA. Why's that, Mama?

PAULINE. Peter Nicolayevitch asked to sleep in Kostya's room.

MASHA. Let me — (*She makes the bed.*)

PAULINE. (*Sighing*) Old people, what children — (*Goes to the desk. Leaning on her elbows she gazes at the manuscript. A pause.*)

MEDVEDENKO. So I'm going. Goodbye, Masha. (*Kisses her hand.*) Goodbye, Mother. (*Tries to kiss her hand.*)

PAULINE. (*With annoyance*) Well, go if you're going.

MEDVEDENKO. Goodbye, Constantine Gavrilovitch.

(*TREPLEFF without speaking gives him his hand.* MEDVEDENKO *goes out.*)

PAULINE. (*Gazing at the manuscript*) Nobody ever thought or dreamed that some day,

Kostya, you'd turn out to be a real author. But now, thank God, the magazines send you money for your stories. (*Passing her hand over his hair*) And you've grown handsome — dear, good Kostya, be kind to my little Masha.

MASHA. (*Making the bed*) Let him alone, Mama.

PAULINE. She's a sweet little thing. (*A pause.*) A woman, Kostya, doesn't ask much — only kind looks. As I well know.

(TREPLEFF *rises from the desk and without speaking goes out.*)

MASHA. You shouldn't have bothered him.

PAULINE. I feel sorry for you, Masha.

MASHA. Why should you?

PAULINE. My heart aches and aches for you. I see it all, I understand everything.

MASHA. It's all foolishness! Hopeless love — that's only in novels. No matter. Only you mustn't let yourself go, and be always waiting for something, waiting for fine weather by the sea. If love stirs in your heart, stamp it out. Now they've promised to transfer my husband to another district. As soon as we get there — I'll forget it all — I'll tear it out of my heart by the roots.

(*Two rooms off is heard a melancholy waltz.*)

PAULINE. Kostya is playing. That means he's feeling sad.

MASHA. (*Waltzes silently a few turns.*) The great thing, Mama, is to be where I don't see him. If only my Semyon could get his transfer, I promise you I'd forget in a month. It's all nonsense.

(*Door on Left opens.* DORN *and* MEDVEDENKO *come in, wheeling* SORIN *in his chair.*)

MEDVEDENKO. I have six souls at home now. And flour at seventy kopecks.

DORN. So it just goes round and round.

MEDVEDENKO. It's easy for you to smile. You've got more money than the chickens could pick up.

DORN. Money! After practicing medicine thirty years, my friend, so driven day and night that I could never call my soul my own, I managed to save up at last two thou-

sand rubles; and I've just spent all that on a trip abroad. I've got nothing at all.

MASHA. (*To her husband*) Aren't you gone yet?

MEDVEDENKO. (*Apologizing*) How can I, when they won't let me have a horse?

MASHA. (*Under her breath angrily*) I wish I'd never lay eyes on you again.

(SORIN's *wheel chair remains Left Center.* PAULINE, MASHA, *and* DORN *sit down beside him.* MEDVEDENKO *stands to one side gloomily.*)

DORN. Look how many changes they have made here! The drawing room is turned into a study.

MASHA. Constantine Gavrilovitch likes to work in here. He can go into the garden whenever he likes and think.

(*A watchman's rattle sounds.*)

SORIN. Where's my sister?

DORN. She went to the station to meet Trigorin. She'll be right back.

SORIN. If you thought you had to send for my sister, that shows I'm very ill. (*Reflecting*) Now that's odd, isn't it? I'm very ill, but they won't let me have any medicine around here.

DORN. And what would you like? Valerian drops? Soda? Quinine?

SORIN. So it's more philosophy, I suppose. Oh, what an affliction! (*He motions with his head toward the sofa.*) Is that for me?

PAULINE. Yes, for you, Peter Nicolayevitch.

SORIN. Thank you.

DORN. (*Singing sotto voce*) " The moon drifts in the sky tonight."

SORIN. Listen, I want to give Kostya a subject for a story. It should be called: " The Man Who Wanted To " — *L'homme qui a voulu.* In my youth long ago I wanted to become an author — and never became one; wanted to speak eloquently — and spoke execrably (*Mimicking himself*) and so on and so forth, and all the rest of it, yes and no, and in the résumé would drag on, drag on, till the sweat broke out; wanted to marry — and never married; wanted always to live in town — and now am ending up my life in the country, and so on.

DORN. Wanted to become a State Counsellor — and became one.

SORIN. (*Laughing*) For that I never longed. That came to me of itself.

DORN. Come now, to be picking faults with life at sixty-two, you must confess, that's not magnanimous.

SORIN. How bullheaded you are! Can't you take it in? I want to live.

DORN. That's frivolous; it's the law of nature that every life must come to an end.

SORIN. You argue like a man who's had his fill. You've had your fill and so you're indifferent to living, it's all one to you. But at that even you will be afraid to die.

DORN. The fear of death — a brute fear. We must overcome it. The fear of death is reasonable only in those who believe in an eternal life, and shudder to think of the sins they have committed. But you in the first place don't believe, in the second place what sins have you? For twenty-five years you served as State Counsellor — and that's all.

SORIN. (*Laughing*) Twenty-eight.

(TREPLEFF *enters and sits on the stool beside* SORIN. MASHA *never takes her eyes off his face.*)

DORN. We are keeping Constantine Gavrilovitch from his work.

TREPLEFF. No, it's nothing.

(*A pause.*)

MEDVEDENKO. Permit me to ask you, Doctor, what town in your travels did you most prefer?

DORN. Genoa.

TREPLEFF. Why Genoa?

DORN. Because of the marvelous street crowd. When you go out of your hotel in the evening you find the whole street surging with people. You let yourself drift among the crowd, zigzagging back and forth, you live its life, its soul pours into you, until finally you begin to believe there might really be a world spirit after all, like that Nina Zaretchny acted in your play. By the way, where is Nina just now? Where is she and how is she?

TREPLEFF. Very well, I imagine.

DORN. I've been told she was leading rather an odd sort of life. How's that?

TREPLEFF. It's a long story, Doctor.

DORN. You can shorten it.

(*A pause.*)

TREPLEFF. She ran away from home and joined Trigorin. That you knew?

DORN. I know.

TREPLEFF. She had a child. The child died. Trigorin got tired of her, and went back to his old ties, as might be expected. He'd never broken these old ties anyhow, but flitted in that backboneless style of his from one to the other. As far as I could say from what I know, Nina's private life didn't quite work out.

DORN. And on the stage?

TREPLEFF. I believe even worse. She made her debut in Moscow at a summer theater, and afterward a tour in the provinces. At that time I never let her out of my sight, and wherever she was I was. She always attempted big parts, but her acting was crude, without any taste, her gestures were clumsy. There were moments when she did some talented screaming, talented dying, but those were only moments.

DORN. It means, though, she has talent?

TREPLEFF. I could never make out. I imagine she has. I saw her, but she didn't want to see me, and her maid wouldn't let me in her rooms. I understood how she felt, and never insisted on seeing her. (*A pause.*) What more is there to tell you? Afterward, when I'd come back home here, she wrote me some letters. They were clever, tender, interesting; she didn't complain, but I could see she was profoundly unhappy; there was not a word that didn't show her exhausted nerves. And she'd taken a strange fancy. She always signed herself the sea gull. In "The Mermaid" the miller says that he's a crow; the same way in all her letters she kept repeating she was a sea gull. Now she's here.

DORN. How do you mean, here?

TREPLEFF. In town, staying at the inn. She's already been here five days, living there in rooms. Masha drove in, but she never sees anybody. Semyon Semyonovitch declares that last night after dinner he saw her in the fields, a mile and a half from here.

MEDVEDENKO. Yes, I saw her. (*A pause.*) Going in the opposite direction from here, toward town. I bowed to her, asked why she had not been out to see us. She said she'd come.

TREPLEFF. Well, she won't. (*A pause.*) Her father and stepmother don't want to know her. They've set watchmen to keep her off the grounds. (*Goes toward the desk with* DORN.) How easy it is, Doctor, to be a philosopher on paper, and how hard it is in life!

SORIN. She was a beautiful girl.

DORN. How's that?

SORIN. I say she was a beautiful girl. State Counsellor Sorin was downright in love with her himself once for a while.

DORN. You old Lovelace! [1]

(*They hear* SHAMREYEFF's *laugh.*)

PAULINE. I imagine they're back from the station.

TREPLEFF. Yes, I hear Mother.

(*Enter* MADAME ARCADINA *and* TRIGORIN, SHAMREYEFF *following.*)

SHAMREYEFF. We all get old and fade with the elements, esteemed lady, but you, most honored lady, are still young — white dress, vivacity — grace.

ARCADINA. You still want to bring me bad luck, you tiresome creature!

TRIGORIN. (*To* SORIN) Howdy do, Peter Nicolayevitch. How is it you are still indisposed? That's not so good. (*Pleased at seeing* MASHA) Masha Ilyinishna!

MASHA. You know me? (*Grasps his hand.*)

TRIGORIN. Married?

MASHA. Long ago.

TRIGORIN. Are you happy? (*Bows to* DORN *and* MEDVEDENKO, *then hesitatingly goes to* TREPLEFF.) Irina Nicolayevna tells me you have forgotten the past and given up being angry.

(*TREPLEFF holds out his hand.*)

ARCADINA. (*To her son*) Look, Boris Alexeyevitch has brought you the magazine with your last story.

[1] the seducer in Richardson's novel, *Clarissa Harlowe;* hence, a rake

TREPLEFF. (*Taking the magazine. To* TRIGORIN) Thank you. You're very kind.

(*They sit down.*)

TRIGORIN. Your admirers send their respects to you. In Petersburg and in Moscow, everywhere, there's a great deal of interest in your work, and they all ask me about you. They ask: what is he like, what age is he, is he dark or fair? For some reason they all think you are no longer young. And nobody knows your real name, since you always publish under a pseudonym. You're a mystery, like the Man in the Iron Mask.

TREPLEFF. Will you be with us long?

TRIGORIN. No, tomorrow I think I'll go to Moscow. I must. I'm in a hurry to finish a story, and besides I've promised to write something for an annual. In a word it's the same old thing.

(MADAME ARCADINA *and* PAULINE *have set up a card table.* SHAMREYEFF *lights candles, arranges chairs, gets box of lotto from a cupboard.*)

TRIGORIN. The weather's given me a poor welcome. The wind is ferocious. Tomorrow morning if it dies down I'm going out to the lake to fish. And I want to look around the garden and the place where — do you remember? — your play was done. The idea for a story is all worked out in my mind, I want only to refresh my memory of the place where it's laid.

MASHA. Papa, let my husband have a horse! He must get home.

SHAMREYEFF. (*Mimics.*) A horse — home. (*Sternly*) See for yourself: they are just back from the station. They'll not go out again.

MASHA. They're not the only horses — (*Seeing that he says nothing, she makes an impatient gesture.*) Nobody can do anything with you —

MEDVEDENKO. I can walk, Masha. Truly —

PAULINE. (*Sighs.*) Walk, in such weather! (*Sits down at card table.*) Sit down, friends.

MEDVEDENKO. It's only four miles — Goodbye. (*Kisses wife's hand.*) Goodbye,

Mama. (*His mother-in-law puts out her hand reluctantly.*) I should not have troubled anybody, but the little baby — (*Bowing to them*) Goodbye. (*He goes out as if apologizing.*)

SHAMREYEFF. He'll make it. He's not a general.

PAULINE. (*Taps on table.*) Sit down, friends. Let's not lose time, they'll be calling us to supper soon.

(SHAMREYEFF, MASHA, *and* DORN *sit at the card table.*)

ARCADINA. (*To* TRIGORIN) When these long autumn evenings draw on we pass the time out here with lotto. And look: the old lotto set we had when my mother used to play with us children. Don't you want to take a hand with us till suppertime? (*She and* TRIGORIN *sit down at the table.*) It's a tiresome game, but it does well enough when you're used to it. (*She deals three cards to each one.*)

TREPLEFF. (*Turns magazine pages.*) He's read his own story, but mine he hasn't even cut. (*He lays the magazine on the desk; on his way out, as he passes his mother, he kisses her on the head.*)

ARCADINA. But you, Kostya?

TREPLEFF. Sorry, I don't care to. I'm going for a walk. (*Goes out.*)

ARCADINA. Stake — ten kopecks. Put it down for me, Doctor.

DORN. Command me.

MASHA. Has everybody bet? I'll begin. Twenty-two.

ARCADINA. I have it.

MASHA. Three.

DORN. Here you are.

MASHA. Did you put down three? Eight! Eighty-one! Ten!

SHAMREYEFF. Not so fast.

ARCADINA. What a reception they gave me at Kharkoff! Can you believe it, my head's spinning yet.

MASHA. Thirty-four.

(*A sad waltz is heard.*)

ARCADINA. The students gave me an ovation, three baskets of flowers, two wreaths

and look — (*She takes off a brooch and puts it on the table.*)

SHAMREYEFF. Yes, that's the real —

MASHA. Fifty!

DORN. Fifty, you say?

ARCADINA. I had a superb costume. Say what you like, but really when it comes to dressing myself I am no fool.

PAULINE. Kostya is playing. The poor boy's sad.

SHAMREYEFF. In the papers they often abuse him.

MASHA. Seventy-seven.

ARCADINA. Who cares what they say?

TRIGORIN. He hasn't any luck. He still can't discover how to write a style of his own. There is something strange, vague, at times even like delirious raving. Not a single character that is alive.

MASHA. Eleven!

ARCADINA. (*Glancing at* SORIN) Petrusha, are you bored? (*A pause.*) He's asleep.

DORN. He's asleep, the State Counsellor.

MASHA. Seven! Ninety!

TRIGORIN. Do you think if I lived in such a place as this and by this lake, I would write? I should overcome such a passion and devote my life to fishing.

MASHA. Twenty-eight!

TRIGORIN. To catch a perch or a bass — that's something like happiness!

DORN. Well, I believe in Constantine Gavrilovitch. He has something! He has something! He thinks in images, his stories are bright and full of color, I always feel them strongly. It's only a pity that he's got no definite purpose. He creates impressions, never more than that, but on mere impressions you don't go far. Irina Nicolayevna, are you glad your son is a writer?

ARCADINA. Imagine, I have not read him yet. There's never time.

MASHA. Twenty-six!

(TREPLEFF *enters without saying anything, sits at his desk.*)

SHAMREYEFF. And, Boris Alexeyevitch, we've still got something of yours here.

TRIGORIN. What's that?

SHAMREYEFF. Somehow or other Constantine Gavrilovitch shot a sea gull, and you asked me to have it stuffed for you.

TRIGORIN. I don't remember. (*Reflecting*) I don't remember.

MASHA. Sixty-six! One!

TREPLEFF. (*Throwing open the window, stands listening.*) How dark! I don't know why I feel so uneasy.

ARCADINA. Kostya, shut the window, there's a draft.

(TREPLEFF *shuts window.*)

MASHA. Ninety-eight.

TRIGORIN. I've made a game.

ARCADINA. (*Gaily*) Bravo! Bravo!

SHAMREYEFF. Bravo!

ARCADINA. This man's lucky in everything, always. (*Rises.*) And now let's go have a bite of something. Our celebrated author didn't have any dinner today. After supper we'll go on. Kostya, leave your manuscript, come have something to eat.

TREPLEFF. I don't want to, Mother, I've had enough.

ARCADINA. As you please. (*Wakes* SORIN.) Petrusha, supper! (*Takes* SHAMREYEFF's *arm.*) I'll tell you how they received me in Kharkoff.

(PAULINE *blows out candles on table. She and* DORN *wheel* SORIN's *chair out of the room. All but* TREPLEFF *go out. He gets ready to write. Runs his eye over what's already written.*)

TREPLEFF. I've talked so much about new forms, but now I feel that little by little I am slipping into mere routine myself. (*Reads.*) " The placards on the wall proclaimed " — " pale face in a frame of dark hair " — frame — that's flat. (*Scratches out what he's written.*) I'll begin again where the hero is awakened by the rain, and throw out all the rest. This description of a moonlight night is too long and too precious. Trigorin has worked out his own method, it's easy for him. With him a broken bottleneck lying on the dam glitters in the moonlight and the mill wheel casts a black shadow — and there before you is the moonlit night; but with me it's the shimmering light, and the silent twinkling of the stars, and the far-off sound of a piano dying away in the still, sweet-scented air. It's painful. (*A pause.*) Yes, I'm coming more and more to the conclusion that it's a matter not of old forms and not of new forms, but that a man writes, not thinking at all of what form to choose, writes because it comes pouring out from his soul. (*A tap at the window nearest the desk*) What's that? (*Looks out.*) I don't see anything. (*Opens the door and peers into the garden.*) Someone ran down the steps. (*Calls.*) Who's there? (*Goes out. The sound of his steps along the veranda. A moment later returns with* NINA.) Nina! Nina! (*She lays her head on his breast, with restrained sobbing.*)

TREPLEFF. (*Moved*) Nina! Nina! It's you — you. I had a presentment, all day my soul was tormented. (*Takes off her hat and cape.*) Oh, my sweet, my darling, she has come! Let's not cry, let's not.

NINA. There's someone here.

TREPLEFF. No one.

NINA. Lock the doors. Someone might come in.

TREPLEFF. Nobody's coming in.

NINA. I know Irina Nicolayevna is here. Lock the doors.

TREPLEFF. (*Locks door on Right. Goes to door on Left.*) This one doesn't lock. I'll put a chair against it. (*Puts chair against door.*) Don't be afraid, nobody's coming in.

NINA. (*As if studying his face*) Let me look at you. (*Glancing around her*) It's warm, cozy — This used to be the drawing room. Am I very much changed?

TREPLEFF. Yes — you are thinner and your eyes are bigger. Nina, how strange it is I'm seeing you. Why wouldn't you let me come to see you? Why didn't you come sooner? I know you've been here now for nearly a week. I have been every day there where you were, I stood under your window like a beggar.

NINA. I was afraid you might hate me. I dream every night that you look at me and don't recognize me. If you only knew! Ever since I came I've been here walking about — by the lake. I've been near your house often, and couldn't make up my mind to come in. Let's sit down. (*They sit.*) Let's sit down and let's talk, talk. It's pleasant here, warm, cozy — You hear — the wind? There's a place in Turgenev: " Happy is he who on such a night is under his own roof, who has a warm corner." I — a sea gull — no, that's not it. (*Rubs her forehead.*) What was I saying? Yes — Turgenev. " And may the Lord help all homeless wanderers." It's nothing. (*Sobs.*)

TREPLEFF. Nina, again — Nina!

NINA. It's nothing. It will make me feel better. I've not cried for two years. Last night I came to the garden to see whether our theater was still there, and it's there still. I cried for the first time in two years, and my heart grew lighter and my soul was clearer. Look, I'm not crying now. (*Takes his hand.*) You are an author, I — an actress. We have both been drawn into the whirlpool. I used to be as happy as a child. I used to wake up in the morning singing. I loved you and dreamed of being famous, and now? Tomorrow early I must go to Yelets in the third class [2] — with peasants, and at Yelets the cultured merchants will plague me with attentions. Life's brutal!

TREPLEFF. Why Yelets?

NINA. I've taken an engagement there for the winter. It's time I was going.

TREPLEFF. Nina, I cursed you and hated you. I tore up all your letters, tore up your photograph, and yet I knew every minute that my heart was bound to yours forever. It's not in my power to stop loving you, Nina. Ever since I lost you and began to get my work published, my life has been unbearable — I am miserable — All of a sudden my youth was snatched from me, and now I feel as if I'd been living in the world for ninety years. I call out to you, I kiss the ground you walk on, I see your face wherever I look, the tender smile that shone on me those best years of my life.

NINA. (*In despair*) Why does he talk like that? Why does he talk like that?

TREPLEFF. I'm alone, not warmed by any-

[2] the cheapest coach on European railways

body's affection. I'm all chilled — it's cold like living in a cave. And no matter what I write it's dry, gloomy, and harsh. Stay here, Nina, if you only would! And if you won't, then take me with you.

(NINA *quickly puts on her hat and cape.*)

TREPLEFF. Nina, why? For God's sake, Nina. (*He is looking at her as she puts her things on. A pause.*)

NINA. My horses are just out there. Don't see me off. I'll manage by myself. (*Sobbing*) Give me some water.

(*He gives her a glass of water.*)

TREPLEFF. Where are you going now?

NINA. To town. (*A pause.*) Is Irina Nicolayevna here?

TREPLEFF. Yes. Thursday my uncle was not well, we telegraphed her to come.

NINA. Why do you say you kiss the ground I walk on? I ought to be killed. (*Bends over desk.*) I'm so tired. If I could rest — rest. I'm a sea gull. No, that's not it. I'm an actress. Well, no matter — (*Hears* ARCADINA *and* TRIGORIN *laughing in the dining room. She listens, runs to door on the Left and peeps through the keyhole.*) And he's here too. (*Goes to* TREPLEFF.) Well, no matter. He didn't believe in the theater, all my dreams he'd laugh at, and little by little I quit believing in it myself, and lost heart. And there was the strain of love, jealousy, constant anxiety about my little baby. I got to be small and trashy, and played without thinking. I didn't know what to do with my hands, couldn't stand properly on the stage, couldn't control my voice. You can't imagine the feeling when you are acting and know it's dull. I'm a sea gull. No, that's not it. Do you remember, you shot a sea gull? A man comes by chance, sees it, and out of nothing else to do, destroys it. That's not it — (*Puts her hand to her forehead.*) What was I — ? I was talking about the stage. Now I'm not like that. I'm a real actress, I act with delight, with rapture, I'm drunk when I'm on the stage, and feel that I am beautiful. And now, ever since I've been here, I've kept walking about, kept walking and thinking, thinking and

The Sea Gull, Act Four. See page 358. Alfred Lunt as Trigorin, Lynn Fontanne as Mme. Arcadina. Photo by Vandamm.

believing my soul grows stronger every day. Now I know, I understand, Kostya, that in our work — acting or writing — what matters is not fame, not glory, not what I used to dream about, it's how to endure, to bear my cross, and have faith. I have faith and it all doesn't hurt me so much, and when I think of my calling I'm not afraid of life.

TREPLEFF. (*Sadly*) You've found your way, you know where you are going, but I still move in a chaos of images and dreams, not knowing why or who it's for. I have no faith, and I don't know where my calling lies.

NINA. (*Listening*) Ssh — I'm going. Goodbye. When I'm a great actress, come and look at me. You promise? But now — (*Takes his hand.*) It's late. I can hardly stand on my feet, I feel faint. I'd like something to eat.

TREPLEFF. Stay, I'll bring you some supper here.

NINA. No, no — I can manage by myself. The horses are just out there. So, she brought him along with her? But that's all one. When you see Trigorin — don't ever tell him anything. I love him. I love him even more than before. "An idea for a short story." I love, I love passionately, I love to desperation. How nice it used to be, Kostya! You remember? How gay and warm and pure our life was; what things we felt, tender, delicate like flowers. Do you remember? "Men and beasts, lions, eagles and partridges, antlered deer, mute fishes dwelling in the water, starfish and small creatures invisible to the eye — these and all life have run their sad course and are no more. Thousands of creatures have come and gone since there was life on the earth. Vainly now the pallid moon doth light her lamp. In the meadows the cranes wake and cry no longer; and the beetles' hum is silent in the linden groves." (*Impulsively embraces* TREPLEFF, *and runs out by the terrace door.*)

(*A pause.*)

TREPLEFF. Too bad if anyone meets her in the garden and tells Mother. That might upset Mother. (*He stands for two minutes tearing up all his manuscripts and throwing them under the desk, then unlocks door on Right, and goes out.*)

DORN. (*Trying to open the door on the Left*) That's funny. This door seems to be locked. (*Enters and puts chair back in its place.*) A regular obstacle race —

(*Enter* MADAME ARCADINA *and* PAULINE, *behind them* YAKOV *with a tray and bottles;* MASHA, *then* SHAMREYEFF *and* TRIGORIN.)

ARCADINA. Put the claret and the beer for Boris Alexeyevitch here on the table. We'll play and drink. Let's sit down, friends.

PAULINE. (*To* YAKOV) Bring the tea now, too. (*Lights the candles and sits down.*)

SHAMREYEFF. (*Leading* TRIGORIN *to the cupboard*) Here's the thing I was telling you about just now. By your order.

TRIGORIN. (*Looking at the sea gull*) I don't remember. (*Reflecting*) I don't remember.

(*Sound of a shot off stage Right. Everybody jumps.*)

ARCADINA. (*Alarmed*) What's that?

DORN. Nothing. It must be — in my medicine case — something blew up. Don't you worry. (*He goes out Right, in a moment returns.*) So it was. A bottle of ether blew up. (*Sings.*) "Again I stand before thee."

ARCADINA. (*Sitting down at the table*) Phew, I was frightened! It reminded me of how — (*Puts her hands over her face.*) Everything's black before my eyes.

DORN. (*Turning through the magazine, to* TRIGORIN) About two months ago in this magazine there was an article — a letter from America — and I wanted to ask you among other things — (*Puts his arm around* TRIGORIN'S *waist and leads him toward the front of the stage.*) since I'm very much interested in this question. (*Dropping his voice*) Get Irina Nicolayevna somewhere away from here. The fact is Constantine Gavrilovitch has shot himself.

THE EMPEROR JONES

A PLAY IN EIGHT SCENES

by Eugene O'Neill

CHARACTERS

BRUTUS JONES, emperor

HENRY SMITHERS, a Cockney trader

LEM, a native chief

SOLDIERS, adherents of Lem

AN OLD NATIVE WOMAN

The Little Formless Fears

Jeff

The Negro Convicts

The Prison Guard

The Planters

The Auctioneer

The Slaves

The Congo Witch Doctor

The Crocodile God

The action of the play takes place on an island in the West Indies as yet not self-determined by White Marines. The form of native government is, for the time being, an empire.

SCENE ONE

SCENE — *The audience chamber in the palace of the Emperor — a spacious, high-ceilinged room with bare, white-washed walls. The floor is of white tiles. In the rear, to the left of center, a wide archway giving out on a portico with white pillars. The palace is evidently situated on high ground, for beyond the portico nothing can be seen but a vista of distant hills, their summits crowned with thick groves of palm trees. In the right wall, center, a smaller arched doorway leading to the living quarters of the palace. The room is bare of furniture with the exception of one huge chair made of uncut wood which stands at center, its back to rear. This is very apparently the Emperor's throne. It is painted a dazzling, eye-smiting*
scarlet. *There is a brilliant orange cushion on the seat and another smaller one is placed on the floor to serve as a footstool. Strips of matting, dyed scarlet, lead from the foot of the throne to the two entrances.*

It is late afternoon, but the sunlight still blazes yellowly beyond the portico and there is an oppressive burden of exhausting heat in the air.

As the curtain rises, a native Negro woman sneaks in cautiously from the entrance on the right. She is very old, dressed in cheap calico, bare-footed, a red bandana handkerchief covering all but a few stray wisps of white hair. A bundle bound in colored cloth is carried over her shoulder on the end of a stick. She hesitates beside the doorway, peering back as if in extreme dread of being discovered. Then she begins to glide

359

noiselessly, a step at a time, toward the doorway in the rear. At this moment, SMITHERS *appears beneath the portico.*

SMITHERS *is a tall, stoop-shouldered man about forty. His bald head, perched on a long neck with an enormous Adam's apple, looks like an egg. The tropics have tanned his naturally pasty face with its small, sharp features to a sickly yellow, and native rum has painted his pointed nose to a startling red. His little, washy-blue eyes are red-rimmed and dart about him like a ferret's. His expression is one of unscrupulous meanness, cowardly and dangerous. He is dressed in a worn riding suit of dirty white drill, puttees, spurs, and wears a white cork helmet. A cartridge belt with an automatic revolver is around his waist. He carries a riding whip in his hand. He sees the woman and stops to watch her suspiciously. Then, making up his mind, he steps quickly on tiptoe into the room. The woman, looking back over her shoulder continually, does not see him until it is too late. When she does* SMITHERS *springs forward and grabs her firmly by the shoulder. She struggles to get away, fiercely but silently.*

SMITHERS. (*Tightening his grasp — roughly*) Easy! None o' that, me birdie. You can't wriggle out now. I got me 'ooks on yer.

WOMAN. (*Seeing the uselessness of struggling, gives way to frantic terror, and sinks to the ground, embracing his knees supplicatingly*) No tell him! No tell him, Mister!

SMITHERS. (*With great curiosity*) Tell 'im? (*Then scornfully*) Oh, you mean 'is bloomin' Majesty. What's the gaime, any 'ow? What are you sneakin' away for? Been stealin' a bit, I s'pose. (*He taps her bundle with his riding whip significantly.*)

WOMAN. (*Shaking her head vehemently*) No, me no steal.

SMITHERS. Bloody liar! But tell me what's up. There's somethin' funny goin' on. I smelled it in the air first thing I got up this mornin'. You blacks are up to some devil-ment. This palace of 'is is like a bleedin' tomb. Where's all the 'ands? (*The woman keeps sullenly silent.* SMITHERS *raises his whip threateningly.*) Ow, yer won't, won't yer? I'll show yer what's what.

WOMAN. (*Coweringly*) I tell, Mister. You no hit. They go — all go. (*She makes a sweeping gesture toward the hills in the distance.*)

SMITHERS. Run away — to the 'ills?

WOMAN. Yes, Mister. Him Emperor — Great Father. (*She touches her forehead to the floor with a quick mechanical jerk.*) Him sleep after eat. Then they go — all go. Me old woman. Me left only. Now me go too.

SMITHERS. (*His astonishment giving way to an immense, mean satisfaction*) Ow! So that's the ticket! Well, I know bloody well wot's in the air — when they runs orf to the 'ills. The tom-tom 'll be thumping out there bloomin' soon. (*With extreme vindictiveness*) And I'm bloody glad of it, for one! Serve 'im right! Puttin' on airs, the stinkin' nigger! 'Is Majesty! Gawd blimey! I only 'opes I'm there when they takes 'im out to shoot 'im. (*Suddenly*) 'E's still 'ere all right, ain't 'e?

WOMAN. Yes, him sleep.

SMITHERS. 'E's bound to find out soon as 'e wakes up. 'E's cunnin' enough to know when 'is time's come. (*He goes to the doorway on right and whistles shrilly with his fingers in his mouth. The old woman springs to her feet and runs out of the doorway, rear.* SMITHERS *goes after her, reaching for his revolver.*) Stop or I'll shoot! (*Then stopping — indifferently*) Pop orf then, if yer like, yer black cow. (*He stands in the doorway, looking after her.*)

(JONES *enters from the right. He is a tall, powerfully-built, full-blooded Negro of middle age. His features are typically negroid, yet there is something decidedly distinctive about his face — an underlying strength of will, a hardy, self-reliant confidence in himself that inspires respect. His eyes are alive with a keen, cunning intelligence. In manner he is shrewd, suspicious, evasive. He wears a light blue uniform coat, sprayed with brass buttons, heavy gold chevrons on his shoulders, gold braid on the collar, cuffs, etc. His pants are bright red with a light blue stripe down the side. Patent-leather laced boots with brass spurs, and a belt with a long-barreled, pearl-handled revolver in a holster complete his make-up. Yet there is something not altogether ridicu-*

comfiture) Don't yer notice nothin' funny today?

JONES. (*Coldly*) Funny? No. I ain't perceived nothin' of de kind!

SMITHERS. Then yer ain't so foxy as I thought yer was. Where's all your court? (*Sarcastically*) The Generals and the Cabinet Ministers and all?

JONES. (*Imperturbably*) **Where dey**

The Emperor Jones, Scene One. Theater Collection, New York Public Library.

lous about his grandeur. He has a way of carrying it off.)

JONES. (*Not seeing anyone — greatly irritated and blinking sleepily — shouts*) Who dare whistle dat way in my palace? Who dare wake up de Emperor? I'll git de hide fravled off some o' you niggers sho'!

SMITHERS. (*Showing himself — in a manner half-afraid and half-defiant*) It was me whistled to yer. (*As* JONES *frowns angrily*) I got news for yer.

JONES. (*Putting on his suavest manner, which fails to cover up his contempt for the white man*) Oh, it's you, Mister Smithers. (*He sits down on his throne with easy dignity.*) What news you got to tell me?

SMITHERS. (*Coming close to enjoy his dis-*

mostly runs de minute I closes my eyes — drinkin' rum and talkin' big down in de town. (*Sarcastically*) How come you don't know dat? Ain't you sousin' with 'em most every day?

SMITHERS. (*Stung but pretending indifference — with a wink*) That's part of the day's work. I got ter — ain't I — in my business?

JONES. (*Contemptuously*) Yo' business!

SMITHERS. (*Imprudently enraged*) Gawd blimey, you was glad enough for me ter take yer in on it when you landed here first. You didn' 'ave no 'igh and mighty airs in them days!

JONES. (*His hand going to his revolver like a flash — menacingly*) Talk polite, white man! Talk polite, you heah me! I'm boss heah now, is you fergettin'? (*The Cockney seems about to challenge this last statement with the facts but something in the other's eyes holds and cows him.*)

SMITHERS. (*In a cowardly whine*) No 'arm meant, old top.

JONES. (*Condescendingly*) I accepts yo' apology. (*Lets his hand fall from his revolver.*) No use'n you rakin' up ole times. What I was den is one thing. What I is now 's another. You didn't let me in on yo' crooked work out o' no kind feelin's dat time. I done de dirty work fo' you — and most o' de brain work, too, fo' dat matter — and I was wu'th money to you, dat's de reason.

SMITHERS. Well, blimey, I give yer a start, didn't I — when no one else would. I wasn't afraid to 'ire yer like the rest was — 'count of the story about your breakin' jail back in the States.

JONES. No, you didn't have no s'cuse to look down on me fo' dat. You been in jail you'self more'n once.

SMITHERS. (*Furiously*) It's a lie! (*Then trying to pass it off by an attempt at scorn*) Garn! Who told yer that fairy tale?

JONES. Dey's some tings I ain't got to be tole. I kin see 'em in folk's eyes. (*Then after a pause — meditatively*) Yes, you sho' give me a start. And it didn't take long from dat time to git dese fool woods' niggers right where I wanted dem. (*With pride*) From stowaway to Emperor in two years! Dat's goin' some!

SMITHERS. (*With curiosity*) And I bet you got yer pile o' money 'id safe some place.

JONES. (*With satisfaction*) I sho' has! And it's in a foreign bank where no pusson don't ever git it out but me no matter what come. You didn't s'pose I was holdin' down dis Emperor job for de glory in it, did you? Sho'! De fuss and glory part of it, dat's only to turn de heads o' de low-flung, bush niggers dat's here. Dey wants de big circus show for deir money. I gives it to 'em an' I gits de money. (*With a grin*) De long green, dat's me every time! (*Then rebukingly*) But

you ain't got no kick agin me, Smithers. I'se paid you back all you done for me many times. Ain't I pertected you and winked at all de crooked tradin' you been doin' right out in de broad day? Sho' I has — and me makin' laws to stop it at de same time! (*He chuckles.*)

SMITHERS. (*Grinning*) But, meanin' no 'arm, you been grabbin' right and left yourself, ain't yer? Look at the taxes you've put on 'em! Blimey! You've squeezed 'em dry!

JONES. (*Chuckling*) No, dey ain't *all* dry yet. I'se still heah, ain't I?

SMITHERS. (*Smiling at his secret thought*) They're dry right now, you'll find out. (*Changing the subject abruptly*) And as for me breakin' laws, you've broke 'em all yerself just as fast as yer made 'em.

JONES. Ain't I de Emperor? De laws don't go for him. (*Judicially*) You heah what I tells you, Smithers. Dere's little stealin' like you does, and dere's big stealin' like I does. For de little stealin' dey gits you in jail soon or late. For de big stealin' dey makes you Emperor and puts you in de Hall o' Fame when you croaks. (*Reminiscently*) If dey's one thing I learns in ten years on de Pullman ca's listenin' to de white quality talk, it's dat same fact. And when I gits a chance to use it I winds up Emperor in two years.

SMITHERS. (*Unable to repress the genuine admiration of the small fry for the large*) Yes, yer turned the bleedin' trick, all right. Blimey, I never seen a bloke 'as 'ad the bloomin' luck you 'as.

JONES. (*Severely*) Luck? What you mean — luck?

SMITHERS. I suppose you'll say as that swank about the silver bullet ain't luck — and that was what first got the fool blacks on yer side the time of the revolution, wasn't it?

JONES. (*With a laugh*) Oh, dat silver bullet! Sho' was luck! But I makes dat luck, you heah? I loads de dice! Yessuh! When dat murderin' nigger ole Lem hired to kill me takes aim ten feet away and his gun misses fire and I shoots him dead, what you heah me say?

SMITHERS. You said yer'd got a charm so's no lead bullet'd kill yer. You was so strong only a silver bullet could kill yer, you told 'em. Blimey, wasn't that swank for yer — and plain, fat-'eaded luck?

JONES. (*Proudly*) I got brains and I uses 'em quick. Dat ain't luck.

SMITHERS. Yer know they wasn't 'ardly liable to get no silver bullets. And it was luck 'e didn't 'it you that time.

JONES. (*Laughing*) And dere all dem fool, bush niggers was kneelin' down and bumpin' deir heads on de ground like I was a miracle out o' de Bible. Oh Lawd, from dat time on I has dem all eatin' out of my hand. I cracks de whip and dey jumps through.

SMITHERS. (*With a sniff*) Yankee bluff done it.

JONES. Ain't a man's talkin' big what makes him big — long as he makes folks believe it? Sho', I talks large when I ain't got nothin' to back it up, but I ain't talkin' wild just de same. I knows I kin fool 'em — I *knows* it — and dat's backin' enough fo' my game. And ain't I got to learn deir lingo and teach some of dem English befo' I kin talk to 'em? Ain't dat wuk? You ain't never learned ary word er it, Smithers, in de ten years you been heah, dough yo' knows it's money in yo' pocket tradin' wid 'em if you does. But you'se too shiftless to take de trouble.

SMITHERS. (*Flushing*) Never mind about me. What's this I've 'eard about yer really 'avin' a silver bullet molded for yourself?

JONES. It's playin' out my bluff. I has de silver bullet molded and I tells 'em when de time comes I kills myself wid it. I tells 'em dat's 'cause I'm de on'y man in de world big enuff to git me. No use'n deir tryin'. And dey falls down and bumps deir heads. (*He laughs.*) I does dat so's I kin take a walk in peace widout no jealous nigger gunnin' at me from behind de trees.

SMITHERS. (*Astonished*) Then you 'ad it made — 'onest?

JONES. Sho' did. Heah she be. (*He takes out his revolver, breaks it, and takes the silver bullet out of one chamber.*) Five lead an'

dis silver baby at de last. Don't she shine pretty? (*He holds it in his hand, looking at it admiringly, as if strangely fascinated.*)

SMITHERS. Let me see. (*Reaches out his hand for it.*)

JONES. (*Harshly*) Keep yo' hands whar dey b'long, white man. (*He replaces it in the chamber and puts the revolver back on his hip.*)

SMITHERS. (*Snarling*) Gawd blimey! Think I'm a bleedin' thief, you would.

JONES. No, 'tain't dat. I knows you'se scared to steal from me. On'y I ain't 'lowin' nary body to touch dis baby. She's my rabbit's foot.

SMITHERS. (*Sneering*) A bloomin' charm, wot? (*Venomously*) Well, you'll need all the bloody charms you 'as before long, s' 'elp me!

JONES. (*Judicially*) Oh, I'se good for six months yit 'fore dey gits sick o' my game. Den, when I sees trouble comin', I makes my getaway.

SMITHERS. Ho! You got it all planned, ain't yer?

JONES. I ain't no fool. I knows dis Emperor's time is sho't. Dat why I make hay when de sun shine. Was you thinkin' I'se aimin' to hold down dis job for life? No, suh! What good is gittin' money if you stays back in dis raggedy country? I wants action when I spends. And when I sees dese niggers gittin' up deir nerve to tu'n me out, and I'se got all de money in sight, I resigns on de spot and beats it quick.

SMITHERS. Where to?

JONES. None o' yo' business.

SMITHERS. Not back to the bloody States, I'll lay my oath.

JONES. (*Suspiciously*) Why don't I? (*Then with an easy laugh*) You mean 'count of dat story 'bout me breakin' from jail back dere? Dat's all talk.

SMITHERS. (*Skeptically*) Ho, yes!

JONES. (*Sharply*) You ain't 'sinuatin' I'se a liar, is you?

SMITHERS. (*Hastily*) No, Gawd strike me! I was only thinkin' o' the bloody lies you told the blacks 'ere about killin' white men in the States.

JONES. (*Angered*) How come dey're lies?

SMITHERS. You'd 'ave been in jail if you 'ad, wouldn't yer then? (*With venom*) And from what I've 'eard, it ain't 'ealthy for a black to kill a white man in the States. They burns 'em in oil, don't they?

JONES. (*With cool deadliness*) You mean lynchin'd scare me? Well, I tells you, Smithers, maybe I does kill one white man back dere. Maybe I does. And maybe I kills another right heah 'fore long if he don't look out.

SMITHERS. (*Trying to force a laugh*) I was on'y spoofin' yer. Can't yer take a joke? And you was just sayin' you'd never been in jail.

JONES. (*In the same tone — slightly boastful*) Maybe I goes to jail dere for gettin' in an argument wid razors ovah a crap game. Maybe I gits twenty years when dat colored man die. Maybe I gits in 'nother argument wid de prison guard was overseer ovah us when we're wukin' de roads. Maybe he hits me wid a whip and I splits his head wid a shovel and runs away and files de chain off my leg and gits away safe. Maybe I does all dat an' maybe I don't. It's a story I tells you so's you knows I'se de kind of man dat if you evah repeats one word of it, I ends yo' stealin' on dis yearth mighty damn quick!

SMITHERS. (*Terrified*) Think I'd peach on yer? Not me! Ain't I always been yer friend?

JONES. (*Suddenly relaxing*) Sho' you has — and you better be.

SMITHERS. (*Recovering his composure — and with it his malice*) And just to show yer I'm yer friend, I'll tell yer that bit o' news I was goin' to.

JONES. Go ahead! Shoot de piece. Must be bad news from de happy way you look.

SMITHERS. (*Warningly*) Maybe it's gettin' time for you to resign — with that bloomin' silver bullet, wot? (*He finishes with a mocking grin.*)

JONES. (*Puzzled*) What's dat you say? Talk plain.

SMITHERS. Ain't noticed any of the guards or servants about the place today, I 'aven't.

JONES. (*Carelessly*) Dey're all out in de garden sleepin' under de trees. When I sleeps, dey sneaks a sleep, too, and I pretends I never suspicions it. All I got to do is to ring de bell and dey come flyin', makin' a bluff dey was wukin' all de time.

SMITHERS. (*In the same mocking tone*) Ring the bell now an' you'll bloody well see what I means.

JONES. (*Startled to alertness, but preserving the same careless tone*) Sho' I rings. (*He reaches below the throne and pulls out a big, common dinner bell which is painted the same vivid scarlet as the throne. He rings this vigorously — then stops to listen. Then he goes to both doors, rings again, and looks out.*)

SMITHERS. (*Watching him with malicious satisfaction, after a pause — mockingly*) The bloody ship is sinkin' an' the bleedin' rats 'as slung their 'ooks.

JONES. (*In a sudden fit of anger flings the bell clattering into a corner*) Low-flung, woods' niggers! (*Then catching Smithers' eye on him, he controls himself and suddenly bursts into a low chuckling laugh.*) Reckon I overplays my hand dis once! A man can't take de pot on a bob-tailed flush all de time. Was I sayin' I'd sit in six months mo'? Well, I'se changed my mind den. I cashes in and resigns de job of Emperor right dis minute.

SMITHERS. (*With cool admiration*) Blimey, but you're a cool bird, and no mistake.

JONES. No use'n fussin'. When I knows de game's up I kisses it goodbye widout no long waits. Dey've all run off to de hills, ain't dey?

SMITHERS. Yes — every bleedin' man jack of 'em.

JONES. Den de revolution is at de post. And de Emperor better git his feet smokin' up de trail. (*He starts for the door in rear.*)

SMITHERS. Goin' out to look for your 'orse? Yer won't find any. They steals the 'orses first thing. Mine was gone when I went for 'im this mornin'. That's wot first give me a suspicion of wot was up.

JONES. (*Alarmed for a second, scratches his head, then philosophically*) Well, den I hoofs it. Feet, do yo' duty! (*He pulls out a gold watch and looks at it.*) Three-thuty. Sundown's at six-thuty or dereabouts. (*Puts his watch back — with cool confidence.*) I got plenty o' time to make it easy.

SMITHERS. Don't be so bloomin' sure of it. They'll be after you 'ot and 'eavy. Ole Lem is at the bottom o' this business an' 'e 'ates you like 'ell. 'E'd rather do for you than eat 'is dinner, 'e would!

JONES. (*Scornfully*) Dat fool no-count nigger! Does you think I'se scared o' him? I stands him on his thick head more'n once befo' dis, and I does it again if he come in my way. . . . (*Fiercely*) And dis time I leave him a dead nigger fo' sho'!

SMITHERS. You'll 'ave to cut through the big forest — an' these blacks 'ere can sniff and follow a trail in the dark like 'ounds. You'd 'ave to 'ustle to get through that forest in twelve hours even if you knew all the bloomin' trails like a native.

JONES. (*With indignant scorn*) Look-a-heah, white man! Does you think I'se a natural bo'n fool? Give me credit fo' havin' some sense, fo' Lawd's sake! Don't you s'pose I'se looked ahead and made sho' of all de chances? I'se gone out in dat big forest, pretendin' to hunt, so many times dat I knows it high an' low like a book. I could go through on dem trails wid my eyes shut. (*With great contempt*) Think dese ign'rent bush niggers dat ain't got brains enuff to know deir own names even can catch Brutus Jones? Huh, I s'pects not! Not on yo' life! Why, man, de white men went after me wid bloodhounds where I come from an' I jes' laughs at 'em. It's a shame to fool dese black trash around heah, dey're so easy. You watch me, man! I'll make dem look sick, I will. I'll be 'cross de plain to de edge of de forest by time dark comes. Once in de woods in de night, dey got a swell chance o' findin' dis baby! Dawn tomorrow I'll be out at de oder side and on de coast whar dat French gunboat

is stayin'. She picks me up, takes me to Martinique when she go dar, and dere I is safe wid a mighty big bankroll in my jeans. It's easy as rollin' off a log.

SMITHERS. (*Maliciously*) But s'posin' somethin' 'appens wrong an' they do nab yer?

JONES. (*Decisively*) Dey don't — dat's de answer.

SMITHERS. But, just for argument's sake — what'd you do?

JONES. (*Frowning*) I'se got five lead bullets in dis gun good enuff fo' common bush niggers — and after dat I got de silver bullet left to cheat 'em out o' gittin' me.

SMITHERS. (*Jeeringly*) Ho, I was forgettin' that silver bullet. You'll bump yourself orf in style, won't yer? Blimey!

JONES. (*Gloomily*) You kin bet yo' whole roll on one thing, white man. Dis baby plays out his string to de end and when he quits, he quits wid a bang de way he ought. Silver bullet ain't none too good for him when he go, dat's a fac'! (*Then shaking off his nervousness — with a confident laugh*) Sho'! What is I talkin' about? Ain't come to dat yit and I never will — not wid trash niggers like dese yere. (*Boastfully*) Silver bullet bring me luck anyway. I kin outguess, outrun, outfight, an' outplay de whole lot o' dem all ovah de board any time o' de day er night! You watch me! (*From the distant hills comes the faint, steady thump of a tomtom, low and vibrating. It starts at a rate exactly corresponding to normal pulse beat — 72 to the minute — and continues at a gradually accelerating rate from this point uninterruptedly to the very end of the play.*)

(*JONES starts at the sound. A strange look of apprehension creeps into his face for a moment as he listens. Then he asks, with an attempt to regain his most casual manner.*) What's dat drum beatin' fo'?

SMITHERS. (*With a mean grin*) For you. That means the bleedin' ceremony 'as started. I've 'eard it before and I knows.

JONES. Cer'mony? What cer'mony?

SMITHERS. The blacks is 'oldin' a bloody meetin', 'avin' a war dance, gettin' their courage worked up b'fore they starts after you.

JONES. Let dem! Dey'll sho' need it!

SMITHERS. And they're there 'oldin' their 'eathen religious service — makin' no end of devil spells and charms to 'elp 'em against your silver bullet. (*He guffaws loudly.*) Blimey, but they're balmy as 'ell!

JONES. (*A tiny bit awed and shaken in spite of himself*) Huh! Takes more'n dat to scare dis chicken!

SMITHERS. (*Scenting the other's feeling — maliciously*) Ternight when it's pitch black in the forest, they'll 'ave their pet devils and ghosts 'oundin' after you. You'll find yer bloody 'air'll be standin' on end before ter-morrow mornin'. (*Seriously*) It's a bleedin' queer place, that stinkin' forest, even in day-light. Yer don't know what might 'appen in there, it's that rotten still. Always sends the cold shivers down my back minute I gets in it.

JONES. (*With a contemptuous sniff*) I ain't no chicken-liver like you is. Trees an' me, we'se friends, and dar's a full moon com-in' bring me light. And let dem po' niggers make all de fool spells dey'se a min' to. Does yo' s'pect I'se silly enuff to b'lieve in ghosts an' ha'nts an' all dat ole woman's talk? G'long, white man! You ain't talkin' to me. (*With a chuckle*) Doesn't you know dey's got to do wid a man was member in good standin' o' de Baptist Church? Sho' I was dat when I was porter on de Pullmans, befo' I gits into my little trouble. Let dem try deir heathen tricks. De Baptist Church done per-tect me and land dem all in hell. (*Then with more confident satisfaction*) And I'se got little silver bullet o' my own, don't for-git.

SMITHERS. Ho! You 'aven't give much 'eed to your Baptist Church since you been down 'ere. I've 'eard myself you 'ad turned yer coat an' was takin' up with their blarsted witch doctors, or whatever the 'ell yer calls the swine.

JONES. (*Vehemently*) I pretends to! Sho' I pretends! Dat's part o' my game from de fust. If I finds out dem niggers believes dat black is white, den I yells it out louder 'n deir loudest. It don't git me nothin' to do missionary work for de Baptist Church. I'se after de coin, an' I lays my Jesus on de shelf for de time bein'. (*Stops abruptly to look at his watch — alertly*) But I ain't got de time to waste no more fool talk wid you. I'se gwine away from heah dis secon'. (*He reaches in under the throne and pulls out an expensive Panama hat with a bright multi-colored band and sets it jauntily on his head.*) So long, white man! (*With a grin*) See you in jail sometime, maybe!

SMITHERS. Not me, you won't. Well, I wouldn't be in yer bloody boots for no bloomin' money, but 'ere's wishin' yer luck just the same.

JONES. (*Contemptuously*) You're de frightenedest man evah I see! I tells you I'se safe's 'f I was in New York City. It takes dem niggers from now to dark to git up de nerve to start somethin'. By dat time, I'se got a head start dey never kotch up wid.

SMITHERS. (*Maliciously*) Give my regards to any ghosts yer meets up with.

JONES. (*Grinning*) If dat ghost got money, I'll tell him never ha'nt you less'n he wants to lose it.

SMITHERS. (*Flattered*) Garn! (*Then curiously*) Ain't yer takin' no luggage with yer?

JONES. I travels light when I wants to move fast. And I got tinned grub buried on de edge o' de forest. (*Boastfully*) Now say dat I don't look ahead an' use my brains! (*With a wide, liberal gesture*) I will all dat's left in de palace to you — and you better grab all you kin sneak away wid befo' dey gits here.

SMITHERS. (*Gratefully*) Righto — and thanks ter yer. (*As* JONES *walks toward the door in rear — cautioningly*) Say! Look 'ere, you ain't goin' out that way, are yer?

JONES. Does you think I'd slink out de back door like a common nigger? I'se Em-peror yit, ain't I? And de Emperor Jones leaves de way he comes, and dat black trash don't dare stop him — not yit, leastways. (*He stops for a moment in the doorway, lis-tening to the far-off but insistent beat of the tom-tom.*) Listen to dat roll-call, will you? Must be mighty big drum carry dat far. (*Then with a laugh*) Well, if dey ain't no whole brass band to see me off, I sho' got de drum part of it. So long, white man. (*He puts his hands in his pockets and with studied carelessness, whistling a tune, he saunters out of the doorway and off to the left.*)

SMITHERS. (*Looks after him with a puzzled admiration.*) 'E's got 'is bloomin' nerve with 'im, s'elp me! (*Then angrily*) Ho — the bleedin' nigger — puttin' on 'is bloody airs! I 'opes they nabs 'im an' gives 'im what's what! (*Then putting business before the pleasure of this thought, looking around him with cupidity*) A bloke ought to find a 'ole lot in this palace that'd go for a bit of cash. Let's take a look, 'Arry, me lad. (*He starts for the doorway on Right.*)

SCENE TWO

SCENE — *Nightfall. The end of the plain where the Great Forest begins. The fore-ground is sandy, level ground dotted by a few stones and clumps of stunted bushes cowering close against the earth to escape the buffeting of the trade wind. In the rear the forest is a wall of darkness dividing the world. Only when the eye becomes ac-customed to the gloom can the outlines of separate trunks of the nearest trees be made out, enormous pillars of deeper blackness. A somber monotone of wind lost in the leaves moans in the air. Yet this sound serves but to intensify the impression of the forest's relentless immobility, to form a background throwing into relief its brooding, implaca-ble silence.*

(JONES *enters from the Left, walking rapidly. He stops as he nears the edge of the forest, looks around him quickly, peering into the dark as if searching for some famil-iar landmark. Then, apparently satisfied that he is where he ought to be, he throws him-self on the ground, dog-tired.*)

Well, heah I is. In de nick o' time, too! Little mo' an' it'd be blacker'n de ace of spades heahabouts. (*He pulls a bandana handkerchief from his hip pocket and mops off his perspiring face.*) Sho'! Gimme air! I'se tuckered out sho' 'nuff. Dat soft Em-peror job ain't no trainin' fo' a long hike ovah dat plain in de brilin' sun. (*Then with a chuckle*) Cheah up, nigger, de worst is yet to come. (*He lifts his head and stares at the forest. His chuckle peters out abruptly. In a tone of awe*) My goodness, look at dem woods, will you? Dat no-count Smithers said dey'd be black an' he sho' called de turn. (*Turning away from them quickly and looking down at his feet, he snatches at a chance to change the subject — solicitously.*) Feet, you is holdin' up yo' end fine an' I sutinly hopes you ain't blisterin' none. It's time you git a rest. (*He takes off his shoes, his eyes studiously avoiding the forest. He feels of the soles of his feet gingerly.*) You is still in de pink — on'y a little mite fever-ish. Cool yo'selfs. Remember you done got a long journey yit befo' you. (*He sits in a weary attitude, listening to the rhythmic beating of the tom-tom. He grumbles in a loud tone to cover up a growing uneasiness.*) Bush niggers! Wonder dey wouldn't git sick o' beatin' dat drum. Sound louder, seem like. I wonder if dey's startin' after me? (*He scrambles to his feet, looking back across the plain.*) Couldn't see dem now, nohow, if dey was hundred feet away. (*Then shaking himself like a wet dog to get rid of these depressing thoughts*) Sho', dey's miles an' miles behind. What you gittin' fidgety about? (*But he sits down and begins to lace up his shoes in great haste, all the time muttering reassuringly.*) You know what? Yo' belly is empty, dat's what's de matter wid you. Come time to eat! Wid nothin' but wind on yo' stumach, o' course you feels jiggedy. Well, we eats right heah an' now soon's I gits dese pesky shoes laced up! (*He finishes lacing up his shoes.*) Dere! Now le's see. (*Gets on his hands and knees and searches the ground around him with his eyes.*) White stone, white stone, where is you? (*He sees the first white stone and crawls to it — with satisfaction.*) Heah you is! I knowed dis was de right place. Box of grub, come to me. (*He turns over the stone and feels in under it — in a tone of dismay.*) Ain't heah! Gorry, is I in de right place or isn't I? Dere's 'nother stone. Guess dat's it. (*He scrambles to the next stone and turns it over.*) Ain't heah, neither! Grub whar is you? Ain't heah. Gorry, has I got to go hungry into dem woods — all de night? (*While he is talking he scrambles from one stone to another, turning them over in frantic haste. Finally, he jumps to his feet excitedly.*) Is I lost de place? Must have! But how dat happen when I was followin' de trail across de plain in broad daylight? (*Almost plaintively*) I'se hungry, I is! I gotta git my feed. Whar's my strength gonna come from if I doesn't? Gorry, I gotta find dat grub high an' low somehow! Why it come dark so quick like dat? Can't see nothin'. (*He scratches a match on his trousers and peers about him. The rate of the beat of the far-off tom-tom increases perceptibly as he does so. He mutters in a bewildered voice.*) How come all dese white stones come heah when I only remembers one? (*Suddenly, with a frightened gasp, he flings the match on the ground and stamps on it.*) Nigger, is you gone crazy mad? Is you lightin' matches to show dem whar you is? Fo' Lawd's sake, use yo' haid. Gorry, I'se got to be careful! (*He stares at the plain behind him apprehensively, his hand on his revolver.*) But how come all dese white stones? And whar's dat tin box o' grub I had all wrapped up in oil cloth?

(*While his back is turned, the* LITTLE FORMLESS FEARS *creep out from the deeper blackness of the forest. They are black, shapeless, only their glittering little eyes can be seen. If they have any describable form at all it is that of a grubworm about the size of a creeping child. They move noiselessly, but with deliberate, painful effort, striving to raise themselves on end, failing and sinking prone again.* JONES *turns about to face the forest. He stares up at the tops of the trees, seeking vainly to discover his whereabouts by their conformation.*)

Can't tell nothin' from dem trees! Gorry, nothin' 'round heah look like I evah seed it

befo'. I'se done lost de place sho' 'nuff! (*With mournful foreboding*) It's mighty queer! It's mighty queer! (*With sudden forced defiance — in an angry tone*) Woods, is you tryin' to put somethin' ovah on me?

(*From the formless creatures on the ground in front of him comes a tiny gale of low mocking laughter like a rustling of leaves. They squirm upward toward him in twisted attitudes.* JONES *looks down, leaps backward with a yell of terror, yanking out his revolver as he does so — in a quavering voice.*) What's dat? Who's dar? What is you? Git away from me befo' I shoots you up! You don't? . . .

(*He fires. There is a flash, a loud report, then silence broken only by the far-off, quickened throb of the tom-tom. The formless creatures have scurried back into the forest.* JONES *remains fixed in his position, listening intently. The sound of the shot, the reassuring feel of the revolver in his hand, have somewhat restored his shaken nerve. He addresses himself with renewed confidence.*)

Dey're gone. Dat shot fix 'em. Dey was only little animals — little wild pigs, I reckon. Dey've maybe rooted out yo' grub an' eat it. Sho, you fool nigger, what you think dey is — ha'nts? (*Excitedly*) Gorry, you give de game away when you fire dat shot. Dem niggers heah dat fo' su'tin! Time you beat it in de woods widout no long waits. (*He starts for the forest — hesitates before the plunge — then urges himself in with manful resolution.*) Git in, nigger! What you skeered at? Ain't nothin' dere but de trees! Git in! (*He plunges boldly into the forest.*)

SCENE THREE

SCENE — *Nine o'clock. In the forest. The moon has just risen. Its beams, drifting through the canopy of leaves, make a barely perceptible, suffused, eerie glow. A dense low wall of underbrush and creepers is in the nearer foreground, fencing in a small triangular clearing. Beyond this is the massed blackness of the forest like an encompassing barrier. A path is dimly discerned leading down to the clearing from Left, rear, and winding away from it again toward the Right. As the scene opens nothing can be distinctly made out. Except for the beating of the tom-tom, which is a trifle louder and quicker than in the previous scene, there is silence, broken every few seconds by a queer, clicking sound. Then gradually the figure of the Negro,* JEFF, *can be discerned crouching on his haunches at the rear of the triangle. He is middle-aged, thin, brown in color, is dressed in a Pullman porter's uniform, cap, etc. He is throwing a pair of dice on the ground before him, picking them up, shaking them, casting them out with the regular, rigid, mechanical movements of an automaton. The heavy, plodding footsteps of someone approaching along the trail from the Left are heard and* JONES' *voice, pitched in a slightly higher key and strained in a cheering effort to overcome its own tremors.*

De moon's rizen. Does you heah dat, nigger? You gits more light from dis out. No mo' buttin' yo' fool head agin' de trunks an' scratchin' de hide off yo' legs in de bushes. Now you sees whar yo'se gwine. So cheer up! From now on you has a snap. (*He steps just to the rear of the triangular clearing and mops off his face on his sleeve. He has lost his Panama hat. His face is scratched, his brilliant uniform shows several large rents.*) What time's it gittin' to be, I wonder? I dassent light no match to find out. Phoo'. It's wa'm an' dat's a fac'! (*Wearily*) How long I been makin' tracks in dese woods? Must be hours an' hours. Seems like fo'evah! Yit can't be, when de moon's jes' riz. Dis am a long night fo' yo', yo' Majesty! (*With a mournful chuckle*) Majesty! Der ain't much majesty 'bout dis baby now. (*With attempted cheerfulness*) Never min'. It's all part o' de game. Dis night come to an end like everything else. And when you gits dar safe and has dat bankroll in yo' hands you laughs at all dis. (*He starts to whistle but checks himself abruptly.*) What yo' whistlin' for, you po' dope! Want all de worl' to heah you? (*He stops talking to listen.*) Heah dat

ole drum! Sho' gits nearer from de sound. Dey're packin' it along wid 'em. Time fo' me to move. (*He takes a step forward, then stops — worriedly.*) What's dat odder queer clickety sound I heah? Dere it is! Sound close! Sound like — sound like — Fo' God sake, sound like some nigger was shootin' crap! (*Frightenedly*) I better beat it quick when I gits dem notions. (*He walks quickly into the clear space — then stands transfixed as he sees* JEFF — *in a terrified gasp.*) Who dar? Who dat? Is dat you, Jeff? (*Starting toward the other, forgetful for a moment of his surroundings and really believing it is a living man that he sees — in a tone of happy relief.*) Jeff! I'se sho' mighty glad to see you! Dey tol' me you done died from dat razor cut I gives you. (*Stopping suddenly, bewilderedly*) But how you come to be heah, nigger? (*He stares fascinatedly at the other, who continues his mechanical play with the dice.* JONES' *eyes begin to roll wildly. He stutters.*) Ain't you gwine — look up — can't you speak to me? Is you — is you — a ha'nt? (*He jerks out his revolver in a frenzy of terrified rage.*) Nigger, I kills you dead once. Has I got to kill you again? You take it den. (*He fires. When the smoke clears away* JEFF *has disappeared.* JONES *stands trembling — then with a certain reassurance.*) He's gone, anyway. Ha'nt or no ha'nt, dat shot fix him. (*The beat of the far-off tom-tom is perceptibly louder and more rapid.* JONES *becomes conscious of it — with a start, looking back over his shoulder.*) Dey's gittin' near! Dey's comin' fast! And heah I is shootin' shots to let 'em know jes' whar I is. Oh, Gorry, I'se got to run. (*Forgetting the path he plunges wildly into the underbrush in the rear and disappears in the shadow.*)

SCENE FOUR

SCENE — *Eleven o'clock. In the forest. A wide dirt road runs diagonally from Right, front, to Left, rear. Rising sheer on both sides the forest walls it in. The moon is now up. Under its light the road glimmers ghastly and unreal. It is as if the forest had stood aside momentarily to let the road pass through and accomplish its veiled purpose. This done, the forest will fold in upon itself again and the road will be no more.* JONES *stumbles in from the forest on the Right. His uniform is ragged and torn. He looks about him with numbed surprise when he sees the road, his eyes blinking in the bright moonlight. He flops down exhaustedly and pants heavily for a while. Then with sudden anger:*

I'm meltin' wid heat! Runnin' an' runnin' an' runnin'! Damn dis heah coat! Like a strait-jacket! (*He tears off his coat and flings it away from him, revealing himself stripped to the waist.*) Dere! Dat's better! Now I kin breathe! (*Looking down at his feet, the spurs catch his eye.*) And to hell wid dese high-fangled spurs. Dey're what's been a-trippin' me up an' breakin' my neck. (*He unstraps them and flings them away disgustedly.*) Dere! I gits rid o' dem frippety Emperor trappin's an' I travels lighter. Lawd! I'se tired! (*After a pause, listening to the insistent beat of the tom-tom in the distance*) I must 'a put some distance between myself an' dem — runnin' like dat — and yit — dat damn drum sound jes' de same — nearer, even. Well, I guess I a'most holds my lead anyhow. Dey won't never catch up. (*With a sigh*) If on'y my fool legs stands up. Oh, I'se sorry I evah went in for dis. Dat Emperor job is sho' hard to shake. (*He looks around him suspiciously.*) How'd dis road evah git heah? Good level road, too. I never remembers seein' it befo'. (*Shaking his head apprehensively*) Dese woods is sho' full o' de queerest things at night. (*With a sudden terror*) Lawd God, don't let me see no more o' dem ha'nts! Dey gits my goat! (*Then trying to talk himself into confidence*) Ha'nts! You fool nigger, dey ain't no such things! Don't de Baptist parson tell you dat many time? Is you civilized, or is you like dese ign'rent black niggers heah? Sho'! Dat was all in yo' own head. Wasn't nothin' dere. Wasn't no Jeff! Know what? You jus' get seein' dem things 'cause yo'

belly's empty and you's sick wid hunger inside. Hunger 'fects yo' head and yo' eyes. Any fool know dat. (*Then pleading fervently*) But bless God, I don't come across no more o' dem, whatever dey is! (*Then cautiously*) Rest! Don't talk! Rest! You needs it. Den you gits on yo' way again. (*Looking at the moon*) Night's half gone a'most. You hits de coast in de mawning! Den you'se all safe.

(*From the Right forward a small gang of Negroes enter. They are dressed in striped convict suits, their heads are shaven, one leg drags limpingly, shackled to a heavy ball and chain. Some carry picks, the others shovels. They are followed by a white man dressed in the uniform of a prison guard. A Winchester rifle is slung across his shoulders and he carries a heavy whip. At a signal from the* GUARD *they stop on the road opposite where* JONES *is sitting.* JONES, *who has been staring up at the sky, unmindful of their noiseless approach, suddenly looks down and sees them. His eyes pop out, he tries to get to his feet and fly, but sinks back, too numbed by fright to move. His voice catches in a choking prayer.*)

Lawd Jesus!

(*The* PRISON GUARD *cracks his whip — noiselessly — and at that signal all the convicts start to work on the road. They swing their picks, they shovel, but not a sound comes from their labor. Their movements, like those of* JEFF *in the preceding scene, are those of automatons — rigid, slow, and mechanical. The* PRISON GUARD *points sternly at* JONES *with his whip, motions him to take his place among the other shovelers.* JONES *gets to his feet in a hypnotized stupor. He mumbles subserviently.*)

Yes, suh! Yes, suh! I'se comin'.

(*As he shuffles, dragging one foot, over to his place, he curses under his breath with rage and hatred.*)

God damn yo' soul, I gits even wid you yit, sometime.

(*As if there were a shovel in his hands he goes through weary, mechanical gestures of digging up dirt, and throwing it to the road-*

side. *Suddenly the* GUARD *approaches him angrily, threateningly. He raises his whip and lashes* JONES *viciously across the shoulders with it.* JONES *winces with pain and cowers abjectly. The* GUARD *turns his back on him and walks away contemptuously. Instantly* JONES *straightens up. With arms upraised as if his shovel were a club in his hands he springs murderously at the unsuspecting* GUARD. *In the act of crashing down his shovel on the white man's skull,* JONES *suddenly becomes aware that his hands are empty. He cries despairingly.*)

Whar's my shovel? Gimme my shovel till I splits his damn head! (*Appealing to his fellow convicts*) Gimme a shovel, one o' you, fo' God's sake!

(*They stand fixed in motionless attitudes, their eyes on the ground. The* GUARD *seems to wait expectantly, his back turned to the attacker.* JONES *bellows with baffled, terrified rage, tugging frantically at his revolver.*)

I kills you, you white debil, if it's de last thing I evah does! Ghost or debil, I kill you again!

(*He frees the revolver and fires point blank at the* GUARD's *back. Instantly the walls of the forest close in from both sides, the road and the figures of the convict gang are blotted out in an enshrouding darkness. The only sounds are a crashing in the underbrush as* JONES *leaps away in mad flight and the throbbing of the tom-tom, still far distant, but increased in volume of sound and rapidity of beat.*)

SCENE FIVE

SCENE — *One o'clock. A large circular clearing, enclosed by the serried ranks of gigantic trunks of tall trees whose tops are lost to view. In the center is a big dead stump worn by time into a curious resemblance to an auction block. The moon floods the clearing with a clear light.* JONES *forces his way in through the forest on the Left. He looks wildly about the clearing with hunted, fearful glances. His pants are in tatters, his shoes cut and misshapen, flapping about his feet. He slinks cautiously to the* stump *in the center and sits down in a tense position, ready for instant flight. Then he holds his head in his hands and rocks back and forth, moaning to himself miserably.*

Oh Lawd, Lawd! Oh Lawd, Lawd! (*Suddenly he throws himself on his knees and raises his clasped hands to the sky — in a voice of agonized pleading.*) Lawd Jesus, heah my prayer! I'se a po' sinner, a po' sinner! I knows I done wrong, I knows it! When I cotches Jeff cheatin' wid loaded dice my anger overcomes me and I kills him dead! Lawd, I done wrong! When dat guard hits me wid de whip, my anger overcomes me, and I kills him dead. Lawd, I done wrong! And down heah whar dese fool bush niggers raises me up to the seat o' de mighty, I steals all I could grab. Lawd, I done wrong! I knows it! I'se sorry! Forgive me, Lawd! Forgive dis po' sinner! (*Then beseeching terrifiedly*) And keep dem away, Lawd! Keep dem away from me! And stop dat drum soundin' in my ears! Dat begin to sound ha'nted, too. (*He gets to his feet, evidently slightly reassured by his prayer — with attempted confidence.*) De Lawd'll preserve me from dem ha'nts after dis. (*Sits down on the stump again.*) I ain't skeered o' real men. Let dem come. But dem odders. . . . (*He shudders — then looks down at his feet, working his toes inside the shoes — with a groan.*) Oh, my po' feet! Dem shoes ain't no use no more 'ceptin' to hurt. I'se better off widout dem. (*He unlaces them and pulls them off — holds the wrecks of the shoes in his hands and regards them mournfully.*) You was real, A-One patin' leather, too. Look at you now. Emperor, you'se gittin' mighty low!

(*He sits dejectedly and remains with bowed shoulders, staring down at the shoes in his hands as if reluctant to throw them away. While his attention is thus occupied, a crowd of figures silently enter the clearing from all sides. All are dressed in Southern costumes of the period of the fifties of the last century. There are middle-aged men who are evidently well-to-do planters. There is one*

spruce, authoritative individual — the AUC-
TIONEER. *There is a crowd of curious spectators, chiefly young belles and dandies who
have come to the slave-market for diversion.
All exchange courtly greetings in dumb show
and chat silently together. There is something stiff, rigid, unreal, marionettish about
their movements. They group themselves
about the stump. Finally a batch of slaves are
led in from the left by an attendant — three
men of different ages, two women, one with
a baby in her arms, nursing. They are placed
to the left of the stump, beside* JONES.

*The white planters look them over ap-
praisingly as if they were cattle, and exchange judgments on each. The dandies
point with their fingers and make witty remarks. The belles titter bewitchingly. All
this in silence save for the ominous throb of
the tom-tom. The* AUCTIONEER *holds up his
hand, taking his place at the stump. The
group strain forward attentively. He touches*
JONES *on the shoulder peremptorily, mo-
tioning for him to stand on the stump — the
auction block.*

JONES *looks up, sees the figures on all sides,
looks wildly for some opening to escape, sees
none, screams and leaps madly to the top of
the stump to get as far away from them as
possible. He stands there, cowering, paralyzed with horror. The* AUCTIONEER *begins
his silent spiel. He points to* JONES, *appeals to
the planters to see for themselves. Here is a
good field hand, sound in wind and limb as
they can see. Very strong still in spite of his
being middle-aged. Look at that back. Look
at those shoulders. Look at the muscles in his
arms and his sturdy legs. Capable of any
amount of hard labor. Moreover, of a good
disposition, intelligent and tractable. Will any
gentleman start the bidding? The* PLANTERS
*raise their fingers, make their bids. They are
apparently all eager to possess* JONES. *The
bidding is lively, the crowd interested. While
this has been going on,* JONES *has been
seized by the courage of desperation. He dares
to look down and around him. Over his face
abject terror gives way to mystification, to
gradual realization — stutteringly.)*

What you all doin', white folks? What's all
dis? What you all lookin' at me fo'? What
you doin' wid me, anyhow? (*Suddenly con-
vulsed with raging hatred and fear*) Is dis a
auction? Is you sellin' me like dey uster
befo' de war? (*Jerking out his revolver just
as the* AUCTIONEER *knocks him down to one
of the planters — glaring from him to the
purchaser*) And *you* sells me? And *you* buys
me? I shows you I'se a free nigger, damn yo'
souls! (*He fires at the* AUCTIONEER *and at
the* PLANTER *with such rapidity that the
two shots are almost simultaneous. As if this
were a signal the walls of the forest fold in.
Only blackness remains and silence broken
by* JONES *as he rushes off, crying with
fear — and by the quickened, ever louder
beat of the tom-tom.*)

SCENE SIX

SCENE — *Three o'clock. A cleared space in
the forest. The limbs of the trees meet over
it forming a low ceiling about five feet
from the ground. The interlocked ropes of
creepers reaching upward to entwine the
tree trunks give an arched appearance to the
sides. The space thus enclosed is like the dark,
noisome hold of some ancient vessel. The
moonlight is almost completely shut out and
only a vague, wan light filters through.
There is the noise of someone approaching
from the Left, stumbling and crawling
through the undergrowth.* JONES' *voice is
heard between chattering moans.*

Oh, Lawd, what I gwine do now? Ain't
got no bullet left on'y de silver one. If mo' o'
dem ha'nts come after me, how I gwine skeer
dem away? Oh, Lawd, on'y de silver one
left — an' I gotta save dat fo' luck. If I
shoots dat one I'm a goner sho'! Lawd, it's
black heah! Whar's de moon? Oh, Lawd, don't
dis night evah come to an end? (*By the
sounds, he is feeling his way cautiously forward.*) Dere! Dis feels like a clear space. I
gotta lie down an' rest. I don't care if dem
niggers does cotch me. I gotta rest.

(*He is well forward now where his figure
can be dimly made out. His pants have been*

so torn away that what is left of them is no better than a breech cloth. He flings himself full length, face downward on the ground, panting with exhaustion. Gradually it seems to grow lighter in the enclosed space and two rows of seated figures can be seen behind JONES. They are sitting in crumpled, despairing attitudes, hunched, facing one another with their backs touching the forest walls as if they were shackled to them. All are Negroes, naked save for loin cloths. At first they are silent and motionless. Then they begin to sway slowly forward toward each other and back again in unison, as if they were laxly letting themselves follow the long roll of a ship at sea. At the same time, a low, melancholy murmur rises among them, increasing gradually by rhythmic degrees which seem to be directed and controlled by the throb of the tom-tom in the distance, to a long, tremulous wail of despair that reaches a certain pitch, unbearably acute, then falls by slow gradations of tone into silence and is taken up again. JONES starts, looks up, sees the figures, and throws himself down again to shut out the sight. A shudder of terror shakes his whole body as the wail rises up about him again. But the next time, his voice, as if under some uncanny compulsion, starts with the others. As their chorus lifts he rises to a sitting posture similar to the others, swaying back and forth. His voice reaches the highest pitch of sorrow, of desolation. The light fades out, the other voices cease, and only darkness is left. JONES can be heard scrambling to his feet and running off, his voice sinking down the scale and receding as he moves farther and farther away in the forest. The tom-tom beats louder, quicker, with a more insistent, triumphant pulsation.)

SCENE SEVEN

SCENE — Five o'clock. The foot of a gigantic tree by the edge of a great river. A rough structure of boulders, like an altar, is by the tree. The raised river bank is in the nearer background. Beyond this the surface of the river spreads out, brilliant and un-

ruffled in the moonlight, blotted out and merged into a veil of bluish mist in the distance. JONES' voice is heard from the Left rising and falling in the long, despairing wail of the chained slaves, to the rhythmic beat of the tom-tom. As his voice sinks into silence, he enters the open space. The expression of his face is fixed and stony, his eyes have an obsessed glare, he moves with a strange deliberation like a sleepwalker or one in a trance. He looks around at the tree, the rough stone altar, the moonlit surface of the river beyond, and passes his hand over his head with a vague gesture of puzzled bewilderment. Then, as if in obedience to some obscure impulse, he sinks into a kneeling, devotional posture before the altar. Then he seems to come to himself partly, to have an uncertain realization of what he is doing, for he straightens up and stares about him horrifiedly — in an incoherent mumble.

What — what is I doin'? What is — dis place? Seems like — seems like I know dat tree — an' dem stones — an' de river. I remember — seems like I been heah befo'. (Tremblingly) Oh, Gorry, I'se skeered in dis place! I'se skeered! Oh, Lawd, pertect dis sinner!

(Crawling away from the altar, he cowers close to the ground, his face hidden, his shoulders heaving with sobs of hysterical fright. From behind the trunk of the tree, as if he had sprung out of it, the figure of the CONGO WITCH DOCTOR appears. He is wizened and old, naked except for the fur of some small animal tied about his waist, its bushy tail hanging down in front. His body is stained all over a bright red. Antelope horns are on each side of his head, branching upward. In one hand he carries a bone rattle, in the other a charm stick with a bunch of cockatoo feathers tied to the end. A great number of glass beads and bone ornaments are about his neck, ears, wrists, and ankles. He struts noiselessly with a queer prancing step to a position in the clear ground between JONES and the altar. Then with a preliminary, summoning stamp of his foot on the earth, he begins to dance and to chant. As if in response to his summons the beating of the tom-tom grows to a fierce, exultant boom whose throbs seem to fill the air with vibrating rhythm. JONES looks up, starts to spring to his feet, reaches a half-kneeling, half-squatting position and remains rigidly fixed there, paralyzed with awed fascination by this new apparition. The WITCH DOCTOR sways, stamping with hands and sways his body to and fro from the waist. The whole spirit and meaning of the dance has entered into him, has become his spirit. Finally the theme of the pantomime halts on a howl of despair, and is taken up again in a note of savage hope. There is a salvation. The forces of evil demand sacrifice. They must be appeased. The WITCH DOCTOR points with his wand to the sacred tree, to the river beyond, to the altar, and finally to JONES with a ferocious command.

The Emperor Jones, Scene Seven. Theater Collection, New York Public Library.

his foot, his bone rattle clicking the time. His voice rises and falls in a weird, monotonous croon, without articulate word divisions. Gradually his dance becomes clearly one of a narrative in pantomime, his croon is an incantation, a charm to allay the fierceness of some implacable deity demanding sacrifice. He flees, he is pursued by devils, he hides, he flees again. Ever wilder and wilder becomes his flight, nearer and nearer draws the pursuing evil, more and more the spirit of terror gains possession of him. His croon, rising to intensity, is punctuated by shrill cries. JONES has become completely hypnotized. His voice joins in the incantation, in the cries, he beats time with his JONES seems to sense the meaning of this. It is he who must offer himself for sacrifice. He beats his forehead abjectly to the ground, moaning hysterically.)

Mercy, Oh Lawd! Mercy! Mercy on dis po' sinner.

(The WITCH DOCTOR springs to the river bank. He stretches out his arms and calls to some god within its depths. Then he starts backward slowly, his arms remaining out. A huge head of a crocodile appears over the bank and its eyes, glittering greenly, fasten upon JONES. He stares into them fascinatedly. The WITCH DOCTOR prances up to him, touches him with his wand, motions with hideous command toward the waiting monster. JONES *squirms on his belly nearer and nearer, moaning continually.*)

Mercy, Lawd! Mercy!

(*The crocodile heaves more of his enormous bulk onto the land.* JONES *squirms toward him. The* WITCH DOCTOR'S *voice shrills out in furious exultation, the tom-tom beats madly.* JONES *cries out in a fierce, exhausted spasm of anguished pleading.*)

Lawd, save me! Lawd Jesus, heah my prayer!

(*Immediately, in answer to his prayer, comes the thought of the one bullet left him. He snatches at his hip, shouting defiantly.*)

De silver bullet! You don't git me yit!

(*He fires at the green eyes in front of him. The head of the crocodile sinks back behind the river bank, the* WITCH DOCTOR *springs behind the sacred tree and disappears.* JONES *lies with his face to the ground, his arms outstretched, whimpering with fear as the throb of the tom-tom fills the silence about him with a somber pulsation, a baffled but revengeful power.*)

SCENE EIGHT

SCENE — *Dawn. Same as Scene Two, the dividing line of forest and plain. The nearest tree trunks are dimly revealed but the forest behind them is still a mass of glooming shadows. The tom-tom seems on the very spot, so loud and continuously vibrating are its beats.* LEM *enters from the Left, followed by a small squad of his soldiers, and by the Cockney trader,* SMITHERS. LEM *is a heavy-set, ape-faced old savage of the extreme African type, dressed only in a loin cloth. A revolver and cartridge belt are about his waist. His soldiers are in different degrees of rag-concealed nakedness. All wear broad palm-leaf hats. Each one carries a rifle.* SMITHERS *is the same as in Scene One. One of the soldiers, evidently a tracker, is peering about keenly on the ground. He grunts and points to the spot where* JONES *entered the forest.* LEM *and* SMITHERS *come to look.*

SMITHERS. (*After a glance, turns away in disgust*) That's where 'e went in right enough. Much good it'll do yer. 'E's miles orf by this an' safe to the Coast, damn 'is 'ide! I tole yer yer'd lose 'im, didn't I? — wastin' the 'ole bloomin' night beatin' yer bloody drum and castin' yer silly spells! Gawd blimey, wot a pack!

LEM. (*Gutturally*) We cotch him. You see. (*He makes a motion to his soldiers who squat down on their haunches in a semi-circle.*)

SMITHERS. (*Exasperatedly*) Well, ain't yer goin' in an' 'unt 'im in the woods? What the 'ell's the good of waitin'?

LEM. (*Imperturbably — squatting down himself*) We cotch him.

SMITHERS. (*Turning away from him contemptuously*) Aw! Garn! 'E's a better man than the lot o' you put together. I 'ates the sight o' 'im but I'll say that for 'im. (*A sound of snapping twigs comes from the forest. The soldiers jump to their feet, cocking their rifles alertly.* LEM *remains sitting with an imperturbable expression, but listening intently. The sound from the woods is repeated.* LEM *makes a quick signal with his hand. His followers creep quickly but noiselessly into the forest, scattering so that each enters at a different spot.*)

SMITHERS. (*In the silence that follows — in a contemptuous whisper*) You ain't thinkin' that would be 'im, I 'ope?

LEM. (*Calmly*) We cotch him.

SMITHERS. Blarsted fat 'eads! (*Then after a second's thought — wonderingly*) Still an' all, it might 'appen. If 'e lost 'is bloody way in these stinkin' woods 'e'd likely turn in a circle without 'is knowin' it. They all does.

LEM. (*Peremptorily*) Sssh! (*The reports of several rifles sound from the forest, followed a second later by savage, exultant yells. The beating of the tom-tom abruptly ceases.* LEM *looks up at the white man with a grin of satisfaction.*) We cotch him. Him dead.

SMITHERS. (*With a snarl*) 'Ow d'yer know it's 'im an' 'ow d'yer know 'e's dead?

LEM. My mens dey got 'um silver bullets. Dey kill him shore.

SMITHERS. (*Astonished*) They got silver bullets?

LEM. Lead bullet no kill him. He got um strong charm. I cook um money, make um silver bullet, make um strong charm, too.

SMITHERS. (*Light breaking upon him*) So that's wot you was up to all night, wot? You was scared to put after 'im till you'd molded silver bullets, eh?

LEM. (*Simply stating a fact*) Yes. Him got strong charm. Lead no good.

SMITHERS. (*Slapping his thigh and guffawing*) Haw-haw! If yer don't beat all 'ell! (*Then recovering himself — scornfully*) I'll bet yer it ain't 'im they shot at all, yer bleedin' looney!

LEM. (*Calmly*) Dey come bring him now. (*The soldiers come out of the forest, carrying* JONES' *limp body. There is a little reddish-purple hole under his left breast. He is dead. They carry him to* LEM, *who examines his body with great satisfaction.* SMITHERS *leans over his shoulder — in a tone of frightened awe.*) Well, they did for yer right enough, Jonesy, me lad! Dead as a 'erring! (*Mockingly*) Where's yer 'igh an' mighty airs now, yer bloomin' Majesty? (*Then with a grin*) Silver bullets! Gawd blimey, but yer died in the 'eighth o' style, any'ow! (LEM *makes a motion to the soldiers to carry the body out Left.* SMITHERS *speaks to him sneeringly.*)

SMITHERS. And I s'pose you think it's yer bleedin' charms and yer silly beatin' the drum that made 'im run in a circle when 'e'd lost 'imself, don't yer? (*But* LEM *makes no reply, does not seem to hear the question, walks out Left after his men.* SMITHERS *looks after him with contemptuous scorn.*) Stupid as 'ogs, the lot of 'em! Blarsted niggers!

PART THREE

PLAYS FOR ANALYSIS

FUENTE OVEJUNA
(THE SHEEP WELL)

by Lope De Vega
TRANSLATED BY JOHN GARRETT UNDERHILL

꙳꙳꙳꙳꙳꙳꙳꙳꙳꙳꙳꙳꙳꙳꙳꙳꙳꙳꙳꙳꙳꙳꙳꙳꙳꙳꙳꙳꙳꙳꙳꙳

CHARACTERS

THE KING, FERDINAND OF ARAGON

QUEEN ISABELLA OF CASTILE

DON MANRIQUE, Master of Santiago [1]

RODRIGO TÉLLEZ GIRÓN, Grand Master of Calatrava [1]

FERNÁN GÓMEZ DE GUZMÁN, Commander of Calatrava

FLORES }
ORTUÑO } his retainers

CIMBRANOS, a soldier

A Judge

Two Regidors [2] of Ciudad Real

ESTEBAN }
ALONSO } Alcaldes [3] of Fuente Ovejuna

JUAN ROJO }
CUADRADO } Regidors

Another Regidor of Fuente Ovejuna

FRONDOSO }
MENGO } peasants
BARRILDO }

LEONELO, a student

A Farmer

A Soldier

LAURENCIA }
PASCUALA } peasant girls
JACINTA }

A Boy

Musicians, Soldiers, Farmers, Villagers, and Attendants

The scene is laid in Almagro, the village of Fuente Ovejuna, the country round about Ciudad Real, and at the itinerant Royal Court in Castile
Time: 1476

ACT ONE

A street in Almagro. The COMMANDER *enters with* FLORES *and* ORTUÑO, *servants.*

COMMANDER. Does the Master know I have come to town?

---
[1] religious and military orders of knighthood
[2] councilmen
[3] mayors

FLORES. He does, sir.

ORTUÑO. The years will bring discretion.

COMMANDER. I am Fernán Gómez de Guzmán.

FLORES. Today youth may serve as his excuse.

COMMANDER. If he is ignorant of my name, let him respect the dignity of the High Commander.

379

ORTUÑO. He were ill advised to fail in courtesy.

COMMANDER. Or he will gain little love. Courtesy is the key to favor while discourtesy is stupidity that breeds enmity.

ORTUÑO. Should a rude oaf hear how roundly he was hated, with the whole world at his heels not to bark but to bite, he would die sooner than convict himself a boor.

FLORES. Slight no man. Among equals pride is folly, but toward inferiors it becomes oppression. Here neglect is want of care. The boy has not yet learned the price of favor.

COMMANDER. The obligation which he assumed with the sword the day that the cross of Calatrava was fixed upon his breast, bound him to humility and love.

FLORES. He can intend no despite that his quick spirit shall not presently make appear.

ORTUÑO. Return, sir, not stay upon his pleasure.

COMMANDER. I have come to know this boy.

(*Enter the* MASTER OF CALATRAVA *and Attendants.*)

MASTER. A thousand pardons, Fernán Gómez de Guzmán! I am advised of your arrival in the city.

COMMANDER. I had just complaint of you, for my affection and our birth are holy ties, being as we are the one Master of Calatrava, and the other Commander, who subscribes himself yours wholly.

MASTER. I had no thought of this purposed honor, Fernando, hence a tardy welcome. Let me embrace you once again.

COMMANDER. Vying in honor. I have staked my own on your behalf in countless causes, even answering during your minority before the Pope at Rome.

MASTER. You have indeed. By the holy token that we bear above our hearts, I repay your love, and honor you as I should my father.

COMMANDER. I am well content.

MASTER. What news of the war at the front?

COMMANDER. Attend and learn your obligation.

MASTER. Say I am already in the field.

COMMANDER. Noble Master
Don Rodrigo Téllez Girón,
To power and rule exalted
Through bravery of a mighty sire
Who eight years since
Renounced the Mastership,
Devising it to you,
As was confirmed by oaths and surety
Of Kings and High Commanders,
Even the Sovereign Pontiff,
Pius the Second,
Concurring by his bull,
And later Paul, succeeding him,
Decreeing holily
That Don Juan Pacheco,
Noble Master of Santiago,
Should co-adjutor be
With you to serve,
Till now, his death recorded,
All government and rule
Descend upon your head,
Sole and supreme
Despite your untried years.
Wherefore take counsel,
Harkening to the voice of honor,
And follow the commitment
Of kin and allies, wisely led.
Henry the Fourth is dead.
Let all his lieges
Bend the knee forthwith
To Alonso, King of Portugal,
Heir by right in Castile
Through his wife
In tie of marriage,
Though Ferdinand,
Lord of Aragon,
Like right maintains
By title of his wife,
Isabella.
Yet to our eyes
The line of her succession is not clear,
Nor can we credit
Shadow of deception
In the right descent
Of Juana,[4] now secure

---

[4] wife of Alonso

Under the protection of your cousin,
Who loves you as a brother.
Therefore summon all the Knights
Of Calatrava to Almagro,
Thence to reduce
Ciudad Real,
Which guards the pass
Dividing Andalusia from Castile,
On both
Frowning impartially.
Few men will gain the day.
For want of soldiers
The people mount the walls,
Aided by errant knights
Faithful to Isabella,
And so pledged to Ferdinand
As King.
Strike terror, Rodrigo,
To the hearts of those who say
That this great cross
Rests heavily
Upon the sagging bosom of a child.
Consider the Counts of Ureña,
From whom you spring,
Flaunting the laurels of their might
Upon the heights of fame,
Nor neglect to emulate
The Marquises of Villena,
With other gallant captains
Whose names in manifold
Brighten the outstretched wings
Of reputation.
Unsheathe your virgin sword
Till in battle, like the cross,
It drip with blood.
Of this red cross,
Blasoned on the breast,
Breathes there no votary
Whose drawn sword flashes white.
At the breast the one,
At the side the other
Must glow and flame with red!
So crown, valiant Girón,
With deeds
The immortal temple
Reared stone by stone
By your great ancestors.
MASTER. Fernán Gómez,

I shall march with you
Because our cause is just,
And with my kin bear arms.
If I must pass,
Then shall I pass at Ciudad Real
As a lightning stroke,
Cleaving as I pass,
While my scant years proclaim
To friend and foe alike
That when my uncle died
Was no mortality of valor.
I draw my sword
That men may see it shine,
Livid with the passion of the cross,
Maculately red.
Where hold you residence?
Send on your vassals
To combat in my train.
COMMANDER. Few but faithful serve,
    Who will contend like lions
    In battle.
    Fuente Ovejuna [5] is a town
    Of simple folk,
    Unskilled in warfare,
    Rather with plough and spade
    Tilling the fields.
MASTER. Fuente Ovejuna, glebe of peace!
COMMANDER. Favored possession
    In these troubled times,
    Pastoral, serene!
    Gather your men;
    Let none remain unarmed.
MASTER. To-day I spur my horse
    And level my eager lance.

The Square of Fuente Ovejuna. PASCUALA
and LAURENCIA *enter.*

LAURENCIA. I prayed he would never
come back.

PASCUALA. When I brought the word I
knew it would grieve you.

LAURENCIA. Would to God he had never
seen Fuente Ovejuna!

PASCUALA. Laurencia, many a girl has
made a pretense of saying no, yet all the
while her heart has been as soft as butter
in her.

---

[5] i.e., the village of the Sheep Well

LAURENCIA. I am a live-oak, gnarled and twisted.

PASCUALA. Yes, but why refuse a drink of water?

LAURENCIA. I do, be the sun never so hot, though you may not believe it. Why love Fernando? He's no husband.

PASCUALA. No, woman.

LAURENCIA. And amen! Plenty of girls in the village have trusted the Commander to their harm.

PASCUALA. It will be a miracle if you escape.

LAURENCIA. You are blind, because I have avoided him a full month now, Pascuala, and no quarter. Flores, who lays his snares, and that villain Ortuño, offered me a waist, a necklace, and a head-dress. They praised Fernando, their master, and pictured him so great that I blushed at his very glory, but for all that they could not move me.

PASCUALA. But where was this?

LAURENCIA. Down by the brook there, a week gone yesterday.

PASCUALA. You're already lost, Laurencia.

LAURENCIA. No, no, no!

PASCUALA. Maybe the priest might believe your story.

LAURENCIA. I am too innocent for the priest. In His Name, Pascuala, but of a morning rising early I had rather set me a slice of ham on the fire to munch with a crust of bread of my own kneading, filching a glass meanwhile out of the old stopped butt, once mother's back is turned, to wet my thirst, and then climb up to watch the cow thrash through the cabbages, all foaming at the mouth come noonday, while I hearten myself with a bit of eggplant and a strip of bacon after hard walking, and return weary toward suppertime to nibble the raisins, home-grown in our own vineyard, which God fend the hail from, sitting me down with a dish of salad and pepper and olive oil, and so to bed tired at nightfall, in contentment and peace, with a prayer on my lips to be preserved from the men, devils, God knows, every one, than I would deliver myself to their wiles for all their love and fury.

What they want is to undo us, joy in the night and at dawning a maid's mourning.

PASCUALA. You are right, Laurencia, for a sated lover flies faster than a farm sparrow. In the winter when the fields are bare they sing " tweet " under the eaves till they come by the crumbs from the farmer's board, but when the fields are green and frost has been forgotten, instead of fluttering down to sing " tweet " they hop up to the roof-tree and cry " twit," and " twit " it is at you standing down below, make the most that you can of their twitting. Men are the same. When they need us we are their very lives, their heart, their soul, their entire being, but their hunger satisfied, off they fly and leave us, too, with the echo of their twitting. So I say no man can be trusted.

(MENGO, BARRILDO and FRONDOSO enter.)

FRONDOSO. You defeat yourself, Barrildo.

BARRILDO. Two judges are here who can decide between us.

MENGO. Agree upon the forfeit and then we'll call in the girls. If they favor me, you hand me both your shirts, with whatever else you have on your backs, in meed of victory.

BARRILDO. Agreed. But what will you give if you lose?

MENGO. My rebeck of old box, which is worth more than a granary, for God knows its like cannot be bought in the village.

BARRILDO. Fairly said and offered.

FRONDOSO. Done! — God save you, ladies.

LAURENCIA. Frondoso calls us ladies.

FRONDOSO. The flattery of the age.
  The blind we say are one-eyed,
  The cross-eyed merely squint,
  Pupils equal masters
  While cripples barely limp;
  The spendthrift fools call " open,"
  The dumb now hold their tongues,
  Bullies out-vie brave men,
  Shouters shame the grave men,
  And as for saving,
  Praise the miser —
  None so active as the meddler
  To promote the common good.
  Gossips will " talk freely,"
  While concede we must

The quarrelsome are just.
Boasters display their courage,
The shrinking coward " retires,"
The impudent grow witty,
The taciturn sit pretty,
All hail the idiot.
Gamblers, pray, " look forward,"
The bald deserve respect,
Admit the ass is graceful,
That large feet proclaim the faithful,
While a blotched and pimpled face-full
Is a scientific indication
Of a sluggish circulation.
The lie today a truth is,
Rudeness clever youth is,
And if you have a hump,
Why follow your bent
All the way over,
Without stooping
Moreover,
And so to conclude
I call you ladies,
For otherwise there is no telling what names
   I might call you.

LAURENCIA. In the city praise may be the fashion, Frondoso, but by my faith we have a contrary custom in the country, where words are sharp and barbed, upon tongues that are calloused to use them.

FRONDOSO. Who speaks knows.

LAURENCIA. Turn all in reverse.

Know and be a bore,
Work and you have luck,
The prudent are faint-hearted,
The upright reek with muck.
Advice today spells insult,
Charity rank waste,
Be fair and painted ugly,
Be good, what wretched taste!
Truth is made for boobies,
No purity wins rubies,
While as for giving,
'Tis a veil for sinful living,
Fie, fie the hypocrite!
Disparage true worth always.
Dub simple faith imbecility,
Flat cowardice amiability,
Nor ever be fearful
Against the innocent
To speak an ear-full.
No woman is honest,
No beauty is chaste,
And as for virtue
There is not enough to hurt you,
For in the country
A curse
Turns merit to reverse.

MENGO. Devil of a girl!

BARRILDO. On my soul, she is too quick for us!

MENGO. A pinch of spice plashed into the holy water the day of her christening.

LAURENCIA. Well, well, since you question us, let us have it without delay and judge truly.

FRONDOSO. I'll set out the argument.

LAURENCIA. Plant in season, then, and begin.

FRONDOSO. Attend, Laurencia.

LAURENCIA. Oh, I'll have an answer for you some day.

FRONDOSO. Be fair, be just.

LAURENCIA. What is this wager?

FRONDOSO. Barrildo and I oppose Mengo.

LAURENCIA. Mengo is right. So, there!

BARRILDO. A fact is certain and plain which he denies.

MENGO. I deny it because it's a lie and they wander from the mark.

LAURENCIA. Explain.

BARRILDO. He maintains there is no such thing as love.

LAURENCIA. Then it takes hold of one mightily.

BARRILDO. Yes, though it be blind, for without love the world would never go on.

MENGO. I say little, not being able to read, though I could learn, but if the elements make the world and our bodies are made of the elements which war against each other unceasingly, causing anger and discord, then where is love?

BARRILDO. Mengo, the world is love, here and hereafter, not discord. Harmony is love. Love is a reaching out.

MENGO. A pulling in, according to nature, which governs all things through the resemblances that are. Love is a looking to its own, its preservation. I raise my hand to my face to prevent the blow, I move my feet to remove me from danger to my body, my eye-lids close to shield my sight through the attraction of a mutual love.

PASCUALA. He admit's it's love, so what then? There's an end.

MENGO. We love ourselves, no one else, that's flat.

PASCUALA. Mengo, what a lie! And God forgive me. The love a man bears for a woman, or a beast for its mate, is a fierce, consuming passion.

MENGO. Self-love, interest, not pure love. What is love?

LAURENCIA. A running after beauty.

MENGO. But why run after beauty?

LAURENCIA. For the thrill and the pleasure, boy.

MENGO. True. And the pleasure a man seeks for himself.

LAURENCIA. True again.

MENGO. So that self-love seeks its own delight?

LAURENCIA. Granted.

MENGO. Therefore there is no love, only we like what we like, and we intend in all things to get it, to seek delight, our delight.

BARRILDO. One day the priest preached in the village about a man named Plato who had taught men how to love, but what Plato loved, he said, was the soul and the virtue that was hidden in it.

PASCUALA. So the fathers teach the children in 'cademies and schools.

LAURENCIA. Yes, and don't you listen to any nonsense, either. Mengo, thank God you never knew the curse of love.

MENGO. Were you ever in love?

LAURENCIA. In love with my honor, always.

FRONDOSO. Come, come, ladies! Decide, decide.

BARRILDO. Who wins?

PASCUALA. Let the priest or the sacristan cook up a reply, for Laurencia loves too much and I not a little, so how can we, siding both ways, decide?

FRONDOSO. They laugh at us.

(*Enter* FLORES.)

FLORES. God guard the fair!

PASCUALA. This man is from the Commander.

LAURENCIA. Why so brash, old goshawk, in the village?

FLORES. You meet me as a soldier.

LAURENCIA. From Don Fernando?

FLORES. The war is done, though it has cost us blood, and armies of our friends.

FRONDOSO. Say what of note our band achieved.

FLORES. I will, and that better than another, having seen it with my own eyes.
Beleaguering the city
Of Ciudad Real,
By charter royal,
The valiant Master mustered in
Two thousand foot,
Bravest among his vassals,
Beside three hundred horse,
Churchmen and laymen,
For the crimson cross
Summons to its aid
Those who profess it on their breasts
Though robed and habited for prayer,
Crusading oft in holy cause,
Ruthless to slay the Moor.
Boldly the lad rode forth,
His tunic green
Embroidered with golden scrolls,
While silken cords
Caught up his sleeves,
Stayed sixfold
Above his iron gauntlets.
His steed was sturdy stout,
A dappled roan
Bred beside the Betis,
Drinking of the willing stream
And pasturing on lush meadows,
But now in panoply of white
Bedecked, patterns of net
Flecking the snowy pools
That gemmed his mottled hide
From plumèd crest
Down to the buckskin tailpiece.
At equal pace
The Commander Fernán Gómez
Bestrid a piebald charger,

Black of mane, the tail coal black,
White foaming at the nostril.
A Turkish coat of mail he wore,
Breastplate and corselet
Glowing bright orange,
Relieved with pearls and gold.
White plumes
Topped off his helmet,
Pallid plumes wind-blown,
Striking dismay,
The while his puissant arm
Banded now red, now white,
Brandished an ash-tree,
Famous as his lance
Even to Granada.
The city flew to arms,
Vain boasts of loyalty
With greed contending,
Some fearful for their homes,
Some of their treasure.
The Master breached those walls,
Flung back those surly churls,
And the heads
Of the rebel leaders,
As of those conspiring there
Against his dignity,
With a blow
Severed from the body.
We gagged the common folk,
Then beat them openly,
So in that town
The Master is feared and praised
Conjointly.
Though few in years,
By deeds, by valor and by victory
Nature in him has forged
A bolt from heaven
To rive Africa,
Her blue moon senescent
To the red cross bowed,
Obeisant.
Rich the promise
Of the rape of this fair city,
With apportionment
Of present gain
To him and the Commander
Now hear the music sound, for zest in vic-
    tory adds sweetest savor.
(*The* COMMANDER *enters with* ORTUÑO *and*

Musicians, accompanied by JUAN ROJO,
Regidor, ESTEBAN *and* ALONSO, *Alcaldes.*)

SONG

Welcome, great Commander,
Many times a victor,
Men and fields mowed down!
Guzmáns, arm, to battle!
Girones, strike, to battle!
Doves in peace,
Mighty in repose.
Forward to the conflict,
Strong of limb as oak trees,
Drive the Moors before you
From Ciudad Real.
Flaunt your pennons proudly
In Fuente Ovejuna,
Valiant Fernán Gómez,
Glorious Conqueror!
COMMANDER.   Acknowledgement   and
    thanks in this our town
Receive in token of the love you show.
    ALONSO. Accept this rustic tribute to re-
        nown,
    Proffered how simply. These poor meadows
        grow
Scant sustenance of woe.
    ESTEBAN. Welcome accept
To Fuente Ovejuna, whose elders glow
    With pride, offering homely gifts, yet ept
To please, as pod or sprout or root, in carts
Heaped high with ruddy fruits, the produce
    rept
    From field and orchard, ripening in our
        hearts,
Mellowed in crib and barnyard. First, car one
Twin hampers bears of jars, baked for these
    marts,
    Whereto are added geese that sleekly run
Long necks from tangling nets, and shrilly
    shriek
Cackles of praise, paeans of booty won.
    Ten salted hogs bid the next wagon creak,
Bulging with fatty trimmings and dried
    meat;
The skins like amber shine, side, haunch and
    breek.
    A hundred pair of capon follow, treat

For the belly, plump hens torn from the
    cock
Through all the eager farms, tender and
    meet
  For axing. Arms we lack, nor bring we
    stock
Of blooded steeds, nor harness for the bold,
For such in rustic hands were cheat and mock
  Of love's pure gold which in our hearts is
    told.
Twelve wine-skins next appear, with beady
    wine
Filled full, in winter enemy of cold
  And friendly to the soldier, ally in line
Of battle, or on defense trusty like steel,
Tempering courage, for temper springs of
    wine.
  Unnumbered cheeses, last, jounce past
    awheel,
With products of the churn and dairy days,
  True tokens of the love the people feel
Toward you and yours, harvests of heart-felt
    praise.

COMMANDER. Thanks and be gone, Alcaldes of this town. Be gone assured of favor.

ALONSO. Rest, Master, in enjoyment of
our love. These cat-tails before the door and
this coarse sedge grass should bear pearls to
match your deserving, as indeed we pray,
and yet fall short of the devotion of the
village.

COMMANDER. I accept the gifts right
gladly. So get you gone.

ESTEBAN. The singers will repeat the refrain.

SONG

  Welcome, great Commander,
  Many times a victor,
  Men and fields mowed down!
                        (*Exeunt.*)

COMMANDER. The girls stay behind.

LAURENCIA. No, Your Excellency.

COMMANDER. By the Lord you do! No airs
nor graces! These are soldiers here.

LAURENCIA. Pascuala, he looks your way.

PASCUALA. Do you teach me to be modest?

COMMANDER. I look your way, little
chuck with the crook, and tend to this burr
of the pasture, till she open to me.

PASCUALA. We grew here, Master.

COMMANDER. Pass into the house where
my men will keep you safe.

LAURENCIA. If the Alcaldes go in so will
we, because one is my father, but a girl by
herself is just a girl and must be careful.

COMMANDER. A word, Flores.

FLORES. Master?

COMMANDER. How? What mean these
green-briers?

FLORES. Walk straight in, girls. Come!

LAURENCIA. You let go!

FLORES. Any fool can walk.

PASCUALA. You'll lock the door if we do
go in.

FLORES. Pass and taste the spoils of war.
Come!

COMMANDER. (*Aside to* ORTUÑO) Throw
the bolt, Ortuño, once they're inside.
                        (*Exit.*)

LAURENCIA. You hurt us, Flores.

ORTUÑO. These cheeses came in no cart.

PASCUALA. No, and we are not for you,
either, so get out!

FLORES. What can you do with a girl?

LAURENCIA. Your master has his fill today for one stomach.

ORTUÑO. He's a judge of meat and prefers you, though the carts pass.

LAURENCIA. Then let him burst!
                        (*The girls go out.*)

FLORES. What will the Master say with
never a sight of a woman for good cheer?
They laugh at us.

ORTUÑO. Blows reward service, mostly
given for villainy, so there's no cure. It's
desert.

A tent prepared for audience. Enter the
KING DON FERDINAND OF ARAGON *and*
QUEEN ISABELLA, *accompanied by* DON
MANRIQUE *and Attendants.*

ISABELLA. To prepare is wise. Sire, harry
Alonso of Portugal where he has pitched his
tents, for a ready offense averts the threatened injury.

THE KING. Navarre and Aragon despatch
swift aid and succor. Under my command

the Castilian bands shall be formed. Success
lies in prevention.

ISABELLA. Majesty, prevail by strategy.

DON MANRIQUE. Two Regidors of Ciudad
Real crave audience.

THE KING. Admit them to our presence.
(*Enter two Regidors of Ciudad Real.*)

FIRST REGIDOR. Great Ferdinand the Cath-
olic our King,
Posting from Aragon to high Castile
On warlike service and the common weal,
Humble petition to thy sword we bring
For vengeance, urging here the patent royal
Bestowed on Ciudad Real, thy city,
Foully wronged. To be thy city was our joy,
Thy will our law, proclaimed in kingly char-
ter;
But blows of fate laid low our fealty.
A froward youth, Rodrigo Téllez Girón,
Master of Calatrava, with naked sword
Carves out addition to his wide domain,
Wasting our homes, our lands and revenues.
We met his treacherous assault, and force
Opposed to force, by threat and fear un-
daunted,
Till blood in rivers ran adown our streets,
Alas but vainly! The day we lost, and he,
Pricked on by the Commander Fernán Gó-
mez,
Cunning in council, governs the city,
While we, enslaved, lament our injuries.

THE KING. Where dwells this Fernán Gómez?

FIRST REGIDOR. Sire, Fuente Ovejuna is his
seat,
Wherein he rules amid his seignories.
He governs there, there does he his will,
Raining down blows upon his abject thralls
Beyond endurance.

THE KING. Name your captain.

SECOND REGIDOR. Sire,
None lives. Not one, alas, of noble blood
Survives unwounded, untaken or unslain.

ISABELLA. This cause demands an instant
remedy.
The walls may be surrendered to the foe,
Who thus will boldly dominate the pass,
Entering Extremadura from the side
Of Portugal.

THE KING. Set forth at once, Manrique,
And with two chosen companies chastise
This arrogance, denying let or stay.
The Count of Cabra shall by our command
As swiftly follow, bravest of the house
Of Córdoba.
The front of tyranny must bow
And pride lie low
In the presence of our majesty.

ISABELLA. Depart ambassador of victory.
(*Exeunt.*)

*A river bank near Fuente Ovejuna. Trees
and bushes.* LAURENCIA *and* FRONDOSO *enter.*

LAURENCIA. I had not wrung the sheets,
you saucy Frondoso, when you drove me
from the river bank with spying. While we
gaze the countryside talks and waits on tiptoe. The sturdiest of our lads, your jacket is
the gayest and the costliest, so others note
what you do, and not a girl in the village
nor herdsman on the hills nor down in the
river bottoms but swears we are one and of
right ought to be joined, while Juan Chamor-
ro, the sacristan, leaves his piping to publish
the banns, for love, they say, goes first to
church. Ah, wine burst the vaults in August,
and burst every pot with must but I heed
them not nor attend to their chatter, though
it be time, methinks, and time soon for our
own good to put an end to all this idle talk
and pother.

FRONDOSO. Laughing Laurencia, I die
while you smile. Though I say nothing you
will not hear me, till at last I have scarcely
strength even to mutter. I would be your
husband but you repay with taunts my faith
and loyalty.

LAURENCIA. I encourage you all I can.

FRONDOSO. It's not enough. When I think
of you I cannot eat, drink or sleep. I starve
yet love an angel. God knows I die.

LAURENCIA. Cross yourself, Frondoso, or
else bethink you of some charm.

FRONDOSO. There's a charm for two doves
at the church, love, that makes them one.
God set us beak to beak!

LAURENCIA. Speak to your master, Juan

Rojo, if you will, and can summon the courage, else I must, since he is my uncle. Pray for the day, and hope.

FRONDOSO. Look! The Commander!

LAURENCIA. Stalking deer. Hide in the bushes.

FRONDOSO. Big bucks are hard to hide.

(*The* COMMANDER *enters.*)

COMMANDER. Aha! Following the fawn, I hit upon the doe.

LAURENCIA. I was resting from washing and return to the brookside now, Commander.

COMMANDER. Sweet Laurencia, stay, nor obscure the beauty heaven has granted to my sight. If you have escaped my hand till now, the woods and the fields will befriend us, for they are accomplices of love. Bend your pride and let your cheek flush as it has never done yet in the village. Sebastiana, who was Pedro Redondo's wife, has been mine, and so has the chit who wedded Martín del Pozo. I came upon her two nights a bride, and she opened to me fondly.

LAURENCIA. My lord, they had opened to so many that their fondness was no longer in question. Ask the village. God grant you luck with the deer. The cross on your breast proclaims you are no tempter of women.

COMMANDER. You protest too much, lass. I put down my crossbow. With my hands I will subdue these pretty wiles.

LAURENCIA. No, no! What would you? Let go!

(FRONDOSO *re-enters and seizes the crossbow.*)

COMMANDER. Struggle is useless.

FRONDOSO. (*Aside*) I take the bow. Heaven grant I do not shoot.

COMMANDER. Yield! Have done!

LAURENCIA. Heaven help me now!

COMMANDER. We are alone, no one will hear —

FRONDOSO. Noble Commander, loose that girl, or your breast shall be my mark, though the cross shine clear upon it.

COMMANDER. The dog insults me!

FRONDOSO. Here is no dog. Laurencia, flee!

LAURENCIA. Frondoso, you take care.

FRONDOSO. Go!

(LAURENCIA *goes.*)

COMMANDER. Only a fool deprives himself of his sword, which I, god or devil, put by, fearing to fright the chase!

FRONDOSO. By God above, Commander, if I loose this string I'll gyve you like a hawk!

COMMANDER. Betrayed! Traitorous hind, deliver up that crossbow. Dog, set down!

FRONDOSO. To be shot through? Hardly. Love is a warrior that yields his throne to none.

COMMANDER. Shall a knight valiant in battle be foiled by a dumb peasant? Stay, wretch! On guard! — for I forget my rank and station.

FRONDOSO. I do not. I am a swain, but since I will to live, I take the crossbow with me.

COMMANDER. Ignominy, shame! I will have vengeance to the hilt. Quickly I vanish.

ACT TWO

Square in Fuente Ovejuna. ESTEBAN *enters with a Regidor.*

ESTEBAN. Better touch the reserve no further. The year bodes ill with threat of foul weather, so let the grain be impounded though there be mutiny among the people.

REGIDOR. I am of your mind if the village may be governed in peace.

ESTEBAN. Then speak to Fernán Gómez. These astrologers with their harangues pretend they know secrets God only knows. Not a scrap can they read of the future, unholy fabricators of what was and what shall be, when to their eyes even the present is blank,

For their ignorance is rank.

Can they bring the clouds indoors and lay the stars upon the table? How do they peer into heaven and yet come down with such dire disasters? These fellows tell us how and when to sow, here with the grain, there with the barley and the vegetables, the squash, mustard, and cucumber —

As squashes add them to the number.

Next they predict a man will die and one does in Transylvania, or the vineyards shall suffer drought, or people take to beer in far-off Germany; also cherries will freeze and impoverish the neighbors in Gascony, while there will be a plague of tigers in Hyrcania. So or not so, pray remember.

The year ends with December.

(LEONELO, *a student, enters with* BARRILDO.)

LEONELO. I grant this town nothing, upon a re-view, but as the plain seat of stupidity.

BARRILDO. How did you fare in Salamanca?

LEONELO. That is no simple story.

BARRILDO. By this you must be a complete Bártulo.[1]

LEONELO. Not even a barber by this. In our faculty few trim knowledge from the course.

BARRILDO. You return to us a scholar.

LEONELO. No, but I have learned what it is wise to know.

BARRILDO. With all the printing of books nowadays a man might pick up a few and be wise.

LEONELO. We know less than we did when there was less knowledge, for the bulk of learning is so great no man can compass it. Confusion results from excess, all the stir goes to froth, while those who read befuddle their heads with endless pages and become literal slaves. The art of printing has raised up a thousand geniuses overnight. To be sure it spreads and conserves the Holy Scriptures, that they may be known of all and endure, but this invention of Gutenberg, that famous German of Mayence, has in fact devitalized glory. Many a man of repute has proved a very fool when his books have been printed, or else suffered the mortification of having simpletons issue theirs in his name. Others have set down arrant nonsense and credited it to their enemies out of spite, to whose undoing it circulates and appalls the world.

BARRILDO. I can find no words to argue with you.

LEONELO. The ignorant have the learned at their mercy.

BARRILDO. Leonelo, on every account printing is a mighty invention.

LEONELO. For centuries the world did very well without it, and to this hour it has not produced one Jerome nor a second Augustine. The men were saints.

BARRILDO. Sit down and rest, for my head is dizzy opposing you.

(JUAN ROJO *and a Farmer enter.*)

JUAN ROJO. There is not a dower on four of these farms if the fields continue as they are, and this may be seen on all sides, far and near, for all is one.

FARMER. What word of the Commander?

JUAN ROJO. Would Laurencia had never set foot by the river!

FARMER. I could dangle him gladly from that olive tree, savage, unbridled and lewd!

(*The* COMMANDER *enters with* ORTUÑO *and* FLORES.)

COMMANDER. Heaven for the just!

REGIDOR. Commander!

COMMANDER. God's body, why do you stand?

ESTEBAN. Señor, where the custom is to sit, we stand.

COMMANDER. I tell you to sit down.

ESTEBAN. As honorable men we cannot do you honor, having none.

COMMANDER. Sit down while I talk with you!

ESTEBAN. Shall we discuss my hound, sir?

COMMANDER. Alcalde, these true men of mine praise the rare virtue of the animal.

ESTEBAN. The beast is swift. In God's name but he can overtake a thief or harry a coward right cruelly.

COMMANDER. I would set him on a graceful hare that these days lopes before me.

ESTEBAN. Done, if you will lead us to the hare.

COMMANDER. Oh, speaking of your daughter —

ESTEBAN. My daughter?

COMMANDER. Yes, why not? The hare.

ESTEBAN. My daughter is not your quarry.

---

[1] wise man

COMMANDER. Alcalde, pray you prevail upon her.

ESTEBAN. How?

COMMANDER. She plumes herself before me. A wife, and a proud one, of a councillor who attends before me now and listens, at my every look darts kindling glances.

ESTEBAN. She does ill. You, Señor, do ill also, speaking thus freely.

COMMANDER. Oh, what rustic virtue! Here, Flores, get him the book of *Politics*, and let him perfect himself in Aristotle.

ESTEBAN. Señor, the town would live in the reflection of your honor. There be men in Fuente Ovejuna.

LEONELO. I never read of such a tyrant.

COMMANDER. What have I said, in faith, to which you take exception, Regidor?

JUAN ROJO. You have spoken ill. Speak well, for it is not meet you level at our honor.

COMMANDER. Your honor? Good! Are we importing friars to Calatrava?

REGIDOR. There be those that be content to wear the cross, though the heart be not too pure.

COMMANDER. I do not injure you, mingling my blood with yours.

JUAN ROJO. A smirch is no hidden stain.

COMMANDER. In doing my will I accord your wives honor.

ESTEBAN. The very words spell dishonor, while your deeds pass all remedy.

COMMANDER. Obstinate dolt! Ah, better the cities where men of parts and renown wreak their will and their pleasure! There husbands give thanks when their wives sacrifice upon the altar.

ESTEBAN. They do no such service, if with this you would move us. God rules, too, in the cities, and justice is swift.

COMMANDER. Get up and get out.

ESTEBAN. We have said what you have heard.

COMMANDER. Out of the square straight! Let not one remain behind!

ESTEBAN. We firmly take our leave.

COMMANDER. What? In company?

FLORES. By the rood, hold your hand!

COMMANDER. These hinds would slander me, defiling the square with lies, departing together.

ORTUÑO. Pray be patient.

COMMANDER. I marvel that I am so calm! Walk each one by himself, apart. Let no man speak till his door has shut behind him!

LEONELO. Great God, can they stomach this?

ESTEBAN. My path lies this way.

(ESTEBAN, JUAN ROJO, *Regidor*, LEONELO *and the Peasants go out, leaving the* COMMANDER, FLORES *and* ORTUÑO.)

COMMANDER. What shall we do with these knaves?

ORTUÑO. Their speech offends you and you by no means hide your unwillingness to hear it.

COMMANDER. Do they compare themselves with me?

FLORES. Perversity of man.

COMMANDER. Shall that peasant retain my crossbow and not be punished while I live?

FLORES. Last night we took him, as we thought, at Laurencia's door, and I gave an oaf who was his double a slash that married his two ears.

COMMANDER. Can you find no trace of that Frondoso?

FLORES. They say he remains in these parts still.

COMMANDER. And dares remain, who has attempted my life?

FLORES. Like a silly bird or a fish, a decoy will tempt him and he will fall into the lure.

COMMANDER. That a laborer, a stripling of the soil should aim a crossbow at a captain before whose sword Córdoba and Granada tremble! Flores, the end of the world has come!

FLORES. Blame love, for it knows no monopoly of daring.

ORTUÑO. Seeing he lived, I took it as a token of your kindly disposition.

COMMANDER. Ortuño, the smile is false. Dirk in hand, within these two hours would I ransack the place, but vengeance yields the rein to reason until the hour shall come. Which of you had a smile of Pascuala?

FLORES. She says she intends to marry.

COMMANDER. How far is she prepared to go?

FLORES. She will advise you anon when she can accept a favor.

COMMANDER. How of Olalla?

ORTUÑO. Fair words.

COMMANDER. Buxom and spirited! How far?

ORTUÑO. She says her husband has been uneasy these past days, suspicious of my messages, and of your hovering about, attended. As soon as his fears are allayed, you shall have a sign.

COMMANDER. On the honor of a knight 'tis well! These rustics have sharp eyes and commonly are evil-minded.

ORTUÑO. Evil-minded, ill-spoken and ill-favored.

COMMANDER. Say not so of Inés.

FLORES. Which one?

COMMANDER. Antón's wife. Aha!

FLORES. Yes, she will oblige any day. I saw her in the corral, which you can enter secretly.

COMMANDER. These easy girls we requite but poorly. Flores, may women never learn the worth of the wares they sell!

FLORES. No pain wipes out the sweetness wholly. To prevail quickly, cheats the expectation, but, as philosophers agree, women desire the men as they are desired, nor can form be without substance, at which we should not complain, nor wonder.

COMMANDER. A man who is fiercely swept by love finds solace in a speedy yielding to desire, but afterward despises the object, for the road to forgetfulness, even under the star of honor, is to hold oneself cheap before love's importuning.

(CIMBRANOS, *a Soldier, enters, armed.*)

CIMBRANOS. Where is the Commander?

ORTUÑO. Behold him, if you have the faculty of sight.

CIMBRANOS. Oh, gallant Fernán Gómez, Put off the rustic cap

For the morion [2] of steel
And change the cloak
For armor!
The Master of Santiago
And the Count of Cabra,
By title of the Castilian Queen,
Lay siege to Don Rodrigo Girón,
In Ciudad Real,
And short his shrift unaided
Before their approaching powers,
Forfeiting the spoils so dearly won
At cost of blood of Calatrava.
Already from the battlements
Our sentinels descry
Pennons and banners,
The castles and the lions,
Quartered with the bars of Aragon.
What though the King of Portugal
Heap on Girón vain honors?
Vanquished, the Master must creep home
To Almagro, wounded,
Abandoning the city.
To horse, to horse, Señor!
At sight of you
The enemy will fly
Headlong into Castile,
Nor pause this side surrender.

COMMANDER. Hold and speak no more!
        Stay for me.
        Ortuño, sound the trumpet
        Here in the square.
        What soldiers
        Are billeted with me?

ORTUÑO. A troop of fifty men.

COMMANDER. To horse every one!

CIMBRANOS. Spur apace or Ciudad Real
        Falls to the King.

COMMANDER. That shall never be.
                        (*Exeunt.*)

Open country, fields or meadow. MENGO *enters with* LAURENCIA *and* PASCUALA, *running.*

PASCUALA. Don't leave us.

MENGO. What's the matter?

LAURENCIA. Mengo, we seek the village

---

[2] helmet

in groups, when there's no man to go with us, for fear of the Commander.

MENGO. How can the ugly devil torment so many?

LAURENCIA. He is upon us night and day.

MENGO. Oh, would heaven send a bolt to strike him where he stands!

LAURENCIA. He's an unchained beast, poison, arsenic and pestilence throughout the land.

MENGO. Laurencia, they say Frondoso pointed an arrow at his breast for your sake, here in this very meadow.

LAURENCIA. Mengo, I hated all men till then, but since that day I relent. Frondoso had courage; it will cost him his life.

MENGO. He must fly these fields, that's sure.

LAURENCIA. I love him enough to advise it, but he'll have no counsel of me, storming and raging and turning away. The Commander swears he will hang him feet upward.

PASCUALA. I say hang the Commander.

MENGO. Stone him I say. God knows but I will up and at him with a rock I saved at the sheep-fold that will land him a crack that will crush his skull in! He's wickeder than Gabalus, that old Roman.

LAURENCIA. The one that was so wicked was Heliogabalus. He was a man.

MENGO. Whoever he was, call him Gab or Gal, his scurvy memory yields to this. You know history. Was there ever a man like Fernán Gómez?

PASCUALA. No, he's no man. There must be tigers in him.

(JACINTA enters.)

JACINTA. Help in God's name, if you are women!

LAURENCIA. Why, what's this, Jacinta?

PASCUALA. We are all your friends.

JACINTA. The Commander's men, on their way to Ciudad Real, armed with villainy when it should be steel, would seize me and take me to him.

LAURENCIA. God help you, Jacinta! With you, pray he be merciful, but I choose rather to die than be taken!   (Exit.)

PASCUALA. Jacinta, being no man I cannot save you.   (Exit.)

MENGO. I can because I am a man in strength and in name. Jacinta, stand beside me.

JACINTA. Are you armed?

MENGO. Twice. I have two arms.

JACINTA. You will need more.

MENGO. Jacinta, the ground bears stones.

(FLORES and ORTUÑO enter.)

FLORES. Did you think you could run away from us?

JACINTA. Mengo, I am dead with fear!

MENGO. Friends, this is a poor peasant girl.

ORTUÑO. Do you assume to defend her?

MENGO. I do, so please you, since I am her relative and must protect her, if that may be.

FLORES. Kill him straightway!

MENGO. Strike me heaven, but I am in a rage! You can put a cord around my neck but, by God, I'll sell my life dear!

(The COMMANDER and CIMBRANOS enter.)

COMMANDER. Who calls? What says this turd?

FLORES. The people of this town, which we should raze for there is no health in it, insult our arms.

MENGO. Señor, if pity can prevail in the face of injustice, reprove these soldiers who would force this peasant girl in your name, though spouse and parents be bred to honor, and grant me license straight to lead her home unharmed.

COMMANDER. I will grant them license straight to harm you for your impudence. Let go that sling.

MENGO. Señor —

COMMANDER. Flores, Ortuño, and Cimbranos, it will serve to tie his hands.

MENGO. Is this the voice of honor?

COMMANDER. What do these sheep of Fuente Ovejuna think of me?

MENGO. Señor, have I offended you, or mayhap the village, in anything?

FLORES. Shall we kill him?

COMMANDER. It would soil your arms which we shall stain with redder blood.

ORTUÑO. We wait your orders, sir.

COMMANDER. Flog him without mercy. Tie him to that oak-tree, baring his back, and with the reins —

MENGO. No, no, for you are noble!

COMMANDER. Flog him till the rivets start from the straps!

MENGO. My God, can such things be?

(*They lead him off.*)

COMMANDER. Pretty peasant, draw near daintily. Who would prefer a farmer to a valiant nobleman?

JACINTA. But will you heal my honor, taking me for yourself?

COMMANDER. Truly I do take you.

JACINTA. No, I have an honorable father, sir, who may not equal you in birth, but in virtue he is the first.

COMMANDER. These are troubled days, nor will this rude peasantry salve my outraged spirit. Pass with me under the trees.

JACINTA. I?

COMMANDER. This way.

JACINTA. Look what you do!

COMMANDER. Refuse and I spurn you. You shall be the slut of the army.

JACINTA. No power of lust can overcome me.

COMMANDER. Silence and go before.

JACINTA. Pity, Señor!

COMMANDER. Pity have I none.

JACINTA. I appeal from your wickedness to God!

(*Exit the* COMMANDER, *haling her out.*)

Room in JUAN ROJO'S *house.* LAURENCIA *and* FRONDOSO *enter.*

LAURENCIA. Through fields of danger
My love comes to me.

FRONDOSO. The hazard bear witness
To the love that I bear.
The Commander has vanished
O'er the brow of the hill
And I, the slave of beauty,
Lose all sense of fear,
Seeing him disappear.

LAURENCIA. Speak ill of no man.
To pray for his end
Postpones it, my friend.

FRONDOSO. Eternally.
And may he live a thousand years,
And every one bear joy!
I'll pray for his soul also
And may the pious litany
Bite, sear, and destroy!
Laurencia, if my love
Live in your heart,
Let me enter there, love,
To dwell loyally.
The town counts us one,
Yet by the book we are twain.
Will you, I wonder,
Say yes,
Compulsion under?

LAURENCIA. Say for me to the town
Oh yes, yes and yes
Again and again!

FRONDOSO. I kiss your feet
For this new miracle of mercy.
Beauty grants me joy
In words grace conjures.

LAURENCIA. Flatter me no more,
But speak to my father
And win my uncle's praise.
Oh, speak,
Frondoso,
Oh may we marry, oh Frondoso,
It will be heaven
To be your wife!

FRONDOSO. In God we trust.

(*Hides himself. Enter* ESTEBAN *and* JUAN ROJO, *Regidor.*)

ESTEBAN. His departure outraged the square, and indeed it was most unseemly behavior. Such tyranny stuns as a blow; even poor Jacinta must pay the price of his madness.

JUAN ROJO. Spain turns already to the Catholic Kings, a name by which our rulers have come to be known, and the nation renders obedience to their laws. They have appointed the Master of Santiago Captain General of Ciudad Real, despatching him forthwith against Girón's oppression of the town. But my heart aches for Jacinta, being as she is an honest girl.

ESTEBAN. They beat Mengo soundly.

JUAN ROJO. I never saw dye, black or red, to rival his flesh.

ESTEBAN. Peace and no more, for my blood boils, or else congeals at his name. Have I authority or a staff of office?

JUAN ROJO. The man cannot control his servants.

ESTEBAN. On top of all this they chanced on Pedro Redondo's wife one day in the very bottom of the valley, and after he insulted her she was turned over to the men.

JUAN ROJO. Who is listening concealed?

FRONDOSO. I, a petitioner.

JUAN ROJO. Granted, Frondoso. Your father brought you to be, but I have brought you to be what you are, a prop and support, who is my very son in the house.

FRONDOSO. Assured, Alcalde, of permission, I speak as one by birth honorable, and not obscure.

ESTEBAN. You have suffered wrong at the hand of Fernán Gómez?

FRONDOSO. More than a little.

ESTEBAN. My heart records it. The man is surely mad.

FRONDOSO. Señor, appealing to a father,
Serving a daughter,
I beg her hand
Not all a stranger.
Pardon presumption though it be extreme;
Boldly I speak for men shall count me bold.

ESTEBAN. By that word, Frondoso,
You renew my life,
Brushing aside
The apprehension of the years.
Now heaven be praised, my son,
For your proposal seals our honor,
Which may love guard jealously.
Apprise your father straight
Of this new promised joy,
For my consent stays
But his approbation,
In whose fair prospect
Beams my happiness.

JUAN ROJO. The maid must consent also.

ESTEBAN. Her consent should precede
And has preceded indeed,
Because a faithful lover
Is prophet and recorder.

I have taken an oath to bestow some right good maravedis [3] upon a good young man.

FRONDOSO. I seek no dower. Gold, they say, makes the day dull.

JUAN ROJO. So long as he does not court the wine-skins, you may dower him without stint or mercy.

ESTEBAN. I will speak to my daughter that assurance may be doubly sure.

FRONDOSO. Do, pray, for violence has no part in love.

ESTEBAN. Dearest daughter Laurencia!

LAURENCIA. Oh, father?

ESTEBAN. She approves for she answers before I speak! — Dearest daughter Laurencia, step apart a moment. Frondoso, who is an honest lad, if one there be in Fuente Ovejuna, inquires of me as to your friend Gila, whom he would honor as a wife.

LAURENCIA. Gila a wife?

ESTEBAN. Is she a fitting mate, a proper wife?

LAURENCIA. Yes, father, oh she is! Of course!

ESTEBAN. Of course she is ugly, as ugly as they come, which led me to suggest, Laurencia, that Frondoso look at you.

LAURENCIA. Father, be serious as becomes your office.

ESTEBAN. Do you love him?

LAURENCIA. I have favored him and am myself favored. But you knew!

ESTEBAN. Shall I say yes?

LAURENCIA. Yes, father, for me.

ESTEBAN. The yes will do for us both. Come, we will seek his father,

JUAN ROJO. Instantly.

ESTEBAN. My boy, to return to the dower. I can afford, yes, and I pledge, four thousand maravedis.

FRONDOSO. Señor, I am your son now and you offend me.

ESTEBAN. A day and pride abates, lad, but if you marry without a dower, by my faith, many a day will succeed and the abatement not be mended.

(*Exeunt* ESTEBAN *and* JUAN ROJO.)

[3] money

LAURENCIA. Frondoso, bliss!

FRONDOSO. Yes, triply.

    In a single moment
    I feel so happy
    I could die with pleasure!
    Bliss it must be
    Shared among three.
    I look at you and laugh,
    Laugh my heart out.
    Oh, what treasure
    I drink in at a glance
    Now love comes to me,
    Laurencia!   (*Exeunt.*)

Ciudad Real. The walls. The MASTER, *the* COMMANDER, FLORES, *and* ORTUÑO *enter.*

COMMANDER. Fly, sir! There is no remedy.

MASTER. The wall giving way, the weight of the enemy undoes us.

COMMANDER. We have bled them and cost them many lives.

MASTER. The banner of Calatrava shall not trail among their spoils, though it were recompense turning all to glory.

COMMANDER. Our league, Girón, crumbles and lies lifeless.

MASTER. Can we outstrip fortune, though she be blind, favoring us today, today, to leave us?

VOICES. (*Within*) Hail, Victory! Hail, the Crown of Castile!

MASTER. The pennons show upon the battlements while all the windows of the tower thrust banners forth, proclaiming the victory.

COMMANDER. Much joy may they have of the day! By my soul, a day of slaughter!

MASTER. Fernán Gómez, I'll to Calatrava.

COMMANDER. And I to Fuente Ovejuna. Stay upon your cousin of Portugal, or, weighing adversity, yield allegiance to the Catholic King.

MASTER. I shall apprise you with despatch.

COMMANDER. Time is a hard general.

MASTER. God grant me few years like this, fertile in undeception.   (*Exeunt.*)

Esteban's house in Fuente Ovejuna. Enter the wedding-train, Musicians, MENGO, FRONDOSO, LAURENCIA, PASCUALA, BARRILDO, ESTEBAN *and* JUAN ROJO.

MUSICIANS. Joy to the bride
    And long life beside!
        Long life!

MENGO. A clever boy thought that up! Oh, that boy is clever!

BARRILDO. He could troll it out at any wedding.

FRONDOSO. Mengo sings only to the lash because he says it has more tang to it.

MENGO. Yes, and I know a young chap in the valley, not meaning you of course, who would make a nice dish for the Commander.

BARRILDO. Enough of gloom and amen, seeing that a ferocious barbarian offers at our honor.

MENGO. I believe a hundred soldiers whipped me that day, and all I had was a sling that I gave up to protect me. However, I know a man, not mentioning names, who was full of honor and pursued with a syringe loaded with dye and some herbs that caused him great pain, and oh my, the pain that they caused him! How that man did suffer!

BARRILDO. By way of jest. It was done as a laughing matter.

MENGO. As it came out afterwards. At the time he never laughed nor even suspected, but felt much better without the dye, though while it was in, death was preferable.

FRONDOSO. A song would be preferable, or anything. Come, let it be a good one, Mengo.

MENGO. Good! Do you invite me?
    Bride and groom
    Must dwell together.
    Pray God neither one of them
    Dare fight or row it.
    Let both die
    Just too tired out to live
    A long time after
    They have forgotten all about it —
    I mean the wedding.

FRONDOSO. God help the poet who made that up!

BARRILDO. He needs more help.

MENGO. Oh, that reminds me! Did you ever see a baker baking buns? He dips the dough into the oil until the pot is full, and then some swell up, some come out askew and twisted, leaning to the right, tumbling to the left, some scorched, some burned, some uneatable. Well, a poet's subject is his dough, he plops a verse onto the paper hoping it will turn out sweet, and his friends all tell him so, but when he tries to sell it he has to eat it himself, for the world is too wise to buy or else hasn't the money.

BARRILDO. You came to the wedding so as not to give the bride and groom a chance to talk.

LAURENCIA. Uncle, you must be kissed. And you, too, Father —

JUAN ROJO. Not on the hand. May your father's hand be your protection, and Frondoso's also, in the hour of need.

ESTEBAN. Rojo, heaven protect her and her husband on whom I invoke an everlasting benison.

FRONDOSO. Ever to share with you.

JUAN ROJO. Come all now, play and sing, for they are as good as one.

MUSICIANS. O maiden fair
    With the flowing hair,
  Shun Fuente Ovejuna!
    A warrior knight
    Awaits thee there,
  Waits the maid with the flowing hair
  With the Cross of Calatrava.
    Oh, hide in the shade
    By the branches made!
    Why, lovely maiden,
    Why afraid?
    Against desire
    No wall may aid
  'Gainst the Knight of Calatrava.

    Thou grim knight spare
    Frail beauty there
  By Fuente Ovejuna!
    No screen can hide,
    No mountain bare,

  No ocean bar love anywhere
  'Gainst the Knight of Calatrava.
    Here in the shade,
    Shall love's debt be paid.
    O peerless maiden,
    Why afraid?
    Against desire
    No wall may aid
  'Gainst the Knight of Calatrava.

(*The* COMMANDER, FLORES, ORTUÑO *and* CIMBRANOS *enter.*)

COMMANDER. Let all in the house stand still on pain of death.

JUAN ROJO. Señor, though this be no play, your command shall be obeyed. Will you sit down? Why all these arms and weapons? We question not, for you bring home victory.

FRONDOSO. I am dead unless heaven helps me.

LAURENCIA. Stand behind me, Frondoso.

COMMANDER. No, seize and bind him.

JUAN ROJO. Surrender, boy, 'tis best.

FRONDOSO. Do you want them to kill me?

JUAN ROJO. Why, pray?

COMMANDER. I am no man to take life unjustly, for, if I were, my soldiers would have run him through ere this, forward or rearwards. Throw him into prison where his own father shall pronounce sentence upon him, chained in his dank cell.

PASCUALA. This is a wedding, Señor.

COMMANDER. What care I for weddings? Is this your occupation in the village?

PASCUALA. Pardon him, Señor, if he has done wrong, being who you are.

COMMANDER. Pascuala, he has done no wrong to me, but offense to the Master, Téllez Girón, whom God preserve. He has mocked his law, scoffed at his rule, and punishment must be imposed as a most dire example, or there will be those to rise against the Master, seeing that one afternoon, but shortly gone, flower of these loyal and faithful vassals, he dared take aim, pointing the crossbow at the bosom of the High Commander.

ESTEBAN. If a father-in-law may offer a word of excuse, his dudgeon was not strange but manly, taking umbrage as a lover. You would deprive him of his wife. Small wonder the man should defend her!

COMMANDER. Alcalde, the truth is not in you.

ESTEBAN. Be just, Señor.

COMMANDER. I had no thought to deprive him of his wife, nor could so have done, he having none.

ESTEBAN. But you had the thought, which shall suffice. Henceforth enough! A King and Queen rule now in Castile whose firm decrees shall bring this rioting to cease, nor will they stay their hands, these wars once ended, nor suffer arrogance to overpower their towns and villages, crucifying the people cruelly. Upon his breast the King will place a cross, and on that royal breast it shall be the symbol, too, of honor!

COMMANDER. Death to presumption! Wrest the staff from him.

ESTEBAN. Señor, I yield it up, commanded.

COMMANDER. Beat him with it while he capers about this stable. Have at him smartly!

ESTEBAN. Still we suffer your authority. I am ready. Begin!

PASCUALA. They beat an old man?

LAURENCIA. Yes, because he is my father. Beat him, avenging yourself on me!

COMMANDER. Arrest her, and let ten soldiers guard this sinful maid!

(*Exeunt* COMMANDER *and Train.*)

ESTEBAN. Justice, descend this day from heaven! (*Exit.*)

PASCUALA. No wedding but a shambles. (*Exit.*)

BARRILDO. And not a man of us said a word!

MENGO. I have had my beating already and you can still see purple enough on me to outfit a Cardinal, without the trouble of sending to Rome. Try, if you don't believe it, what a thorough job they can do.

JUAN ROJO. We must all take counsel.

MENGO. My counsel, friends, is to take nothing but forget it. I know which side I am on, though I don't say, for it's scaled like a salmon. Never again will any man get me to take it. Nor woman either.

ACT THREE

A room in the Town Hall at Fuente Ovejuna. ESTEBAN, ALONSO, *and* BARRILDO *enter.*

ESTEBAN. Is the Town Board assembled?

BARRILDO. Not a person can be seen.

ESTEBAN. Bravely we face danger!

BARRILDO. All the farms had warning.

ESTEBAN. Frondoso is a prisoner in the tower and my daughter Laurencia in such plight that she is lost save for the direct interposition of heaven.

(JUAN ROJO *enters with the Second Regidor.*)

JUAN ROJO. Who complains aloud when silence is salvation? Peace, in God's name, peace!

ESTEBAN. I will shout to the clouds till they re-echo my complaints while men marvel at my silence.

(*Enter* MENGO *and Peasants.*)

MENGO. We came to attend the meeting.

ESTEBAN. Farmers of this village, an old man whose grey beard is bathed in tears, inquires what rites, what obsequies we poor peasants, assembled here, shall prepare for our ravished homes, bereft of honor? And if life be honor, how shall we fare, since there breathes not one among us whom this savage has not offended? Speak! Who but has been wounded deeply, poisoned in respect? Lament now, yes, cry out! Well? If all be ill, how then say well? Well, there is work for men to do.

JUAN ROJO. The direst that can be. Since by report it is published that Castile is subject now to a King who shall presently make his entrance into Córdoba, let us despatch two Regidors to that city to cast themselves at his feet and demand remedy.

BARRILDO. King Ferdinand is occupied with the overthrow of his enemies, who are not few, so that his commitments are warlike entirely. It were best to seek other succor.

REGIDOR. If my voice have any weight, I declare the independence of the village.

JUAN ROJO. How can that be?

MENGO. On my soul, my back tells me the Town Board will be informed as to that directly.

REGIDOR. The tree of our patience has been cut down, the ship of our joy rides storm-tossed, emptied of its treasure. They have rept the daughter from one who is Alcalde of this town in which we dwell, breaking his staff over his aged head. Could a slave be scorned more basely?

JUAN ROJO. What would you have the people do?

REGIDOR. Die or rain death on tyrants! We are many while they are few.

BARRILDO. Lift our hands against our Lord and Master?

ESTEBAN. Only the King is our master, save for God, never these devouring beasts. If God be with us, what have we to fear?

MENGO. Gentlemen, I advise caution in the beginning and ever after. Although I represent only the very simplest laborers, who bear the most, believe me we find the bearing most unpleasant.

JUAN ROJO. If our wrongs are so great, we lose nothing with our lives. And end, then! Our homes and vineyards burn. Vengeance on the tyrants!

(*Enter* LAURENCIA, *her hair disheveled.*)

LAURENCIA. Open, for I have need of the support of men! Deeds, or I cry out to heaven! Do you know me?

ESTEBAN. Martyr of God, my daughter?

JUAN ROJO. This is Laurencia.

LAURENCIA. Yes, and so changed that, gazing, you doubt still!

ESTEBAN. My daughter!

LAURENCIA. No, no more! Not yours.

ESTEBAN. Why, light of my eyes, why, pride of the valley?

LAURENCIA. Ask not, reckon not,
Here be it known
Tyrants reign o'er us,
We are ruled by traitors,
Justice is there none.
I was not Frondoso's,

Yours to avenge me,
Father, till the night
I was yours
Though he was my husband,
You the defender
Guarding the bride.

As well might the noble pay for the jewel lost in the merchant's hand!

I was lost to Fernán Gómez,
Haled to his keep
Abandoned to wolves.
A dagger at my breast
Pointed his threats,
His flatteries, insults, lies,
To overcome my chastity
Before his fierce desires.

My face is bruised and bloody in this court of honest men. Some of you are fathers, some have daughters. Do your hearts sink within you, supine and cowardly crew? You are sheep, sheep! Oh, well-named, Village of Fuente Ovejuna, the Sheep Well! Sheep, sheep, sheep! Give me iron, for senseless stones can wield none, nor images, nor pillars — jasper though they be — nor dumb living things that lack the tiger's heart that follows him who steals its young, rending the hunter limb from limb upon the very margin of the raging sea, seeking the pity of the angry waves.

But you are rabbits, farmers,
Infidels in Spain,
Your wives strut before you
With the cock upon their train!
Tuck your knitting in your belts,
Strip off your manly swords,
For, God living, I swear
That your women dare
Pluck these fearsome despots,
Beard the traitors there!
No spinning for our girls;
Heave stones and do not blench.
Can you smile, men?
Will you fight?
Caps we'll set upon you,
The shelter of a skirt,
Be heirs, boys, to our ribbons,
The gift of the maidenry,

For now the Commander will hang Frondoso from a merlon of the tower, without let or trial, as presently he will string you all, you race of half-men, for the women will leave this village, nor one remain behind! Today the age of Amazons returns, we lift our arms and strike against this villainy, and the crash of our blows shall amaze the world!

ESTEBAN. Daughter, I am no man to bear names calmly, opprobrious and vile. I will go and beard this despot, though the united spheres revolve against me.

JUAN ROJO. So will I, for all his pride and knavery.

REGIDOR. Let him be surrounded and cut off.

BARRILDO. Hang a cloth from a pike as our banner and cry " Death to Monsters! "

JUAN ROJO. What course shall we choose?

MENGO. To be at them, of course. Raise an uproar and with it the village, for every man will take an oath and be with you that to the last traitor the oppressors shall die.

ESTEBAN. Seize swords and spears, crossbows, pikes and clubs.

MENGO. Long live the King and Queen!

ALL. Live our lords and masters!

MENGO. Death to cruel tyrants!

ALL. To cruel tyrants, death!

(*Exeunt all but* LAURENCIA.)

LAURENCIA. March on, and heaven march before you!

(*At the door*)

Hello! Ho, women of this town! Draw near!
    Draw near for the salvation of your honor!

(PASCUALA, JACINTA *and various Women enter.*)

PASCUALA. Who calls us? Where are the men today?

LAURENCIA. Behold them down that street, marching to murder Fernán Gómez. Yes, old men, young men, and troops of eager boys, like furies run to meet him! Shall they share all the glory of this mighty day, when we women can boast wrongs that match and outstrip theirs?

JACINTA. What can we do?

LAURENCIA. Fall in behind me and we will do a deed that shall re-echo round the sphere! Jacinta, you have been most deeply wronged; lead forth a squadron of our girls.

JACINTA. You have borne no less.

LAURENCIA. Oh, Pascuala, for a flag!

PASCUALA. Tie a cloth upon this lance to flourish. We shall have our banner.

LAURENCIA. Stay not even for that, for now it comes to me: — Every woman her headdress! Wave, banners, wave!

PASCUALA. Name a captain and march!

LAURENCIA. We need no captain.

PASCUALA. No? Wave, banners!

LAURENCIA. When my courage is up I laugh at the Cid and pale Rodomonte! [1]

(*Exeunt.*)

Hall in the Castle of the Commander. FLORES, ORTUÑO, CIMBRANOS *and the* COMMANDER *enter. Also* FRONDOSO, *his hands bound.*

COMMANDER. And by the cord that dangles from his hands
Let him be hung until cut down by death.

FRONDOSO. My lord, you shame your worth.

COMMANDER. String him up on the battlements without further word.

FRONDOSO. I had no thought, my lord, against your life.

(*Noise and uproar.*)

FLORES. What is this noise outside?

COMMANDER. I hear voices.

FLORES. Do they threaten your justice, sire?

(*Knocking and blows.*)

ORTUÑO. They are breaking down the gates.

COMMANDER. The gate of my castle, the seat of the Commandery?

FLORES. The people fill the court.

JUAN ROJO. (*Within*) Push, smash, pull down, burn, destroy!

ORTUÑO. I like not their numbers.

COMMANDER. Shall these hinds come against me?

---

[1] leaders famous in Spanish and Italian epics

FLORES. Such passing fury sweeps them that all the outer doors are already beaten in!

COMMANDER. Undo this bumpkin. Frondoso, speak to this Alcalde. Warn him of his peril.

FRONDOSO. Sire, what they do, remember is done in love.   (*Exit.*)

MENGO. (*Within*) Hail, Ferdinand and Isabella, and let the traitor die!

FLORES. Señor, in God's name you had best conceal your person.

COMMANDER. If they persevere we can hold this room, for the doors are strong. They will turn back as quickly as they came.

FLORES. When the people rise and screw their courage to the point, they never stop short of rapine and blood.

COMMANDER. Behind this grating as a barricade we can defend ourselves right stoutly.

FRONDOSO. (*Within*) Free Fuente Ovejuna!

COMMANDER. What a leader for these swine! I will out and fall upon them.

FLORES. I marvel at your courage.

ESTEBAN. (*Entering*) Now we meet the tyrant and his minions face to face! Death to the traitor! All for Fuente Ovejuna!

(*Enter the Peasants.*)

COMMANDER. Hold, my people! Stay!

ALL. Wrongs hold not. Vengeance knows no stay!

COMMANDER. Tell your wrongs, and on the honor of a knight I'll requite them, every one.

ALL. Fuente Ovejuna! Long live Ferdinand, our King! Death to traitors and unbelievers!

COMMANDER. Will you not hear me? I lift my voice. I am your lord and master.

ALL. No, our lords and masters are the Catholic Kings!

COMMANDER. Stay a little.

ALL. All for Fuente Ovejuna! Die, Fernán Gómez!

(*Exeunt after breaking through the bars. The Women enter, armed.*)

LAURENCIA. Stop here and challenge fortune, no women but an army.

PASCUALA. Any that shows herself a woman by mercy, shall swallow the enemy's blood!

JACINTA. We shall spit his body on our pikes.

PASCUALA. As one we stand behind you.

ESTEBAN. (*Within*) Die, traitor though Commander!

COMMANDER. I die! O God, have pity in Thy clemency!

BARRILDO. (*Within*) Flores next!

MENGO. Have at him, for he landed on me with a thousand whacks.

FRONDOSO. I'll draw his soul out like a tooth!

LAURENCIA. They need us there!

PASCUALA. Let them go on! We guard the door.

BARRILDO. (*Within*) No prayers, no mercy, vermin!

LAURENCIA. Pascuala, I go with my sword drawn, not sheathed!   (*Exit.*)

BARRILDO. (*Within*) Down with Ortuño!

FRONDOSO. Slash him across the cheek.

(*FLORES enters, fleeing, pursued by MENGO.*)

FLORES. Pity, Mengo! I was not to blame.

MENGO. To be a pimp was bad enough, but why the devil lay on me?

PASCUALA. Mengo, give this man to the women. Stay! Stay!

MENGO. 'Fore God I will! And no punishment could be worse.

PASCUALA. Be well avenged!

MENGO. Believe me!

JACINTA. Run him through!

FLORES. What? Pity, women!

JACINTA. His courage well becomes him.

PASCUALA. So he has tears?

JACINTA. Kill him, viper of the vile!

PASCUALA. Down, wretch, and die!

FLORES. Pity, women, pity!

(*ORTUÑO enters, pursued by LAURENCIA.*)

ORTUÑO. I am not the man, I was not guilty!

LAURENCIA. In, women, and dye your conquering swords in traitor's blood. Prove all your courage!

PASCUALA. Die dealing death!

ALL. All for Fuente Ovejuna! Hail, King
Ferdinand!   (*Exeunt.*)

Near Ciudad Real. Enter the KING DON
FERDINAND OF ARAGON *and* QUEEN ISA-
BELLA OF CASTILE, *accompanied by* DON
MANRIQUE, *Master of Santiago.*
   MANRIQUE. Convenient haste hard follow-
      ing on command,
The victory was gained at little cost,
With show of slight resistance. Eagerly
We crave a fresh assault to try our prowess.
The Count of Cabra consolidates the front
And fends a counter-stroke, keeping the field.
   KING. The troops are well disposed. By our
      decree
He shall continue in his tents, the line
Reforming, holding the pass. An evil wind
Sweeps up from Portugal, where armed Al-
   fonso
Levies further powers. Cabra shall remain
The head and forefront of our valor here,
Watchful as diligent, that men may see
The danger fly before the sentinel
And peace return with plenty to the land.
         (*Enter* FLORES, *wounded.*)
   FLORES. King Ferdinand the Catholic,
   By right acclaim in Castile crowned,
   In token of thy majesty
   Oh hear the foulest treachery
   Done yet by man from where the sun
   Springs in the wakening east
   To the lands of westering night!
   KING. If there be warrant, speak.
   FLORES. O thou great King, my wounds
      speak,
   Admitting no delay
   To close my story
   With my life.
   I come from Fuente Ovejuna,
   Where the wretched hinds of the village
   Have basely murdered their liege lord
   In one general mutiny.
   Perfidious folk,
   They slew Fernán Gómez
   As vassals moving upon slight cause,
   Fixing upon him
   The name of Tyrant,
   Thenceforward their excuse.

They broke down his doors,
Closing their ears
To his free knightly pledge
To do each and all
Full justice,
Steeling their hearts against him,
And with unseemly rage
Tearing the cross from his breast,
Inflicting cruel wounds.
After which they cast him from a high win-
dow to the ground where he was caught on
pikes and swordpoints by the women. They
bore him in dead and the most revengeful
pulled at his beard and hair, defacing every
feature, for their fury waxed to such extremity that they sliced off his ears neatly.
They beat down his scutcheon with staves
and boast outright that they will set the
royal arms above the portal where their lord's
should be, full in the square of the village.
They sacked the keep as a fallen foe's, and,
exulting, raped his goods and properties.
These things I saw, hidden — unhappy was
my lot! — and so remained till nightfall, es-
caping to lay my prayer before you. Justice,
Sire, that swift penalty may fall upon these
offending churls! Bloodshed this day cries
out to God and challenges your rigor!
   KING. No violence, no cruelty so dire
Escapes the inquest of our royal eye.
I marvel greatly at this villainy,
Wherefore to-day a judge shall be despatched
To verify the tale, and punishment
Mete out unto the guilty as example.
A captain, too, shall march in his escort
Securing the sentence, for mutiny
The bolder grown, bolder the chastisement.
Look to his wounds.   (*Exeunt.*)

*The Square in Fuente Ovejuna. The Peasants
enter, men and women, bearing the head of
Fernán Gómez on a pike.*
   MUSICIANS. Hail, Ferdinand!
            Isabella, hail!
            Death, tyrant band!
   BARRILDO. Let's hear from Frondoso.
   FRONDOSO. I've made a song and, if it's
wrong, you correct it as it goes along.

Hail, Isabella!
'Tis plain to be seen
Two can make one,
A King and a Queen.
When they die —
This to you, Saint Michael —
Just lift them both up to the sky.
Sweep the land clean,
O King and Queen!

LAURENCIA. See what you can do, Barrildo.

BARRILDO. Silence, then, while I get a rhyme in my head.

PASCUALA. If you keep your head it will be twice as good.

BARRILDO. Hail to the King and Queen,
For they are very famous!
They have won
And so they will not blame us.
May they always win,
Conquer giants
And a dwarf or two.
Down with tyrants!
And now I'm through.

MUSICIANS. Hail, Ferdinand!
Isabella, hail!
Death, tyrant band!

LAURENCIA. Mengo next!

FRONDOSO. Now Mengo!

MENGO. I'm a poet that is one.

PASCUALA. You're the back of the belly.

MENGO. Oh, one Sunday morning
The rascal beat me
From behind!
'Twas no way to treat me,
Most unkind.
How it hurt to seat me!
Glory to the Christian Kings! —
The wife must mind.

MUSICIANS. Hail, Ferdinand!
Isabella, hail!
Death, tyrant band!

ESTEBAN. You can take the head off the spear now.

MENGO. He might have been hung for his looks. Phew!

(JUAN ROJO enters with a shield bearing the royal arms.)

REGIDOR. Here come the arms!

ESTEBAN. Let all the people see.

JUAN ROJO. Where shall the arms be set?

REGIDOR. Before the town-hall, here, above the door.

ESTEBAN. Noble escutcheon, hail!

BARRILDO. That is a coat of arms!

FRONDOSO. I see the light today, for the sun begins to shine.

ESTEBAN. Hail Castile and hail León!
Hail the bars of Aragon!
May tyrants die!
Hear, Fuente Ovejuna,
Follow counsel of the wise,
Nor hurt shall lie;
King and Queen must needs inquire
Right and wrong as they transpire,
Passing nearby.
Loyalty our hearts inspire.

FRONDOSO. That's a problem too. What shall our story be?

ESTEBAN. Let us all agree to die, if it must be, crying *Fuente Ovejuna*, and may no word of this affair pass beyond that ever.

FRONDOSO. Besides it is the truth, for what was done, Fuente Ovejuna did it, every man and woman.

ESTEBAN. Then that shall be our answer?

ALL. Yes!

ESTEBAN. Now I shall be the Judge and rehearse us all in what we best had do. Mengo, put you to torture first.

MENGO. Am I the only candidate?

ESTEBAN. This is but talk, lad.

MENGO. All the same let's get through with it, and quickly.

ESTEBAN. Who killed the Commander?

MENGO. Fuente Ovejuna killed him.

ESTEBAN. I'll put you to the torture.

MENGO. You will on your life, sir.

ESTEBAN. Confess, conscienceless hind!

MENGO. I do. What of it?

ESTEBAN. Who killed the Commander?

MENGO. Fuente Ovejuna.

ESTEBAN. Rack him again! Turn the wheel once more.

MENGO. You oblige me.

ESTEBAN. Reduce him to carrion and let him go.

(Enter CUADRADO, Regidor.)

CUADRADO. What is this meeting?

FRONDOSO. Why so grave, Cuadrado?

CUADRADO. The King's Judge is here.

ESTEBAN. All to your homes, and quickly!

CUADRADO. A Captain comes with him also.

ESTEBAN. Let the devil appear! You know what you are to say?

CUADRADO. They are going through the village prepared to take a deposition of every soul.

ESTEBAN. Have no fear. — Mengo, who killed the Commander?

MENGO. Fuente Ovejuna. Ask me who!

(*Exeunt.*)

Almagro. A room in the Castle. The MASTER *enters with a Soldier.*

MASTER. Such news cannot be! To end like this? I have a mind to run you through for your insolence.

SOLDIER. I was sent, Master, without malice.

MASTER. Can a mad handful of louts be moved to such fury? I will take five hundred men forthwith and burn the village, leaving no memory of those paths that were so basely trod.

SOLDIER. Master, be not so moved, for they have committed themselves to the King, whose power is not to be gainsaid lightly.

MASTER. How can they commit themselves to the King when they are vassals of Calatrava?

SOLDIER. That, Master, you will discuss with the King.

MASTER. No, for the land is his and all that it contains. I do obeisance to the Crown, and if they have submitted to the King I will subdue my rage and betake me to his presence as to a father's. My fault is grievous, in whose palliation I plead my untried years. I hang my head at this mischance of honor, but again to stumble were clear dishonor, yes, and certain death. (*Exeunt.*)

The Square of Fuente Ovejuna. Before the Town Hall. Enter LAURENCIA.

LAURENCIA. Loving, that the beloved should suffer pain
A grinding sorrow fastens on the heart,
Fearing the loved must bear alone the smart
Care weighs the spirit down and hope lies slain.
The firm assurance, watchful to attain,
Doubting falters, and hastens to depart,
Nor is it folly in the brave to start
And tremble, promised boon transformed to bane.
I love my husband dearly. Now I see
Harpies of Vengeance rise before my sight
Unshapely, and my hope breathes a faint breath.
Only his good I seek. Oh, set him free
Ever with me to tremble in the night,
Or take him from me, so you take me, death!

(*Enter* FRONDOSO.)

FRONDOSO. Linger not, Laurencia.

LAURENCIA. My dear husband, fly danger, for I am its very heart.

FRONDOSO. Are you one to reject the homage of a lover?

LAURENCIA. My love, I fear for you, and you are my constant care.

FRONDOSO. Laurencia, I am so happy, that surely this moment heaven smiles upon us both.

LAURENCIA. You see what has happened to the others, and how this judge proceeds firmly, with all severity? Save yourself before it is too late. Fly and avoid the danger!

FRONDOSO. What do you expect in such an hour? Shall I disappear and leave the peril to others, besides absenting myself from your sight? No, counsel me courage, for in danger a man betrays his blood, which is as it should be, come what may.

(*Cries within.*)

I hear cries. They have put a man to the torture unless my ears deceive me. Listen and be still!

(*The* JUDGE *speaks within and Voices are heard in response.*)

JUDGE. Old man, I seek only the truth. Speak!

FRONDOSO. An old man tortured?

LAURENCIA. What barbarity!

ESTEBAN. Ease me a little.

JUDGE. Ease him. Who killed Fernando?

ESTEBAN. Fuente Ovejuna.

LAURENCIA. Good, father! Glory and praise!

FRONDOSO. Praise God he had the strength!

JUDGE. Take that boy there. Speak, you pup, for you know! Who was it? He says nothing. Put on the pressure there.

BOY. Judge, Fuente Ovejuna.

JUDGE. Now by the King, carls, I'll hang you to the last man! Who killed the Commander?

FRONDOSO. They torture the child and he replies like this?

LAURENCIA. There is courage in the village.

FRONDOSO. Courage and heart.

JUDGE. Put that woman in the chair. Give her a turn for her good.

LAURENCIA. I can't endure it.

JUDGE. Peasants, be obstinate and this instrument brings death. So prepare! Who killed the Commander?

PASCUALA. Judge, Fuente Ovejuna.

JUDGE. Have no mercy.

FRONDOSO. I cannot think, my mind is blank!

LAURENCIA. Frondoso, Pascuala will not tell them.

FRONDOSO. The very children hold their peace!

JUDGE. They thrive upon it. — More! More!

PASCUALA. Oh, God in heaven!

JUDGE. Again, and answer me! Is she deaf?

PASCUALA. I say Fuente Ovejuna.

JUDGE. Seize that plump lad, half undressed already.

LAURENCIA. It must be Mengo! Poor Mengo!

FRONDOSO. He can never hold out.

MENGO. Oh, oh, oh!

JUDGE. Let him have it.

MENGO. Oh!

JUDGE. Prod his memory.

MENGO. Oh, oh!

JUDGE. Who slew the Commander, slave?

MENGO. Oh, oh! I can't get it out! I'll tell you —

JUDGE. Loosen that hand.

FRONDOSO. We are lost!

JUDGE. Let him have it on the back!

MENGO. No, for I'll give up everything!

JUDGE. Who killed him?

MENGO. Judge, Fuente Ovejuna.

JUDGE. Have these rogues no nerves that they can laugh at pain? The most likely, too, lie by instinct. I will no more today. To the street!

FRONDOSO. Now God bless Mengo! I was afraid, transfixed, but that lad is a cure for fear.

(BARRILDO and the Regidor enter with MENGO.)

BARRILDO. Good, Mengo, good!

REGIDOR. You have delivered us.

BARRILDO. Mengo, bravo!

FRONDOSO. We cheer you.

MENGO. Oh, oh! Not much.

BARRILDO. Drink, my friend, and eat. Come, come!

MENGO. Oh, oh! What have you got?

BARRILDO. Sweet lemon peel.

MENGO. Oh, oh!

FRONDOSO. Drink, drink. Take this.

BARRILDO. He does, too.

FRONDOSO. He takes it well. Down it goes.

LAURENCIA. Give him another bite.

MENGO. Oh, oh!

BARRILDO. Drink this for me.

LAURENCIA. Swallowed without a smile.

FRONDOSO. A sound answer deserves a round drink.

REGIDOR. Another, son?

MENGO. Oh, oh! Yes, yes!

FRONDOSO. Drink, for you deserve it.

LAURENCIA. He collects for every pang.

FRONDOSO. Throw a coat around him or he will freeze.

BARRILDO. Have you had enough?

MENGO. No, three more. Oh, oh!

FRONDOSO. He is asking for the wine.

BARRILDO. Yes, let him drink as much as

he likes for one good turn begets another. What's the matter now?

MENGO. It leaves a taste in my mouth. Oh, I'm catching cold!

FRONDOSO. Another drink will help. Who killed the Commander?

MENGO. Fuente Ovejuna.

(*Exeunt the Regidor,* MENGO *and* BARRILDO.)

FRONDOSO. He has earned more than they give him. Ah, love, as you are mine confess to me. Who killed the Commander?

LAURENCIA. Love, Fuente Ovejuna.

FRONDOSO. Who?

LAURENCIA. Don't you think you can torture me. Fuente Ovejuna.

FRONDOSO. It did? How did I get you, then?

LAURENCIA. Love, I got you. (*Exeunt.*)

The open country. Enter the KING *and* QUEEN, *meeting.*

ISABELLA. Meeting, Sire, we crown our fortune gladly.

KING. In union lies a more enduring glory.
Passing to Portugal the direct path
Leads me to you.

ISABELLA. To my heart, Majesty,
Turning away from conquest gratefully.

KING. What news of the war in Castile?

ISABELLA. Peace succeeds and the land lies ready, expecting the plough.

KING. Now my eyes light upon a living miracle, the consummation of a queenly peace.

(*Enter* DON MANRIQUE.)

MANRIQUE. The Master of Calatrava begs audience, having journeyed to your presence from his seat.

ISABELLA. I have a mind to greet this gentleman.

MANRIQUE. Majesty, his years are few, yet they have proved his valor great.

(*Exit. Enter the* MASTER.)

MASTER. Rodrigo Téllez Girón,
Master of Calatrava,
Humbly kneels repentant
And pardon begs, foredone.
False counsels proffered one

By one seduced my heart
To deeds disloyal and rash;
Now end all as begun
When a too ready ear
In Fernando placed its trust,
That false and unjust knight.
Pardon, Sire, past fear!
In mercy hold me dear,
Oh grant me royal favor,
To pay in loyalty
Forever rendered here!
Upon Granada's plain
When sounds the wild alarm
My valor shall wreak harm,
My sword-strokes fall amain
And through that fell champaign
Dart wounds to the enemy
Till the cross of victory
Red o'er the merlons reign.
Five hundred men in steel
I shall lead to smite your foes
Upon my life and oath, or close
My eyes in death! Here I kneel,
Never to displease you more.

KING. Rise, Master. Having tendered your allegiance you shall be received royally.

MASTER. Every word is balm.

ISABELLA. Few speak as bravely as they fight.

MASTER. Esther has returned to earth to wed a Christian Xerxes.[2]

(DON MANRIQUE *enters.*)

MANRIQUE. Sire, the Judge that was despatched to Fuente Ovejuna has arrived with the process to report to Your Majesty.

KING. (*To the* MASTER) These aggressors, being of the Commandery, fall within your province.

MASTER. Sire, I yield to you, else were bloody vengeance taken for the death of the Commander.

KING. (*To the* QUEEN) Then the decision rests with me?

ISABELLA. I grant it willingly though the right were mine of God.

---

[2] i.e., Ahasuerus, first ruler of a *united* Persia (521 B.C.). Esther was his Jewish queen, a model of courage, wisdom, beauty, and patriotism. See the *Book of Esther* in The Old Testament.

(*Enter* JUDGE.)

JUDGE. I journeyed to Fuente Ovejuna in prosecution of your command probing all with due diligence and care. Having verified the crime, no writ or indictment has issued, inasmuch as with one accord and most singular fortitude, to all my questions as to the murderer the answer was Fuente Ovejuna. Three hundred were put to torture, to the degree that forced them each to speak, without profit, Sire, of one word other than I have told you. Boys of ten were delivered to the rack, without yielding so much as a whisper, nor could they be moved by flattery or gold. Wherefore, this is my report, the evidence having failed: either you must pardon the village or wipe it out to the last man. They have followed me to your feet that in your own person you may pronounce judgment.

KING. If they seek our presence, let them appear before us, every one.

(*Enter* ESTEBAN *and* ALONSO, *Alcaldes,* JUAN ROJO *and* CUADRADO, *Regidors,* LAURENCIA, FRONDOSO, MENGO *and Peasants, both men and women.*)

LAURENCIA. Are those the King and Queen?

FRONDOSO. The power and majesty of Castile!

LAURENCIA. How beautiful, how wonderful! Saint Antonio, bless them both!

ISABELLA. Are these the people of the village?

ESTEBAN. Majesty, Fuente Ovejuna humbly kneels at your feet in allegiance. The mad tyranny and fierce cruelty of the dead Commander, raining insults through the farms, themselves provoked his death. He ravished our homes, forced our daughters, and knew no heart nor mercy.

FRONDOSO. This simple girl, O Queen, who is mine by rite of heaven, and has brought me all happiness which surely must be matchless, on my wedding-night, as if it had been his very own, he bore off to his keep, and but that she is secure in honor, basely that night he had deflowered her.

MENGO. I know something as to that, with your permission, Queen, because you must be anxious to hear from me, seeing the bloody tanning that I got. I stood up for a girl in the village when the Commander went along the way to her undoing, the scurvy Nero, and then he took it out on me, and there never was a more thorough job at bottom. Three men paid it their attention, good pay all three, since when, if you ask the explanation, I paid more for balm and ointment, with the powder and the myrtle I applied, than I could sell my sheepcot for.

ESTEBAN. Sire, we yield ourselves to you. You are our King, and in witness of submission we have placed your arms above our doors. Have mercy, Sire, for our excuse is our extremity, which deserves your clemency.

KING. As no indictment is set down, although the fault be grave, it shall be pardoned. Since you yield yourselves to me, I further take the town under my protection, for in the Crown henceforth its charter shall abide, until such time as God in His mercy shall vouchsafe you a new Commander.

FRONDOSO. When His Majesty speaks
    His voice we obey.
    " Fuente Ovejuna " ends.
    Friends, approve the play.

OEDIPUS REX
(KING OEDIPUS)

by Sophocles

AN ENGLISH VERSION BY DUDLEY FITTS
AND ROBERT FITZGERALD

CHARACTERS

OEDIPUS
A PRIEST
CREON
TEIRESIAS

IOCASTE (JOCASTA)
MESSENGER
SHEPHERD OF LAÏOS
SECOND MESSENGER

CHORUS OF THEBAN ELDERS

THE SCENE. *Before the palace of Oedipus, King of Thebes. A central door and two lateral doors open onto a platform which runs the length of the façade. On the platform, right and left, are altars; and three steps lead down into the* orchestra, *or chorus-ground. At the beginning of the action these steps are crowded by* SUPPLIANTS *who have brought branches and chaplets of olive leaves and who lie in various attitudes of despair.* OEDIPUS *enters.*

OEDIPUS

My children, generations of the living
In the line of Kadmos,[1] nursed at his ancient
  hearth:
Why have you strewn yourselves before these
  altars
In supplication, with your boughs and gar-
  lands?
The breath of incense rises from the city
With a sound of prayer and lamentation.

[1] legendary founder of Thebes.

                           Children,
I would not have you speak through mes-
  sengers,
And therefore I have come myself to hear
  you —
I, Oedipus, who bear the famous name.
         (To a PRIEST)
You, there, since you are eldest in the com-
  pany,
Speak for them all, tell me what preys upon
  you,
Whether you come in dread, or crave some
  blessing:
Tell me, and never doubt that I will help you
In every way I can; I should be heartless
Were I not moved to find you suppliant here.

PRIEST

Great Oepidus, O powerful King of Thebes!
You see how all the ages of our people
Cling to your altar steps: here are boys
Who can barely stand alone, and here are
  priests
By weight of age, as I am a priest of God,

And young men chosen from those yet un-
    married;
As for the others, all that multitude,
They wait with olive chaplets in the squares,
At the two shrines of Pallas, and where
    Apollo
Speaks in the glowing embers.
                        Your own eyes
Must tell you: Thebes is in her extremity
And cannot lift her head from the surge of
    death.
A rust consumes the buds and fruits of the
    earth;
The herds are sick; children die unborn,
And labor is vain. The god of plague and
    pyre
Raids like detestable lightning through the
    city,
And all the house of Kadmos is laid waste,
All emptied, and all darkened: Death alone
Battens upon the misery of Thebes.

You are not one of the immortal gods, we
    know;
Yet we have come to you to make our prayer
As to the man of all men best in adversity
And wisest in the ways of God. You saved
    us
From the Sphinx,[2] that flinty singer, and the
    tribute
We paid to her so long; yet you were never
Better informed than we, nor could we teach
    you:
It was some god breathed in you to set us
    free.

Therefore, O mighty King, we turn to you:
Find us our safety, find us a remedy,
Whether by counsel of the gods or men.
A king of wisdom tested in the past
Can act in a time of troubles, and act well.
Noblest of men, restore
Life to your city! Think how all men call
    you

[2] A monster, half-woman, half-beast, who destroyed all who failed to answer her riddle: what is it
that walks on four legs in the morning, two legs at
midday, and three legs at night. Oedipus guessed the
answer (man) and was made King of Thebes and
husband of its widowed queen Iocaste.

Liberator for your triumph long ago;
Ah, when your years of kingship are remem-
    bered,
Let them not say *We rose, but later fell* —
Keep the State from going down in the
    storm!
Once, years ago, with happy augury,
You brought us fortune; be the same again!
No man questions your power to rule the
    land:
But rule over men, not over a dead city!
Ships are only hulls, citadels are nothing,
When no life moves in the empty passage-
    ways.

OEDIPUS

Poor children! You may be sure I know
All that you longed for in your coming here.
I know that you are deathly sick; and yet,
Sick as you are, not one is as sick as I.
Each of you suffers in himself alone
His anguish, not another's; but my spirit
Groans for the city, for myself, for you.

I was not sleeping, you are not waking me.
No, I have been in tears for a long while
And in my restless thought walked many
    ways.
In all my search, I found one helpful course,
And that I have taken: I have sent Creon,
Son of Menoikeus, brother of the Queen,
To Delphi, Apollo's place of revelation,
To learn there, if he can,
What act or pledge of mine may save the
    city.
I have counted the days, and now, this very
    day,
I am troubled, for he has overstayed his time.
What is he doing? He has been gone too long.
Yet whenever he comes back, I should do ill
To scant whatever hint the god may give.

PRIEST

It is a timely promise. At this instant
They tell me Creon is here.

OEDIPUS

                    O Lord Apollo!
May his news be fair as his face is radiant!

Laurence Olivier as Oedipus. Courtesy Eileen Darby, Graphic House.

PRIEST

It could not be otherwise: he is crowned with
    bay,
The chaplet is thick with berries.

OEDIPUS

                We shall soon know;
He is near enough to hear us now.
        (*Enter* CREON.)
                        O Prince:
Brother: son of Menoikeus:
What answer do you bring us from the god?

CREON

It is favorable. I can tell you, great afflic-
    tions
Will turn out well, if they are taken well.

OEDIPUS

What was the oracle? These vague words
Leave me still hanging between hope and
    fear.

CREON

Is it your pleasure to hear me with all these
Gathered around us? I am prepared to speak,
But should we not go in?

OEDIPUS

                Let them all hear it.
It is for them I suffer, more than for myself.

CREON

Then I will tell you what I heard at Delphi.

In plain words
The god commands us to expel from the land
    of Thebes
An old defilement that it seems we shelter.
It is a deathly thing, beyond expiation.
We must not let it feed upon us longer.

OEDIPUS

What defilement? How shall we rid ourselves
    of it?

CREON

By exile or death, blood for blood. It was
Murder that brought the plague-wind on the
    city.

OEDIPUS

Murder of whom? Surely the god has named
    him?

CREON

My lord: long ago Laïos was our king,
Before you came to govern us.

OEDIPUS

                I know;
I learned of him from others; I never saw
    him.

CREON

He was murdered; and Apollo commands us
    now
To take revenge upon whoever killed him.

OEDIPUS

Upon whom? Where are they? Where shall
    we find a clue
To solve that crime, after so many years?

CREON

Here in this land, he said.
                If we make enquiry,
We may touch things that otherwise escape
    us.

OEDIPUS

Tell me: Was Laïos murdered in his house,
Or in the fields, or in some foreign country?

CREON

He said he planned to make a pilgrimage.
He did not come home again.

OEDIPUS

                And was there no one,
No witness, no companion, to tell what hap-
    pened?

CREON

They were all killed but one, and he got away
So frightened that he could remember one
    thing only.

OEDIPUS

What was that one thing? One may be the
    key
To everything, if we resolve to use it.

CREON

He said that a band of highwaymen attacked
them,
Outnumbered them, and overwhelmed the
King.

OEDIPUS

Strange, that a highwayman should be so
daring —
Unless some faction here bribed him to do it.

CREON

We thought of that. But after Laïos' death
New troubles arose and we had no avenger.

OEDIPUS

What troubles could prevent your hunting
down the killers?

CREON

The riddling Sphinx's song
Made us deaf to all mysteries but her own.

OEDIPUS

Then once more I must bring what is dark
to light.
It is most fitting that Apollo shows,
As you do, this compunction for the dead.
You shall see how I stand by you, as I should,
To avenge the city and the city's god,
And not as though it were for some distant
friend,
But for my own sake, to be rid of evil.
Whoever killed King Laïos might — who
knows? —
Decide at any moment to kill me as well.
By avenging the murdered king I protect
myself.

Come, then, my children: leave the altar
steps,
Lift up your olive boughs!
                         One of you go
And summon the people of Kadmos to gather
here.
I will do all that I can; you may tell them
that.   (*Exit a* PAGE.)
So, with the help of God,

We shall be saved — or else indeed we are
lost.

PRIEST

Let us rise, children. It was for this we came,
And now the King has promised it himself.
Phoibos [3] has sent us an oracle; may he de-
scend
Himself to save us and drive out the plague.
(*Exeunt* OEDIPUS *and* CREON *into the palace
by the central door. The* PRIEST *and the* SUP-
PLIANTS *disperse R and L. After a short
pause the* CHORUS *enters the* orchestra.)

CHORUS

[STROPHE [4] 1]

What is the god singing in his profound
Delphi of gold and shadow?
What oracle for Thebes, the sunwhipped
city?

Fear unjoints me, the roots of my heart
tremble.

Now I remember, O Healer, your power,
and wonder:
Will you send doom like a sudden cloud, or
weave it
Like nightfall of the past?

Ah no: be merciful, issue of holy sound:
Dearest to our expectancy: be tender!

[ANTISTROPHE [5] 1]

Let me pray to Athenê, the immortal daughter of Zeus,
And to Artemis her sister
Who keeps her famous throne in the market
ring,

And to Apollo, bowman at the far butts of
heaven —

O gods, descend! Like three streams leap
against

---

[3] Apollo
[4] i.e., stanza
[5] i.e., a stanza corresponding in pattern to the
strophe. It is thought that *strophe* and *antistrophe*
may indicate portions of the ode to be sung by semi-
choruses, or groups within the whole chorus.

The fires of our grief, the fires of darkness;
Be swift to bring us rest!

As in the old time from the brilliant house
Of air you stepped to save us, come again!

[STROPHE 2]

Now our afflictions have no end,
Now all our stricken host lies down
And no man fights off death with his mind;

The noble plowland bears no grain,
And groaning mothers can not bear —

See, how our lives like birds take wing,
Like sparks that fly when a fire soars,
To the shore of the god of evening.

[ANTISTROPHE 2]

The plague burns on, it is pitiless,
Though pallid children laden with death
Lie unwept in the stony ways,

And old grey women by every path
Flock to the strand about the altars

There to strike their breasts and cry
Worship of Zeus in wailing prayers:
Be kind, God's golden child!

[STROPHE 3]

There are no swords in this attack by fire,
No shields, but we are ringed with cries.

Send the besieger plunging from our homes
Into the vast sea-room of the Atlantic
Or into the waves that foam eastward of
    Thrace —

For the day ravages what the night spares —

Destroy our enemy, lord of the thunder!
Let him be riven by lightning from heaven!

[ANTISTROPHE 3]

Phoibos Apollo, stretch the sun's bowstring,
That golden cord, until it sing for us,
Flashing arrows in heaven!
                    Artemis, Huntress,
Race with flaring lights upon our moun-
    tains!

O scarlet god, O golden-branded brow,
O Theban Bacchos [6] in a storm of Maenads,
                    (*Enter* OEDIPUS, *Center.*)
Whirl upon Death, that all the Undying
    hate!
Come with blinding cressets, come in joy!

OEDIPUS

Is this your prayer? It may be answered.
    Come,
Listen to me, act as the crisis demands,
And you shall have relief from all these
    evils.

Until now I was a stranger to this tale,
As I had been a stranger to the crime.
Could I track down the murderer without a
    clue?
But now, friends,
As one who became a citizen after the mur-
    der,
I make this proclamation to all Thebans:

If any man knows by whose hand Laïos, son
    of Labdakos,
Met his death, I direct that man to tell me
    everything,
No matter what he fears for having so long
    withheld it.
Let it stand as promised that no further
    trouble
Will come to him, but he may leave the land
    in safety.

Moreover: If anyone knows the murderer to
    be foreign,
Let him not keep silent: he shall have his re-
    ward from me.
However, if he does conceal it; if any man
Fearing for his friend or for himself dis-
    obeys this edict,
Hear what I propose to do:

I solemnly forbid the people of this country,
Where power and throne are mine, ever to
    receive that man
Or speak to him, no matter who he is, or let
    him

---

[6] Dionysos

Join in sacrifice, lustration, or in prayer.
I decree that he be driven from every house,
Being, as he is, corruption itself to us: the Delphic
Voice of Zeus has pronounced this revelation.
Thus I associate myself with the oracle
And take the side of the murdered king.

As for the criminal, I pray to God —
Whether it be a lurking thief, or one of a number —
I pray that that man's life be consumed in evil and wretchedness.
And as for me, this curse applies no less
If it should turn out that the culprit is my guest here,
Sharing my hearth.

     You have heard the penalty.

I lay it on you now to attend to this
For my sake, for Apollo's, for the sick
Sterile city that heaven has abandoned.
Suppose the oracle had given you no command:
Should this defilement go uncleansed for ever?
You should have found the murderer: your king,
A noble king, had been destroyed!

        Now I,
Having the power that he held before me,
Having his bed, begetting children there
Upon his wife, as he would have, had he lived —
Their son would have been my children's brother,
If Laïos had had luck in fatherhood!
(But surely ill luck rushed upon his reign) —
I say I take the son's part, just as though
I were his son, to press the fight for him
And see it won! I'll find the hand that brought
Death to Labdakos' and Polydoros' child,
Heir of Kadmos' and Agenor's line.
And as for those who fail me,
May the gods deny them the fruit of the earth,
Fruit of the womb, and may they rot utterly!
Let them be wretched as we are wretched, and worse!

For you, for loyal Thebans, and for all
Who find my actions right, I pray the favor
Of justice, and of all the immortal gods.

CHORAGOS [7]

Since I am under oath, my lord, I swear
I did not do the murder, I cannot name
The murderer. Might not the oracle
That has ordained the search tell where to find him?

OEDIPUS

An honest question. But no man in the world
Can make the gods do more than the gods will.

CHORAGOS

There is one last expedient —

OEDIPUS

      Tell we what it is.
Though it seem slight, you must not hold it back.

CHORAGOS

A lord clairvoyant to the lord Apollo,
As we all know, is the skilled Teiresias.
One might learn much about this from him, Oedipus.

OEDIPUS

I am not wasting time:
Creon spoke of this, and I have sent for him —
Twice, in fact; it is strange that he is not here.

CHORAGOS

The other matter — that old report — seems useless.

[7] leader of the chorus (also spelled Choregus)

OEDIPUS

Tell me. I am interested in all reports.

CHORAGOS

The King was said to have been killed by
highwaymen.

OEDIPUS

I know. But we have no witnesses to that.

CHORAGOS

If the killer can feel a particle of dread,
Your curse will bring him out of hiding!

OEDIPUS

No.
The man who dared that act will fear no
curse.
(*Enter the blind seer* TEIRESIAS, *led by a*
PAGE.)

CHORAGOS

But there is one man who may detect the
criminal.
This is Teiresias, this is the holy prophet
In whom, alone of all men, truth was born.

OEDIPUS

Teiresias: seer: student of mysteries,
Of all that's taught and all that no man
tells,
Secrets of Heaven and secrets of the earth:
Blind though you are, you know the city lies
Sick with plague; and from this plague, my
lord,
We find that you alone can guard or save us.

Possibly you did not hear the messengers?
Apollo, when we sent to him,
Sent us back word that this great pestilence
Would lift, but only if we established clearly
The identity of those who murdered Laïos.
They must be killed or exiled.
Can you use
Birdflight or any art of divination
To purify yourself, and Thebes, and me
From this contagion? We are in your hands.
There is no fairer duty
Than that of helping others in distress.

TEIRESIAS

How dreadful knowledge of the truth can be
When there's no help in truth! I knew this
well,
But did not act on it: else I should not have
come.

OEDIPUS

What is troubling you? Why are your eyes
so cold?

TEIRESIAS

Let me go home. Bear your own fate, and I'll
Bear mine. It is better so: trust what I say.

OEDIPUS

What you say is ungracious and unhelpful
To your native country. Do not refuse to
speak.

TEIRESIAS

When it comes to speech, your own is neither temperate
Nor opportune. I wish to be more prudent.

OEDIPUS

In God's name, we all beg you —

TEIRESIAS

You are all ignorant.
No; I will never tell you what I know.
Now it is my misery; then, it would be
yours.

OEDIPUS

What! You do know something, and will
not tell us?
You would betray us all and wreck the
State?

TEIRESIAS

I do not intend to torture myself, or you.
Why persist in asking? You will not persuade me.

OEDIPUS

What a wicked old man you are! You'd try
a stone's
Patience! Out with it! Have you no feeling
at all?

TEIRESIAS

You call me unfeeling. If you could only see
The nature of your own feelings . . .

OEDIPUS

Why,
Who would not feel as I do? Who could endure
Your arrogance toward the city?

TEIRESIAS

What does it matter!
Whether I speak or not, it is bound to come.

OEDIPUS

Then, if " it " is bound to come, you are
bound to tell me.

TEIRESIAS

No, I will not go on. Rage as you please.

OEDIPUS

Rage? Why not!
And I'll tell you what I think:
You planned it, you had it done, you all but
Killed him with your own hands: if you had
eyes,
I'd say the crime was yours, and yours alone.

TEIRESIAS

So? I charge you, then,
Abide by the proclamation you have made:
From this day forth
Never speak again to these men or to me;
You yourself are the pollution of this country.

OEDIPUS

You dare say that! Can you possibly think
you have
Some way of going free, after such insolence?

TEIRESIAS

I have gone free. It is the truth sustains me.

OEDIPUS

Who taught you shamelessness? It was not
your craft.

TEIRESIAS

You did. You made me speak. I did not want
to.

OEDIPUS

Speak what? Let me hear it again more
clearly.

TEIRESIAS

Was it not clear before? Are you tempting
me?

OEDIPUS

I did not understand it. Say it again.

TEIRESIAS

I say that you are the murderer whom you
seek.

OEDIPUS

Now twice you have spat out infamy. You'll
pay for it!

TEIRESIAS

Would you care for more? Do you wish to
be really angry?

OEDIPUS

Say what you will. Whatever you say is
worthless.

TEIRESIAS

I say that you live in hideous love with her
Who is nearest you in blood. You are blind
to the evil.

OEDIPUS

It seems you can go on mouthing like this
for ever.

TEIRESIAS

I can, if there is power in truth.

OEDIPUS

There is:
But not for you, not for you,
You sightless, witless, senseless, mad old
man!

TEIRESIAS

You are the madman. There is no one here
Who will not curse you soon, as you curse
me.

OEDIPUS

You child of endless night! You cannot hurt
me
Or any other man who sees the sun.

TEIRESIAS

True: it is not from me your fate will come.
That lies within Apollo's competence,
As it is his concern.

OEDIPUS

Tell me:
Are you speaking for Creon, or for yourself?

TEIRESIAS

Creon is no threat. You weave your own
doom.

OEDIPUS

Wealth, power, craft of statesmanship!
Kingly position, everywhere admired!
What savage envy is stored up against these,
If Creon, whom I trusted, Creon my friend,
For this great office which the city once
Put in my hands unsought — if for this
power
Creon desires in secret to destroy me!

He has bought this decrepit fortune-teller,
this
Collector of dirty pennies, this prophet
fraud —
Why, he is no more clairvoyant than I am!

Tell us:
Has your mystic mummery ever approached
the truth?
When that hellcat the Sphinx was perform-
ing here,
What help were you to these people?
Her magic was not for the first man who
came along:
It demanded a real exorcist. Your birds —
What good were they? or the gods, for the
matter of that?
But I came by,
Oedipus, the simple man, who knows noth-
ing —
I thought it out for myself, no birds helped
me!

And this is the man you think you can destroy,
That you may be close to Creon when he's
king!
Well, you and your friend Creon, it seems to
me,
Will suffer most. If you were not an old
man,
You would have paid already for your plot.

CHORAGOS

We cannot see that his words or yours
Have been spoken except in anger, Oedipus,
And of anger we have no need. How can
God's will
Be accomplished best? That is what most
concerns us.

TEIRESIAS

You are a king. But where argument's con-
cerned
I am your man, as much a king as you.
I am not your servant, but Apollo's;
I have no need of Creon to speak for me.

Listen to me. You mock my blindness, do
you?
But I say that you, with both your eyes, are
blind:
You cannot see the wretchedness of your
life,
Nor in whose house you live, no, nor with
whom.
Who are your father and mother? Can you
tell me?
You do not even know the blind wrongs
That you have done them, on earth and in
the world below.
But the double lash of your parents' curse
will whip you
Out of this land some day, with only night
Upon your precious eyes.
Your cries then — where will they not be
heard?
What fastness of Kithairon will not echo
them?
And that bridal-descant of yours — you'll
know it then,

The song they sang when you came here to
Thebes
And found your misguided berthing.
All this, and more, that you cannot guess at
now,
Will bring you to yourself among your chil-
dren.

Be angry, then. Curse Creon. Curse my
words.
I tell you, no man that walks upon the earth
Shall be rooted out more horribly than you.

OEDIPUS

Am I to bear this from him? — Damnation
Take you! Out of this place! Out of my
sight!

TEIRESIAS

I would not have come at all if you had not
asked me.

OEDIPUS

Could I have told that you'd talk nonsense,
that
You'd come here to make a fool of yourself,
and of me?

TEIRESIAS

A fool? Your parents thought me sane
enough.

OEDIPUS

My parents again! — Wait: who were my
parents?

TEIRESIAS

This day will give you a father, and break
your heart.

OEDIPUS

Your infantile riddles! Your damned abra-
cadabra!

TEIRESIAS

You were a great man once at solving riddles.

OEDIPUS

Mock me with that if you like; you will find
it true.

TEIRESIAS

It was true enough. It brought about your
ruin.

OEDIPUS

But if it saved this town?

TEIRESIAS

(To the PAGE)
            Boy, give me your hand.

OEDIPUS

Yes, boy; lead him away.
                        — While you are here
We can do nothing. Go; leave us in peace.

TEIRESIAS

I will go when I have said what I have to
say.
How can you hurt me? And I tell you again:
The man you have been looking for all this
time,
The damned man, the murderer of Laïos,
That man is in Thebes. To your mind he is
foreign-born,
But it will soon be shown that he is a The-
ban,
A revelation that will fail to please.
                        A blind man,
Who has his eyes now; a penniless man, who
is rich now;
And he will go tapping the strange earth
with his staff.
To the children with whom he lives now he
will be
Brother and father — the very same; to her
Who bore him, son and husband — the very
same
Who came to his father's bed, wet with his
father's blood.

Enough. Go think that over.
If later you find error in what I have said,
You may say that I have no skill in proph-
ecy.

(Exit TEIRESIAS, led by his PAGE.
OEDIPUS goes into the palace.)

CHORUS

[STROPHE 1]

The Delphic stone of prophecies
Remembers ancient regicide
And a still bloody hand.
That killer's hour of flight has come.
He must be stronger than riderless
Coursers of untiring wind,
For the son of Zeus armed with his father's
    thunder
Leaps in lightning after him;
And the Furies follow him, the sad Furies.

[ANTISTROPHE 1]

Holy Parnassos' peak of snow
Flashes and blinds that secret man,
That all shall hunt him down:
Though he may roam the forest shade
Like a bull gone wild from pasture
To rage through glooms of stone.
Doom comes down on him; flight will not
    avail him;
For the world's heart calls him desolate,
And the immortal Furies follow, forever
    follow.

[STROPHE 2]

But now a wilder thing is heard
From the old man skilled at hearing Fate in
    the wing-beat of a bird.
Bewildered as a blown bird, my soul hovers
    and cannot find
Foothold in this debate, or any reason or rest
    of mind.
But no man ever brought — none can bring
Proof of strife between Thebes' royal house,
Labdakos' line, and the son of Polybos [8];
And never until now has any man brought
    word
Of Laïos' dark death staining Oedipus the
    King.

[ANTISTROPHE 2]

Divine Zeus and Apollo hold
Perfect intelligence alone of all tales ever
    told;
And well though this diviner works, he
    works in his own night;

[8] supposed father of Oedipus

No man can judge that rough unknown or
    trust in second sight,
For wisdom changes hands among the wise.
Shall I believe my great lord criminal
At a raging word that a blind old man let
    fall?
I saw him, when the carrion woman faced
    him of old,
Prove his heroic mind! These evil words are
    lies.

(*Enter* CREON.)

CREON

Men of Thebes:
I am told that heavy accusations
Have been brought against me by King
    Oedipus.

I am not the kind of man to bear this
    tamely.

If in these present difficulties
He holds me accountable for any harm to
    him
Through anything I have said or done —
    why, then,
I do not value life in this dishonor.

It is not as though this rumor touched
    upon
Some private indiscretion. The matter is
    grave.
The fact is that I am being called disloyal
To the State, to my fellow citizens, to my
    friends.

CHORAGOS

He may have spoken in anger, not from his
    mind.

CREON

But did you not hear him say I was the one
Who seduced the old prophet into lying?

CHORAGOS

The thing was said; I do not know how seri-
    ously.

CREON

But you were watching him! Were his eyes
    steady?
Did he look like a man in his right mind?

CHORAGOS
                    I do not know.
I cannot judge the behavior of great men.
But here is the King himself.
                    (*Enter* OEDIPUS.)

OEDIPUS
                    So you dared come back.
Why? How brazen of you to come to my
    house,
You murderer!
                    Do you think I do not know
That you plotted to kill me, plotted to steal
    my throne?
Tell me, in God's name: am I coward, a fool,
That you should dream you could accom-
    plish this?
A fool who could not see your slippery
    game?
A coward, not to fight back when I saw it?
You are the fool, Creon, are you not? hoping
Without support or friends to get a throne?
Thrones may be won or bought: you could
    do neither.

CREON
Now listen to me. You have talked; let me
    talk, too.
You cannot judge unless you know the
    facts.

OEDIPUS
You speak well: there is one fact; but I find
    it hard
To learn from the deadliest enemy I have.

CREON
That above all I must dispute with you.

OEDIPUS
That above all I will not hear you deny.

CREON
If you think there is anything good in being
    stubborn
Against all reason, then I say you are wrong.

OEDIPUS
If you think a man can sin against his own
    kind

And not be punished for it, I say you are
    mad.

CREON
I agree. But tell me: what have I done to
    you?

OEDIPUS
You advised me to send for that wizard, did
    you not?

CREON
I did. I should do it again.

OEDIPUS
                    Very well. Now tell me:
How long has it been since Laïos —

CREON
                    What of Laïos?

OEDIPUS
Since he vanished in that onset by the road?

CREON
It was long ago, a long time.

OEDIPUS
                    And this prophet,
Was he practicing here then?

CREON
                    He was; and with honor, as now.

OEDIPUS
Did he speak of me at that time?

CREON
                    He never did;
At least, not when I was present.

OEDIPUS
                    But . . . the enquiry?
I suppose you held one?

CREON
                    We did, but we learned nothing.

OEDIPUS
Why did the prophet not speak against me
    then?

CREON

I do not know; and I am the kind of man
Who holds his tongue when he has no facts
    to go on.

OEDIPUS

There's one fact that you know, and you
    could tell it.

CREON

What fact is that? If I know it, you shall
    have it.

OEDIPUS

If he were not involved with you, he could
    not say
That it was I who murdered Laïos.

CREON

If he says that, you are the one that knows
    it! —
But now it is my turn to question you.

OEDIPUS

Put your questions. I am no murderer.

CREON

First, then: You married my sister?

OEDIPUS

                    I married your sister.

CREON

And you rule the kingdom equally with her?

OEDIPUS

Everything that she wants she has from me.

CREON

And I am the third, equal to both of you?

OEDIPUS

That is why I call you a bad friend.

CREON

No. Reason it out, as I have done.
Think of this first: Would any sane man
    prefer

Power, with all a king's anxieties,
To that same power and the grace of sleep?
Certainly not I.
I have never longed for the king's power —
    only his rights.
Would any wise man differ from me in this?
As matters stand, I have my way in every-
    thing
With your consent, and no responsibilities.
If I were king, I should be a slave to policy.

How could I desire a sceptre more
Than what is now mine — untroubled influ-
    ence?
No, I have not gone mad; I need no honors,
Except those with the perquisites I have
    now.
I am welcome everywhere; every man salutes
    me,
And those who want your favor seek my
    ear,
Since I know how to manage what they ask.
Should I exchange this ease for that anxiety?
Besides, no sober mind is treasonable.
I hate anarchy
And never would deal with any man who
    likes it.

Test what I have said. Go to the priestess
At Delphi, ask if I quoted her correctly.
And as for this other thing: if I am found
Guilty of treason with Teiresias,
Then sentence me to death! You have my
    word
It is a sentence I should cast my vote for —
But not without evidence!
                    You do wrong
When you take good men for bad, bad men
    for good.
A true friend thrown aside — why, life it-
    self
Is not more precious!
                    In time you will know this well:
For time, and time alone, will show the just
    man,
Though scoundrels are discovered in a day.

CHORAGOS

This is well said, and a prudent man would
    ponder it.

Judgments too quickly formed are dangerous.

OEDIPUS

But is he not quick in his duplicity?
And shall I not be quick to parry him?
Would you have me stand still, hold my
peace, and let
This man win everything, through my inac-
tion?

CREON

And you want — what is it, then? To banish me?

OEDIPUS

No, not exile. It is your death I want,
So that all the world may see what treason
means.

CREON

You will persist, then? You will not believe
me?

OEDIPUS

How can I believe you?

CREON

        Then you are a fool.

OEDIPUS

To save myself?

CREON

      In justice, think of me.

OEDIPUS

You are evil incarnate.

CREON

     But suppose that you are wrong?

OEDIPUS

Still I must rule.

CREON

     But not if you rule badly.

OEDIPUS

O city, city!

CREON

     It is my city, too!

CHORAGOS

Now, my lords, be still. I see the Queen,
Iocaste, coming from her palace chambers;
And it is time she came, for the sake of you
both.
This dreadful quarrel can be resolved through
her.

(*Enter* IOCASTE.)

IOCASTE

Poor foolish men, what wicked din is this?
With Thebes sick to death, is it not shame-
ful
That you should rake some private quarrel
up?
     (*To* OEDIPUS)
Come into the house.

     — And you, Creon, go now:
Let us have no more of this tumult over
nothing.

CREON

Nothing? No, sister: what your husband
plans for me
Is one of two great evils: exile or death.

OEDIPUS

He is right.
   Why, woman I have caught him squarely
Plotting against my life.

CREON

         No! Let me die
Accurst if ever I have wished you harm!

IOCASTE

Ah, believe it, Oedipus!
In the name of the gods, respect this oath of
his
For my sake, for the sake of these people
here!

CHORAGOS

        [STROPHE 1]
Open your mind to her, my lord. Be ruled
by her, I beg you!

OEDIPUS

What would you have me do?

CHORAGOS

Respect Creon's word. He has never spoken
  like a fool,
And now he has sworn an oath.

OEDIPUS

      You know what you ask?

CHORAGOS

                    I do.

OEDIPUS

            Speak on, then.

CHORAGOS

A friend so sworn should not be baited so,
In blind malice, and without final proof.

OEDIPUS

You are aware, I hope, that what you say
Means death for me, or exile at the least.

CHORAGOS

            [STROPHE 2]
No, I swear by Helios, first in Heaven!
  May I die friendless and accurst,
The worst of deaths, if ever I meant that!
  It is the withering fields
    That hurt my sick heart:
  Must we bear all these ills,
    And now your bad blood as well?

OEDIPUS

Then let him go. And let me die, if I must,
Or be driven by him in shame from the land
  of Thebes.
It is your unhappiness, and not his talk,
That touches me.
        As for him —
Wherever he is, I will hate him as long as I
  live.

CREON

Ugly in yielding, as you were ugly in rage!
Natures like yours chiefly torment themselves.

OEDIPUS

Can you not go? Can you not leave me?

CREON

                    I can.
You do not know me; but the city knows
  me,
And in its eyes I am just, if not in yours.
                (*Exit* CREON.)

CHORAGOS

            [ANTISTROPHE 1]
Lady Iocaste, did you not ask the King to
  go to his chambers?

IOCASTE

First tell me what has happened.

CHORAGOS

There was suspicion without evidence; yet it
  rankled
As even false charges will.

IOCASTE

            On both sides?

CHORAGOS

                  On both.

IOCASTE

        But what was said?

CHORAGOS

Oh let it rest, let it be done with!
Have we not suffered enough?

OEDIPUS

You see to what your decency has brought
  you:
You have made difficulties where my heart
  saw none.

CHORAGOS

            [ANTISTROPHE 2]
Oedipus, it is not once only I have told
  you —
  You must know I should count myself
    unwise
To the point of madness, should I now for-
  sake you —
  You, under whose hand,
    In the storm of another time,
    Our dear land sailed out free.
    But now stand fast at the helm!

IOCASTE

In God's name, Oedipus, inform your wife
as well:
Why are you so set in this hard anger?

OEDIPUS

I will tell you, for none of these men deserves
My confidence as you do. It is Creon's work,
His treachery, his plotting against me.

IOCASTE

Go on, if you can make this clear to me.

OEDIPUS

He charges me with the murder of Laïos.

IOCASTE

Has he some knowledge? Or does he speak
from hearsay?

OEDIPUS

He would not commit himself to such a
charge,
But he has brought in that damnable soothsayer
To tell his story.

IOCASTE

      Set your mind at rest.
If it is a question of soothsayers, I tell you
That you will find no man whose craft gives
knowledge
Of the unknowable.

    Here is my proof:

An oracle was reported to Laïos once
(I will not say from Phoibos himself, but
from
His appointed ministers, at any rate)
That his doom would be death at the hands
of his own son —
His son, born of his flesh and of mine!

Now, you remember the story: Laïos was
killed
By marauding strangers where three highways meet;

But his child had not been three days in this
world
Before the King had pierced the baby's ankles
And had him left to die on a lonely mountain.

Thus, Apollo never caused that child
To kill his father, and it was not Laïos' fate
To die at the hands of his son, as he had
feared.
This is what prophets and prophecies are
worth!
Have no dread of them.
                It is God himself
Who can show us what he wills, in his own
way.

OEDIPUS

How strange a shadowy memory crossed my
mind,
Just now while you were speaking; it chilled
my heart.

IOCASTE

What do you mean? What memory do you
speak of?

OEDIPUS

If I understand you, Laïos was killed
At a place where three roads meet.

IOCASTE

              So it was said;
We have no later story.

OEDIPUS

          Where did it happen?

IOCASTE

Phokis, it is called: at a place where the
Theban Way
Divides into the roads toward Delphi and
Daulia.

OEDIPUS

When?

IOCASTE

We had the news not long before you came
And proved the right to your succession here.

OEDIPUS

Ah, what net has God been weaving for me?

IOCASTE

Oedipus! Why does this trouble you?

OEDIPUS

Do not ask me yet.
First, tell me how Laïos looked, and tell me
How old he was.

IOCASTE

He was tall, his hair just touched
With white; his form was not unlike your
own.

OEDIPUS

I think that I myself may be accurst
By my own ignorant edict.

IOCASTE

You speak strangely.
It makes me tremble to look at you, my
King.

OEDIPUS

I am not sure that the blind man cannot see.
But I should know better if you were to tell
me —

IOCASTE

Anything — though I dread to hear you ask
it.

OEDIPUS

Was the King lightly escorted, or did he ride
With a large company, as a ruler should?

IOCASTE

There were five men with him in all: one
was a herald;
And a single chariot, which he was driving.

OEDIPUS

Alas, that makes it plain enough!
But who —
Who told you how it happened?

IOCASTE

A household servant,
The only one to escape.

OEDIPUS

And is he still
A servant of ours?

IOCASTE

No; for when he came back at last
And found you enthroned in the place of the
dead king,
He came to me, touched my hand with his,
and begged
That I would send him away to the frontier
district
Where only the shepherds go —
As far away from the city as I could send
him.
I granted his prayer; for although the man
was a slave,
He had earned more than this favor at my
hands.

OEDIPUS

Can he be called back quickly?

IOCASTE

Easily.
But why?

OEDIPUS

I have taken too much upon myself
Without enquiry; therefore I wish to consult
him.

IOCASTE

Then he shall come.
But am I not one also
To whom you might confide these fears of
yours?

OEDIPUS

That is your right; it will not be denied you,
Now least of all; for I have reached a pitch
Of wild foreboding. Is there anyone
To whom I should sooner speak?

Polybos of Corinth is my father.
My mother is a Dorian: Meropê.
I grew up chief among the men of Corinth
Until a strange thing happened —
Not worth my passion, it may be, but
strange.

At a feast, a drunken man maundering in
    his cups
Cries out that I am not my father's son!

I contained myself that night, though I felt
    anger
And a sinking heart. The next day I visited
My father and mother, and questioned them.
    They stormed,
Calling it all the slanderous rant of a fool;
And this relieved me. Yet the suspicion
Remained always aching in my mind;
I knew there was talk; I could not rest;
And finally, saying nothing to my parents,
I went to the shrine at Delphi.

The god dismissed my question without re-
    ply;
He spoke of other things.
                   Some were clear,
Full of wretchedness, dreadful, unbearable:
As, that I should lie with my own mother,
    breed
Children from whom all men would turn
    their eyes;
And that I should be my father's murderer.

I heard all this, and fled. And from that day
Corinth to me was only in the stars
Descending in that quarter of the sky,
As I wandered farther and farther on my way
To a land where I should never see the evil
Sung by the oracle. And I came to this coun-
    try
Where, so you say, King Laïos was killed.

I will tell you all that happened there, my
    lady.

There were three highways
Coming together at a place I passed;
And there a herald came towards me, and a
    chariot
Drawn by horses, with a man such as you
    describe
Seated in it. The groom leading the horses
Forced me off the road at his lord's command;
But as this charioteer lurched over towards
    me

I struck him in my rage. The old man saw
    me
And brought his double goad down upon my
    head
As I came abreast.
              He was paid back, and more!
Swinging my club in this right hand I
    knocked him
Out of his car, and he rolled on the ground.
                     I killed him.

I killed them all.
Now if that stranger and Laïos were — kin,
Where is a man more miserable than I?
More hated by the gods? Citizen and alien
    alike
Must never shelter me or speak to me —
I must be shunned by all.
               And I myself
Pronounced this malediction upon myself!

Think of it: I have touched you with these
    hands,
These hands that killed your husband. What
    defilement!

Am I all evil, then? It must be so,
Since I must flee from Thebes, yet never
    again
See my own countrymen, my own country,
For fear of joining my mother in marriage
And killing Polybos, my father.
                     Ah,
If I was created so, born to this fate,
Who could deny the savagery of God?

O holy majesty of heavenly powers!
May I never see that day! Never!
Rather let me vanish from the race of men
Than know the abomination destined me!

CHORAGOS

We too, my lord, have felt dismay at this.
But there is hope: you have yet to hear the
    shepherd.

OEDIPUS

Indeed, I fear no other hope is left me.

IOCASTE

What do you hope from him when he comes?

OEDIPUS

This much:
If his account of the murder tallies with
   yours,
Then I am cleared.

IOCASTE

What was it that I said
Of such importance?

OEDIPUS

Why, " marauders," you said,
Killed the King, according to this man's
   story.
If he maintains that still, if there were sev-
   eral,
Clearly the guilt is not mine: I was alone.
But if he says one man, singlehanded, did it,
Then the evidence all points to me.

IOCASTE

You may be sure that he said there were
   several;
And can he call back that story now? He
   cannot.
The whole city heard it as plainly as I.
But suppose he alters some detail of it:
He cannot ever show that Laïos' death
Fulfilled the oracle: for Apollo said
My child was doomed to kill him; and my
   child —
Poor baby! — It was my child that died first.

No. From now on, where oracles are concerned,
I would not waste a second thought on any.

OEDIPUS

You may be right.
But come: let someone go
For the shepherd at once. This matter must
   be settled.

IOCASTE

I will send for him.
I would not wish to cross you in anything,
And surely not in this. — Let us go in.

(*Exeunt into the palace.*)

CHORUS

[STROPHE I]

Let me be reverent in the ways of right,
Lowly the paths I journey on;
Let all my words and actions keep
The laws of the pure universe
From highest Heaven handed down.
For Heaven is their bright nurse,
Those generations of the realms of light;
Ah, never of mortal kind were they begot,
Nor are they slaves of memory, lost in sleep:
Their Father is greater than Time, and ages
   not.

[ANTISTROPHE I]

The tyrant is a child of Pride
Who drinks from his great sickening cup
Recklessness and vanity,
Until from his high crest headlong
He plummets to the dust of hope.
That strong man is not strong.
But let no fair ambition be denied;
May God protect the wrestler for the State
In government, in comely policy,
Who will fear God, and on His ordinance
   wait.

[STROPHE 2]

Haughtiness and the high hand of disdain
Tempt and outrage God's holy law;
And any mortal who dares hold
No immortal Power in awe
Will be caught up in a net of pain:
The price for which his levity is sold.
Let each man take due earnings, then,
And keep his hands from holy things,
And from blasphemy stand apart —
Else the crackling blast of heaven
Blows on his head, and on his desperate heart;
Though fools will honor impious men,
In their cities no tragic poet sings.

[ANTISTROPHE 2]

Shall we lose faith in Delphi's obscurities,
We who have heard the world's core
Discredited, and the sacred wood
Of Zeus at Elis praised no more?
The deeds and the strange prophecies
Must make a pattern yet to be understood.

Zeus, if indeed you are lord of all,
Throned in light over night and day,
Mirror this in your endless mind:
Our masters call the oracle
Words on the wind, and the Delphic vision
    blind!
Their hearts no longer know Apollo,
And reverence for the gods has died away.
                (*Enter* IOCASTE.)

IOCASTE

Princes of Thebes, it has occurred to me
To visit the altars of the gods, bearing
These branches as a suppliant, and this in-
    cense.
Our King is not himself: his noble soul
Is overwrought with fantasies of dread,
Else he would consider
The new prophecies in the light of the old.
He will listen to any voice that speaks dis-
    aster,
And my advice goes for nothing.
        (*She approaches the altar, Right.*)
                    To you, then, Apollo,
Lycean lord, since you are nearest, I turn in
    prayer.

Receive these offerings, and grant us deliver-
    ance
From defilement. Our hearts are heavy with
    fear
When we see our leader distracted, as helpless
    sailors
Are terrified by the confusion of their helms-
    man.
            (*Enter* MESSENGER.)

MESSENGER

Friends, no doubt you can direct me:
Where shall I find the house of Oedipus,
Or, better still, where is the King himself?

CHORAGOS

It is this very place, stranger; he is inside.
This is his wife and mother of his children.

MESSENGER

I wish her happiness in a happy house,
Blest in all the fulfillment of her marriage.

IOCASTE

I wish as much for you: your courtesy
Deserves a like good fortune. But now, tell
    me:
Why have you come? What have you to say
to us?

MESSENGER

Good news, my lady, for your house and
    your husband.

IOCASTE

What news? Who sent you here?

MESSENGER

                    I am from Corinth.
The news I bring ought to mean joy for you,
Though it may be you will find some grief
    in it.

IOCASTE

What is it? How can it touch us in both
    ways?

MESSENGER

The people of Corinth, they say,
Intend to call Oedipus to be their king.

IOCASTE

But old Polybos — is he not reigning still?

MESSENGER

No. Death holds him in his sepulchre.

IOCASTE

What are you saying? Polybos is dead?

MESSENGER

If I am not telling the truth, may I die my-
    self.

IOCASTE

            (*To a* MAIDSERVANT)
Go in, go quickly; tell this to your master.

O riddlers of God's will, where are you now!
This was the man whom Oedipus, long ago,
Feared so, fled so, in dread of destroying
    him —
But it was another fate by which he died.
            (*Enter* OEDIPUS, *Center.*)

OEDIPUS

Dearest Iocaste, why have you sent for me?

IOCASTE

Listen to what this man says, and then tell
    me
What has become of the solemn prophecies.

OEDIPUS

Who is this man? What is his news for me?

IOCASTE

He has come from Corinth to announce
    your father's death!

OEDIPUS

Is it true, stranger? Tell me in your own
    words.

MESSENGER

I cannot say it more clearly: the King is dead.

OEDIPUS

Was it by treason? Or by an attack of illness?

MESSENGER

A little thing brings old men to their rest.

OEDIPUS

It was sickness, then?

MESSENGER

              Yes, and his many years.

OEDIPUS

Ah!
Why should a man respect the Pythian
    hearth, or
Give heed to the birds that jangle above his
    head?
They prophesied that I should kill Polybos,
Kill my own father; but he is dead and
    buried,
And I am here — I never touched him, never,
Unless he died of grief for my departure,
And thus, in a sense, through me. No. Poly-
    bos
Has packed the oracles off with him under-
    ground.
They are empty words.

IOCASTE

              Had I not told you so?

OEDIPUS

You had; it was my faint heart that betrayed
    me.

IOCASTE

From now on never think of those things
    again.

OEDIPUS

And yet — must I not fear my mother's bed?

IOCASTE

Why should anyone in this world be afraid,
Since Fate rules us and nothing can be fore-
    seen?
A man should live only for the present day.

Have no more fear of sleeping with your
    mother:
How many men, in dreams, have lain with
    their mothers!
No reasonable man is troubled by such things.

OEDIPUS

That is true; only —
If only my mother were not still alive!
But she is alive. I cannot help my dread.

IOCASTE

Yet this news of your father's death is won-
    derful.

OEDIPUS

Wonderful. But I fear the living woman.

MESSENGER

Tell me, who is this woman that you fear?

OEDIPUS

It is Meropê, man; the wife of King Polybos.

MESSENGER

Meropê? Why should you be afraid of her?

OEDIPUS

An oracle of the gods, a dreadful saying.

MESSENGER

Can you tell me about it? or are you sworn to silence?

OEDIPUS

I can tell you, and I will.
Apollo said through his prophet that I was the man
Who should marry his own mother, shed his father's blood
With his own hands. And so, for all these years
I have kept clear of Corinth, and no harm has come —
Though it would have been sweet to see my parents again.

MESSENGER

And is this the fear that drove you out of Corinth?

OEDIPUS

Would you have me kill my father?

MESSENGER

As for that
You must be reassured by the news I gave you.

OEDIPUS

If you could reassure me, I would reward you.

MESSENGER

I had that in mind, I will confess: I thought
I could count on you when you returned to Corinth.

OEDIPUS

No: I will never go near my parents again.

MESSENGER

Ah, son, you still do not know what you are doing —

OEDIPUS

What do you mean? In the name of God tell me!

MESSENGER

— If these are your reasons for not going home.

OEDIPUS

I tell you, I fear the oracle may come true.

MESSENGER

And guilt may come upon you through your parents?

OEDIPUS

That is the dread that is always in my heart.

MESSENGER

Can you not see that all your fears are groundless?

OEDIPUS

How can you say that? They are my parents, surely?

MESSENGER

Polybos was not your father.

OEDIPUS

Not my father?

MESSENGER

No more your father than the man speaking to you.

OEDIPUS

But you are nothing to me!

MESSENGER

Neither was he.

OEDIPUS

Then why did he call me son?

MESSENGER

I will tell you:
Long ago he had you from my hands, as a gift.

OEDIPUS

Then how could he love me so, if I was not his?

MESSENGER

He had no children, and his heart turned to you.

OEDIPUS

What of you? Did you buy me? Did you find me by chance?

MESSENGER

I came upon you in the crooked pass of
    Kithairon.

OEDIPUS

And what were you doing there?

MESSENGER

                    Tending my flocks.

OEDIPUS

A wandering shepherd?

MESSENGER

                But your saviour, son, that day.

OEDIPUS

From what did you save me?

MESSENGER

            Your ankles should tell you that.

OEDIPUS

Ah, stranger, why do you speak of that child-
    hood pain?

MESSENGER

I cut the bonds that tied your ankles to-
    gether.

OEDIPUS

I have had the mark as long as I can remem-
    ber.

MESSENGER

That was why you were given the name you
    bear.[9]

OEDIPUS

God! Was it my father or my mother who
    did it?
Tell me!

MESSENGER

I do not know. The man who gave you to me
Can tell you better than I.

OEDIPUS

It was not you that found me, but another?

[9] *Oedipus* was thought to mean " Swollen-footed."

MESSENGER

It was another shepherd gave you to me.

OEDIPUS

Who was he? Can you tell me who he was?

MESSENGER

I think he was said to be one of Laïos' peo-
    ple.

OEDIPUS

You mean the Laïos who was king here years
    ago?

MESSENGER

Yes; King Laïos; and the man was one of his
    herdsmen.

OEDIPUS

Is he still alive? Can I see him?

MESSENGER

                        These men here
Know best about such things.

OEDIPUS

                    Does anyone here
Know this shepherd that he is talking about?
Have you seen him in the fields, or in the
    town?
If you have, tell me. It is time things were
    made plain.

CHORAGOS

I think the man he means is that same shep-
    herd
You have already asked to see. Iocaste perhaps
Could tell you something.

OEDIPUS

                    Do you know anything
About him, Lady? Is he the man we have
    summoned?
Is that the man this shepherd means?

IOCASTE

                    Why think of him?
Forget this herdsman. Forget it all.
This talk is a waste of time.

OEDIPUS

How can you say that,
When the clues to my true birth are in my
hands?

IOCASTE

For God's love, let us have no more question-
ing!
Is your life nothing to you?
My own is pain enough for me to bear.

OEDIPUS

You need not worry. Suppose my mother a
slave,
And born of slaves: no baseness can touch
you.

IOCASTE

Listen to me, I beg you: do not do this thing!

OEDIPUS

I will not listen; the truth must be made
known.

IOCASTE

Everything that I say is for your own good!

OEDIPUS

My own good
Snaps my patience, then; I want none of it.

IOCASTE

You are fatally wrong! May you never learn
who you are!

OEDIPUS

Go, one of you, and bring the shepherd here.
Let us leave this woman to brag of her royal
name.

IOCASTE

Ah, miserable!
That is the only word I have for you now.
That is the only word I can ever have.

(*Exit into the palace.*)

CHORAGOS

Why has she left us, Oedipus? Why has she
gone
In such a passion of sorrow? I fear this silence:
Something dreadful may come of it.

OEDIPUS

Let it come!
However base my birth, I must know about
it.
The Queen, like a woman, is perhaps ashamed
To think of my low origin. But I
Am a child of Luck; I cannot be dishon-
ored.
Luck is my mother; the passing months, my
brothers,
Have seen me rich and poor.

If this is so,
How could I wish that I were someone else?
How could I not be glad to know my birth?

CHORUS

[STROPHE]

If ever the coming time were known
To my heart's pondering,
Kithairon, now by Heaven I see the torches
At the festival of the next full moon,
And see the dance, and hear the choir sing
A grace to your gentle shade:
Mountain where Oedipus was found,
O mountain guard of a noble race!
May the god who heals us lend his aid,
And let that glory come to pass
For our king's cradling-ground.

[ANTISTROPHE]

Of the nymphs that flower beyond the years,
Who bore you, royal child,
To Pan of the hills or the timberline Apollo,
Cold in delight where the upland clears,
Or Hermes for whom Kyllenê's heights are
piled?
Or flushed as evening cloud,
Great Dionysos, roamer of mountains,
He — was it he who found you there,
And caught you up in his own proud
Arms from the sweet god-ravisher
Who laughed by the Muses' fountains?

OEDIPUS

Sirs: though I do not know the man,
I think I see him coming, this shepherd we
want:
He is old, like our friend here, and the men

Bringing him seem to be servants of my
house.
But you can tell, if you have ever seen him.
(*Enter* SHEPHERD *escorted by servants.*)

CHORAGOS

I know him, he was Laïos' man. You can
trust him.

OEDIPUS

Tell me first, you from Corinth: is this the
shepherd
We were discussing?

MESSENGER

This is the very man.

OEDIPUS

(*To* SHEPHERD)

Come here. No, look at me. You must answer
Everything I ask. — You belonged to Laïos?

SHEPHERD

Yes: born his slave, brought up in his house.

OEDIPUS

Tell me: what kind of work did you do for
him?

SHEPHERD

I was a shepherd of his, most of my life.

OEDIPUS

Where mainly did you go for pasturage?

SHEPHERD

Sometimes Kithairon, sometimes the hills
near-by.

OEDIPUS

Do you remember ever seeing this man out
there?

SHEPHERD

What would he be doing there? This man?

OEDIPUS

This man standing here. Have you ever seen
him before?

SHEPHERD

No. At least, not to my recollection.

MESSENGER

And that is not strange, my lord. But I'll
refresh
His memory: he must remember when we
two
Spent three whole seasons together, March to
September,
On Kithairon or thereabouts. He had two
flocks;
I had one. Each autumn I'd drive mine home
And he would go back with his to Laïos'
sheepfold. —
Is this not true, just as I have described it?

SHEPHERD

True, yes; but it was all so long ago.

MESSENGER

Well, then: do you remember, back in those
days,
That you gave me a baby boy to bring up as
my own?

SHEPHERD

What if I did? What are you trying to say?

MESSENGER

King Oedipus was once that little child.

SHEPHERD

Damn you, hold your tongue!

OEDIPUS

No more of that!
It is your tongue needs watching, not this
man's.

SHEPHERD

My King, my Master, what is it I have done
wrong?

OEDIPUS

You have not answered his question about
the boy.

SHEPHERD

He does not know . . . he is only making
trouble . . .

OEDIPUS

Come, speak plainly, or it will go hard with you.

SHEPHERD

In God's name, do not torture an old man!

OEDIPUS

Come here, one of you; bind his arms behind him.

SHEPHERD

Unhappy king! What more do you wish to learn?

OEDIPUS

Did you give this man the child he speaks of?

SHEPHERD

                                        I did.

And I would to God I had died that very day.

OEDIPUS

You will die now unless you speak the truth.

SHEPHERD

Yet if I speak the truth, I am worse than dead.

OEDIPUS

Very well; since you insist upon delaying —

SHEPHERD

No! I have told you already that I gave him the boy.

OEDIPUS

Where did you get him? From your house? From somewhere else?

SHEPHERD

Not from mine, no. A man gave him to me.

OEDIPUS

Is that man here? Do you know whose slave he was?

SHEPHERD

For God's love, my King, do not ask me any more!

OEDIPUS

You are a dead man if I have to ask you again.

SHEPHERD

Then . . . then the child was from the palace of Laïos.

OEDIPUS

A slave child? or a child of his own line?

SHEPHERD

Ah, I am on the brink of dreadful speech!

OEDIPUS

And I of dreadful hearing. Yet I must hear.

SHEPHERD

If you must be told, then . . .

                    They said it was Laïos' child;

But it is your wife who can tell you about that.

OEDIPUS

My wife! — Did she give it to you?

SHEPHERD

                              My lord, she did.

OEDIPUS

Do you know why?

SHEPHERD

                              I was told to get rid of it.

OEDIPUS

An unspeakable mother!

SHEPHERD

                    There had been prophecies . . .

OEDIPUS

Tell me.

SHEPHERD

          It was said that the boy would kill his own father.

OEDIPUS

Then why did you give him over to this old man?

SHEPHERD

I pitied the baby, my King,
And I thought that this man would take him
    far away
To his own country.
        He saved him — but for what a fate!
For if you are what this man says you are,
No man living is more wretched than Oedi-
    pus.

OEDIPUS

Ah God!
It was true!
    All the prophecies!
                — Now,
O Light, may I look on you for the last time!
I, Oedipus,
Oedipus, damned in his birth, in his marriage
    damned,
Damned in the blood he shed with his own
    hand!

        (*He rushes into the palace.*)

CHORUS

Alas for the seed of men.   [STROPHE 1]

What measure shall I give these generations
That breathe on the void and are void
And exist and do not exist?

Who bears more weight of joy
Than mass of sunlight shifting in images,
Or who shall make his thought stay on
That down time drifts away?

Your splendour is all fallen.

O naked brow of wrath and tears,
O change of Oedipus!
I who saw your days call no man blest —
Your great days like ghosts gone.

                [ANTISTROPHE 1]
That mind was a strong bow.

Deep, how deep you drew it then, hard arch-
    er,
At a dim fearful range,
And brought dear glory down!

You overcame the stranger —
The virgin with her hooking lion claws —
And though death sang, stood like a tower
To make pale Thebes take heart.

Fortress against our sorrow!

Divine king, giver of laws,
Majestic Oedipus!
No prince in Thebes had ever such renown,
No prince won such grace of power.

                [STROPHE 2]
And now of all men ever known
Most pitiful is this man's story:
His fortunes are most changed, his state
Fallen to a low slave's
Ground under bitter fate.

O Oedipus, most royal one!
The great door that expelled you to the light
Gave at night — ah, gave night to your
    glory:
As to the father, to the fathering son.

All understood too late.

How could that queen whom Laïos won,
The garden that he harrowed at his height,
Be silent when that act was done?

                [ANTISTROPHE 2]
But all eyes fail before time's eye,
All actions come to justice there.
Though never willed, though far down the
    deep past,
Your bed, your dread sirings,
Are brought to book at last.

Child by Laïos doomed to die,
Then doomed to lose that fortunate little
    death,
Would God you never took breath in this air
That with my wailing lips I take to cry:

For I weep the world's outcast.

Blind I was, and cannot tell why;
Asleep, for you had given ease of breath;

A fool, while the false years went by.
(*Enter, from the palace,* SECOND MESSEN-
GER.)

SECOND MESSENGER

Elders of Thebes, most honoured in this land,
What horrors are yours to see and hear, what
weight
Of sorrow to be endured, if, true to your
birth,
You venerate the line of Labdakos!
I think neither Istros nor Phasis, those great
rivers,
Could purify this place of the corruption
It shelters now, or soon must bring to
light —
Evil not done unconsciously, but willed.

The greatest griefs are those we cause ourselves.

CHORAGOS

Surely, friend, we have grief enough already;
What new sorrow do you mean?

SECOND MESSENGER

The Queen is dead.

CHORAGOS

Iocaste? Dead? But at whose hand?

SECOND MESSENGER

Her own.
The full horror of what happened you can-
not know,
For you did not see it; but I, who did, will
tell you
As clearly as I can how she met her death.

When she had left us,
In passionate silence, passing through the
court,
She ran to her apartment in the house,
Her hair clutched by the fingers of both
hands.
She closed the doors behind her; then, by that
bed
Where long ago the fatal son was con-
ceived —

That son who should bring about his father's
death —
We heard her call upon Laïos, dead so many
years,
And heard her wail for the double fruit of
her marriage,
A husband by her husband, children by her
child.

Exactly how she died I do not know:
For Oedipus burst in moaning and would
not let us
Keep vigil to the end: it was by him
As he stormed about the room that our eyes
were caught.
From one to another of us he went, begging
a sword,
Cursing the wife who was not his wife, the
mother
Whose womb had carried his own children
and himself.
I do not know: it was none of us aided him,
But surely one of the gods was in control!
For with a dreadful cry
He hurled his weight, as though wrenched
out of himself,
At the twin doors: the bolts gave, and he
rushed in.
And there we saw her hanging, her body
swaying
From the cruel cord she had noosed about
her neck.
A great sob broke from him, heartbreaking
to hear,
As he loosed the rope and lowered her to the
ground.

I would blot out from my mind what happened next!
For the King ripped from her gown the
golden brooches
That were her ornament, and raised them,
and plunged them down
Straight into his own eyeballs, crying, " No
more,
" No more shall you look on the misery
about me,
" The horrors of my own doing! Too long
you have known

" The faces of those whom I should never
        have seen,
" Too long been blind to those for whom I
        was searching!
" From this hour, go in darkness! " And as
        he spoke,
He struck at his eyes — not once, but many
        times;
And the blood spattered his beard,
Bursting from his ruined sockets like red
        hail.

So from the unhappiness of two this evil has
        sprung,
A curse on the man and woman alike. The
        old
Happiness of the house of Labdakos
Was happiness enough: where is it today?
It is all wailing and ruin, disgrace, death —
        all
The misery of mankind that has a name —
And it is wholly and for ever theirs.

CHORAGOS

Is he in agony still? Is there no rest for him?

SECOND MESSENGER

He is calling for someone to lead him to the
        gates
So that all the children of Kadmos may look
        upon
His father's murderer, his mother's — no,
I cannot say it!
                And then he will leave Thebes,
Self-exiled, in order that the curse
Which he himself pronounced may depart
        from the house.
He is weak, and there is none to lead him.
So terrible is his suffering.
                        But you will see:
Look, the doors are opening; in a moment
You will see a thing that would crush a heart
        of stone.
(*The central door is opened;* OEDIPUS,
blinded, is led in)

CHORAGOS

Dreadful indeed for men to see.
Never have my own eyes
Looked on a sight so full of fear.

Oedipus!
What madness came upon you, what daemon
Leaped on your life with heavier
Punishment than a mortal man can bear?
No: I cannot even
Look at you, poor ruined one.
And I would speak, question, ponder,
If I were able. No.
You make me shudder.

OEDIPUS

God. God.
Is there a sorrow greater?
Where shall I find harbour in this world?
My voice is hurled far on a dark wind.
What has God done to me?

CHORAGOS

Too terrible to think of, or to see.

OEDIPUS

O cloud of night,   [STROPHE I]
Never to be turned away: night coming on,
I cannot tell how: night like a shroud!

My fair winds brought me here.
                        O God. Again
The pain of the spikes where I had sight,
The flooding pain
Of memory, never to be gouged out.

CHORAGOS

This is not strange.
You suffer it all twice over, remorse in pain,
Pain in remorse.

OEDIPUS

Ah dear friend   [ANTISTROPHE I]
Are you faithful even yet, you alone?
Are you still standing near me, will you stay
        here,
Patient, to care for the blind?
                        The blind man!
Yet even blind I know who it is attends me,
By the voice's tone —
Though my new darkness hide the comforter.

CHORAGOS

Oh fearful act!
What god was it drove you to rake black
Night across your eyes?

OEDIPUS

Apollo. Apollo. Dear   [STROPHE 2]
Children, the god was Apollo.
He brought my sick, sick fate upon me.
But the blinding hand was my own!
How could I bear to see
When all my sight was horror everywhere?

CHORAGOS

Everywhere; that is true.

OEDIPUS

And now what is left?
Images? Love? A greeting even,
Sweet to the senses? Is there anything?
Ah, no friends: lead me away.
Lead me away from Thebes.
           Lead the great wreck
And hell of Oedipus, whom the gods hate.

CHORAGOS

Your fate is clear, you are not blind to that.
Would God you had never found it out!

OEDIPUS

           [ANTISTROPHE 2]
Death take the man who unbound
My feet on that hillside
And delivered me from death to life! What
   life?
If only I had died,
This weight of monstrous doom
Could not have dragged me and my darlings
   down.

CHORAGOS

I would have wished the same.

OEDIPUS

Oh never to have come here
With my father's blood upon me! Never
To have been the man they call his mother's
   husband!
Oh accurst! Oh child of evil,
To have entered that wretched bed —
           the selfsame one!
More primal than sin itself, this fell to me.

CHORAGOS

I do not know how I can answer you.
You were better dead than alive and blind.

OEDIPUS

Do not counsel me any more. This punish-
   ment
That I have laid upon myself is just.
If I had eyes,
I do not know how I could bear the sight
Of my father, when I came to the house of
   Death,
Or my mother: for I have sinned against
   them both
So vilely that I could not make my peace
By strangling my own life.
           Or do you think my children,
Born as they were born, would be sweet to
   my eyes?
Ah never, never! Nor this town with its high
   walls,
Nor the holy images of the gods.
             For I,
Thrice miserable! — Oedipus, noblest of all
   the line
Of Kadmos, have condemned myself to enjoy
These things no more, by my own maledic-
   tion
Expelling that man whom the gods declared
To be a defilement in the house of Laïos.
After exposing the rankness of my own guilt,
How could I look men frankly in the eyes?
No, I swear it,
If I could have stifled my hearing at its
   source,
I would have done it and made all this body
A tight cell of misery, blank to light and
   sound:
So I should have been safe in a dark agony
Beyond all recollection.
           Ah Kithairon!
Why did you shelter me? When I was cast
   upon you,
Why did I not die? Then I should never
Have shown the world my execrable birth.

Ah Polybos! Corinth, city that I believed
The ancient seat of my ancestors: how fair

I seemed, your child! And all the while this evil
Was cancerous within me!
                    For I am sick
In my daily life, sick in my origin.

O three roads, dark ravine, woodland and way
Where three roads met: you, drinking my father's blood,
My own blood, spilled by my own hand: can you remember
The unspeakable things I did there, and the things
I went on from there to do?
                    O marriage, marriage!
The act that engendered me, and again the act
Performed by the son in the same bed —
                    Ah, the net
Of incest, mingling fathers, brothers, sons,
With brides, wives, mothers: the last evil
That can be known by men: no tongue can say
How evil!
        No. For the love of God, conceal me
Somewhere far from Thebes; or kill me; or hurl me
Into the sea, away from men's eyes forever.

Come, lead me. You need not fear to touch me.
Of all men, I alone can bear this guilt.
(*Enter* CREON.)

CHORAGOS

We are not the ones to decide; but Creon here
May fitly judge of what you ask. He only
Is left to protect the city in your place.

OEDIPUS

Alas, how can I speak to him? What right have I
To beg his courtesy whom I have deeply wronged?

CREON

I have not come to mock you, Oedipus,
Or to reproach you, either.

(*To* ATTENDANTS)
                    — You, standing there:
If you have lost all respect for man's dignity,
At least respect the flame of Lord Helios: [10]
Do not allow this pollution to show itself
Openly here, an affront to the earth
And Heaven's rain and the light of day. No, take him
Into the house as quickly as you can.
For it is proper
That only the close kindred see his grief.

OEDIPUS

I pray you in God's name, since your courtesy
Ignores my dark expectation, visiting
With mercy this man of all men most execrable:
Give me what I ask — for your good, not for mine.

CREON

And what is it that you would have me do?

OEDIPUS

Drive me out of this country as quickly as may be
To a place where no human voice can ever greet me.

CREON

I should have done that before now — only,
God's will had not been wholly revealed to me.

OEDIPUS

But his command is plain: the parricide
Must be destroyed. I am that evil man.

CREON

That is the sense of it, yes; but as things are,
We had best discover clearly what is to be done.

OEDIPUS

You would learn more about a man like me?

CREON

You are ready now to listen to the god.

[10] the sun

OEDIPUS

I will listen. But it is to you
That I must turn for help. I beg you, hear
  me.

The woman in there —
Give her whatever funeral you think proper:
She is your sister.
                    — But let me go, Creon!
Let me purge my father's Thebes of the
  pollution
Of my living here, and go out to the wild
  hills,
To Kithairon, that has won such fame with
  me,
The tomb my mother and father appointed
  for me,
And let me die there, as they willed I should.
And yet I know
Death will not ever come to me through
  sickness
Or in any natural way: I have been preserved
For some unthinkable fate. But let that be.

As for my sons, you need not care for them.
They are men, they will find some way to
  live.
But my poor daughters, who have shared my
  table,
Who never before have been parted from
  their father —
Take care of them, Creon; do this for me.
And will you let me touch them with my
  hands
A last time, and let us weep together?
Be kind, my lord,
Great prince, be kind!
                    Could I but touch them,
They would be mine again, as when I had
  my eyes.
(*Enter* ANTIGONE *and* ISMENE, *attended.*)
Ah, God!
Is it my dearest children I hear weeping?
Has Creon pitied me and sent my daughters?

CREON

Yes, Oedipus: I knew that they were dear to
  you

In the old days, and know you must love
  them still.

OEDIPUS

May God bless you for this — and be a
  friendlier
Guardian to you than he has been to me!

Children, where are you?
Come quickly to my hands: they are your
  brother's —
Hands that have brought your father's once
  clear eyes
To this way of seeing —
                    Ah dearest ones,
I had neither sight nor knowledge then, your
  father
By the woman who was the source of his
  own life!
And I weep for you — having no strength to
  see you — ,
I weep for you when I think of the bitterness
That men will visit upon you all your lives.
What homes, what festivals can you attend
Without being forced to depart again in
  tears?
And when you come to marriageable age,
Where is the man, my daughters, who would
  dare
Risk the bane that lies on all my children?
Is there any evil wanting? Your father killed
His father; sowed the womb of her who bore
  him;
Engendered you at the fount of his own ex-
  istence!

That is what they will say of you.

                                   Then, whom
Can you ever marry? There are no bride-
  grooms for you,
And your lives must wither away in sterile
  dreaming.

O Creon, son of Menoikeus!
You are the only father my daughters have,
Since we, their parents, are both of us gone
  forever.
They are your own blood: you will not let
  them

Fall into beggary and loneliness;
You will keep them from the miseries that
    are mine!
Take pity on them; see, they are only chil-
    dren,
Friendless except for you. Promise me this,
Great Prince, and give me your hand in
    token of it.
            (CREON *clasps his right hand.*)
Children:
I could say much, if you could understand
    me,
But as it is, I have only this prayer for you:
Live where you can, be as happy as you
    can —
Happier, please God, than God has made
    your father!

                    CREON

Enough. You have wept enough. Now go
    within.

                    OEDIPUS

I must; but it is hard.

                    CREON

                    Time eases all things.

                    OEDIPUS

But you must promise —

                    CREON

                    Say what you desire.

                    OEDIPUS

Send me from Thebes!

                    CREON

                    God grant that I may!

                    OEDIPUS

But since God hates me . . .

                    CREON

    No, he will grant your wish.

                    OEDIPUS

You promise?

                    CREON

    I cannot speak beyond my knowledge.

                    OEDIPUS

Then lead me in.

                    CREON

    Come now, and leave your children.

                    OEDIPUS

No! Do not take them from me!

                    CREON

                    Think no longer
That you are in command here, but rather
    think
How, when you were, you served your own
    destruction.
(*Exeunt into the house all but the* CHORUS;
the CHORAGOS *chants directly to the audi-
ence.*)

                    CHORAGOS

Men of Thebes: look upon Oedipus.

This is the king who solved the famous riddle
And towered up, most powerful of men.
No mortal eyes but looked on him with envy,
Yet in the end ruin swept over him.

Let every man in mankind's frailty
Consider his last day; and let none
Presume on his good fortune until he find
Life, at his death, a memory without pain.

THE PLAYWRIGHTS

AESCHYLUS (525–456 B.C.)

The first of the three major tragic poets of the ancient world, Aeschylus was born of noble parentage and served his country as a warrior and as a playwright. Since only fragments of the pre-Aeschylean drama exist, it is difficult to know how much of the form and technique of focussed tragedy he " invented." However, within the body of his surviving work there is such rapid development in structure, unity, and the use of the playwright's tools that it is probably not unjust to call him " the founder of Greek tragedy." Of his ninety plays, seven survive, from the primitive *Suppliant Maidens* to the *Oresteia*, a trilogy examining the nature of justice. His plays are deeply religious and philosophical, but in the trilogy, as in *Prometheus Bound*, his skill as a playwright is so masterly that abstract ideas and problems of great intellectual and spiritual magnitude are translated into actions of the sharpest conflict and tension. He is credited with introducing the second speaking actor, permitting the extension of the episode, and with the refinement of masks and costumes to particularize his characters.

There are many translations of his complete works into English. Particular attention should be called to the translation of the *Oresteia* by Richmond Lattimore (Chicago, 1953), with a useful commentary. For further information and criticism, see: Gilbert Murray, *Aeschylus, The Creator of Tragedy*, Oxford, 1940; H. W. Smyth, *Aeschylean Tragedy*, Berkeley, 1924; George Thomson, *Aeschylus and Athens*, London, 1941.

CHEKHOV, ANTON (1860–1904)

Chekhov was born in the south of Russia and trained at the University of Moscow for a doctor of medicine. He began his literary career as a writer of naturalistic short stories, a medium of which he continued to be a master even after turning to the theater. Elements from his medical career and his practice of fiction give his plays their characteristic subject matter and tone: he appears to be an objective, almost disinterested reporter of the Russian life of his day. Yet, although he rejected both the well-made play and the meticulous construction of Ibsen, in his dramatic work Chekhov is a highly conscious manipulator of his naturalistic materials. The conflicts are single and strong (generally between one generation and another, or one social group and another) and he has developed the use of the dominant symbol (a sea gull, an orchard) to perhaps an even greater degree than Ibsen. Since his most successful plays were associated with productions by the Moscow Art Theater, it is important to observe the close connection between his (unwritten) theories of playwrighting and the theories of naturalistic acting and production advanced by Constantin Stanislavsky.

A convenient translation of Chekhov's major plays by Constance Garnett will be found in the Modern Library. For further criticism and information, see: S. D. Balukhaty, *The Sea Gull Produced by Stanislavsky*, London, 1952; William Gerhardi, *Anton Chekhov, A Critical Study*, London, 1926; Ronald Hingely, *Chekhov, A Biographical and Critical Study*, London, 1950; David Magarshack, *Chekhov the Dramatist*, London, 1952.

IBSEN, HENRIK (1828–1906)

After a youth spent in poverty and frustrated attempts to become a painter and a scholar, Ibsen turned to the writing of plays and was rewarded with the post of manager of the newly-formed National Theater in Oslo. Here he came to know first-hand the practical problems of the theater as well as the major works of contemporary European playwrights. His own early plays were romantic in content and panoramic in structure. Under the influence of the well-made play and the revolutionary intellectual currents of the time, he eventually began writing social-problem plays (*A Doll's House, Ghosts, An Enemy of the People*) which mark the rebirth of serious drama in the modern world. At heart a poet and true citizen of the world, he soon developed the mechanically proficient well-made problem play into a symbolic drama (*Rosmersholm, Master Builder Solness, John Gabriel Borkman*) capable of both deep insight and broad vision. Bernard Shaw's portrait of him (*The Quintessence of Ibsenism*) as a destroyer of false ideals is a good place to begin in understanding Ibsen, but a study of his symbolic techniques reveals that he was, as he himself said, more the poet and less the social critic than his contemporaries recognized.

Ibsen's complete works, translated by William Archer and others, are available in twelve volumes (New York, 1929). A convenient selection of eleven plays may be found in the Modern Library. For further information and criticism, see: M. E. Bradbrook, *Ibsen the Norwegian*, London, 1946; B. W. Downs, *Ibsen, The Intellectual Background*, Cambridge (Eng.), 1948; John Northam, *Ibsen's Dramatic Method*, London, 1953; P. F. D. Tennant, *Ibsen's Dramatic Technique*, Cambridge (Eng.), 1948; H. J. Weigand, *The Modern Ibsen, A Reconsideration*, New York, 1929.

MARLOWE, CHRISTOPHER (1564–1593)

The brief, hectic, and many-faceted career of Christopher Marlowe is almost an epitome of the aspirations and failures of Renaissance Man as he himself crystallized them in *Doctor Faustus*. Son of a Canterbury shoemaker,

he was educated at the local church school and displayed such brilliance that he was sent on to Cambridge. He came into the artistic circles of London with a reputation as a scholar, a philosopher, and a freethinker, became celebrated as a poet and playwright, and was murdered in a tavern brawl under circumstances which suggest that he had spent at least a part of his short life as a government agent. The first of the great English playwrights, his action, his characters, and his dialogue share in common a magnificence and a headlong rush that has by turns appealed to and appalled later critics. As the bridge between the medieval panoramic drama (he retains many of the conventions of the morality play) and the great tragedy of the Elizabethan and Jacobean theater (he made blank verse the conventional medium of expression and secular history acceptable subject matter for tragedy), he has been endlessly fascinating to scholars. His theatrical power is attested by the frequent revivals of *Doctor Faustus* on the modern stage.

For further information and criticism, see: John Bakeless, *The Tragicall History of Christopher Marlowe*, 2 vols., Cambridge (Mass.), 1942; F. S. Boas, *Christopher Marlowe, A Biography and Short Critical Study*, Oxford, 1940; P. H. Kocher, *Christopher Marlowe, A Study of His Thought, Learning, and Character*, Chapel Hill, 1946; Harry Levin, *The Overreacher*, Cambridge (Mass.), 1952.

MOLIÈRE (1622–1673)

Molière is the stage-name adopted by Jean Baptiste Poquelin, manager and chief actor of a provincial group of players who came to Paris in 1658. The company seems to have been organized along the lines of the Italian *commedia dell'arte* troupes, each actor having his assigned line of business or character, and the plays devised to employ the stock company in a series of burlesque, comic, or satiric actions. Molière was, in addition, supplier of plays for his company, at first little farces of considerable skill, then comedies satirizing the foibles of contemporary society, and finally plays which attack the weaknesses of mankind in general with such seriousness that some French critics have been reluctant to class them as comedies (*The Misanthrope,* for example). *Tartuffe* illustrates him at his best, and his most typical, manipulating a group of stock characters (a clever servant, a stern parent, young lovers) through a stereotyped action (gulling the parent who would stand in the way of young love), but turning the conventional materials into a frontal assault, not on hypocrisy, but on the irrational behavior of the hero, Orgon. The plays are written in prose, or a careless rhyming verse. Molière is not a witty writer, and his dialogue is more facile than comic. The humor of his plays lies in the situation, the comic business which he devised, and the over-all pattern of the action.

Molière's plays have been frequently translated into English, but the translations generally fail to give much notion of his theatrical effectiveness. A complete translation, with French text, was made by H. van Laun in six volumes (Edinburgh, 1876). Single plays, *The Miser* and *The Mock Doctor,* were skillfully adapted by Henry Fielding, and *The Would-Be Invalid,* by Morris Bishop. For further information and criticism, see: Brander Matthews, *Molière, His Life and His Works,* New York, 1910; John Palmer, *Molière,* New York, 1930.

O'NEILL, EUGENE (1888–1952)

Eugene O'Neill was the son of a famous American actor, and grew up in the theater when it was at its most theatrical, the theater of melodrama and romance. During his young manhood he attempted to escape from his background by putting to sea on a series of freighters, but inevitably he was drawn back to the stage and his days of vagabonding were transmuted into materials for drama. After studying with George Pierce Baker at the 47 Workshop, a playwrighting course at Harvard which gave early training to many of the most important dramatists in the revival of the American theater, he be-

gan producing with the Provincetown Players. While his subject matter and his themes reflect the stresses and confusions of contemporary life and while his view of life and man's fate is conditioned always by the intellectual enthusiasms of the 'twenties, his theatrical heritage was so strong that many of his plays have succeeded in breaking the bonds of the fads and limited vision of their period. A restless experimenter, O'Neill explored the possibilities of the modern theater as an expressive medium more thoroughly than any of his contemporaries, and has been the mentor to all who have followed him in time if not in attitude.

For further information and criticism, see: B. H. Clark, *Eugene O'Neill, The Man and His Plays,* New York, 1927; Edward Engel, *The Haunted Heroes of Eugene O'Neill,* Cambridge (Mass.), 1953; R. D. Skinner, *Eugene O'Neill, A Poet's Quest,* New York, 1935.

SHAKESPEARE, WILLIAM (1564–1616)

The son of a provincial tradesman, Shakespeare came to London with the conventional classical education of his day, but without the university training which had made skeptics of so many of his fellows. Consequently his plays reflect accurately the accepted beliefs of his time in theology, politics, and sociology. By his poetic power he was able to translate his own age into an image so vivid and lifelike that it has endured for all time. He was a practical man of the theater as well as a poet and playwright, an actor and part owner of an acting company. Much of his work must have been written on demand, to supply the needs of the repertory; he wrote comedy, history, tragedy, tragicomedy, and all with such success that he was able to retire from active life some years before his death. For men of the theater he must always remain an idol: with his eye only on his work, on his audience and their tastes and capacities, and on the box-office receipts, he nonetheless composed at least 36 plays, most of which have achieved a permanent place on the stages of the world.

They are a part of the priceless heritage of mankind.

For further information and criticism, see: Ann Bradby, *Shakespeare Criticism*, Oxford, 1936 (an anthology); E. K. Chambers, *William Shakespeare*, 2 vols., Oxford, 1930; Marchette Chute, *Shakespeare of London*, New York, 1949; E. L. Hubler, *The Sense of Shakespeare's Sonnets*, Princeton, 1952 (an introduction to the basic ideas and attitudes of the playwright); A. C. Sprague, *Shakespearean Players and Performances*, Cambridge (Mass.), 1953.

SOPHOCLES (495–406 B.C.)

As the younger contemporary of Aeschylus, Sophocles is generally accepted as the master dramatist of the Greek theater. He seems to have devoted the whole of his life to his art, expanding the capabilities of the focussed form to such an extent that he became the model, not just for Aristotle in his analysis of dramatic art, but to the playwrights who were to revive the form during the Renaissance. Perhaps his greatest innovation was the addition of a third speaking actor, multiplying the number of characters available (by doubling) to the playwright, and so increasing the importance and extensiveness of the episodes. In his plays the chorus is less important dramatically than in the plays of Aeschylus, though their lyrics are among the greatest of antiquity. Sophocles abandoned the trilogy and made of five complexly constructed episodes a single dramatic unit, independent of the other plays presented on the same program. Of his 120 plays, seven survive, and have been repeatedly translated into English. The standard translation, by R. C. Jebb, accurate but conveying no notion of the poetic power of the original and only a suggestion of the dramatic experience, exists in many editions. A particularly interesting approach to his technique is to be found in *The Imagery of Sophocles' Antigone*, by R. H. Goheen (see *A List of Suggested Readings*, E 4).

For further information and criticism, see: A. J. A. Waldock, *Sophocles the Dramatist*, Cambridge (Eng.), 1951; C. H. Whitman, *Sophocles: A Study of Heroic Humanism*, Cambridge (Mass.), 1951.

VEGA, LOPE DE (1562–1635)

In the melodramatic life of Lope de Vega, perhaps no fact is more startling than that he claimed to have written 2,000 plays, of which almost 500 actually exist in print or manuscript. His biography reads like an historical novel, the story of a humble scholar who took part in the Armada, was entangled in dozens of intrigues, twice married, a priest, a father, a wit, a novelist, poet, and playwright. His plays, obviously written at top speed, were produced in a theater much like those of Shakespearian London, with many playing areas but no scenery. He drew his subject matter from romance, history, and the Bible, and his verse dialogue is a mingling of ballad meter, sonnet form, and various lyric measures. As is necessary for such mass production, he had a clearly formulated theory of drama, which he set forth in *The New Art of Writing Plays* (Publications of the Dramatic Museum of Columbia University, New York, 1914). Few of his plays have been translated into English: *Four Plays by Lope de Vega*, translated by J. G. Underhill, New York, 1936; *Discovery of the New World by Christopher Columbus*, translated by Frieda Fligelman, Berkeley, 1950. *The Star of Seville*, credited to him by several translators, is spurious.

For further information and criticism, see: Angel Flores, *Lope de Vega, Monster of Nature*, New York, 1930; H. A. Rennert, *The Life of Lope de Vega*, Philadelphia, 1904; Rudolph Schevill, *The Dramatic Art of Lope de Vega*, Berkeley, 1918. See also C. E. Anibal, "The Historical Elements of Lope de Vega's *Fuente Ovejuna*," *PMLA*, LXIX (1934), 657ff.; Jacinto Benevente, Critical Essay appended to Underhill's translation.

A List of Suggested Readings

A. THEORY OF DRAMA

Harley Granville-Barker, *On Dramatic Method*, London, 1931.

——, *The Use of the Drama*, Princeton, 1945.

Barrett H. Clark, ed., *European Theories of the Drama*, New York, 1947. [An anthology of selections from the major theorists and critics of the drama from Aristotle to the present.]

Francis Fergusson, *The Idea of a Theatre*, Princeton, 1949. [Anchor Books Edition, New York, 1953.]

Allardyce Nicoll, *The Theory of Drama*, London, 1931.

B. HISTORY OF DRAMA

Sheldon Cheyney, *The Theatre: Three Thousand Years of Drama, Acting, and Stagecraft*, New York, 1929. [A convenient introductory work, written with enthusiasm and well illustrated.]

John Gassner, *Masters of the Drama*, New York, 1954. [The basic single-volume study of the world's major playwrights and their works.]

Allardyce Nicoll, *World Drama*, New York, 1950.

Donald C. Stuart, *The Development of Dramatic Art*, New York, 1928.

C. HISTORY OF THEATER AND STAGING

George Freedley and J. A. Reeves, *A History of the Theater*, New York, 1941.

Phyllis Hartnoll, ed., *The Oxford Companion to the Theatre*, New York, 1951. [A dictionary and encyclopedia of the stage.]

Allardyce Nicoll, *The Development of the Theatre*, New York, 1927.

D. SPECIAL TOPICS — HISTORY OF DRAMATIC FORMS

1. Classical Theater and Drama

J. T. Allen, *Stage Antiquities of the Greeks and Romans*, New York, 1921. [The best introduction for the novice.]

Margarete Bieber, *The History of the Greek and Roman Theater*, Princeton, 1939. [A magnificent and inclusive picture book.]

H. D. F. Kitto, *Greek Tragedy*, New York, Anchor Books, 1954. [A rare combination of scholarship, critical taste, and theater sense.]

2. Medieval Theater and Drama

E. K. Chambers, *The Medieval Stage*, 2 vols., Oxford, 1903.

Willard Farnham, *The Medieval Heritage of Elizabethan Tragedy*, Berkeley, 1936.

445

Karl Young, *The Drama of the Medieval Church*, Oxford, 1933. [Texts and Commentary.]

3. Panoramic Theater and Drama

Alan S. Downer, *The British Drama*, New York, 1950.
Harley Granville-Barker, *Prefaces to Shakespeare*, Princeton, 1946–47.
C. W. Hodges, *The Globe Restored*, London, 1953.
R. G. Moulton, *Shakespeare as a Dramatic Artist*, Oxford, 1929.

E. SPECIAL TOPICS — ELEMENTS OF DRAMATIC ART

1. Theater

Mordecai Gorelik, *New Theaters for Old*, New York, 1941.
Robert Edmond Jones, *The Dramatic Imagination*, New York, 1941.
Lee Simonson, *The Stage is Set*, New York, 1932.

2. Scenes and Machines

E. Gordon Craig, *On the Art of the Theater*, London, 1911.
John Gassner, ed., *Producing the Play*, New York, 1952.
George Kernodle, *From Art to Theater*, Chicago, 1944.
Lee Simonson, *The Art of Scenic Design*, New York, 1950.

3. Actors and Acting

Toby Cole and H. K. Chinoy, *Actors on Acting*, New York, 1949.
G. H. Lewes, *On Actors and the Art of Acting*, London, 1875.
Michael Redgrave, *The Actor's Ways and Means*, London, 1953.
Arthur Colby Sprague, *Shakespeare and the Actors*, Cambridge (Mass.), 1944.
Constantin Stanislavsky, *On the Art of the Stage*, London, 1950. [With a long essay elucidating the famous " method of acting " by David Magarshack.]

4. The Playwright and the Written Record

William Archer, *Playmaking*, New York, 1912.
G. P. Baker, *Dramatic Technique*, Boston, 1919.
J. H. Lawson, *Theory and Technique of Playwrighting*, New York, 1949.

W. H. Clemen, *The Development of Shakespeare's Imagery*, Cambridge (Mass.), 1951
A. S. Downer, " The Life of Our Design," *The Hudson Review*, II (1949), 242 ff.
R. F. Goheen, *The Imagery of Sophocles' Antigone*, Princeton, 1951.

Erich Auerbach, *Mimesis*, Princeton, 1953.
Eric Bentley, *The Playwright as Thinker*, New York, 1946.
Suzanne Langer, *Feeling and Form*, New York, 1953.

F. COLLECTIONS OF PLAYS

John Gassner, *A Treasury of the Theater*, 2 vols., New York, 1951. [65 plays from Aeschylus to Arthur Miller.]

Dudley Fitts, *Greek Plays in Modern Translation*, New York, 1947. [11 plays, translated by Fitts, Richmond Lattimore, Edith Hamilton, W. B. Yeats, etc.]

Whitney Oates and Eugene O'Neill, Jr., *The Complete Greek Drama*, 2 vols., New York, 1938. [All the surviving plays of Aeschylus, Sophocles, Euripides, Aristophanes, and Menander in standard translations.]

J. Q. Adams, *Chief Pre-Shakespearean Dramas*, Boston, 1924. [63 plays, including examples of liturgical, mystery, morality, and Tudor professional drama.]

Hazelton Spencer, *Elizabethan Plays*, Boston, 1933. [28 plays from Marlowe to Shirley.]

Gerald E. Bentley, *The Development of English Drama*, New York, 1950. [23 plays from the craft cycles to Pinero.]

A. H. Quinn, *Representative American Plays*, New York, 1917 (and later revised editions). [31 plays from 1767 to the present.]

John Gassner, *Best Plays of the Modern American Theater*, 4 vols., New York, 1939 — [About 80 plays covering the first fifty years of the twentieth century. Title varies slightly from volume to volume.]

S. M. Tucker and Alan S. Downer, *25 Modern Plays*, 3rd ed., New York, 1953. [Representative English, European, and American plays from Ibsen to the present.]

INDEX

449